A LIBRARY OF LITERARY CRITICISM

*A Library
of Literary Criticism*

THE HEBREW BIBLE *in* *Literary* *Criticism*

Compiled and edited by
ALEX PREMINGER
and EDWARD L. GREENSTEIN

Ungar • New York

1986
The Ungar Publishing Company
370 Lexington Avenue, New York, N.Y. 10017

Library of Congress Cataloging-in-Publication Data

The Hebrew bible in literary criticism.

   (A Library of literary criticism)
   Includes index.
   1. Bible. O.T.—Criticism, interpretation, etc.
I. Preminger, Alex. II. Greenstein, Edward L.
III. Series.
BS1171.2.H43   1986   221.6′6   86-16069
ISBN 0-8044-3266-X

To Augusta Friedman Preminger
and in memory of Saly, Lea, and Felix Preminger

To Batsheva Greenstein

CONTENTS

PART 4: APOCRYPHA   587

PREFACE

A note near the end of the book of Ecclesiastes cautions: "Of the making of many books there is no end." The present book, we confess, confirms that ancient admonition. We have here drawn from several hundred books and periodicals and made yet another book. It documents and represents the literary criticism of the Hebrew Bible from ancient to modern times, from classical exegesis to deconstruction. We divide our selections among four parts: The Bible in General, which by and large comprises comments of a broad scope; Literary Features, which includes various topics pertinent to the Hebrew Bible; The Texts, in which comments are correlated with specific literary passages in the Bible; and Apocrypha (on which, see below).

Although the literary study of the Bible has come into fashion of late, our attention to the Bible's artistic and rhetorical side has, we believe, independent merit. Since antiquity, readers have sought to find significance, and even some sort of pleasure, in the Hebrew Bible, the great foundation of Western religion and classic of Western culture. They have relied upon many different methods for deriving meaning from the biblical text. Ancient and medieval rabbis, for example, applied special interpretive techniques toward deciphering the arcane messages they believed God had encoded into the sacred scripture. The Christian gospel writers searched the Hebrew Bible for prophetic allusions that would foretell and legitimize the ministry of Jesus. In more recent times, historians have regarded the Biblical text as a composite of diverse strata and ideological strains. Through painstaking analysis of the text into documents and traditions they have endeavored to retrieve the sources of the Bible and reconstruct the history of ancient Israel by placing those sources in their original contexts. Others compare the languages and literatures of contemporary ancient civilizations—Amorites, Assyrians, Babylonians, Canaanites, Moabites, Egyptians, Hittites, Hurrians, and more—in order better to understand the words, idioms, grammar, motifs, genres, and other literary conventions of the Bible. Archaeology, sociology, anthropology—all these disciplines throw light on different facets of the Biblical text. Each has yielded meanings that another discipline would not.

Since the beginning of the Common Era readers have been impressed with the rhetorical force and artistic, poetic qualities of the Hebrew Bible. Such readers have called attention to the literary figures and tropes of the Scriptures both to admire them and to emulate them. As the Bible served as a fountainhead of religious truth, so did it serve as a model of metaphor and style, of literature. Yet the Hebrew Bible originated in a Near Eastern society whose conventions reflected oriental traditions and tastes. With the impact of Hellenistic, Roman, Islamic, and other cultures, readers of the Bible grew more and more remote from the literary and social mind-set out of which the Bible emerged. Thus, while some literary critics have held the Bible up to the standards of a particular society and assessed its artistic merit on the basis of their own canons and concerns, others have attempted to bridge the cultural gap between contemporary readers and biblical literature by familiarizing them with the Bible's own rhetorical features. Literary criticism has therefore tended to demystify the Bible's forms and formulations and to reclaim it for a contemporary audience as a kind of once-lost but recently recovered treasure. When certain Jews of the early Middle Ages and certain Christians of the Enlightenment identified parallelism, for example, as a major principle of biblical versifying, they sought not only to appreciate the rhetoric of ancient Hebrew prosody but also to understand the poetry through its rhetoric.

More recent literary critics of the Hebrew Bible have maintained, in fact, that by laying bare the literary structure and workings of biblical literature one discerns indispensable clues to the meaning of the text. The form of a text, insofar as it can be isolated from the substance of that text, shapes and produces meaning as crucially as the semantic content. Literary analysis, then, takes its place among all the various strategies that readers and students have exploited to interpret and find significance in the Bible.

We have assembled here excerpts of the many types of literary comment on the Hebrew Bible, from the more impressionistic literary appreciation of some readers to the more complex analysis of various critics. We have taken the liberty of identifying literary comment even in texts in which such comment does not purport to be literary criticism. A rabbinic midrash, to take one example, and a monologue in a modern novel, to take another, do not correspond to what we would regard as criticism, or even as appreciation. As a discipline, literary criticism of the Bible does not substantially begin until the eighteenth century. Indeed, some literary critics today maintain that proper literary analysis of the Bible did not develop until well into the twentieth century. Nevertheless, it has been our object to represent all types of literary comment on the Hebrew Bible, the implicit as well as the explicit. We have, in fact, included statements about the Bible that do barely more than evaluate it. Such opinions may sometimes do little to illumine the biblical text. They do, however, register the influence of the Hebrew Bible on later writing. For this reason we have incorporated selections by major authors and others, even some whose names do not usually appear in histories of literary criticism and whose views on biblical literature now seem somewhat less than sophisticated.

The amount of literary criticism written on the Hebrew Bible is astonishing.

Of the material we have collected alone, we have had to omit nearly half for the sake of space. Because we cannot be comprehensive, we have necessarily been selective. As far as possible we have tried to include, even on a single text or topic in many cases, perspectives from different periods and places and contrasting positions and methodologies. Virtually all literary approaches are represented, among them new criticism, formalist poetics, psychoanalysis, structuralism, and even the recently blooming deconstruction. Unfortunately, certain interesting criticism could not be included on account of its detailed and extremely technical nature. We have sought to present the best material available that could be understood by the interested reader. In addition, much excellent writing on biblical literature could not be included, either because of insurmountable copyright problems or because it did not lend itself to excerpting. Excerpts range from about a hundred words to about a thousand. Under each topic we arrange excerpts chronologically, revealing shifts in critical attitudes, ideas, and evaluation.

Two other important considerations have influenced our choices. The retrospective nature of this anthology has often led us to prefer earlier works over more recent ones. We hope that this historical concern will make our selection of interest to the contemporary specialist as well as the more general reader. We have also made a special effort to include significant works in foreign languages, many excerpts of which we have translated for this volume (these are indicated by daggers in their bibliographic citations). We have attempted to represent in particular the very extensive Hebrew literary writing on the Bible, from ancient to modern times. Few such works have been translated into Western languages, and their quality and extent lends them unusual import.

One other factor, this one beyond our control, tilts the anthology a bit out of balance. For reasons too complex to discuss here, certain topics (such as prosody) have been treated widely, whereas others (such as plot) have been scarcely developed. The fact that we may include twenty excerpts on one topic and only four on another does not necessarily reflect the relative importance of those topics for the literary study of the Bible. Similarly, certain subjects (such as rhetoric) have been essayed from early on; others (such as informational or narrative gaps) were not expressly treated until the twentieth century. We have been limited by the material that has been written, but the areas that have been little explored may prove fertile for further cultivation.

At this point we wish to clarify three items that relate to the contents of the book. First, we deal here only with the Hebrew Bible or Scriptures. The Hebrew Bible comprises three parts: *Torah* ("Teaching," the Pentateuch), *Nevi'im* ("Prophets," including the "historical" books of Joshua, Judges, Samuel, and Kings), and *Ketuvim* ("Writings," or Hagiographa). The Hebrew Bible contains the same books as the so-called Old Testament of the Christian Bible, but the Hebrew Bible and the Old Testament differ in the sequence of books. Primarily, in the Hebrew Bible the prophetic books are placed in the center; in the Old Testament they are at the end. In addition, some Christian churches include certain

Jewish books that were not included in the Jewish Bible: the Apocrypha. Because these books often fall clearly within the Hebrew literary tradition and because many authors speak of these books in direct relation to those of the Hebrew Bible proper, we have included here some comments on four Apocryphal texts (Ecclesiasticus, or Ben Sira; Judith; Tobit; and the Wisdom of Solomon).

Second, we follow nearly all modern scholars in distinguishing two books within the biblical text of Isaiah. The first, chapters 1–39, we designate as Isaiah I; the second, chapters 40–66, as Isaiah II. Isaiah I is ascribed in the Bible to Isaiah son of Amoz; the prophecies of Isaiah II are anonymous, but their author is conventionally called Deutero-Isaiah or the Second Isaiah.

The third item involves the figures David, Moses, and Samuel. Each is a central character in the biblical narrative and therefore heads a section of excerpts. In traditional, precritical, or noncritical writing about these characters it is assumed that they composed parts of the Bible. Hence, some excerpts discuss not only the characters but also the supposed authors David (Psalms), Moses (Pentateuch), and Samuel (Samuel).

A word of explanation is in order concerning the many quotations from the Bible. Whenever feasible, we have attempted to supply chapter and verse for quotations, although it has not always been possible to determine the Bible version used. In those cases, citations generally have been from the King James Version and occasionally from the Holy Scriptures according to the Masoretic Text (Jewish Publication Society of America, 1962–82), where that seemed to be the most likely source.

Finally, we wish to acknowledge the encouragement and assistance we have received in the several years in which we have worked on this book. A special note of appreciation is due Meir Sternberg and Robert Alter for their early interest, advice, and concrete suggestions. We are also grateful for their professional advice to Isaac Barzilay, Adele Berlin, Shaye J.D. Cohen, Avraham Holtz, Yochanan Muffs, Adina Ofek, Joel Rosenberg, and Moshe Sokolow; and, for their assistance, to Professor Menahem Haran, Ora Horn Prouser, Rosemarie Tiedeman, and Ernesto Yattah. To those librarians—especially Herman Dicker and Linda Lerman of the Jewish Theological Seminary Library, Darleen Podolny of the West Palm Beach Public Library, and Hilda Volker and Doris Mizell of the Volusia County (Florida) Library Center—who provided through interlibrary loan much of the source material for this book, we express our thanks. A fellowship grant for 1980–81 awarded to Alex Preminger by the Memorial Foundation for Jewish Culture greatly expedited this work; and Winifred and Tom Herlihy graciously hosted Mr. Preminger during his stay in New York. Last but hardly least, we thank our publisher, Mr. Frederick Ungar, for his constant support, and Rita Stein for her invaluable work as editor in seeing the manuscript through press.

THE EDITORS

ABBREVIATIONS

Am.	Amos
AV	Authorized Version (1611)
B.C.E.	Before the Common Era
c.	century, centuries
ca.	*circa*, about
C.E.	Common Era
ch., chs.	chapter(s)
Chron.	Chronicles
col., cols.	column(s)
cp.	compare
Dan.	Daniel
Deut.	Deuteronomy
E	Hypothetical written source of various narrative and legal portions of the Pentateuch. Named for its use of the divine name *Elohim*, its provenience is commonly held to be North Israel, 8th c. B.C.E.
Eccl.	Ecclesiastes
Ecclus.	Ecclesiasticus
Exod.	Exodus
Ezek.	Ezekiel
Gen.	Genesis
H.	Hebrew Bible
Hab.	Habakkuk
Hos.	Hosea
Isa.	Isaiah
J	Hypothetical written source of various narrative and legal portions of the Pentateuch. Named for its use of the divine name *YHWH*, its provenience is commonly held to be Judah, 10th–9th c. B.C.E.
J.B.	Jerusalem Bible
Jer.	Jeremiah

Jon.	Jonah
Josh.	Joshua
Jud.	Judith
Judg.	Judges
Kgs.	Kings
KJV	King James Version (AV)
Lam.	Lamentations
Lev.	Leviticus
LXX	Septuagint, various Greek translations of the Hebrew scriptures made in the late pre-Christian centuries and first Christian centuries, used as the official version of the Bible by the early Church
Mal.	Malachi
Mic.	Micah
Nah.	Nahum
Neh.	Nehemiah
NJPS	New Jewish Publication Society translation of the Bible
Num.	Numbers
Obad.	Obadiah
P	Hypothetical written source of priestly (hence *P*) legal and narrative material in the Pentateuch, dated to just before, during, or after the Babylonian exile of Judah in the 6th c. B.C.E.
Prov.	Proverbs
Ps., Pss.	Psalm(s)
pt.	part
r	recto (folio), right-hand (leaf or page)
RSV	Revised Standard Version
RV	Revised Version
Sam.	Samuel
sig., sigs.	signature(s)
Song	Song of Songs
sq.	*sequens, sequentes*, following
Tob.	Tobit
v., vv.	verse(s)
v	verso (folio), left-hand (leaf or page)
Wisd.	Wisdom
Zech.	Zechariah
Zeph.	Zephaniah

Part 1
THE HEBREW BIBLE IN GENERAL

THE BIBLE

We find, then, that in the sacred oracles delivered by the prophet Moses, there are three separate characters; for a portion of them relates to the creation of the world, a portion is historical, and the third portion is legislative. Now the creation of the world is related throughout with exceeding beauty and in a manner admirably suited to the dignity of God, taking its beginning in the account of the creation of the heaven, and ending with that of the formation of man; the first of which things is the most perfect of all imperishable things, and the other of all corruptible and perishable things. And the Creator, connecting together immortal and mortal things at the creation, made the world, making what he had already created the dominant parts, and what he was about to create the subject parts.

The historical part is a record of the lives of different wicked and virtuous men, and of the rewards, and honours, and punishments set apart for each class in each generation.

The legislative part is sub-divided into two sections, one of which has a more general object proposed to it, laying down accordingly a few general comprehensive laws; the other part consists of special and particular ordinances. And the general heads of these special ordinances are ten, which are said not to have been delivered to the people by an interpreter, but to have been fashioned in the lofty region of the air, and to have been connected by a rational distinctness and utterance. While the others, I mean the particular and minute laws, were delivered by the prophet. [1st c.]

> Philo Judaeus. *The Works of Philo Judaeus.* Vol. III. Tr. from the Greek by C. D. Yonge (London, Henry C. Bohn, 1855), pp. 456–66

I must copy out a good part of the writings of David and Isaiah, if I would represent the poetical Excellencies of their Thoughts and Stile: Nor is the Language of the lesser Prophets, especially in some Paragraphs, much inferior to these.

Now while they paint human Nature in its various Forms and Circumstances, if their designing be so just and noble, their Disposition so artful, and their colouring so bright beyond the most fam'd human Writers, how much more must their Descriptions of God and Heaven exceed all that is possible to be said by a meaner Tongue? . . . How meanly do the best of the *Gentiles* talk and trifle upon this Subject, when brought into Comparison with Moses, whom Longinus himself, a *Gentile* Critic, cites as a Master of the sublime Stile, when he chose to use it? . . . [God's] Wonders of Providence for the Terror and Ruin of his Adversaries, and for the Succour of his Saints, is set before our Eyes in the Scripture with equal Magnificence, and as becomes Divinity. . . .

Nor did the blessed Spirit which animated these Writers forbid them the use of Visions, Dreams, the opening of Scenes dreadful and delightful, and the Introduction of Machines upon great occasions: The Divine License in this respect is admirable and surprizing, and the Images are often too bold and dangerous for an uninspir'd Writer to imitate.

> I. Watts. Preface to *Horae Lyricae*. 5th ed. corr. (London, Printed for John Clark and Richard Hett, 1727), pp. xi, xiv, xvi

No writers abound so much in passionate Exclamation, in that striking way of communicating sentiments, Interrogation, or in metaphors taken from sublime objects, and from action, of all others the most animated. Unincumbered by Critical manacles, they gave their imaginations an unlimited range, called absent objects before the sight, gave life to whole inanimate creation, and in every period, snatched the grace which is beyond the reach of art, and which, being the genuine offspring of elevated Genius, finds the shortest passage to the human soul. With all this license no writers have so few faulty passages. "But" says the Critic "they don't describe *exactly according* to *our rules*." True sir; and when you can convince me that *Homer* and *Virgil*, from whom you gather those rules, were sent into the world to give Laws to all other authors; when you can convince me that every beauty of fine writing is to be found, in its highest perfection, in their works, I will allow the beauties of the divine writers to be faults. 'Till that can be demonstrated, I must continue to admire the most shining instances of Genius, unparallell'd in force, or sublimity. . . . The account of Creation,—of *Eliezer* and *Rebekah*,—of the *Israelites'* passage thro' the Red sea—& of the Law given at Sinai— . . . of David and Jonathan— . . . Each of these is handled in a manner masterly and inimitable; each of these is treated with that peculiar simplicity, which is a grand characteristic of every species of inspired writing, & which affects the mind more than all the artful, studied flourishes of Rhetoric.

> Timothy Dwight. *A Dissertation on the History, Eloquence, and Poetry of the Bible* (New Haven, Conn., Printed by Thomas and Samuel Green, 1772), pp. 4–5, 9

For pathos of narrative; for the selections of incidents that go directly to the heart; for the picturesque of character and manner; the selection of circumstances that mark the individuality of persons; for copiousness, grandeur, and sublimity of imagery; for unanswerable cogency and closeness of reasoning; and for irresistible force of persuasion: no book in the world deserves to be so unceasingly studied, and so profoundly meditated upon as the Bible. [Sept., 1811]

> John Quincy Adams. *Letters to His Son on the Bible and Its Teachings* (Auburn, N.Y., Derby, Miller, 1849), pp. 118–19

A large part of the Old Testament is enthusiastically written in an exalted frame of mind and belongs to the realm of poetic art. . . . For example, let us recall the Book of Ruth, which has as its noble purpose the creation of decent, interesting ancestors for a king of Israel; at the same time it can be considered as the most charming little complete piece of writing that has been handed down to us in epic and idyllic form.

Let us then linger for a moment to consider the Song of Solomon, which has come down to us as the most tender and inimitable expression of love, passionate and full of grace. To be sure, we deplore the fact that the poems—fragmentary, jumbled, and in confused disorder—do not afford us a pure and full pleasure; and yet we are delighted in sensing ourselves transported into those conditions in which the poets lived. Throughout there is a gentle breeze blowing from the loveliest district of Canaan: a rustic, familiar setting, vineyards, gardens, the growing of spices, some urban restriction; but then, in the background a regal court with its splendors. The chief theme, however, remains the ardent affection of youthful hearts that seek, find, repel, and attract one another in various extremely simple situations.

Often we have thought of singling out some of the verses of this lovely confusion and arranging them in order, but it is precisely this puzzling, insoluble quality that gives these pages their charm and special character. How often have well-meaning, order-loving spirits been enticed into trying to find or to inject a reasonable coherence! But the very same task remains for the next person.

In just this way the Book of Ruth has already exercised its invincible charm upon many a worthy man, so that he succumbed to the illusion that the events described so laconically could gain to some degree by a detailed paraphrase.

And so, book for book, the Book of all Books would seem to prove that it has been given to us so that we may have our experience with it, as if it were another world, and lose ourselves in it, be enlightened and educated.

> Johann Wolfgang von Goethe. *West-östlicher Divan*, 1819, in *Goethe's Werke*. Vol. XXI (Vienna and Stuttgart, 1820), pp. 231–33†

What a book! Big and wide as the world, with its roots in the abysses of creation and towering up into the blue mysteries of the heavens. . . . Sunrise and sunset, promise and fulfillment, birth and death, the whole drama of mankind, everything is in this book. . . . It is the Book of Books, *biblia* [the Bible]. Jews should easily be consoled for having suffered the loss of Jerusalem and the Temple and the Ark of the Covenant and the golden utensils and Solomon's precious objects

. . . such a loss is trifling compared with the Bible, the indestructible treasure that they rescued. If I am not mistaken, it was Mohammed who named the Jews "the people of the Book," a name by which they are called to this very day in the Orient and one that is profoundly significant. A Book is their fatherland, their possessions, their sovereign, their fortune, and their misfortune. They live within the enclave whose boundaries are this Book; here they practice their inalienable civil rights; from here no one can drive them away, here no one can hold them in disdain, here they are strong and worthy of admiration. Absorbed in the reading of this Book, they noticed little of the changes that occurred around them in the real world; peoples sprang up and disappeared; nations rose up, flourished, and faded away; revolutions stormed across the surface of the earth. . . . They, however, the Jews, sat stooped over their Book and noticed nothing of time's wild chase that swept past above their heads! [Letter to Ludwig Börne, July 8, 1830]

> Heinrich Heine. *Sämtliche Werke*. Vol. VII. Ed. by Ernst Elster (Leipzig and Vienna, Bibliographisches Institut, 1890), p. 46†

In the Jewish "Old Testament," the book of divine justice, there are men, things, and sayings on such an immense scale, that Greek and Indian literature has nothing to compare with it. One stands with fear and reverence before those stupendous remains of what man was formerly, and one has sad thoughts about old Asia and its little out-pushed peninsula Europe, which would like, by all means, to figure before Asia as the "Progress of Mankind." . . .

The taste for the Old Testament is a touchstone with respect to "great" and "small"; perhaps [the cultured man of today] will find that the New Testament, the book of grace, still appeals more to his heart (there is much of the odour of the genuine, tender, stupid beadsman and petty soul in it). To have bound up this New Testament (a kind of *rococo* of taste in every respect) along with the Old Testament into one book, as the "Bible," as "The Book in Itself," is perhaps the greatest audacity and "sin against the Spirit" which literary Europe has upon its conscience. [1886]

> Friedrich Nietzsche. *Beyond Good and Evil*. Tr. by Helen Zimmern (New York, Macmillan, 1907), pp. 59–60

French critics, particularly those of the classical school, are wont to assert that in French literature the intellect, or reason, is supreme, other faculties being kept in strict subordination to this one. In Carlyle, on the other hand, we might say that the pure intellect is somewhat in abeyance; in much of Shelley's verse that both the intellect and the will are comparatively disregarded. With the Bible it is otherwise. Speaking broadly, it is pervaded at once by a rational element, a sensuous element, an imaginative element, and an animating or motive element. It is the union of these in due proportions which constitutes full and perfect naturalness, and such union we have in many parts of the Bible.

The Scriptures everywhere postulate intellect—or the absence of it; but only in a small minority of instances is it dealt with in what may be called the way of argument, or reasoning. There is no attempt to convert men from their errors by ratiocinative or philosophical processes. A right state of mind is denoted by such words as understanding, or wisdom. This is conceived as the direct gift of God, and connotes much besides clearness of intellectual vision. To the perfection of wisdom a right state of the will and affections is assumed as necessary, and thus we are led back to a consideration of human nature in its totality.

The presence of imagination in the Bible will need no proof. Who that has read the Psalms, or the Prophets, or the Apocalypse, can doubt it for a moment? And who will have any more hesitation in recognizing that the guidance of the will is perhaps the primary purpose which underlies history and precept, proverb, hymn, and vision of seer?

The sensuous element is perceptible in the metaphoric language and in the rhythm. However lofty or sublime be the sentiment, the diction is concrete, never abstract. Every chapter—with comparatively few exceptions—is a gallery of word-pictures; and it is this picturesqueness which makes the Bible always attractive and usually intelligible. To the great bulk of readers the abstract is identical with the dry, and but few persons could be won to a perusal, much less imitation, of the Bible, were it couched in the phraseology of an Aristotle. The picturesqueness of Scriptural language addresses the mind's eye; its simple, regular, natural harmony addresses the ear. Its harmony is simple, because it depends mainly on parallelism, or, as it has been called, antiphony; with this may be contrasted the intricate symphonic effects of a Pindaric ode, or of its most felicitous imitations in English, and, in prose, the now accelerated, now delayed and regressive footing of a prolonged Ciceronian period. It is regular, because the ear, when ever so little accustomed to it, knows just what to expect. The verses fall into a march-tune; their movement is disciplinary, first of the emotions, and through them of life and conduct. It is natural, because the emphatic syllable of the word—and this alike in Hebrew and English—coincides with the natural stress of the rhythm, and both with the pulse of the thought itself. In other words, that syllable which is fullest of meaning gets at the same time the rhythmical stroke within the word and within the verse. If this principle be compared with the quantitative laws of Latin and Greek—which apply to the harmonies of prose no less than to those of poetry—the difference will be apparent. Moreover, the balance of clauses is natural in another sense, in that their length coincides approximately with that of a single expiration of the breath. And this, as it is closely related with the pulse of the blood, with the beat of the heart, elucidates and justifies the remark of Dean Stanley in his *History of the Jewish Church* (2. 165): "'The rapid stroke as of alternate wings,' 'the heaving and sinking as of the troubled heart,' which have been beautifully described as the essence of the parallel structure of Hebrew verses, are exactly suited for the endless play of human feeling, and for the understanding of every age and nation."

Sensibility . . . has a large place assigned it in the Bible. Every emotion is comprised in the mighty gamut. Is it friendship? Behold the love of David for

Jonathan. Is it righteous anger? Consider the imprecations of the Psalmist. Is it exultation? Read over the Song of Deborah. Is it reverence, joy, hope, faith, grief, pity? Each one finds a tongue, and speaks the expressive language of the heart.

> Albert S. Cook. *The Bible and English Prose Style* (Boston, Heath, 1892), pp. xviii–xx

The Bible is full of both passion and sentiment, but it has no sentimentality. It is rather remarkable that there is, so far as I can remember, not one touch of false sentiment. In nearly all old books, the pathos that drew tears from contemporary readers often obtains either smiles or yawns from later generations; but the scenes of sentiment in the Bible are so deeply founded on human nature, that they impress the twentieth century with as much force as in the time when they were written. Four supreme instances, out of an uncountable number, may be given—illustrating the love of man to woman, the love of brother to brother, the love of man to man, and the grief of a father for a dead son.

And Jacob served seven years for Rachel; and they seemed unto him but a few days, for the love he had to her.

In the marvellous story of Joseph and his brethren, when Joseph saw the lad Benjamin, his own brother, the situation is enough to tax the power of the most consummate artist; but the simplicity and dignity of the Bible narrative leave nothing to add, change, or omit. . . .

When David was informed of the death of Saul and Jonathan, his lament for the latter is unsurpassed in literature as a tribute to the strength of men's friendships. . . .

When King David awaits the news of the decisive battle of the civil war, he has only one question for both messengers, *Is the young man Absalom safe?* Ahimaaz did not dare to tell the truth, when he saw where his master's interest centered; Cushi replied with matchless diplomatic tact, but to no avail. The king's passion of grief for his cruel son seemed merely an enigma to the two messengers, whilst to that seasoned fighting-hack, Joab, it seemed ridiculous and disgusting. But to us it is not only impressive beyond words, it reveals one of the qualities of the king that make us love him.

> William Lyon Phelps. *Reading the Bible* (New York, Macmillan, 1919), pp. 23–25

To begin with, we have in the Old Testament *an almost illimitable wealth of artistic stimulation.* It was one of the German classical writers who discovered the beauty of the Old Testament, and Goethe, who, like Bacon, "took all knowledge for his province," followed that discovery with sympathy and interest. In his notes to the *Westöstlichen Divan,* he writes: "When we recall the time when Herder and [Johann Gottfried] Eichhorn pointed this out to us, we are reminded of a great delight comparable to a veritable Oriental sunrise." In the Prologue to his greatest poem, Goethe had in mind the Prologue to the book of Job; and in the concluding act of the second part of the same poem, where angels and devils fight for Faust's soul, we have an echo of a Jewish legend, in which a similar fight takes place for the dead body of Moses, so that a brilliant writer of modern days has even called Moses both the prototype and antitype of Faust. Everyone knows also how devotedly Goethe from early youth read the Old Testament, how greedily he drank in Luther's glorious translation, and how, by making his own Luther's powerful Bible German, he invigorated the German literary language of his time, which had degenerated to insipidity. Our educated people, even our lovers of aesthetics, seem to have forgotten what living streams of poetical beauty are found in the Old Testament. Our pious people are wont to say that the Bible walks abroad in the guise of a slave, wearing the humble garments of a beggar. To be sure, by no means everything in the Old Testament is of equal aesthetic value; there is much in it that is, from this point of view, arid and desolate enough. But looking at it as a whole we may nevertheless say that the Old Testament wears no beggar's dress, but the royal robe that befits it.

In the first place, among the best known aesthetic creations of the Bible are those glorious *poetical narratives,* of marvellous insight and unique feeling for beauty of form, composed with truly classical sense of style, and therefore the delight of artists down through the ages and the theme of ever new creations, imitated again and again, in poetry and on canvas—narratives which bring the life of early days vividly before our eyes, a well of rejuvenescence for a civilization grown old, intelligible at sight to our children, beloved by them, and embodying for them lofty and eternal thoughts. Think of the force with which, in the Cain story, murder is set forth as the basal crime; the charm of the Joseph story, eloquent of fraternal envy and fraternal love, and full of faith in an overruling Providence; the attractiveness of the Ruth idyl, exhibiting a widow's love lasting beyond death and the grave; the magnificent solemnity of the Creation narrative; the wondrous story of Paradise, naïve yet profound. Old Testament Science has only begun to apply itself to the study of this aesthetic side of the narratives. One should imagine that philologists, historians of civilization, and all interested in aesthetics would vie with us in holding up to view these golden treasures, and that even our poets would study these ancient narratives and learn from them the secret of compact power, unity of construction, and graphic clearness. We hope this will ere long be the case. Meantime, however, we would say to teachers: Realize what valuable material you have in these narratives. How much poorer in poetical materials our schools would be if these were absent from them! Nay, it would mean ruin to our aesthetic civilization if adults, not having learned the Old Testament at school, should be unable to understand at once allusions to those Old Testament narratives which former times have bequeathed to us in lavish abundance.

Again, there are the prophets—many of them also poets of the first rank, using a language full of power and energy and majestic elevation—trumpets of God, uttering notes of such strength that our ears can hardly bear them, filled with overwhelming anger and overflowing with rapture, or at other times melting into pity, torn by grief and sorrow, and withal rising to defiant faith. Here, too, is a marvellously varied world—only partially, it is true, intelligible to our children—unlike any modern literature, but just because of its strangeness, its bizarre, rugged greatness, full of attractiveness to our older pupils. And in this poetical dress, which no one who has known it can ever forget, we have the highest thoughts of the human race; above all, the imperishable power of the Moral Idea.

Hermann Gunkel. *What Remains of the Old Testament, and Other Essays*. Tr. from the German by A. K. Dallas (New York, Macmillan, 1928), pp. 19–21

When we consider the earliest stages of Biblical literature, we are confronted by an amazing phenomenon. They do not give the impression of having an embryonic character, or of being literary first fruits; nor are there any signs of experimentation or of searching for the right path discernible in them. On the contrary, they present us with finished and perfected writings that bear witness to a well-established artistic tradition, as though they had been preceded by a centuries-old process of development. But Israel's history does not provide sufficient time for such development, since the beginning of Biblical literature coincides with the commencement of the life of the nation. How then can we explain this phenomenon?

At the first blush, it was possible to suppose that the Israelites learnt the techniques of literary art from what they found ready to hand among the great nations in whose midst they dwelt—the Egyptians on the one hand, and on the other, the Assyrians and Babylonians. It is a fact that the essential elements of poetry, such as the rhythm of the verse and the structure of the sentence, the principle of parallelism and its special rules, were common to all the peoples of the ancient East; and that even in prose the forms of rhetoric and the methods of expression were largely similar in all the literatures of these peoples. Hence it was feasible, on the face of it, to assume that there existed in antiquity a process not unlike that which obtained in the Middle Ages, when the Jewish poets learnt from their Arab neighbours the art of poetry in all its details—the rules of metre, the structure and arrangement of poems, the choice of themes and the use of traditional motifs, the embellishments and images of poesy—and before fifty years had passed from the time when "they began to twitter," as Judah Alharizi expressed it, they had already attained a very high degree of artistic perfection.

However, such a process may appear probable and reasonable only at the first glance. After profounder study we are forced to the conclusion that the matter could not possibly have evolved in this way. . . .

The correct way to solve the problem is to be found in the hypothesis that Biblical literature was but the continuation of the *antecedent Canaanite literature*. Just as Hebrew is only one of the dialects that grew from the ancient Canaanite stock, and just as it is the successor, with certain dialectical changes that arose through the ramification and evaluation of the various Canaanite dialects in the second millennium B.C.E., of the most ancient and most homogeneous Canaanite tongue, so Hebrew literature is a sequel to the Canaanite literary tradition, which had already taken shape among the Canaanite-speaking population before the rise of the people of Israel. . . .

It is clear why Biblical literature is already at a stage of artistic completeness when it first originates. Its rules of literary expression and its path among the Canaanite dialects were already firmly established in the past. Therefore our ancestors, when they first came to express their thoughts in literary form, did not have to fashion techniques of expression; these were quite ready to hand, and it was easy to use them in order to create a new literature, a literature new in truth, in its content and spirit, but a continuation of the old in its forms—new wine, so to speak, in an old flagon. [1942–43]

> Umberto Cassuto. *Biblical and Oriental Studies*. Vol. II. Tr. from the Hebrew by I. Abrahams (Jerusalem, Magnes Press, 1975), pp. 17–18

The Bible is unquestionably the most beautiful book in the world. Allow everything you please for the barbaric history in the Old Testament and the silly Little Bethel theology in the New, and there remains a series of poems so overwhelmingly voluptuous and disarming that no other literature, old or new, can offer a match for it. Nearly all of it comes from the Jews, and their making of it constitutes one of the most astounding phenomena in human history. Save for a small minority of superior individuals, nearly unanimously agnostic, there is not much in their character, as the modern world knows them, to suggest a genius for exalted thinking. . . .

Yet these same rude, unpopular and often unintelligent folk, from time almost immemorial, have been the chief dreamers of the Western world, and beyond all comparison its greatest poets. It was Jews who wrote the magnificent poems called the Psalms, the Song of Solomon, and the Books of Job and Ruth; it was Jews who set platitudes to deathless music in Proverbs; and it was Jews who gave us the Beatitudes, the Sermon on the Mount, the imcomparable ballad of the Christ Child, and the twelfth chapter of Romans. I incline to believe that the scene recounted in John 8:3–11, is the most poignant drama ever written in the world, as the Song of Solomon is unquestionably the most moving love song, and the Twenty-third Psalm the greatest of hymns. All these transcendent riches Christianity inherits from a little tribe of sedentary Bedouins, so obscure and unimportant that secular history scarcely knows them. No heritage of modern man is richer and none has made a more brilliant mark upon human thought, not even the legacy of the Greeks.

> H. L. Mencken. *Treatise on the Gods*. 2d ed. corrected and rewritten (New York, Knopf, 1946), pp. 286–87

We come back to where we started this section, then, to the Bible, the only form which unites the architectonics of Dante with the disintegration of Rabelais. From one point of view, the Bible presents an epic structure of unsurpassed range, consistency and completeness; from another, it presents a seamy side of bits and pieces which makes the *Tale of a Tub, Tristram Shandy,* and *Sartor Resartus* look as homogeneous as a cloudless sky. Some mystery is here which literary criticism might find it instructive to look into.

When we do look into it, we find that the sense of unified continuity is what the Bible has as a work of fiction, as a definitive myth extending over time and space, over invisible and visible orders of reality, and with a parabolic dramatic structure of which the five acts are creation, fall, exile, redemption, and restoration. The more we study this myth, the more its descriptive or sigmatic aspect seems to fall into the background. For most readers, myth, legend, historical reminiscence, and actual history are inseparable in the Bible; and even what is historical fact is not there because it is "true" but because it is mythically significant. The begats in Chronicles may be authentic history; the Book of Job is clearly an imaginative drama, but the Book of Job is more important. . . . The priority of myth to fact is religious as well as literary; in both contexts the significance of the flood story is in its imaginative status as an archetype, a status which no layer of mud on top of Sumeria will ever account for. . . .

At this point the analytic view of the Bible begins to come into focus as the thematic aspect of it. In proportion as the continuous fictional myth begins to look illusory, as the text breaks down into smaller and smaller fragments, it takes on the appearance of a sequence of epiphanies, a discontinuous but rightly ordered series of significant moments of apprehension or vision. The Bible may thus be examined from an aesthetic or Aristotelian point of view as a single form, as a story in which pity and terror, which in this context are the knowledge of good and evil, are raised and cast out. Or it may be examined from a Longinian point of view as a series of ecstatic moments or points of expanding apprehension — this approach is in fact the assumption on which every selection of a text for a sermon is based. Here we have a critical principle which we can take back to literature and apply to anything we like, a principle in which the "holism," as it has been called, of Coleridge and the discontinuous theories of Poe, Hulme, and Pound are reconciled. Yet the Bible is "more" than a work of literature, so perhaps the principle has a wider range of extension even than literature.

> Northrop Frye. *Anatomy of Criticism* (Princeton, N.J.,
> Princeton University Press, 1957), pp. 325–26

The nobility and eternal relevance of the Bible is heightened by its superb literary form. The Bible is a library of masterpieces written by men who are artists not for art's sake, a conception which they would not have favored had they known it, but for life's sake. They were impelled by a single purpose, to tell their message as directly and effectively as possible. With the sure instinct of genius, they utilized the literary techniques and forms of their day and developed them to perfection. Unbeknown to themselves, they produced a gallery of classics in which deceptive simplicity conceals the highest art.

Tolstoy has called the Joseph saga in Genesis the greatest narrative in the world, unrivaled for dramatic power and psychological finesse. Throughout the four books of the Torah in which Moses is the guiding spirit, no formal description of the great leader is to be met with, except for one brief passage where he is described as the "humblest of men" (Num. 12:3). Nonetheless, the character of Moses is one of the most vivid ever drawn. The trajectory of his career is traced through mounting trials and crises with an art as consummate as it is unconscious, an art that Boswell might well have envied but could not surpass.

Over and beyond the sheer perfection of its elements is the architectural structure of Genesis. The majestic opening verse, "In the beginning, God created the heaven and the earth," takes the cosmos as its background. Immediately thereafter, with characteristic Jewish realism, heaven is let alone and the narrative turns to the earth. Concerning itself with the human race, it traces the origin of mankind, its trials and sins culminating in the Flood, from which only Noah and his family survive (2–9). The offspring of two of his sons, Ham and Japhet, are briefly listed and dismissed (10:1–20), so that the descendants of Shem may be treated at greater length (10:21ff.; 11:10ff.) This serves as a preface to the career of Abraham, with whom the history of Israel begins (12–24). Of his two sons, Ishmael's descendants are briefly noted (25:12ff.), and the narrative concentrates on Isaac (25:19–27). He, too, has two sons, Esau whose stock is dismissed in one chapter (36), and Jacob, whose personal fortunes and family misfortunes become the fundamental theme of the rest of the book. The Joseph saga then prepares the way for the bondage in Egypt, the liberation by Moses and the giving of the Law at Sinai. With unsurpassed literary art, the Book of Genesis has thus linked Creation and Revelation.

The historian-author of Samuel has painted an unforgettable portrait in the life story of Saul, with its bright early promise and the cloud of mental instability and ruin later descending upon him. At least equally notable is the vivid narrative of David's life with its bright ascendancy, its glorious noonday and its tragic dusk. Surrounding these two principal figures stands an immortal gallery of human nature, Samuel and Jonathan, Michael and Bath-Sheba, Nathan and Solomon, Absalom and Barzillai. Ruth has been described as the most perfect short story ever written. Jonah has been justly called by [German Protestant Bible scholar] C. H. Cornill the "noblest book in the Old Testament." For sheer storytelling art, it belongs with the Elijah cycle and Esther. The memoirs of Nehemiah are a revealing picture of the period of the Restoration, with the problems strikingly similar to our own. Oratory has suffered in esteem in modern times, but the tenderness of Deuteronomy, the majesty of Isaiah, and the heartrending pathos of Jeremiah will never lose their power, because they speak from the heart and deep calls to deep.

The poetry of the Bible is perhaps its crowning glory. The moral fervor of the prophets, the passionate tenderness of the love lyrics in the Song of Songs, the grief of Lamentations, and all the human impulses reflected in the Book of Psalms have never been surpassed and rarely equaled. Faith and doubt, victory and defeat, hatred and doom, rebellion and submission, all find matchless expression in the Psalter, the world's most beloved songster. The nature poetry in Psalms (19 and 104) and the great God-speeches in Job have been acclaimed by figures as various as Herder and von Humboldt. The common sense of Proverbs will never cease to charm as well as to instruct young and old, while mature minds grappling with the mystery of life and the existence of evil will find both comradeship and comfort in Ecclesiastes and Job. The one was called by [Ernest] Renan "the most charming book ever written by a Jew." The other was pronounced by [Thomas] Carlyle "the grandest book ever written with pen."

> Robert Gordis. In *The Jews*. Vol. I. Ed. by Louis Finkelstein. 3rd ed. (New York, Harper, 1960), pp. 816–18

It is so easy to lose sight of the planning, the execution, the skill, the artistry, the tremendous fashioning of the Pentateuch. It is not so much the deeds of the Hebrews that are important, but the way in which these deeds are recorded in Scripture that makes them important. The recording becomes significant because the writers were men of utmost skill. Completely human, they had time to laugh, they had time to be outraged by violence, they had the foibles of occasional arrogance and parochialism and triumphalism, and yet they rose to set a standard and to establish criteria for ethical living that shaped civilization for good for hundreds, indeed thousands, of years. No event in Hebrew history is as important as the writing of the Pentateuch. It is worthwhile to master source analysis and tradition history and form criticism if only to see what a tremendous achievement is the writing of this book.

Chief in importance, however, is the literary conception itself. Respecting the latter, one cannot fault the Pentateuch. The inherent idea of tracing "history" is an exalted one. In execution, the characters are drawn with such fidelity to human beings that we are never at a loss to understand them. The stakes are high, never trivial. Sometimes incidents are a bit obscure, and sometimes we flounder in this or that tiny item, as, for example, the curious account of the circumcision of Moses' son in Exodus 4. Yet the over-riding skill is there. I sometimes wonder whether it is the holiness of the Pentateuch that has made it live as literature, and I suppose there is truth in that; yet I often think that it is the literary quality of the Pentateuch that has made it appeal to men as holy.

> Samuel Sandmel. *Judaism*. Fall, 1973, p. 467

[The Pentateuch's] significance as story is readily apparent. Time is its first, not its fourth, dimension. Commencing, not *in medias res*, not with the birth of a hero, nor *ab urbe condita* [from the founding of the city], but with unconditioned "beginning" (*reshit*) and moving through antediluvian lifetimes, through genealogical tables and patriarchal biographies, down to time-scales of forty years and of forty days and until the particular "this day" of Deuteronomy, the Pentateuch encompasses all time as a sequence that moves inexorably in one direction toward a single goal. And more than most stories, more even than most epics, the Pentateuch refuses to leave the goal unspecified or to allow it to be only gradually unveiled; in the Pentateuch the goal is explicit from the beginning in the promises that call for fulfilment. Especially if Genesis 12 is read as a recapitulation and redefinition of the primal intentions of God for man (land, descendants, a divine-human relationship), the Pentateuch gives its hand away at its very beginning—not, indeed, to foreshorten the enormous distance between Genesis 1 and Deuteronomy 34 or to dissipate the sense of movement, but precisely to signify that the reality it portrays, of relentless movement toward a goal, is the major significance this vast segment of human history holds. Most remarkably, from the standpoint of the nature of story, the Pentateuch's determined movement towards a goal is matched only by its failure to reach that goal. It has a beginning and a middle, but no end. True, the death of Moses provides a formal end for the Pentateuch, but this is no hero's death that rounds off the story, and this cannot be the end to which the Pentateuchal promises have been driving. How different the mood of Deuteronomy 34 is from the last lines, let us say, of *Samson Agonistes*:

> All is best, though we oft doubt,
> What th' unsearchable dispose
> Of highest wisdom brings about,
> And ever best found in the close . . .
> His servants he with new acquist
> Of true experience from this great event
> With peace and consolation hath dismiss'd,
> And calm of mind all passion spent.

For the Pentateuch, far from concluding with "all passion spent," presses beyond itself to a goal that lies still in the future even when its story is over. To the reader of conventionally structured narratives the Pentateuch's conclusion is frustrating. But therein a question about the reader's perception of reality or one's preferred shape of reality is posed: must one have stories that spend themselves in the telling, or can one live with a story that remains incomplete? That question about story may well be a question, or challenge, about life—and not merely about life in general, but about one's own life. The Pentateuch as story confronts us existentially, that is, with a probing of our own existence.

> David J. A. Clines. *The Theme of the Pentateuch*
> (Sheffield, England, JSOT Press, 1978), pp. 105–7

BIBLICAL AND OTHER LITERATURES COMPARED

There are not in all the world so eloquent Books as the Scriptures; and . . . nothing is more demonstrable, then [*sic*] that if we would take all those Figures, and Tropes, which are collected out of secular Poets, and Orators, we may give higher, and livelier examples, of every one of those Figures, out of the Scriptures, then out of all the Greek and Latine Poets, and Orators. [1640]

> John Donne. *Donne's Sermons*. Selected Passages with an Essay by Logan Pearsall Smith (Oxford, Clarendon Press, 1919), p. 28

[The Hebrews'] Phrases are certainly more ardent and intense than Those in any *Europaean* Language, and the Figures more bold and vehement. Tho' Their Poetry was less artificial, 'twas more nervous, lively, and expressive than ours. They have Nothing of the *Finesse*, Nothing that is over-wrought. This renders them so vivid, beautiful, and affecting.

In a Word, there seems to be the same Difference between the *Oriental* and *Europaean* Poetry, as between their Gardens and Plantations. Ours perhaps are disposed with greater Elegance, Order, and Regularity; but the inartificial Beauties, and agreeable Rudeness of Theirs, where Nature appears in all her Charms, and unsubdu'd by Art, give a wild, and perhaps more forcible, pleasure to the Mind.

> John Husbands. Preface to *A Miscellany of Poems by Several Hands* (Oxford, J. Husbands, 1731), sigs. f1ᵛ–f2ʳ

It is a curious spectacle to behold the competition of the two most ancient languages in the world, the languages in which Moses and Lycurgus published their laws, and David and Pindar chanted their hymns. The Hebrew, concise, energetic, with scarcely any inflexion in its verbs, expressing twenty shades of a thought by the mere apposition of a letter, proclaims the idiom of a people, who, by a remarkable combination, unite primitive simplicity with a profound knowledge of mankind.

The Greek, probably formed from the Hebrew (as may be reasonably conjectured from its roots and its ancient alphabet), displays in its intricate conjugations, in its endless inflexions, in its diffuse eloquence, a nation of an imitative and social genius; a nation elegant and vain, fond of melody and prodigal of words.

Would the Hebrew compose a verb? He needs but know the three radical letters which form the third person singular in the preterite. He then has at once all the tenses and all the moods, by introducing certain *servile* letters before, after or between those three radical letters.

The Greek meets with much greater embarrassments. He is obliged to consider the *characteristic*, the *termination*, the *augment*, and the *penultima* of certain *persons* in the *tenses* of the verbs; things the more difficult to be discovered, as the characteristic is lost, transposed or takes up an unknown letter, according to the very letter before which it happens to be placed. . . .

The simplicity of the Bible is more concise and more solemn; the simplicity of Homer more diffuse and more lively. The former is sententious and employs the same locutions to express new ideas. The latter is fond of expatiating, and often repeats in the same phrases what has been said before. . . .

The narrative of Homer is interrupted by digressions, harangues, descriptions of vessels, garments, arms and sceptres, by genealogies of men and things. Proper names are always surcharged with epithets; a hero seldom fails to be *divine*, *like the immortals*, or *honoured by the nations as a God*. A princess is sure to have *handsome arms*; her shape always resembles the *trunk of the palmtree of Delos*, and she owes her locks to *the youngest of the graces*.

The narrative of the Bible is rapid, without digression, without circumlocution; it is broken into short sentences, and the persons are named without flattery. These names are incessantly recurring, and the pronoun is scarcely ever used instead of them; a circumstance which, added to the frequent repetition of the conjunction *and*, indicates by this extraordinary simplicity, a society much nearer to the state of nature, than that sung by Homer. All the selfish passions are awakened in the characters of the Odyssey; whereas they are dormant in those of Genesis. . . .

The descriptions of Homer are prolix, whether they be of the pathetic or terrible character, melancholy or cheerful, energetic or sublime.

The Bible, in all its different species of descriptions, gives in general but one single trait; but this trait is striking and distinctly exhibits the object to our view. . . .

The comparisons of Homer are lengthened out by relative circumstances; they are little pictures hung round an edifice to refresh the eye fatigued with the elevation of the domes, by calling it to natural scenery and rural manners.

The comparisons of the Bible are almost all given in few words: a lion, a torrent, a storm, a conflagration, roars, falls, ravages, consumes. It is, however, no stranger to mere circumstantial similes, but then it adopts an oriental turn and suddenly personifies the object, as height in the cedar, &c. . . .

Finally, the sublime in Homer commonly arises from the general combination of the parts, and arrives by degrees at its acme.

In the Bible it is always unexpected; it bursts upon you like lightning, and you are left wounded by the thunderbolt, before you know how you were struck by it.

In Homer again, the sublime consists in the magnificence of the words harmonizing with that of the ideas.

In the Bible, on the contrary, the highest degree of sublimity always proceeds from a vast discordance between the majesty of the ideas, and of the littleness of the word that expresses it. [1802]

> François René de Chateaubriand. *The Beauties of Christianity*. Vol. II. Tr. by Frederic Shoberl (London, Printed for Henry Colburn, 1813), pt. 2, pp. 204, 207–9

The grand store-house of enthusiastic and meditative Imagination, of poetical, as contradistinguished from human and dramatic Imagination, is the prophetic and lyrical parts of the holy Scriptures, and the works of Milton, to which I cannot forbear to add those of Spenser. I select these writers in preference to those of ancient Greece and Rome because the anthropomorphitism [*sic*] of the Pagan religion subjected the minds of the greatest poets in those countries too much to the bondage of definite form; from which the Hebrews were preserved by their abhorrence of idolatry.

> William Wordsworth. Preface to *Poems* Vol. I. (London, Printed for Longman, Hurst, Rees, Orme, and Brown, 1815), pp. xxix–xxx

It cannot be necessary to say that from that memorable centre of intellectual activity have emanated the great models in art and literature, which, to Christendom, when recasting her mediaeval forms, became chiefly operative in controlling her luxuriance, and in other negative services, though not so powerful for positive impulse and inspiration. Greece was in fact *too* ebullient with intellectual activity—an activity too palestric, and purely human—so that the opposite pole of the mind, which points to the mysterious and the spiritual, was, in the agile Greek, too intensely a child of the earth, starved and palsied; whilst in the Hebrew, dull and inert intellectually, but in his spiritual organs awake and sublime, the case was precisely reversed. Yet, after all, the result was immeasurably in favor of the Hebrew. Speaking in the deep sincerities of the solitary and musing heart, which refuses to be duped by the whistling of names, we must say of the Greek that—*laudatur et alget* [he is praised but neglected]—he has won the admiration of the human race, he is numbered amongst the chief brilliancies of earth, but on the deeper and more abiding nature of man he has no hold. He will perish when any deluge of calamity overtakes the libraries of our planet, or if any great revolution of thought remoulds them, and will be remembered only as a generation of flowers is remembered; with the same tenderness of feeling, and with the same pathetic sense of a natural predestination to evanescence. Whereas the Hebrew, by introducing himself to the secret places of the human heart, and sitting there as incubator over the awful germs of the spiritualities that connect man with the unseen worlds, has perpetuated himself as a power in the human system: he is co-enduring with man's race, and careless of all revolutions in literature or in the composition of society. The very languages of these two races repeat the same expression of their intellectual differences, and of the differences in their missions. The Hebrew, meagre and sterile as regards the numerical wealth of its ideas, is infinite as regards their power; the Greek, on the other hand, rich as tropic forests, in the polymorphous life, the life of the dividing and distinguishing intellect, is weak only in the supreme region of thought. The Hebrew has scarcely any individuated words. As a Hebrew scholar if he has a word for a *ball* (as a tennis ball, *pila lusoria*); he says, "Oh yes." What is it then? Why he gives you the word for *globe*. Ask for *orb*, for *sphere*, &c., still you have the same answer; the individual circumstantiations are swallowed up in the generic outline. But the Greek has a felicitous parity of wealth in the abstract and the concrete. Even as *vocal* languages, the Hebrew and the Greek obey the same prevailing law of difference. The Hebrew is a sublime monochord, uttering vague vowel sounds as indistinct and shy as the breathings of an Aeolian harp when exposed to a fitful breeze. The Greek is more firmly articulated by consonants, and the succession of its syllables runs through a more extensive compass of sonorous variety than can be matched in any other known language.

Thomas De Quincey. *De Quincey's Writings*. Vol. XV
(Boston, Ticknor, Reed and Fields, 1854), pp. 166–67

It is worthy of note that Hebrew literature, its noble prophecies, its more spiritual Psalms, its blazing apocalyptic visions, its supreme words of comfort and hope, grew directly out of tragedy and disaster. In this it contrasts quite strongly with the literature of the Greeks, which was for the most part the fruitage of prosperity. Out of the victory of the Greeks over the Trojans came the songs of Homer; after the defeat of Persia came the brilliant day of Aeschylus, Sophocles, Euripides; in the fullness of Athens' glory Socrates questioned and Plato philosophized with a mind serene. Even Demosthenes spoke when there was a chance for victory; destruction was not inevitable.

More than any other literature in the world the Hebrew is the outgrowth of tragic experience. The fiercer the storm, the deeper it sent its roots downward to lay hold of the foundations of the world. The genial sunlight was not its inspiration. Poets and prophets wrote their great works down in the depths near the elemental flames.

Charles A. Dinsmore. *The English Bible as Literature*
(Boston, Houghton Mifflin, 1931), pp. 70-71

We hear much nowadays about Egyptian literature and Babylonian literature. Can anyone who reads those scanty, broken fragments, which are called "literature" because they are undoubtedly in writing, ever dream of putting them beside the contribution of the Hebrew race to real literature? Why the Hebrews reached this preeminence no one can possibly tell; it is part of the mystery of race and national endowment. But when all is said and the dust of learned controversy has cleared away there survive for us only two real literatures in the ancient Mediterranean world, those in Hebrew and in Greek. There may have been others; we know nothing of them; and the surviving records do not suggest that they need be considered. There is even an element of pathos in watching Assyriologists and Egyptologists gathering up the scraps of literature left by those most unliterary peoples and trying to make it rival the literature of the Hebrews. In a single one of the stories about David as told by these there is more of genuine literature than in all the Egyptian and Assyrian annals. . . .

Across the minds of the Hebrews there came the mystery of creative genius in words, and the things which they so created were of the kind that refuses to die. Songs of the emotion of a moment they may have been, but they still live in the fellowship of Homer and Pindar. Deborah and Barak sang of some obscure little victory in the plain of Esdraelon, but they did it in words that ring still in our ears and with pictures that are part of the literary inheritance of the human race. The Mother of Sisera still looks from her lattice and still asks her ladies her fatal question. She is as abiding as any tragic figure of Euripides or Aeschylus. Of which of the odes of victory of Egypt or Assyria can this be said? And when David laments for Jonathan, "O mountains in Gilboa!" we are carried down many centuries to Byron's heart-cry, "Hills of Annesley!"

Is it possible even now to rescue our Book of Genesis from the archeologists and claim it as the work of a great artist and philosopher? Cannot we read it with his eyes and mind who tried to make it an expression of what for him were the fundamental institutes of human life, of what were the psychological characteristics of the family which began his race and of how that race stood over against the non-Hebrew world? Can we trace out, following him, the varying philosophies of the Hebrew thinkers who were face to face with exactly the same problems as we ourselves, and not recognize in them the breathings and leadings of the one Spirit? We can see how different were their schemes of life and how varying were their methods of meeting life. But life was in every word that they wrote and their life was ours. The rough utilitarian philosophy of the Book of Proverbs is exactly reproduced in the crass moralizing and practical wisdom of Dorothy Dix, and its sententious sayings are not far removed from the wisecracks of our own homely moralists. And if Proverbs seems often to ignore the real facts of life, the Book of Job abundantly treats, from many viewpoints, the problem of unmerited suffering, and the Book of Ecclesiastes faces with a triumphant *élan vital* a horribly pessimistic faith. We know that Job as the mouthpiece of humanity, is on a higher level and nearer to us than Prometheus on his crag, and that Ecclesiastes preached a practical philosophy richer and nobler than that of any Stoic.

> Duncan B. MacDonald. *The Hebrew Literary Genius* (Princeton, N.J., Princeton University Press, 1933), pp. 218–19

Its chronicles are better reading than most of our fashionable histories, and less intentionally mendacious. In revolutionary invective and Utopian aspiration it cuts the ground from under the feet of Ruskin, Carlyle, and Karl Marx; and in epics of great leaders and great rascals it makes Homer seem superficial and Shakespear unbalanced. And its one great love poem is the only one that can satisfy a man who is really in love. Shelley's Epipsychidion is, in comparison, literary gas and gaiters. [1932]

> George Bernard Shaw. Preface to *The Adventures of the Black Girl in Her Search for God* (New York, Dodd, Mead, 1933), p. 67

The claim of the Old Testament stories to represent universal history, their insistent relation—a relation constantly redefined by conflicts—to a single and hidden God, who yet shows himself and who guides universal history by promise and exaction, gives these stories an entirely different perspective from any the

Homeric poems can possess. As a composition, the Old Testament is incomparably less unified than the Homeric poems, it is more obviously pieced together—but the various components all belong to one concept of universal history and its interpretation. If certain elements survived which did not immediately fit in, interpretation took care of them; and so the reader is at every moment aware of the universal religio-historical perspective which gives the individual stories their general meaning and purpose. The greater the separateness and horizontal disconnection of the stories and groups of stories in relation to one another, compared with the *Illiad* and the *Odyssey*, the stronger is their general vertical connection, which holds them all together and which is entirely lacking in Homer. Each of the great figures of the Old Testament, from Adam to the prophets, embodies a moment of this vertical connection. God chose and formed these men to the end of embodying his essence and will—yet choice and formation do not coincide, for the latter proceeds gradually, historically, during the earthly life of him upon whom the choice has fallen. How the process is accomplished, what terrible trials such a formation inflicts, can be seen from our story of Abraham's sacrifice. Herein lies the reason why the great figures of the Old Testament are so much more fully developed, so much more fraught with their own biographical past, so much more distinct as individuals, than are the Homeric heroes. Achilles and Odysseus are splendidly described in many well-ordered words, epithets cling to them, their emotions are constantly displayed in their words and deeds—but they have no development, and their life-histories are clearly set forth once and for all. So little are the Homeric heroes presented as developing or having developed, that most of them—Nestor, Agamemnon, Achilles—appear to be of an age fixed from the very first. Even Odysseus, in whose case the long lapse of time and the many events which occurred offer so much opportunity for biographical development, shows almost nothing of it. Odysseus on his return is exactly the same as he was when he left Ithaca two decades earlier. But what a road, what a fate, lie between the Jacob who cheated his father out of his blessing and the old man whose favorite son has been torn to pieces by a wild beast!—between David the harp player, persecuted by his lord's jealousy, and the old king, surrounded by violent intrigues, whom Abishag the Shunnamite warmed in his bed, and he knew her not! The old man, of whom we know how he has become what he is, is more of an individual than the young man; for it is only during the course of an eventful life that men are differentiated into full individuality; and it is this history of a personality which the Old Testament presents to us as the formation undergone by those whom God has chosen to be examples. Fraught with their development, sometimes even aged to the verge of dissolution, they show a distinct stamp of individuality entirely foreign to the Homeric heroes. Time can touch the latter only outwardly, and even that change is brought to our observation as little as possible; whereas the stern hand of God is ever upon the Old Testament figures; he has not only made them once and for all and chosen them, but he continues to work upon them, bends them and kneads them, and, without destroying them in essence, produces from them forms which their youth gave no grounds for anticipating. The objection that the biographical element of the Old Testament often springs from the combination of several legendary personages does not apply; for this combination is a part of the development of the text. And how much wider is the pendulum swing of their lives than that of the Homeric heroes! For they are bearers of the divine will, and yet they are fallible, subject to misfortune and humiliation—and in the midst of misfortune and in their humiliation their acts and words reveal the transcendent majesty of God. There is hardly one of them who does not, like Adam, undergo the deepest humiliation—and hardly one who is not deemed worthy of God's personal intervention and personal inspiration. Humiliation and elevation go far deeper and far higher than in Homer, and they belong basically together. The poor beggar Odysseus is only masquerading, but Adam is really cast down, Jacob really a refugee, Joseph really in the pit and then a slave to be bought and sold. But their greatness, rising out of humiliation, is almost superhuman and an image of God's greatness. The reader clearly feels how the extent of the pendulum's swing is connected with the intensity of the personal history—precisely the most extreme circumstances, in which we are immeasurably forsaken and in despair, or immeasurably joyous and exalted, give us, if we survive them, a personal stamp which is recognized as the product of a rich existence, a rich development. And very often, indeed generally, this element of development gives the Old Testament stories a historical character, even when the subject is purely legendary and traditional.

> Erich Auerbach. *Mimesis.* Tr. by Willard Trask (Princeton, N.J., Princeton University Press, 1953), pp. 16–18

This basic difference between ancient Hebrew literature and Greek, Persian or Arabic literatures is, first of all, due to sociological reasons. An elaborate and rigid system of prosody and composition in poetry develops where there is an idle or semi-idle class of men who have leisure enough to enjoy it. The Book of Esther tells us that the King of Persia made a feast for his princes and servants which lasted 180 days. This statement is not as grotesque as it sounds, for, according to the Persian epos, the nobleman's time was divided between "*rezm ubezm,*" war and feasts. However, when one has a great deal of time at one's disposal, one looks for some pleasant way of passing it. This is where the poet comes in. The poet, in his turn, having plenty of time for the display of his art, cannot always produce something original. He has to develop a fixed routine on which he can rely for producing mechanically rather lengthy pieces of poetry. Thus there develops a metre and a more or less stereotyped poetic style with expletives and stop-gaps—as in Homer. In the Persian epos we have the same thing: a lady could hardly make her appearance without having an adjective attached to her name to the effect that her arms were like silver, or that her face was like a moon—adjectives the poet also needed for filling up his verse as required by the metre.

In Israel there was no leisure class of any size or, if one did emerge, now and then, it was short lived. Most of the people were farmers who worked with their own hands or at least supervised personally the work of the younger members of the family, servants or seasonal laborers. "The sun rises" . . . says Psalm 104. . . . "Man goeth forth unto his work and to his labor until the evening" (22–23). Only on the holidays, the Sabbaths and possibly also during the long winter evenings was there leisure available for listening to poets and prophets. This largely explains why Biblical literature is so natural and straightforward: it is the creation of a working people, who, having little time to spare, waste no words.

This sociological aspect of Biblical literature also accounts, to a certain degree, for another of its most salient characteristics: its general human appeal. The Bible could be translated into hundreds of languages and brought to the remotest peoples because of the unique human touch which appeals to everyone. Most classical literatures are the creation of a class. We have already spoken of the Persian epos and its atmosphere of the Court and noblemen. Similarly, the Greek epos pictured the life of the petty kings and warriors of the Hellenic islands. The literature of Athens was the product of a bourgeoisie living largely on slave labor. The literature of Rome represented a certain upper class exploiting an empire. People of leisure who live at the expense of others can produce more abundantly and more exquisitely refined products than a nation of farmers. But a class is confined to certain limits of time and space. Its literature can be fully understood only by those who take the trouble to thoroughly study its peculiarities of life. The case is quite other with Israel's literature, which is that of an essentially classless people. Working people, leading a simple life, constitute the majority of mankind. That is why the literature of Israel, which is itself the creation of such a people, has had so wide an appeal.

S. D. Goitein. *Judaism*. Winter, 1954, p. 74

The heroes of the Old Testament were in a process of becoming, whereas the heroes of Greek narrative were in a state of being. Process in Greek narrative was confined to the action of a plot. And even so, the action exemplified unchanging, universal laws; while the agents of the action, the characters, became as the plot unfolded only more and more consistent ethical types. Abraham, Jacob, David, and Samson, on the other hand, are men whose personal development is the focus of interest.

Robert Scholes and Robert Kellogg. *The Nature of Narrative* (New York, Oxford University Press, 1966), p.123

LANGUAGE

It is a rule with those who speak the Holy Tongue that they will sometimes speak very explicitly and sometimes convey their intent through elliptical expressions, from which the listener must figure out the sense. Know: Words are like bodies and meanings are like souls, and the body is like a vessel for the soul. Accordingly, as a rule all scholars of language will attend to the general sense without concerning themselves with variations in words, since they are equivalent in meaning. Let me give you some examples. The Lord said to Cain: "Cursed may you be from the ground, for when you work the ground it will cease to give you its yield. A migrant and meanderer will you be on the land" (Gen. 4:11–12). Cain, however, said: "Look, you have expelled me today from the face of the land" (Gen. 4:14). Only someone who has no mind would think that the sense is not equivalent on account of a variation in the words. . . . The principle is: in every instance of variation, as in the dream of Pharaoh, [the dream] of Nebuchadnezzar, and of others, you will find different words, yet the sense is equivalent. [ca. 1150]

> Abraham ibn Ezra. *Miqra'ot gedolot* (Venice, Bomberg, 1524). No pagination [commentary on Exod. 20:1]†

So the language, that abounds in verbs, which present a vivid expression and picture of their objects, is a poetical language. The more too it has the power of forming its nouns into verbs, the more poetical it is. The noun always exhibits objects only as lifeless things, the verb gives them action, and this awakens feeling, for it is itself as it were animated with a living spirit. Recollect what [Gotthold Ephraim] Lessing has said of Homer, that in him all is bustle, motion, action, and that in this the life, the influence, the very essence of all poetry consists. Now with the Hebrew the verb is almost the whole of the language. In other words every thing lives and acts. The nouns are derived from verbs, and in a certain sense are still verbs. They are as it were living beings, extracted and moulded, while their radical source itself was in a state of living energy. Observe in modern languages, what an effect it has in poetry, when verbs and nouns are still nearly related, and one may be formed into the other. Think of the English, the German. The language, of which we are speaking, is an abyss of verbs, a sea of billows, where motion, action, rolls on without end. [1782]

> Johann Gottfried von Herder. *The Spirit of Hebrew Poetry*. Vol. I. Tr. by James Marsh (Burlington, Vt., Edward Smith, 1833), p. 29

Hebrew, in point of force and purity, seems at its height in Isaiah. It is most corrupt in Daniel, and not much less so in Ecclesiastes; which I cannot believe to have been actually composed by Solomon, but rather suppose to have been so attributed by the Jews, in their passion for ascribing all works of that sort to their *grand monarque*.

Hebrew is so simple, and its words are so few and near the roots, that it is impossible to keep up any adequate knowledge of it without constant application. The meanings of the words are chiefly traditional. . . . Brute animals have the vowel sounds; man only can utter consonants. It is natural, therefore, that the consonants should be marked first, as being the framework of the word; and no doubt a very simple living language might be written quite intelligibly to the natives without any vowel sounds marked at all. The words would be traditionally and conventionally recognized as in short hand—thus—*Gd crtd th Hvn nd th Rth.*

> Samuel Taylor Coleridge. *Specimens of the Table Talk* (London, John Murray, 1835), Vol. I, p. 56; Vol. II, pp. 246–47

And in spite of his turn for personification, his want of a clear boundary line between poetry and science, his inaptitude to express even abstract notions by other than highly concrete terms,—in spite of these scientific disadvantages, or rather, perhaps, because of them, because he had no talent for abstruse reasoning to lead him astray,—the spirit and tongue of Israel kept a propriety, a reserve, a sense of the inadequacy of language in conveying man's ideas of God, which contrast strongly with the licence of affirmation in our Western theology. "The high and holy One that inhabiteth eternity, whose name is holy" [Isa. 57:15], is far more proper and felicitous language than "the moral and intelligent Governor of the universe," just because it far less attempts to be precise, but keeps to the language of poetry and does not essay the language of science. As he had developed his idea of God from personal experience, Israel knew what we, who have developed our idea from his words about it, so often are ignorant of: that his words were but *thrown out* at a vast object of consciousness, which he could not fully grasp, and which he apprehended clearly by one point alone,—that it made for the great concern of life, *conduct.* . . .

The language of the Bible, then, is literary, not scientific language; language *thrown out* at an object of consciousness not fully grasped, which inspired emotion. Evidently, if the object be one not fully to be grasped, and one to inspire emotion, the language of figure and feeling will satisfy us better about it, will cover more of what we seek to express, than the language of literal fact and science, the language of science about it will be *below* what we feel to be the truth.

> Matthew Arnold. *Literature and Dogma* (London, Smith, Elder, 1873), pp. 38, 41

Hebrew may be called primarily a language of the senses. The words originally expressed concrete or material things and movements or actions which struck the senses or started the emotions. Only secondarily and in metaphor could they be used to denote abstract or metaphysical ideas. There is a prevalence in them of the harder, heavier consonants, including a greater variety of gutturals, than Western alphabets contain. Much use is made of the explosive letters, and the doubled consonant exerts its full value both for phonetic and grammatical reasons. Thus, though the liquids and softer gutturals also abound in the vocabulary, it is urgency more than beauty, emphasis more than melody, which strike the ear as characteristic of Hebrew. So far the language was suited to a people who first heard the voice of their God in thunder and tempest, who primitively were warriors and minstrels of war, excited to battle-cries, curses, and prayers for vengeance on their foes; and who were destined to become a people of prophets and enforcers of truth as well as of poets and singers. One remembers the summons to the prophet to *call with the throat*.

Few abstract terms exist in ancient Hebrew and no compound words. Abstraction and constructive power are almost as absent from the grammar and the syntax as from the vocabulary. That subordination of clause to clause in which the subtlety and flexibility of other languages appears is hardly found, but to the end, both in prose and verse, the clauses are almost invariably strung together by the bare copulas *and* and *then* in a co-ordination which requires both skill and spirit to redeem it from monotony.

Such were the means of expression afforded to the poets, prophets, and historians of Israel. What change they made in the vocabulary and grammar we are without enough material to trace. Signs of literary genius are rather to be traced in the growing deftness of their use of so defective an instrument, and in the high styles of verse and prose which they ultimately achieved with it. Up to at least the end of the exile their literature proves a growing fineness of ear and mastery of poetic form, with increasing power to mould so concrete and sensuous a dialect to the utterance both of the subtler thoughts of man and the sublimest truths about God.

> George A. Smith. In *The Legacy of Israel*. Ed. by Edwyn R. Bevan and Charles Singer (Oxford, Clarendon Press, 1927), pp. 10–11

An attempt to evaluate the impress left by the Bible on the mind of Western man would be equivalent to an analysis of our entire civilization. Less ambitious, but almost equally difficult, would be an examination of the Biblical influence, in translation, on the languages of the modern nations, and particularly on English. It is an extraordinary circumstance that a translation should have played the leading role in forming the style of writers whose names are synonymous with the highest achievement in literature, and this not by virtue of thematic material —which would be comprehensible enough in view of the unique importance of the contents of the Bible—but rather by virtue of the subtler effect of style.

The question rises at once to the mind: What are the qualities of that remarkable language which penetrates the heavy integument of translation to find its way into the manner of thought of so many peoples? And a second question rises with it: What is the secret of its amazing virility, and whence comes the resilience that enables this language to reassume, after many centuries, all the characteristics of youth—its freshness, its energy, and its youthfulness? To neither question do we find even the beginnings of an answer in the family history of the language in question. Its relatives of the Middle Semitic branch, the various Canaanite dialects—Phoenician, Punic, Moabite, Edomite, Ugaritic—have long been dead. From what we can reconstruct of them they seem to have been, even in their halcyon days, dull and unimaginative. The East Semitic branch, the

Assyrian-Babylonian cuneiform, makes a scarcely better impression. It is the language of the army, the countinghouse, and the lawcourt; it is boastful, efficient, and precise; but where it attempts to rise to the aesthetic and spiritual its posture is ungainly, its flight low. Aramaic, of the North Semitic branch, once dominated the commerce of the whole Near East and enjoyed great prestige. It added a few chapters to the Hebrew Bible and has left us several important translations of the whole and of various parts; it provided the Babylonian and Palestinian Jewish teachers with a convenient vehicle for Israel's law and folklore. And this is all. It showed more vitality than its cousins of the Middle and East branches; but it is expiring today unnoticed and unlamented in a degenerate dialect spoken by a few Jews and Christians in Mesopotamia and Kurdistan.

The only other virile surviving Semitic language is Arabic, a member of the South branch. But we shall not find in it the clue to the riddle of Hebrew. . . . Despite its abounding wealth and its high refinement, Arabic is deficient in energy. All its fire is contained in its flame, and even the flame flickers at times, as in the pages of the Koran. But the energy of Hebrew is not exhausted by the flame; a deeper source of heat and power lies in the foundations of the language, like the latent fires heaped in the bowels of the volcano.

The mystery of Hebrew deepens when we approach the technical side of its structure. "It is impossible to conceive anything more simple and unadorned" than the Hebrew language. Its grammatical resources are meager in the extreme. Etymologically it is no better off. It cannot boast of more than five hundred root words. Its vowel system is confined to three primary sounds, its verb to two tense forms. The formation of compounds, verbs or nouns, and the construction of rolling periods in such a medium is virtually impossible. The direct conquests of the Hebrew language, as distinguished from the indirect influence it has exerted through the translation of its supreme utterance, are nil. It never became the language of more than one people, and throughout the major part of its history, that people made Hebrew a sanctity walled off from the invigorating effects of secular usage. We are not even sure that the original pronunciation has been preserved correctly. The very name by which the language is now known, Ivrit, or Hebrew, is absent from the Bible, and remained unmentioned for fifteen hundred years after the records began.

Solomon Goldman. The Book of Books. (Philadelphia,
Jewish Publication Society of America, 1948), pp. 1–3

The Bible in Hebrew is far more a different thing from the Bible in any translation than the original Homer, say, is from the best of the translations of Homer, because the language in which it is written is more different from English than Greek is. To speak merely from the point of view of style, the writing of the earliest books is a good deal tighter and tougher—[Ernest] Renan calls it a twisted cable—than is easy to imitate with the relatively loose weave of English. It is also much more poetic, or, rather, perhaps—since the King James Version does partly take care of this with its seventeenth-century rhythms—poetic in a more primitive way. [Some passages are actually] in a kind of verse, and even the prose has a metrical basis. The first verse of Genesis, for instance, almost corresponds to a classical hexameter, and we soon feel we are reading an epic or a saga or something of the sort. The progress of the chronicle is interspersed with old prophecies and fragments of ballads that have evidently been handed down by word of mouth and that stand out from the background of the narrative by reason of their oracular obscurity and their "parallelistic" form. There are many plays on words and jingles that disappear in our solemn translations, and the language itself is extremely expressive, full of onomatopoetic effects. The word for "to laugh" is *tsakháq* ("kh" as in "Chekhov"), and thus Isaac is called Isaac (*Yitskháq*) because Sarah, in her delightful scene with God, cannot refrain from laughing when He tells her she shall yet bear a child; a light rain is called *matár*, a heavier downpour *géshem* (it was a *géshem* that caused the Deluge). The words for the emotions are likely to come from the physical states that accompany them. The verbs for "to love" and "to hate" are both based on heavy breathing: *aháv* and *ayáv*. Patience and impatience are rendered as the taking of long or short breaths.

The Hebrew language is also emphatic to a degree with which our language can hardly compete. The device for affirming something strongly is to repeat the important word, and God's warning to Adam that he will "dying, die," if he disobeys His orders, seems weakened in our vision—"thou shalt surely die"—as does Joseph's assertion that "stolen, I was stolen out of the land of the Hebrews" by "indeed I was stolen." Nor can we match the vehement expression of the violent Hebrew emotions. When Jehovah, about to invoke the Flood, has become disgusted with man, it is not adequate to say that the thoughts of man's heart were "only evil continually"; in the "*raq ra kol hayyóm*" of the text, we seem to hear the Creator actually spitting on his unworthy creation. "And Isaac trembled very exceedingly" is the rendering of the King James Version of the passage in which Isaac discovers that Jacob has deceived him, which falls short of "Isaac trembled mightily a great trembling," and in the next verse we read that Esau "cried mightily a great and bitter cry." This violence and vehemence of the Hebrews is implicit in the structure of the language itself. They did not conjugate their verbs for tenses, as the modern Western languages do, since our modern conception of time was something at which they had not yet arrived—a significant feature of the language that I want, in a later section of this article, to discuss by itself at length. What the Hebrews had instead of tenses were two fundamental conjugations for perfect and imperfect—that is, for action completed and action uncompleted. And both of these two "aspects" theoretically exist in seven variations for every verb (though actually the complete set is rare) that have nothing to do with time. The primary form of the verb is known as the "light" or simple form, and the second is the passive of this. [This seems plain sailing enough,] but what follow are three intensive forms—active, passive and reflexive—and two causatives—active and passive.

These verbs, which take little account of time, are the instruments, then, of a people who, at the period when this language was formed, must have been both passionate and energetic. It is not a question of *when* something happens, but whether the thing is completed or certain to be completed. There are special forms, the causatives, for getting things done: "I will multiply your descendants," "They made Joseph take off his coat." The intensives are unexpected to the non-Semitic reader, who has difficulty in getting the hang of them, but feels a dynamic element in the very bone of the language, and soon begins to find them fascinating. The translator of these strange verb forms, which double the middle consonant and vary the pattern of vowels, is obliged to resort to an adverb or a stronger verb. The intensive form of [one of] the word[s] for "to kill," the paradigm verb that the student learns, is given in the grammars as "kill brutally." So you have "break" and "break to pieces," "grow" and "grow luxuriantly." A curious example, which occurs in Genesis 24:21, illustrates the problems of translators. When the emissary of Abraham meets Rebecca at the well and watches her attentively in silence, to see whether she will behave in the way by which he has proposed to God that the wife appointed for Isaac may be made to reveal herself, a verb that means "to look at" is put in the intensive form. The old Revised Version made it "And the man looked steadfastly on her"; the new Revised Version has it "gazed at her"—the first of these, that is, adds an adverb, the second tries to find an appropriate verb, and the nuances conveyed are different.

> Edmund Wilson. *New Yorker*. May 15, 1954, pp. 130–32

In ancient Israel language possessed a primitive vitality that is relatively alien to the modern Western mind. The relation between sound and meaning was grasped with an immediacy and directness that are best understood by children and poets. The elemental situations in which words are spoken and heard are intuitively recognized. Exclamations, commands, direct address, dialogue, question and answer, the use of names, and climax—all reflect the functions which words perform in life. Much of the Old Testament has its origin in words that are spoken, rather than in written literature. Men participate in them and surrender themselves to them in an interior and responsible way. Words are alive. They have within them the power and vitality of the speaker, and they are transmitted to those who hear with ears attuned to their living sources. They tend to arrange themselves in all kinds of patterns. They succeed one another in series and thus produce a climactic effect. They balance each other in many different ways, whether as words or clauses or more extended units, and give rise to what is known as parallelism. They are repeated again and again in fresh contexts to give them emphasis and force. This attitude toward language was congenial to the production of poetic expression.

> James Muilenburg. *The Interpreter's Bible*. Vol. V (Nashville, Abingdon Press, 1956), p. 386

The efficacy of word and gesture springs from the fact that they are thought to contain in themselves the reality to which they give expression. For it is not the mind of man which creates the relationship between the token and the thing signified; this relationship pertains to the object, even when it seems to be a purely formal one, even when we can see nothing but a play on words: "What seest thou, Amos? And I said: A hook to draw down fruit (*qāyits*). And the Lord said to me: The end (*qēts*) is come upon my people Israel" (Am. 8:2). Similarly, in the Book of Jeremias, we read: "And the word of the Lord came to me, saying: What seest thou, Jeremias? And I said: I see a rod watching (a branch of almond blossom—*shāqēd*). And the Lord said to me: Thou hast seen well, for I will watch over (*shōqēd*) my word to perform it" (Jer. 1:11–12).

A comparison, therefore, will not appear to be merely the result of any author's poetic fancy; it forms part of the thing seen; everything springs from this objective reality which, at the first impact of sensation, compels recognition in the observer, to such an extent that Renan wrote: "What distinguishes the Semitic family is that the primitive close relationship between sensation and idea has always been maintained, that one of the two terms has never excluded the other, that, in a word, the process of idealization has never fully operated; so much so that, in each word, can be heard, as it were, an echo of the primitive sensations which determined the choice of the earliest appellations." [*Histoire générale et système comparé des langues sémitiques*, Paris, 1863, pp. 23–24]

Our biblical language, therefore, is inapt to serve a free, creative imagination; it is intended to express only things which have been actually experienced. This does not, of course, mean that it is never artificial, as when the sacred authors indulge too freely in clichés or exaggerate beyond measure accepted figures of speech. They do not, in fact, feel the need to be always creating a new expression, but are quite content to recall the image, for example, of a hidden lion as it lies in wait for its prey, or that of a starving bear, deprived of its cubs. In order to meet new situations, they will simply take up old themes, to which they will give unexpected proportions; thus the apocalypses will construct rambling edifices with borrowed materials; an examination of the detail of their background will, fundamentally, reveal nothing but simple, traditional images: storm, thunder, earthquake, darkened skies. This disjointedness is evidence of a lack, rather than an excess, of imagination. Thus, even when it is inflated, the language of the Bible remains close to concrete reality and never turns into a language of escape. It is created by a reality from which it is unable to break away and over which it claims to have control.

> Evode Beaucamp. *The Bible and the Universe* (London, Burns & Oates, 1963), pp. 151–52

The focus of the Biblical narrative is the recording of acts. The joining of one act to another is what imparts to the Biblical narrative its dramatic character. . . . In this, in the presentation of happenings, the authors of the Bible rely upon a linguistic feature unique to the Semitic languages.

We have already dealt with the limited descriptive vocabulary used by the Hebrew writers. We have noted the paucity of adjectives and especially of adverbs. This creates hardships for the modern Hebrew idiom, which has scuttled the condensed abbreviation characteristic of the Bible's style and has struggled for this reason with the relative poverty of modifiers in the Hebrew lexicon.

The dynamism in the Biblical story is achieved by means of the accentuated use of one part of speech, the verb. The Hebrew verb is distinguished in one respect: It can vary its nuances through relatively slight morphological changes. I am referring to the system of conjugations. By means of a change in vocalization (indicated by pointing), or by means of adding a letter, the transition from active to passive or from an intransitive to a transitive action is accomplished, or a one-time action is transformed into a recurring one. The very same verb can signify something and its opposite, for example: *hata'* ["he sinned"]—*hitte'* ["he rid of sin"]; *saqal* ["he stoned"]—*siqqel* ["he rid of stones"]; *sheresh* ["he uprooted"]—*hishrish* ["he rooted"]; and so forth. And at the same time the verb, the predicate of the sentence, expresses within it the subject, too. In only one word a grammatically and semantically complete sentence can be concentrated —*shamarti* ["I kept watch"];*'akhal* ["he ate"]; *yelekhu* ["they will go"]. This concentration becomes apparent when you translate a Hebrew sentence into one in a foreign language. The number of foreign words will of necessity exceed the Hebrew by thirty percent or more. Moreover, the Hebrew verb can subsume even the object, by means of which a complete transitive sentence can be expressed in only one word: *seqaluhu* ["they stoned him"]; *he'ekhiluhu* ["they fed him"]; etc. Again, by means of a formal alteration, which we call the "conversive *waw,*" it is possible to transfer an action from one tense to another: *yishmor* ["he will watch"]—*wayyishmor* ["he watched"]; "Joseph fell (*wayyippol*) on his father's face, and he wept (*wayyevk*), and he kissed (*wayyishaq*) him" (Gen. 50:1). . . . We may understand that these diverse possibilities, packed into the Hebrew verb, are what make it the part of speech given to transformation and developing various strategies.

Verbs can be adjoined with no space between them because the subject can be contained in the predicate. This is what endows the Biblical story with an air of dynamism, of activity, and of constant happening that is the inner secret of drama. In sentences like the one in which the actions of Esau are recorded—"He ate, he drank, he got up, and he went" (Gen. 25:34)—the aural impression is automatically translated into a visual impression. And the sensation of action and activity does not abate. In a similar fashion we receive a distinct visual impression from the action of Yael in murdering Sisera: "She struck Sisera, smashed his head, bashed and beat in his temple. Between her legs he bent and fell, he lay between her legs, he bent, he fell, where he bent over, he fell plundered" (Judg. 5:27). The words themselves and their combinations possess an overwhelming degree of motion, achieved by highlighting the verbs against a background of a minimum of other parts of speech, which is in this instance not even extreme.

The multiplication of verbs in speech and in described action in the biblical story produce an extra urgency in the described chain of events. The words of Ruth that consummate the argument between her and her mother-in-law seem to jump us ahead on the journey of the two women from Moab: "Ruth said, 'Do not implore me to abandon you and leave you; rather, where you go, I shall go, and where you lodge, I shall lodge, your people is my people, and your God my God; where you die, I shall die and be buried there'" (Ruth 1:16–17). Our feet are already standing in Bethlehem of Judah, their destination.

We find that even when the author is not taken with an unlimited conjoining of a verb to a second and a third (as in the actions of Esau and Yael), the verbs make up a substantial percentage of the words in the sentence. Thus in the binding of Isaac: "Abraham rose early in the morning, he saddled his ass, he took his two lads with him, and Isaac his son, he split wood for the offering, he got up, and he went to the place of which God had told him" (Gen. 22:3). Even in passages like this the number of verbs reaches about a quarter or a third of the words in the sentence.

> Shemaryahu Talmon. *Darkhei hassippur bammiqra'*. Ed. by Gavriel Gil (Jerusalem, Hebrew University, 1965), pp. 50–52†

Just because parataxis happens to be a mark of colloquial speech in many languages, it does not follow that it is a proof of naiveté when we find it in literary Hebrew. It is simply not true that the Hebrew speaker was unable to express logical connections. What is true is that Hebrew idiom prefers the paratactical style in which such connections are implicit and taken for granted.

The Hebrew word for "and" is the single letter waw added to the beginning of a word, phrase or sentence. Here is a set of waw-sentences literally translated, from which it may be seen that the logical connections (supplied in parentheses) are not very hard to detect:

Explicative:	Abel brought an offering from the firstborn of his flock, and (i.e.) their fat portions (Gen. 4:4).
Concessive:	You have said, "You shall have peace, and (although) the sword is at your throats" (Jer. 4:10).
Circumstantial:	I saw Adonai enthroned and (with) his train filling the temple (Isa. 6:1).
Causal:	Do not detain me and (since) the Lord has made my journey successful (Gen. 24:56).
Comparative:	(As) a door turns on its hinges and (so) a sluggard turns on his bed (Prov. 26:14).
Final:	Bring it to me and (so that) I may eat it (Gen. 27:4).
Conditional:	(If you) cherish her and (then) she will lift you high (Prov. 4:8). . . .

Anyone who habitually employs parataxis in expression will be sure to think paratactically as well. He will set two ideas side by side and allow the one to qualify the other without bothering to spell out in detail the relation between them. An excellent example is provided by the psalmist in his hymn on the eloquence of the celestial bodies.

"They have no speech or language, / their voice is not heard; / Their music goes out through all the earth, / their words reach to the end of the world" (Ps. 19:3–4). In the Age of Reason it took Joseph Addison eight lines to say [in "The Spacious Firmament on High"] what the psalmist had said more succinctly in four.

G. B. Caird. *The Language and Imagery of the Bible* (Philadelphia, Westminster Press, 1980), pp. 118–19

TRANSLATION

It has long been the practice of learned men to exercise their minds by rendering into Latin the works of Greek writers, and, what is more difficult, to translate the poems of illustrious authors though trammelled by the farther requirements of verse. . . .

It is hard to follow another man's lines and everywhere keep within bounds. It is an arduous task to preserve felicity and grace unimpaired in a translation. Some word has forcibly expressed a given thought; I have no word of my own to convey the meaning; and while I am seeking to satisfy the sense I may go a long way round and accomplish but a small distance of my journey. Then we must take into account the ins and outs of transposition, the variations in cases, the diversity of figures, and, lastly, the peculiar, and, so to speak, the native idiom of the language. A literal translation sounds absurd; if, on the other hand, I am obliged to change either the order or the words themselves, I shall appear to have forsaken the duty of a translator. . . .

How difficult the task is, the sacred records testify; for the old flavour is not preserved in the Greek version [of the Hebrew Bible] by the Seventy. It was this that stimulated Aquila, Symmachus, and Theodotion [who also translated the Hebrew Bible into Greek]; and the result of their labors was to impart a totally different character to one and the same work; one strove to give word for word, another the general meaning, while the third desired to avoid any great divergency from the ancients. A fifth, sixth, and seventh edition, though no one knows to what authors they are to be attributed, exhibit so pleasing a variety of their own that, in spite of their being anonymous, they have won an authoritative position. Hence, some go so far as to consider the sacred writings somewhat harsh and grating to the ear; which arises from the fact that the persons of whom I speak are not aware that the writings in question are a translation from the Hebrew, and therefore, looking at the surface not at the substance, they shudder at the squalid dress before they discover the fair body which the language clothes. In fact, what can be more musical than the Psalter? Like the writings of our own Flaccus [i.e., Horace] and the Grecian Pindar it now trips along in iambics, now flows in sonorous alcaics, now swells into sapphics, now marches in half-foot metre. What can be more lovely than the strains of Deuteronomy and Isaiah? What more grave than Solomon's words? What more finished than Job? All these, as [Flavius] Josephus and Origen [the church father] tell us, were composed in hexameters and pentameters, and so circulated amongst their own people. When we read these in Greek they have *some* meaning; when in Latin they are utterly incoherent. But if any one thinks that the grace of language does not suffer through translation, let him render Homer word for word into Latin. I will go farther and say that, if he will translate this author into the prose of his own language, the order of the words will seem ridiculous, and the most eloquent of poets almost dumb. [382]

> Saint Jerome. "Preface to the Chronicle of Eusebius." *A Select Library of Nicene and Post-Nicene Fathers of the Christian Church*. 2nd series, Vol. VI. Ed. by Philip Schaff and Henry Wace (New York, Christian Literature Co., 1893), pp. 483–84

The public translators had only in their view the rendering the *Hebrew* text as fully and close as they possibly could, without endeavouring at the smooth and polish'd expression that should give their words a numerousness, and an agreeable sound to the ear. By this means they have retain'd a much more valuable quality, that is, the sense, the spirit, the elevation, and the divine force of the original; whereas those gentlemen, who have attempted any part of the Old Testament in rhime, have either, by the natural effeminacy of those identical sounds which we call rhime, or by a pursuit of a smooth and flowing versification, or by expressing paraphrastically what is said simply in the original, lost the force and energy of the divine song, in the weak ornaments of modern poetry; at least, this I can say for my self, that I never found my soul touch'd by the best of these performances (even from [Abraham] *Cowley* himself down to this day) tho' it has been scarce able to support the violent emotions, and excessive transports raised by the common translation.

> Charles Gildon. *The Laws of Poetry* (London, Printed for W. Hinchliffe and J. Walthoe, 1721), p. 120.

It must indeed be admitted that many beauties of the sacred volume, and particularly its poetical beauties, have not been transmitted to us, from the difficulty which naturally exists in representing in a comparatively new language those forms of expression so peculiarly germane to the original, as to be incapable of transfusion. Besides, it is more than doubtful that the learned translators of the Bible now in use among us recognized all the poetical fragments existing in the Pentateuch; but although they treated these sublime compositions as mere prose, they have nevertheless frequently exhibited their beauties with singular felicity and admirable truth. The very circumstance of our authorized translation having been made by so many hands . . . naturally renders it the more complete; an assumption which will be confirmed by the following judicious remarks of Miles Coverdale in his translation of the Bible, bearing date 1535, and dedicated to King Henry the Eighth.

"Now, whereas the most famous interpreters of all geve sondrye judgmentes on the texte (so far as it is donne by the spiryte of knowledge in the Holye Gooste) methynke no man shoulde be offended thereat, for they referre theyr doynges in mekenes to the spiryte of trueth in the congregation of God: and sure I am that there commethe more knowledge and understondinge of the Scripture by their sondrye translacions, than by all the gloses of our sophisticall doctours. For that one interpreteth somthynge obscurely in one place, the same translateth another (or els he himselfe) more manifestly, by a more playne vocable of the same meaning, in another place."

This passage shows the liberal temper and unbiassed spirit of that truly great but ill-used man.

> John Hobart Caunter. *The Poetry of the Pentateuch.* Vol. I (London, E. Churton, 1839), pp. 434–35

Whoever wants to know, without understanding Hebrew, what the Old Testament is must read it in the Septuagint, the most accurate, most genuine and, at the same time, most beautiful of all translations; there it has an entirely different tone and color. The style of the Septuagint is for the most part both noble and naïve; there is nothing ecclesiastical about it and there is no trace of anything Christian. Compared with it, the Lutheran translation appears to be both vulgar and pious; it is also often inaccurate, at times intentionally, and throughout maintains a canonical and edifying tone. In [certain] passages . . . Luther has permitted himself some modifications that could be called falsifications. [1851]

> Arthur Schopenhauer. "Über Religion," in *Sämtliche Werke.* Vol. XI (Stuttgart, Cotta, 1897?), p. 41†

And the effect of Hebrew poetry can be preserved and transferred in a foreign language, as the effect of other great poetry cannot. The effect of Homer, the effect of Dante, is and must be in great measure lost in a translation, because their poetry is a poetry of metre, or of rhyme, or both; and the effect of these is not really transferrable. A man may make a good English poem with the matter and thoughts of Homer or Dante, may even try to reproduce their metre, or to reproduce their rhyme; but the metre and rhyme will be in truth his own, and the effect will be his, not the effect of Homer or Dante. Isaiah's, on the other hand, is a poetry, as is well known, of parallelism; it depends not on metre and rhyme, but on a balance of thought, conveyed by a corresponding balance of sentence; and the effect of this can be transferred to another language. Hebrew poetry has in addition the effect of assonance and other effects which cannot perhaps be transferred; but its main effect, its effect of parallelism of thought and sentence, can.

> Matthew Arnold. Introduction to *Isaiah of Jerusalem* in the Authorized English Version (London, Macmillan, 1883), pp. 4–5

A book could be written on the long series of concessions in matter of territory which verse has made to prose; but no sensible critic will allow these transfers to

prove that poetry has ceased to be rhythmic utterance. The most obvious transfer, of course, is translation; is not the English Bible as noble poetry, one asks,
as can be found in any time or clime? Mr. Theodore Watts is sure of the rhythmic
test until he faces the claims of this noblest prose. Yet surely what appeals to us
here is not poetry, but the genius of the English tongue at its greatest and best,
flinging its full strength upon a task which at the time lay close to the heart of the
English people. The Bible is not the masterpiece of our poetry, but of our prose;
it beats not only with the divine pulse of its original, but also with that immense
vitality and energy of English religious life in days when to many Englishmen
life and religion were identical. That does not make it poetry. One must not open
the gates of poetry to this or that passage of prose, and shut them, through whim
or shame, upon a thousand other passages. Let in that great chapter of Job, and
anon *Werther* is there, *Silas Marner*, *Tom Jones*,—we have marshalled this rout
already. No, if the Bible be poetry, it is because it is rhythmic utterance, not because it is sublime. That tremendous reach of emotion borne on the cadence of a
style majestic and clear, the voice of a solitary desolation crying to the desolation
of all mankind, the wail of an eternal and unanswered question—

> Wherefore is light given to him that is in misery,
> And life unto the bitter in soul? [Job 3:20]

—is not this a poem? It is almost certainly a poem in the original; it might be a
poem in English, provided the rhythm of the lines, printed as they now are, with
parallelism and cadence properly brought out, seemed to the reader to have a recurrent regularity which could take it into the sphere of rhythmic law; otherwise
it is prose, the prose of great literature, indeed, but prose. It must be granted,
too, that the latter view is preferable. As great literature, the book of Job belongs
with Dante, and Milton, and with a few passages, where Goethe touches the
higher levels, in *Faust*; but it is not poetry in the sense that Dante and Milton and
Goethe impress upon one when one reads their great passages. Longinus writes
on the sublime in literature, and he is within his rights when he puts Thucydides
and Homer and Moses upon one plane; but it is the plane of sublimity in thought
and phrase, and it is not the plane of poetry.

Francis B. Gummere. The Beginnings of Poetry (New
York, Macmillan, 1901), pp. 57–58

It is in the Scriptures alone that meaning has ceased to be the watershed for the
flow of language and the flow of revelation. Where the text, in its literalness and
without the mediation of meaning, belongs directly to the true language, to truth
or dogma, it is unreservedly translatable. No longer, however, is the translation
required for the sake of the text but because of the multitude of languages. Such
boundless trust vis-à-vis the text is demanded of the translation that, just as in
the original language and revelation must fuse without tension, so literalness and
freedom must unite without strain in the translation in the form of the interlinear
version. For to some degree all great writings, but the sacred to the highest de-

gree, contain their virtual translation between the lines. The interlinear version of the Scriptures is the prototype or ideal of all translation.

> Walter Benjamin. Foreword to Charles Baudelaire, *Tableaux parisiens*. German tr. with a foreword by W. Benjamin (Heidelberg, Richard Weissbach, 1923), p. xvii†

The Old Testament is a collection of Oriental books, Oriental in thought as well as in form. No translation can hope to be faithful and forcible unless it manages to preserve as much as possible of the Oriental flavour of the original texts, and yet there must be an effort to bring this far-off world nearer to the modern mind, an effort which may occasionally forbid the translator to be literal.

Again, several of the most characteristic Hebrew terms, religious, social, and psychological, have no English equivalent which exactly corresponds to their original meaning. Something is dropped as they are passed from Hebrew into English. Even the rhythm of the prose as well as of the verse cannot be carried over into our modern language without a certain amount of alteration, if the version is not to be pedantic. Furthermore, the habit of playing upon words, acrostics, euphemisms, paranomasia, and verbal tropes of this kind, baffles the translator, who may be reduced to the desperate expedient of suggesting within brackets (as, for example, at Genesis 3:20 and Micah 1:10, 11) the point of some allusion or piece of popular etymology.

One crucial instance of the difficulty offered by a Hebrew term lies in the prehistoric name given at the exodus by the Hebrews to their God. Strictly speaking, this ought to be rendered "Yahweh," which is familiar to modern readers in the erroneous form of "Jehovah." Were this version intended for students of the original, there would be no hesitation whatever in printing "Yahweh." But almost at the last moment I have decided with some reluctance to follow the practice of the French scholars and of Matthew Arnold (though not exactly for his reasons), who translate this name by "the Eternal," except in an enigmatic title like "the Lord of hosts." There is a distinct loss in this, I fully admit; to drop the racial, archaic term is to miss something of what it meant for the Hebrew nation. On the other hand, there is a certain gain, especially in a book of lyrics like the Psalter.

> James Moffatt. *The Holy Bible Containing the Old and New Testaments: A New Translation* (New York, George H. Doran, 1926), pp. xviii–xix

[Martin] Luther was able to translate the Bible because it is possible to reproduce in the German language the characteristic features of Hebrew as well as the Hebraisms in New Testament Greek: for instance, the coordinate rather than the subordinate construction of sentences. If he had wanted to translate the Bible into the language of his own publications that reveal him to be the thoroughly humanistically schooled master of language, the result would have been an [Emil F.] Kautzsch–[Karl H. von] Weizsäcker [19th-c. German scholarly Bible translation] or something even worse—but not the Luther Bible. He had the courage, however, to introduce into German the Hebrew sentence structure that even at that time for the educated German language consciousness was cyclopean; and in this way he created a work that outlasted the language consciousness of the period. To the realm of the German language of his time he added his conquest: the new province of Bible German that within the history of the German language could now have its own history; and therefore it was not simply swept along without resistance by the further development of the total body of the language, but, actively participating, impinged upon this development and in that way maintained itself in its own characteristic features. . . .

And Luther had to translate because the German people then needed this spiritual influx of an alien language. Of all books, the Bible is the one whose destiny it is to be translated, and consequently it is the one that was translated the earliest and the most frequently. What the meaning is of all translating, the coming of "that day," that is for the Bible, with its intermingling of narrative, challenge, and promise—unique in all literature—actually the ring that holds these elements together. Thus, the first appearance of a people in world history is marked by the moment when it translates the Bible and appropriates it for itself. This entrance into world history invariably also demands a sacrifice of ethnic isolation, a sacrifice reflected in the people's language as it undergoes the recasting necessarily linked with a translation of the Bible. For whereas translations of other works always touch upon only a part of life—for example, a translation of Shakespeare alludes only to the theater—a translation of the Bible reaches into all spheres of life: There is no "religious sphere." . . . The Reformation is the first German event that affected the outside world and never again vanished from it. Ever since then, German destiny has been interwoven with world destiny. Luther's act of translation designates this point in time.

Franz Rosenzweig. Afterword to his translation of Jehuda Halevi, *Fünfundneunzig Hymnen und Gedichte* (Berlin, Lambert Schneider, 1927), pp. 155–57†

The century during which the English translation slowly grew, was also a period of great spiritual stress. [William] Tyndale's heroic life ended in martyrdom; John Rogers died at the stake; none of the earlier translators counted their lives dear unto themselves. Translation and original alike came through the furnace, and those who first wrote and those who last rendered were inspired by an intensity of feeling which found inevitable expression, among other ways, in the very cadences of their speech. For the prose of the King James Version is not rhythmic without cause. We are dealing, as in the matter of the diction, with a development, and the very mould in which the familiar words are cast—the actual rhythms of the majestic English prose which we have just read—are what they are through influences active for centuries before the Jacobean translators were born.

One of those influences lay in the very nature of Hebrew poetry itself, the formative principle of which, as everybody knows, was what has been called "the rhythm of meaning"—a parallelism of thought, as well as of form, which was susceptible of infinite variety. "'The rapid stroke as of alternate wings,'" says Dean Stanley, in a well-known passage, "'the heaving and sinking as of the troubled heart,' which have been beautifully described as the essence of the parallel structure of Hebrew verse, are exactly suited for the endless play of human feeling, and for the understanding of every age and nation." And again, as in the case of the diction, we have to observe a peculiar circumstance. Poetic rhythms, as a rule, are incorrigibly untranslatable; the luckless fate of innumerable "translations in the metres of the original" bears eloquent witness to that mournful truth. But here was a rhythm dependent upon an inner impulse rather than upon external rule—ebbing and flowing, rising and falling with the fluctuations of thought or mood, and carrying, through its powerful beat, the impelling emotion into the reader's mind, to stir in turn the springs of rhythm there. The sixteenth- and seventeenth-century translators of the Bible were happily untroubled by pedantic theories of the technique of Hebrew verse; what they felt was this deep inner rhythm—this alternating surge of thought or feeling; and untrammelled by any attempt to reproduce with technical exactness its outward form, they responded to its inner spirit in a prose whose rhythms, so moulded, have a flexibility, a stateliness, a grand freedom, which even the original does not always share.

> J. L. Lowes. *Essays in Appreciation* (Boston, Houghton, Mifflin, 1936), pp. 26–27

A translation which renders every word and construction of the source, even with rectified verbal linkage, will still not sound anything like an original piece in the receptor language because it does not follow the stylistic habits of that language. It may be too paratactic, or too hypotactic, link sentences too much or too little, be too emphatic or too "flat," too rhetorical or too artless, too forthright in matters that are taboo in society, and so forth. . . . In the case of the Bible, the very dignity of the book made it at certain periods undesirable that it should sound like any other book in the language. Taste changes a great deal, partly as a function of translation activity (number and type of works translated). While today a lot of thought is given to ways of making Bible translations read like traditional native stories, and New Testaments are provided in simplified language, the British public steadfastly refuses to accept modernized versions instead of the archaic and hebraizing Authorized (King James) Version. The degree of acceptability expected from a translated work is thus a matter of fashion and literary practice of the moment. Thus it is also the main theme of the voluminous literature on literary translation, and that which lends direct interest to the history of translation as an art.

> Chaim Rabin. *Textus*. 6, 1968, pp. 11–12

[The King James Version's] language is not really that of the Jacobean scholars and churchmen who compiled it. It is slightly archaic, as if the editors had wished to give to Scripture a lofty strangeness. Yet at the same time, it was produced at that moment in which the English language lived in singular excellence and vitality. Where the editors of 1604–1611 chose to improve on their predecessors, they did so with the instrument of [Edmund] Spenser, [Richard] Hooker, [Philip] Sidney, [John] Florio, Shakespeare, [Ben] Jonson, [Francis] Bacon, and [John] Donne.

The King James is the only great thing in this world ever done by a committee. Divided into six panels—two at Westminster and two each at Oxford and Cambridge—some fifty linguists and divines collaborated on the final text. There were notables among them: Lancelot Andrewes, Richard Thomson (renowned both as linguist and drunkard), Thomas Holland, and Richard Brett, reputed to know Arabic, Hebrew, and Aramaic. There are many reasons for the supremacy of the AV: progress in the interpretation of the Hebrew and Greek meanings; the plurality of judgment brought to bear on every word; the tradition of previous English texts. Yet there is much about the King James that still seems wondrous. Countless times, one marvels at the felicity of phrase and the evenness of tone—the more striking in view of the number of editors involved. It is truly as if tongues of fire had spoken.

No other work has played a comparable role in determining the habits of feeling and imagination of the English-speaking world. None has done as much to ingrain in the English sensibility uses of speech which we feel to be, in some central way, native to the language. Wherever English prose has a natural excellence, whether in Swift or George Eliot or Lincoln, there sounds inside it the regal simplicity, the alternance of Anglo-Saxon and Latin, the graphic imagery and narrative pace of the King James.

> George Steiner. *Language and Silence* (New York, Atheneum, 1970), pp. 191–92

Because translation is not a surface phenomenon, it follows that linguistic devices such as puns and plays on words which depend heavily on surface similarities are not usually translatable. Once in a while there will be an appropriate corresponding possibility in the receptor language, but usually not. [Ellis E.] Pierce [*The Bible Translator*, 5 (1954), pp. 62–73] . . . tries his hand at some plays on words in the translation of Micah 1:10ff.:

> Tell it not in Telltown (Gath)
> In Weeptown (Bochim), weep.
> Grovel in dust in Dusttown (Beth le-Ophrah).

The effort reveals the otherwise unsuspected play on words, but there is nothing remotely "natural" about it for English, and the breaking or stretching of the English rules is not particularly effective. It is usually impossible to get a natural equivalent of surface structure phenomena.

The situation becomes worse when Pierce (and [James] Moffatt) add an imitation of the Hebrew alliteration in verses 11, 13:

> Fare forth naked, O fair ones of Fairtown (Shaphir). . . .
> Harness the horses, O habitants of Horsetown (Lachish).

There are times, of course, when surface forms in two languages do carry the same function, and so the source and the translation are somewhat similar in this respect. When the surface forms are successfully similar, however, it is because the deep structure can be realized effectively in such forms in both languages. This may be coincidence, or it may represent some fairly common pattern from language to language.

Moffatt (1922) translates some jingles in the book of Judges by restructuring as English jingles:

> If you hadn't used my heifer for your plough
> You wouldn't have guessed my riddle now. (Judg. 14:18)

> Our God has now put
> the foe in our hands,
> who wasted our lands
> and slew us in bands! (Judg. 16:24)

Moffatt did this because these are two of the rare instances of elaborate rhyme in the Hebrew verse of the Old Testament. . . . By the principles of dynamic equivalence translation the motive may have been wrong (matching rhyme with rhyme), but the effect was not too bad because the original function works out well with a jingle-like effect in English.

> William A. Smalley. *On Language, Culture, and Religion.* Ed. by Matthew Black and W. A. Smalley (The Hague, Mouton, 1974), p. 356

Obviously, one main reason for the "untranslatableness" of poetry is its formal qualities. It is more patterned than prose. And this form of pattern is typically of sounds: rhyme, rhythm, accent, alliteration, quantity, line length, stanza length, and so on. But the Hebrew poetry of the Old Testament is not typical in this way. Unquestionably there are some elements of sound pattern in Hebrew verse; most certainly, paronomasia, or wordplay of the punning sort. But on other matters of sound pattern, learned opinion is much divided. . . . There is no question at all, however, that the supreme operational formal principle is a system of parallelism, of lines, or members, or *stichoi* as they are variously called; and also of parallelism within the lines, and less conspicuously of groups of lines in related clusters, with chiasmus frequent both in small units and in large, sometimes with refrains, and often with an *inclusio,* or a return at the end to the beginning, marking what is sometimes called ring structure. . . .

It is true that there are some qualities of the Hebrew language other than poetic structure that tend to work for a high degree of congruence in translations. One is a strong tendency toward the concrete. The formulation of the Law is the extent, perhaps, of the Hebrew abstractive genius; Hebrew "Wisdom," as in other Near Eastern wisdom literatures, consists of discrete proverbs, in series. Israel was a poet, as [Matthew] Arnold says. And so he anthropomorphosized, and reified, and dealt in figures. Not for him the-force-not-ourselves-that-makes-for-righteousness, or the stream-of-tendency-by-which-all-things-seek-to-fulfill-the-law-of-their-being, but a burning bush, the voice from the whirlwind, a father, a shepherd, a pillar of fire, a fortress, a refiner's fire, the wielder of the plumb line, the winnower. [Eugene A.] Nida proposes that the Bible is accessible in translation because the culture it is based in is the most widespread type, both temporally and like other cultures geographically. I suppose one might agree: the various cultural phases—nomadic herdsman, slave, subsistence farmer—these are basic and widespread modes of life. But I think the point is that the Hebrew used these basics as metaphors for abstract things, and it is that which helps to keep the texts translatable and accessible. That—along with the device of self-glossing that the parallelism affords. [Psalm 24] gives us "He that hath clean hands and a pure heart"; the difficult abstraction of *pure heart* is unequivocally explained by the very accessible metaphor of *clean hands*. In ritual, literal hand-washing efficiently symbolizes spiritual cleansing. . . .

To sum up: these differences between Greek and Hebrew, which of course have been much explored and commented on, reveal the Hebrew as comparatively translatable—its short statements, its preponderance of simple nouns and verbs, its concreteness, its parataxis—all these things transfer comparatively easily into another language. . . .

What, then, of the formal element common to all these translations [English: King James Version, New English Bible, Book of Common Prayer; French: *La Bible de Jérusalem*; German: Luther's version; Latin: Jerome's version; Greek: *Septuagint exemplar vaticanum*; Hebrew: Hebrew Prayer Book] of Psalm 24. The sound patterns, obviously, are not transferable, language to language, except when there are actual repetitions within the poem itself—refrains, that is, and, of course, proper nouns. And yet the essential pattern prevails, the parallelisms that are the radical formal element of Hebrew verse. By these patterns, the poem refers back to itself, sets up expectations within itself, and resolves itself. Those who are familiar with traditional musical form will recognize a strong similarity here: repetitions with variations, paired phrases, refrains, da capos, resolutions, and tonality. But the remarkable thing is that although the form is "musical" the patterns are not of sound but of meaning. The sense unit coincides with the form unit, constitutes, in fact, the form unit. It is what Ernest Renan called a *rime des pensées*, a rhyme of thoughts, or a music of ideas. It all lends itself to music supremely well—witness a thousand psalm settings now in scores in Western music—and it is hard to imagine that it did not originally move to music, most probably dance as well. . . .

We are agreed, and have been for years, on the great beauty of these translated poems. They are, I think, somewhat neglected now by literary scholars, and yet their influence and importance are incalculably great. Secular culture loses when it leaves these great texts to the theologians. By means of their meta-phors and structures they extend our consciousness. While in Eastern culture there is the persistent idea that the most important things are unsayable, in West-ern culture I believe there is more of a sense of unlimited possibilities in poetry, just because these translated Hebrew poems have achieved the "impossible" so often.

Ruth apRoberts. PMLA. Oct., 1977, pp. 987–88, 997, 999, 1002

The Old and New Testaments are unremittingly physical in their articulation, like most other sane human narrations—action follows and is generally caused by sensory perception of some previous action. Failure to convey that reality is fail-ure to tell the story, failure to confront and recreate (in a language like English, equally capable of the reality) the embarrassing and demanding corporeality of the original.

It is a failure endemic to most contemporary translations. . . .

In Exodus 4 when Yahweh tells Moses to return to Egypt and demand his people's freedom from Pharaoh, Moses replies that he is not an appropriate mes-senger. Berry's literal translation is "O Lord, not a man of words [am] I, both from yesterday and from the third day, and since thy speaking unto thy servant; for heavy of mouth and heavy of tongue [am] I." But Yahweh insists, "And now go, and I will be with thy mouth, and will teach thee what thou shalt speak." King James preserves the physical claustrophobia implicit in the Hebrew image —"I will be with thy mouth"—and the Revised Standard follows. But Knox again violates both Hebrew and his Latin original (*ego ero in ore tuo*) by giving "I will speak with thy mouth"; and the New English collapses into its usual ex-planation and abstract commonness, "I will help your speech and tell you what to say."

What the abstractionists are saying is plain—"The original of course em-ployed its resources of limited vocabulary and primitive imagery to the limit, but what we must tell you is what they *meant* to say." In its fidelity not to what was meant but to what was actually seen and said (and *therefore* meant), the King James and its English predecessors achieved their triumph—for close study will show that the qualities of vision, narrative vigor, style, and rhythm which have made King James not only the most influential work in our literature but unshak-ably the Bible for three centuries of believers are not the product of supreme lit-erary skill in the translators or of the benevolent *Zeitgeist* of Elizabethan-Jaco-bean England but of loyalty to a simple principle. In the general assumption that almost every word of a narrative or lyric original may be transmuted, however mysteriously, into a close visual equivalent in the vernacular, the King James awarded itself an enduring distinction—a continuous poetry rooted in and blos-soming from our only means of knowledge: the human body and its fragile organs.

That is not to claim that the King James is any longer a satisfactory translation of the originals, as we now have them. The Hebrew and Greek texts available in seventeenth-century England were sadly inaccurate; and hundreds of matters (linguistic, rhythmic, historical) now comprehended or clarified were dark then—especially the Koiné Greek of the New Testament, so imperfectly understood by scholars trained in classical Greek and lacking the mass of papyrus and scroll unearthed in the nineteenth and twentieth centuries. The Revised Standard, in its redaction of King James, is the closest contemporary approach to a satisfactory conversion of the original in its own terms of bone and sinew, though in their moments of independence the translators reveal a middling command of plain English. An adequate attempt on the whole, in its range of genres and effects, would require the service not only of the linguists, textual critics, and theologians who labored on the Revised Standard, the New English, and the Jerusalem versions but of writers by nature and experience, men and women who would not attempt to apply an external beauty to originals which are often rough but who might catch the tones of ancient voices, their indelible copies of sightings of a power content to approach us in our human shape, the figure He honored enough to create.

Reynolds Price. *A Palpable God* (New York, Atheneum, 1978), pp. 53–55

The translation of the Hebrew Bible presents its own unique problems. . . . The tradition preserved in the Masoretic Text, abbreviated MT by scholars, is not . . . the only extant textual tradition of the Bible. The Dead Sea Scrolls, dating from the late third century B.C. to the first century A.D., preserve many readings which vary from the MT. The early translations of the Bible into Greek, Latin, Aramaic and Syriac, completed in the late centuries B.C. and the early centuries A.D., sometimes contain a text different from the MT. Sometimes early rabbinic midrashim (expositions of the Biblical text) quote Hebrew texts which also differ from the MT.

Although the MT is the earliest complete vocalized Hebrew text of the Bible, and it incorporates the efforts of Jewish scholars over the centuries to preserve the correct reading tradition of their sacred text, it does contain readings that are inaccurate. Sometimes, better readings are contained in the earlier Dead Sea Scrolls or in the ancient translations. This presents the Bible translator with a fundamental problem in every verse rendered—which text, the Masoretic Text, the Dead Sea Scroll text, or the text of an ancient translation, should serve as the basis for translations and interpretations?

Marc Brettler. *Biblical Archaeology Review*. Nov.– Dec., 1982, p. 63

A work of literary art is essentially an arrangement of words, as music comprises tones and silences and as sculpture comprises matter and space. If one loses the words, one loses the art, just as one loses the music if one loses the tones or the silences. But aside from a purist's devotion to words, there are two other founda-

tions supporting more literal translation. The one is stylistic. The meaning of a
biblical passage may hinge on the repetition of a word or an allusion. For example, in II Samuel 7 the word *bayit* "house" interweaves three themes: King David
had already established his kingship and was dwelling in a royal *house*; the Lord,
his god, was then dwelling in a tent-shrine, not in stable *house;* David will build
for the Lord a *house,* and the Lord will assure the enduring prosperity of David's
dynasty, which is expressed in Hebrew by *bayit* "house." The more literal rendering of the King James (or Authorized) Version (KJV) of 1611 translates *bayit*
consistently as "house" so that the literary device of verbal repetition reaches the
English reader. The more idiomatic rendering of the British New English Bible
(NEB) of 1970 translates *bayit* as "house" when it refers to the king's palace or
the future temple but as "family" when it refers to David's dynasty. The superidi-
omatic Today's English Version (TEV, entitled the *Good News Bible*) of the
American Bible Society (1976) renders *bayit* as "palace," "temple," and "dynasty" in its respective references, completely obliterating the thematic connections of the original. . . .

Meaning in literature entails tone, mood, attitude, feeling, the voice of a
speaker, not merely information. "Style," as an eighteenth-century French natu-
ralist put it, "is the man." In contemporary criticism the style is the art. It imparts
meaning to the whole by infusing the parts with thematic coherence. Psalm 19,
as [Michael] Fishbane has shown, develops the motif of *speaking* in each of its
three segments. The motif is introduced in the very first verse:

> The sky *relates* the glory of God,
> of the work of his hands the vault *tells*.

The TEV buries the motif in its "idiomatic" rendering:

> How clearly the sky *reveals* god's glory!
> How plainly it *shows* what he has done!

The inseparability of form and content informed above all the translation method
of Martin Buber and Franz Rosenzweig, who began to render the Hebrew Bible
into German in 1925, and it accounts in part for what at first blush has appeared
to many as a literal, word-for-word version. In their essays on Bible translation,
both Buber and Rosenzweig exploded the false division between content and
form.

That style constitutes an essential component of the text is nowhere more apparent than in repetitive patterns in which it is the fact and manner of repetition,
not the semantic content—which remains the same—that is the point. With
Gertrude Stein we may concede that "there is no such thing as repetition," for a
stimulus has a different effect each time it is presented. For example, a unique
pattern in biblical (and Ugaritic) prosody is the so-called "staircase," a three- (or
more) line figure in which the material of the first line is interrupted, then repeated and completed or extended in the second line. It is the suspense-produc-
ing interruption of the first line, in its position just prior to the repeated material,

that creates the effect. Consider the famous example in Psalm 92:10. The classic, more "literal" KJV renders:

> For lo, thine enemies, O LORD
> for lo, thine enemies shall perish;
> all the workers of iniquity shall be scattered.

The "idiomatic" versions of the NEB and TEV render:

> Thy foes will surely perish,
> all evildoers will be scattered.

> We know that your enemies will die,
> and all the wicked will be defeated.

They dissolve the pattern altogether.

A second basis supporting the literal mode of translation, in addition to the stylistic, is anthropological. Instead of telling us how we would say it, a literal translation tells us how they would say it. . . .

A more literal reproduction of imagery can often shed light on the realia of an alien society. Consider the following case, in which even the KJV simplifies, and blurs, the realia of the imagery in Lamentations 2:4a:

> He [the Lord] hath bent his bow like an enemy;
> he stood with his right hand as an adversary.

The Hebrew says *darakh qashto* "he stepped on his bow," which depicts the ancient technique of grasping the longbow with one's left hand, securing it at bottom with one's foot, and pulling the arrow back in the bowstring with one's right hand.

Edward L. Greenstein. Prooftexts. Jan., 1983, pp. 11–14

Part 2

LITERARY FEATURES

CHARACTER

How wonderfully beautiful is the delineation of the characters of the three patriarchs in Genesis! To be sure, if ever man could, without impropriety, be called,
or supposed to be, "the friend of God," Abraham was that man. We are not surprised that Abimelech and Ephron seem to reverence him so profoundly. He was
peaceful, because of his conscious relation to God; in other respects, he takes
fire, like an Arab sheikh, at the injuries suffered by Lot, and goes to war with the
combined kinglings immediately.

Isaac is, as it were, a faint shadow of his father Abraham. Born in possession
of the power and wealth which his father had acquired, he is always peaceful and
meditative; and it is curious to observe his timid and almost childish imitation of
Abraham's stratagem about his wife. Isaac does it beforehand, and without any
apparent necessity.

Jacob is a regular Jew, and practises all sorts of tricks and wiles, which according to our modern notions of honour, we cannot approve. But you will observe that all these tricks are confined to matters of prudential arrangement, to
worldly success and prosperity (for such, in fact, was the essence of the birthright); and I think we must not exact from men of an imperfectly civilized age the
same conduct as to mere temporal and bodily abstinence which we have a right to
demand from Christians. Jacob is always careful not to commit any violence; he
shudders at bloodshed. See his demeanour after the vengeance taken on the
Shechemites. He is the exact compound of the timidity and gentleness of Isaac,
and of the underhand craftiness of his mother Rebecca. No man could be a bad
man who loved as he loved Rachel. I dare say Laban thought none the worse of
Jacob for his plan of making the ewes bring forth ring-streaked lambs.

Samuel Taylor Coleridge. *Specimens of the Table Talk*
(New York, Harper, 1835), pp. 100–101

A comparison has often been made between the great trek of Abram across the
desert from Ur of the Chaldees to Palestine and the voyage of Aeneas and the
Trojans through the Mediterranean from Troy to Latium, and, therefore, between the Aeneid and this part of Genesis. But they have very little in common

and the treatment is essentially different. Virgil was possessed by the idea of the founding of the Roman State and his characters meant little to him; they were carried on upon a flood of destiny. But in this story of Abram the Hebrew subjectivity had full play and used what events there were to bring out the characters which were everything. And the psychological material in those characters every preacher knows, or used to know. Yet that material is not given to us directly. There are no characteristics of Abraham rehearsed to us in an anaysis of him; we are only told some stories about him and he stands there before us. So, and perhaps still more, Sarah stands and talks. Beside her we have the figure of Hagar —Arabia's mother—who does not talk; but we get her nevertheless, in her story of suffering and eternal pity. And there we see another strange thing in those stories—how the women stand out, separate and clear, Sarah, Rebekah, Rachel and all their kind and rivals besides. We hear much of the suppression and nonentity of oriental women from those who do not know either the East or their Bibles. These women are the equals of the men and, for better or for worse, are their rulers. And how distinct the men, too, are; take the three, Jacob, Esau, Laban. With what zest and interest this keen psychologist works each out. He does not take sides as the modern preacher does; he is an artist and likes them all equally well and knows them all from the inside out. He liked Rebekah and even Jacob as Thackeray liked Becky Sharpe and as Galsworthy liked all the multitude of figures in his *Forsyte Saga*. Just so this philosopher-artist balances and rounds all his characters. Consider that perfect bit of characterization not only personal but racial, pronounced by Isaac on Jacob and Esau. "By thy sword wilt thou live; yet thy brother wilt thou serve. And it will happen, when thou wanderest free, thou wilt break his yoke from thy neck." (Gen. 27:40.) So, to this day, if the nomad Arab enters the cultivated lands he is enslaved by his blood-kin and their different life. To save his soul he must return to his deserts and his wanderings; whatever the life there is it is a free life. That the philosopher had seen and knew. Consider, too that these men and women with whom he is thus impartially dealing are the founders of his race; the pilgrim fathers and mothers of a people that for him meant everything in the world. Yet his instinct as an artist will not permit him to idealize them; he takes them as the stories give them and simply makes plain of what manner they must have been. It is a family chronicle like the family annals in which Thackeray loved to work from Esmond down and like Thackeray, too, he knew well the persistence to type of the women of a family. It is with such novelists as Thackeray and Galsworthy of the older, direct type that his kinship lies, rather than with the more modern novel of psychological character analysis. Yet he is as subtle in his little touches as Henry James and a great deal clearer. And in it all the marvel is that he was able to produce such living men and women out of the given material of a folk-tale. Does this throw doubt on the historic reality of these people and their lives? Are they only like those vague pre-patriarchal figures—Adam and Eve, Cain and Abel, Noah and his descendants—out of which he drew the foundations of all human life? The very characterization shows that for him there was a difference; that these earlier figures were no such real persons, were, at best, types. Our "Adam" is not a proper name, but mankind in a single person, and our Eve is the Living One, only personified. But with Abram all that changes. The philosopher knew that Abram was an historic man and he treats him accordingly. Are we, then, only under the spell of his art when we feel that Abram and Sarah and all the rest lived lives, then and there, as true as those of David, Saul, and Jonathan? That is a hard question and is not really of the matter of this book. But if they were not real how explain the people who sprang from them and who felt sure about them? How explain, above all else, the evidently complete faith in them of their rehearser in these pages of Genesis? His own attitude was plainly that of the modern historian who tries to re-create, freely but truly, the figures of his history.

Duncan B. MacDonald. *The Hebrew Literary Genius* (Princeton, N.J., Princeton University Press, 1933), pp. 117–19

We repeatedly mention the "Biblical type"—what is it? Is it Abigail, when she speaks to David after sending the present, or Abraham when he prepares the wood to sacrifice his son Isaac? Is it a brutal and primitive character like Abimelech, or a human, gentle and tender character like Hannah? All these are Biblical types, not only because they are to be found in the Bible, but because to many of us they seem typical of the world of the Bible. Many other characters may be mentioned besides Hannah, Abimelech and Abigail, but which of them is more Biblical? Perhaps we had better speak, not of the Biblical character but of groups and types of Biblical heroes.

At the same time it should be remembered that the great heroes of the Bible are not completely presented through one particular situation. In one chapter we can learn all we need to know about Abimelech or Abigail, but after all these are only subsidiary heroes in the Bible. When we come to the principal, central heroes, we must consider them in their different aspects, and sometimes there is all the difference in the world between the various aspects of the one hero. You find the main lines of Abraham's character in the story of the binding of Isaac, but even this story does not completely exhaust his character. Is there a single story that gives us the whole of Jacob: the theft of the blessing or the night in Bethel, the flight from Laban's house or the confrontation with the angel? These stories, indeed, express widely different, almost opposed characteristics, and perhaps there is something both of Abraham and Abigail in Jacob. The individual stories bring out different characteristics, which save them from both monotony and naïveté; and when we pass on to the story-cycle we find variety of another kind, the variety that resides in one character.

Zvi Adar. *The Biblical Narrative* (Jerusalem, Department of Education and Culture, World Zionist Organization, 1959), pp. 52–53

In the Bible, character is commonly given and does not develop or exfoliate as it does in Shakespeare or the Greeks. We know Jacob, Esau, Samson, Abraham, Solomon, Joshua, Ruth, and others immediately, as they are introduced to us, and we grasp at once the strong, simple lines of their characters, usually shaped by ethical presuppositions. The exceptions, like Saul, David . . . and Moses, are among the most interesting personages in the book. . . . Usually the biblical figure, impressive though he may be, is linear, not in the round. If we compare women in the Bible with Helen, Andromache, Clytemnestra, and Electra, we must, I think, concede the superiority of the Greeks in the dynamics of character portrayal. The reason is clear: the writers of the Bible were not . . . essentially interested in persons, but in ethics, and the ethical equation is, if I may say so, linear, not geometrical as figure. Biblical personages do not speak in idiosyncratic terms as Homer's people do; they speak, in the main, for moral ends. Exceptions, of course, will occur to every one, but consider the converstations of Pharaoh with Moses and Aaron. His speech is without individual flavor because, since we know that God hardened his heart, he can speak only as an automaton. We do not overhear his speech to understand his psychology as in the case of Achilles or Odysseus; his utterances are simply part of the algebra of a providential situation. In general, I think, the motivation of biblical personages is less interesting than is the case with the Greeks because in most instances what they do is immediately inspired by God or, negatively, God-defying, and therefore they do not make their own decisions. Compare in this connection the complex revelations of Oedipus of the wrongs he has done with the simple parable of the vineyard by which Nathan convinces David that he is the murderer of Uriah. Since we have been previously informed through Nathan that the Lord has promised, "If he commit iniquity, I will chasten him . . . But my mercy shall not depart away from him, as I took it from Saul," [II Sam. 7:14–15] simple repentance serves, and David, twenty verses later, engenders Solomon upon the body of Bath-sheba, Uriah's wife. The agonized search for meaning and for reconciliation that distinguishes *Oedipus Rex* and informs *Oedipus at Colonnos* can have no part in this frame of reference.

Howard Mumford Jones. Five Essays on the Bible (New York, American Council of Learned Societies, 1960), pp. 57–58

The narrator does not customarily delineate his characters' personality traits: that is to say, he does not himself add to what is reflected or what is not reflected by the situations as they are given. Thus, for example, Isaac is given no definition at all outside the framework of the action itself. The narrator does not summarize his opinion of Esau in his own words. The same is true for Jacob and his adversary Laban. We are all convinced that Laban is crafty, but the text does not say so explicitly. Potiphar's wife was, we assume, a light-headed woman. Thus does the reader assess her. But no such thing is stated in the narrative.

This lack of sketching of the personalities of the characters in the plot drew the attention of people of the postbiblical periods, both earlier and later. Various authors found here material by which to distinguish themselves. They would endeavor to fill the gap that the first narrator left in his story. They would insinuate into the story their own ideas and the ideas of their age. Biblical personalities would take on a form and shed a form according to each interpreter's conception. Biblical characters were easily adapted to any perception because those who created them did not nail them down. Thus, an explicator can interpret the name "Laban the Aramaean" as "Laban the *Rammai*" [Deceiver]. And thus, Thomas Mann could present Potiphar's wife in his great book *Joseph and His Brothers* actually as a tragic figure. For this reason one generation will adore David as a tender and pleasant youth, singer of Israel's songs and composer of the psalms, but another generation will see in him the hero, the one who expanded Israel's borders. One will be impressed by Solomon the author of proverbs, wisest of men; in another's memory, his image will be fixed as the great organizer, the acute and clever builder of the state.

Only occasionally is one of the personalities delineated in his most salient features. Thus, for example, Ishmael is introduced as "a wild man, his hand on everyone, and everyone's hand on him" (Gen. 16:12). Up to this point, the narrator reveals his own opinion: from this point on he is silent. We find with Moses a handbreadth's disclosure that is accompanied by two handbreadths' obstruction: "And the man Moses was very humble" (Num. 12:3). No more than this will the author say about the central leader of the people of Israel for all ages, to the recording of whose activities most of the books of the Torah are devoted. We are not informed whether he was intemperate or gentle, patient or impetuous. You may get a hint one way or the other, but explicit words you will not hear.

Sometimes the definition of a fellow character will be placed in the mouth of one of the personalities in the story. Thus may we interpret the words of David to his army commanders, Joab and Abishai, after their assassination of Abner, son of Ner: "And I, today, am limp, though the anointed king, and these men, the sons of Zeruiah, are too tough for me. May the Lord pay back the doer of evil according to his evil!" (II Sam. 3:39). Nevertheless, instances of this sort are few. Normally a man will be known through his deeds. The figure of Esau has been shaped once and for all by the series of verbs, "He ate, he drank, he got up, and he went" (Gen. 25:34), which come to complement his own words, "Pray, let me gulp from this red, red stuff" [Gen. 25:30]. Our opinion of Laban has been fixed by the excitement aroused in him at the sight of the jewelry on his sister's arms (Gen. 24:30), a sight that motivates him to offer hospitality, suspect in its excess, to the man distributing these trinkets: "Laban ran outside to the man at the well. When he saw the nose-ring and the bracelets on his sister's arms, and when he heard the words of his sister Rebekah, saying 'Thus did the man say to me,' he approached the man, standing by the camels at the well. He said, 'Come, O blessed one of the Lord! Why are you standing outside when I have made room for you in my house, and a place for the camels.'" The character of Laban that is here delineated in the detail of his actions furnishes a nuance similar to that in the parallel episode of the reception of Jacob: "When Laban heard the report of Jacob the son of his sister, he ran to greet him, he embraced him, he hugged him, and he brought him to his house" (Gen. 29:13). We see here Laban putting up a front in the hope that this messenger from the house of Abraham is also loaded with valuables, as was his predecessor.

However, it does not suffice for the biblical narrator to characterize his heroes with only one trait. The personalities of the narrative are living personalities, in their virtues and in their deficiencies. They are not "types" embodying a well-defined form or a single central feature. The tangle of diverse emotions in a man's heart and his diverse, often contradictory qualities the author raises before our eyes when he ties the personalities of the narrative into relationships that keep changing with the world that surrounds them. The Jacob who steals his brother's blessing in stealth and at the same time seeks to rid himself of responsibility for his actions is revealed as a devoted lover in his relationship with Rachel: "Jacob worked for seven years for Rachel, and they were in his eyes like a few days since he loved her" (Gen. 29:20). And this man, who would not hesitate to exploit his father's blindness in order to deceive him, is himself a father full of love and compassion for his sons, Joseph and Benjamin. The same Joseph the braggart—dreamer of dreams, alert and clever—reveals an almost unexpected strong stance against the seductive Egyptian woman. In various life situations, which confront him with many diverse people, his personality is illuminated in varied, changing aspects.

> Shemaryahu Talmon. *Darkhei hassippur bammiqra'*.
> Ed. by Gavriel Gil (Jerusalem, Hebrew University, 1965), pp. 36–38†

The most intensely individual characters in the Bible are always put into vital relation with their communities as well as with their God, for the consistent patterns of Biblical characterization indicate that personalities can be firmly grounded only in these terms. Thus Moses is not called to a solitary communion with God, but rather to the freeing and establishment of his people. His relationships to God and to the community are of course distinct, but they are never dissociated, and when he claims as his own prerogative that power to work wonders which has been delegated to him by God, he is incapacitated from leading into the land of promise the people whom he had already freed. With David, the next great leader of Israel, the relationship to community and to God are similarly close, but David's great sin is in usurping the place of a man while Moses' was in usurping the powers of God. When David becomes infatuated with Uriah's wife, Bathsheba, he does not hesitate to have Uriah placed where he will be killed in battle, and he proceeds to marry the woman whose chastity he had already violated. By this infringement of human rights and human integrity, David is incapacitated from building the temple just as Moses had earlier been incapacitated from leading the people into Canaan.

Both Moses and David stand out among the most clearly delineated characters in human history and literature. In the Bible they are painted, as Oliver Cromwell wanted himself painted, "warts and all." But even more remarkable is the fact that in times when magic power and royal power were extravagantly honored, Moses was condemned for his misuse of the one and David for his abuse of the other. And these two men, we must remember, were the greatest heroes of Israel. The presentation of their faults and weaknesses and defeats is therefore all the more interesting, and it indicates from but another point of view the fact that in the Bible the real hero is not any man—no matter how heroic or noble—but rather the Lord God.

The development of the characterization of God as the protagonist of the Bible is cumulative. His character cannot be understood on the basis of any one book of the Bible, much less on the basis of an isolated verse or two. We see him first as the creator of the universe in the magnificent opening of Genesis, but here the universe is obviously only a backdrop against which the drama of man is to be played out. The initial panorama of humanity shows Everyman and Everywoman endowed with a harmonious existence in a garden, an existence which they can maintain by accepting the primacy of God. When they repudiate this primacy, chaos replaces harmony and they find themselves in a wilderness rather than a garden. God's first attempt to provide mankind with a good existence has failed, because man refused to accept it. The second attempt comes after the flood, and it too fails for essentially the same reason.

At this point God turns from attempting to create a righteous, harmonious, and peaceful order for all mankind, and begins to concentrate upon one race —the race of Abraham—and the Bible focuses upon the experience of this one people. The chosen people became a kind of laboratory school for the development of a conception of human personality and human society which may serve as a pattern to all of mankind. The dramatic movement then is this: a concern for all mankind is narrowed in focus—without losing its universal intent in the mind of God—to one segment of mankind, whose experiences and insights will later be used as a means of enlightening the entire human race as to the meaning and purpose of true humanity.

Roland M. Frye. Introduction to *The Reader's Bible*
(Princeton, N.J., Princeton University Press, 1979),
pp. xx–xxi

Four Women—Michal, Bathsheba, Abishag, and Abigail—have been presented here, and we have seen how differently they are characterized. Michal and Bathsheba in I Kings 1–2 are full-fledged characters in the modern sense. They are realistically portrayed; their emotions and motivations are either made explicit or are left to be discerned by the reader from hints provided in the narrative. We feel that we know them, understand them, and can, to a large extent, identify with them. Abigail, on the other hand, is much more of a type than an individual; she represents the perfect wife. Different from both the character and the type is what I have called the agent. Examples of agents are Bathsheba in II Samuel 11–12 and Abishag. Both of these women appear in the narrative as functions of the plot or as part of the setting. They are not important for themselves, and nothing of themselves, their feelings, etc., is revealed to the reader.

The reader cannot relate to them as people. They are there for the effect that they have on the plot or its characters. They are necessary for the plot, or serve to contrast with or provoke responses from the characters.

There is no real line separating these three types; the difference is a matter of the degree of characterization rather than the kind of characterization. One might think of them as points on a continuum: 1) the agent, about whom nothing is known except what is necessary for the plot; the agent is a function of the plot or part of the setting; 2) the type, who has a limited and stereotyped range of traits, and who represents the class of people with these traits; 3) the character, who has a broader range of traits (not all belonging to the same class of people), and about whom we know more than is necessary for the plot.

It is interesting to note that none of the characters analyzed here is really a main character in the broad sweep of the stories in Samuel and Kings. The main concern of all of the episodes is the king and the kingship, yet David is the dominant character only in II Samuel 11–12. In the Michal story in I Samuel 19 his role is secondary to Michal's; he is not even given any words to say. The scene does not shift away from Michal after David has exited, but remains focused on Michal and the encounter with her father. The same is true of the Abigail story, in which David is a supporting actor for the leading lady. Again, most of the action takes place at Abigail's home, in the absence of David. The scene shifts to David's location only when Abigail is there. In I Kings 1–2 David is barely alive. To be sure, it is his extreme condition that motivates the struggle for succession, and his word that confirms the winner, but he is hardly a main character in the narrative. It is Bathsheba who emerges as the main character even though the story is really not about her.

The result in all of these cases is an indirect presentation of David, in which various aspects of his character emerge naturally, outside of the glare of direct scrutiny. These episodes are then combined, in the mind of the reader, with the episodes in which David is the main character. D. M. Gunn has already shown how the David stories alternate between a presentation of the private man and the public figure, so that in the end family affairs and affairs of state are intermingled, each having an effect upon the other. What has not been observed is that there is also an alternation in the narratives between David as main character and David as subordinate character, and that these correspond roughly to the public and private domains. Furthermore, there is a correspondence between the public and private stages in David's life in terms of his responses to his wives:

| Michal | emotionally cold, but uses her to political advantage | *the cold, calculated gaining of power* |
| Abigail | eager but gentlemanly response | *self-assurance as a popular leader* |

| Bathsheba | lust, grasping what is not his | *desire to increase his holdings, expand his empire* |
| Abishag | impotence | *loss of control of the kingship* |

The David stories have been woven into a masterful narrative in which all facets of the hero's complex personality are allowed to emerge. This is accomplished by highlighting him at times, and by showing him in the reflection of lesser characters at other times. This shift in focus and in clarity of presentation produces a narrative which has depth, which is credible to the reader, and which never fails to engage his interest.

> Adele Berlin. *Poetics and Interpretation of Biblical Narrative* (Sheffield, England, Almond Press, 1983), pp. 31–33

INNER LIFE

Whereas in principle personal moods can be variegated without limit, the summarizing penetration (of the narrator into a character's interior) is concentrated in the Bible into a representation of a very limited number of conditions (experiences, processes), establishing what may be called the repertoire of basic feelings. Because the psychological repertoire is essentially constituted by statistical frequencies, one can argue, of course, about its composition and its precise boundaries. But there is no doubt that it is limited, and there is also no doubt that at its center are the areas of feeling of love, hate, fear, anger, discovery, and recognition—omitting, for example, admiration, shame, ambition—among which most of the above-cited summaries are distributed.

In and of itself, the limitedness of the psychological repertoire can point up concentration of interest in certain areas of the interior world at the expense of others, more than paucity of interest in the interior world in general. On the contrary, the history of literature teaches of the frequency of such repertoires without any connection to the status of the psyche, of their significance in the comparative definition of various poetics, and of differences in their arrangement and hierarchical organization corresponding to changes at the core of interior concern—as in the transition from Homeric epic to ancient written literature, from the romance to the novel, or from the classical novel to the modern one. Only in the Bible the effect of condensing (in breadth) the psychological repertoire per se is joined by the flattening (in depth) effect of the linguistic repertoire. Every one of the feelings or basic areas of feeling is indicated for the most part by means of a fixed penetration formula: for example, "he loved" for loving, "he dreaded" for fear, "his wrath burned" for anger, "he knew" or "he saw" for recognition. These feelings are transmitted in miniature form, forced into structural procrustean beds, undergoing deconcretizations, repesented by a minus sign to indicate the empty part of the cup of consciousness. Yet, it is as though all these were not enough—and all the features are apt to appear at one and the same time: "And the people did not know that Jonathan went" (I Sam. 14:4)—for with respect to lexical-linguistic form, still attached to them is this or that predetermined marker from the small stock of formulaic markers. . . .

Laying bare the basic feelings and experiences of the Biblical world (love, hate, anger, fear) is customarily organized in pairs—and sometimes, in principle, also in triads—graded on a clear ladder of potency. In every such opposition the number that is undistinguished per se is the standard or the stylized minimum while the member distinguished per se by the potency of feeling is characterized by the addition of reinforcers, in the form predicate + adjective and/or adverb, chiefly "very much" [me'od]. A regularization of compositional structure is thereby created:

(31a)   [All the people] came to Egypt for they dreaded the Chaldeans (II Kgs. 25:26)

(31b)   All the people very much dreaded the Lord and Samuel (I Sam. 12:18)

(31c)   They very very much dreaded [Jehu] and said (II Kgs. 10:4)

The structure of gradation of reinforcers is a very delicate and sophisticated instrument in that the thing is seen from a first glance. The discriminating use of reinforcers, aside from the nuancing in it, refers of course to a feeling more potent than the usual or expected. But this does not mean that the gradation is absolute—for every such discriminating penetration automatically indicates a greater potency than any undiscriminated penetration of the same area of feeling. For example, it is likely that the trembling of Isaac that reveals the theft of the birthright from his beloved son was truly more awesome than the trembling of the Israelites upon hearing the thunder and lightning at Mount Sinai, or that the House of Ahab's fear of Jehu surpassed the people's fear of the Chaldeans; and in light of the fact that there is revealed in these gradations a double linguistic reinforcer, and hence an extraordinary extreme ("very much great," "they very very much dreaded"), it is perhaps reasonable to assume so. But it is not only that this sort of conclusion is uncertain, on account of the many contextual variables they possess for fortifying the weak and deepening the visibly flat, it is not especially interesting, because there is neither a basis nor an intention for making such a specific comparison. Even when the comparison lays bare distinct calibrators of gradation in some passage, their meaning is liable to be less psychological than stylistic and compositional.

The Book of Jonah, for example, tends to run in largeness of all sizes. So it is in its exterior descriptions ("Nineveh, the big city," "a big wind," "a big storm," "a big fish") and in its interior descriptions ("The men dreaded a big dread," "Jonah was upset a big upset," "Jonah enjoyed over the gourd a big joy"). But from here to the conclusion that this is the Dostoevsky of the Bible is still a great distance: the scale of choices on the first gradation of reinforcement can instruct us in the characteristic narrative patterns of the Book of Jonah . . . more than in the behavorial patterns of its characters.

Meir Sternberg. Ha-sifrut. Dec., 1979, pp. 119–20†

The argument has occasionally been made that the biblical narrator is wont to describe the inner life of the characters not directly but by means of their actions and dialogue, and that the reader must infer the inward situation from the outward behavior. It is correct that this is the narrator's tack in most instances, but . . . in not a few instances the narrator penetrates directly into the psyche of the characters and delineates explicitly their thoughts and feelings, their aspirations and motivations. . . .

The most unequivocal evidence of the unlimited knowledge of the narrator is certainly in what he relates about God. The narrator pretends to know the Lord's feelings, thoughts, intentions, attitudes, and judgment:

> The Lord was sorry that he made the human in the land, and he was pained at the heart (Gen. 6:6).
>
> But Noah found favor in the Lord's eyes (Gen. 6:8).
>
> God saw the Israelites, and God cared (Exod. 2:25)
>
> The Lord was enraged against Moses (Exod. 4:14).
>
> The thing that David did was bad in the Lord's eyes (II Sam. 11:27).
>
> And the Lord commanded to confound the good advice of Ahitophel so that the Lord could bring Absalom to harm (II Sam. 17: 14). . . .

As was explained, the narrator's penetration into the psyche of the protagonists is neither a rare phenomenon nor in the least exceptional. Nevertheless, it cannot be overlooked that all the inward views indicate concisely and quintessentially a specific psychic state and do not describe the genesis of this state. The psychic life of the characters is not made into a theme unto itself, and the narrator hardly ever conveys to us directly the process that goes on within the characters' psyche; in vain would we search the Bible's stories for direct descriptions of internal deliberation, psychic struggle, inner grappling and wrestling. The narrator suffices with quick and hurried glances and from time to time informs us of the situation at that moment in the psyche of the characters.

Shimeon Bar-Efrat. Ha'itsuv ha'omanuti shel hassippur bammiqra' (Tel Aviv, Sifriat Poalim, 1979), pp. 48–50, 52†

The inner life of Joseph, in the first part of the story of Joseph and his brothers, is steeped in mistiness. We have no data of the nature of his feelings toward his brothers in his dreams, of what dismay he felt when he was thrown into the pit. However, the fact that the narrator could examine the recesses of his heart in later scenes of the story indicates that the initial reticence was intentional, to achieve some didactic, artistic goal.

Already when Joseph's brothers come to bow down to him, the narrator first reveals the inner state of Joseph, who recognizes his brothers yet "acted the stranger to them and spoke to them harshly" ([Gen.] 42:7). And in ironic opposition to the theatrical scene of the brothers bowing down to him, the narrator descends to draw from the wellsprings of Joseph's heart that "Joseph recalled the dreams which he dreamt of them" (42:9), an assessment that only an all-knowing narrator, descending into the secret soul of his characters, has the authority to describe.

The opposing stances between Joseph and his brothers warrant again and again a baring of inner states. Joseph's compassion toward his brother Benjamin was heated up, and he wanted to cry. He therefore hurried into his chamber to cry there (43:30). Afterward, Joseph washes his face and this time succeeds at stifling himself when he goes out (ibid.:31).

Which is not so of the stance described after the tense speech of Judah. This time the narrator first reveals that "Joseph could stifle himself before all those attending him" (45:1).

The selectivity in the degree of baring matters of the soul becomes evident to us as the product of the author-narrator's intention by the fact that while in the first scene of confrontation in the story, between the brothers and Joseph, which takes place in the land of Canaan, the inner state of Joseph is steeped in mistiness, in the scenes of confrontation on the soil of Egypt it is the inner world of the brothers that remains in a covering of mist. Only after the flurry of getting reacquainted does the narrator find it proper to reveal that "his brothers could not speak to him, for they shuddered before him" (45:3).

Naftali Tucker. Beth Mikra. July–Sept., 1982, pp. 230–31†

CONVENTIONS

In the great periods of later literatures, literary history must necessarily take the form of biographies of the great writers and their works must be interpreted through their personal experiences. But in ancient Israel personality, even in the case of an author, was far less developed. In the Psalms, for instance, we find an extraordinary sameness of content—in different Psalms we find the same thoughts, moods, forms of expression, metaphors, rhetorical figures, phrases. Even the very greatest writers in Israel, the prophets, frequently exhibit the most striking uniformity. This is due to the fact that in antiquity the power of custom was far greater than it is in the modern world, and besides, like everything else connected with religion, religious literature—and the writings contained in the Old Testament are almost exclusively religious—is very conservative. Therefore a history of Hebrew literature, if it is to do justice to its subject-matter, has comparatively little concern with the personality of the writers. That has, of course, a place of its own, but Hebrew literary history should occupy itself more with the literary type that lies deeper than any individual effort. Hebrew literary history is therefore the history of the literary types practised in Israel, and it is perfectly possible to produce such a history from the sources that are available. . . .

Some of the main literary types may be briefly mentioned. There is first the broad classification into Prose and Poetry. Narrative is usually found in prose form, and the following different kinds of narrative can be distinguished: stories about the deities, i.e. Myths; primitive Folk-tales (of these two, only fragments are found in Israel); the popular Saga; the longer Romance; the religious Legend; and, lastly, Historical Narrative in the stricter sense. Poetical literary types include: the oracular wisdom, the prophetic oracular saying, the Lyric—the two last mentioned being specially frequent. Lyric poetry is again subdivided into (a) secular lyrics, such as the Dirge, the Love Song, the scornful lay, the song of carouse, the wedding song, the song of victory, the royal song, and (b) spiritual lyrics, including the Hymn, the Thanksgiving, the Dirge (both private and public, the Eschatological Psalm, etc. Numerous types are found conjoined in the prophetic writings—the Vision in narrative form, the Prophetic Oracle, the Discourse (in many forms). Among these last mentioned the oldest is that which foretells the future, and may either be the Threat or the Promise; the Invective, upbraiding sin; the Exhortation, calling to well-doing, and many others. Most of these types have long been recognized, and it is the task of Literary History to study them systematically and scientifically. Each type must be studied in order to show the materials with which it deals and the forms which it necessarily assumes. It will be found that a particular literary type is distinguished by a certain form of exordium. Just as the fairy-tale of to-day usually opens with "Once upon a time," a letter with "Dear Sir," a sermon with "Brethren," so the Hebrew Hymn frequently opens with "Sing unto the Lord," the Dirge with "Ah! How," the Prophetic Invective with "Ha! Ye." It is possible that students who are still unfamiliar with these ancient types will at first find it difficult to recognize them, definite and distinct as they are, but we must remember that this difficulty did not exist for the ancient world. To the people of Israel the laws of literary form were as familiar as the rules of Hebrew grammar. They obeyed them unconsciously and lived in them; it is only we who have to learn to understand them.

Hermann Gunkel. *What Remains of the Old Testament and Other Essays*. Tr. from the German by A. K. Dallas (New York, Macmillan, 1928), pp. 58–61

The ancient Hebrew poets escaped the prelogical jungles into which many of the greatest modern poets have strayed on occasion precisely because of their close attachment to transmitted forms of verse and poetic clichés. Even today few biblical scholars have an adequate appreciation of the importance of the strictly formal element in ancient literary composition. Hermann Gunkel, Eduard Norden, and Martin Dibelius, followed closely by many others, have indeed created a different approach to the interpretation of ancient literature, but there are still a great many scholars—probably a majority, in fact—who continue to emphasize individual style and to treat each line of a Hebrew poem as though it were the reflection of some psychological idiosyncracy of the poet, instead of being an example of a given genre or category of compostion.

> William F. Albright. *Hebrew Union College Annual.*
> 23, 1950–51, p. 2

When we ask why poets, who were capable of the most original, profound, and moving thoughts world literature has ever known, should have had such regular and continual traffic with clichés, the answer must lie in an understanding of their dependence upon, and regard for, tradition. Reliance upon tradition, in turn, must find its *raison d'être* in some particular need to which it answered. This need, it may be suggested, had its genesis at a time when poetry was being composed without the aid of writing tools, that is to say when poetic composition was an oral art. The poet had to construct his verses "on his feet," as it were, and to retain them in his memory. He was therefore forced to rely upon some mnemonic device, in this case upon a conventional diction and traditional patterns of composition. Syro-Palestinian poets, who formed their verses primarily in parallel lines, apparently found it expedient to employ conventionally fixed pairs of words. Such stylization enabled the poet more readily to compose and to retain his verses; for, once he had set forth a line of two, three, or four words or phrases, the formation of the parallel line was virtually at hand since the parallel terms, which would complete the thought, were already determined. The fixed pairs, therefore, constituted for the Syro-Palestinian poet what we have termed one of the "essentials of his craft." He doubtless acquired these through listening to the poems of his contemporaries and adapting for his own poetic needs those patterns of diction and verse structure that most pleased. New patterns could be, and were, formed; and as they conformed to the traditional modes of versification, and struck the poets' fancies as apt, would tend by repeated use to find their way into the repertory of poetic diction.

This phenomenon of dependence upon a traditional diction has recently been found to have obtained among the early Greeks as well. By careful analyses of epithets and phrases that find recurrent expression in the Homeric epics, the *Iliad* and the *Odyssey*, Professor Milman Parry was able to show conclusively what many had apparently suspected for some time, namely that such repetitions of stock expressions were not the result of accident, nor yet of an impoverished imagination, but of a long-established tradition. So extensive in Homer's work did Parry find the use of such formulas, as he termed them, that the poems have come to be recognized by all subsequent students as having been composed almost entirely, if not entirely, of set phrases. . . .

Unlike the Greek, the Hebrew poet structured his verses not with whole formulaic phrases (though on occasion, as we shall indicate, this technique also was employed) but with fixed pairs of parallel terms. If these pairs were fitted into the lines in accordance with some principle of meter, it has yet to be discovered. That metrical considerations played a role is highly probable, but a demonstration of it—as clear as that for Greek verse—is not at hand. . . .

Awareness of, and emphasis upon, the stylization of early verse, important as it is for an appreciation of the poets' craft, must not be permitted to obscure the uniqueness of the individual poem's vitality, which may be sought only in the imaginative utilization of tradition toward particular poetic ends. Again we may find instruction in the analogy of the Homeric epics. So heavy, to the modern student, seems the hand of tradition at work in these poems that it would appear to have stifled any poetic creativity. That this is not the case is evident from the power and appeal the *Iliad* and the *Odyssey* have ever exerted. The creativity of the poet clearly, therefore, must lie elsewhere than in his subject matter or in his diction, both of which, by scholarly consensus, were his by inheritance and not by invention. As a recent critic has written,

> There is no evidence at all that the poet of the *Iliad* invented a single character or episode in his whole poem. He may not even have invented a single phrase. His invention was the *Iliad*. [Cedric H. Whitman. *Homer and the Homeric Tradition*, 1958, p. 14.]

So too the creativity of the Hebrew poet will not be found by the application of any modern requirement for "originality." Rather is it in the reworking of old themes by means of conventional phraseology, in traditional manner, to reproduce familiar actions uniquely and poetically significant that the poet's genius is to be sought. Since his tradition, for the most part, demanded the construction of verses in parallel cola by means of traditionally fixed word-pairs, it is in the poet's arrangement of these with one another, his ability in so doing to give to the lines composed of the conventionally correspondent terms distinctive meaning, and his harmonious setting of these in a larger whole—fashioning thereby a unity, with part answering to part—that the impact of his poem's force will have been felt. Clearly, the more skillful or gifted the poet, the more intense the emotional response of his audience and the greater its appreciation.

Stanley Gevirtz. *Patterns in the Early Poetry of Israel* (Chicago, University of Chicago Press, 1963), pp. 10–12, 14

In the [Ugaritic] Baal Epic, the goddess Anath catches sight of the messengers Vineyard and Field, and reacts violently: "No sooner espies she the gods, / Than Anath's feet do stumble. / Behind, her loins do break; / Above, her face doth sweat: / Bent are the joints of her loins, / Weakened those of her back." [Tr. by

H. L. Ginsberg. In *Ancient Near Eastern Texts Relating to the Old Testament*. Ed. by James B. Pritchard, 1955, pp. 136–37]

This description of dismay at the approach of bad news was a commonplace in Ugaritic literature. Asherah's response to the approach of Baal and Anath is identical. . . . When word is brought to Dan'el of Aqhat's death, his reaction is the same, though it is depicted in a slightly shortened form. . . . A brief variant of this convention appears in the Keret Epic . . . : "As soon as she (Thitmanet) sees her brother, Her [loins] to the ground do break" [tr. Ginsberg, op. cit., p. 147].

H. L. Ginsberg has called attention to this literary convention, and has pointed out one biblical parallel, Ezekiel 21:11–12. The present study will show, in the first place, that in biblical Hebrew literature there is a widespread literary convention depicting the reaction to bad news, conceptually similar to that in the Canaanite poem, though there are few verbal correspondences. Secondly, it will be pointed out that certain passages which have been quoted as descriptions of prophetic ecstasy are actually examples of this commonplace depiction of dismay.

In Jeremiah 6:22–23, the prophet announces the coming of the enemy from the north. In verse 24 he continues: "We heard the news of it: / our hands grew weak (*rafu yadeinu*) / Anguish seized us, / pains like those of a woman in labor (*hil kayyoleda*)."

Jeremiah 50:43 is nearly identical: "The king of Babylon heard news of them / and his hands grew weak. / Anguish seized him, / pains like those of a woman in labor."

Jeremiah 49:23 is longer, and partly obscure, but the same pattern and vocabulary can be recognized in it. . . .

Isaiah 13 describes the mustering of the hosts of the Lord for attack on Babylon. The day of the Lord is coming and the sound of the hosts is heard (vv. 1–6). Verses 7 and 8 depict the reaction: "Therefore all hands will grow weak / and every man's heart will melt (*yimmas*), / and they will be dismayed . . . . / Anguish and pains will seize them; / they will writhe like a woman in labor. . . ."

To summarize, the following are the principal elements of the convention: (1) approach of the bad news or, in Isaiah 13, of the foe; (2) the hands' falling helpless (*rafa*), present in four of the five examples cited above; (3) pains in the loins like labor pains, mentioned explicitly in four of five examples and alluded to in the fifth by *shivron motnayim* ["breaking of the loins"]; (4) melting of the heart (*masas, mug*), three examples.

Other passages can be identified as examples of the same convention, though somewhat less stereotyped in form. . . .

Elements of this convention are also used in Hebrew prose to describe the reaction to bad news. Thus II Samuel 4:1: "When Saul's sons heard that Abner was dead in Hebron, his hands grew weak (*rafu*), and all Israel was troubled." Compare also Deuteronomy 2:25; Joshua 2:9 and 5:1.

Delbert R. Hillers. *Zeitschrift für Alttestamentliche Wissenschaft*, 77, no. 1, 1965, pp. 86–88

Ancient Israelite literature reflects the notion that divine justice is often of a highly poetic variety. That is to say, divine retribution often exhibits a measure for measure correspondence between a crime and its punishment. Thus one is to be punished specifically through that with which one sins. A particularly striking case in point is afforded by the depiction of Haman suspended from the very gallows he had erected for Mordecai.

The doctrine in question is most explicitly formulated in the so-called Wisdom material of the Bible, and appears in various psalms and proverb collections. When reduced to proverbial form the idea is quite consistently expressed by essentially two distinct figures of speech, or sets of images. It is the aim of this study to examine the particular imagery that has seemingly attached itself to the notion of poetic justice. This will involve discussion of some of the individual associations and nuances of each set of images, as well as the combined effect of their appearance together. To this end, the imagery will be viewed both from the standpoint of internal biblical usage, and in relation to its affinities to attested ancient near eastern literary conventions.

The most frequently encountered representation of poetic justice at work employs the imagery of pits, nets and traps, e.g. Psalm 7:16, "He dug out a pit, excavated it, / May he fall into the very pit he made"; Psalm 9:16, "The nations have sunk down into the pit they made, / their foot has been caught in the very net they concealed"; Psalm 35:8, ". . . and may the net he concealed catch hold of him"; Psalm 57:7, ". . . They have dug a pit before me, / they themselves have fallen into it"; Proverbs 26:27a, "One who digs a pit will fall into it"; Proverbs 28:10a, "As for one who diverts the upright onto an evil course, he will fall into his very own pit"; Ecclesiastes 10:8a, "One who digs a pit will himself fall into it."

The survival and perpetuation of this particular mode of expressing poetic justice form a most fascinating chapter in the literary history of biblical poetry. The biblical imagery and terminology are taken over intact in Ben Sira 27:26, "One who digs a pit will fall into it, / one who sets up a trap will be caught in it." So too, the same figurative representation is preserved in the Thanksgiving Scroll of the Dead Sea sect: "And as for them, may the net they have spread for me seize their own foot, / and may they fall into the very traps they have concealed for my person." . . .

The image of the entrapped trapper as expressed in proverbial form enjoyed even further longevity and considerable geographical diffusion by virtue of its consistent inclusion in the many versions and translations comprising the Aḥiqar literature. The latter, being built around a moralizing tale of treachery and its recompense, effectively employs our figurative maxim as a motto summarizing the story as a whole. For purposes of convenience, the Syriac version of the proverb may be taken as fairly typical of its appearance in the various Aḥiqar versions: "Whoever digs a pit for his fellow man fills it with his own figure."

Ultimate punishment through such devices as pits, nets and traps may be appreciated as most fitting, since the biblical evildoer is quite often portrayed as initially employing these very contrivances. This usage is evident, for example, in

Jeremiah 18:22 (cf. v. 20) where the prophet complains: "For they have dug a pit to hold me fast, / and concealed traps at my feet." The figurative description employed here is amply paralleled elsewhere in biblical poetry. Moreover, this conventional representation of the wicked in action would also seem to have been assumed in Psalm 94:13b where divine punishment for some otherwise unspecified crime is indicated by the phrase: "Until He digs [. . .] a pit for the wicked." Similarly, Job 18:8–10 and 22:10a enumerate elaborate punishments for the wicked which all involve entanglement in various types of nets and traps. Such punishments may be properly understood in terms of exact retribution for the stereotyped activity ascribed to the evildoer. . . .

The conceptualization of the evildoer as a predatory hunter is succinctly expressed in Psalm 10:9 (cf. v. 8): "He lies in ambush in a concealed place like a lion in his lair; / he lies in ambush to seize a poor man, / he seizes a poor man, dragging him along in his net." The combination here of the evildoer and his hunting net with the lion in ambush is highly evocative. The lion is elsewhere depicted as the hunter *par excellence* in passages which stress his cunning use of ambush. Indeed, the use of ambush by the predator is little different from the setting of traps, both being seen as particularly treacherous ploys of the hunter. . . .

Alongside the constellation of entrapment images there exists a less frequently encountered set of images also employed to express figuratively the notion of poetic justice. This second grouping is comprised of various throwing and striking weapons, some employed in hunting but, as a group, associated most closely with warfare. The specific usage in terms of portraying exact retribution may be seen, for example, in Psalm 37:14–15: "The wicked have whetted a sword / and they have bent their bow / to fell the poor and wretched / to slaughter the righteous; May their sword enter their own insides / and may their bows be broken." . . .

Like the associated images of sword, bow and arrow, the stone is employed to depict the workings of poetic justice, as in Proverbs 26:27b: "And as for one who rolls a stone, it returns back to him." Similarly, in Ben Sira 27:25a the very same figurative portrayal appears: "One casting a stone on high is really casting (it) upon his own head."

The imagery of the sword, arrow and stone expresses poetic justice by concretely depicting the physical reversal of weapons in motion. . . .

In the context of biblical literature, poetic justice is divine retribution, and thus implicit in the imagery of the recoiling weapon is the active intervention of the Deity.

Murray H. Lichtenstein. *Journal of the Ancient Near Eastern Society of Columbia University*, 5 (1973), pp. 255–58, 260–62

A number of passages in the narrative of Judges and Samuel may be shown to exhibit an interesting measure of conventionality or stereotyping. This characteristic, it will be argued, is not only likely to reflect traditional composition but also quite possibly *oral* traditional composition. The discussion presented here is intended as a contribution to our understanding of narrative technique in the Old Testament; its conclusions also have a bearing upon questions regarding the composition of the books of Judges and Samuel, with respect to both the particular passages concerned and the larger blocks of material to which these belong. . . .

The first group of passages, all from I and II Samuel, has as its subject matter the account of a battle: I Samuel 4:10, from the story of the capture of the ark and the death of Eli; I Samuel 4:17, the report of the battle of Aphek by the messenger who comes to Eli; I Samuel 31:1, the defeat of Saul at Gilboa; II Samuel 1:4, the description of the course of that battle by the man who brings the news to David; II Samuel 2:17, the confrontation between the men of David and those of Ishbosheth; and II Samuel 18:6f., from the account of Absalom's rebellion. There is a special circumstance shared by these battles—they are all accounts of *defeats* suffered by Israel (or the "men of Israel"). . . .

Now to the passages themselves. There is first, in those accounts which are not messenger's reports, a simple statement that the battle was joined, and second, in all passages, (a) an equally brief mention of the outcome (in terms of the flight/defeat of one side), (b) a mention of casualties, usually described as large, on the side of the defeated, and (c) an account of the death of a person or persons of importance usually on the defeated side, an exception being II Samuel 2 where it is Asahel, on the winning side, whose death is detailed. At its most basic, this last element takes the form of a brief mention of the fact of the death, in I Samuel 31 this is followed by a more detailed account, while in II Samuel 2 and 18 the elaboration alone is given without any initial summary expression. . . .

As far as the linguistic affinities between the various instances of the pattern are concerned they are fairly complex. . . .

What are we to make of these patterns? For a start it is important to clear up two basic issues. Following Wolfgang Richter and John Van Seters I have tended to talk of "patterns" if not of "forms." But is it not possible that the similarities noted among the passages are simply fortuitous. After all, one could perhaps argue that given a large enough number of short accounts of battles, some are bound to coincide to some extent—a point that is perhaps even more pertinent in relation to Richter's delineation of "form" than it is in the case of the particular battle accounts under discussion.

It is hard to dismiss this possibility out of hand. Nevertheless one can weigh some of the factors involved and remain sceptical. The parallels between the "Battle" scenes not only involve subject matter in common but an economy of subject matter. It is not only a matter of what is said but of what is not said. One can imagine a great many features of a battle that might have claimed the narrator's attention but which receive no mention at all. Moreover, the rather terse sequence, in markedly circumscribed language, occurs in the face of some important variables, viz. the relative length and particular details of the stories in which it occurs.

It is noticeable also that in I Samuel 31 the pattern in what seems to be its basic form (with virtually a single clause sufficing for each element), while remaining an integral part of the narrative as a whole, rather spoils its flow since it anticipates the more detailed (and aesthetically more satisfying) account of the death of Saul and his sons which immediately follows upon it. In other words, it could be argued that element (c) in its simplest form is narrated in I Samuel 31 *despite* the subsequent development of the passage, just because it *is* part of a regularly employed sequence.

David M. Gunn. *Vetus Testamentum.* July, 1974, pp. 286, 288–89, 292–93

One of the chief difficulties we encounter as modern readers in perceiving the artistry of biblical narrative is precisely that we have lost most of the keys to the conventions out of which it was shaped. The professional Bible scholars have not offered much help in this regard, for their closest approximation to the study of convention is form criticism, which is set on finding recurrent regularities of pattern rather than the manifold variations upon a pattern that any system of literary convention elicits; moreover, form criticism uses these patterns for excavative ends—to support hypotheses about the social functions of the text, its historical evolution, and so forth. . . .

The most crucial case in point is the perplexing fact that in biblical narrative more or less the same story often seems to be told two or three or more times about different characters, or sometimes even about the same character in different sets of circumstances. Three times a patriarch is driven by famine to a southern region where he pretends that his wife is his sister, narrowly avoids a violation of the conjugal bond by the local ruler, and is sent away with gifts (Gen. 12:10–20; Gen. 20; Gen. 26:1–12). Twice Hagar flees into the wilderness from Sarah's hostility and discovers a miraculous well (Gen. 16; Gen. 21:9–21), and that story itself seems only a special variation of the recurrent story of bitter rivalry between a barren, favored wife and a fertile co-wife or concubine. That situation, in turn, suggests another oft-told tale in the Bible, of a woman long barren who is vouchsafed a divine promise of progeny, whether by God himself or through a divine messenger or oracle, and who then gives birth to a hero.

Different repeated episodes have elicited different explanations, but the most common strategy among scholars is to attribute all ostensible duplication in the narratives to a duplication of sources, to a kind of recurrent stammer in the process of transmission, whether written or oral. . . .

I should like to propose that there is a series of recurrent narrative episodes attached to the careers of biblical heroes that are analogous to Homeric type-scenes in that they are dependent on the manipulation of a fixed constellation of predetermined motifs. Since biblical narrative characteristically catches its protagonists only at the critical and revealing points in their lives, the biblical type-scene occurs not in the rituals of daily existence but at the crucial junctures in the lives of the heroes, from conception and birth to betrothal to deathbed. Not every

type-scene will occur for every major hero, though often the absence of a particular type-scene may itself be significant. Some of the most commonly repeated
biblical type-scenes I have been able to identify are the following: the annunciation (and I take the term from Christian iconography precisely to underscore the
elements of fixed convention) of the birth of the hero to his barren mother; the
encounter with the future betrothed at a well; the epiphany in the field; the initia-
tory trial; danger in the desert and the discovery of a well or other source of sustenance; the testament of the dying hero.

> Robert Alter. *The Art of Biblical Narrative* (New York,
> Basic Books, 1981), pp. 47–51

A listing convention shared among these literatures involves the use of sequential
numbers in story-telling and wisdom recitation. The author of Proverbs 30, a
chapter full of number sayings, explains: "Under three things the earth shudders,
/ There are four it cannot tolerate: / A slave who has become king; / An obstinate
fool when he is filled with food; / An unpopular woman when she gets a husband; / And a slave girl when she supplants her mistress." (Prov. 30:21–23; tr.
R. B. Y. Scott)

Similarly the god Baal in an Ugaritic story uses numbers in stating his pet
peeves (he refers to himself in the third person). "Baal hates two sacrifices /
Three, the Rider of Clouds [that is, Baal again]: / The sacrifice of shame / And
the sacrifice of baseness / And the sacrifice of the abuse of handmaids." . . . (tr.
C. H. Gordon)

The use of the pair x and $x + 1$ in story-telling is not surprising. Children put
billion after million as often as they add jillion after billion. But the convention
endures strongly in the Near East and its cultural dependencies. A modern Palestinian Arab storyteller tells of a young man who, when asked how many children
he has, says, "Three or four." The force of verbal habit that aided the author of
Proverbs has apparently overpowered the storyteller. In a recent *New Yorker*
piece, James Stevenson related a breakfast-time incident from a diner in rural
Virginia.

> Old customer says something derogatory about cook; waitress
> concurs. Cook: "They's three things I can't stand—and you's two
> of them."

The cook here has bested the tradition, if unwittingly. Whether she was consciously quoting the language of Proverbs or not, she bears out the truth of C. H.
Gordon's remark, "What the Greek and Latin classics are to modern European
literature, Ugaritic is to the Old Testament."

> Michael P. O'Connor. In *The Bible and Its Traditions*.
> Ed. by Michael P. O'Connor and David N. Freedman.
> Special issue of *Michigan Quarterly Review*. Summer,
> 1983, pp. 209–10.

Description. *See* Narrator: Description

DIALOGUE

Another feature of the best short stories of all ages is natural use of dialogue. The extent to which it is used in the Bible stories is remarkable, and adds much to their verisimilitude. Take, as an example, the little story of Elijah's dealing with the widow of Zarephath (I Kgs. 17:8–24). It opens with the explicit direction under compulsion of which Elijah went to Zarephath: "Arise, get thee to Zarephath, which belongeth to Zidon, and dwell there: behold, I have commanded a widow woman there to sustain thee."

Thus we plunge without elaboration into the story. Sixteen verses comprise this tale: only five are indirect speech, and the result is a most realistic narrative. The extensive use of dialogue, which can be illustrated from any of the stories studied, has two important consequences. The first is, that superfluous details drop off and a delightful simplicity results. The other is, that the characters live from the first moment. There is no need for the narrator to tell us what the people are like. Their own words reveal it. Even when we isolate this little story from the rest of the Elijah stories, we can infer a great deal about his character. He is a man directly under the guidance of the unseen, and he obeys the direction simply and unquestioningly. Equally simply, he issues his commands, and in faith utters his prayer for the recovery of the child. The widow of Zarephath is a very natural character. She realises the prophet's greatness and she gives way before the dominating certainty of his commands; but when her son falls ill, she is ready to turn round and blame him, till the miracle of the child's recovery clears away her doubts. The narrative then reverts to the account of the relations between Elijah and Ahab, which had been momentarily broken by the throwing into relief of this human little story. "The widow's curse" has become proverbial and the tale is known wherever the Bible is read.

> Kathleen E. Innes. *The Bible as Literature* (London, Jonathan Cape, 1930), pp. 36–37

The character of religion as it appears in both Old and New Testament makes the dialogue an inevitable form of rhetorical expression. God is known as one who speaks, addresses, calls, initiates agreements or covenants, engages in public trial-scenes, as well as one who invites to mutual converse and understanding. It is he who says, "Come now, let us reason together" (Isa. 1:18), or, "Son of man, stand upon your feet, and I will speak with you" (Ezek. 2:1). The Bible is therefore full of dialogue and of a most searching kind. And it is not only a dialogue between God and man. For where man is so defined it follows that the mutual relation of man and man is charged with significance. The Psalmist can say of a friend who, indeed, later betrayed him: "We took sweet counsel together" (55:14).

The implicit dialogue in all biblical religion comes to rhetorical expression in the Old Testament in striking ways. We naturally think first of the primordial interchanges between God and Adam and Eve, between God and Cain; the covenant-agreements with the patriarchs and Moses; the great colloquies of the Book of Job. There are passages in the Psalms where the common worshipper is overheard in silent converse with God, it may be in expostulation and pleading on his bed in the night watches. We have also the dramatic court-scenes in which God and Israel occupy the changing roles of plaintiff and accused. In the forty-first chapter of Isaiah, indeed, God convokes all the nations of the earth to be witnesses to the validity of his case:

> Listen to me in silence, O coastlands:
>   let the peoples renew their strength;
>   let them approach, then let them speak;
>   let us draw near for judgment (41:1).

As with the dialogue between God and man, so with that between his messengers and their hearers. The style of the Bible often bears witness to the rejoinders, protests, even blasphemies of the human interlocutors. Hans Walter Wolff [20th c. German Old Testament scholar] observes that the Book of Hosea is made up of reports by the prophet's disciples, who "preserved his words soon after each discussion with his hearers." The words of Hosea as transmitted to us still convey the opposition and self-justification of those addressed by the prophet, and sometimes their very words.

Amos N. Wilder. *Early Christian Rhetoric* (Cambridge, Mass., Harvard University Press, 1971), pp. 44–45

Alongside the wealth of dialogue literature which we know from ancient Egypt and Mesopotamia, the didactic literature of Israel has only the dialogue of Job with his friends which, however, far surpasses its companion pieces outside Israel. Whether the much simpler dialogues in the fables, for example in the Jotham fable or in the dispute between the Tamarisk and the Date Palm, are literary precursors of the great dialogue poems still has to be decided. One is particularly conscious of the lack of a study of the specific nature of the thought-process which is at work in the great dialogues. Such a study would lead us out of what is, in any case, an erroneous comparison with Greek or even with modern dialogues. It is not surprising that these dialogues lack any personal, psychological delineation of the protagonists. More difficult for the modern reader is the lack of any genuine contact of the speakers with each other. In the case of Job, one often has the impression that he has not listened properly. Often, indeed, both protagonists get excited about the same thing, thus, for example, in the Job dialogue when they come to discuss the theme of divine freedom. With this lack there is connected the greatest difficulty, the lack of a clear statement of the subject of the debate and the lack of any clearly marked progress in the thought. When Job begins a lament (Job 7:14), he finds himself at once in the conventional *Gattung* of the individual lament and follows its conventional topics which often do not fit his biographical situation, so that for a while one loses sight of the problem. Now the Job dialogue certainly does not move in a circle; a progress in the thought can be discerned, but here not only one question but several are tackled and these are passed back and forth at will in the course of the speeches. However, caution is advised. Perhaps this movement of thought is strange to us rather than defective; for, after all, even we can still perceive that here questions are, rather, circled around and that precisely in this way a depth and a breadth are achieved in the discussion of the problem which could never have been intuited to this extent if the discussion had moved towards a solution by way of a linear progression. It is the intuition that is important above all. It is more important than a perception which can be formulated conceptually and then expressed in a sentence. As far as this intuition is concerned, the poet always aims at an effect of totality.

In a later period—we mention only the main points—there was composed in Israel another dialogue, one of the finest things ever written there, namely the conversation between Ezra and the interpreting angel in II(4) Esdras, which stems directly from the wisdom tradition.

Gerhard von Rad. Wisdom in Israel (Nashville, Abing-
don Press, 1972), pp. 40–41

The dramatic instinct for dialogue pervades biblical literature. Strictly speaking, there is no pure drama in the Bible, and Hebrew culture produced no theater. Most biblical writers, however, display a strong tendency to achieve concreteness of presentation through the use of dialogue. Most biblical stories depend heavily on dialogue rather than summarized narrative as a way of describing the action. The book of Job, although it is a narrative told by a narrator, is structured like a play. And many lyric poems in the Bible are dramatic in structure, with the speaker addressing a mute but implied listener.

Several things account for the prevalence of dialogue in biblical literature. It is evidence of the literary impulse to be concrete in presentation. When a writer gives the actual words of characters, it is obvious that he is not simply offering an abstract summary about an event but is actually presenting the event in all its experiential immediacy. Secondly, the prominence of dialogue reflects the fact that originally much of the Bible existed as oral literature. When literature is chiefly spoken rather than written, storytellers or poets naturally have a high regard for uttered speech, and it is not surprising that their literary works would make frequent use of speech patterns. Finally, the frequent use of dialogue is rooted in the biblical view of man and God. In biblical literature man achieves full meaning only in relationship—relationship to God and the human community. Similarly, the God of the Bible is the God who communicates—who speaks, calls, and invites human response. Dialogue is the natural and inevitable rhetorical mode for this view of man and God, for dialogue is the language of relationship and encounter. It is small wonder, therefore, that biblical literature is full of voices speaking and replying.

Leland Ryken. The Literature of the Bible (Grand Rap-
ids, Mich., Zondervan, 1974), pp. 20–21

Because dialogues have a very high frequency in the narratives of the Bible, they impress their stamp upon them decisively.

In many instances the dialogue is the lion's share of the story, taking a much larger space than the words of the narrator, so that almost everything that happens is borne upon its shoulders, for example, in the Garden of Eden story (Gen. 3) and in the story of Saul and the she-asses (I Sam. 9–10), which are constructed largely of dialogues. Sometimes everything that happens is conveyed by means of dialogue, the narrator's words being no more than a framework, for example, in the story of David's withdrawal from the Philistine camp before the battle at Gilboa (I Sam. 29) and in the episode about passing on word of Absalom's death to David (II Sam. 18:19–32).

Despite the large place dialogue occupies in most narratives of the Bible, the dialogues in these stories are not lengthy. Not only do the characters express themselves in concentrated, crystallized form, but even the number of statements in each dialogue does not generally exceed two or three. There are only a few exceptions: In the dialogue between David and the woman of Tekoa (II Sam. 14:4–20) there are no fewer than fifteen statements. The woman speaks eight times and David seven times; in addition, the woman's words are spoken expansively, comfortably. In a not very large number of instances a lengthy discourse, a speech, is presented, such as, for example, the speech of Rab-shakeh (II Kgs. 18:19–25, 28–35), which in its two parts takes no fewer than fifteen verses.

Dialogue fulfills two principal functions in Biblical narratives. On the one hand it advances the plot, since it does not generally contain rumination and thought but deals, rather, with actions and deeds, and in most instances looks toward the future. It mainly brings up plans and aspirations, or it attempts to persuade or influence.

On the other hand, dialogue serves to illuminate the human dimension, revealing personal factors such as motives and intentions, points of view and attitudes, positions and reactions. The very narratives mentioned above, the Garden of Eden story, the story of Saul and the she-asses, the story of David's withdrawal from the Philistine camp, the episode of the messengers, and many other stories, of course, may serve as illustrations. . . .

In dialogue the speed of the telling approximates the speed of what is told. Approximates, but does not match. For dialogue in biblical narrative is never a precise naturalistic imitation of actual conversation. The biblical dialogue is concentrated and stylized to a high degree. It has no idle chatter. Rather, all the details that are conveyed have been well calculated and perform a clear function. Moreover, the dialogue is so condensed that frequently details we would like or expect to find are missing.

Here [is an example that shows] that the dialogue in the biblical narrative is much more compressed than a real conversation or, in other words, that the time of the telling goes on for less than the time of what is being told.

> Absalom arose early and stood beside the Way of the Gate, and any man who had a case to bring to the king for judgment— Absalom would call out to him,
> and he said: "From what town are you?" and he said: "Your ser-

vant is from one of the tribes of Israel."
Absalom said to him: "See, your words are good and valid, but
you get no hearing from the king" (II Sam. 15:2–3).

In this concentrated dialogue, which illustrates the debased manner in which
Absalom went out to win popularity for himself among the people, the litigant
gives Absalom an answer that is not possible in reality. For to Absalom's question "From what town are you?" he should have answered by mentioning the
name of the town, perhaps with the addition of the name of the tribe, but here we
find a sort of homogenization of all the answers given by respondents in the
course of time (as it is written in the continuation: "Absalom did this thing to all
the Israelites who would come for the king's judgment").

This and more. It would make sense that in the continuation of the conversation Absalom would ask the man what distresses him and for what purpose he is
coming for judgment from the king, and that the man would tell him the details
of the case, explaining the evolution of events and the sides involved in the dispute. All this has been deleted from the dialogue before us. The man himself and
the essence of his litigation are of no interest and significance to the subject of
the narrative. In contrast, more significant is the reaction of Absalom, both for
his characterization and for the development of the plot: "See, your words are
good and valid, but you get no hearing from the king." So, too, the continuation
in his words: "If someone would appoint me judge in the land, every man who
had a case for judgment would come to me, and I would vindicate him." Out of
strict selectivity, then, only what is germane to the story is presented in dialogue,
with drastic deletion of the remainder.

Shimeon Bar-Efrat. *Ha'itsuv ha'omanuti shel hassip-*
pur bammiqra' (Tel Aviv, Sifriat Poalim, 1979), pp.
157–58 †

Everything in the world of biblical narrative ultimately gravitates toward dialogue—perhaps, as I have had occasion to suggest, because to the ancient Hebrew writers speech seemed the essential human faculty: by exercising the capacity of speech man demonstrated, however imperfectly, that he was made in the
image of God. This "gravitation" often means that phrases or whole sentences
first stated by the narrator do not reveal their full significance until they are repeated, whether faithfully or with distortions, in direct speech by one or more of
the characters. It also means that, quantitatively, a remarkably large part of the
narrative burden is carried by dialogue, the transactions between characters typically unfolding through the words they exchange, with only the most minimal intervention of the narrator. As a rule, when a narrative event in the Bible seems
important, the writer will render it mainly through dialogue, so the transitions
from narration to dialogue provide in themselves some implicit measure of what
is deemed essential, what is conceived to be ancillary or secondary to the main
action. Thus, David's committing adultery with Bathsheba is reported very
rapidly through narration with brief elements of dialogue, while his elaborate
scheme first to shift the appearance of paternity to Uriah, and when that fails, to

murder Uriah, is rendered at much greater length largely through dialogue. One may infer that the writer means to direct our attention to the murder rather than to the sexual transgression as the essential crime.

If, then, the very occurrence of extended dialogue should signal the need for special attentiveness as we read, there is a set of more specific questions we might ask ourselves about the way the dialogue emerges and develops. Is this the first reported speech for either or both of the two interlocutors? If so, why did the writer choose this particular narrative juncture to make the character reveal himself through speech? How does the kind of speech assigned to the character—its syntax, tone, imagery, brevity or lengthiness—serve to delineate the character and his relation to the other party to the dialogue? In looking for answers to this last question, it will be especially helpful to keep in mind the tendency of the biblical writers to organize dialogue along contrastive principles—short versus long, simple versus elaborate, balanced versus asymmetrical, perceptive versus obtuse, and so forth. Finally, we should be alert to the seeming discontinuities of biblical dialogue and ponder what they might imply. When do characters ostensibly answer one another without truly responding to what the other person has said? When does the dialogue break off sharply, withholding from us the rejoinder we might have expected from one of the two speakers?

To the extent that we can reasonably imagine how speakers of Hebrew some three thousand years ago really might have addressed one another, biblical dialogue would seem to exhibit many fine touches of persuasive mimesis, from Esau's crudeness and Judah's desperate eloquence to Hushai's cunning rhetorical contrivance. Virtually everywhere, however, dialogue in the Bible shows the clearest signs of using manifestly stylized speech, and it is always worth trying to see how the stylization makes the dialogue a more elegantly effective vehicle of meaning. Perhaps the most common feature of stylization in these spoken interchanges is the fact that the characters often repeat whole sentences or even series of sentences of each other's speech almost verbatim: A will tell B something regarding C, and B will then proceed to march off to C and say to him, You know, A instructed me . . . and go on to quote A's words. Whenever we encounter this convention—and, of course, there are many variations on the little schematic paradigm of it I have constructed here—it behooves us to watch for the small differences that emerge in the general pattern of verbatim repetition. To be sure, there are times when these differences may be quite inconsequential, as context and common sense should be able to warn us. But frequently enough, the small alterations, the reversals of order, the elaborations or deletions undergone by the statements as they are restated and sometimes restated again, will be revelations of character, moral, social, or political stance, and even plot. Often, such revelations will be matters of piquant or instructive nuance, but sometimes they can be quite momentous. In either case, the reliance on this particular technique suggests how much the biblical writers like to lead their readers to inferences through oblique hints rather than insisting on explicit statement.

Robert Alter. The Art of Biblical Narrative (New York, Basic Books, 1981), pp. 182–83

DICTION

To use interchangeable nouns and verbs whose meaning is the same is permitted [in Hebrew poetry] because the words are varied; and some scholars of language think that this usage is one of the modes of elegance and rhetoric, as in "Who has made and done" [Isa. 41:4], "I created him, I fashioned him, and I made him" [Isa. 43:7], "That they may see and know and pay mind and recognize at once" [Isa. 41:20]. Some of our older interpreters think that [in Isa. 43:7] the word "I-created-him" refers to insemination, while "I fashioned him" refers to the formation of the limbs and veins and "I made him" refers to the skin. But this interpretation is far from reasonable. It actually intends only to reinforce the sense. Similarly: "tired and weary" [Deut. 25:18], "he expired and died" (if one says "he expired" one need not say "he died") [Gen. 25:8]; the words "and he is defiled until evening" rendering superfluous the word "and he is pure" [in Lev. 17:15]. But the verse "your wives will become widows and your sons orphans" [Exod. 22:23] does not belong to this category (which opposes the opinion that if one says "Your wives will become widows" one need not say "and your sons orphans") for there can be a widow without sons and orphans without a mother. Sometimes a word will be used in varied ways but having one meaning, such as "you do not give water to the tired to drink" [Job 22:7]. The word "tired" here connotes "thirsty"; but elsewhere it connotes "hungry," as in "for tired am I" [Gen. 25:30]. It is also said, "And the wine is for the tired in the wilderness to drink" [II Sam. 16:2], [where "tired"] substitutes for "thirsty." . . . Sometimes interchangeable nouns and verbs are used a great deal, such as "O Lord, my allotment, my portion and my cupfill, you determine my destiny" [Ps. 16:5]. In this verse four words with one meaning vary. . . . Nevertheless, interpreters who find the nouns in the verse "from your land, and from your birthplace, and from your father's house" [Gen. 12:1] to be interchangeable are in error because each noun here has a distinctive meaning. "Your land" refers to Ur of the Chaldeans; "your birthplace" is his city; "your father's house"—this is his house and his family. Interchangeable nouns, however, are of a different type: they occur in a single place without any new information, as in "The roar of a lion and the voice of a mountain lion, and the teeth of young lions are shattered, a ravaging panther without prey, and lion cubs will be dispersed" [Job 4:10–11]. We know the meaning of all these nouns from their parallelism, as they have no cognates. . . . Interchangeable nouns, that is to say, different words that have a single meaning, are numerous in [Hebrew], such as "to extort" and "to embezzle." . . . Similarly, "usury" and "interest" are used the same way in the Bible, having a single sense. [ca. 1135]

Moses ibn Ezra. *Shirat Yisra'el*. Tr. from the Arabic by Ben-Zion Halper (Leipzig, Abraham Joseph Stybel Publishing, 1924), pp. 125–28, 130†

There is a *graceful* and *dignify'd* Simplicity, as well as a *bald* and *sordid* one, which differ as much from each other as the Air of a *plain* Man from that of a *Sloven:* 'Tis one thing to be tricked up, and another not to be dress'd at all. Simplicity is the Mean between Ostentation and Rusticity.

This pure and noble Simplicity is no where in such Perfection as in the *Scripture* and our Author [Homer]. One may affirm with all respect to the inspired Writings, that the *Divine Spirit* made use of no other Words but what were intelligible and common to Men at that Time, and in that Part of the World; and as *Homer* is the Author nearest to those, his Style must of course bear a greater Resemblance to the sacred Books than that of any other Writer.

This Consideration . . . may methinks induce a Translator on the one hand to give into several of those general Phrases and Manners of Expression, which have attain'd a Veneration even in our Language from their Use in the *Old Testament*; as on the other, to avoid those which have been appropriated to the Divinity, and in a Manner consign'd to Mystery and Religion.

> Alexander Pope. Preface to *The Iliad of Homer*. Vol. I. Tr. by Mr. Pope (London, Printed by W. Bowyer, 1715), sigs. H1^{v}–H2^{r}

The style is never more simple and restrained than when the ways of God are being described, as, for instance, in the creation, "*the spirit of God moved upon* the face of the waters." Or again, "God said, Let there be light, and there was light." (Gen. 1:2, 3) In the crossing of the Red Sea, "it came to pass in the morning watch, that the Lord *looked forth* upon the host of the Egyptians through the pillar of fire and of cloud, and *discomfited* the host of the Egyptians." (Exod. 14:24) One look of God overwhelms hosts, which may have inspired Byron's fine lines on the destruction of Sennacherib's forces. . . .

The compactness and vigour of the diction are less easy to appreciate in a translation. A fair impression may be gained by following the Authorized Version, and omitting words in italics, when it will be noticed that certain features of the Hebrew verb-forms, and the omission of the verb "to be" and of many of the pronouns and prepositions, make the original even more concise than the translation. For example,

> Where shall wisdom be found. . . ?
> The depth saith, Not in me . . . (Job 28:12, 14)

Metaphor also helps to make the diction vigorous and concise. E.g. "If thou doest not well, sin *croucheth* at the door." (Gen. 4:7) The Authorized Version had "lieth," but the word refers to the attitude of a wild beast waiting to spring. In Jonah (1:13), where the Revised Version says "the men rowed hard to get them back to land," the Hebrew has "they *dug the sea*." . . .

A good instance of compactness of diction is furnished by Job 3:3 ff.:

> Let the day perish wherein I was born,
> And the night *which said,* There is a man child conceived.

This is the fierce curse of a man overwhelmed with tragedy. Jeremiah waters it down into a pitiful complaint, by lengthening the lines and drawing them out into two couplets:

> Cursed be the day wherein I was born:
> Let not the day wherein my mother bare me be blessed.
> Cursed be the man who brought tidings to my father,
> Saying, A man child is born unto thee; making him very glad.
>
> (Jer. 20:14 f.)

The difference between the vigorous, compressed couplet of Job and the drawn-out version of Jeremiah has been expressed as follows: "the first sounds the note of tragedy, the second that of elegy."

The concentration of the diction upon a single idea, to impress that idea more firmly on the mind, may be illustrated by the famous passage of the "Man of Sorrows" or "the righteous servant" in Isaiah 53.

In English and Latin literature this result is achieved by the concentration of noun, verb, and epithet in the same sentence upon one idea, as in the following examples:

> With music *lulled* his *indolent repose*.
> Wordsworth, *Excursion* 1:720 [i.e., 4:853]

> *Sollicitam* timor *anxius angit*.
> Vergil, *Aeneid* 9:89
> (*Anxious* fear *wrings* my *troubled* heart.) . . .

In these examples the epithets at least are not wholly necessary to the meaning, but they help to drive it home, or, so to say, to make atmosphere. The Old Testament writers use epithets more rarely, but they do collect words of similar meaning to create an atmosphere round a central idea. They play skilfully upon words of similar import, with a certain amount of repetition and delicate variations. It is difficult otherwise to account for the effectiveness of the following sentences describing trustfulness from Isaiah 26:3–4:

> A *stedfast* mind thou *keepest* in *peace, peace,* because it *trusteth*
> in thee. *Trust* ye in the Lord *for ever*, for in the Lord Jehovah is an
> *everlasting* rock. . . .

The literary beauty which now [ch. 53] concerns us does not this time spring from the imagery, though the passage is relieved by the simile of the dumb sheep in verse 7. It is due, as was said above, to the skilful play upon words of similar meaning, expressing suffering, delicately varied and sometimes repeated (notice especially v. 5). There are nine different verbs, three of them repeated, and seven different nouns, one of them repeated, to express the treatment meted out to the man of sorrows, besides phrases of similar effect. These culminate in "the grave," verse 9, and in the fine expression of verse 12, a suitable climax, "he poured out his soul unto death." There is a similar play upon sin, iniquities, and transgression, and the English translators, by reserving the longer words for the cadences, preserved the sonority of the rhythm. The passage is thus a kind of mournful but majestic requiem, with a burst of more joyous music at the close,

> I will divide him a portion with the great,
> And he shall divide the spoil with the strong,

sinking again on the last chord into the strains which composed the main theme,

> and he bare the sin of many,
> and made intercession for the transgressors. [v. 12]

Percy C. Sands. *Literary Genius of the Old Testament* (Oxford, Clarendon Press, 1924), pp. 85–88

The well-known parallelism of clauses is present in a certain measure in the poetry of many ancient and modern peoples. (It is very prominent, for example, in the national epic of the Finns!) But in the ancient Orient, it is only in Canaanite poetry that its use attains the same, sometimes monotonous, regularity as in Hebrew. In order to meet the exigencies of such a prosody, the Canaanite and Hebrew poets have some fixed pairs of synonymous words or phrases for certain concepts which poets have frequent occasion to express (e.g.: head, eternity, to fear, to rejoice). Many such fixed pairs are common to Ugaritic and biblical poetry (though of course the words were not pronounced exactly alike in the two languages). Moreover, the members of such a pair are—with apparently no exceptions in Ugaritic poetry and with very few in Hebrew—always employed in the same order, and that order is also nearly always the same in both literatures. Common to both is the rule that it is the more usual expression that comes first, the second in some cases being hardly used at all except precisely for the purpose of balancing the first. For example, the ordinary Hebrew word for "eternity" is *'olam* (or *'olamim*), and if the poet wishes to express this concept a second time in a parallel clause he uses "generation and generation," *dor wador* (or *dor dor*, or *dor dorim*). And except for the pronunciation, it is the same in Ugaritic. Thus, the continuation of the encouragement of Baal . . . is, literally:

> Thou wilt win thy kingdom of eternity [*'lm* = Heb. *'olam*],
> thy dominion of all generations [*dr dr* = Heb. *dor dor*];

with which compare (Ps. 145:13):

> Thy kingdom is a kingdom of all eternity [*'olamim*],
> and thy dominion endureth through all generations [*dor wa-dor*].

H. L. Ginsberg. *Biblical Archaeologist,* May, 1945, pp. 55–56

Let us look at a . . . pair of lines, where we can observe how the movement from ordinary to literary term is associated with an allied developmental pattern. Here, too, we will see emphatic interlinear parallelism, which goes on to an intriguing third line, but I must resist the temptation to use a third line as well because it hinges on a word found only here that is uncertain in meaning. The verses are from Isaiah 59:9–10: "We hope for light and look! darkness, / for effulgence, and in gloom we go. / / We grope like blind men a wall, / like the eyeless we grope." The first line follows the pattern of moving from ordinary to poetic term for both the nouns in each verset—from simple light and darkness to the more literary *negohot* and *'afeilot,* effulgence and gloom, which, moreover, are cast in the feminine plural form, elsewhere used to give nouns an abstract or adverbial force, and which seems to endow the words here (I would guess) with an aura of vastness. The second line intensifies the assertion of the first line by making the outer darkness an inner darkness, the total incapacity to see, and transforming the general image of walking in the dark of the preceding verset into a more concrete picture of a blind man groping his way along a wall. The "blind men" of the first verset become "no-eyes" (*'ein 'eynaim*) in the second verset, which is not the substitution of a term from literary diction but of a kind of kenning or epithet. The effect, however, is like that in the move from "grave" to "Perdition"—a realization of the first term (or, as [the Russian writer Isaac V.] Shklovsky would have put it, a defamiliarization of it) which calls our attention to its essential meaning.

Again and again, the biblical poets will introduce a common noun in the first verset and match it with a kind of explanatory epithet—or, more interestingly, a metaphorical substitution—in the second verset. Sometimes, the substitution would appear to be rather automatic and not particularly strong in expressive effect, as in these two separate lines from the prophet Joel (Joel 1:5 and 13): "Rise, drunkards, and weep, / and wail all *drinkers of wine.*" "Gird yourselves and keen, you priests, / wail, you *ministrants of the altar.*" In other instances, it is hard to be sure whether the term in the second verset represents a "realization" of its counterpart in the first because we don't know to what extent a particular kenning may have become an automized substitution for the Hebrew listener. Thus, when Micah (6:7) says, "Shall I give my firstborn for my trespass, / *the fruit of my loins* for my own sins?" perhaps the kenning of the second verset communicates nothing more than the idea of offspring, though I would be inclined to suspect that it reinforces the sense of intimate bodily connection between parent and child. A similar pairing occurs in Job (15:14), where, however, the likelihood of dynamic progression from the first term to the second may be somewhat higher. "What is man that he should be guiltless, / that he should be in the right, *he born-of-woman?*" At any rate, the replacement of the general term *'enosh,* man, by the kenning, *yelud 'ishah,* born-of-woman, would seem to stress man's creaturely frailty, his dependence upon the cycle of biological reproduction, which fits in with the emphasis the speaker (Eliphaz) goes on to make, that the very heavens are not innocent before God, and how much more so lowly man.

Robert Alter. *Hebrew University Studies in Literature and the Arts.* Spring 1983, pp. 86–87

It has been widely assumed that there existed a stock of fixed pairs which belonged to the poetic tradition of Canaan and Israel, and that poets, specially
trained in their craft, drew on this stock to aid in the oral composition of parallel
lines. If, for example, a poet generated a line containing the word *ksp* ["silver"],
his next line would be formed around its fixed pair, *ḥrṣ* ["gold"].

There are actually two separate issues involved here. One is the issue of oral
composition, which remains a hypothesis for biblical poetry. The other is the issue of the existence of fixed pairs as opposed to non-fixed pairs. The connection
made between theories of oral composition and word pairs is an accident of intellectual history. The discovery of Ugaritic word pairs and their similarity to Hebrew word pairs came at the same time that the Parry-Lord theory was in ascend-
ence. Scholars simply linked newly emerging evidence with newly emerging
theories. Since it proved impossible to find in Hebrew poetry the same kinds of
metrical formulae that were present in Greek poetry, biblical scholars substituted
what they had in abundance—parallel word pairs—and declared them to be the
functional equivalents of formulae. Word pairs existed, according to this line of
thought, to enable a poet to compose orally.

But, of course, this leaves much unaccounted for. For one thing, it does not
explain how the rest of the line, besides the word pairs, was composed. For another, the same word pairs occur in poetry that was almost certainly not composed orally. For these reasons, as well as because of recent doubts about the
Parry-Lord theory, the time has come, as others have already suggested, to remove the issue of oral composition from the discussion of word pairs.

That leaves us with the notion of a stock of fixed pairs—the poet's dictionary, as it has been called. This was presumably a poetic substratum of biblical
Hebrew and Ugaritic, the privileged knowledge of trained poets. But this stock
of pairs, once numbering a few dozen, is now approaching a thousand and still
growing. Moreover, the same pairs that occur in poetic parallelism also occur in
prose—in juxtaposition, collocation, and even in construct with one another. If
these pairs were, indeed, reserved for poets, then they threaten to leave the ordinary speaker without a vocabulary. It seems obvious that we cannot separate
them from the total lexicon of Hebrew. Having said that, it becomes clear that
there is no qualitative difference between the so-called "fixed" pairs and pairs
that have not been so labelled. The only difference is that fixed pairs are attested
more often than non-fixed pairs. Since it serves the present study no purpose to
make this quantitative distinction, we will speak only of word pairs.

If word pairs are not part of a poetic substratum, where do they come from? I
would contend that they are simply the products of normal word associations that
are made by all competent speakers. This has been stated or hinted at, at least in
part, by W. Watters, J. Kugel, P.C. Craigie, and M. O'Connor. Watters says
that "many recurring pairs may be ascribed . . . to borrowing, coincidence, or idiom," and "pairs which are deemed 'rare associations' by modern scholarship,
were but common associations to the poet and the public" [William R. Watters,
Formula Criticism and the Poetry of the Old Testament, 1976, pp. 73, 75]. The

implicit assumption here, although it is developed no further, is that both common and rare pairings derive from commonly held associations of terms. Kugel echoes this when he states that "Hebrew and Ugaritic, like most languages, had their stock of conventionally associated terms, of synonyms and near-synonyms, and of antonyms and near-antonyms" [James L. Kugel, *The Idea of Biblical Poetry*, 1981, p. 33]. But, although both Watters and Kugel are on the right track, they do not pursue it far enough. Kugel still holds on to the idea of a "stock of conventionally associated terms," as if certain words had handy associations which facilitated pairing, and others did not. (The terms "synonyms" and "antonyms" also need to be replaced, for they do not aptly describe most word pairs.) . . .

The poetic pairings are the same as those in prose. All of these associations belong to the same linguistic phenomenon. Much of this was already sensed by biblicists but there was no model around which to structure the discussion. The linguistic theory of word association provides that model.

This approach to word pairs leads to the conclusion that they were not specially invented to enable the composition of parallel lines. Word pairs exist, at least potentially, in all languages, whether or not they use parallelism; and in those that do use parallelism, the word pairs are not restricted to parallel lines but may occur in non-parallelistic writing as well. *It is not word pairs that create parallelism. It is parallelism that activates word pairs.* Since parallelism is essentially a form of coupling, it produces coupling on all linguistic levels. On the lexical level the coupling takes the form of the realization of two or more words which are normally (or sometimes not so frequently) associated by speakers of the language. The lists of pairs that scholars have collected are not part of a poetic or even literary tradition. They are much more: they are a window into what psycholinguists would call the language behavior, and ultimately the whole conceptual world, of speakers of biblical Hebrew and Ugaritic. They evince mundane connections like *ox* and *ass* and ethnic prejudices like *Philistine* and *uncircumcised*. Not only should we continue to collect them, but we should document their frequencies and patterns to the extent that textual remains permit. This is the linguistic task.

The literary task is to see how a given author or verse uses a specific pair for his own purpose—to create his own emphasis or meaning. Does he use an unexpected or rare association to shock his readers? Does he originate a new association of words much as he does in a simile or metaphor? Or does he give new life to a common association? Poets, after all, use the same language and the same linguistic rules as their audience, but it is the way in which they use these that makes them poets.

Adele Berlin. Ugarit-Forschungen, 15, 1983, pp. 7–8,
16

HUMOR

The Hebrew Bible rightly deserves to be termed the Book of Books in the world of letters: it is distinguished from other literary productions by the richness of its sentences, its charm of style and diction, its pathos, and also by the flashes of genuine humour, which here and there illuminate its pages. Naturally its humour differs materially from the broad, rich humour of Sterne, Cervantes, Voltaire or Heine, but it has a stamp of its own, which is in some respects akin to that found in certain passages of the ancient classics. One or two examples will serve.

In the first book of the *Iliad,* Homer describes a scene on Mount Olympus, in which the Greek gods and goddesses are represented as seated at a banquet, and waited upon by the lame Hephaestus. Observing his halting gait, they burst into peals of laughter. Comparable, perhaps, with this is the description of the well-known scene on Mount Carmel, when Elijah, the true prophet of God, gathered round him the false prophets of Baal. After they had leapt on the altar from morning unto even, crying incessantly, "Oh, Baal, hear us," Elijah stepped forth, and exclaimed mockingly, "Cry ye louder, for he is a god; perhaps he talketh or walketh, or is on a journey; or peradventure he sleepeth and must be awaked" (1 Kgs. 18:27). The Aristophanic punning on proper names is paralleled not infrequently in the Bible. Thus, for example, the Hebrew word *Nabal* (1 Sam. 25:3), which means "rogue," is well applied as the proper name of a man, who was noted for the baseness of his character. Characteristic, too, is the name of one of Job's fair daughters, *Qeren-happukh* (Job 42:14), which literally means "a horn (or box) of cosmetics," suggesting the means by which the owner of that name may occasionally have embellished her charms. To the same class belongs the term *Tsara* . . . which has the double designation of "a rival wife," living in a country where polygamy is in vogue, and also of "misery." The humour hidden in these three words is certainly not brought into prominence in the authorized English version, where they are respectively translated by "folly," "Qeren-happukh," and "adversary." From these examples it will be seen that an acquaintance with the idiom of the Hebrew tongue is essential to the thorough understanding of the Bible, and as Biblical critics have hitherto paid but little attention to this particular subject, the remarks to be offered on it in the present essay may, perhaps, be of some interest. . . .

The greatest satirist among them was undoubtedly the prophet Isaiah, whose orations combine the pungency of satire with the charm of an exquisite poetical style. Somewhat in the manner of Demosthenes and Cicero, Isaiah often wages war against the vices which prevailed among the higher and lower classes of his people. He frequently derides princes and leaders for not preserving and upholding that true spirit of patriotism, which generally helps to make a country secure from external invasion. "Ye are," he exclaims with bitter irony, "Ye are only *mighty to drink wine,* and men of *strength* to pour out *strong drinks*" (Isa.

5:22). Isaiah's orations frequently contain graphic and satirical descriptions of how things will be when that fatal day—the *dies irae, dies illa*—comes, on which the enemy will reign supreme within the capital of the Judaeans, bringing with them the suffering of famine, sickness, and pestilence. These poorly clad and careworn men will surround the lucky owner of a decent garment, saying: "Thou hast still clothing, be thou our ruler, and let this ruin be under thine hand." But he will decline the proffered honour with the humiliating remark: "I will *not* be an healer; for in my house is neither bread nor clothing: make me not a ruler of the people" (ibid. 3:6 and 7). The then prevailing need and distress will not be less felt by the Jewish women, most of whom the disastrous war will have deprived of their husbands and natural protectors. The consequence of this will be that "On the day *seven* women will take hold of *one* man, saying, We will eat our own bread, and wear our own apparel: only let us be called by thy name, and thus take away our reproach" (ibid. 4:1). . . .

The burlesquing of idols and idolatry always afforded a ready mark for the sarcasm of the prophets. As Aristophanes in *The Birds* ridicules the Greek gods and goddesses, so Isaiah satirizes the sham gods of *his* country, which were held in great estimation by not a few of his own people. His description of the origin and manufacture of an idol is certainly full of humour. "He" (the pious idolater) "heweth down a tree (he says) and burneth part thereof in a fire; one part serves him as firewood, by means of which he roasteth meat and is satisfied; yea, he warmeth himself therewith, and saith: Aha, I am warm; I have seen the fire. And out of the residue thereof he maketh a god, even his graven image: he falleth down before it, and worshippeth it, and prayeth unto it, and saith: Deliver me, for thou art my god" (ibid. 44:17).

With equal humour Isaiah makes merry over the false prophets of Israel, whom he compares to blind watchmen and to dumb dogs. "His (Israel's) watchmen," he says, "are blind: they are all ignorant, they are all dumb dogs, they cannot even bark; they lie down as if dreaming, and are fond of slumber" (ibid. 56:10).

Joseph Chotzner. Hebrew Humour and Other Essays
(London, Luzac, 1905), pp. 1–4

That the Bible . . . contains humor has certainly simply been overlooked before because from a purely theological perspective this light-hearted literary genre was not held to be worthy of the Bible. The scientific approach to biblical scripture, though, has pointed out the purely worldly character of many passages. When Jacob took advantage of Esau's extreme hunger in order to get him to hand over his birthright (Gen. 25:29ff); when he disguised himself in order to filch the blessing designated by Isaac for Esau (Gen. 27); when he then, through great cunning, got rich through Laban (Gen. 30:25ff.); when Rachel in a rude scene stole and hid her father's household gods (Gen. 31:19ff.); when Samson performed pranks like [Till] Eulenspiegel (Judg. 13ff.); when the prophet Elijah mocked the priests of Baal with incomparable humor (I Kgs. 18:27); when one hears of the ostentation of the Judean women transformed [metaphorically] into the dressing table of an elegant lady in the obloquy of Isaiah (Isa. 3:18ff.); when one thinks one is reading a chapter from Dante's *Divine Comedy* in [Isaiah's] description of Nebuchadnezzar's appearance in the netherworld (ibid. 14:9ff.); when he made fun of the craftsman who carved himself a god out of a block of stone, another part of which he used for preparation for his food (ibid. 44:13ff.); when Hosea found irony in the idolators "who offer up human beings and kiss calves" (Hos. 13:2); when the Book of Esther is full of astonishing shifts of situation (for example, the minister Haman as herald in front of the Jew Mordecai)—listeners or readers laugh at these popular stories, in which many elements of humor, like those occurring in other literatures, too, are at hand.

> J. K. Kohn and L. Davidsohn, In *Jüdisches Lexikon*. Vol. II. Ed. by Georg Herlitz and Bruno Kirschner (Berlin, Jüdischer Verlag, 1928), col. 1687†

Certainly, the Bible bears no resemblance to a joke book. There are only a few passages clearly designed to cause readers to laugh. But there is deep and pervasive concern with laughter as a complex and very important human activity.

Taking into account the many varieties of laughter, there are more than 250 biblical references to it. They are most heavily concentrated in "wisdom literature": Job, Psalms, Proverbs, and Ecclesiastes. Isaiah and Jeremiah make many allusions to laughter, and the topic is of great significance to gospel writers. . . .

Deliberate exploitation of verbal plasticity underlies many forms of humor. It is basic to both the pun and the riddle. While both may be employed in modern life purely for the sake of a laugh, near-sacredness of words in Hebrew thought made word play solemn as well as amusing.

Guests invited to Samson's wedding feast were challenged by a riddle. Their inability to solve it made them the target of Samson's laughter; they were defeated in an intellectual struggle. Seriousness of the matter is indicated by Delilah's reaction. Her husband, she said, could not possibly love her because he gave the wrong answer in response to her pleading (Judg. 16:10, 15). Personally as well as in sympathy with her countrymen, she resented the triumphant laughter of her bridegroom.

> Gary Webster. *Laughter in the Bible* (St. Louis, Bethany Press, 1960), pp. 9, 19

An unusual measure of critical agreement has been realized in descriptions of the Bible's lack of humor. Yet the opinion represented by such statements as [Alfred North] Whitehead's that "the total absence of humor from the Bible is one of the most singular things in all literature" relies on evidence which is at best equivocal. The need for a re-evaluation of this evidence will be asserted here; it can be effectively demonstrated that the Comic is a relevant category of analysis to the understanding of the Bible, and that failure to acknowledge this must inevitably distort that understanding and any theoretical inferences based on it. The implications of Whitehead's comment, for instance, are neither covert nor irenic: what Professor Salo Baron has diagnosed as the "lachrymose conception of Jewish history"—Jewish history as desperate grimness—has been applied to the earliest moments of that history; and it casts as fragmented a shadow over that time as does the analysis of more recent periods which would take its cue exclusively from the motifs of persecution and exile.

The pun seem too slight an element on which to build such an argument. But precisely because it is the most informal expression of the literary Comic do certain of its appearances in the Bible lend emphasis to the claim made here. For although the pun frequently appears spontaneous and unmediated, it can also mark the focus of a situation carefully and artistically contrived; and where this is the case, the contrast with its appearance elsewhere is sharpened. We are informed, in short, that the intention it must then be admitted to represent is integral to the design of the text.

Two puns found in Genesis become especially telling for this reason. The builders of the Tower of Babel find themselves blocked not only from the *bab' el* —"gateway to God"—which they had wanted to enter, but also from each other: "The Lord did there confound [*balal*] their language" (11:8). Again, in the Joseph story, Joseph interprets the dream of a fellow-prisoner who had been Pharaoh's cup-bearer: "Yet within three days shall Pharaoh lift up [*yissa'*] thine head, and restore thee unto thy place; and thou shalt deliver Pharaoh's cup into his hand. . . ." The royal baker, a third inmate, is encouraged by this response to relate a dream which he has had, and Joseph's second reply mimics the first: "Yet within three days shall Pharaoh lift up [*yissa'*] thy head—from off thy shoulders and shall hang thee from a tree; and the birds shall eat thy flesh from off thee." The sardonic twist of word and fate recurs as the outcome of Joseph's predictions is announced: "And it came to pass the third day, which was Pharaoh's birthday, that he made a feast unto all his servants: and he lifted up the head of the chief butler and the chief baker among his servants. And he restored the chief butler unto his butlership again . . . but he hanged the chief baker . . ." (Gen. 40:10–20).

These puns are symptomatic. For one thing, they constitute strong evidence that the narrative is "serious" in its adaptation of humor: the textual design of both incidents, at least in this one respect, seems beyond dispute. Secondly, they provide an indication of the themes of the Biblical Comic—what the narrative considers funny or risible. The Tower of Babel incident, whatever else it does, offers an opportunity to poke fun at idolators and their version of the way to God. The same motif, it will be noted, recurs in other appearances of the Comic in Genesis. When Jacob flees with his family from the house of Laban, Rachel, unknown to her husband, abducts the Teraphim, Laban's household gods. Laban pursues the group and, overtaking them, demands an accounting. Challenged by Jacob, he fruitlessly searches the camp, finally confronting Rachel who remains seated as he approaches her: "Let it not displease my Lord," Rachel calms him, "that I cannot rise up before thee; for the custom of women is upon me" (31:34).

She happens, of course, to be sitting on the Teraphim—and we have a glimpse of unclerical ribaldry in oblique defense of the Biblical God.

The latter episode also counts as one of several variations on the narrative's "trickster" theme, in which the situation represented turns on a battle—and ensuing loss—of wits. Thus, Abraham, to protect himself from their rivalry for her favors, twice misleads his hosts into believing that Sarah is his sister (Gen. 12:10–20; 20:2–16). The trickster finds himself undone in both attempts, compounding the deception of the second occasion with the lame excuse that Sarah really *is* his half-sister—who also happens to be his wife. The chronicle of Jacob, especially in describing his commerce with Laban, remarks a number of episodes in which the lines of contest are similarly drawn. In one of these, Jacob, after serving Rachel's father seven years to gain her hand, anticipates the bounty of his bride and his wedding night. Suspecting nothing (and knowing, we wonder, how much), he awakens in the hard light of morning to find himself bound instead to the "tender-eyed" Leah and to seven more years in the service of the wily Laban (Gen. 13:15–28). Prior to this, the first meeting between Jacob and Esau after Isaac's death provides a near-farcical variation on the trickster theme. Jacob fears the worst at the hands of his brother who had threatened to kill him. Esau surprises Jacob, however, with a welcome which becomes so effusive that the scene closes as Jacob, still suspicious of the turn of events, anxiously but delicately attempts to escape Esau's importunements.

Dov B. Lang. Judaism. Summer, 1962, pp. 249–50

The Hebrew Scriptures are filled with a sense of playfulness, especially with the language. Often, the point of a passage depends on the reader's appreciation of an outrageous pun. Satire, gentle wit and even farce abound in almost every book. . . .

Many of the most famous scenes in the Hebrew Scriptures rely on puns, which we often miss in the English. The name "Adam," for example, is formed from the Hebrew word for "earth" or "clay." In Genesis 2, the name indicates Adam's origin, man's earthiness. It would thus appeal to the Semitic sense of irony that the ground, not Adam himself, is cursed after the forbidden fruit is eaten. The name "Eve" is in the Hebrew *Hawwah*, or "she who makes live," indicating her motherhood of the human race. . . .

God, for the Hebrews, is not only a master punster. The divine allows him or herself to become involved in numerous comic scenes. The judgment scene in the garden is typical. When God asks the man whether he has eaten of the forbidden tree, Adam tries to throw the blame back on God: "The woman you gave me, she gave me of the tree and I ate" (Gen. 3:12). The woman in turn shifts the blame to the serpent. God, however, cuts this Gordian knot of blame-shifting and breaks up the conspiracy for good by placing enmity between the conspirators: woman and serpent, woman and man, man and earth. This solution is highly ironic and is used by God again in defeating the conspiracy of Babel.

Humanity plans to build a tower "whose top may reach unto heaven" (Gen.

11:14). Here God splits up the conspirators by confounding their language. Again, a pun figures prominently in the story. The Hebrew word for "to confuse" (Gen. 11:9) that is used is similar to the name "Babel," and is the origin for the English word" to babble." . . .

The book of Judges preserves ancient oral material which often shows an earthly sense of humor. The saga of Ehud is practically farce. In it, the hero gains access to the king of Moab's inner chambers by claiming to have "a message from God." He does, but not in the way the king expects. Left-handed, Ehud stabs the king with a dagger concealed on his right thigh. The author makes great play of the fact that the king was so fat that "the hilt too went in after the blade, and the fat closed over the blade [Judg. 3:22]." Our hero loses his knife in the fat, but escapes through a window. His escape is made possible by the fact that the servants thought that the king was "probably covering his feet in the inner part of the cool room," a thinly disguised but creative euphemism for sitting on the toilet. Though crude to our ears, the tale of Ehud is indubitably a comic one.

The ancient mind enjoyed the interplay of wit. Samson puts Delilah off three times with false clues about the source of his strength before she finally wheedles it out of him. Jacob toils for seven years for the hand of Rachel, only to be deceived into marrying her less marriageable sister. But Jacob is a master trickster, having tricked Esau out of his inheritance. He asks his father-in-law only for the rarest of animals: black sheep and spotted goats. Laban quickly agrees, feeling that he has once again made out better than his son-in-law. But Jacob breeds Laban's flocks to produce such strains. "Laban thus got the feeble and Jacob the sturdy, and he grew extremely rich." Jacob's cleverness is rewarded.

Joseph's practical jokes on his brothers (Gen. 42–46) can also be put into this category of comedy. Prophets as well as patriarchs can be tricksters. Nathan tells King David of a rich man who took a lamb, the only possession of a poor man. Touched, David cries that the man deserves to die. Then Nathan interprets the story: the poor man is Uriah, Bathsheba's husband, whom David has had killed so that he could steal his wife. In an ironic twist, the king has pronounced his own sentence!

Eugene J. Fisher. Religious Education, Nov.–Dec., 1977, pp. 571–72, 574, 577–78

Hyperbole. *See* Rhetoric: Hyperbole

IMAGERY

It is undoubtedly clear and evident that most prophecies are given in images, for this is the characteristic of the imaginative faculty, the organ of prophecy. We find it also necessary to say a few words on the figures, hyperboles, and exaggerations that occur in Scripture. They would create strange ideas if we were to take them literally without noticing the exaggeration which they contain, or if we were to understand them in accordance with the original meaning of the terms, ignoring the fact that these are used figuratively. Our Sages say distinctly Scripture uses hyperbolic or exaggerated language; and quote as an instance, "cities walled and fortified, rising up to heaven" (Deut. 1:28). As a hyperbole our Sages quote, "For the bird of heaven carries the voice" (Eccl. 10:20); in the same sense it is said, "Whose height is like that of cedar trees" (Am. 2:9). Instances of this kind are frequent in the language of all prophets; what they say is frequently hyperbolic or exaggerated, and not precise or exact. What Scripture says about Og, "Behold, his bedstead was an iron bedstead, nine cubits its length," etc. (Deut. [3:11]), does not belong to this class of figures, for the bedstead (*eres,* comp. *arsenu,* Song of Sol. 1:16) is never exactly of the same dimensions as the person using it; it is not like a dress that fits round the body; it is always greater than the person that sleeps therein; as a rule, is it by a third longer. If, therefore, the bed of Og was nine cubits in length, he must, according to this proportion, have been six cubits high, or a little more. The words, "by the cubit of a man," mean, by the measure of any ordinary man, and not by the measure of Og; for men have the limbs in a certain proportion. Scripture thus tells us that Og was double as long as an ordinary person, or a little less. This is undoubtedly an exceptional height among men, but not quite impossible. As regards the Scriptural statement about the length of man's life in those days, I say that only the persons named lived so long, whilst other people enjoyed the ordinary length of life. The men named were exceptions, either in consequence of different causes, as e.g., their food or mode of living, or by way of miracle, which admits of no analogy.

We must further discuss the figurative language employed in Scripture. In some cases this is clear and evident, and doubted by no person; e.g., "The mountains and hills shall break forth in song before you, and all the trees of the wood clap their hands" (Isa. 55:12); this is evidently figurative language; also the following passage—"The fir-trees rejoice at thee," etc. (*ibid.* 14:8), which is rendered by Jonathan, son of Uzziel, "The rulers rejoice at thee, who are rich in possessions." This figure is similar to that used in the phrase, "Butter of kine and milk of sheep," etc. (Deut. 32:14).

And these figures are very frequent in the books of the prophets. Some are easily recognized by the ordinary reader as figures, others with some difficulty. Thus nobody doubts that the blessing, "May the Lord open to thee his good treasure, the heavens," must be taken figuratively; for God has no treasure in which He keeps the rain. The same is the case with the following passage—"He opened the doors of heaven, he rained upon them manna to eat" (Ps. 78:23, 24). No person assumes that there is a door or gate in heaven, but every one understands that this is a simile and figurative expression. In the same way must be understood the following passages—"The heavens were opened" (Ezek. 1:1); "If not, blot me out from thy book which thou hast written" (Exod. 32:32); "I will blot him out from the book of life" (*ibid.* v. 33). All these phrases are figurative; and we must not assume that God has a book in which He writes, or from which

He blots out, as those generally believe that do not find figurative speech in these passages. They are all of the same kind. [ca. 1195]

Moses Maimonides. *Guide for the Perplexed.* Tr. from the Arabic by M. Friedländer. 2d ed., rev. (London, Routledge & Kegan Paul, 1904), pp. 247–48.

Generally speaking there is so exact an Analogy between the *Scripture-Comparisons,* and Things compared, as Strikes Us at first Sight. As they never shou'd be used but to cast some new Light upon the Thing to which they are applied, so in [Song of Songs] they are taken from sensible and familiar Objects, with which those, to whom the sacred Authors wrote, were daily conversant. Palm-Trees, Cedars, Lions, Eagles, are common in *Palestine.* The Comparison of God to the Latter is at the same time one of the most exact Descriptions, and apt Similies imaginable. *As an Eagle stirreth up her nest, fluttereth over her young, spreadeth abroad her Wings, taketh them, beareth them on her Wings,* so the Lord alone *did lead him, and there was no strange God with him.* (Deut. 32:11, 12) . . .

The *Ancients* differ'd from the *Moderns* in the use and application of the Simile. The Art and Design of adapting every Particular in the *Comparison,* so as to make it exactly correspond, seems peculiar to the *Moderns.* The *Ancients* thought it sufficient to hit the general Resemblance, and draw the out-lines just and strong. They were so employ'd about the principal Features—and *essential* Beauties of the Piece, that they oftentimes neglected the Drapery and *ornamental.* . . .

The Old Testament affords Instances [of allegory] in abundance. The most ancient extant is That of *Jotham* in the Ninth Chapter of the Book of Judges, which with the utmost Simplicity is very artfully contrived, to rebuke the Treachery of *Abimelech,* and the Revolt and Folly of the *Shechemites.* Indeed Allegory is peculiarly proper for Reproof. 'Tis commonly said, that few Persons know how to *take* Reproof, but (as Lord Shaftsbury somewhere observes) 'tis because few Persons know how to *give* it. Some Colouring and Disguise is often necessary to conceal it from the Eyes of the Person reprov'd, till it has touch'd his Heart. . . . Of this We have a remarkable Instance in the *Parable* of Nathan to David, after He had kill'd *Uriah,* and taken his Wife. How artfully is the Story framed to raise the just Indignation of the King against the Offender? (II Sam. 12) . . . The Circumstances of the Story greatly add to the Beauty of it. The Comparison of the Subject to a poor Man, of the Monarch to an oppressive rich one; of *Uriah's* Wife to a little favourite Ew-Lamb that had been always fondled with, and of *David's* Passion to a Traveller that was come to him, is very apt, just, and delicate.

John Husbands. Preface to *A Miscellany of Poems by Several Hands* (Oxford, J. Husbands, 1731), sigs. f3ᵛ– f4ʳ, g2ʳ–g2ᵛ, grᵛ

Now we shall find, that the Metaphors and Comparisons of the Hebrew Poets, present to us a very beautiful view of the natural objects of their own country, and of the arts and employments of their common life. . . .

They were a people chiefly occupied with agriculture and pasturage. These were arts held in high honour among them; not disdained by their patriarchs, kings, and prophets. Little addicted to commerce; separated from the rest of the world by their laws and their religion; they were, during the better days of their state, strangers in a great measure to the refinements of luxury. Hence flowed, of course, the many allusions to pastoral life, to the "green pastures" and the "still waters," and to the care and watchfulness of a shepherd over his flock, which carry to this day so much beauty and tenderness in them, in the 23rd Psalm, and in many other passages of the Poetical Writings of Scripture. Hence, all the images founded upon rural employments, upon the wine-press, the threshing-floor, the stubble and the chaff. To disrelish all such images, is the effect of false delicacy. Homer is at least as frequent, and much more minute and particular, in his similes, founded on what we now call low life; but, in his management of them, far inferior to the Sacred Writers, who generally mix with their comparisons of this kind somewhat of dignity and grandeur, to ennoble them. What inexpressible grandeur does the following rural image in Isaiah, for instance, receive from the intervention of the Deity: "The nations shall rush like the rushings of many waters; but God shall rebuke them, and they shall fly far off; and they shall be chased as the chaff of the mountain before the wind, and like the down of the thistle before the whirlwind." [Isa. 17:13] . . .

From all this it results, that the imagery of the Sacred Poets is, in a high degree, expressive and natural; it is copied directly from real objects, that were before their eyes; it has this advantage, of being more complete within itself, more entirely founded on national ideas and manners, than that of most other Poets. In reading their works, we find ourselves continually in the land of Judea. The palm-trees, and the cedars of Lebanon, are ever rising in our view. The face of their territory, the circumstances of their climate, the manners of the people, and the august ceremonies of their religion, constantly pass under different forms before us.

The comparisons employed by the Sacred Poets are generally short, touching on one point only of resemblance, rather than branching out into little Episodes. In this respect, they have perhaps an advantage over the Greek and Roman Authors; whose comparisons, by the length to which they are extended, sometimes interrupt the narration too much, and carry too visible marks of study and labour. Whereas, in the Hebrew Poets, they appear more like the glowings of a lively fancy, just glancing aside to some resembling object, and presently returning to its track.

Hugh Blair. *Lectures on Rhetoric and Belles Lettres.* 2nd. ed., corr. Vol. III. (London, Printed for W. Strahan, T. Cadell, 1785), pp. 185, 189–91

The greater part of the imagery of the Old Testament is drawn from nature.

We shall not expect to find in the Old Testament those feelings towards the beauty of natural objects which Wordsworth felt. With Wordsworth it was a "cult" to look for beauty in nature and find it and talk about it. Take for instance the smile about the maiden:

A violet by a mossy stone / Half hidden from the eye,
Fair as a star, when only one / Is shining in the sky. ["Lucy Gray"]

A Hebrew might have used the violet by way of comparison, as he used the lily and the rose of Sharon, but he would not have stopped to analyse the special beauty of a violet "half hidden by a mossy stone." The lily was beautiful and that was enough. Three British poets [Shelley, James Hogg, Wordsworth] have given us studies of skylarks. The only thing a Hebrew poet would have found time to notice in a skylark is its special qualifications for praising its Maker. If there were any song birds in Palestine they are not mentioned. Shelley again compares something with "mountain springs under the morning sun." A Hebrew poet does indeed notice the brightness of the morning sun free from clouds [II Sam. 23:4], but would not, one feels, have noticed the particular effect of it upon water.

The Hebrew saw in nature the work of a strong hand rather than the beauty and variety that the modern eye has been trained to see. Allowance must also be made for the difference in scenery. But to the Hebrew each natural object seems to have suggested a single purity or characteristic, and that quality was rarely beauty. For instance, to him the chief feature of a flower was its rapid fading, and it appears as an image only of the shortness of human life. Contrast the following verdict:

A lily of a day / Is fairer far, in May,
Although it fall and die that night,
It was the plant and flower of light. (Ben Jonson)

The lily here does not simply point a moral about "change and decay," it is the "thing of beauty (that) is a joy for ever."

Natural objects in the Old Testament are images or reflections of God, and are noticed for some single prominent feature:

Mountains suggested strength and durability: God's "righteousness is like the strong mountains." (Ps. 36:6) "As the mountains are round about Jerusalem, so the Lord is round about his people." (Ps. 125:2) "Before the mountains were brought forth . . . from everlasting to everlasting thou art God." (Ps. 90:2, cf. Job 15:7, Deut. 33:15) "By his strength setteth fast the mountains." (Ps. 65:6) The beautiful outlines, rolling slopes, and light effects of the mountains are not noticed, only their strength and durability.

Rivers, such as the Nile, suggest strength in motion. The following metaphor shows the terrible advance of the Assyrians:

> The Lord bringeth up upon them the waters of the River, strong and many, and he shall come up over all his channels, and go over all his banks: and he shall sweep onward into Judah . . . he shall reach even to the neck. (Isa. 8:7–8). . . .

Animals also are noticed for their strength or wonderful motion as things of terror rather than of beauty. It is the strong and wild animals that are mentioned most frequently, the lion, the wild ass, the unicorn, the wild ox ("canst thou bind him?"), behemoth ("his limbs are like bands of iron"), leviathan ("in his neck abideth strength, and terror danceth before him"). Even the horse is mentioned only for its strength, and the fine description of one in Job is of the warhorse ("the glory of his snorting is terrible"). [Job 39–41]

So it is with *birds*. The eagle is quoted numberless times for its strength of flight or its terror as a bird of prey, and its habits and those of doves have been keenly noted, but the song and plumage of birds are rarely noticed.

It will be found then that (1) one prominent feature is selected for comparison from all natural objects, e.g. the eagle's swiftness, the mountain's strength, the ant's wisdom, the stream's instability; (2) it is the stern side of nature that comes under observation as a rule. This would largely be due to the nature of the scenery in Palestine; (3) nature is merely a mirror of God's strength, majesty, and power.

Percy C. Sands. Literary Genius of the Old Testament
(Oxford, Clarendon Press, 1924), pp. 73–76

The Bible achieves its vividness by means of what might be called "picture language." It rarely resorts to abstract ideas or theoretical phrasing. Although the thoughts which it expresses are often profound and sometimes extremely delicate in their distinctions, the language is the visual language which is found in the simple eloquence of simple people. In this way, the great Biblical thoughts are brought right down to earth and poured into the vessel of objects that can be seen and handled. The Bible could almost be painted as well as it was written, so visual is it.

For example, the Prophet Jeremiah wishes to indicate that the people of Israel have turned away so long from God to many idolatries and have become so accustomed to the injustices of their daily life, that by now it seems hopeless for them ever to rid themselves of their sinfulness. Instead of speaking, as we would of a "deep-rooted habit of sin which cannot be easily discarded," the Prophet expresses the idea in an image that leaps immediately to the eye. He says: "Can the leopard change his spots, or the Ethiopian his skin?" (13:23.)

When Isaiah desires to describe the ideal future, when a righteous king will usher in a period of peace and when violence will disappear as a motive for human action, he does not speak as we would do, using the vague terms "era" and "violence" and "human cooperation." He says vividly and concretely: "The wolf shall dwell with the lamb and a little child shall lead them." (11:6.)

Such picture language is very close to metaphor. A spiritual idea is compared to a physical fact. It is often unconscious metaphor. But the Bible is also full of conscious metaphor, apt and impressive. When the Prophet Isaiah wants to say that God will forgive the people their sins, that He will afford them an opportunity for repentance so that they may be righteous once more, he thinks of the contrast between sinfulness and righteousness in the metaphor of two brilliant colors, and he says: "Though your sins be as scarlet, they shall be as white as snow." (1:18.)

The Prophets seek to explain why a people chosen by God should yet be so sinful. Both Jeremiah and Isaiah use the same metaphor to explain this difficulty. It is a word picture that was familiar to the people of Palestine who worked in their vineyards, and who knew how important it is to have the proper stock for the vine, and who also found to their sorrow that often a good breed of vine somehow degenerates. So the Prophet Jeremiah says of Israel:

> Yet I had planted thee a noble vine,
> Wholly a right seed;
> How then art thou turned into the degenerate plant?
>   (2:21.)

So too Isaiah uses the same metaphor: "For the vineyard of the Lord of hosts is the house of Israel." (5:7.)

In a prose portion of the Bible, when the lawgiver desires to make clear to the people the punishments that will be theirs for their sinfulness, he makes use of a vivid agricultural metaphor. Instead of saying that they will suffer drought and that nothing will grow and there will be sandstorms instead of rain, he says: "And thy heaven that is over thy head shall be brass and the earth that is under thee shall be iron. The Lord will make the rain of thy land powder and dust." (Deut. 28:23, 24.) When, in a similar passage in Leviticus, the author wants to say that part of God's punishment will be that the people will lose their inner confidence and become terror-stricken and nervous, he says that they will be terrified at the sound of a leaf rustling behind them in a wind and they will run away when no one drives them. But he says it much more vividly and pictorially than we moderns would express it. He says: "And the sound of a driven leaf shall chase them; and they shall flee as one fleeth from the sword; and they shall fall when none pursueth." (26:36.) It is thus through concrete image and clear meaningful metaphors that the Bible achieves everywhere its brilliant vividness.

Solomon B. Freehof. *Preface to Scripture* (Cincinnati, Union of American Hebrew Congregations, 1950), pt. 1, pp. 80–83

It must be obvious that there are many "iterative" themes and images and symbols in the Old Testament . . . which might reveal something of the unity binding together in their imaginative experience psalmist, prophet, and historian. There is, for instance, the image of Israel as God's vineyard (cp. Isa. 5 &c.) which clearly has a more than functional purpose. The vine and the fruit of the vine have, in the religion of Israel, a special ritual value, as can be seen from the restrictions, especially in the case of the Nazirite, which surround them. The analogy is thus neither superficial nor fortuitous; it is on the contrary organic and reciprocal. A religious significance enters into both sides of it. . . .

The image of bride and bridegroom expressing the relation of God to Israel has likewise a rich and mysterious significance which makes the language of Jeremiah 2:2f. the language of the Covenant in a unique sense. Again, the relationship is an organic and reciprocal one in which each side of the analogy is illuminated by the other. In Hosea the analogy, rooted as it is in the prophet's own experience of marriage, takes on an almost obsessive character. In the expression ["I shall betroth you to me in faith, and you shall know the Lord"] (Hos. 2:22) he attains a potent ambiguity through the use of a term *y-d-'* ["know"] which signifies at once marital union, spiritual intimacy, and revelation. In the immediately preceding verse in Hosea, the term *raḥamim* ["mercy"] likewise retains in its context part of its original concrete force as a word denoting the affective biological link between the mother (and by extension, the father) and the issue of her womb. The image is made more explicit later in 11:2 and in such passages as Psalm 103:13. Here again the Father-Son relationship in the sphere of God-Israel does not nullify or displace the parent-child relation in the human sphere. On the contrary it is rooted in it and in turn gives it additional meaning and depth.

The iterative image to which I wish to devote the remainder of this article, however, is the image of the *natural order* as analogous to the character and function of law in the sphere of God-Israel. This may reveal better than any other example something of the structure and dimension of Old Testament imagery in general as well as something of the Israelite response to nature which needs to be understood in terms of the imaginative categories of Israel itself rather than those of a natural theology built up on the thought-forms of ancient Greece. . . .

We may now proceed directly to the analogy as it is displayed in the nineteenth Psalm and in related passages in the Psalter, namely Psalms 119:89, 147:14–20, and 33:6. In the first seven verses of Psalm 19 we have a description of the natural order; the sun, the most powerful and prominent symbol of that order, marking out the rhythmic alternation of day and night. This is no mechanical process of masses in motion as in the Newtonian cosmology; for nature has its own vital properties and the creatures express their joy in carrying out their allotted tasks. "He is as a bridegroom coming out of his chamber, And rejoiceth as a strong man to run his course." These verses are followed by five more in which the imagery of the natural order is transferred to the sphere of Law which, like the sun, enlightens the eyes, makes joyful the heart, is "bright" (*barah:* cp. Song 6:10) and "stands perpetually." Again, it is golden, or rather, "more desirable than gold." In verse 12 I detect a truly metaphysical ambiguity in the word *nizhar* which means at once "warned" or "taught" (cp. Eccl. 4:13; Ezek. 3:21) and also "enlightened" or "gleaming," its fundamental signification as in *zohar,* "splendour" (Dan. 12:3). The "splendour" would of course refer back to the sun passage, verses 1–7. In the remaining three verses the poet draws out the spiritual conclusion of his meditation and makes use of further ambiguously compressed phrases: the word *nistarot* ["hidden things"] echoes *nistar* ["hidden"] in verse 7; *hasokh* ["cover"] may have been suggested by *nistar* and the linked idea of *hoshekh* ["darkness"] which would constitute a kind of implied paronomasia. *Eitam* ["strong"] goes back to *tamim* ["perfect"] (v. 8) which in turn is suggested by the picture of the sun's perfect movement, its accomplished design. . . .

The witness in the sky, on the seas, and on the earth, is an integral part of the religion of Israel—the imagery of nature is no mere addition for poetical adornment or rhetorical illustration but is rather an organic part of the metaphysical insight of prophet and psalmist. It is a revelation parallel to that of God's direct revelation to Israel; it illuminates it, and is in turn illuminated by it.

Harold Fisch. *Journal of Theological Studies*. Oct.,
1955, pp. 164–65, 171–73

The most striking characteristic of biblical poetry, the feature which more than any other makes it the supreme lyrical literature that it is, are the images and figures which the poet employs to embody his feelings and thoughts. There is scarcely a poem within the entire corpus of Old Testament literature which does not bear witness to Israel's genius for imagery. The poet scales the loftiest heights and plumbs the lowest depths for his images. He enlists every aspect of nature, every human emotion and experience, every fragment drawn from daily life to translate his thoughts into living reality. The Book of Psalms has for that reason often been said to be the supreme lyrical literature of the world. Such books as Hosea and Jeremiah are monuments to the imagination of Israel, excelled only by the sublime poetry of Job and the superlative lyrical sequences of Deutero-Isaiah. The supremacy of Israel's poetry has but one explanation: its poets addressed themselves to the loftiest themes that ever inspired the mind and heart of man, the themes that concern man ultimately, kindle their highest aspirations, and demand their deepest devotion.

James Muilenburg. In *Encyclopedia Judaica*. Vol. XIII
(Jerusalem, Keter, 1972), cols. 680–81

God as a dragon, or a leopard, or lye [*sic*], or a hunter, or a woman in labor. God's people as stubborn oxen, dry rot, pottery, silver, soil, dew, a bride. God's relationship with his people as that of a lover wooing his sweetheart, a ferocious bear ready to tear up his prey, a parent teaching a toddler how to walk, a mother breast-feeding her baby. Outlandish comparisons? The extravagance of some modern paraphraser? No. A translation as dignified as the King James has them.

This figurative strain is an important dimension of biblical language. Some readers of Scripture may look upon it as a decorative device or a nice poetic touch. Others may consider the figurative language something that we have to look through or around or over in order to get the real meaning. I doubt whether those evaluations do justice to the biblical Word. Metaphor, simile, and image are central to scriptural language. . . .

We can easily find figurative language in the Psalms. The Lord is my shepherd. The godly man is like a tree planted beside the river. The Old Testament saint's wife is a fruitful vine and his children are like olive shoots around his table. (I'm not sure if we have here a hybrid plant or a mixed metaphor.) The gates of death. Mountains skipping like rams.

The historical sections of the Bible are usually straightforward, discursive prose. But even here we find incidents or reflections described metaphorically, as in Jacob's farewell speech: "[Judah] washes his garments in wine and his vesture in the blood of grapes," and several of the other sons are likened to lion, donkey, serpent, and hind (Gen. 49). In Deuteronomy 32 Moses uses an extended metaphor (teaching is like rain/dew/shower) and then praises the Lord with a series of anthropomorphisms and metaphors, including the beautiful one of the eagle flying under its young.

How about the teaching portions of Scripture? Certainly Proverbs is rich in moral teaching—and it is also an inexhaustible source of metaphoric language. In the opening chapters Wisdom is personified as a woman, and in chapter 8 Wisdom, again as a woman, is created before the world and is God's co-worker and co-enjoyer of creation. A man consorting with massage-parlor girls is like an ox going to the slaughter (7:22), and a contentious woman reminds the proverb maker of a leaky faucet (27:15).

There is also a figurative strain in many of the prophetic writings. The sheep of Isaiah 53, the wine, milk, and bread, and the seed-producing rain and singing mountains of Isaiah 55, the strange creatures of Ezekiel and Revelation, can be read in an other-than-common-sense meaning. In Hosea the Lord compares himself to a husband, moth, lion, showers, farmer, parent, dew, heated oven, garden, and a cake not turned. Ezekiel abounds in metaphoric and symbolic language; the wheels within wheels and the skeleton of dry bones are only a small part of the wealth of imagery.

Harry Boonstra. *Christianity Today*. Dec. 17, 1976, p. 22

The natural images of the Bible are a primarily poetic feature of it. . . . There are two levels of nature: the lower one, expressed in God's contract with Noah, presupposes a nature to be dominated and exploited by man; the higher one, expressed in an earlier contract with Adam in Paradise, is the nature to which man essentially belongs, and the Eden story prefigures the redemption which takes him back to this upper level. On the way from the lower level to the higher one we meet the images of the world of work, the pastoral, agricultural, and urban imagery that suggest a nature transformed into a humanly intelligible shape. The Bible's structure of imagery, then, contains, among other things, the imagery of sheep and pasture, the imagery of harvest and vintage, the imagery of cities and temples, all contained in and infused by the oasis imagery of trees and water that suggests a higher mode of life altogether.

These images constitute part of what I call the apocalyptic world, the ideal world (looking at it from one point of view) which the human creative imagination envisages, which human energy tries to bring into being, and which the Bible presents also as a form of "revelation": the vision, the model, the blueprint that gives direction and purpose to man's energies.

Northrop Frye. *The Great Code: The Bible and Literature* (New York, Harcourt Brace Jovanovich, 1982), pp. 139–40

While the ancient Israelite was forbidden to make any concrete and plastic image of God, it would have been strange indeed if God, the source and creator of the human personality, did not Himself have a real and concrete personhood, something which He so generously bestowed upon man, His creation.

And if God is somehow a person, He must logically have a form which can be seen even though this form was free from substantiality. Thus, Moses and the elders actually see the physical manifestation of the Lord sitting on a throne supported by a dais of lapis lazuli. Similarly, Ezekiel sees the Lord as a man sitting astride his movable throne made of fiery angelic beings. What profoundly shocking, mysterious images dance before our eyes, enough to stimulate and nourish the imaginations of a thousand painters and poets. If the ancient Israelite did not paint the image of God on canvas, he did depict the divine image most graphically and concretely with the winged words of his religious poetry. The more monotheism repressed plastic representation of God and of man, the more daring and concrete were the modes of literary depiction. Thus, for example, in His relationship to sinful Israel, God compares Himself to a ferocious lion, a leopard, and a bereaved bear:

> So I am become like a lion to them.
> Like a Leopard I lurk on the way;
> Like a bear robbed of her young I attack them
> and rip open the casing of their hearts. (Hos. 13:7–8)

Describing His nourishing treatment of the righteous, God calls Himself a fruitful tree:

> When I respond and look to Him,
> I become like a verdant cypress.
> Your fruit is provided by Me. (Hos. 14:9)

One would have thought that God or the prophet would have avoided such an image because of its possible misleading similarity to idolatrous nature worship. But the image is not repressed. In Second Isaiah, the divine sense of urgency to bring about the delayed redemption of Israel from the Babylonian exile is expressed by the startling image of a woman in labor:

> I have kept silent for too long,
> Kept still and restrained Myself;
> Now I will scream like a woman in labor,
> I will pant and I will gasp. (42:14)

These few examples clearly illustrate the difference between the bloodless philosophical abstractions concerning the nature of the ultimate principle and the graphic, concrete, imagaic mode of thinking that is typical of the Hebrew Bible.

Yochanan Muffs. In *J. James Tissot: Biblical Paintings* (New York, The Jewish Museum, 1982), pp. 8–9

Informational Gaps. *See* Narrator: Informational Gaps and Redundancy

Informational Redundancy. *See* Narrator: Informational Gaps and Redundancy

LINE

Every line is divided into two parts; unable to escape from our classical training, we commonly call this a caesura. It often happens that each part is a complete sentence in itself, e.g. in Isaiah 1:2b, 3b. In the latter case it will be noted that we have what [G. B.] Gray called "complete parallelism," and it is evidently lines of this kind which led to [Robert] Lowth's adoption of the term. In some ways this is unfortunate, for it suggests to the casual reader or hearer that there is always some more or less exact correspondence in thought between the two parts of the line; indeed the second may be taken to be a simple repetition of the first. It is, however, comparatively seldom that we meet with so perfect a correspondence, and some word like "balance" might more accurately describe the fact. It is the essence of poetic form in every language that it should first create an expectation in the mind of the hearer, and then more or less completely satisfy that expectation. In the forms of poetry best known to us the mind normally fastens on the sound, but in a *Sinnrhythmus* the thought will most impress the listener. It may or may not be a reproduction of ideas in other words, though this is probably the most elementary form; it may be simply the *number* of significant ("selbstän-dige") ideas which serves to satisfy the mind of the listener. . . .

In any case, the outstanding fact is that the caesura is a real break, both in the sense and in the sound. The last word in the first part is always to be read more closely with that which precedes than with that which follows. There are apparent exceptions; it happens from time to time that where a line contains five significant terms the third seems to belong to the second part rather than to the first. Gray has suggested that this may be a deliberate effort to emphasise a word by holding it, as it were, in suspense. Thus in Psalm 42:5a the verb *'eshpekha* gains greatly in force if there is a slight pause after it, and at the same time there is additional emphasis on those which follow in the second part of the line: "Let me remember these things and pour out—my soul upon me". . . .

Quite often the general sense runs straight on, but even so there is a pause between the two parts of the line. The poet may keep the hearer waiting before he satisfies the expectation which he has aroused. The caesura, then, may appear in the middle of a sentence, but a division is always possible; the final test is that the first part can never end with a construct depending on the first word of the second part.

The number of words on each side of the caesura may vary as between two and three. We sometimes find a line which appears to have four significant words in one part or in both; it may be followed by a 3, as in the great Chaos vision of Jeremiah [Jer. 4:23–26]. But as a rule it will be found that there is a lesser break within the 4, and it is, in fact a 2:2.

It would seem, then, that both the sense and the sound played a part in Hebrew verse-form. The analogy of the Arabic *saj'* gives some ground (so far as analogy ever can) to the view that primitive Hebrew poetry relied rather on the sense than on the sound for its structure. But, through their very nature, the Semitic languages make possible a close connection between the two.

T. H. Robinson. *Vetus Testamentum, Supplement.* 1, 1953, pp. 140–41

Although the corpus of classical Hebrew poetry—comprising at least one third of the Hebrew Bible—spans a period of roughly 800 years, from the twelfth to the fourth century B.C.E., Hebrew poetic form and vocabulary appear to have remained fairly stable. Throughout this time the basic structural unit within the poem was the line, which was usually divided into two parts or cola by a caesura, although it was sometimes divided into three cola by two caesuras. Normally the caesura was marked by both semantic and syntactic juncture, each colon being essentially an independent unit. This customary lack of enjambment is a striking feature of Hebrew poetry. These features of the poetry are illustrated by Hosea 11:8: "How can-I-give-you-up, O-Ephraim ‖ how can-I-hand-you-over, O-Israel." The caesura is clearly marked, the second colon being a repetition both semantically and syntactically of the first.

The caesura, however, does not always fall in the middle of the line, as in this example. More commonly it occurs after the middle, only rarely before. Lamentations 3:11 is an example of such an unbalanced line with the caesura coming after the middle: "He-led-me-off my-way and-tore-me-to-pieces ‖ he-has-made-me desolate." Although the line is unbalanced (three words in the first colon, two in the second), the caesura is no less clearly marked by syntax and semantics than in the balanced line quoted above.

Some lines, however, do not contain such semantic and syntactic breaks, and it may be doubted whether in such cases caesuras do in fact occur; for example, Amos 1:3: "Because-they-have-threshed Gilead with-threshing-sledges of-iron." Unlike the English translation, the Hebrew places "Gilead" at the end of the line, preceded by the sign of the accusative. By this formal arrangement, the poet presumably is indicating the unity of the line. A further example is provided by Jeremiah 5:17, whose different structural nature is readily apparent when seen in juxtaposition to the segmented line that precedes it in the text:

> They-shall-eat-up your-flocks and-your-herds ‖ they-shall-eat-up your-vines and-your-fig-trees. (v.16)

> Your-fortified cities in which you trust they-shall-destroy with-the-sword. (v.17)

In the first line (16) the placement of the caesura is clearly marked, while in the second (17) there is neither semantic nor syntactic reduplication to mark the occurrence of a caesura. Furthermore, the placing of the instrument "sword" at the end of the line, while the verb "destroy" in the Hebrew, begins the line, would seem again to indicate the unitary, unsegmented nature of the line.

But such long lines, segmented or unsegmented, were not the only structural units used by the poet in constructing a poem. Units of less than line length, often having the length of a colon or half a line, are also found. Sometimes these short lines are introductory, as the phrase "Thus says the-LORD" often is. A short line may also be used in an exclamatory or rhetorical manner as in Amos 2:11: "Is-it not indeed-so, O-people of-Israel?"

In Hebrew poetry, then, we need to reckon with three different types of line: the segmented, the unsegmented, and the short. The great majority of lines in Hebrew poetry are segmented, either balanced or unbalanced.

Perry B. Yoder. In *Versification*. Ed. by W. K. Wimsatt
(New York, Modern Language Association/New York
University Press, 1972), pp. 52–53

A small number of constraints determine the shape of the line in Hebrew verse. The first refers to the interrelations of clauses, the second to their components, and the third to their components' components. These three are the clause, constituent, and unit constraints. All three have the same range of variation, a range of four:

clause constraint	$\emptyset$	1	2	3
constituent constraint	1	2	3	4
unit constraint	2	3	4	5

This group of constraints refers to the line entire and we call these the overall constraints. They are complemented by the nominal phrase constraints which require that no nominal phrase of more than four units be line internal, and that no nominal phrase of more than three units occur in a line unless the line contains either only one clause and two constituents, or no clauses and one constituent. The overall constraints are further supplemented by the major clause predicator constraints, which require that no line contain three major clause predicators unless it contains nothing else; and that no line contain two major clause predicators unless only one of the predicators has dependent nominal phrases.

A line of Hebrew poetry is a passage of poetic discourse which obeys the overall constraints, i.e., which contains no fewer than no clause predicators and no more than three in its base structure, no fewer than one constituent and no more than four constituents in its surface structure, and no fewer than two units and no more than five in its surface structure; and which obeys the nominal phrase constraints and the major clause predicator constraints. . . .

The four constraints which together define the Hebrew verse line correctly suggest the availability of a great diversity of line structures. Not all actualizations of the three overall constraints are equally common. . . . The clause constraint allows between zero and three clauses in a line, but 898 lines [in the corpus studied] (75%) have one clause; the other three possibilities are much less frequently used. One hundred and thirty eight cases (11%) have no clauses, 157 lines (13%) have two, and 7 have three.

Of the range of constituent groupings, two dominate: there are 571 2-constituent lines (48%) and 485 3-constituent lines (40%). There are, in contrast, 98 1-constituent lines (8%) and only 46 with 4 constituents (4%). A majority of lines, 690 (57%) have three units; 298 (25%) have two units, 190 (16%) have four, while only 22 (2%) have five.

Michael O'Connor. *Hebrew Verse Structure* (Winona Lake, Ind., Eisenbrauns, 1980), pp. 315–16

In poetry, the basic unit must be the smallest segment of verse that a poet must employ to allow that segment to be recognized by his audience as poetry. It is the essential compositional unit of verse, its molecule. It is also clearly a matter of perceptions, involving author and audience. A purely mechanical determination of the basic unit is therefore impossible.

[Michael] O'Connor maintains that the basic unit of Biblical verse is not the couplet but the *single line [Hebrew Verse Structure* (Eisenbrauns, Winona Lake, Ind., 1980)]. He is firm on this point. In prosodies with exacting meters the line is indeed the basic unit; although even there a sequence of two such lines is really needed to prove the point. O'Connor has, of course, abolished meter for Biblical verse; but his [syntactic] "constriction" has inherited, as it were, the single line from its deceased predecessor. Since that line is to be described solely in terms of syntax, and with circular clarity is fully describable syntactically, a firm basis for Hebrew prosody would seem to have been established.

However, as we have seen, "constriction" is quite irrelevant in the context of a "replacement" for meter; and, consequently, the single line has no perceptual reality at all in Biblical verse of the sort required of a basic unit. It is merely an "atom" of a couplet, as it were. Of course, if a strict meter could be established for Biblical verse, the single line would succeed to the throne. Until then, parallelism with its couplet is, if not the king of Hebrew poetry, at least its regent.

Stephen A. Geller. *Jewish Quarterly Review.* July, 1982, p. 71

LYRIC

Those frequent songs throughout the law and prophets beyond all these, not in their divine argument alone, but in the very critical art of composition may be easily made appear over all the kinds of Lyrick poesy, to be incomparable. These abilities, wheresoever they be found, are the inspired guift of God rarely bestow'd, but yet to some (though most abuse) in every Nation: and are of power beside the office of a pulpit, to inbreed and cherish in a great people the seeds of vertu, and publick civility, to allay the perturbations of the mind, and set the affections in right tune, to celebrate in glorious and lofty Hymns the throne and equipage of Gods Almightinesse, and what he works.

> John Milton. *The Reason of Church-Governement Urg'd against Prelaty* (London, Printed by E. G. for John Rothwell, 1641), p. 39

In Hebrew lyrick poetry, simplicity, in this development of it, is especially necessary, since of all poetry it was least constructed by rule, and as a work of art, and was rather poured forth spontaneously, as genuine feeling wells up from a heart filled with lively emotions.

Would that we had an edition of the Psalms, in which David was treated merely as Horace is! in which, without casuistick subtleties, the poet should be shown as a poet, his beauty not indeed, cried into our ears, but at the same time not defaced by the patchwork of languages and versification foreign to its nature. In higher criticism upon the poetry of the Hebrews we are still but children. We either stifle ourselves with various readings, or embellish the simplicity of the original with the modish attire of modern languages. [1783]

> Johann Gottfried von Herder. *The Spirit of Hebrew Poetry*. Vol. II Tr. by James Marsh (Burlington, Vt., Edward Smith, 1833), p. 230

It would be impossible to discuss adequately here the Hebrew poets, who have produced a lyric so different in kind from all other lyrics to stand in a class by itself. As it is equal in importance to the Great Drama of Shakespeare, Aeschylus, and Sophocles, we may perhaps be allowed to call it the "Great Lyric." The Great Lyric must be religious—it must, it would seem, be an outpouring of the soul, not towards man but towards God, like those of the God-intoxicated prophets and psalmists of Scripture. Even the lyric fire of Pindar owes much to the fact that he had a child-like belief in the myths to which so many of his contemporaries had begun to give a languid assent. But there is nothing in Pindar, or indeed elsewhere in Greek poetry, like the rapturous song, combining unconscious power with unconscious grace, which we have called the Great Lyric. It might perhaps be said indeed that the Great Lyric is purely Hebrew.

> Theodore Watts. In *Encyclopaedia Britannica*. Vol. XIX. 9th ed. (Edinburgh, Black, 1885), pp. 269–70

It is thus convenient to indicate three landmarks in the development of biblical lyrics. One is the Processionary Ode. The second is the Anthem, in which, without the full procession, there is some suggestion of elaborate performance, such (for example) as provision for two or more performers. There is, thirdly, the Song or Meditation, which is nothing more than the musical outpouring of a single performer.

Of the full processional ode the Bible contains two magnificent examples. One is the triumphal song put into the mouth of Israel in the moment of its deliverance at the Red Sea; here the text distinctly states how Miriam "took a timbrel in her hand, and all the women went out after her with timbrels and with dances." [Exod. 15:20] The structure of this Song of Moses and Miriam is very simple: the Men, in successive stanzas, celebrate the fact of the deliverance itself, the mystic manner in which it has been brought about, the panic falling upon all the foes who guard the approach to Canaan; between the stanzas the Women dance and sing the refrain: —

> Sing ye to the LORD, for he hath triumphed gloriously;
> The horse and his rider hath he thrown into the sea. [Exod. 15:21]

The other is the similar Song of Deborah in triumph over the fall of Sisera. . . . The two odes are supreme examples of early lyric poetry. And they can be fully appreciated only by reading them with the same antiphonal rendering with which they were originally performed. . . .

The anthems of Temple service include all the more elaborate ascriptions of praise to God of which the psalter is full. They breathe the joyous spirit of a sacred feast day, or express vows of thanksgiving. They especially abound towards the end of The Book of Psalms, where, to a general refrain of "Hallelujah," psalm after psalm calls upon the heights and the depths, all orders of nature and all classes of men, with all instruments of music and everything that hath breath, to join in praising Jehovah. Perhaps the point where the ritual anthem most nearly resembles the original processionary ode is found in the hundred and eighteenth psalm. . . .

The songs and meditations of the psalter are a treasury of the richest gems in lyric poetry. They celebrate such themes as the providence of God [Pss. 103, 104] exhibited in the salvation of the individual or the nation, or in the Divine judgment between the righteous and wicked [Pss. 52, 58, 75, 83, 94]. They give expression to the spirit of trust, or consecration [Pss. 11, 16, 42, 90, 91]; to every aspect of the devout life.

Richard G. Moulton. *A Short Introduction to the Literature of the Bible* (Boston, Heath, 1903), pp. 220–21, 225–26, 231–32

The Hymns also exalt *the doings of Jahveh in the past*. In Babylonian and Egyptian hymns dealing with this subject, mythological allusions are frequent, and similar material is not altogether absent from the Hebrew Hymn.

Rahab Thou didst crush   like carrion
  with strong arm   Thou scatteredst Thy foes:
Thine are the heavens   Thine the earth;
The world and what fills it   Thou hast founded.

(Ps. 89:11.)

In the previous verse we read:

Thou abidest Lord   over the insolence of the sea
at the tumult of its waves   Thou stillest them.

Here Rahab is the sea-monster whom Jahveh subdued before the creation and from whose power He delivered the world. There is another mythical echo in the majestic 19th Psalm, where the glory of the solar ball is likened to that of a youthful hero. And there are other similar allusions.

It is no mere chance that the Creation Myth should find such a prominent place in this Hymn type of poetry. The creation of the world by God is one of the chief themes of the Hymns even among other peoples, because in that work the omnipotence of God is especially revealed.

This supplies a clue to a part of the history of the religion of Israel. The Hebrew mind, *pari passu* with its development along its own lines, took up an attitude increasingly antagonistic to myth, and that element became fainter and fainter till it ultimately disappeared. Its place was taken by the *Sacred Legend*. We have a whole series of hymns which sing the praise of the God who led Israel in the days of old, and which borrow their material for this purpose from the narrative books which were by that time in existence and contained many traditional and legendary elements. Examples are Psalm 105:14, Exodus 15. We see here how the great thought—proclaimed with such zest by the prophets—that the history of Israel was a fellowship between Jahveh and His people, edified and helped later generations. This adoption of the Legend into the Hymn is a phenomenon peculiar to Hebrew hymnody. There is nothing like it in the hymns of Babylon or Egypt. The recurrent theme of such legendary hymns is the story of the Passover—a proof of the deep impression made by that feast on the religious mind in Israel.

But the Hymns have also much to say about *Jahveh in the future*. He is the God who was and is, and is to come. The heart of the pious Hebrew thrills when he thinks of the time that is to come, when Jahveh will reveal Himself in His true majesty and ascend the throne of the world. This is another manifest proof how the preaching of the prophets influenced the hymns. The favourite method followed by the singer when thinking of this theme was to project himself into these latter days, with the result that to him the coming event was as if it had already happened. This impressive figure, exemplified in Psalms 46 and 149, was borrowed by the hymn-singer from the prophets.

Hermann Gunkel. *What Remains of the Old Testament, and Other Essays*. Tr. from the German by A. K. Dallas (New York, Macmillan, 1928), pp. 77–79

The poetical genius of the Hebrews was lyrical, and in this field they were unsurpassed. . . . May it not be possible that the very reason the Hebrews did not develop the drama is to be found in that propensity for the subjective which made them the great lyricists of religion, thus giving voice to the sublime spiritual experiences of their race. What grips us in the psalms is the universality of the aspirations and hopes expressed in them. "The Lord is *my* shepherd" must be parsed as in the singular number and the present tense, but it is expressive of an attitude of trust which is theirs for the taking by all men. Let any of us pore over the confession of sin in Psalm fifty-one in a conscience-stricken moment and we feel that it is our sin, too, over which the singer of Israel is weeping vicariously. These personal songs have as nation-wide a meaning and appeal as have prophetic utterances, such as Isaiah 1:16–18. Indeed, the prophets used the personal dirge to express national grief over the death or decay of the kingdom.

The greatest danger of lyric poetry is the risk which it runs of being preoccupied with the petty. This is especially true of the religious lyric, as the unwholesome sentimentalism of most mystic effusions demonstrates. In these there is a weak copying of the form while all weighty significance is lacking. But Hebrew lyric poetry never falls into this pit. The poets mount as on eagles' wings to a vantage point in the empyrean. The love of God and the sin of man confront one another; while there is room for joy the things of sorrow are not forgotten; the contrasts and realities of life are held in clear perspective.

Arthur J. Culler. *Creative Religious Literature* (New York, Macmillan, 1930), pp. 120–21

There is no Hebrew poetry but lyric poetry. Yet the Hebrews were face to face with life in all its multiplicity of suggestion and situation and their poetry, like all true poetry, had to be a criticism of life. So their lyric had, by one device or another, to fill all the functions filled in other literatures by the drama, the epic, and the didactic poem. The result was an immense extension of the possibilities of the lyric. They developed an epic lyric, a dramatic lyric, a didactic lyric, preserving in each the true singing, emotional, subjective note of the lyric. English poetry, being strongly lyric and strongly dramatic, has recognized and named the dramatic lyric in a series of poems by [Robert] Browning. . . .

The dramatic action [in the monologues of Job] is really in Job's mind, the conflict between his conception of the friendly God as he thought he had known him in the past and the hostile God who had now struck him down with ruin, grief, and disease. The skirmishing of his speeches with the Friends is not the action and only helps the action as it stimulates Job's mind to wider impressions and possibilities. Each of his speeches is in essence a conversation with himself, after he has brushed away the importunate Friend who has spoken last. The case is the same with the epic lyric. In Greek poetry it would be an Ode of Victory, but the Hebrew singer can put into it far more description and narrative than the Greek would have thought permissible. Yet the elements of description and narrative are all framed to carry the exulting emotion of the singer and the pictures and events in all their detail have no point or meaning apart from the singer. The great example of this in the surviving Hebrew literature is the Song of Deborah; and the song itself in the fifth chapter of Judges should be carefully contrasted with the plain historical narrative in the fourth chapter. Neither is made out of the other; they are independent ways of rendering one event. And the song has a wealth of detail that is not in the history, detail steeped in emotion and given only to develop emotion. The coming of Jehovah; the gathering of the clans; those that came not; the fight in the valley; the winding river of Kishon; blessed be Jael! the Mother of Sisera at her lattice; why lingers his chariot?—all render the exulting joy of the victorious singers. There is the material here for a Book of the Iliad, but Homer would have handled it with a clear objectivity, as an epic artist who stood outside his work and shaped it into form. Deborah and Barak sang and praised Jehovah out of the fullness of their joy and triumph. Yet there are moments in it of the most objective vividness; there is the sudden dramatizing of that scene between the Mother of Sisera and her ladies; she looked forth from her lattice and she still looks and listens—an abiding picture. Such flashes of drama the Hebrew could reach; for a moment, in an historic present, he could put himself into her at her lattice—but no more. The Mother of Sisera is not built up into the figure of tragic ignorance which Homer would have given us. . . .

The case of the didactic lyric is much simpler. A great proportion of the Psalms fall into this class and we all know what their essence is. Impassioned self-confession, a record of personal experience, whether addressed to Jehovah in penitence, or to the Psalmist's soul in upbraiding, or to his fellow man in direct exhortation, is turned into moral arousing and guidance. The Psalmist has learned in suffering what he teaches in song, and so he pours out his emotional experience and his resultant ideas and reactions, and they go to form what is still the greatest manual for the personal religious life.

Duncan B. MacDonald. *The Hebrew Literary Genius*
(Princeton, N.J., Princeton University Press, 1933), pp.
15–16, 18–19

The lyric is preeminently an utterance that is overheard. The lyric poet usually speaks in his own voice, using the "I" form of the pronoun. The significant aspect of the poem is the expression of the speaker, who in the Psalms is often in the act of addressing God directly. In large measure we can say that whereas the prophet's utterance is the words of God to man, the Psalms contain the thoughts and feelings of man addressed to God. Even if the speaking voice in a psalm is plural ("we," "us"), it is important to remember that the poem was written by a single person, expressing sentiments that were first of all his own. There is no such thing as a communal emotion; there is instead a group of individuals who have the same personal feelings. If the sentiments expressed in a lyric poem are so obviously the private feelings of the poet, we might ask how we should read the Psalms. The answer is that we should read them as giving expression to a shared religious experience. It is an example of the commonplace that the poet is a spokesman and representative, saying what others want said and saying it better than they could. Like a public prayer, the psalmists' outpourings of religious thought and feeling are at once private and public: they are spoken by a single person but express what an entire group feels.

The emotional element in a lyric poem is often considered its chief identifying trait—its differentia. Although a lyric poem may contain thought or reflection, it is above all an utterance of intense emotion. It is not easy to convey emotion in poetry. The means of doing so include the use of an exclamatory idiom, the use of hyperbole (conscious exaggeration for the sake of communicating strong feeling), the use of emotive words, and the vivid description of the stimulus to the emotion (thereby evoking a similar feeling in the reader). Mainly, however, the psalmists make religious feelings the subject matter of their poetry. Praise, adoration, awe, joy, sorrow, depression—these are the emotional subjects that recur throughout the Psalms. As a result, we should come to the Psalms with the expectation of finding there the expression of religious feelings. We should not expect to find an account of historical events, since ordinarily a lyric poem will make use only of so much history or narrative as is necessary to make clear the nature and source of the emotion being presented. Nor should we expect to find an exposition of theological doctrine. Theological doctrine can be deduced from the Psalms, but that is not their main business. The Psalms, being lyric poetry, exist primarily to give expression to the emotional side of religious experience. . . .

Because of their brevity, the Psalms must be regarded as self-contained units. They are not chapters in a continuing sequence but are complete entities, separate from the psalms that precede and follow them. Lyrics usually have a single controlling topic or theme. Unless one is aware of the unifying theme, an individual psalm has a tendency to remain a series of fragments, a kind of misreading somewhat fostered by the conventional division of the Psalms into verses. The unifying theme may be a thought or an emotion that controls all of the details in the poem and unifies them into a single whole. The unifying theme is usually stated early in the poem, functioning as the stimulus or point of departure and exercising a formative influence on the development of the poem.

Leland Ryken. *The Literature of the Bible* (Grand Rapids, Mich., Zondervan, 1974), pp. 122–24

METAPHOR

Metaphor is found in such abundance in our Holy Scriptures that one cannot count the passages quickly. . . . I shall adduce here a few examples from the many, which should suffice for you. For my aim is to demonstrate the validity of my claim through clear vision and not to cloud the issue with superfluous verbiage. Here are examples [in alphabetical order according to Hebrew] for you: "mother of the road" [crossroads, Ezek. 21:26], "pupil of the night" [nighttime, Prov. 7:9], "sons of his quiver" [arrows, Lam. 3:13], "the wings of the city heights" [the highest locations, Prov. 9:3], "an iron sinew is your neck" [Isa. 48:4], "the doors of his face" [Job 41:6], "grain of heaven" [manna, Ps. 78:24], "echo of the mountains" [Ezek. 7:7], "the multitude of your bowels" [your mercies, Isa. 63:15], "the teat of her glory" [her bounteous glory, Isa. 66:11], "the heat waves of famine" [Lam. 5:10], "the fat of the land" [Gen. 45:18], "the dew of your youth" [Ps. 110:3], "the navel of the earth" [Judg. 9:37], "a day will give birth" [Prov. 27:1], "wine of treachery" [Prov. 4:17], "turban of victory" [Isa. 59:17], "wings of dawn" [Ps. 139:9], "bread of slothfulness" [Prov. 31:27], "tongue of gold" [bar of gold, Josh. 7:24], "cloak of triumph" [Isa. 61:10], "staff of bread" [Lev. 26:26], "the waterskins of heaven" [Job 38:37], "twilight of my desire" [Isa. 21:4], "the jubilation of your salvation" [Ps. 51:14], "lip of the curtain" [edge, Exod. 26:4], "eyeballs of dawn" [Job 3:9], "cords of love" [Hos. 11:4], "the fruit of their machinations" [consequences, Jer. 6:19], "face of warfare" [II Sam. 10:9], "a diamond fingernail" [point, Jer. 17:1], "mighty steps" [big plans, Job 18:7], "the horn of his anointed" [his honor, I Sam. 2:10], "spider's web" [tangled argument, Isa. 59:5], "a wind of jealousy" [Num. 5:14], "flames of the bow" [arrows, Ps. 76:4], "the rod of my wrath" [Isa. 10:5], "a sun of triumph" [Mal. 3:20], "a teaching of kindness" [Prov. 31:26], "columns of smoke" [Joel 3:3].

The Arabs have spoken extensively on the virtue of such tropes and have let everyone know that they esteem them, that they are, in their opinion, the splendor of the linguists; and they have praised all poets who use them. In fact, their Koran contains many tropes like them. . . .

The essence of metaphor is that you describe an unknown thing with a known one. And if you would only regard it with a sensible eye and weigh it on just scales, you will see it has a special value. There are two sorts of metaphor: one in which the proposition is explicit and clear, and another in which the intended sense is hidden and concealed. The explicit proposition is like the examples I adduced above, and the hidden is like "The heavens tell of the honor of God" [Ps. 19:2]. The very next verse proves that the poet is using these words metaphorically and not literally, for it is written there: "There is no speech, and there are no words, etc." [Ps. 19:3]. [ca. 1135]

Moses ibn Ezra. *Shirat Yisra'el.* Tr. from the Arabic by Ben-Zion Halper (Leipzig, Abraham Joseph Stybel Publishing, 1924), pp. 160–62†

[1] Metaphor is diction in which certain words are taken as parable and in a transferred sense, because some resemblance obtains between the literal and transferred meanings which allows this appropriately to be done. For example: The wilderness and the parched land shall be glad; and the desert shall rejoice,

and blossom as the rose [Isa. 35:1]. Gladness is properly attributable only to man, but appears here through resemblance; for the bringing forth of the flowers is indicative of great good in the case of a desert and parched land, just as gladness is an indication of a man's good. Similarly: All flesh is grass, and all the goodliness thereof is as the flower of the field [40:6]; the prophet has likened the flesh, which quickly wastes away, to the grass and the flower of the field whose brief hour is soon done.

[2] The aim in using Metaphor is sometimes conciseness, as in: For ye have consumed the vineyard; the spoil of the poor is in your houses [Isa. 3:14]. The reference to the consumption of the vineyard was intended to mean that they had stripped the poor man in question of his possessions, just as nothing is left in a vineyard after it has been consumed by fire; the use of such language thus enables the prophet to be brief. Sometimes the aim is decency of language, as in: And the man knew Eve his wife [Gen. 4:1], and in: Then let my wife grind unto another [Job 31:10]; each of these is a euphemistic description of the sexual act. Sometimes the intention is to magnify a matter, as in: Woe unto them that draw iniquity with cords of vanity, and sin as it were with a cart rope [Isa. 5:18]. Sometimes it is meant to minify: Ye conceive chaff, ye shall bring forth stubble [33:11]; Ephraim shepherdeth wind, and chaseth after the east wind [Hos. 12:2]. And sometimes its sole purpose is elegance: that put darkness for light, and light for darkness, that put bitter for sweet and sweet for bitter! [Isa. 5:20]. [1475]

> Messer David ben Judah Leon. *The Book of the Honeycomb's Flow*. Ed. and tr. by Isaac Rabinowitz (Ithaca, N.Y., Cornell University Press, 1983), pp. 511, 513

[Cleanth] Brooks and [Robert Penn] Warren exemplify the function of the metaphor with an image from the Book of Ecclesiastes 7:6: "For as the crackling of thorns under a pot, so is the laughter of the fool" [King James Version]. This comparison, they write, utilizes the crackling sound of the dry thorns when they catch fire to describe the laughter of the fool. Indeed, there is no denying that there is a realistic similarity from the aural standpoint between the sound of the thorns under the pot and the sound of the hollow laughter of the fool. . . . This metaphor, however, has much greater force than—and many features beyond—the phonetic description. There is also an evaluation of this laughter: The laughter of the fool is hollow and empty, devoid of any meaning. "As the sound of thorns under the pot" tells us: The refuse of trimmed thorns is devoid of value, it perishes in smoke and is no more, wind carries off the smoke. In this metaphor is contained justification for the affirmation at the end of the verse: "This also is vanity." And even more: The metaphor is not only an illustration of "vanity"; it is vanity. Vanity is embodied in it: clear light to the eyes, a sound reaching many ears, yet its content is empty, its essence is nothing.

> Meir Weiss. *Hammiqra' kidmuto* (Jerusalem, Bialik Institute, 1967), pp. 80–81†

To the metaphor systems which are common to all cultures the Bible adds one or two of its own. By far the most important and extensive of these is the metaphorical use of Exodus language. The Exodus from Egypt marked the beginning of Israel's nationhood, and was commemorated by successive generations as the ground of their faith. Their God was distinguished from the gods of other nations as "Yahweh your God who brought you out of Egypt, out of the land of slavery" (Exod. 20:1). Thus Egypt became the symbol for any enslavement to tyranny: to become vassals to Assyria was to return to Egypt (Hos. 11:5). Yahweh was an out-of-Egypt-bringing God, who could be trusted to rescue Israel from affliction and sin.

> For in the Lord is love unfailing,
> And great is his power to set men free.
> He alone will set Israel free
> from all their sins
>
> (Ps. 130:7–8).

When the Israelites looked forward to a new age, they envisaged it as a new Exodus (Isa. 11:12–16; 43:16–20). . . .

Another important biblical metaphor system is derived from the ritual of the temple, and especially from sacrifice. In connexion with the evolution of the priesthood . . . we have already taken note of the spiritualisation of sacrifice in the Old Testament. But this phenomenon could equally well be described as metaphor, the transfer of sacrificial terms from their original referents, the lambs, bulls, pigeons and meal-offering of the levitical code, to new referents such as loyalty, obedience and thanksgiving. . . .

There is one metaphor system which is not peculiar to the Bible, but which deserves special mention because of its frequent and varied use there. To the modern ear the biblical writers seem inordinately fond of law-court language. Often God is the judge who condemns the wicked and upholds the cause of the weak and helpless (I Sam. 24:15; Ps. 9:4; 43:1; 140:12; Lam. 3:58; Mic. 7:9). The sentences passed in a human court may be reversed in God's court of appeal (Prov. 22:22–23). But sometimes instead God appears in court as advocate, the guardian of orphans (Prov. 23:11), or as the defending counsel pleading Israel's cause against her aggressors (Ps. 119:154; Isa. 50:8–9; 51:22; Jer. 50:34; 51:36). On other occasions God is himself the litigant, pressing his case against injustice (Ps. 74:22), against the gods of Babylon (Isa. 41:21; 43:9), against all nations (Jer. 25:9), and above all against the rebellious Israel (Ps. 103:9; Isa. 3:13–15; Jer. 2:9; Hos. 4:1–4; 12:2; Mic. 6:1–5). Job constantly returns to the idea that his predicament is to be regarded as a lawsuit between himself and God: he demands that God should state the grounds for his complaint (10:2), rebukes his friends for thinking that God's case needs the support of their dishonest arguments (13:6–8), laments that he cannot meet God face to face and settle with him out of court (23:3–6), takes a solemn oath of innocence (31:5–40), and finally insists that his accuser ought to have put the indictment in writing (31:35). In an ancient court of law the primary aim of a litigant was not to convince judge and jury, but to convince the adversary, so that he would withdraw his own case and acknowledge defeat by placing a finger on his lips; and this Job does when God's voice has questioned him out of the whirlwind (40:4).

The reason for this frequent recourse to forensic metaphor was not that the Israelites were excessively litigious, nor that law was their religion, but simply that the law-court was the only context in which they experienced a systematic quest for truth governed by rules of procedure. Truth, like justice, was for them something to be discovered and maintained in court. It was natural for them, therefore, to see through the lens of legal metaphor any attempt to arrive at religious truth. Today, when we talk about verification, we are inclined to think in terms of scientific method, even if we hear scientists speaking of evidence, probably unaware that they are using a metaphor taken from the processes of law. But most of the truths that Israel was interested in had to rest on the testimony of witnesses; and the law laid down that "a charge must be established on the evidence of two or three witnesses" (Deut. 19:15).

G. B. Caird. *The Language and Imagery of the Bible*
(Philadelphia, Westminster Press, 1980), pp. 155–58

The Song of Songs may be chosen as an illustration of the role of a sustained *cluster of metaphor* in Old Testament poetry. Country (with its flocks, vineyards, sun, flowers, hills, fields and villages) and court (with its king, chambers, curtains, maidens, jewels, couches, perfumes, banquets, streets and squares) function as a brilliant but transparent metaphoric system for the disjunction of the lovers that is always striving towards union. The imagery is everywhere sensuous, with fragrances, breezes, natural beauty, delights of food and wine; and the emotional language is highly pitched, with ravishment of heart, lovesickness, desperate longing, exultation, and its images of animal energy and grace (gazelle, stag, goats, raven, doves, fawns). Again, the imagery of enclosed gardens, walls, doors, of absence and presence, of losing and finding, pervades the poem with the tension of sexual desire, frustration, and fulfillment. It is not the explicit reference to breasts and kissing that creates the erotic quality of this poem, but the consistent play of metaphor. The language is rarely direct and explicit (hence the difficulties in reconstructing a drama from the poem, or even in some places of assigning speeches); rather it is "subtle and seductive, leaving many things unspoken but nonetheless present." [Roland E. Murphy. *Biblical Theology Bulletin,* 9, 1979, p. 104]

David J. A. Clines. *Interpretation.* April, 1980, p. 124

METER

Well, then, from the beginning of the book to the words of Job, the Hebrew version is in prose. Further, from the words of Job where he says, "May the day perish wherein I was born, and the night in which it was said, a man-child is conceived" [3:3] to the place where before the close of the book it is written, "Therefore I blame myself and repent in dust and ashes" [42:6] we have hexameter verses running in dactyl and spondee: and owing to the idiom of the language other feet are frequently introduced not containing the same number of syllables, but the same quantities. Sometimes, also, a sweet and musical rhythm is produced by the breaking up of the verses in accordance with the laws of metre, a fact better known to prosodists than to the ordinary reader. But from the aforesaid verse to the end of the book the small remaining section is a prose composition. And if it seem incredible to any one that the Hebrews really have metres, and that, whether we consider the Psalter or the Lamentations of Jeremiah, or almost all the songs of Scripture, they bear a resemblance to our Flaccus [i.e., Horace] and the Greek Pindar, and Alcaeus, and Sappho, let him read Philo, Josephus, Origen, Eusebius of Caesarea, and with the aid of their testimony he will find that I speak the truth. [392]

> Saint Jerome. "Preface to Job." *A Select Library of Nicene and Post-Nicene Fathers of the Christian Church.* 2nd series. Vol. VI. Ed. by Philip Schaff and Henry Wace (New York, Christian Literature Co., 1893), p. 491

There are without doubt metrical arrangements to the sacred poems we have mentioned [Deut. 32, Isa. 5, Psalms, Job, Lamentations], but they do not depend on the number of syllabic feet, whether complete or incomplete, like the poems to which we are accustomed today—for these, in the words of the Kuzari [of Judah Halevi], are the procedures of poetry in Arabic, which is a distortion of our language [Hebrew]. Rather, their metrical arrangements are in the number of propositions and their components—subject, predicate, and their modifiers—in each written utterance or phrase. Sometimes the utterance will have two feet, and with the second one that is attached to it there will be four. And sometimes it will have three, and with the second one [that is attached to it] there will be six perfect feet, such as: "Your-right-hand, O-Lord"—this is an utterance unto itself possessing two units, or, you might say, two feet. "Awesome in strength" [Exod. 15:6]—this resembles it and is attached to it so that together they are four [feet]. So, too, the second "Your-right-hand" [loc. cit.] are another two [feet], "smashes the-enemy" are two more, so that they are four. In the same pattern is: "The-enemy said / I-shall-pursue, I-shall-overtake / I-shall-divide the-spoil / Myself will-be-sated-with-them / I-shall-brandish my-sword / My-hand will-dispossess-them / You-have swept with-your-wind" [Exod. 15:9–10], etc. However, the poem "Give-ear" [Deut. 32] is three-three, which are six, that is: "Give-ear, O-heaven, that-I-may-speak / and-hear, O-land, the-utterance-of-my-mouth / Let-my-lesson fall like-rain / Let-my-sayings drip like-dew" [Deut. 32:1–2], etc.

And sometimes in a single verse, even more so in an entire poem, there will be both kinds of meters, that of two-two and that of three-three, according to how the Spirit alighted on the prophet, and because the variations are suited to the meaning, such as "By-the-wind of-your-nostrils / the-water piled-up," they are two-two; "it-stood-up like-a flowing column / the-depths froze in-the-heart-of-the-sea," three-three [Exod. 15:8]. And so, too, in the Song of the Well [Num. 21:17], it begins three-three and is followed by two-two, and similarly in the Prayer of Habakkuk [Hab. 3] . . . it goes in the three-three pattern: "God comes from-Teiman / and-the-Holy-One from-Mount-Paran, *selah* / his-glory covers the-sky / and-his-praise fills the-land" [Hab. 3:3].

Now in some of these utterances the enlightened person will need to recognize some words that, for whatever reason, do not enter into these meters, as in the poem "Give-ear": "He-said, 'Let-me-hide my-face from-them'" [Deut. 32:20]. The word "he-said" is a distinct statement. Thus, "Let-me-hide my-face from-them" are three feet. "Let-me-see what-is their-future" are three more, etc. . . .

You should not count the syllables or the words, only the ideas. And for this reason many times a small word is joined to the one beside it. Thus do the verses of Psalms observe the order that we have mentioned: "Be-gracious-to-me, O-God, according-to-your-love"—three [feet]—"according-to-the-greatness-of [a small, attached word in Hebrew] your-compassion blot-out my-transgressions" [Ps. 51:3]. . . .

Now it is not too wondrous for me to see that there are many verses that I do not know how to fit into the above-mentioned patterns, and perhaps those which break out [of the pattern] are more numerous than those which hold. Nonetheless, with the scheme of my words enlightened persons will grow wise and find out further what I have not conceived. For in any case we should believe that all the poems that are found in the Holy Scriptures—the Song at the Sea [Exod. 15], and of the Well [Num. 21:17–18], and "Give-ear" [Deut. 32], and of Deborah [Judg. 5], and the Song of David, and the Books of Job, Proverbs, and Psalms—all of them without doubt observe an order and arrangement, this one in one style and that one in another. Or a single one itself possesses diverse meters. For indeed, when we read them aloud, we feel a wonderful exaltation, even if our knowledge of their arrangements does not penetrate completely—just as we speak, rise, and sit, even without knowing with precisely which muscles or natural organs our movements are accomplished. . . .

Especially with respect to the songs of David that were said before the Lord's altar, there is no doubt, as the Kuzari stated in the second discourse, that they were set to music. . . . And do not be surprised at our saying that a single poem could possess diverse meters, for if you knew the nature of the poems of the sages of the nations of the world . . . it would become clear to you that they do the same thing. [ca. 1560]

Azariah dei Rossi. Me'or 'einayim. 2nd printing (Berlin, Youth Education Society, 1794), pp. 257b–58a†

While parallelism is a genuine and compelling feature of Hebrew poetry, meter is detectable mainly by analogy with other poetry and by implication from the balanced lines. As a result, certain stress patterns can be formulated on the assumption that a stress should be granted to each of the major words in a distich (or tristich). But the metric hypotheses rest upon a combination of inference from parallelism and application of the Masoretic accents, rather than on any intrinsic evidence from biblical Hebrew.

In the Masoretic accentual system, each word, no matter what its length, receives one stress (except for proclitics joined to following words by the "binder" or *maqqēf*). Since, in the average Hebrew word, the accent is on the last syllable, the "meter" tends to be a rising one. Ordinarily a word posesses two or three syllables, and this produces a pattern analogous to the classical iambic foot (a short unstressed and a long stressed syllable) and the anapaestic foot (two shorts unstressed and a long stressed syllable).

The classical analogies are entirely misleading, however, because in Hebrew the number of unstressed syllables allowable between stresses is variable. It appears that between two stressed syllables an unstressed syllable is not absolutely necessary (e.g., in successively accented monosyllables) and that there can be as many as four or five unstressed syllables (about the maximum length of a Hebrew word). It is a matter of debate whether longer words require or permit a second stress. It is also problematic whether on occasion two short terms may receive a single stress, while terms joined by the "binder" may be permitted separate stresses. Where such accentual flexibility existed—or is suspect of existing—the application of rigid classical meters only obscures the true poetry with an imposed and artificial orderliness.

The most common pattern is a six-stress distich which, taking into account the caesura between stichs, is represented as a 3 + 3 meter. It is the predominant meter in Deutero-Isaiah, Job, and Proverbs. Its parallelisms are largely synonymous and antithetic, with many complete parallelisms. Occasionally the sense requires that a six-stress line be read as a tristich, and thus a 2 + 2 + 2 pattern emerges. Less frequent, but not always to be emended as errors, are instances of 4 + 4 and 2 + 2, which appear usually as variants of 3 + 3 and 3 + 2 patterns.

Of the unequal or balancing meters, 3 + 2 is most widespread. It has been dubbed the Qinah or lament meter because it is dominant in Lamentations [q.v.] . . . and in many of the laments appearing in the Psalms and the Prophets. It is doubtless a product of intense emotion, with the second stich breaking short, like a catch in the throat. Yet it cannot be insisted that the emotion was always grief, since the 3 + 2 rhythm is dominant in some compositions expressing praise and joy (e.g., Ps. 65). A common variant of 3 + 2 is 2 + 2, and there are some lines that can be scanned only as 2 + 3.

While there are poems and strophes within poems where the fundamental meter of 3 + 3 or 3 + 2 is undisturbed, a majority of Hebrew poems have lines of mixed metric length. In many cases the meters are so hybrid that it is impossible to locate the fundamental pattern. With the help of the versions some lines may be restored to a more consistent metric pattern. In other cases we can be fairly certain of disorder but cannot restore the original with any sense of confidence. But a large number of these metrically hybrid poems must be accepted as normal Hebrew poetic practice.

All that we know of ancient Near Eastern poetry supports the principle of metrical fluidity. Babylonian poetry has a prevailing 2 + 2 meter, but is interspersed with lines that can be read only as threes, often to be scanned as 2 + 2 + 3. Sometimes a six-stress line seems to require 2 + 2 + 2. The ancient Canaanite literature from Ugarit reveals a frequent 3 + 3 pattern, but there are innumerable variations. Especially noticeable is the tristich, in 3 + 3 + 3 or 2 + 2 + 2 schemes. In view of its frequency at Ugarit, it cannot be denied that Hebrew poets purposely used tristichs. . . . These Canaanite discoveries in particular, dating from the fourteenth century B.C. and in a tongue dialectically related to biblical Hebrew, argue strongly the futility of seeking metrical exactness in the poetry of the Old Testament. Emendation of the text for metrical reasons and without syntactic or versional support, is a dubious practice. Yet there is consistency in Hebrew poetry to the extent that parallel stichs seldom range beyond a variation of one stress in length; thus, e.g., 4 + 2 or 2 + 4 rhythms are distinct rarities.

Meter, insofar as it exists in Hebrew poetry, is actually the rhythmical counterpart of parallellism of thought. Rhythm is not due to syllabic quantities but to the less definable instinct of balancing parts whose exact accentual values are not measurable and probably never were. Ordinarily the conceptual or semantic parallelism is matched by numerical or structural parallelism. The stichs tend to be nearly the same length, but this similar fulness of line is not a metric phenomenon any more than balanced masses in painting are metrical. Both parallelism and meter obey an impulse to regular repetition, but in Hebrew poetry regularity of stress is subordinated to regularity of balanced ideas. Thus the tendency to fill out lines with incomplete parallelisms by means of compensation . . . is not metrical (i.e. the necessity of having two three-stress stichs) but rather is due to the desire to oppose word masses of about the same weight while varying and emphasizing the thought. The concept is closer to a spatial concern with "mass" than to a temporal concern with "stress."

Norman Gottwald. In *The Interpreter's Dictionary of the Bible*. Vol. III (Nashville, Abingdon Press, 1962), p. 834

The lines of Hebrew poetry, as we have just seen, can be described as conforming to one of two patterns, either XX (balanced) or XX − 1 (unbalanced), X representing the number of terms in the first cola, usually varying from two to four. Since most lines of Hebrew poetry follow one of these two patterns, the poets, presumably, had as one of their objectives to produce lines whose cola conformed to these patterns. This appearance of measuredness strongly supports the contention that meter is a prosodic feature of Hebrew poetry. In fact, some Hebrew poetry has admitted a quite regular metrical scansion.

In previous centuries, under the influence of classical models, metrical theories based on syllable length (quantity) were developed, but in modern times the consensus among those who allow meter in Hebrew poetry is that it is accentual.

Opinion differs, however, as to what type of accentual meter is present. Some theorists hold that the word is the basic metrical unit; others count the number of major accents and see the number of unaccented syllables as relatively unimportant. Yet others argue that Hebrew poetry had "feet," and that thus the number of unaccented syllables is important. Within this last group there is a further controversy as to the type of foot, some contending it is a two-syllable foot with alternating accented and unaccented syllables, others, that it is a three-syllable anapestic foot.

In contrast, then, to parallelism, the occurrence and basic nature of which are recognized by all, there is little consensus regarding meter. Its very existence is denied; among those who affirm it there is only limited agreement as to its nature; and it is argued that it must have changed in the course of time through changes in the pronunciation of the language.

Much of this debate results from our ignorance of the pronunciation of classical Hebrew and its changes during the period when the poetry was composed. Even if such data could be reconstructed, the manner in which the poetry was read or recited, with elisions, wrenched accents, and the like, would remain unknown.

> Perry B. Yoder. In *Versification*. Ed. by W. K. Wimsatt (New York, Modern Language Association/New York University Press, 1972), p. 58

Hebrew poetry . . . is metered, and although meter does not in itself guarantee an effective expressive use of language, its skillful use may contribute greatly to expressive quality. The regularity of meter helps to make the language move smoothly and easily. The regular occurrences of stressed syllables (or long syllables in those languages which work on that system) helps to accentuate the key words. And the changes in meter, when skillfully handled, may highlight shifts, bring something to attention, or alter the mood.

Hebrew meter is based on the regular occurrence of stressed syllables, with the varying numbers of unstressed syllables between being read so as to take roughly the same amount of time, no matter how many there are . . . a phenomenon which can be referred to as stress-timed meter rather than syllable-timed meter.

> William A. Smalley. In *On Language, Culture, and Religion*. Ed. Matthew Black and W. A. Smalley (The Hague, Mouton, 1974), p. 346

The most common meter in the Bible and in Ugarit is that of three stresses to a stich and of two stichs to a line (conventional symbol: 3 + 3). An example of a long chapter written almost entirely in this meter is the song "Give ear" [Deut. 32]. . . . Other examples are Isaiah 58; Psalm 104; Proverbs 8; and Job 9. This meter prevails in most of the poetic chapters, though not necessarily consistently: Stichs of two stresses, or four, are mixed with stichs of three.

The 3 + 2 meter has earned the name *qina* ["lament"] meter, as we have found it in Lamentations chapter 3:

> *'ani-haggéver ra'à 'oní / beshévet 'evrató*
> *'otí nahág wayyólakh / hóshekh welo'-'ór* [vv. 1–2].

But it is doubtful that this meter is unique to laments. Of the five chapters of the Book of Lamentations only one is written in it. By contrast it appears in various poems that are not laments, for example:

> *zakhárti-lakh hésed ne'uráyikh / 'ahavát kelulotáyikh*
> *lekhtékh 'aharáy bammidbár / be'érets lo'-zeru'à*
> *qódesh yisra'él laYHẂH / re'shít tevu'ató* (Jer. 2:2–3).

In the 4 + 4 meter the poets of the Bible sometimes achieve an effect of heaviness:

> *yó'vad yóm 'iwwáled bó / wehalávla 'amár hóra gáver* (Job 3:2).

This meter predominates in the Song at the Sea (Exod. 15) even though many lines within it are written in a different meter. It gives it a festive sound:

> *'ashíra laYHẂH ki-ga'ó ga'à / sús werokhevó ramá vayyám* [v. 1].

And similarly:

> *tsalelú ka'oféret bemáyim 'addirím* [v. 10].

In fact, it is possible to view these examples as combinations of two-word stichs ([2 + 2] + [2 + 2]: *'ashíra laYHẂH / ki ga'ó ga'à /*—etc.). Such a breakdown into shorter stichs is especially evident in the lines:

> *'amár 'oyév / 'erdóf 'assíg / 'ahalléq shalál / timla'émo nafshí /*
> *'aríq harbí / torishémo yadí* [v. 9].

A meter of short stichs sometimes appears in lines of six stresses, constructed in a pattern of 2 + 2 + 2:

> *'urí 'urí / livshí 'óz / zerbá' YHẂH* (Isa. 51:9).

The 2 + 2 + 2 meter can endow the poem with a slow and very free movement, and with an air of reflectiveness:

> When-the-Lord returned / the-captivity-of Zion / we-were like-dreamers
> Then filled / our-mouths with-laughter / and-our-tongues with-song
> Then-said the-nations / "The-Lord has-done-greatly / in-dealing with-these"
> The-Lord has-done-greatly / in-dealing with-us / we-were joyful
> Return, O Lord / our captivity / like-streams in-the-Negev
> Those-who-sow in-tears / in-song will-reap
> He-who-goes walking and-crying / carrying the-sack-of seed
> Will-come, come in-song / carrying his sheaves (Ps. 126).

At the end of the poem, the meter changes in accord with the change in mood.

A precise analysis of Psalm 42–43 would show that its meter can best be defined as based on lines of 5 + 5 stresses.

The value of metrical analysis: It has already been explained that it is possible to propose several metrical patterns for one poem, for it is impossible to reach certainty on this matter, and few are the chapters whose rhythm is really unitary. Moreover, whoever engages in this endeavor frequently encounters exceptional poetic verses that can in no way be analyzed metrically according to the proposed method. . . . Indeed, we should always remember that in this area the obscure is greater than the apparent. The proposed method (accepted by biblical scholarship) is no more than a tool that enables us to study the form of the Bible's poems, to discriminate among poems, and to perceive something of their charm. A declamation of the poems with extra enunciation of their meter (scansion) according to the proposed method will sound forced, but reciting them on the basis of an understanding of their meter (according to this method) gives insight into the beauty of their sounds. In other words, we have not reconstructed the original biblical prosody, whether it was recognized or whether it was an undefined matter of practice; the scholars who thought they could make a reconstruction failed. But by virtue of their efforts we have a tool, be it a substitute for the original prosody or an imprecise reflection of it.

> Israel Yeivin. *'Entsiqlopedya miqra'it*. Vol. VII. Ed. by Benjamin Mazar et al. (Jerusalem, Bialik Institute, 1976), cols. 641–42†

The heart of the metrical crux in Hebrew is now, and always has been, the assumptions of the metricists. Some writers, like G[eorge] B. Gray, have at least been moved to investigate the relationship between parallelism and line length, suspicious that the latter's apparent regularity might somehow be related to the former; but hampered by a faulty notion of parallelism, all that he and later writers have been able to come up with is the observation of "compensation," the apparent attempt of biblical authors to include some compensatory extra word or phrase in the B half to make up for an unparalleled term in A and so preserve the equality of clause length. This, instead of challenging their narrow idea of what "parallelism" embraces, has only implied the inscrutable workings of some metrical principle in addition to parallelism.

Surely an objective look at the origins and fruits of metrical speculation should long ago have resulted in a rejection of the whole idea. For, as we have seen, the Bible and rabbinic literature describe musical instruments and singing arrangements, antiphony and cantillation; but there is nothing about meter. An elaborate system, nay three systems, were developed to punctuate the biblical text, and these reflected the slightest nuances of possible conjunction and disjunction in public performance; but nothing in the systems has any sort of regularity that might be associated with meter. Those who first attributed meter to the Bible were Hellenized Jews, and later, Greek-speaking Christians, whose desire to parallel the excellencies of Greek poetry with their own sacred texts is all too easy to document. The meters they attributed, hexameters and pentameters, are no longer invoked; all that has been retained is their erroneous assumption of metricality. Over the years, meter, rhyme, and other trappings of poetry have all been "discovered" in the Bible, ever defined according to traditions current in the writer's own tongue. Meter has been quantitative in the Greco-Roman manner, with or without rules of position and elision; quantitative in the Judeo-Arabic manner; syllabic as in the vernacular poetries of Europe; accentual-syllabic, as in English; pure accentual, as in English and German; *Wortrhythmus; vers libre;* "irregular"; and so forth. . . .

There is indeed an answer to this age-old riddle: no meter has been found because none exists. Or, as others have urged, *parallelism is the only meter of biblical poetry*—but even for this statement to be correct, each of these terms must be understood in a nontraditional manner. For by "parallelism" what we really mean is the subjoining, "seconding" form of emphasis, abstracted and generalized to our pause sequence; and by "meter" is meant only a loose and approximate regularity, sometimes, to be sure, clearly cultivated, so that sentence after epigrammatic sentence in Job or Isaiah rings true with the click of a couplet. Finally, we must recall that the building-block of this meter, the "seconding" clause, was not imported from another planet, but grew organically out of ordinary speech and remained an everyday trope of emphasis, so that its "irregular" use in certain passages is not to be (and surely was not) read as a breakdown of the "meter," nor yet a residue or fragment of some more truly "metrical" subtext, but simply as a less intense, less consciously rhetorical, form of expression. "Prose" and "poetry" are a matter of degree.

> James L. Kugel. *The Idea of Biblical Poetry: Parallelism and Its History* (New Haven, Conn., Yale University Press, 1981), pp. 300–302

Motifs and Themes. *See* Themes and Motifs

NARRATIVE

The narrative of the Bible shows a combination of two sets of qualities: on the one hand it has a simplicity and a limpid and vivid clearness which make it appeal to all sorts and conditions of men; on the other hand through its whole range it has an undercurrent of earnestness and strong feeling. Thus the style clothes and transfigures even homely events with beauty and spiritual power; and the concreteness and clearness crystallize the deep feeling expressed by the strong rhythm and the varied music of the style. . . .

The type of narrative that springs most readily to one's mind when one speaks of the Biblical narrative is the vivid kind of story which for the most part fills Genesis, Samuel, and Kings. For swiftness, for the unerring sense of effective detail, these stories are our standard in English. The story of the Garden of Eden, and the fall of man, and the stories of Abraham, Isaac, and Jacob show us this vivid narrative at its clearest and simplest. Even in this vivid and simple narrative, however, there is considerable variety. The stories of this type in Genesis are pastoral, almost idyllic, in contrast to the histories of the bloody Joab and his slaughter of Amasa and Absalom, or of the primitive feuds of Gideon and Jephthah in Judges, or of Elisha and Jehu and their merciless extermination of the worshippers of Baal. These later stories produce an effect of a stern reality, beside which the stories of the patriarchs have, as has been said, "the freshness of the elder world." . . .

Let us consider more carefully the simple and vivid narrative. It is characterized by a lively and naïve interest in the affairs of human life, and by natural and unpremeditated story-telling. Such are the simpler of the stories of the patriarchs, the story of Rebecca at the well, of Jacob and his tortuous dealings with his brother Esau and his father-in-law Laban, and the stories of Joseph, with that most touching scene of all where he could no longer refrain from disclosing himself to his brethren. In other books of the Bible we come to examples of this style with its full human interest in the stories of Jephthah and of Samson, in the story of Saul seeking his father's asses, in the various stories of David and Saul, in the story of David and Bathsheba, and of the rebellion of the arrogant Absalom. . . . In all these stories the interest lies almost wholly in the actions and in the people. They show no evidence of any pondering on the meaning of history; the events and the actors in them are sufficient for the narrators. The narrative moves directly and rapidly, yet with extraordinary vividness of characterization. The contrast between Jacob and Esau is perhaps the best example of this compact portrayal of character: Jacob farsighted and wily in a peculiarly Oriental way, yet withal sobered and deepened by his foresight of the great future which the promises of Jehovah had laid out for his race; Esau bluff and honest, but reckless of any good beyond that of the present moment. . . .

Yet if we knew only these stories in the Old Testament, we should miss a notable element of what makes up our impression of the Biblical narrative. For after all, that narrative is not merely a standard for vividness; it is also a standard for depth of meaning and a solemn stateliness of style. For these qualities one must turn to the other two of these three types of narrative. The latest of these, which is found chiefly in the Pentateuch, and which we may call the priestly, is bare of vivifying detail. The first chapter of Genesis in comparison with the second is austere and abstract: by itself and beside the warm human interest of the other stories it seems lacking in life. It does not scintillate with the words and the movement of living beings; it sets forth the newly created universe and the world of the patriarchs as an empty expanse in which the Lord God of Israel stands at a remote and awful distance. And if one follows out the passages in which this type of narrative occurs through the Pentateuch one gets only an outline of the history, and an outline in which religious institutions and ceremonies overshadow the individuals of the race. Examples of this bare but solemn narrative are the story of the creation in Genesis 1, of God's covenant with Noah after the Flood, of the covenant and promise to Abraham in Genesis 17, of Abraham's purchase of the field of Ephron the Hittite at Machpelah for a buryingplace in Genesis 23, and of the Lord's commission to Moses to lead the children of Israel out of Egypt in Exodus 6. Besides these and many other passages of narrative, the great mass of laws and liturgical prescriptions and the exhaustive genealogies and chronology scattered through these books of the Pentateuch belong to the same priestly source, and add their solemn precision and formality to the general effect. Yet throughout this bare and unimaginative type of narrative is marked by a dignity and elevation which go a long way to color one's impression of the Biblical narrative as a whole. . . .

The third type of narrative which must be taken into account in forming an estimate of the Biblical narrative as a whole is that of Deuteronomy and the analogous passages in the other histories; in time of origin this is intermediate between the other two. [*See also* Deuteronomy.]

> J. H. Gardiner. *The Bible as English Literature* (New York, Scribner's, 1906), pp. 34, 37, 42–45, 48

To the narratives great tribute has been paid by modern masters of their art. Especially memorable are Goethe's admiration of the tales of the Patriarchs and Tolstoy's judgement that the story of Joseph is the model of what story-telling should be. The originality of these narratives cannot be doubted. Their style bears no marks of foreign influence and all that has been recovered of the Egyptian literature of travel and adventure is not comparable to them—does not approach them in simplicity, charm, or dramatic power, far less in moral feeling and insight. For their main lines the Hebrew narratives have the careers and fortunes of individuals, and when separated from the additions that later editors have imposed on them they prove marvellously true transcripts of human life and character. With equal faithfulness they reflect the primitive morality of the times with which they deal, and record the vices as well as the virtues of their heroes, aware of the complexities of human character and showing a fine sense of proportion in portraying these. Even in the story of Balaam, the governing aim of which is a national one, namely to contrast the irresistible purpose of Israel's God for His people with the futile endeavour of the powers, from Pharaoh to Balak, to frustrate it, what subtlety is shown in depicting this conflict in the mind and conduct of Balaam, with all the mixed religious experience and fluctuating conscience of that ambiguous and most interesting pagan! This is worked out with a simplicity that must not be allowed to hide from us the psychological power by which it is informed.

But the richest flowering of the Hebrew genius for narrative is found in the histories of Saul and David, originally (as is admitted) by a contemporary writer or writers, but subsequently edited into their present form. When they have been relieved of the dogmatic additions imposed upon them, their natural beauty and piety become fully apparent.

The stories reveal a very rare combination of equal intimacy and detachment. There is no sparing of the faults and errors of their heroes, and the keen insight into the complex characters of these and the sympathy felt for them develop through a simple tale of the consequences they brought upon themselves to the outlines of a great tragedy, or rather of two tragedies, of which they are the central figures, while surrounded by lesser personalities whose passions and blunders contribute to the general effect. There is no intrusion of miracle nor arbitrary interference by the Deity, but a simple faith in God's justice and His discipline of families and individuals; and things work themselves out naturally as the issues of men's right or wrong actions yet conditioned by forces over which the men themselves have no control. Thus throughout we have that mingling of sternness and of pathos, of the rigid development of moral consequence and the inevitable addition of accident or fate which form the essence of great tragedy. Let us keep in mind that all this vivid recital of events, this revelation of character and its consequences, with their tragic culminations, were accomplished through a medium of expression so defective in construction and flexibility as we have seen the Hebrew language to be.

George A. Smith. In The Legacy of Israel. Ed. by Edwyn R. Bevan and Charles Singer (Oxford, Clarendon Press, 1927), pp. 15–17

In a kind of a way what has made the Old Testament such permanently good reading is that really in a way in the Old Testament writing there really was not any such thing there was not really any succession of anything and really in the Old Testament there is really no sentence existing and no paragraphing, think about this thing, think if you have not really been knowing this thing and then let us go on telling about what paragraphs and sentences have been what prose and poetry has been. So then in the Old Testament writing there is really no actual conclusion that anything is progressing that one thing is succeeding another thing, that anything in that sense in the sense of succeeding happening is a narrative of anything, but most writing is based on this thing most writing has been a real narrative writing a telling of the story of anything in the way that thing has been happening and now everything is not that thing there is at present not a sense of anything being successively happening, moving is in every direction beginning and ending is not really exciting, anything is anything, anything is happening and anybody can know anything at any time that anything is happening and so really and truly is there any sentence and any paragraphing is there prose and poetry as the same thing or different things is there now any narrative of any successive thing.

Gertrude Stein. Narration: Four Lectures (Chicago, University of Chicago Press, 1935), p. 19

The Old Testament stories are concerned mainly with the figures of Hebrew tradition, and they are, primarily at least, figures of real life. It may be, in order to achieve the purpose of the narrator, that these figures, when they become characters of a story, are at times redrawn or overdrawn, that the setting in which they live and move may be idealized and the incidents in which they take part idyllized, and that the action, in the course of its detailing, may be elaborated or even exaggerated. There can, however, be no doubt that the Old Testament stories, in varying degree of course, are so skilfully composed that they attract and retain the interest and attention of the reader. There is probably no group of stories in world literature whose effect has been so striking and so permanent. The plot, the characters, and the phrasing are the joy and the abiding possession of millions.

What, then, can be described as the characteristic features of Old Testament story-telling? The worldwide appreciation accorded to the stories, shows that there must be something precious and durable in their content and structure. Even a superficial examination of a number of the stories with which the Old Testament records are so liberally embellished leads easily to the recognition of some marked features. An outstanding feature, and one which leaps to the eye everywhere, is the economy of words and the paucity of descriptive matter. Characters are introduced and drawn and scenes are depicted with remarkable brevity. Beyond the fact that Abraham was the son of Terah and took a wife Sarai and moved from Ur of the Chaldees to Haran and dwelt there we are told nothing more by way of introduction to Abraham. Elijah is introduced even more baldly. "Elijah the Tishbite, who was of the sojourners of Gilead." Of David we are merely told, "Now he was ruddy and withal of a beautiful countenance and goodly to look upon." The reader is thus left to form his estimate of the characters in the account given of their utterances and their deeds.

It follows that where there is such studied crystallization, each small detail becomes of account, and every word may be accounted of value. An example of the masterly fashion in which drama and pathos can be packed into a brief compass is given in this moving description of the death of the Shunammite child. "And when the child was grown it fell on a day that he went out to his father to the reapers. And he said unto his father, My head, my head. And he said to his servant, Carry him to his mother. And when he had taken him and brought him to his mother, he sat on her knees until noon and then died" [II Kgs. 4:18–20].

Edward Robertson. *John Rylands Library Bulletin.*
Dec., 1944, pp. 454–56

The basic unit of the narrative literature of the Bible is the individual story, which is one or two ordinary pages long. These stories were at first passed on by word of mouth from generation to generation, and from this point of view they are therefore typical folk-tales, and like most folk-tales they pay much attention to the ancestors and leaders of the people (or the tribe). The later in date these leaders are, the more exact the stories are from the historical point of view; it is not historical accuracy that is the main thing, however, but the pleasure of the story and education through literature. Hence it contains both typical folk-lore themes and basic human ideas. The folklore themes do not, indeed, dominate the story, but it, like all great literature, dominates them. The human aspect subordinates them to itself, and therefore from each story there emerges a living personality and not a formular personality acting according to a folkloristic theme. From this realistic and living description of the individual and his fate there emerges some idea. The Biblical story, like the folk-tale, is always a story of action, but the progress of the action, according to the characteristic dramatic lines of complication and denouement, expresses some idea, which gives significance to the plot and to the fate of its central character. This idea is generally a particular variation on the idea of requital, and in this way it is parallel with the characteristic popular preference for a happy ending; but the end is not always a happy one in the simple meaning of the term. The idea of requital is bound up with the idea of Providence, i.e. the hidden force that is the cause of the action in the Biblical stories is not Fate but God; but the ways of God are not always clear and simple. God, who is the hidden hero, does not force himself on the story or take an active part in the course of events. The supreme Providence is behind the scenes, while the stage is occupied by a complete and pretty complicated human world, an apparently independent world, presented to us as it is. No character in the stories is distorted in consequence of the fact that Jotham's prophecy is fulfilled, and Hannah bears a son, and David marries Abigail, and Abraham does not kill Isaac—and yet, in all these stories we have passed beyond the simple folk tale and reached the domain of deliberate literature, based on a realistic conception of man and his acts, presenting living human beings in situations possessing a human and moral significance, and creating as a product of all this, a vision of human life. The source of the Biblical story is the folk-tale, but it contains much more than does the folk-tale as commonly understood; it is real literature, great literature, classic literature. . . .

It should be specially emphasized that there are numerous shades of colour in the individual scriptural story, a multiplicity of colours that arises both from differences of approach and from differences in the types of hero. Sometimes the Biblical story is light in character, as in the episode of David and Abigail, and sometimes it hints at profound depths in the human soul, as in the story of the binding of Isaac. The difference in tone, moreover, results in a difference in values, for it is a long way from the emphasis on practical shrewdness and cleverness to the emphasis on the extreme faith in God which contains no element of shrewdness at all, while both the practical cleverness and the great faith are fundamental values in the Biblical narrative. It is difficult to see the combination in an individual story, but it can be clearly seen by anyone who follows a central Biblical character through a series of stories. It seems that specific combinations of shrewdness and faith are the key to the understanding of such characters as Jacob and David. Practical wisdom implants the "Biblical type" in the soil of everyday reality, while faith leads him across the frontiers of the everyday—and anyone who wishes to understand the nature of the Biblical type and the scriptural narrative must be aware of both of these qualities at the same time.

Zvi Adar. *The Biblical Narrative* (Jerusalem, Department of Education and Culture, World Zionist Organization, 1959), pp. 49–50, 52

Hebrew fiction—that is, narrative contrived to resemble reality—can offer us, on a small scale, the sorts of aesthetic pleasure we derive from modern novels. Equally important, it can allow us to see—from a slightly different vantage point—how the "God-obsessed" consciousness of the Hebrew people leaves its mark on fairly free imaginative creations.

Two motives interplay in these stories: the desire to instruct and the desire to entertain. Our own reading of fiction tells us that these are not always a well-matched team. The lead horse (edification or propaganda) pulls too hard, and the off horse (aesthetic satisfaction or delight) refuses to follow. American fiction is full of novels like Upton Sinclair's *The Jungle* or his later "Lanny Budd" series where, quite obviously, social and political propaganda takes precedence over elements of entertainment and over truth to life. . . .

The initial problem we face in reckoning the artistic success or failure of Hebrew "fiction" is the same. Drawing on a variety of materials—fragments of history, legend, folklore, their own invention—the authors seldom overlook their primary duty; at least, there is not an H. Allen Smith among them. More seriously, there is not among them a writer like the great modern French novelist, Marcel Proust. Proust, in his monumental and detailed *Remembrance of Things Past,* showed that he felt his chief duty lay in giving a harmonious, detailed, and aesthetically pleasing picture of the reality he knew. He is plainly not concerned with the "moral" or lesson we may draw from his work. The Hebrew writers of Esther, Daniel, and the others were all moralists in the first place and artists only in the second place. In fact, the very elements in these stories that give us pleasure—the brief but sharp pictures of ancient custom, the sudden sense that human motives we still know are fleetingly revealed—are not the chief ones for these old "novelists." Their aim is to urge home a godly point; the other effects are incidental by-products. Thus, in Tobit, our delight with the parting comment of the mother to her son-in-law is a delight with something on the periphery of the book. (The mother says, at the end of Chapter 10, ". . . behold, I commit my daughter unto thee in special trust, vex her not.") Likewise, the subtlety in the character drawing of the heroine Judith and the noble colloquy of Ruth and Naomi in the first chapter of Ruth can give the reader a keen pleasure. But reactions of pleasure to isolated "gems" ignore the writers' central intent: a drive toward edification. These sections of the Bible offer us not merely a collection of colored stones to hold in the memory. If we but see them so, they have their places in a larger handiwork.

This larger handiwork—the complete narratives and what lay behind their creation—sometimes merits the modern term of praise, "a work of art"; and often it does not. It is not surprising that the least aesthetically successful stories are those in which the lead horse of edification pulls too hard.

Harold H. Watts. The Modern Reader's Guide to the Bible. Rev. ed. (New York, Harper, 1959), pp. 160–62

Any artistic treatment of the biblical theme whose aim is to portray the Bible's characters as tragic heroes is made possible only by forsaking *the artistic-sacral basis upon which the biblical narrative is founded.* That is to say, only a denial of the truth that is the soul of the biblical narrative makes possible the transformation of a biblical character into a tragic hero. In other words, desacralization is a presupposition of tragic interpretation. But desacralization of a sacral text is an arbitrary, illegitimate act, transforming sacral reality—the document of sacral faith—into "fiction." . . .

Only in an age that has ceased to understand the peculiar spiritual data of sacral literature was an attempt born to view biblical characters as tragic characters, able to serve as subjects for the heroes of modern tragedy. The biblical story itself, without the arbitrary secular exegesis that undermines its authenticity, delimits itself, both with respect to the world of ancient tragedy and with respect to the possibilities of modern drama and of modern literature in general. It is distinguished qualitatively from ancient tragedy in that it is founded upon a set of values that leaves no room for relativism. So, too, biblical narrative does not know the concept of the hero who is enfolded within his selfhood. The existence of *differing, opposing truths,* more or less equal in value, opposes the spirit of the biblical narrative. On the other hand, a situation devoid of salvation, devoid of hope for redemption, for the mercy of God, cannot obtain in biblical narrative. Salvation always awaits a biblical personality, and repentance redounds to him, as we have seen even in the most extreme case of Cain, who admits and confesses: "My sin is too great to bear." And Job submits only after the possibility of dialogue had been opened to him: "By the ear's hearing have I heard you, and now has my eye seen you. Therefore do I repudiate and repent, in dust and ashes" [Job 42:5–6]. This sort of thing is unimaginable in the world of Greek tragedy, and in European tragedy since the sixteenth century, too. The redemption of man through the mercy of God does not allow tragic knowledge to prevail over a man who does not admit of true tragedy, for true tragedy has no way out. But where there is faith in redemption—there is a way out.

This and more: Greek tragedy stands under the sign of myth. And even if it must be admitted that biblical narrative, too, is saturated with mythical elements, these elements have been overwhelmed by the pervasive idea of a single, unique God who is absolute. His omnipotence and truths preclude the existence of differing and relative truths. The autonomy of the myths has been broken in the biblical world: "Such is the nature of myth: life that admits of nothing above it or below it. This life is devoid of lordship over objects (*ohne beherrschte Dinge*), without gods imposing rule (*ohne beherrschende Götter*). And it makes no difference if the bearers of this life are gods, humans, or objects. This life is in itself naked" [Franz Rosenzweig. *Der Stern der Erlösung* (Frankfurt, 1921), Vol. I, p. 130]. This sort of myth is the very antithesis of biblical narrative. And it is again apropos to dilate on Aeschylus' *Prometheus* in order to appreciate how great is the distance between the world of Greek myth, to the degree to which it consists in tragedy, and biblical narrative. Prometheus' great indictment expresses his anxiety over the relativism that pretends to appear as the supreme value. This is the meaning of Prometheus' cry against Zeus. Zeus is *"a new ruler on the throne of rule,"* "the son of Cronos has become a tyrant *without law*" (emphasis not in the original). . . . "When this arrogant one falls, the curse of his father Cronos will befall him," ". . . *I am undone without judgment.*" One may accordingly stress again: the book of Job and the books of the Bible in general are distinguished from tragedy to the degree to which the biblical God is distinguished from the Greek myths or from the neomodern myths.

And biblical narrative is separated from modern tragedy or modern literature and art in general by the gaping chasm between sacral art and the art of secular fiction. . . .

Biblical narrative, like any sacral art, can be approached from two antithetical primary assumptions: from the assumption of one who believes in the sacral reality of the narrative, or of the artistic testimony; or from the skeptical assumption of desacralization, which transforms the testimony into the subject of fiction. . . . One can formulate the primary difference between sacral art and secular fiction in a paradoxical manner. *Sacral art knows no religious subject,* because its entire reality, its entire world, is holy. The religious theme, as a theme among all the other themes, is the distinctive mark of secular art, of the art of fiction, emerging and cutting its way out of an autonomous world.

Baruch Kurzweil. Iyyun. July 1961, pp. 153–55†

In the biblical narration no significant dimensions are scanted. The private and the public are interrelated, the psychological and the social, the empirical and the metaphysical. And there is a robust reality-sense, a power in being, and it is related to the fact that man in Scripture, precisely in his total perspectives, is still linked with the archaic hidden roots and fibres of his pre-historical and biological inheritance. This test is a challenge to any kind of truncation of man, whether naturalistic or spiritualizing or solipsist. It exposes particularly one dominant feature of modern letters, that which can be generally characterized as the "epiphany." For the epiphany moment in modern experience and the modern novel, which often has to carry the whole burden of meaning, represents a highly fragmentary grasp of reality. The momentary vision in question may have a romanticist, an existentialist or a surrealist character, but in whatever form it evidences a forfeiture of relationships and so of holism. It testifies, indeed, to an impoverishment of vitality in the visionary rather than the contrary. For when epiphany is powerful it orders reality. . . .

There is one further challenge presented by the biblical epos. It is difficult to state it without seeming to involve theology. We have already had it in view when discussing the "dialogical" dimension of that narrative. The question raised is that of doing justice to the full mystery of the self and its aliveness at the level of inter-personal encounter and mutuality. The unique humanism of the Old Testament would appear to rest upon some momentous cultural drama that moved the race along towards the personal.

Its narrative, therefore, evokes something more than the usual suspenseful turns of fortune of men and societies and something more than the joys and sorrows, hopes and disappointments of life. In such classic epic and fictions the deeper enigma of man is hardly touched. What is missing is some sense of that secret of his being where he is a mixture of freedom and helplessness, of loneliness and entanglement, and where all this carries with it a consciousness of responsibility, and where man is sensitive not only to external approval or disapproval but to internal peace or shame. It is a question of the dramas of the heart, and of the share of men's willing and choosing in the fatefulness of the world.

I can do no better to suggest this special awakening of the self than by noting how in the biblical episodes, in the Old Testament stories, God, as it were, looks man in the eye. . . . "Eyeball to eyeball," we say. This kind of naked confrontation and searching of the human self can mean a calling to account . . . we think of Nathan's words to David: "Thou art the man!" . . . But such moral reverberations of a positive character can also be evoked in the narrative: Joseph disclosing himself to his brothers, or the mutual magnanimity of David and the three mighty men who at the risk of their lives brought him water from the well which was by the gate of Bethlehem, to solace him at a moment of homesickness and dereliction. Quite apart from theology, all this represents a deeper kind of humanism, an existential kind of realism, such that the narrative pierces to the heart's core of the reader and binds us hand and foot. . . .

The dimension of involvement of which we have been speaking refers first of all to the characters in the given narrative. But the reader is also involved. We are reminded of Berthold Brecht therefore. For if it was his view that there must be a distance between the audience and the action it was to ensure that the spectator's responsibility was demanded. Transferred to the arts of narration this means that the hearer or reader should not be a victim of hypnotic compulsion or sorcery. Brecht spoke significantly therefore of a dialectical or epic theatre. The biblical epic has this character. It is not seductive, subjective, romantic. It does not work by a depersonalizing enchantment. When one finds sentiment in the Old Testament—as, for example, in the sacrifice of Isaac or the immolation of Jephthah's daughter—any evasion into common pathos is blocked by a high art of austerity, or any consent to disguised forms of masochism or sadism such as are invited in current novels and plays. The sufferer in such episodes is not a victim but an actor at a sacrifice.

Amos N. Wilder. *The New Voice: Religion, Literature, Hermeneutics* (New York, Herder and Herder, 1969), pp. 70–73

We may speak of *didactic narrative* when the presentation dispenses with puzzling literary devices and when a specific context of events is presented quite openly as far as its outward sequence is concerned. In the ways in which the didactic purpose of the narrator is expressed there are considerable differences. In this respect, the Joseph narrative shows great restraint, both at its climax and in its individual features; for example, in the description of Joseph's innocence only the person who is capable of listening sensitively really feels himself addressed. Similarly in the prose narrative in Job, it is the events, the spoken word, which instruct. Only in the summary sentences (Job 1:22; 2:10b) does the narrator address the reader from outside of the narrative. Much more powerful are the didactic emphases in a narrative which has been placed there by an event which a wise man has observed in the street (Prov. 7:6ff.). The story of Tobit also releases its teachings directly and openly, for here it is not just the events themselves which instruct; in addition, the narrator places voluminous instructions on the lips of the protagonists. Such didactic narratives have, of course, rarely been "written" *ad hoc*; as a rule they cast old narrative material in a new form. In the case of the Tobit narrative this is generally acknowledged. In the case of the Joseph narrative it cannot be proved; but it is fairly certain that the story of the vizier who climbed to power and honour must have had its earlier stages. Already, for the narrator of Genesis, it lay in the distant past.

The level of ancient Israelite narrative art can be recognized in the mastery with which narrative expositions were composed. If this is already true of literary narratives such as those in the books of Samuel, then it is certainly true also of didactic narratives. The exposition of the Joseph story sets the reader, with its very first sentences, in the centre of a scene agitated with passions, on the one hand the father's love, on the other the brothers' hatred. This is followed by Joseph's two dreams, which direct one's gaze into a still veiled future. The exposition closes with the sentence, "And his brothers were jealous of him, but his father kept the thing in mind" (Gen. 37:11). Events as such come into play only when the father sends the defenceless Joseph to the brothers who are busy far away with their herds. The most artistic of all expositions has been achieved by the narrator of the book of Tobit. It consists of two sections which run parallel to each other and which correspond from the point of view of their form. The first deals with the old man Tobit who has buried a corpse which lay near his house and who is completely impoverished by adverse circumstances which have a connection with this occurrence. The other deals with a young girl whose suitors were each strangled on their wedding night by a wicked demon. These two people, independently of each other and widely separated from each other, ask God to let them die. God, however, hears the prayers of these two, who do not know each other, and links their destinies for good (Tob. 1–3). The real action begins only in Tobit 4.

A sharp differentiation of didactic narrative from other types of narrative is naturally impossible. The points of transition are fluid. Does the militant book of Judith belong more with historical narratives? From the point of view of its material it leads the reader into the military and political sphere and, tricked out with a whole load of partly confused, historical reminiscences, tells of a woman's heroism. Nevertheless, this narrative, too, will have to be credited with a didactic purpose which goes beyond the communication of sensational events, for the theme of the book is the uniqueness of Israel's God, the questioning of it and its historical proof. Much more obviously, in this respect, are the Daniel narratives to be classified here, especially Dan. 1; 3–6. They certainly do not come from that period of terrible religious persecution by Antiochus Epiphanes (167 B.C.), but from a much earlier time, namely from a Diaspora situation in which the

Jews were certainly not persecuted but in which, on the contrary, the way to high offices of state lay open to them. But this very loyalty to the great king concealed the possibility of quite specific religious conflicts.

Gerhard von Rad. *Wisdom in Israel* (Nashville, Abingdon Press, 1972), pp. 46–47

Anyone who saw "The Pawnbroker" knows that a major cause of the film's effectiveness was the visual flashback scenes in which the pawnbroker perceived and interpreted the present through analogous experiences from the past. The Bible story creates added dimensions of meaning through the same allusive device, which, because it is verbal, has more of an "overlay" effect than "flashback." As has been noted, the first of the seven sections established the cosmic setting in Creation and the Flood for the mundane events which follow, preparing us to find other allusions to the primeval stories. In [Exod.] 1:8–14 there are clear references to the arrogance of the Tower of Babel story, and 2:1–10 presses back to the preserving ark of the Noah story. If we move further back in the sequence of primeval narratives, the preceding story is that of Cain and Abel; 2:11–15 talks of Moses as his brothers' keeper, defending one who is being beaten to death, then intervening to prevent one brother from smiting another. Preceding Cain and Abel is the Garden of Eden. Do we have an allusion to that in 2:15–22 when it talks about the daughters being driven away (a theme emphasized by the naming of "Gershom") from the water, the source of life (cf. Gen. 3:24)? Is the narrative, moving back with its allusions through the primeval story sequence, portraying a God who, through Moses and the people of Israel, is in the process of reversing the alienation and broken community which had been man's condition since earliest times?

We can only briefly touch on the implications of these allusions. Pharaoh's Babel-like building activity is doomed to fail because bondage crushes the human spirit. Moses in the ark is, like Noah, the preserver of life for mankind because he will point the way to freedom. His intervention to prevent one Hebrew brother from smiting another is an attempt to overcome the hostility between brothers which had existed since Cain killed Abel. Paradoxically, the seven daughters are driven away by the shepherds because God, confirming the new situation of pride and hostility embodied in man's disobedience, had driven Adam and Eve out of Eden, away from the tree of life. Is Moses' returning the driven-out daughters to the well a symbolic act for the new life which will be made possible through Israel's covenant relationship with God?

James S. Ackerman. In *Literary Interpretations of Biblical Narratives*. Ed. by Kenneth R. R. Gros Louis et al. (Nashville, Abingdon Press, 1974), pp. 114–15

The Hebrew short story is a distinct and discrete form, with its own ground rules, its own purposes, its own range of content (which could be quite varied, by the way, and could include much valuable historical information), and its own style. Included in it were rhythmic elements which are characteristic of the style and probably at least partially mnemonic in purpose. As examples we can include a number of the patriarchal narratives, especially Genesis 24 and 38; the Joseph story; a number of the Judges narratives, including, for example, Judges 3:15–29 (the Ehud-Eglon episode) and Judges 4; Ruth (minus only its last five verses); and the Job prose story. Quite probably these stories in rhythmic prose had an oral period in that style, and their writing down came not at the end of a process of poetic transmission but at the end of a period of oral transmission in more or less their present rhythmic prose style. Their content, while varied, includes a combination of a certain kind of concern about rather typical people doing rather mundane things which nevertheless turn out to have rather significant results. Their purpose is both entertaining and edifying; it seems too that such narratives are peculiarly Israelite in that the scene of human life where very ordinary human events and figures function is also the scene where God works. And so, while the stories can have all the fun and delight and pathos and violence of common human existence, they also have the dimension of seriousness.

> Edward F. Campbell, Jr. In *Light unto My Path*. Ed. by Howard N. Bream et al. (Philadelphia, Temple University Press, 1974), pp. 90–91

The prominence of narrative as a biblical form arises from the Bible's view of God. The God of the Bible is, above all, the God who acts. He acts not simply in the inner consciousness of people but in the arena of history. Historical narrative is the inevitable mode for writing about the God who acts in history. . . .

It is evident that the story form is uniquely suited to the task of embodying the main outlines of biblical truth. By bringing human characters into interaction with God and with each other, biblical narrative is able to explore the dynamics of relationship that is so central to the biblical view of man. By presenting a double plot in which spiritual and earthly levels of action occur simultaneously, biblical narrative illuminates the spiritual reality that is always the context for human experience. Because narrative is a progression of events moving toward a goal, it is uniquely suited to depicting the dynamic, growing nature of religious experience. And by virtue of its focus on plot conflict, biblical narrative expresses the nature of the continuing struggle between good and evil.

> Leland Ryken. *The Literature of the Bible* (Grand Rapids, Mich., Zondervan, 1974), p. 77

[The narrative mode of the Old Testament] is highly scenic. The story of the Floating Axehead [II Kgs. 6:1–7], for example, contains only one sentence in straight narrative, in the humble function of a link between two scenes: "So he went with them, and they arrived at the Jordan and cut trees." Usually, however, the subject matter is more complex, and cannot all be conveniently told by scenes. The introductions and links are often longish passages in straight narrative, yet they do not deprive the story of its overall scenic character; see, for instance, Genesis 39:1–6, which serves as exposition to the highly scenic story of Joseph and the Egyptian woman. Occasionally a story may be written almost entirely in straight narrative, but the highlights are scenic, nevertheless. Thus in the story of Judah and Tamar (Gen. 38) one finds the sorry sequence of the deaths of Tamar's husbands, which takes a lot of telling, though no elaboration is called for. Consequently it is all in straight narrative. As the story reaches its decisive part—Judah's visit to Tamar, who is disguised as a prostitute, and Tamar's near-execution and triumph—it becomes scenic. Practically all passages of Old Testament prose that have some storytelling importance are scenic.

A sign, or perhaps a consequence, of the tendency to write in the scenic mode is the notorious poverty of Biblical stories in description and comment. In marked contrast to Homer, our story-tellers never tell us what the places and people looked like, what sort of houses they dwelt in, or what the quality of their weapons was. Where information about these things is necessary for the comprehension of the plot, it is given sparingly, by an adjective or a slight remark. Thus we are told that some persons were beautiful (Rachel, Joseph), or wore unusual and significant pieces of clothing (Joseph's striped shirt, Elijah's shaggy cloak). Such bits of information, even where they are more explicit (e.g. Judges 16:26) are not true descriptions, written for their own sake. They are rather the narrator's equivalent of the props and stage sets used in dramatic scenes. The reader is made to imagine things, not told precisely what they were. A remarkable instance of this is the description of Samuel's ghost by the witch of En Dor: "an old man wrapped in a cloak" (I Sam. 28:14). It is hardly sufficient for recognition, and yet we are told that Saul did know it was Samuel, by these words. No shortcoming is felt by the reader, who subconsciously imagines a full description behind the actual words.

Comment is equally brief and rare. The narrator's emotional and moral values are as a rule conveyed indirectly, by the implicit tenor of the stories. People are characterised by their speeches and behaviour, not praised or blamed. However, the narrator does occasionally add an explicit remark. He tells us that the serpent (in the Paradise story) was cunning; that Noah was righteous; that Moses was modest (Num. 12:3); or that David's wooing of Bathsheba and his indirect murder of her husband, was "bad in the Lord's eyes" (II Sam. 11:27)—something of an understatement. Such remarks may be stylistically elaborated, as where it is said of Job that he was "perfect and upright and feared God and shunned evil" (Job 1:1), yet rather slight in the amount of information conveyed. Comment in Biblical stories is always impressive, precisely because of its rarity.

Jacob Licht. *Storytelling in the Bible* (Jerusalem, Magnes Press, 1978), pp. 30–33

NARRATOR

In very many situations where the modern writer would expect a psychological analysis, the primitive story-teller simply presents an action. The spiritual state of the man and woman in Paradise and after the Fall is not analysed, but a single objective touch is given by which we may recognise it. The narrator says nothing of the thoughts of Adam when the woman handed him the forbidden fruit, but merely, that he ate it; he does not discourse to us on Abraham's hospitable disposition, but he tells us how he entertained the three men. He does not say that Shem and Japhet felt chastely and respectfully, but he has them act chastely and respectfully; not that Joseph had compassion upon his brethren, but that he turned away and wept (42:24; 43:30); not that Hagar, when mistreated by Sarah, felt offended in the depths of her maternal pride, but that she ran away from her mistress (16:6); not that Laban was dazzled by the gold of the stranger, but that he made haste to invite him (24:30); not that obedience to God triumphed in Abraham over parental love, but that he arose straightway (22:3); not that Tamar remained faithful to her husband even beyond the grave, but that she took measures to rear up children from his seed (38).

From all this we see on what the story-teller laid the chief emphasis. He does not share the modern point of view that the most interesting and worthy theme for art is the soul-life of man; his childlike taste is fondest of the outward, objective facts. And in this line his achievements are excellent. He has an extraordinary faculty for selecting just the action which is most characteristic for the state of feeling of his hero. How could filial piety be better represented than in the story of Shem and Japhet? Or mother-love better than by the behavior of Hagar? She gave her son to drink—we are not told that she herself drank. How could hospitality be better depicted than in the actions of Abraham at Hebron? And there is nothing less than genius in the simple manner in which the innocence and the consciousness of the first men is illustrated by their nakedness and their clothing.

These simple artists had not learned how to reflect; but they were masters of observation. It is chiefly this admirable art of indirectly depicting men through their actions which makes the legends so vivid. Little as these primitive men could talk about their soul-life, we gain the impression that they are letting us look into the very hearts of their heroes. These figures live before our eyes, and hence the modern reader, charmed by the luminous clearness of these old legends, is quite willing to forget their defects.

But even when the story-teller said nothing of the soul-life of his heroes, his hearer did not entirely fail to catch an impression of it. We must recall at this point that we are dealing with orally recited stories. Between narrator and hearer there is another link than that of words; the tone of the voice talks, the expression of the face or the gestures of the narrator. Joy and grief, love, anger, jealousy, hatred, emotion, and all the other moods of his heroes, shared by the narrator, were thus imparted to his hearers without the utterance of a word. . . .

A further medium of expression for the spiritual life of the personages is articulate speech. Words are not, it is true, so vivid as actions, but to make up for this they can the better reveal the inner life of the personages. The early story-tellers were masters in the art of finding words that suit the mood of the speakers: thus the malice of the cunning serpent is expressed in words, as well as the guilelessness of the childlike woman, Sarah's jealousy of her slave as well as the conciliatoriness of Abraham (16:6), the righteous wrath of Abimelech (20:9), the caution of the shrewd Jacob (32:9), and the bitter lament of Esau (27:36) and of Laban (31:43) when deceived by Jacob. Notable masterpieces of the portrayal of character in words are the temptation of the first couple and the conversation between Abraham and Isaac on the way to the mount of sacrifice.

Hermann Gunkel. *The Legends of Genesis*. Tr. by W. H. Carruth (Chicago, Open Court, 1901), pp. 61–63

It is all very different in the Biblical stories. Their aim is not to bewitch the senses, and if nevertheless they produce lively sensory effects, it is only because the moral, religious, and psychological phenomena which are their sole concern are made concrete in the sensible matter of life. But their religious intent involves an absolute claim to historical truth. The story of Abraham and Isaac is not better established than the story of Odysseus, Penelope, and Euryclea; both are legendary. But the Biblical narrator, the Elohist, had to believe in the objective truth of the story of Abraham's sacrifice—the existence of the sacred ordinances of life rested upon the truth of this and similar stories. He had to believe in it passionately; or else (as many rationalistic interpreters believed and perhaps still believe) he had to be a conscious liar—no harmless liar like Homer, who lied to give pleasure, but a political liar with a definite end in view, lying in the interest of a claim to absolute authority.

To me, the rationalistic interpretation seems psychologically absurd; but even if we take it into consideration, the relation of the Elohist to the truth of his story still remains a far more passionate and definite one than is Homer's relation. The Biblical narrator was obliged to write exactly what his belief in the truth of the tradition (or, from the rationalistic standpoint, his interest in the truth of it) demanded of him—in either case, his freedom in creative or representative imagination was severely limited; his activity was perforce reduced to composing an effective version of the pious tradition. What he produced, then, was not primarily oriented toward "realism" (if he succeeded in being realistic, it was merely a means, not an end); it was oriented toward truth.

Erich Auerbach. *Mimesis*. Tr. by Willard Trask (Princeton, N.J., Princeton University Press, 1953), p. 14

Once the narrator has opened the subject itself he does not stray either to the right or to the left, and only occasionally introduces an incidental remark in so far as it is required for the understanding of what is happening. In the course of the plot itself, each detail is subordinate to the aim; every sentence and every word fulfil the function that is reserved for them in the inner life of the chapter; and from this point of view the Biblical story is a classic example of an organic unity, a true artistic creation. These features, which are outstanding in the story of the binding of Isaac, apply also to the story of Abigail; here, too, the words are carefully thought out, and the length of the narration is not due to any tendency on the part of the narrator, but is a factor in the story. Thus Abigail's speech before David is drawn out for diplomatic reasons, because of the need for David's anger to die down after the flattering words. This writing, intensive and to the point, is characteristic of the narrator who has something definite to say, and who is well aware that his listeners and readers will immediately grasp his essential purpose, if he expresses it briefly and clearly. In this the Biblical story is similar to Greek tragedy, which also vigorously takes hold of the main subject and rejects all adornment and obscurity in order to convey it strongly to the public which is prepared for it. The Biblical narrator does not use "artistic" tricks and "fine writing." The modern author makes one chapter in a Biblical story into a complete novel for the fastidious reader, while the Biblical narrator compresses a complete life history into a single chapter, because he wishes to bring home to his entire public a single clear human subject that emerges from it. The great artistry of the Biblical narrator lies in the fact that he always tells in the shortest possible way about the life of men and momentous happenings, which have a clear and universal significance, and expresses great ideas in simple words.

> Zvi Adar. *The Biblical Narrative* (Jerusalem, Department of Education and Culture, World Zionist Organization, 1959), pp. 55-56

Hebrew narrative style discloses the same tendency to abide in what can be concretely experiential. The characters are stirred by passionate, often conflicting feelings. The divine command to sacrifice his beloved only son must necessarily plunge Abraham into the most grievous inner struggle; whereas the narrative tells only of his silent and conscientious obedience:

> Abraham rose up early in the morning
> and saddled his ass. . . . (Gen. 22:3)

Not a word do we learn about Joseph's behavior in the pit. Yet here would be the opportunity to describe human behavior. Up to this point Joseph had been portrayed as the favorite son who considered himself as the chosen one among the brothers; now, however, he is profoundly humiliated by his own brothers. But the narrator does not make the most of this opportunity. Nevertheless, he is by no means uninterested in human behavior. An outwardly visible gesture aptly characterizes the brothers' conduct:

> They cast him into a pit; but the pit was empty, there was no water
> in it. And they sat down to eat. . . . (Gen. 37:24f.)

Years later, however, in Egypt, when the brothers come into sore straits, the image of Joseph in the pit rises up again—and this time Joseph's plaint is not ignored:

> They said one to another, "We are verily guilty concerning our
> brother. We saw the anguish of his soul when he besought us, and
> we would not listen. . . ." (Gen. 42:21)

The biblical narrators often intend to express more than is present in words. We have to read between the lines. The anguish of the prisoner, to begin with, is not mentioned, because the brothers do not want to admit it, but it remains on their conscience over years.

In a famous comparison, [Erich] Auerbach contrasted Homer's narrative manner with the biblical tales. In the Greek epic the present is fully illuminated; all matters and occurrences are put clearly, comprehensibly, and vividly in the foreground. The biblical story, however, at first passes over Joseph's lament in silence, leaving it to the listener to interpret the brothers' gesture. Only much later does the narrator go back to it; the new situation is seen against the background of what happened long ago; the narrative points to the depth-dimensions of the present events: The threat to Benjamin and the old infamous act against Joseph are connected. The actions and behavior of Homeric heroes, in contrast, are always to be construed entirely from the present situation, from the spontaneous emotion. For them every day is, so to speak, a new beginning. But the people of the biblical stories are stamped by past events and live in the hope of future salvation. Despite the fact that the Hebrew narrator does not succeed in presenting detailed descriptions of fear, hatred, jealousy, and love, and despite the fact that the tales very sparingly use words that deal with what is experienced in mind and spirit, the biblical narrators know how to evoke images of complex psychological situations, and to offer an insight into the enigma and ambivalence of the human spirit. Their listeners are to participate; that is, they are to listen in on what is being passed over in silence and what is expressed only in the gestures, actions, miens, and words of the individuals.

Impressive images of human experience in extremis are found not only in the case of the great figures—Abraham who goes forth to sacrifice his son; Jacob who goes to meet his betrayed brother; David, aging and surrounded by intrigue—but also in the case of peripheral figures: Cast-off Hagar, who distances herself in the desert so far away from her child that she will not have to witness his dying but remains near enough to be with him again immediately, is indeed an unforgettable character. Likewise, too, is Rizpah, Saul's widow, who in the heat of the harvest season watches day and night over the dead bodies of her executed sons; young, swift Asahel, who will not let himself be kept from pursuing the famous commander so that the latter sees himself forced to slay him.

These "images" of human behavior are simply hinted at in a few strokes; important to the narrator is the impression, not the vividness. An exception is the story of left-handed Ehud, who slays fat King Eglon. The exact delineation is important here: the movement of his left hand to his right thigh where the dagger is concealed, the thrust into the belly, the fat in which the dagger disappears up to its haft (Judg. 3:15ff.). Only rarely do biblical authors observe so exactly as does this narrator.

Annemarie Ohler. *Gattungen im Alten Testament* (Düsseldorf, Patmos, 1972), pp. 70–71†

The narrator who appears in most stories in the Bible is the omniscient observer, who is privileged to glimpse acts performed in secret and to hear conversations conducted in a hush, who knows the characters internally, and who unlocks their hearts to us.

Omniscience entails being present everywhere. God is omniscient because he is present in every place at all times. The author resembles God in a number of ways—he, too, creates a world and creates a person, examines his inward parts, and sees the future of a thing at its inception—but he is not privileged to be present in every place at one and the same time. This does not follow from his being human but rather from his being limited by his medium—language. Language allows him to describe only one thing after another, so that one gets the impression that the narrator is now visiting here, now there, looking for a moment into this one's heart and for a moment into that one's, and that he momentarily shifts his vantage point from place to place. . . .

In many stories in the Bible the narrator stays in one place; for example, in the Garden of Eden (Gen. 3), in the story of the purchase of the Machpelah cave (Gen. 23), and in the story of the Queen of Sheba's visit to Solomon (I Kgs. 10). But in many more stories he instantaneously transports himself from place to place: he had been with Abraham in Canaan, but now he is in Aram-Naharaim visiting the house of Bethuel with Abraham's servant (Gen. 24); he had been in Aphek with the armies of Israel and Philistia, but now he is in Shiloh with the elderly Eli (I Sam. 9); he had been with Absalom in Jerusalem, but now he is in Mahanaim with David (II Sam. 17). He jumps back and forth without making a stopover.

The biblical narrator also enters into the innermost chambers; he is privy to the most intimate situations, and he hears tête-à-tête conversations. He is not prevented from knowing that David did not have intercourse with Abishag the Shunammite, the pretty girl who lay in his lap to warm him (I Kgs. 1:4). He remains in Amnon's chamber after the latter ordered everyone out; he is present during the rape, he sees how Amnon overcomes the resisting Tamar, and he hears the exchanges of words between them beforehand and afterward (II Sam. 13). Even the contents of a private letter that David sent to Joab with explicit instructions for disposing of Uriah the Hittite are not concealed from the narrator's vision (II Sam. 11:15). He may even serve as a first-hand witness to conversations conducted in heaven between God and his retinue (Job 1:6–12; 2:1–6). Everything is open and known to him.

> Shimeon Bar-Efrat. *Ha'itsuv ha'omanuti shel hassip-pur bammiqra'* (Tel Aviv, Sifriat Poalim, 1979), pp. 48–49†

Perhaps the most distinctive feature of the role played by the narrator in the biblical tales is the way in which omniscience and inobtrusiveness are combined. The sweep of the biblical narrator's authoritative knowledge extends from the very beginnings of things, which he can report down to the precise language and order of the divine utterances that brought the world into being, to the characters' hidden thoughts and feelings, which he may summarize for us or render in detail as interior speech. He is all-knowing and also perfectly reliable: at times he may choose to make us wonder but he never misleads us. I would suppose that as readers of later fiction most of us tend to associate this sort of emphatic omniscience with narrators like those of Fielding, Balzac, Thackeray, George Eliot, who flaunt their knowledge by stepping out in front of the proscenium arch to chat with or lecture to the audience, making us acutely aware that they are mediating between us and the fictional events. In the Bible, on the other hand, the narrator's work is almost all *récit*, straight narration of actions and speech, and only exceptionally and very briefly *discours*, disquisition on and around the narrated facts and their implications. The assurance of comprehensive knowledge is thus implicit in the narratives, but it is shared with the reader only intermittently and at that quite partially. In this way, the very mode of narration conveys a double sense of a total coherent knowledge available to God (and by implication, to His surrogate, the anonymous authoritative narrator) and the necessary incompleteness of human knowledge, for which much about character, motive, and moral status will remain shrouded in ambiguity.

The practical aspect of all this to be kept in mind as one reads is that the reticence of the biblical narrator, his general refusal to comment on or explain what he reports, is purposefully selective. Why, we should ask ourselves, is a motive or feeling attributed to one character and not to another? Why is one character's attitude toward another stated flatly in one instance, both stated and explained in a second instance, and entirely withheld from us in a third? The Bible's highly laconic mode of narration may often give the impression of presenting the events virtually without mediation: so much, after all, is conveyed through dialogue, with only the minimal "he said" to remind us of a narrator's presence; and even outside of dialogue, what is often reported is absolutely essential action, without obtrusive elaboration or any obvious intervention by the narrator. Against this norm, we should direct special attention to those moments when the illusion of unmediated action is manifestly shattered. Why at a particular juncture does the narrator break the time-frame of his story to insert a piece of expository information in the pluperfect tense, or to jump forward to the time of his contemporary audience and explain that in those days it was the custom in Israel to perform such and such a practice? Why does he pause to make a summarizing statement about the condition of a character, as, for example, in the observation about Joseph's already established viceregal status just as the ten brothers arrive in Egypt? Why at certain points is the regular rapid tempo of narration slowed down to take in details of a kind for which in general no time is allowed?

These various relaxations of reticence are, I suspect, the operation of biblical narrative most resistant to a manageable rule of thumb, but an alertness to their occurrence and a willingness to wonder about their motivation, with the specific contexts as a guide, will help make us better readers of the biblical tales.

Robert Alter. The Art of Biblical Narrative (New York, Basic Books, 1981), pp. 183–85

The narrator's voice can be heard throughout the text in many phrases ranging from the simple "he said" which introduces direct discourse to long passages of summary or description. Often a story opens with a narrated summary, or background, and then proceeds to the scenic section, generally marked by the beginning of dialogue. Obviously, the narrator's presence is felt in the opening summary, but one must remember that his presence can be detected throughout the scenic sections as well.

The most blatant intrusions of the narrator's voice are in etiologies, geographical notes ("He named that place Beth-el; Luz was the city's original name" [Gen. 28:19]), and similar information, like "An *'omer* is a tenth of an *'ephah*" (Exod. 16:36). "A 'prophet' today used to be called a 'seer'" (I Sam. 9:9), "In the first month, that is, the month of Nisan . . . They cast *pur*, that is, the lot" (Esth. 3:7). These are all comments which are external to the story. The narrator steps out of the story, as it were, to say something to his audience. This is known as breaking frame. One of the most common forms of breaking frame is when the narrator leaves the temporal frame of his story, either by giving information from a later time, as in Exodus 16:35: "And the Israelites ate the manna for forty years, until they came to an inhabited land . . ." or by connecting the story to some previous event, as in Genesis 26:1; "And there was a famine in the land besides the first famine that was in the days of Abraham."

Even when the narrator remains within the frame of the story, there are various stances that he may take in relation to it. He may tell the story from an external point of view, as an outside observer looking at a scene or at characters. He would then describe things objectively, seeing what any person present could see. Or he may take an internal point of view, standing among the characters, or telling the story from the perspective of one of them. He could then see more than an outside observer. He becomes a privileged, internal observer, even though he is not involved in the action himself. (The biblical narrator is never a character in the story, except in sections of first-person narrative like parts of the prophetic books or Ezra.) This stance is internal in respect to action. To be internal in respect to a character the narrator must enter the character's mind, telling what the character saw, felt, thought. The point of view may be internal in respect to action and still external in respect to character. This is possible because "internal" and "external" can refer not only to the psychological level, but to all levels.

Adele Berlin. *Poetics and Interpretation of Biblical Narrative* (Sheffield, England, Almond Press, 1983), pp. 57–58

Unlike third-person omniscient narrators in modern fiction, the biblical narrator has a partner in his craft, who, while more powerful and at least equally omniscient, allows the narrator to portray him as a "character" in the story. On a purely literary level the narrator treats God like any other figure, describing his comings and goings, his perspective on creation ("And the Lord saw that it was good"; Gen. 1:10), even God's private musings ("Now the Lord had said, 'Shall I hide from Abraham what I intend to do?'" Gen. 18:17). There is no particular vocabulary, or syntactic features which are indicative of divine speech. Even in the area of quotation, God is no more consistent about literal repetition than other characters. But from an ideological, or theological standpoint, this position is untenable. If the narrator posits an authoritative, omniscient, and exclusive Deity, then he cannot presume to make the claim that he stands outside that creation. This narrator exists not because his advice is requested by God, but by reason of literary necessity. Since, for a variety of reasons, the God of Israel chooses not to relate his own story, it is left to another, or others, to tell the tale. The narrator is omniscient only because God grants him that knowledge and that perspective on the world.

It has been suggested that we understand the relationship between God and the narrator in terms of analogy—as God creates a populated universe, so too the narrator fashions his world. Both God and the narrator know what is in the hearts of their creatures, and both know what the future holds in store for them. I would like to extend this analogy to the area treated above, the question of the style in which narration takes place. We have seen how the narrator is absolutely authoritative within the confines of a literary construct, and, at the same time, passive in terms of the theological universe which he describes. In order to get around this dilemma, the biblical narrator must efface his own presence by remaining anonymous, and by presenting his material in a manner which is ostensibly neutral and objective. But he who appears merely to report the happenings of a divinely ordered cosmos also comments on that story with great subtlety. In an analogous way, the character who acts as narrator in these longer speeches embodies a similar tension between autonomy and dependence. A storyteller such as Abraham's servant is cast precisely in the mold of *his* maker, that equally anonymous, half-hidden, omniscient narrator who brings him to life in the story. And Judah's vulnerability before Joseph, who nonetheless allows him to speak (and to quote him), mirrors, to a certain extent, the relationship between the narrator and God.

George Savran. *Prooftexts*. Jan., 1985, p. 11

DESCRIPTION

To the degree that the narrator becomes involved in matters of dress, he will do so only when he has a thematic need for it. We hear of tearing clothes as a sign of grief. And sometimes he will speak of other symbolic acts connected with clothing, such as spreading the sleeves of a robe over someone seeking protection, especially as a sign of binding a person in marriage (Ruth 3:9). Of Tamar it is said, "She removed the clothes of her widowhood, put on a veil, and wrapped herself up" (Gen. 38:14) so that Judah, her father-in-law, would not recognize her. From the story we learn that widows wore special garb, perhaps during a certain period of their mourning. And we learn further that covering the face with a veil

signifies a woman who can be bought with money. For this reason it says that
when Judah saw the woman, "he reckoned her a harlot" (v. 15). In this same
manner can the verse in Hosea (2:4), "she removed her harlotry from her face,"
be explained. It seems that the veil is what the prophet speaks of as a sign of
harlotry.

In these instances, however, the mention of dress is not just a mere ornament
for the body of the theme. Quite the opposite. We require such observations for
understanding the plot and its development, and to the degree that the thing is
necessary, the author devotes his attention to these matters. Let Joseph's "coat of
many colors" [Gen. 37:3] serve to verify this claim. Interpreters and scholars are
divided about the precise definition of the term. The narrator did not add details
to the term because for the people of those generations it was a routine and commonly used expression and because the importance of the coat was not in its
shape or its colors, but rather in its function in the story. In the sequence of
events in the life of Joseph, the importance of the coat of many colors surpasses
that of any of the mute and anonymous brothers, like Naphtali, Dan, Issachar,
etc. This pertinence is more "active and activating" than any of the passive
personae.

The symbolism of the particular garment that Jacob provided to Joseph was
self-understood to the story's audience in ancient times. If we were to consider
the significance of this gift by way of comparing the story of Joseph with the one
about Tamar, daughter of David, sister of Absalom—"A coat of many colors
was upon her, for thus would the virgin daughters of the king wear tunics" (II
Sam. 13:18)—we learn that a coat of many colors was a sign of royalty. From
this the rage of the brothers is understandable. By giving this garment to Joseph,
Jacob anticipates and confirms Joseph's dream, the dream of his lording over his
brothers.

In this instance, too, the coat is not an enfeebled link in the plot of Joseph and
his brothers, but rather one of those things on which the narrative rests.

Shemaryahu Talmon. Darkhei hassippur bammiqra'.
Ed. by Gavriel Gil (Jerusalem, Hebrew University,
1965), pp. 34–36†

Description creates the setting in which action occurs—the place, the time, the
scenery, the artifacts—and in biblical narrative provides orientation to the characters. In description nouns, adjectives, and other nominal forms have greater
importance than verbs.

In biblical narrative, description plays a subordinate role to narration. Brief
description occurs at the beginning and sometimes at the end of a story. But its
potential is not realized, as a comparison between the Bible and Homer shows.
In the Bible nothing is described which does not contribute to the action. Description of character, scenery, inner feelings, and objects extraneous to the action never distracts the narrator from bringing his story to a rapid climax. Ehud's
sword has two edges and is a cubit in length. No reference is made to how Ehud

formed it or from what metals, even though that sword is the central object in the Ehud/Eglon story. Scenery is never described, as [Hermann] Gunkel noted long ago. Descriptions do often serve the important function of telling the reader how he is to view a character in a story. When a character in introduced, explicit value judgments are given: Deborah is a prophetess, Ehud is a deliverer, Sisera is a cruel oppressor. . . .

The potential of narration, the other constitutive element in biblical stories, is realized completely. The biblical story "centers in action and movement" ([James] Muilenburg). Verbs carry the story, and at its climax they occur in rapid fire, often without connection: "There on the floor their lord lay, dead" (Judg. 3:25). Only the essentials are presented, or obversely, omission is a highly developed skill in this kind of narration. Biblical narration deals "in empty spaces." And the combination of empty space with only those brush strokes essential for creating the narrative line makes biblical narrative so effective.

The suppression of description, rather than giving an effect of incompleteness, gives to biblical stories an air of mystery. The emptiness and silence in the narrative become "fraught with background" ([Erich] Auerbach), like a Japanese painting.

> Leonard L. Thompson. *Introducing Biblical Literature* (Englewood Cliffs, N.J., Prentice-Hall, 1978), pp. 32–33

INFORMATIONAL GAPS AND REDUNDANCY

The Hebrew story-teller differed from the Greek not only in his almost laconic *brevity* and in his total lack of all but the most indispensable detail, but also in his seemingly careful use of *omission* as a literary method and even principle. . . . This omission in the telling of Old Testament stories is very similar to that constantly employed by the unknown composers of the English and Scottish popular ballads. The original writers of *The Wife of Usher's Well* or of *Sir Patrick Spens* depend upon the imagination of their hearers or readers, and therein lies much of the charm of their old tales. . . .

In like manner the Hebrew story-tellers are constantly leaving important events and more important emotions in complete obscurity. Just as time and place are undefined, so thoughts and feelings are unexpressed, suggested only by emptiness and silence or by the most fragmentary speeches. . . .

The Hebrew writers know nothing of the sophistication of the Greek. The language which they employed for their stories was sharp and quick, unfinished, inflexible, fragmentary in comparison. . . . And yet, through its very brevity and bareness and through its empty silences, its writers were able to evoke responses and even understandings impossible to the writers of the epics.

> Mary Ellen Chase. *Life and Language in the Old Testament* (New York, W. W. Norton, 1955), pp. 112–114, 117)

The uniqueness of [the story of David and Bathsheba] becomes evident if we compare it to the Binding of Isaac story, renowned in literary criticism as a story that leaves many details obscure. Indeed, even Abraham's thoughts after loading the wood for the burnt offering onto his son, Isaac, are not expressed in the Bible (Gen. 22). A reader who considers the precise formulation of Abraham's words when he replies to his son's question "But where is the sheep for the burnt offering?" with the words: "God will select the sheep for the burnt offering, my son," will perhaps be able to fill in the gap and reconstruct the father's thoughts (even though this reconstruction will be very vague and truncated, even if the reader exploits the well-known polyvalence of the sentence, deriving from an exploitation of the absence of punctuation marks). But the main thing in the passage is its underscoring of supreme obedience, *dampening all possible thought*, and so the decision on whether Abraham thought about this or that is only of minor significance and does not belong to the central line of the narrative. Reconstructing the turbulent inner world of Abraham would no doubt enrich the story, and the reader who seeks to make the story fully real will perform this act of reconstruction, but in doing so he would add to the story only a minor nuance. The main theme of the story will be understood even without his filling in this gap. The main gaps in the Binding of Isaac story, then, are different from those in the story of David and Bathsheba. . . . We would reach a similar conclusion were we to compare the gaps at the beginning of the Book of Job to the gaps in the story of David and Bathsheba. Different stories are distinguished, then, *through the nature of the array of gaps*.

It should be understood that the way of exploiting the numerous gaps in Biblical narrative should not be taken for granted. It differs from case to case. The Binding of Isaac story exploits a certain array of gaps so that we eliminate anything liable to break our concentration on the main theme; the purpose of these gaps is to build the story's attachment to the venerable action of the father and suppress attention to "all the rest," just as the father himself does. Thus, in the Binding of Isaac story (as opposed to the story of David and Bathsheba) it is precisely the *main theme* that must be related while what appears "marginal" is to be shunted aside. The Binding of Isaac story exploits an array of gaps in order to instill in the reader a hierarchy of importance.

In the David and Bathsheba story, by contrast, it is precisely the main theme that the narrator does not relate: He is a conniver and trickster; he exploits the fact that the reader is obliged to complete in this story what the narrator has not explicitly said, and the array of gaps that has been created in order, first and foremost, to direct attention to what *has not been said* turns out to be the major device by which the narrator step by step sets up the desired ironic tone. The efficacy of the main arrays of gaps depends, therefore, on the privileged nature of the omitted materials and on the connections between them and what is given explicitly. The narrator, who tries as much as possible to variegate his narrative techniques, has here chosen ironic understatement, and the story of David and Bathsheba, for this manner of storytelling evinces it, enables him to use, gladly, narrative techniques that he does not often have occasion to activate. . . .

Does Uriah know of his wife's infidelity? . . .

The sentence "and he did not go down to his house" opens up a gap at another key point. The question—why doesn't Uriah go down to his house?—is connected with a more basic question: *Does Uriah know about his wife's infidelity and pregnancy?* The text does not allow for an answer to this question that is *unequivocal*. Both the hypothesis that answers in the negative and the hypothesis that answers in the affirmative are possible; each of these hypotheses is supported and strengthened by a number of arguments, while other arguments direct attention to the weak spots in it and give support to its rival, and each of the hypotheses casts in another light identical or different details in the text and organizes them in a different manner. The text consciously exploits the inability to decide finally between the two methods of filling the gaps. It obliges us to seize them both, and it profits from the tension between them and from their interrelationships.

> Menakhem Perry and Meir Sternberg. *Ha-sifrut.* Summer, 1968, pp. 267, 271†

There is evidently no greater contrast than that between gap-producing informational reduction and the informational redundancy of repetition structure. Together as one they characterize the narrative art of the Bible, which escalates the contrasts and even erects a mutual relationship between them:

> Actually, before us are two complementary principles, operating by the power of the same poetic logic. It is not only that both operate by indirect means, and not only that the repetition structure directs attention to gaps, and the gaps to the repetition structure, but the repetition structure itself opens up gaps of its own at the same time filling gaps that are not its own (Sternberg [*Ha-sifrut.* Oct., 1977], p. 149).

Covert penetration [into a character's psyche], as in the conveying of inner life in general, is the central arena of operation of this astonishing pair. But there is no need to elaborate here. The subject is discussed in a superficial way throughout my article [ibid.] on the repetition structure: there the interchanges in prospective point of view—and among them the covert prospective montage—were revealed as one of the principal apparatuses for dispelling and rationalizing redundancy of information. The same apparatus (or "strategy") of redundancy is again discussed, and this time, too, within the framework of isolated penetration, in my previous article on the representation of inner life ([*Ha-sifrut.* Dec., 1979], especially pp. 126–32), and it will come up anew in many of the analyses in the following paragraphs. I shall therefore content myself with the main outlines, with the help of some simple examples:

Among its various other roles, the repetition structure operates in two ways to situate and decipher covert penetration into the psyche of the characters—ways that are always symmetrical and are frequently coupled in actuality to the logic of gap-filling. The two ways rest upon the tripartite distinction among the types of components in repetition: the *prospect* component, which looks ahead to the narrative future; the *action* component, which represents the situation or occurrence in the narrative present; and the *report* component, which retrospectively contemplates the narrative past. Yet they differ in the manner and extent of exploitation of the distinction.

In the first way the reader is led to discover in the text covert penetration through the very fact of redundancy, that is to say, through calculating that otherwise he is left with an entirely superfluous component:

(42) Joshua chose thirty thousand men, warriors, and sent them out by night. He commanded them, saying, "[. . .] and when you have seized the city, set fire to the city." [. . .] They came into the city, they captured it, they hastened to set fire to the city. The men of Ai looked behind them, and they saw, behold: the smoke of the city arose to the sky, and they had not the power to flee this way or that (Josh. 8:3–20).

(43) Abimelech and the people with him got up from the ambush. Gaal saw the people and said to Zebul: "Behold: a people is going down from the mountain tops" (Judg. 9:35–36).

In example (42) the appearance of the first two of the three components is easily explained in light of the difference in their standing: The first is the prospect component, relating Joshua's order, while the second is the action component, relating the execution of the order. Both are vital to understanding what happens in the successive stages in the victory over Ai. But in the light of this the redundancy of the third component, the "Behold" sentence, stands out. This is, as was said, properly a part of the framing discourse of the narrator. Yet, even so, it is also the action component, just like what precedes it, so what need is there of two consecutive, parallel action components?

For this reason there is a tendency to dispel the redundancy proper in terms of hidden function. The "Behold" sentence, we conclude, is not a continuation of the framing discourse but embedded within it, and the narrator does not reiterate matters from his own point of view but moves over to join himself to the perspective of the characters. In short, this is no additional, superfluous action component but rather a covert report component by which what has already happened and has been related to us in the preceding stage first reaches the consciousness of those penetrated—the men of Ai. From this standpoint, the same sudden discovery of an existing situation, which is related in example (43) in an externalized, directly quoted "Behold" sentence ("Behold: a people is going down from the mountain tops"), is here related in an interior "Behold" sentence and quoted in a free indirect montage. There the report by the characters is official and here it is unofficial; by this difference the two are informative in varying degrees.

Meir Sternberg. *Ha-sifrut*. July, 1983, p. 106†

POINT OF VIEW

It cannot be said that the biblical narrator is objective in the full sense of the term. In fact, there is no completely objective narrator. For whether he does not hide the negative sides of the protagonists or whether he narrates in reserved and matter-of-fact language, as the biblical narrator is wont to do, that does not mean that he takes no position vis-à-vis his characters. His position may not be articulated by explicit or glaring means, but rather by subtle and subdued means. . . .

The interpretive activity of the narrator is evident wherever we find in the midst of and as an integral part of a narrative sequence words modifying the characters which bear a tone of judgment. For example:

> The lads grew up, and Esau became a man knowing how to hunt, a man of the field, and Jacob was a *simple* man, a dweller of tents (Gen. 25:27).

> They were making merry when men of the town, *useless* men, surrounded the house (Judg. 19:22).

> He had a son and his name was Saul, a young man and *good*, and there was no man of the Israelites better than he (I Sam. 9:2).

> A *wise* woman from the town called out: "Listen, listen, say now to Joab, 'Draw near here that I may speak to you'!" (II Sam. 20:16).

And sometimes the narrator's point of view finds expression by means of the connotations of the words by which he conveys the characters' actions. It might seem that the narrator conveys only the facts of what occurs, but in the baggage of words combined with factual information is conveyed the narrator's attitude toward those facts. For example:

> Sarai *oppressed* (Hagar) and she fled from her (Gen. 16:6).

> It was when Gideon died that the Israelites returned to *whoring* after the Baals (Judg. 8:33).

> The man took hold of his concubine, he brought her outside, and they had intercourse with her, and they *toyed* with her (Judg. 19:25).

> Absalom *stole* the heart of the men of Israel (II Sam. 15:6). . . .

Sometimes the narrator's perspective on events matches the perspective of one of the characters. In this case, even though he narrates in the third person, the narrator appropriates for himself the visual or psychological point of view of that character, and he, so to speak, hides. There follow several examples of this narrative technique.

In many instances where the phrase "and behold!" is found, the narrator adduces a certain detail in conformity with the point of view of one of the characters. This is especially evident when the phrase "and behold!" follows a verb denoting sighting, as in the verses: "Isaac went out to take a stroll in the field toward evening, and he raised his eyes and he saw, *and behold,* camels approaching" (Gen. 24:63); "And he went out, and his servants came in, and they saw, *and behold,* the doors of the roof-chamber were locked" (Judg. 3:24); "The scout went to the parapet of the gate of the city-wall, he raised his eyes, and he saw, *and behold,* a man running alone" (II Sam. 18:24). In these instances the narrator informs us explicitly, for he is describing for us one of the characters from the perspective of that very moment—even though the narrator has shown us that he himself knew beforehand or that he knows more than the perspective of that character at that moment. However, even when "and behold!" is not preceded by a verb denoting sighting, that is, with an explicit statement, . . . in truth matters are frequently conveyed in these instances, too, from the point of view of one of the characters.

> They came there, to Gibeah, *and behold,* a band of prophets to
> meet him (I Sam. 10:10).

> David came to the top, where one would prostrate oneself to God,
> *and behold,* meeting him is Hushai the Arkite, his tunic rent and
> soil upon his head (II Sam. 15:32). . . .

In these examples, "and behold!" refers to the character seeing the thing that is related, and not to the narrator. The narrator perceives, so to speak, the thing—and we, as a consequence, perceive it too—together with the character and his eyes. In the example of Hushai (II Sam. 15:32) the word order is reversed from what is normal in the Bible. In all passages in the Bible in which the word "to meet him" appears, the subject precedes it (see the examples above), but in this example it is not so. Perhaps we are to learn from the irregular word order here that at first David saw someone coming to meet him, but he did not yet perceive who it was, and only afterward he recognized that it was Hushai the Arkite.

Shimeon Bar-Efrat. *Ha'itsuv ha'omanuti shel hassippur bammiqra'* (Tel Aviv, Sifriat Poalim, 1979), pp.
61–64†

The perceptual point of view in Genesis 37 changes several times from that of the narrator, to that of Jacob, to that of the brothers. This allows the reader glimpses of what "really" happened—i.e. what the reliable narrator tells him happened—and how it was perceived by several characters. The characters thereby take on a depth that would be lacking if the narrator's point of view were the only one presented.

The interest point of view is that of Joseph; even though his perceptual point of view is never given. The narrative achieves this by making him the object in every scene (the object of other people's thoughts and actions), and by allowing us to follow him as he moves from one scene to another. This is the significance of the transition scene in which Joseph asks for directions from the stranger near Shechem. It not only serves to show the length of the journey, and the vulnerability of the lost boy, but, even more basic to the narrative technique, also allows Joseph to change location without dropping from the reader's sight.

Because it is told from several perspectives, Genesis 37 is fraught with ambiguity. There is no clear right and wrong. Each character's actions are justified from his point of view. The brothers have reason to hate Joseph, and so their behavior towards him is understandable and thereby less reprehensible. But even amongst the brothers themselves there is ambiguity. Whatever the origin of the Reuben and Judah scenes may be, the result in the present text is to split the monolithic "brothers' point of view" expressed earlier in the chapter into at least two factions. This makes it even more difficult for the reader to condemn them as a group. As for Jacob, his favoritism is largely to blame for the brothers' jealousy and the tragedy that resulted. Yet he suffers from the tragedy more than anyone. It is only from his point of view that Joseph is dead—the brothers (with the possible exception of Reuben), Joseph, and the reader all know otherwise.

Joseph, the "hero," is the least defined of all the characters in this chapter. The little that is shown of him tends to make the reader unsympathetic to his plight. One might conclude that he got what he deserved. Yet, since he appears in every scene until he is sold, and since he is the center of attention of the characters even when he is absent, the reader's interest is constantly focused on him.

Adele Berlin. Poetics and Interpretation of Biblical Narrative (Sheffield, England, Almond Press, 1983), pp. 50–51

PARALLELISM

"Your right hand, O Lord, awesome in strength, / Your right hand, O Lord, shatters the enemy" [Exod. 15:6]. . . . This verse is of the type: "The rivers raise up, O Lord, / The rivers raise up their voice" [Ps. 93:3]; "How long the wicked, O Lord? How long will the wicked rejoice?" [Ps. 94:3]; "Here are your enemies, O Lord, / Here are your enemies perishing" [Ps. 92:10]. Its first half does not consummate its proposition until its latter half comes and completes its proposition; but in its first half it mentions about whom it is speaking. . . . "Who is like you among the mighty, O Lord? Who is like you awesome in holiness?" [Exod. 15:11]. This, too, is of the doubled [patterns] that I explained at "Your right hand, O Lord, awesome in strength" [Exod. 15:6]. [12th c.]

Samuel ben Meir. Perush hattora. Ed. by David Rosín (Breslau, Solomon Sattlander, 1882), p. 102†

"O Lord, in the heaven is your devotion, / Your faithfulness up to the sky" [Ps. 36:6]. For the devotion of God, may he be praised, is as large as it is up to the heaven, as is his faithfulness, for "heaven" and "sky" are one and the same. It is the custom of the language to vary the words where there is doubling of the meaning. Thus [the Psalmist] said in another verse when he exalted devotion and trust [Ps. 57:11]: "For great up to the *heaven* is your devotion, and up to the *sky* your trustworthiness." [13th c.]

> David Kimḥi. *Miqra'ot gedolot.* (Venice, Bomberg, 1515), no pagination [commentary on Ps. 36:6]†

The correspondence of one Verse, or Line, with another I call Parallelism. When a Proposition is delivered, and a second is subjoined to it, or drawn under it, equivalent, or contrasted with it in Sense; or similar to it in the form of Grammatical Construction; these I call Parallel Lines; and the words, or phrases, answering one to another in the corresponding Lines, Parallel Terms.

> Robert Lowth. *Isaiah: A New Translation* (London, Printed by J. Nichols for J. Dodsley and T. Cadell, 1778), pp. 10–11

In Greek and Latin what constitutes verse is a succession of syllables of varying quantity; in Old English it was alliteration, in modern English it is a number of syllables and rhyme that constitute verse. In the Bible, what makes a "verse" is not any particular number or quality of syllables, but the parallelism of two or more clauses:

> Why do the nations rage?
> And the peoples imagine a vain thing? [Ps. 2:1]

The parallelism of which this is the simplest form can be extended to an infinite complexity, the parallelism connecting together not only contiguous lines, but also masses of verse widely separated from one another.

It is to be observed that the word "metre" is used in two different senses. In the broader usage it is almost the equivalent of rhythm in general; in the more particular sense it describes certain kinds of rhythm, especially that depending upon feet and syllables. I use the word in this work in the broad sense, which will include a system founded on parallelism. At the present time it is a subject of discussion among Hebraists whether the Bible in the original has not a metrical system in the other sense; and strophic arrangements of portions of Bible poetry are offered which will be found to be very different from those in the present work. I allude to this subject only to point out that the results of such discussion cannot affect the arrangement offered here. The other metrical arrangement belongs to the original Hebrew, and has not been followed in the received translations. But parallelism of clauses is independent of particular languages, and appears in any adequate translation. . . .

It is necessary to distinguish *Similar* and *Dissimilar Parallelism*. The first obtains where, in a given sequence, all the lines are parallel with one another.

> Yet he commanded the skies above,
> And opened the doors of heaven;
> And he rained down manna upon them to eat,
> And gave them of the corn of heaven.
> Man did eat the bread of the mighty:
> He sent them meat to the full [Ps. 78:23–25].

Dissimilar Parallelism implies that particular lines adhere together with a bond that is closer than the bond which unites them all into sequence [abab].

> The LORD is my light and my salvation;
>   Whom shall I fear?
> The LORD is the strength of my life;
>   Of whom shall I be afraid? [Ps. 27:1]

The passage is obviously a single sequence; and yet the third line is closely parallel with the first, the fourth with the second. . . .

Coming to particular figures of parallelism we may note three different sources of metrical rhythm in biblical poetry, which have contributed three different metrical units. (1) The Traditional poetry preserved in the historical books is for the most part in "Antique Rhythm," which seems to be based upon a unit that may be called a strain. This consists of a couplet, either line of which may be strengthened by an additional line, but not both. . . .

> Take hold of shield and buckler and stand up for mine help:
> Draw out also the spear and stop the way against them that pursue me:
>   Say unto my soul, I am thy salvation . . . [Ps. 35:2–3].

The elasticity of the strain has a special fitness for extemporisation, which figures largely in Traditional poetry. . . .

(2) Wisdom literature is founded on the proverb, which is a couplet (rarely a triplet) of parallel lines: this contributes as a unit the couplet, and aggregates couplets into stanzas.

(3) Dancing with musical accompaniment is a leading feature in primitive poetry: the intricate involutions of the dance reflect themselves in similar involutions of metre, especially by means of antiphony (different singers answering one another), and antistrophic effect (portions of a poem answering one another apart from difference of performers). A glance at Deborah's Song . . . will show to what minuteness these effects can be carried. Thus from the dance we get the single line (i.e. half a parallel) as a unit, and the aggregation of lines into strophes. All these divisions of poetry exercise an influence upon one another: in the psalms all three units obtain—the strain, the couplet, and the single line.

An interesting figure of parallelism is the *Envelope:* the opening line or lines of the sequence are repeated at the close, all that intervenes being read in the light of this common "envelopment." A perfect example is the eighth psalm. . . . Similarly the recurrence of the ejaculation—"Bless the LORD, O my soul"—at the beginning and end of psalms 103 and 104 turns both these into examples of envelope structure.

More frequently a modified form of the Envelope Structure is found, by which the opening and closing lines unite in a single thought of which the intermediate parts are an expansion. Thus in psalm 15, the opening lines of question,

> LORD, who shall sojourn in thy tabernacle?
> Who shall dwell in thy holy hill?

receive an answer in the final line,

> He that doeth these things shall never be moved:

while the intermediate parallels contain the "these things." Compare psalm 26. A fine example is the great psalm 139: here the opening protest, "O LORD, thou hast searched me," etc., concludes as a prayer: "Search me, O LORD," while the whole antistrophic movement of the psalm is occupied with effecting the transition from the one mood to the other. . . . Psalms 23 and 33 are also examples of modified envelopment; the whole device of antistrophic inversion, and the type of psalm described as Dramatic Anthems, are akin to envelopment.

Richard G. Moulton. The Modern Reader's Bible (New York, Macmillan, 1907), pp. 1518–20, 1523

Parallelism was formerly regarded as a form peculiar to Hebrew poetry. Now we know that among Eastern peoples it is in all but universal use. It is a very natural borrowing from the dialogue mode characteristic of primitive folk-song. It rests on profound and universal psychological principles: deep calling to deep, tree to tree, bird to bird, life to life, and thought to thought. The heart of the poet is full of such natural antiphons. In fact, primitive poetry is the art of saying the same thing over and over again in charming ways.

Professor [Louis I.] Newman [Univ. of Calif. Publications. *Semitic Philology*. Vol. I, No. 2 (1918)] has shown that parallelism has passed through three stages of growth: iteration, incremental repetition, and matured parallelism. Iteration was its most primitive form of emotional expression, saying exactly the same thing over and over. In incremental repetition some one of the most daring singers moved by inner impulse ventures to improvise a new unit, which is then repeated over and over if it meets with the approval of the company, thus adding variety and fresh movement to the main thought. The end of this process is the matured parallelism.

Finnish epic poetry is rich in parallel couplets. Longfellow took the meter and parallelism of Hiawatha from the Finnish epic *Kalevala*. Examples of Finnish couplets are:

> "Sea-foam" did thy brother call thee,
> And thy mother called thee "Sunshine."

> Nature was my only teacher,
> Words and water my instructors.

Any number of similar parallelisms may be found in Hiawatha.

There are striking similarities in Chinese literature to the use of parallelism in Hebrew. We have here both the parallelism of thought and in addition a parallelism of tone and grammar which is unique:

> The white stone, unfractured, ranks as most precious,
> The blue lily, unblemished, emits sweet fragrance.

The antithetic couplet is common in Chinese proverbs:

> Unsullied poverty is always happy,
> Impure wealth brings many sorrows. . . .

Parallelism abounded in Babylonian literature, and while not present largely in classic Arabic it does occur frequently in modern Arabic and in Palestinian love songs. . . .

Parallelism occurs in English poems, especially of the ballad type, but we must remember that it is not, as in Hebrew, the dominant principle:

> Old King Cole was a merry old soul,
> And a merry old soul was he. . . .

These examples show how deep-seated is man's instinctive liking for the return swing of the pendulum in saying the same thing over.

> Arthur J. Culler. *Creative Religious Literature* (New York, Macmillan, 1930), pp. 124–26

The distinguishing characteristic of Old Testament verse which unites the rhythmical members of structural units is known as "parallelism." It may be defined as a correspondence in sense and a balance in form between successive lines of a structural unit. Three main types of parallelism in Old Testament verse were recognized by Bishop Lowth, and to these, two or three minor types have been added by later scholars.

Synonymous parallelism. The thought of the first member of a structural unit is repeated in a second and occasionally in a third or a fourth member, the lines in the main resembling closely one another in structure.

> The heavens declare the glory of God;
> And the firmament sheweth his handywork. (Ps. 19:1)

Antithetic parallelism. The thought of the second line is in contrast to that of the first line, the structure of the second line conforming closely to that of the first line.

> A wise son maketh a glad father:
> But a foolish man despiseth his mother. (Prov. 15:20)

Synthetic parallelism. The second member of the structural unit completes or supplements the thought of the first member.

The rich and poor meet together:
The Lord is the maker of them all. (Prov. 22:2)

Introverted parallelism. In a four-line strophe, for instance, the first line corresponds with the fourth and the second with the third.

My son, if thine heart be wise,
My heart shall rejoice, even mine.
Yea, my reins shall rejoice,
When thy lips speak right things. (Prov. 23:15, 16)

Stairlike parallelism. Repetitions of accented words, or of terms standing for such words, occur in a progressive movement in successive lines.

I will lift up mine eyes unto the *hills*,
From *whence* cometh my *help*.
My *help* cometh from the *Lord*
Which made heaven and earth. (Ps. 121:1, 2)

Emblematic parallelism. A statement in one line suggests an application in another line.

As coals are to burning coals, and wood to fire;
So is a contentious man to kindle strife. (Prov. 26:21)

Wilbur O. Sypherd. *The Literature of the English Bible*
(New York, Oxford University Press, 1938), pp. 92–93

All Hebrew poetry is recalcitrant to rigid precepts, aloof to rhyme and assonance, and oblivious of meter. Its magnificent rhythm rolls carelessly, and its line knows no perceptive limit except the reader's breath. Its construction is simple, easy, organic. Its beauty is mediumless even as the God it acclaims is imageless. To seek here for iambic and anapestic rhythms or Sapphic strophes, or a strict poetic code, or anything like an accentual, metrical, or quantitative system is to labor in vain. Here meter is an illusion. Here form is veiled by the thought expressed and evoked. In a word, Hebrew poetry is forever striving, consciously or unconsciously, to shorten the distance between an experience and its expression.

In the attempt to attain this goal Hebrew poetry developed to perfection a literary device much in vogue in Egypt, Babylonia, Phoenicia, and Ugarit, and long ago singled out by the Rabbis for high praise. It was to its exploitation, they said, that Isaiah owed his superiority over all the prophets. The device surnamed parallelism, is basically repetition, that is, the act of repeating in new words what has already been expressed. To the ancients parallelism or repetition must have been a kind of gesturing, dancing, musical accompaniment, or aid to self-expression and communication. It was for them, as indeed it is to this day, a way of speaking eagerly, anxiously, urgently, joyously, triumphantly, under great strain, or in the grip of seething emotions, all as the case might have been. When

Isaiah reported the seraphim calling to one another and saying, "Holy, holy, holy is the LORD of hosts" [6:3], he was accentuating fervor, reverence, and the concept of holiness as applied to the Deity. When Jeremiah was saying, "Trust not in deceptive words, such as 'the temple of the LORD, the temple of the LORD, the temple of the LORD is this!'" [7:4] he was lashing out indignantly against his people and speaking contemptuously of its national shrine. When Ezekiel cried, "A ruin, a ruin, a ruin, will I make it" [21:2], he was expressing anxiety, scorn, apprehension. All three Prophets, it is obvious, resorted to repetition to make their meaning perfectly clear, lend it earnestness, and add to it the greatest possible emphasis.

The rhythm of parallelism, it will have been noted, is simultaneously a rhythm of thought and form. The words repeated have, so to speak, no antonymous existence, no objective of their own. Long before they are uttered they are comprehended in the thought. And they are no sooner uttered but they are submerged by thought.

Solomon Goldman. *From Slavery to Freedom* (New York, Abelard Schuman, 1958), p. 353

In Hebrew poetry, parallelism does not often degenerate into a habit which allows a poet to "grind out" a poem, as did the convention of the heroic couplet in bad eighteenth-century poetry. It is one of the strengths of parallelism as a basic convention that it admits of variations which relieve monotony and remind us that the Hebrew poet was not in the first place a poet, and that his "poem" was not for the sake of art, of isolated aesthetic excellence, but for the sake of the strong, complex insights demanding expression.

The parallelism may consist (and often does) of almost exact repetition of the opening phrase: "Behold, thou art fair, my love: behold, thou art fair" (Song 4:1). "Lord, what is man, that thou takest knowledge of him! or the son of man, that thou makest account of him!" (Ps. 144:3) More often the device consists of a repetition of the given insight in different words: "He delighteth not in the strength of the horse: he taketh not pleasure in the legs of a man" (Ps. 147:10). The use of different words in the second element leads, perhaps insensibly, to the addition of an aspect of the insight not suggested in the first line: "By night on my bed I sought him whom my soul loveth: I sought him, but I found him not" (Song 3:1). "Arise, O God, plead thine own cause: remember how the foolish man reproacheth thee daily" (Ps. 74:22). The first statement occasionally begets the exactly opposite insight, though this is a movement of thought that usually takes place within a Psalm rather than within a verse: "My flesh and my heart faileth: but God is the strength of my heart, and my portion forever" (Ps. 73:26). Finally, although the usual movement of Hebrew poetry is by means of a succession of paired utterances, each one to a degree a unit in itself, there are many places in Psalms and elsewhere where the parallels are allowed to accumulate. A fairly short example of such an accumulation is the address to spring in the Song of Solomon.

Rise up, my love, my fair one, and come away. For lo, the winter is past, the rain is over and gone; the flowers appear on the earth; the time of the singing of birds is come, and the voice of the turtle is heard in our land; the fig tree putteth forth her green figs, and the vines with the tender grape give a good smell. Arise, my love, my fair one, and come away. (2:10–13)

> Harold H. Watts. *The Modern Reader's Guide to the Bible*. Rev. ed. (New York, Harper, 1959), pp. 193–94

The mere fact that parallelism is present in a poem or in an author's work is of little consequence, for it is too ordinary and general a phenomenon. Yet before getting to the special aspects of the individual poem, in the area that it has in common and shares with other individual poems, it is necessary to make distinctions in order to interpret.

The classical division *synonymous-antithetic* is important, and it can reveal many things about the conception of the poem, about the psychology of the author, insofar as it constitutes a "stylistic constant"; when it is an isolated phenomenon, the distinction is obvious and recognized. . . .

We can analyze whether the parallelism has been constructed of a *conventional word-pair* or of an *original word-pair:* "mountains and valleys," "eat and drink," "Lebanon and Bashan" are too familiar to characterize an author, or a poem, to transmit a transcendent meaning; but the pair "fishmongers and casters of fishhooks" (Isa. 19:8) typifies a descriptive penchant for concrete observation, the pair "Red Sea, Jordan" (Ps. 114) realizes a theological synthesis of history, and the pair "stone and rock" applied to God in Isaiah 8:14 is of enormous theological import. The predominance of original parallel pairs is a clear stylistic sign.

The *polar pairs* form a separate group, for they constitute a total and concrete vision: The predominance of polar pairs in Psalm 139 ("whether I sit or stand," "back and front") is most significant, above all in contrast to the synonymy of the terms applied to God (man divides his totality in a series of contingent extremes, while God encompasses him wholly with his perpetual wholeness). Among the polar formulas, we should distinguish between those that divide the whole into two *halves* and those that hold it between two *extremes*. The first appears more immanent and static, the second more transcendent and dynamic.

It can be useful to determine whether the parallelism stands alone or belongs to a *series*: Since it is normal to encounter parallelism in a series, the instances that are distinguished from the normal alternating movement hold particular interest, e.g., Psalm 44:4, where the invocation of Yahweh interrupts the regular binary series with this emotional cry: "But your hand and your arm and the light of your face, for you are gracious to them."

The distinction of Begrich-Horst, too, is interesting: The *piece-by-piece* correspondence of the parts can reveal a style of composition more analytic, artful, intellectual; an *en-bloc* correspondence, a style more synthetic, more creative, more emotional.

Considering the normality of binary parallelism, the *ternary* and *quaternary* gain particular interest. These last are a stylistic constant of Isaiah 40ff. (and 35); the ternaries may have originated in imitation of the foreign, a liturgical usage (Ps. 118), a swelling to serve an alternating movement, etc.

Parallelism can serve to amplify or to concentrate; it may enlarge the image or explain it (Ps. 18: cherubim = wind, thunder = voice, arrows = lightning bolts); it can harmonize two things or put them in tension.

Luis Alonso-Schökel. *Estudios de poética hebrea*
(Barcelona, Juan Flors, 1963), pp. 228–30†

In Hebrew verse, artistic form is subordinated to the subject-matter, and it is the sense of the passage itself which creates the rhythm. Where a Latin poem is invalidated by even one false syllable, Hebrew verse employs a flexible, undulatory rhythm produced neither by syllabic quantity nor by accentuation, but by the antiphonal sense-pattern of the passage. And perhaps even more important is the self-generating emotional force of parallelism, which pulsates in rhythmic unison with the sense.

The distinction between the balance of phrases in parallelism and the apparently similar balance of the neo-classical heroic couplet is subtle, but nonetheless profound. Pope's verse [in *The Rape of the Lock*] exploits the firm metrical framework to create a brilliant series of contrasts and juxtapositions. The pauses dictated by the metre leave the key words echoing in the mind and allow the reader to savour the witty ambivalences.

On her white breast a sparkling Cross she wore,
Which Jews might kiss, and Infidels adore.

We pause at *breast* with its erotic associations. The main accent is next thrown on *Cross*, so that in the following line *kiss* and *adore*, while ostensibly directed at *Cross*, are, of course, really intended for the young lady's bosom. And as we grasp the *double entendre*, at another level we are responding to the pun on the physical and religious meanings of *adore*. In biblical parallelism, however, there is no framework other than the pulsating sense, and the effect is to suggest that the poet has returned to the phrase through sheer joy or sorrow in the statement itself.

The sea saw and fled.
The Jordan turned back. [Ps. 114:3]

Where Pope deliberately gives the impression of playing a game (sometimes the very serious game of ridiculing the absurd), biblical parallelism both reflects and creates an emotional impulse essentially closer to romantic than to neo-classical poetry:

No motion has she now, no force:
  She neither hears nor sees.
  [William Wordsworth. "A Slumber Did My Spirit Seal"]

> Murray Roston. *Prophet and Poet* (Evanston, Ill.,
> Northwestern University Press, 1965), pp. 23–24

With all its intricacy, the structure of parallelistic poetry appears diaphanous [so fine as to be translucent] as soon as it is submitted to a close linguistic analysis, both of the parallel distichs and of their relationship within a broader context. The hexastich 4:8 in the Song of Solomon . . . is said to contain "allusions of unmistakably Canaanite mythological origin" [William F. Albright, in H. H. Rowley, ed., *Studies in Old Testament Prophecy Presented to Theodore H. Robinson*, 1950, p. 7] and to belong to the most archaic poetic texts of the Bible. The following transcription is accompanied by a translation which nearly coincides with Albright's wording.

1. 'itti millevanon kalla	With me from Lebanon, bride,
2. 'itti millevanon tavo'i	with me from Lebanon come!
3. tashuri merosh 'amana	depart from the peak of Amanah,
4. merosh senir wehermon	from the peak of Senir and Hermon,
5. mimme'onot 'arayot	from the lair of lions,
6. meharere nemerim	from the mountains of leopards!

The whole hexastich is cemented by the six occurrences of the preposition "from" and by a noun as the second word unit of every line. Each of the three distichs has its own conspicuous structural properties. The first is the only one which repeats words in identical metrical positions. The first word pair is echoed in 2, and while the third words of the two lines belong to different parts of speech, they still follow the parallelistic pattern, since both the vocative function of the final noun in 1 and the imperative function of the final verb in 2 represent one and the same conative [i.e., oriented toward the addressee] level of language. Thus the first distich, alone in this fragment, fulfills the leading scheme of ancient Hebrew parallelism: $abc — abc$ (or more exactly $abc^1 — abc^2$). . . .

All of the next four lines are syntactically united and differ from the first distich by the presence of nouns in the construct state. The second distich displays characteristic shifts in word position. The two verbs of the hexastich stand out vividly against the background of its twelve nouns; both are similar morphologically and syntactically and polar within the same semantic class—"come" with allative meaning and "depart" with ablative. Together they build an anadiplosis: the first distich is closed by one verb, and the second opens with the other verb; the former verb is preceded, and the latter followed by a prepositional construction. The medial *merosh* of line 3 is repeated at the beginning of 4. In this shift the central place occupied by the second distich within the hexastich finds its clear-cut expression: in an interplay of dichotomy with trichotomy the same preposition "from" which introduces the final, heptasyllabic, pervasively nominal lines is prefixed to the central word in the three initial, longer lines. . . .

Finally, each line contains exactly two contiguous constituents which have isosyllabic correspondents in the parallel line, but both their position in the line and their number of syllables change from distich to distich:

I	II	III
$24\frac{2}{3}$	$\frac{3}{2}23$	43

Both syllabic asymmetries—two against three in the first distich, and three against two in the second—rest upon a confrontation of trisyllabic verbs with disyllabic nominal forms.

The striking trait of the sound texture is the profusion of nasals (21) and their symmetrical distribution: three in each of the first three lines, four in each of the three following lines.

Roman Jakobson. Language. June, 1966, pp. 425–26

From the above examples of parallelistic oral poetry, it is clear that a tradition of fixed pairs is associated with oral tradition and performance. We can thus regard the technique of parallelistic composition by the use of traditional word pairs as a technique developed by oral poetic traditions to meet the needs of oral poets. The needs which this technique solved for the poet were two: first, it bound cola together to form lines, since two cola sharing a traditional word pair would easily be recognized as a unit; and secondly, it aided the poet in providing a second colon, which would be easily recognizable as such when the second colon contained the second term of a word pair whose first term occurred in the first colon. It must be stressed that parallelism in this sense means the sharing of traditional pairs regardless of our semantic concepts of their relationships. As was seen in the examples of Toda poetry, only the first class of traditional word pairs would be considered synonymous in our sense of the term. We must observe from the literary tradition itself what the traditional pairs were.

Since in oral parallelistic poetries the phenomenon of paired words is seen to be the result of oral poetic composition, we may conclude that an oral poetic tradition produced the paired words in the Ugaritic-Hebrew poetry. This also provides a logical explanation for the conservatism and homogeneity of the tradition shared by the two languages. We can see now why [Moshe] Held thought of a "dictionary of parallel words," only it was an oral dictionary, which the poet had in his head, not a written dictionary on his bookshelf.

This is not to say, of course, that every poem containing word pairs represents an oral composition. At some time in the literary tradition there was oral composition, and it was during this time that the fixed pairs were created and used by the oral poets. Whether we have any compositions from the poets of this time remains to be determined. All that seems clear is that fixed pairs give evidence of a period of oral composition at one time in the Hebrew poetic tradition.

Thus far our discussion has centered on formulas-fixed pairs in Hebrew poetry. But formulas are not the only traditional compositional units, for [Milman] Parry also dealt with formulaic expressions. Formulaic expressions are units which have in common the same metrical shape, parts of speech and at least one important word; but as opposed to formulas, the various elements do not recur together elsewhere in the poetry.

I believe that formulaic expressions (pairs which although they occur only once are related to other similar pairs which make up a formulaic system) also exist in Hebrew poetry. In a formulaic system in Hebrew one term remains constant, while the parallel position is occupied by various terms. These variable terms occur elsewhere as parallels and may thus be regarded as analogic substitutes for each other.

For example, *hoshiʿa* (save) occurs once in parallelism to *shafat* (judge) and once parallel to *din* (judge):

> God by thy name *save* me
> and by thy might *judge* me (*din*). (Ps. 54:3)

> Let him *judge* the poor people (*shafat*)
> *save* the needy and crush the oppressor. (Ps. 72:4)

Neither of these sequences is a formula—since they are not repeated elsewhere —but they do form a formulaic system, because *shafat/din* are recognized parallels. (They occur in Ps. 7:9; 9:9; and Prov. 31:9.) In this formulaic system the constant is *hoshiʿa*, the formal condition needing a solution, while the variables *shafat/din*—recognized as analogic variables by their parallel occurrences elsewhere—provide the solution. This formulaic system can be presented schematically as follows:

$$hoshiʿa \ + \ /shafat$$
$$/din$$

or as:

$$hoshiʿa/ \ (shafat/din)$$

This schema illustrates that a formulaic expression may be considered as a constant term plus a parallel word pair. One time the one term of the pair completes the parallelism, another time the other term of the pair provides the parallel.

> Perry B. Yoder. *Vetus Testamentum*. July, 1971, pp. 483–85

The most basic form of poetic expression for Israel, but also for other ancient Near Eastern peoples, was that of *parallelismus membrorum*, where the poet is forced to give expression to the subject-matter from two points of view, that is in two-verse stichoi. Enough has been said, since Herder, in praise of this "thought rhyme," as it has been aptly described. Unquestionably, it offers the poet virtually inexhaustible possibilities of inflection of poetic thought. But is this parallelism also suitable for expressing ideas which have been assimilated? Would the constant reduplication of what is being stated not lead to a certain blurring and thus to a loss of precision? It would indeed, if the stating of these ideas were concerned with achieving as great a conceptual precision as possible. But this is certainly not the case. What is being aimed at is not precision in the concepts, but precision in the reproduction of the subject-matter, if possible over its whole range. As far as that is concerned, the book of Proverbs is full of incomparably vivid and also very precise statements. Ancient Israel, too, was aware of a duty to make a given statement precise, but she demanded this precision not in the coining of terms but in the reproducing of facts.

> Gerhard von Rad. *Wisdom in Israel* (Nashville, Abingdon Press, 1972), pp. 26–27

What is the essence of biblical parallelism? From the beginning our whole presentation has been pitched against the notion that it is actual *paralleling* of any sort that is the point. Save for this last discussion of Psalm 23, our argument has not been based on lack of regularity carried over groups of lines (a phenomenon well known to students of parallelism), but on evidence taken from *within* single parallelistic lines. Sharpness, sequences of actions and cause-effect sequences, differentiation, differences in the *other* words in "fixed pair" parallelism, B's going beyond A in repetitive parallelism, the nonsynonymity of numerical and "self-contradictory" parallelism, the "B-clause *kol*"—each is, in its way, an argument against fixing on the similarity of A and B as central. This is not to say that parelleling is not important—of course it is, it is the most striking characteristic of this style. But focusing on it is just somewhat beside the point.

What then is the essence? In asserting the primacy of our form

$$\underline{\hspace{3cm}} / \underline{\hspace{3cm}} / /$$

we are asserting, basically, a sequence: first part—pause—next part—bigger pause (and only secondarily the rough limits on the length of the clause and their approximate equivalence). But even this sequence is a bit of a shorthand for the real point, for what those pauses actually embody is the *subjoined, hence emphatic*, character of B. The briefness of the brief pause is an expression of B's connectedness to A; the length of the long pause is an expression of the relative disjunction between B and the next line. What this means is simply: B, by being connected to A—carrying it further, echoing it, defining it, restating it, contrasting with it, *it does not matter which*—has an emphatic, "seconding" character, and it is this, more than any aesthetic of symmetry or paralleling, which is at the heart of biblical parallelism.

To state the matter somewhat simplistically, biblical lines are parallelistic not because B is meant to be a parallel of A, but because B typically *supports*

A, carries it further, backs it up, completes it, goes beyond it. This is a slight, but very important, nuance, for it will explain why paralleling is so inconsistent, so *untended:* it was not in itself the point. And this will explain how this basically emphatic sequence could be further abstracted to the series of pauses _____ / _____ // which, as we have seen, was adapted to such unemphatic configurations as "since A, therefore B," "if A, then B," "A happened, and B happened," and so forth—variations that are often disturbingly unparallelistic, but whose filiation with emphatic "seconding" is clear.

> James L. Kugel. *The Idea of Biblical Poetry* (New Haven, Conn., Yale University Press, 1981), pp. 51–52

The analysis of even a short segment of biblical verse soon shows that parallelism is a device more complex in its nature than meter, because, unlike the latter, it involves not only the phonetic level of language, but also the grammatical and semantic. The comprehensiveness of parallelism means that it must constantly be viewed against the background of the language as a whole, including prose. The flow of classical Hebrew prose is marked by pulsations of greater and lesser emphasis in a framework of successive clauses in which the slightest change in word order can have significance. The Hebrew ear must have been trained to perceive these emphases, which provided, in poetry, the essential counterpoints within the regular flow established by meter and the expected binary progression, through parallelism, of the poem's meaning. In such a linguistic environment, poets were able to orchestrate all types and degrees of poetic emphasis in structures from the line to the strophe to the poem as a whole. It should be apparent that the progression of biblical verse is not a matter of primitive flashes of images arranged asyndetically. Rather, the dominant impression of simplicity in poetry is an aspect of the poet's artfulness and his art.

> Stephen A. Geller. *Harvard Theological Review*, Jan., 1982, pp. 37–38

Most significantly, parallelism contributes to the meaning of Biblical verse by structuring the ways in which we perceive its content. The presentation of lines in parallelism has the effect of reinforcing the semantic association between them. It has long been observed that when discrete materials appear to us in similar form, we are led to seek, and find, some meaningful correlation between them. This, for example, is the underpinning principle of rhyme: rhyme creates or tightens an association between two or more words or phrases. Repetition of syntactic structure, which is what I have explained as parallelism, can perform the same function. The psychological nexus between semantic sense and syntactic structure has been demonstrated experimentally. When subjects were presented with a sentence of a particular grammatical form, and were then asked to produce another sentence having the same form, they tended to formulate a sentence that not only mirrored the structure of the model but also echoed something of its semantics. For example, the test sentence *The lazy student failed the exam* elicited such responses as, *The smart girl passed the test, The industrious pupil passed the course, The brilliant boy studied the paper.*

Consider Proverbs 15:20:

> A-wise son gladdens a-father
> and-a-foolish man reviles his-mother.

Here the parallel structure of the two cola binds together two sides of the same coin. For another illustration, see Judg. 5:26a:

> Her-hand to-the-tentpin she-extends
> and-her-right-hand to-the-mallet-of workers.

Here the parallel structure reinforces the nexus of the two distinct actions by which Yael prepares to kill Sisera. That two separate actions are being delineated finds corroboration in the prose version of the episode in the preceding chapter (4:21).

Because the traditional label "'synonymous' parallelism" has been often misleading, it is important to emphasize that more often than not parallelism serves to reinforce the semantic association between two somewhat different concepts or images. For a case in point consider Psalm 23:2.

> In-pastures-of grass he-lays-me-down
> By-water-of tranquility he-guides-me.

Lying in the grass and watering by a pool are clearly distinct events. But of course they share the conceit that the psalmist is a sheep and God its tender shepherd, and it is the common syntactic construction of the two lines that galvanizes their association.

Parallelism also functions to produce a meaningful relation between two propositions that possess no inherent interconnection. An example is Job 5:19:

> In-six straits he-will-save-you
> and-in-seven harm will-not-touch you.

The parallelism associates the distinct propositions that God will save and that harm will not come by linking them: God's salvation is the antidote to calamity. A similar instance is Psalm 119:69:

> They-smear on-me lies, menaces (do)
> I with-full heart shall-guard your-orders.

Note that although these lines have no word-pairs or other stylistic features between them, and although they are far from synonymous, they are precisely parallel:

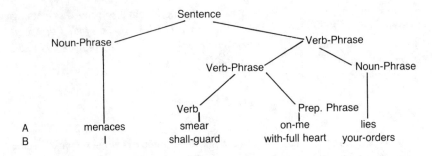

A ... menaces ... smear ... on-me ... lies
B ... I ... shall-guard ... with-full heart ... your-orders

The parallel structure between the two lines reinforces their ideational bond: the psalmist feels secure against his detractors because he trusts that the God whom he obeys will look out for him.

If syntactic symmetry strengthens semantics, a break in the syntactic pattern can reinforce a shift in the thematic flow. The manipulation of syntax to convey meaning is a pronounced feature of Biblical style. For example, a semantic contrast may be underscored by a change in verb-form and word-order. In the following two verses such switches highlight the contradistinction between Rebecca and Isaac and between Ruth and Orpah:

> Isaac loved Esau . . . but Rebecca is-loving Jacob (Gen. 25:28).
> Orpah kissed her-mother-in-law, but Ruth cleaved to-her (Ruth 1:14).

Parallelism can work in the same way. Consider first Psalm 97:1:

> YHWH reigns
> let-rejoice the-land
> Let-be-glad the-many coastlands.

The underlying syntactic structure of each of these three lines is the same. But the second and third lines present responses to the first. A switch in word-order from subject-verb to verb-subject sharpens the semantic shift.

> Edward L. Greenstein. In *A Sense of Text. Jewish Quarterly Review*. 1982 Supplement, pp. 64–67

Paronomasia. *See* Wordplay

PERSONIFICATION

The Hebrew language is full of personifications, and it is undeniable, that this sympathy, this transfer of one's self into the objects around us, and ascription, as it were, of our own feelings to those objects with which we hold converse, has formed not only the inspiring principle of language, of speech, but to a certain extent also the first development and existence of moral principle. Relations of feeling and moral duties cease, where I conceive nothing in a living being analogous to my own being. The more deeply and inwardly I feel this resemblance, and implicitly believe in it, so much the more delightful will be my sympathy, and the exercise of it, in accordance with my own sensibilities. The most ancient poetry, which exerted such a forming influence upon men in their savage state, made use of this fountain of overflowing sensibility to form and cherish in them the feelings of compassion and benevolence. In the blood of Abel his soul cries from the ground. So to Adam, surrounded by the brute creation, all seemed to be animated by his own feelings, and he sought among them all for a help-meet and companion. The sun and moon were kings of heaven, servants of God, rulers of the world. The waving atmosphere was a brooding dove, and God himself, the creator of all, a work-master, after the manner of men, who looked upon his work, rejoiced in and blessed it. . . .

In the book of Job we have unfolded and explained some personifications, on which depends the power of the most affecting discourses, and so it is with the excitement of sympathy in all kinds of emotion. If the poetry of the most ancient times has produced any effect upon the human heart, (and it has undoubtedly produced much), it has the power of doing so by this means alone. Hence, where this flexibility of the heart is wanting, even in our own times, and the man contemplates such personifications and measures them by pure reason, and according to geometrical rules, he will find in the Hebrew and Greek poets only irrational extravagances. In Hebrew the whole language is formed upon the principle of personification; nouns, verbs, and even connecting words are constructed and arranged under its influence. Every thing with them has voice, mouth, hand, countenance, and those relations, which render their representation as son and daughter, one, become necessary for them as for other Orientals a significant and beautiful idiom. An idiom, however, which for the most part has given occasion to the worst misapprehensions, for we may almost affirm it as a general rule "the bolder and more original a poetical conception and figure is, the more it is misunderstood and abused." [1783]

Johann Gottfried von Herder. The Spirit of Hebrew Poetry. Vol. II. Tr. by James Marsh (Burlington, Vt., Edward Smith, 1833), pp. 11–14

The Poetical Figure, which, beyond all others, elevates the Style of Scripture, and gives it a peculiar boldness and sublimity, is Prosopopoeia or Personification. No personifications employed by any Poets, are so magnificent and striking as those of the Inspired Writers. On great occasions, they animate every part of nature, especially, when any appearance or operation of the Almighty is concerned. "Before him went the pestilence—the waters saw thee, O God, and were afraid—the mountains saw thee, and they trembled—The overflowing of the water passed by;—the deep uttered his voice, and lifted up his hands high" [Hab. 3:5, 9, 10]. When enquiry is made about the place of wisdom, Job introduces the "Deep, saying, it is not in me; and the sea saith, it is not in me. Destruction and death say, we have heard the fame thereof with our ears" [28:14, 22]. That noted sublime passage in the Book of Isaiah [ch. 14], which describes the fall of the King of Assyria, is full of personified objects; the fir-trees and cedars of Lebanon breaking forth into exaltation on the fall of the tyrant; Hell from beneath, stirring up all the dead to meet him at his coming; and the dead Kings introduced as speaking, and joining in the triumph. In the same strain, are those many lively and passionate apostrophes to cities and countries, to persons and things, with which the Prophetical Writings every where abound.

Hugh Blair. *Lectures on Rhetoric and Belles Lettres.* 2d ed., corr. Vol. III (London, Printed for W. Strahan, T. Cadell, 1785), pp. 192–93

No one has trouble when, in Western poetry, he encounters the device called *personification*. "Patience on a monument" is conveniently capitalized, and "England" is easily feminized by the pronoun *she*. Our poets "play fair" and let us know when a personification is being brought out. So do the Hebrew poets— sometimes. Often, however, they do not warn us. Orderly personification, to which we are used in poetry, is essentially a *prose* device; it is a studied effort to vivify an abstraction, as in "Patience" and "England." But in Hebrew poetry, a clear line is not drawn between a person and the abstract entity his name stands for. In Jeremiah 31:15, Rachel weeping for her children is a fusion of at least three meanings. Rachel is a person in Hebrew history; she is—the point of transition—a "mother in Israel" because she gave birth to some of the men who fathered the separate tribes; and finally she is also *all* Israel weeping for the downfall of the chosen people. And she is these three things almost at once, not in decent and orderly succession. This confusion—confusion from our point of view—enables the Hebrew poet to reproduce the tension of the time of insight. "Rachel" is, to begin with, three sorts of awarenesses that tend to merge. Indeed, we can sometimes see this process of merging taking place. Thus, in a satiric picture of the vain daughters of Zion sketched by Isaiah, what begins as a character sketch in the style of the "good wife" passage of Proverbs (ch. 31) is suddenly transposed to another level. The "daughters of Zion" are no longer real women; they stand not even for all Hebrew women. They stand for all Israel, male and female. Isaiah's account of the day of disaster lets us see this transformation taking place.

> And it shall come to pass, that instead of sweet smell there shall
> be stink; and instead of a girdle a rent; and instead of well set hair
> baldness; and instead of a stomacher a girding of sackcloth; and
> burning instead of beauty. Thy men shall fall by the sword, and
> thy mighty in the war. And her gates shall lament and mourn; and
> she being desolate shall sit upon the ground. (Isa. 3:24-26)

Harold H. Watts. *The Modern Reader's Guide to the Bible.* Rev. ed. (New York, Harper, 1959), pp. 205–6

[It] is particularly common in proverbial literature. "Wine is an insolent fellow" personifies wine and makes it stand for all addicts (Prov. 20:1; cf. 27:4; 30:15– 16; Ecclus. 10:10). Death is personified in Ecclesiasticus 41:1–4 (cf. Job 28:22; Hos. 13:14), the Lady Stupidity in Proverbs 9:13–18, and the word of God in Wisdom of Solomon 18:14–16. The case of the personified wisdom is more complex, because of the frequency and variety of the imagery. She is represented as a mother, a bride, a taskmaster, and even, by a kaleidoscopic change, as a banquet (Ecclus. 4:11; 15:2; 6:18–31; 24:19–21). More often she is a hostess who presides over a salon of instruction and culture (Prov. 1:20ff.; 8:1ff.; 9:1ff.), and in this guise she is contrasted with the Lady Simplicity, who keeps a house of low repute and hidden danger. But the hostess Wisdom who invites young men to study under her tuition is doing exactly what Jesus ben Sira does at the end of his book (Ecclus. 51:23); and she is thus a metonym standing for all wise teachers. On the other hand, when Wisdom is represented as a master-builder working in the service of God the Creator, this is a metonymic and picturesque way of talking about what God in his wisdom does (Prov. 8:22ff.; Ecclus. 24:1ff.). Because of the illegitimate use which biblical theologians have often made of the personified Wisdom, it cannot be too strongly emphasised that to personify is to treat as a person that which is not a person. In Proverbs and Ecclesiasticus the uses of wisdom as an attribute of God or of wise men, as a way of life, as a gift of God to men and as personification follow one another in rapid proximity; and anyone who takes the trouble to read through these books will need no further proof that their compilers were fully aware of the rhetorical nature of the language they were using.

G. B. Caird. *The Language and Imagery of the Bible*
(Philadelphia, Westminster Press, 1980), pp. 136–37

PLOT

As often in ancient interpretations of venerable texts, be it Bible or Homer, it is not the solution but the problem posed which is important. The ancient readers read seriously and took their texts seriously. Their ear heard every dissonance. The problem of the title of the Book of Esther, once formulated, makes the structure of this book evident. It has two heroes because it has two plots. In the first, Esther, a Jewess, becomes a Persian queen, but the enmity of Haman, the king's vizir, endangers her position and life. She succeeds in saving herself and her people and in bringing Haman to the gallows. In the second, Mordecai, a Jewish courtier, is hated by the vizir Haman. The latter prepares the gallows for his enemy but by accident the king discovers Mordecai's past services and orders Haman to honor his rival. In other words, the book has two heroes and two plots, but the villain is the same in both. The author combined two plots and two tales with extraordinary skill, but some stitches are apparent. Thus, though both the King (6:10) and Haman (5:13; 6:13) know that Mordecai is a Jew, they remain ignorant of the race of Esther, who is the cousin and adopted daughter of Mordecai.

> Elias Bickerman. *Four Strange Books of the Bible* (New York, Schocken, 1967), pp. 171–72

If we define plot in its usual terms as a series of events arranged around a central conflict and possessing a unified development, biblical literature must be regarded as having an overriding plot of which the individual works constitute the various segments. The plot of biblical literature centers in the great spiritual conflict between good and evil. . . .

The presence of the great spiritual conflict makes choice necessary on the part of biblical characters. Every area of human experience is claimed by God and counterclaimed by Satan and the forces of evil. There is no neutral ground. Every human event shows an allegiance toward or against God. The plot of biblical literature has the motif of choice built into its very structure and results in what we might call the drama of the soul's choice. A survey of biblical literature is from this point of view a series of great moral dilemmas and choices. Again and again, characters in biblical literature assume great magnitude as they make the great moral decisions.

In biblical literature decisive action consists of a person's response to external reality and does not reside in external reality itself. Man's problems do not stem from outward events or the hostility of the environment. In contrast to Platonic thought, the material world is not regarded as the great threat to human welfare. Biblical literature instead makes man's moral choices in history the crucial issue. The plot of biblical literature is thus a spiritual plot in which external events provide the *occasion* for significant moral action, good or bad. Given this view of history and human experience, everything that happens to a person is important, representing an opportunity to serve God or rebel against Him.

Plot must have progression as well as conflict. One element of progression in the biblical story is the unfolding of God's purposes throughout history. In this story God is the central character, or the protagonist. . . . From this perspective, the underlying plot of biblical literature is the record of God's acts—in history, in nature, and in the lives of people.

Aristotle formulated the progressive nature of plot in memorable terms when he said that a story must have "a beginning, middle, and end." The biblical view of history adheres to this pattern and provides unity of plot. Underlying biblical literature is a sequence that unfolds as follows: eternity, creation and life before the fall, ordinary human history, the end of history, and the eternal existence of good and evil creatures. This plot unity is reinforced by the fact that the Bible begins with an account of creation and life before the fall and concludes with a description of the consummation of history. Between the beginning and the end stretches history, which is viewed in biblical literature as redemptive for all who accept the salvation of God.

Leland Ryken. *The Literature of the Bible* (Grand Rapids, Mich., Zondervan, 1974), pp. 26–27

Plot develops out of an initial situation in a chain of actions toward a central event, which is the prime instigator of the change, and again out of different events toward a final situation. Were we to draw the line joining these two situations, with its ups and its downs, then there would stand before us the pattern of the plot.

For the most part we find in the narratives of the Bible the classic pattern: The plot line goes up from its activating starting point through the stage of complication to the climax of conflict and tension, and from there rapidly to the point of closure and resolution. This line of development is found, among other places, in the Binding of Isaac story (Gen. 22). . . .

In [the Binding of Isaac story and in the story of Esther] the plot pattern is characterized not only by the line going up to the point of decision and rapidly going down from it but also by a turning point in the direction of the plot development, a turning point that occurs just as the tension reaches its climax. Such a change of direction in the course of the plot is not rare in the narratives of the Bible. . . .

An . . . example of such [change of direction] as turning point may be found in the story of David and Abigail (I Sam. 25). David, who was very hurt by the response of Nabal to his servants, goes out with four hundred men, all girded with swords, to strike against Nabal. Abigail, Nabal's wife, goes out to meet David in an attempt to prevent the revenge, and in her arms are numerous gifts. Just before the decisive encounter the narrator returns to David and conveys to us his thoughts: "And David said, 'For nothing have I watched all of this one's things in the wilderness so that not a thing of his was taken, and he has returned me bad for good. So may God do to the enemies of David, and so may he add, if I by morning's light leave so much as a urinator at the wall of all that is his'" (vv. 21–22). Conveying David's intentions at this moment serves to reinforce the plot line that is developing in the direction of violent revenge. David is brazen in his decision to destroy all that is Nabal's, and he even lends his decision the force of an oath. Right after this the encounter between David and Abigail is related. In this encounter Abigail succeeds in instigating a turning point in David's plans, which is also a turning point in the direction of the plot line. David abrogates the act of revenge, and Nabal receives his punishment at the hands of heaven.

Another structural phenomenon that is found in a number of narratives in the Bible and that determines the plot pattern is that of the dissembled ending. In contrast to the examples adduced above in which the plot line of the story gradually ascends to the point of climax and afterward rapidly descends from it to a resolved ending, here after the gradual ascent to the peak and the rapid descent to the point of resolution, the story does not conclude but rather picks up anew, ascends again to a peak, and only then descends to a true conclusion. . . .

Such a line of development of renewed ascent following descent to the point of resolution may be found in the story of Job. The tension in this story flows from the uncertainty of whether Job will pass the test or not. With the reports of the four catastrophes that befall Job and with the last one in particular (the death of all his children at once), the tension reaches its high point. Job's response, which attests to his firm stance and his steadfast piety, brings us to the point of resolution (end of ch. 1). Here, with the proof that Job has maintained his innocence, the story could have reached its conclusion. But the plot resumes when an additional catastrophe lands upon Job. This time, too, Job passes the test, but the final resolution is not achieved except in the last chapter of the book, when God makes restitution to Job and adds double to all that is his (42:10).

Occasionally the plot in biblical narratives is so constructed that ironic situations are created. I am referring to dramatic irony, that is, irony flowing from a character's knowing less than the reader, or from his unwittingly doing things opposed to his own interests, or from the course of events engendering results opposite to those to which the character aspired.

Sometimes the irony lies in the action, and sometimes it lies in the self-expression of the character. Yet even when it lies in self-expression, we are not speaking of linguistic irony . . . because in contrast to linguistic irony, which is expressed knowingly, with intent from the outset, here the character is not at all aware of the irony in his words. The character speaks naïvely, while the author, who in the final analysis is responsible for formulating the character's words, gives the character's words—without his knowing it—an ironic sense.

> Shimeon Bar-Efrat. *Ha'itsuv ha'omanuti shel hassippur bammiqra'* (Tel Aviv, Sifriat Poalim, 1979), pp. 135–38†

Recurrence, parallels, analogy are the hallmarks of reported action in the biblical tale. The use of narrative analogy, where one part of the story provides a commentary on or a foil to another, should be familiar enough from later literature, as anyone who has ever followed the workings of a Shakespearian double plot may attest. In the Bible, however, such analogies often play an especially critical role because the writers tend to avoid more explicit modes of conveying evaluation of particular characters and acts. Thus, the *only* commentary made on Jacob's getting the firstborn's blessing from his blind father through deception occurs several chapters later in an analogy with a reversal—when he is deceived in the dark and given Leah instead of Rachel, then chided that it is not the law of the land to marry the younger sister before the firstborn.

One kind of recurrence in biblical narrative appears regularly through a long series of events, like the deflection of primogeniture in Genesis, the backslidings of Israel in the Wilderness tales, the periodic intervention of divinely inspired liberators in Judges; and such recurrence works in a way akin to the *Leitwort* [leading word], establishing a kind of rhythm of thematic significance, clearly suggesting that events in history occur according to an ordained pattern. If pattern is decisive in the biblical stress on repeated actions, concatenation is equally important. There is in the biblical view a causal chain that firmly connects one event to the next, link by link, and that, too, accounts for a good deal of recurrence in the narrative shaping of the events; for analogy reinforces this sense of causal connection. One could say that everything that befalls Jacob flows from the fatal moment when he buys the birthright from Esau for a serving of lentil pottage. That event, of course, was itself prefigured in the intrauterine struggle between the twins, and it is followed, both causally and analogically, by the theft of the blessing, Jacob's flight, his various confrontations with the two rival sisters who are his wives, his contentions with his wily father-in-law, his wrestling with the angel, and even his troubles with his sons, who deceive him with a garment, Joseph's tunic, just as he, masquerading as Esau, deceived his own father with a garment.

The two most distinctively biblical uses of repeated action are when we are given two versions of the same event and when the same event, with minor variations, occurs at different junctures of the narrative, usually involving different characters or sets of characters. As a rule, when we can detect two versions of a single event, it is safe to assume that the writer has effected a montage of sources, and the question we might ask is why he should have done this, in what ways do the two narrative perspectives complement or complicate each other. The recurrence of the same event—the sameness being definable as a fixed sequence of narrative motifs which, however, may be presented in a variety of ways and sometimes with ingenious variations—is what I have called "type-scene," and it constitutes a central organizing convention of biblical narrative. Here one has to watch for the minute and often revelatory changes that a given type-scene undergoes as it passes from one character to another. How, for example, we might ask ourselves as readers, does the barren Rebekah's annunciation type-scene differ from Sarah's, from Hannah's, from the wife of Manoah's, from the Shunamite woman's? Occasionally, a type-scene will be deployed in conjunction with a pointed use of narrative analogy by setting two occurrences of the same type-scene in close sequence. Thus, the life-threatening trial in the wilderness first occurs to Abraham's older son, Ishmael (Gen. 21), then to his younger son, Isaac, whom Abraham seems commanded to slaughter (Gen. 22). The alert reader can learn a great deal about the complex meanings of the two stories by studying the network of connections, both in recurring phrases and narrative motifs, that links them—one a tale of a desperate mother driven out into the wilderness with her son, the other a tale of an anguished father silently obeying the injunction to take his son into the wilderness, in both instances an angel's voice calling out from heaven at the critical moment to announce that the boy will be saved. Even the buffer passage between the two stories (Gen. 21:22–34), the tale of a dispute over a well in the desert, reinforces this network of connections, for it involves obtaining a source of life in the wilderness (as explicitly happens in the Ishmael story) and it concludes with Abraham's making a covenant meant to guarantee peace and well-being for his progeny.

Robert Alter. *The Art of Biblical Narrative* (New York, Basic Books, 1981), pp. 180–82

POETRY

And as the oldest, and, I think, the sublimest Poem in the World, is of Hebrew Original, and was made immediately after passing the Red-Sea, at a Time, when the Author had neither Leisure, nor Possibility, to invent a new Art: It must therefore be undeniable, either that the Hebrews brought Poetry out of Egypt, or that Moses receiv'd it from God, by immediate Inspiration. This last, being what a Poet should be fondest of believing, I wou'd fain suppose it probable, that God, who was pleas'd to instruct Moses with what Ceremony he wou'd be worship'd, taught him also a Mode of Thinking, and expressing Thought, unprophan'd by vulgar Use, and peculiar to that Worship. God then taught Poetry first to the Hebrews, and the Hebrews to Mankind in general.

But, however this may have been, there is, apparently, a divine Spirit, glowing forcibly in the Hebrew Poetry, a kind of terrible Simplicity! a magnificent Plainness! which is commonly lost, in Paraphrase, by our mistaken Endeavours after heightening the Sentiments, by a figurative Expression; This is very ill judg'd: The little Ornaments of Rhetorick might serve, fortunately enough, to swell out the Leanness of some modern Compositions; but to shadow over the Lustre of a divine Hebrew Thought, by an Affectation of enliv'ning it, is to paint upon a Diamond, and call it an Ornament.

It is a surprizing Reflection, that these noble Hebrew Poets shou'd have written with such admirable Vigour three Thousand Years ago; and that, instead of improving, we shou'd affect to despise them; as if, to write smoothly, and without the Spirit of Imagery, were the true Art of Poetry, because the only Art we practise. It puts me in Mind of the famous Roman Lady, who suppos'd, that Men had, naturally, stinking Breaths, because she had been us'd to it, in her Husband.

Aaron Hill. Preface to Mr. Pope in *The Creation: A Pindaric Illustration of a Poem, Originally Written by Moses on that Subject* (London, Printed for T. Bickerton, 1720), pp. 4–5

Only the creative thoughts of God, however, are truly objective, have actuality in their outward expression, and stand forth existent and living in the products of creative power. Man can only give names to these creations, arrange and link them together; beyond this, his thoughts remain but lifeless forms, his words and the impulses of his feelings are not in themselves living products. Yet, the clearer the intuition, with which we contemplate and systematize the objects of creation, the more unsophisticated and full the impulse of feeling, which impels us to impress every thing with the purest character and fullest measure of humanity—that which marks the analogy of our being to that of God—the more beautiful, the more perfect, and, let us not doubt, the more powerful will be our poetick art. In this feeling of natural beauty and sublimity the child often has the advantage of the man of gray hairs, and nations of the greatest simplicity have in their natural imagery and expressions of natural feeling, the most elevated and touching poetry. I doubt whether this origin of poetry can be better and more beautifully expressed than it is by the Hebrew *mashal*. The word means *to imprint, to impress,* to impress *a form, a likeness;* and so *to speak in proverbs*, as the *meshalim* of the Hebrew poetry are proverbs, wise sentences of the highest import; and again *to decide, to put in order, to speak* as a king or judge, finally, *to reign, to have dominion, to be powerful by the word of one's mouth*. Here we have the history of the origin of poetry and of the part of it, which is most powerful in its influence.

It would scarcely have been deserving of remark, were it not necessary to prevent frequent misconception and abuse, that the poetical images and feelings of one people, and of one age can never be judged, censured, and rejected according to the standard of another people, and another age. Had the Creator so ordered it, that we had all been born upon the same spot of earth, at the same time, with the same feelings and organs, and under the same outward circumstances, there would have been nothing to object against the uniform standard of taste, of which so much has been said. But since nothing is more susceptible and multifarious than the human heart, since nothing is more subtle and evanescent, than the connecting ties, on which its feelings and passions depend, since it even belongs to the perfection of human nature, that it organize and form itself anew under every climate, in every age, and every peculiar mode of existence, since finally that modicum of articulated air, which we call language, and which yet bears upon its light and butterfly wings all the treasures of poetical imagery and sentiment—since this breath of the mouth, in its manifold variations exhibiting the diversities of every people and every age, is a real Proteus, it seems to indicate either a stupid or a proud presumption to require, that every nation, even of the most ancient times, should think, discourse, feel, and fashion its poetical conceptions in a manner to suit our habits and wants. . . .

Still more incongruous would it be to take a single image or representation out of the connexion, in which it belongs, and compare its style and colouring with those of another, taken from a poet of a different age, of a different nation and language, and of diverse poetical powers. No two things in the world are wholly alike. No one thing is made for the purpose of being compared with another, and the most fresh and delicate growth, when torn from its place, is the first to wither. A poetical image exists only in its connexion with the emotion that prompted it. In losing that it loses every thing, and is only a senseless medley of colours, which only a child values according to the brightness of their tints. Perhaps too no poets lose so much by a comparison of extracted passages and images as the poets of the East. For they are the farthest removed from us, they sung in another world, in part three, four thousand years, before we discoursed about them. Should one compare for example, the picture of a horse in Job with Virgil's description of it, and neglect to remark, who it is that speaks in Job, and for what end, what was the character and estimation of the horse in Virgil's time at Rome, and in the days of Job in Idumaea, and for what purpose it was introduced in these different authors, (to say nothing of language, metre, the genius of the people, and the form of their poetry) would he form a good comparative estimate of them? would they be fairly balanced and compared? [1783]

> Johann Gottfried von Herder. *The Spirit of Hebrew Poetry*. Vol. II. Tr. by James Marsh (Burlington, Vt., Edward Smith, 1833), pp. 8–11

It must occur to every reader that the Greeks in their religious poems address always the Numina Loci [local deities], the Genii, the Dryads, the Naiads, etc., etc. All natural objects were *dead*—mere hollow statues—but there was a Godkin or Goddessling *included* in each. In the Hebrew poetry you find nothing of this poor stuff, as poor in genuine imagination as it is mean in intellect. At best, it is but fancy, or the aggregating faculty of the mind—not imagination or the *modifying* and coadunating faculty. This the Hebrew poets appear to me to have possessed beyond all others, and next to them the English. In the Hebrew poets each thing has a life of its own, and yet they are all our life. In God they move and live and *have* their being; not *had*, as the cold system of Newtonian Theology represents, but *have*. [Letter to William Sotheby, Sept. 10, 1802]

> Samuel Taylor Coleridge. *Letters*. Vol. I. Ed. by Ernest Hartley Coleridge (Boston, Houghton Mifflin, 1895), pp. 405–6

The poetry of the Bible is that of imagination and of faith: it is abstract and disembodied; it is not the poetry of form, but of power; not of multitude, but of immensity. It does not divide into many, but aggrandizes into one. Its ideas of nature are like its ideas of God. It is not the poetry of social life, but of solitude: each man seems alone in the world, with the original forms of nature, the rocks, the earth, and the sky. It is not the poetry of action or heroic enterprise, but of faith in a supreme Providence, and resignation to the power that governs the universe. As the idea of God was removed farther from humanity, and a scattered polytheism, it became more profound and intense, it became more universal, for the Infinite is present to every thing: "If we fly into the uttermost parts of the earth, it is there also; if we turn to the east or the west, we cannot escape from it." Man is thus aggrandised in the image of his Maker. The history of the patriarchs is of this kind; they are founders of a chosen race of people, the inheritors of the earth; they exist in the generations which are to come after them. Their poetry, like their religious creed, is vast, unformed, obscure, and infinite; a vision is upon it—an invisible hand is suspended over it. The spirit of the Christian religion consists in the glory hereafter to be revealed; but in the Hebrew dispensation, Providence took an immediate share in the affairs of his life. Jacob's dream arose out of this intimate communion between heaven and earth; it was this that let down, in sight of the youthful patriarch, a golden ladder from the sky to the earth, with angels ascending and descending upon it, and shed a light upon the lonely place, which can never pass away. The story of Ruth, again, is as if all the depth of natural affection in the human race was involved in her breast. There are descriptions in the book of Job more prodigal of imagery, more intense in passion, than any thing in Homer, as that of the state of his prosperity, and of the vision that came upon him by night. The metaphors are more boldly figurative. Things were collected more into masses, and gave a greater *momentum* to the imagination.

> William Hazlitt. *Lectures on the English Poets* (Philadelphia, Thomas Dobson, 1818), pp. 32–34

It may not, therefore, be altogether beside our purpose to inquire into the causes of the early influence of poetry, and of its application to sacred themes. We shall thus the more readily apprehend why it was so extensively employed by the inspired writers; the book of Job, the Psalms, the Proverbs, Solomon's Song, and by far the larger portion of the prophecies, being decidedly poetical.

"Poetry," says [André] Dacier, a critic of great taste and erudition, "is the offspring of religion"; and Plato affirms of it, that it awakens the spiritual empire of the soul. Such being its character and influence, can we feel surprised that it was employed so largely by the sacred writers, as an agent to infuse such feelings of reverence towards God, and benevolence towards man, as those sublime compositions, of which they were the inspired authors, are so well calculated to engender? Take the poetry of the Hebrew scriptures where you will, and it abounds in these divine records, it incomparably surpasses that of any mere human production. Its variety is unbounded, its richness inexhaustibly copious, and its eloquence sublime. This has been admitted by persons who have denied altogether the inspiration of those scriptures. As one proof of this, among many, I have been assured by a person intimately acquainted with the late Percy Bysshe Shelley, a name deservedly classed among the greatest poets of the nineteenth century, that this highly endowed, but misguided genius, considered the sacred volume as unequalled by any other work, in any language, in the riches of its poetry. He always carried with him a small pocket edition of the Bible when he travelled; and it is said that one was found upon the body when recovered from the waves, in which so unhappy a career was terminated. It is sadly to be lamented that so fine a taste, a mind so exquisitely alive to the beautiful and sublime, should so readily have discovered both in the Bible, and yet have failed to perceive the inspiration of that divine book, the universal presence of the former leading, as it does, so convincingly to the irrefragable proof of the latter . . . .

[Jean Baptiste] Du Bos, an elegant French critic, who died in the early part of the eighteenth century, contends that poetry has been considered in all ages, even by the most accomplished minds, as the fittest agent for preserving the memory of past events, and I am fully disposed to concur with him in this view. "Poetry," says this judicious writer, "is an art in which every thing should please. It is not enough to exhibit nature, which in certain places and circumstances is rude and repulsive, but the poet must choose in her what is beautiful from what is not; whence he ought to select for the subject of imitation something naturally affecting. There is a particular rhetorick for poetry, which consists in discerning very precisely what ought to be said figuratively, and what to be spoken simply; and in knowing where ornament is required and where not; yet the style should be copious, and every species of writing in this art should have a diction proper to itself."

We shall see by-and-by how far these observations will be borne out by the poetry of the Pentateuch, in which those conditions of the art, so judiciously stated by Du Bos, are strictly and beautifully fulfilled. Why so artificial a form of composition was adopted by the prophets, the earlier as well as the later, such as Noah, Isaac, Jacob, Balaam, Moses himself, and the prophetess Deborah, has been already sufficiently answered in the observations which I have sought to press upon the reader's attention. It was but natural that the loftiest forms of speech, the most glowing colouring of language, should be preferred to express the divine communications, and those are more especially the province of poetry. Its being the fittest agent, as Du Bos contends, for preserving the memory of past events, an observation confirmed by the opinion of the great [Johann Georg] Michaelis, formerly professor in the university of Gottingen, is a very weighty reason, among others, why it was employed so largely by the early Hebrew writers. But besides this, it was far better adapted to the character of those deep cryptic revelations which were not intended to be fully proclaimed, but of the eventual consummation of which the particulars were rather suggested than declared.

John Hobart Caunter. *The Poetry of the Pentateuch.*
Vol. I (London, E. Churton, 1839), pp. 5–6, 18–19

It is a characteristic of the poetry of the Hebrews that as a reflex of monotheism it always embraces the universe in its unity, comprising both terrestrial life and the luminous realms of space. It dwells but rarely on the individuality of phenomena, preferring the contemplation of great masses. The Hebrew poet does not depict nature as a self-dependent object, glorious in its individual beauty, but always as in relation and subjection to a higher spiritual power. Nature is to him a work of creation and order, the living expression of the omnipresence of the Divinity in the visible world. Hence the lyrical poetry of the Hebrews, from the very nature of its subject, is grand and solemn, and when it treats of the earthly condition of mankind, is full of sad and pensive longing. It is worthy of remark that Hebrew poetry, notwithstanding its grandeur, and the lofty tone of exaltation

to which it is often elevated by the charm of music, scarcely ever loses the restraint of measure, as does the poetry of India. Devoted to the pure contemplation of the Divinity, it remains clear and simple in the midst of the most figurative forms of expression, delighting in comparisons which recur with almost
rhythmical regularity.

Alexander von Humboldt. *Cosmos*. Vol. II. Tr. from the
German by E. C. Otte (London, Bohn, 1849), p. 412

These sacred poets have but two or three images, two or three notes on the harp,
like the flow of tears that drip in the human heart, and piercing like the cries of
the eagle at which the snake proceeds to embrace its young in its nest. The melancholy of which we so often speak and which is, in effect, the solemn chord and
the fundamental note of the touched soul, dates neither from Vergil, nor from the
Romantic school of our own time, nor from M[onsieur François René] de Chat-
eaubriand, nor from ourselves; it dates from the sacred poetry of the Bible, or
rather it dates from the first tear and from the first contemplation of the infinite
misery of man.

Every element thus seems to have its poet. The Hebrews are the poets of the
rocky heights. Homer, born in an environment of coves, of islands, of foam, of
waves, of the ship sails of maritime Greece, is the poet of the sea. There is no
clash of swords on the beach, no shadow of the ship's head on the tide, no whistling of a wind in the rigging, no clatter of oars on the bulwarks of the ship that
would not be echoed or depicted in his verse. . . .

Vergil and Theocritus are both the poets of the arable or pastoral land. . . .

Dante is the poet of the night and gloom, of apparitions that haunt the darkness . . . .

Milton is the poet of the air . . . . He paints there on a bottomless and endless
canvas the battle between God and rebellious spirits . . . .

As for Job, we repeat again, this is the poet of the desert. But what is the desert? It is space; and of what is space the image? The infinite.

To put it another way, Job is, then, the poet of the infinite.

The desert furnishes him with his subject, his immenseness, his colors, his
images, his style. The infinite concentrated and reverberated in the cavity of a
man's chest—this is Job.

Alphonse Marie Louis de Lamartine. *Cours familier de
littérature*. Vol. II (Paris, published by the author,
1856). pp. 370–73†

There was now witnessed a significant change in Israel. The unexpected and
eventful victories had aroused amongst them the melodious power of song, the
first indication of that talent, without which no nation can attain to a superior degree of culture. The first songs of the Hebrew muse were those of war and victory. The authors (*moshelim*) of warlike hymns rose at once in public estimation,
and their productions were preserved in special collections, as for example, in
the Book of the Wars of God.

Hebrew poetry, in its early stages, was deficient in depth and elegance, but it had two characteristics which in the course of time were developed to the highest stage of refinement. With regard to form, it exhibited a symmetry in the component parts of each verse (*parallelismus membrorum*). The same train of thought was repeated with appropriate variations in two or even three divisions of the verse. In the treatment of a theme, the muse of early Hebrew poetry displayed a tendency to irony, this being the result of a twofold conception, namely, that of the ideal aspect by the side of antithetic reality.

> Heinrich Graetz. *History of the Jews*. Vol. I. Tr. by
> Bella Löwy (Philadelphia, Jewish Publication Society of
> America, 1891), p. 29

All the poems of Orientalism, with the Old and New Testaments at the centre, tend to deep and wide (I don't know but the deepest and widest) psychological development—with little, or nothing at all, of the mere esthetic, the principal verse-requirement of our day. Very late, but unerringly, comes to every capable student the perception that it is not in beauty, it is not in art, it is not even in science, that the profoundest laws of the case have their eternal sway and outcropping.

In his discourse on "Hebrew poets" De Sola Mendes said:

> The fundamental feature of Judaism, of the Hebrew national-
> ity, was religion; its poetry was naturally religious. Its subjects,
> God and Providence, the covenants with Israel, God in Nature,
> and as reveal'd, God the Creator and Governor, Nature in her
> majesty and beauty, inspired hymns and odes to Nature's God.
> And then the checker'd history of the nation furnish'd allusions,
> illustrations, and subjects for epic display—the glory of the sanc-
> tuary, the offerings, the splendid ritual, the Holy City, and lov'd
> Palestine with its pleasant valleys and wild tracts.

Dr. Mendes said that "rhyming was not a characteristic of Hebrew poetry at all. Metre was not a necessary mark of poetry. Great poets discarded it; the early Jewish poets knew it not."

Compared with the famed epics of Greece, and lesser ones since, the spinal supports of the Bible are simple and meagre. All its history, biography, narratives, &c., are as beads, strung on and indicating the eternal thread of the Deific purpose and power. Yet with only deepest faith for impetus, and such Deific purpose for palpable or impalpable theme, it often transcends the masterpieces of Hellas, and all masterpieces. The metaphors daring beyond account, the lawless soul, extravagant by our standards, the glow of love and friendship, the fervent kiss—nothing in argument or logic, but unsurpass'd in proverbs, in religious ecstasy, in suggestions of common mortality and death, man's great equalizers—the spirit everything, the ceremonies and forms of the churches nothing, faith limitless, its immense sensuousness immensely spiritual—an incredible, all-inclusive non-worldliness and dew-scented illiteracy (the antipodes of our Nineteenth Century business absorption and morbid refinement)—no hair-splitting doubts, no sickly sulking and sniffling, no *Hamlet*, no *Adonais*, no *Thanatopsis*, no *In Memoriam*. . . .

Here are the fountain heads of song.

> Walt Whitman. *The Complete Writings*. Vol. VI. Ed. by
> Richard M. Bucke et al. (New York, Putnam's, 1902),
> pp. 104–6, 109

Taken as a whole, all the poetry of the ancient East is much inferior to that of the Hebrews, and the highest praise that can be given to a Babylonian or Egyptian song is that it is not altogether unworthy of being compared with the poems in the Bible. And what a wealth of varied forms is set before us here! The Hebrew poets describe in triumphant strains the majesty of Jahveh. They celebrate His glory in Creation: "The heavens declare the glory of the Eternal" [Ps. 19]; His forgiving grace to Israel: "As a father pitieth his children, so the Lord pitieth them that fear Him" [Ps. 103]. Or they lament with hearts broken by their personal sorrow or by national misfortune, or from their tears they look up confidently to God. Perhaps the most arresting, because the most genuine of all their poems, are those in which in liturgical fashion alternate voices are heard, in which at first, with bell-like tones, the confidence of their faith is strongly expressed, and then the note of pain of the burdened heart is heard—the burdened heart that yearns for those heights of bliss.

Take as an example Psalm 85. In the lofty tone of prophetic vision the first part announces as present actual fact the salvation that is still to come:

> Thou hast, O Jahveh, favoured Thy land,
>   hast turned the fate of Jacob,
> hast remitted the guilt of Thy people,
>   forgiven all their sins;
> hast recalled all Thine anger,
>   and quenched the fire of Thy wrath.

The second part contains a prayer, expressing the yearning of the people for this salvation:

> Restore Thou us, O God of help,
>   let Thy displeasure against us cease!
> Wilt Thou be angry with us always?
>   and prolong Thine anger for ever?
> Wilt Thou not quicken us again,
>   that Thy people may rejoice in Thee?
> Let us, O Jahveh, Thy mercy see
>   and grant us Thy salvation!

The third stanza reverts to the opening note. Out of the circle of singers rises a man accustomed to hear the Divine voice. And he is able to announce that what the downcast hearts so ardently desire is at hand! Salvation is near!

> I will listen to what Jahveh will speak,
>   Verily, He speaks of salvation
> to His people and to His faithful ones,
>   and, to those who turn to Him, of hope.
> Yea, near is His aid to His pious ones,
>   that His glory may dwell in our land.
>
> Mercy and truth meet,
>   Righteousness and peace kiss each other.
> Truth sprouts out of the earth,
>   Grace looks down from heaven.
> Jahveh Himself gives all that is good,
>   Our land yields its fruit.
> Grace goes before Him,
>   and straightness on the path of His steps.

Thus ends the poem in a tone of ecstatic vision: Salvation and Grace on all sides, above and beneath, and everywhere.

Songs like these cry for a composer. They were once meant to be sung; they ought to be set to music once more. Would not Bach have known how to do justice to the varied religious moods of these songs if he had known them in their newer, more vivid interpretation?

Speaking generally, the Hebrew mind had not the type of genius required for lengthy productions, and so the shorter the pieces the more beautiful they are. The Hebrew had a special gift for painting a richly coloured picture in very small compass. But the Hebrew mind succeeded in producing one great poem which is great also in length. I mean the book of Job. Here the author is bold enough to impugn, and even to attack, the strongest base of the whole Hebrew religion, viz. the doctrine of Divine retribution. Sore at heart and afflicted by a horrible and incurable disease—a fate that flatly contradicted the doctrine ardently believed by all good men—he still refuses to give up his conviction of his own innocence. He enters upon a bitter contest with his pious friends, who find their whole religion in this doctrine, and even ventures to call in question the justice of God Himself. Three friends argue with him, but he overthrows all three, and remains alone on the field. Then he rises, and his words sound like an accusation addressed to heaven in the name of all humanity: "Why? Why?" Now comes forth the Eternal One in person, revealing His Divine Majesty in sublime words to the son of earth. All questioning is hushed: "I lay my hand upon my mouth" [40:4]. The book of Job is like a Titan structure towering up to heaven; but at the close all that is of man fades and only God's greatness remains.

Hermann Gunkel. *What Remains of the Old Testament, and Other Essays*. Tr. from the German by A. K. Dallas (New York, Macmillan, 1928), pp. 27–30

As a form of literary composition the poetry of the Bible belongs almost entirely to the Old Testament. There are, to be sure, poetical passages in the New Testament, and some quotations from the poetry of the Old Testament. There are, too, a few songs here and there in the Gospels, notably the songs of Mary and Zacharias in the first chapter of Luke. But in the Old Testament poetry is very prominent indeed. Whole books, as Psalms, Proverbs, Lamentations, Song of Songs, and almost all of the Book of Job are in poetry; and among the prophets, especially Isaiah, Jeremiah, Amos, Hosea, Obadiah, Micah, Nahum, Habakkuk, Zephaniah, Zechariah, and Malachi the form of composition was largely, and in some instances entirely, poetry. Even in the Law and in the more strictly historical books of the Prophets poetry is very abundant in the nature of songs and prayers; as, the prophecy of Jacob, Genesis 49; the songs of Moses, Exodus 15, and Deuteronomy 33; the parable of Balaam, Numbers 24; the song of Deborah, Judges 5; the prayers of Hannah, I Samuel 2; the song of David, II Samuel 22.

The poetry of the Old Testament is distributed over a considerable range of variety. The lyric is abundantly represented in the Psalms and in the isolated songs interspersed among the prose writings. The Songs of Songs, too, is by some critics considered to be a collection of love songs, although the matter of this book has been subjected to such a variety of criticisms and interpretations that it is somewhat hazardous to make positive statements about it. The book of Lamentations is a sublime dirge or elegy, and Proverbs is a collection of aphoristic poems varying in length from two lines, to poems of considerable length, as the poems in praise of Wisdom in the first and second chapters and again in chapters eight and nine. Job is a long symposium of speeches in the form of poetry. It has some of the characteristics of drama, but it is unique in the literature of the world, and must be classed by itself. In the Prophets poetry is quite generally mingled with prose, for the most part representing the more exalted moods of vision, or intenser passion.

> George Sprau. *Literature in the Bible* (New York, Macmillan, 1932), pp. 18–19

Subjective, then, on all sides of their lives the Hebrews assuredly were, whether for better or for worse. It was their strength and their handicap in their thinking and in the expression of their thoughts. But the subjective mind can be either calm in its working or swept by emotional storms. When it is calm, it reasons, narrates, describes—always subjectively—but when high emotion strikes it there is no room for anything but the self swept by its own feelings and rendering itself alone. This was the one essential difference between poetry among the Hebrews and all their other forms of literature. The Hebrew poet was the Hebrew under such strain of emotion; he was the Aoidos, the inspired singer, possessed from within, under divine protection and uttering enchantments; he was not the *poietes*, the "maker" of a poem, separate, objective, as the sculptor with his block of marble. The wide consequences of this for Hebrew poetry can be put most simply in a series of propositions:

(i) The Hebrew poet felt and rendered his emotions; he did not think. Under emotion, quiet thought, the exercise of the logical faculty, was impossible to him.

(ii) Under this strain, he expressed himself. He could not express anything outside of himself.

(iii) He could not even understand anything, or any one, without taking that thing or person into himself, absorbing it and identifying it with himself.

(iv) He could not poetically, that is, emotionally, create without putting himself into the creation. His poetical creation had to be not only a product, but a record of his own emotion.

But all this was only when emotion entered; in prose—narrative, reflective, descriptive—there is not necessarily any emotion. The source and essence of Hebrew poetry was emotion. In this there is nothing new or strange. . . .

But the unique thing about Hebrew poetry is that it never passed beyond this stage or lost this attitude. And this attitude to the end—even through the inartistic absurdities of alphabetic psalms—controlled all Hebrew poetry. The convention of the muse for them had gone far deeper.

It is a singular and significant fact that in our extant Hebrew literature there is no specific word for "poet." There are possible words for "singer," several words for "prophet" on different sides of the prophetic function, words for "wise men" who may have expressed their wisdom in poetical form and metaphor, but none for poet in our or the Greek sense. This can hardly be accident. We shall see hereafter how closely the poet was connected with the prophet; the roots of both lay in a relationship to the Unseen World. The utterances of Wisdom, too, clothed themselves often in poetic form; the Book of Job is both poetry and philosophy. It is therefore probable that, for the Hebrew consciousness, the poet and his poetry had not separated themselves off as a category from the various garbs under which they showed themselves. The poet sang: he was a singer. He manifested from the Unseen World; he was a seer, a prophet. In his song he taught philosophic wisdom; he was a wise man. But the function of poetry, which lay behind them all, had not yet been abstracted. The old Arabs, however, had gone further and their general word for "poet" is deeply significant for the subjective emotionalism of the Hebrews. They called a poet *shāʿir*, a "feeler"—a perceiver, that is, by feeling. This expresses precisely the essence of the Hebrew poet. He "felt" and told in song what he felt. Herein lies the primitive and childlike side of Hebrew poetry. The poet was like a child, sitting and playing by himself; making a song about himself and himself the hero of all that happens in the song. As a child sings in his play of a moment, so the Hebrew race sang to itself, and its songs have remained and have gone round the world.

Duncan B. MacDonald. *The Hebrew Literary Genius* (Princeton, N.J., Princeton University Press, 1933), pp. 13–15

Hebrew poetry has its set of conventions—some easy, some quite demanding—for the reader to deal with. Some readers, unwilling to reckon with them, assert in effect that everything, even in ancient poetry now living on in an English form, should be self-evident. But these same readers are doubtless quite willing to familiarize themselves with the rules of a game of chance in order to watch it or play it with pleasure, and the "rules" governing Hebrew poetry are really much less arbitrary and more closely related to the bedrock of human nature than are the rules governing movements on the football field. . . .

The reading of amorous Hebrew poetry and the reading of the larger collection of religious poetry involve the same problems of apprehension, even to a close parallel of subject matters. Both collections presuppose dramas that run like an endless movie film, offering us a group of scenes again and again. This group of scenes is so familiar to the audiences reached by The Song of Solomon and Psalms that the poet does not need to explain antecedent circumstances as he begins a particular song. Something like this we detect in our own experience when we enter a movie house in the middle of a feature. So well do we know what Hollywood sends us that one glance at the screen tells us the point the story has reached; the sequence of boy meets girl, boy and girl quarrel, boy and girl "reconcile" is utterly familiar. The ancient Hebrew poets could count on a knowledge of a different sort of succession of events; their audience would know at once what point in the endlessly recurring dramas of human love or pursuit of the deity was being taken up.

Harold H. Watts. *The Modern Reader's Guide to the Bible*. Rev. ed. (New York, Harper, 1959), pp. 190–91

As we come to examine the various poetic devices that the prophets or bards used in the poetic parts of the Bible, we ought to begin with their first words, with the openings to their prophecies or their poems and psalms, and to see what devices they used in their opening words in order to adorn and beautify them so as to arouse the attention of those who hear or read their words. . . .

The *first* opening device is the opening as a sort of prelude and preparation for the listener, to arouse his attention to the words being said. This prelude comes in the form of an address of the prophet or bard to heaven and earth, mountains and hills, peoples and nations, kings and regents, or to all people in general, a call to listen.

Thus, the song "Give-ear" opens with this utterance:

> Give-ear, O heaven, that I may speak,
> And let the earth hear the utterances of my mouth. (Deut. 32:1)

And the Song of Deborah:

> Hear, O kings, / Give-ear, O regents. (Judg. 5:3) . . .

And Micah in the opening of his prophecy:

> Hear, O all peoples, / Give heed, O earth and that which fills it.
> (Mic. 1:2)

And in the opening of another prophecy he nicely describes such an address by placing words in the mouth of God, calling him to call upon the mountains and hills to listen to his words; that is, he prefaces an opening to an opening:

> Hear, pray, that which the Lord says:
> Get up, argue with the mountains!
> And let the hills hear your voice:
> Hear, O mountains, the argument of the Lord!
> And you strong-ones, foundations of the earth. (Mic. 6:1-2) . . .

The *second* device of lovely openings in the Bible is the use of a question, which adds life to the words.

The question comes in various ways:

(1) As a *genuine* question, when the one asking does not know the answer, as in the Song of Songs where the daughters of Jerusalem question the shepherd-girl searching for her beloved:

> Whither has your beloved gone?
> O fairest of women!
> Whither has your beloved headed?
> That we may seek him with you. (6:1) . . .

(2) As an *ostensible* question, in which the questioner knows the answer but asks his question anyway in order to demonstrate a lack of right in the one whom he is reproving, as in Isaiah's oracle against Shebna:

> What have you here, and whom have you here,
> That you have hewn for yourself here a grave? (22:16)

That is to say, you have *no* inheritance or property here, nor any relatives, so why have you then hewn out a grave for yourself as though you had planned to live here for the rest of your life, die, and be buried here? . . .

(3) As a question that provokes *another question*, the crucial one, as in Jeremiah:

> Is there no balm in Gilead? / Or is no healer there?
> Then why has the health of my daughter-people not improved? (8:22). . . .

(4) As a question that comes from the beginning *for the sake of the answer*, as in . . . Psalms:

> O Lord! Who will sojourn in your tent?
> Who will dwell on your holy mountain?
> He who walks perfectly and performs justice,
> And speaks truth in his heart. (Ps. 15:1–2) . . .

The *third* device of Biblical openings is the use of a *vocative* or *naming* of the person who is being addressed. The word of exclamation is mostly *hoy* ["Ah!"]. We find this word in the opening of speeches especially in the first part of the Book of Isaiah, as in "Ah, sinful nation!" (1:4) . . .

Sometimes the exclamation of distress "Woe!" is used, as in Ezekiel: "Woe, O city of infamy!" (24:6) . . .

Mentioning a name in the *vocative* at the beginning of discourse is particularly common in the Psalms with regard to the name "Lord," "God," or "my God," which precede a petition, be it plaintive or emotional, such as: "O Lord, do not in your wrath reprove me!" (6:2); "O God, do not be still, do not be quiet or silent, O God!" (83:2). . . .

The *fourth* device of opening is the use of exclamations of *wish* or *desire* for something, as in Jeremiah:

> Would that he would put me in the wilderness,
> A lodging of travelers! (9:1) . . .

And as in the Song of Songs:

> Would that he would make you as my brother,
> Suckling of my mother's breasts! (8:1)

The *fifth* device of biblical openings is the use of the device of the *imperative* in general, apart from the commands that come under the first device, whose basis is a call to listen (*"Hear*, O heaven, and *give-ear*, O land"). God or the prophet or the bard begin their words with a charge or charges that come, of course, in the address. Such a command hardly ever comes by itself but rather in conjunction with another command or commands, a clear sign of the speaker's excitement and rapture. . . .

And sometimes several commands come in this way, as in:

> *Contend*, O Lord, with my contenders, / *Fight* those who fight me.
> *Take hold* of shield and buckler, / And *get up* to my aid.
> And *draw* your dagger and shut off, / In front of my pursuers.
> *Say* to my self: / Your salvation am I. (35:1–3)

David Yellin. *Ketavim nivḥarim*. Vol. II (Jerusalem,
David Yellin Jubilee Committee, 1959), pp. 1–4, 6–8†

If the word "poetry" is to evoke the idea of fantasy and unreality, the adjective "poetic" is unsuitable to qualify a language as factual as that of the Bible. But it is impossible to deny that Holy Writ has a true poetic sense, arising out of a spontaneous perception of movement and of life. For the Semitic genius is more easily inspired by the life and vitality of the universe than by the harmony of its forms and colours. One will here seek in vain colourful, romantic pages, inspired by the sight of a sunrise or sunset, a starry night or the moon rising over a dark mountain-top; nor will one hear the gentle murmur of a clear spring, or the rustle of forests. Ben Sira, for example, when evoking the sun, moon, stars and rainbow (Ecclus. 43:1–12), does not seem to discern any colour; he is unaware of hues or tonalities, perceives only violent contrasts; for him, everything shines and dazzles. As for the psalmist, he is reminded by the sunrise of an exulting runner who sees the track before him, or of a bridegroom coming from his bed in triumph; but of its majestic clearing of the horizon, the author retains nothing more than an impression of growing heat: "His going out is from the end of heaven. And his circuit even to the end thereof: and there is no one that can hide himself from his heat" (Ps. 18:7).

In nature, therefore, the sacred writers are sensitive only to movement. If they have any notion of a possible communion between the universe and the destiny of mankind, it is because they are aware of a common life and rhythm in both. So they will not waste time contemplating the harmony of forms, the splendour or the melancholy of outlines, but will derive their most frequent images from realities which move, change, are born and die: the wind bursting forth, the clouds scudding away, the fire burning up, the water flowing and swallowing up, the withered flower swept away by the storm: "Therefore they shall be as a morning cloud, and as the early dew that passeth away, as the dust that is driven with a whirlwind out of the floor, and as the smoke out of the chimney" (Hos. 13:3). So it is in the evocation of this vitality in things that the reader can discover the poetry of a new and powerful mode of expression; when, for example, he reads of the felled tree which "hath hope . . . If its root be old in the earth, and its stock be dead in the dust: at the scent of water, it shall spring, and bring forth leaves" (Job 14:8–9), or of a thread of tow scorched by fire (Judg. 16:9).

The originality of this poetic sense, compared with our own, is evident in many details. For example, it will be noted that though we may use the same metaphors, we do not attribute exactly the same significance to them. We refer to the "break" of dawn as to a phenomenon which is worthy of retaining our attention by the variable play of its colours—the famous "rosy-fingered dawn"—whereas the prophet will be aware only of the coming invasion of light: "A numerous and strong people as the morning spread among the mountains" (Joel 2:2). And whereas, for us, a shadow suggests the image of a vague presence, the Bible envisages it as the image of something which flees without ever pausing in one place, something after which one runs in vain, something which goes on ahead, with no chance of turning back save by special intervention of God (II Kgs. 20:10–11); it appears here as a "fugitive shadow," whilst for us it is rather a "faint shadow." It is quite understandable that some translators of the Bible should have been mistaken in the matter, as when the original Crampon Bible reads: "*Et tous mes membres ne sont plus qu'une ombre*" ["And all my limbs are no more than a shadow"] (Job 17:7)—a reminiscence, perhaps, of the line of Horace: "*pulvis et umbra sumus*" ["we are dust and shadow (ashes)"]—instead of: "My limbs are vanishing like a shadow."

Evode Beaucamp. *The Bible and the Universe* (London,
Burns and Oates, 1963), pp. 152–54

To speak of "poetry" at all in the Bible will be in some measure to impose a concept foreign to the biblical world. Obviously, there is some ground for this imposition: we have a notion of what poetry's thematic, generic, and organizational characteristics are, and . . . there is a case to be made for the use of the term "poetry" in regard to some parts of the Bible. It has, as noted, an approximate validity, and is sanctioned by a centuries-old tradition. But it is not a perfect fit; and since ancient Israel seems to have gotten along without any corresponding term, it might be better for modern critics to enclose the phrase "biblical poetry," at least mentally, in quotation marks. . . .

In sum, what is called biblical "poetry" is a complex of heightening effects used in combinations and intensities that vary widely from composition to composition even within a single "genre." No great service is rendered here by the concept of biblical poetry, since that term will, if based on the various heightening features seen, include compositions whose genre and subject are most unpoetic by Western standards, and since it will imply a structural regularity and design that are simply not there. The extremes of heightened and unheightened speech in the Bible are visible enough. But the "middle ground" between these extremes is important, and will forever elude a biblical critic equipped only to recognize the maximum of heightening or its total absence. Moreover, such an approach appears to be unfaithful to the Bible's own rhetorical scheme of things. Biblical authors were certainly aware of heightening features, but (judging by the texts themselves) they did not see them as requirements to be applied in prescribed strengths for particular genres and rigorously avoided for others.

> James L. Kugel. *The Idea of Biblical Poetry: Parallelism and Its History* (New Haven, Conn., Yale University Press, 1981), pp. 69, 86, 94

As I read with care not only [James L.] Kugel's work [*The Idea of Biblical Poetry*, 1981] but others and lay them alongside the texts, what is missing in their contributions is a more extended focus on the figurative dimension of poetry. There is considerable confusion in use of terminology, but what I have in mind are more the figures of thought, such as simile, metaphor, personification, metonymy, merismus, and synecdoche, to name the most prominent. This is not a subject that has failed to receive attention in the history of the study of biblical poetry, as Kugel has noted along the way. It certainly was a central concern to Herder, although his treatment is highly unsystematic. And while Robert Lowth's *Lectures on Sacred Poetry* have become a famous classic because of his presentation of parallelism, few remember or note that he began his series with a number of lectures on figurative style with some cogent and continuingly useful analyses of metaphor, allegory, personification, and simile. Our contemporary focus on formal characteristics, figures of speech more than figures of thought, and parallelism has served to obscure the role of figures in biblical poetry. Parallelism is a trope or a figure of speech. Indeed, I would concur with Kugel in describing it as *the* trope and certainly the one most characteristic of or definitive for Hebrew poetry. But is is by no means the only one, and neither aesthetic nor didactic concerns can fail to take into account the role played by other tropes. Here is where one explores the common ground between biblical and other poetry. Northrop Frye speaks of poetry as "a conscious and deliberate use of figures" (*The Great Code* . . . 1982, p. 23) and recently suggested that we "have to consider the possibility that metaphor is not an incidental ornament of biblical language, but one of its controlling modes of thought" (p. 54). One cannot read a Psalm without being literally struck figuratively. To take the one that is before me, Psalm 49, it revolves around the repeated simile that human beings are like the beasts that perish. But the force of that theme is carried even more by other figures: "their graves (Septuagint, Syriac versions) are their homes forever" (v. 12); "like sheep they are set for Sheol; death shepherds them" (v. 15). Or one is confronted, for example in the "Songs of Ascents," with extended similes and metaphors in almost every poem that evoke both emotive and cognitive responses (see 124:1–8; 125:1–2; 126:4–6 127:4–5a; 129:2–7; 131:2; 133: 1–3). The famous Day of Yahweh speech in Amos 5:18–20 conveys its word and its power entirely by the contrast of light and the extended simile of the man who escapes one terrible threat after another only to be done in when he thought himself safe and secure at home.

One could go on indefinitely with illustrations, but that is not really necessary. What I am suggesting is the need for a focus once again on the figures as a major aspect of poetic style. I expect there is some important work to be done not only on the figurative style of individual poems but also by way of classification and analysis of the figures of thought in biblical poetry as a whole or particular blocks of that whole.

> Patrick D. Miller. *Journal for the Study of the Old Testament*. Feb., 1984, pp. 103–4

Poetry and Prose. *See* Prose and Poetry

Point of View. *See* Narrator: Point of view

PROSE AND POETRY

[In the Bible] we have no nonprose texts except for three books: Psalms, Job, and Proverbs. And even these books, as you can see, have neither meter nor rhyme, as in Arabic style. . . . Nevertheless, in a few places there are rhymes, as in: "It cannot be valued with the gold of Ophir (*'ofir*), nor with the precious onyx or sapphire (*vesappir*)" [Job 28:16]; "To turn man from an act (*ma'aseh*), and pride from a man to hide (*yekhasseh*)" [Job 33:17]; "As for me, against a mortal is my complaint (*sihi*); should I not be short of patience (*ruhi*)?" [Job 21:4]. And so on. A few of the songs in the rest of the holy books are also nonprose, as in "Then sang Moses" [Exod. 15], "Give-ear, O heaven" [Deut. 32], "David said" [II Sam. 22], "Deborah sang" [Judg. 5]. I deliberately said "a few of the songs" because there are also prose expressions that are called songs, like the Song of Songs and the Song of the Well [Num. 21:17] and others like them. . . . Rabbinic scholars found the number of these songs to be nine, and most of them in prose. Already the Bible itself has testified that Solomon the Wise, may he rest in peace, composed songs in meter and in prose, which are the proverbs: "He spoke three thousand proverbs" (which are prose) "and his song was five and a thousand" (which are metrical songs) [I Kgs. 5:12]. [ca. 1135]

Moses ibn Ezra. *Shirat Yisra'el*. Tr. from the Arabic by Ben-Zion Halper (Leipzig, Abraham Joseph Stybel Publishing, 1924), p. 57†

The Book of Deuteronomy will afford us a convenient instance; for Moses appears there in the character both of an orator and a poet. In the former character, he addresses a very solemn and interesting oration to the people of Israel (chs. 28, 29, 30, 31), exhorting them, by the most inviting promises, to the observance of the covenant, and dissuading them from the violation of it by threats of the most exemplary punishment: and for the purpose of impressing the same more forcibly on their minds, he afterwards, by the command of God, embellishes the subject with all the elegance of verse (ch. 32), in a poem, which bears every mark of divine inspiration. In these two passages is displayed every excellence of which the Hebrew language is capable in both species of composition; all that is grand, forcible, and majestic, boh in prose and verse: From them too we may be enabled easily to comprehend the difference between the style of oratory among the Hebrews, and that of their poetry, not only in sentiment, but in the imagery, the arrangement, and the language. Whoever wishes, therefore, to satisfy himself concerning the true character and genius of the Hebrew poetry, I would advise carefully to compare the two passages, and I think he will soon discover that the former, though great, spirited, and abounding with ornament, is notwithstanding regular, copious, and diffuse; that, with all its vehemence and impetuosity, it still preserves a smoothness, evenness, and uniformity throughout; and that the latter, on the contrary, consists of sentences, pointed, energetic, concise, and splendid; that the sentiments are truly elevated and sublime, the language bright and animated, the expression and phraseology uncommon; while the mind of the poet never continues fixed to any single point, but glances continually from one subject to another. [1753]

Robert Lowth. *Lectures on the Sacred Poetry of the Hebrews*. Vol. I. Tr. from the Latin by G. Gregory (London, Printed for J. Johnson, 1787), pp. 324–25

That poetry was an art with which the earliest inhabitants of the earth were familiar, may be gathered from the fact, that in the fourth chapter of Genesis, Lamech, the father of Jubal, addresses his wives in verse, the twenty-third and twenty-fourth divisions of that chapter comprising a certain number of hemistichs, or broken verses, so artificially disposed as to produce a clear metrical rhythm, which is, to a certain extent, conveyed in our authorized translation of the Hebrew scriptures. It is the earliest specimen of Hebrew poetry extant. How Moses received it, whether from oral tradition, or from documentary authority, is a matter of no moment. It is sufficient that he has recorded it, and the internal evidence which it bears of being an original fragment of antediluvian poetry, seems to have satisfied all reasonable inquirers. Bishop Jebb, indeed, questions the existence of Hebrew metres, but with all due deference to so respectable a name, the whole structure of the poetical portions of the inspired volume, that is of those portions generally assumed to be poetical, is at once so obviously constructive and artificial, so obedient to certain given laws of composition, that it is impossible not to perceive a distinction so decidedly marked and broad between them and the prose portions as almost to admit of a direct contrast. Let any one, for instance, read the short introduction to the first chapter of Isaiah's prophecies, contained in the first verse of that chapter, according to the division of our English version; let him then proceed to the second verse, and he will be immediately conscious that he has passed from prose to poetry. He cannot fail to perceive quite a different order in the structure of the phraseology; he will, in short, be sensible of the presence of translated verse.

John Hobart Caunter. *The Poetry of the Pentateuch.*
Vol. I (London, E. Churton, 1839), pp. 8–9

Now in Tractate *Nedarim* [of the Babylonian Talmud], page 38, [the statement] "Write yourselves the song *shira*" [Deut. 31:19] has been raised in connection with interpreting the Bible, that it [means] the entire Torah. Evidence is adduced from the end of the verse, "so that this song will be mine as a witness." It is necessary to understand, though, how the entire Torah could be called song [or poetry] when it has not been written in the language of song. Nonetheless, it has the nature and peculiar quality of poetry, that is, discourse in figurative language. For it is known to every intelligent student that poetry is distinguished from prose narrative in two matters, in its nature and in its peculiar quality. (1) In song the subject matter is not clarified as well as in prose narrative, and it is necessary to make annotations on the side that this line refers to this story and that line refers to that story. . . . Such is the nature of the entire Torah, in which no narrative is well clarified, but it is necessary to make annotations and commentaries to explain the language. . . . (2) Song has the peculiar quality of ornamenting with allusions what is not of the song's subject matter, just as it is customary to make the line openings follow the alphabet or the name of the author. This peculiar quality is distinctive of poetry and not of prose narrative. And it is known that this peculiar quality often compels the author almost to twist the language just so that the line openings will begin with the requisite letter. Now this is actually throughout the entire Torah, that in addition to the subject spoken of in the biblical context, each matter also has many secrets and themes hidden, so that the Bible is often in language that is not very precise. And all this is true not only of the holy Torah but of all the holy scriptures.

> Naphtali Zevi Judah Berlin. *Ha'ameq davar.* Vol. I (Vilna, Romm, 1879–80), p. ii†

In none of the great literatures of the world is there so close an intermingling of poetry and prose as in the special literature we call the Bible; and this whether we use the words in the popular usage which confuses "poetry" and "verse," or in the more correct sense as discriminating creative literature and critical. The rhythmic system of Hebrew scripture is peculiar from its overlapping of verse and prose. Old Testament history is an alternation of history and story: the stories are, rhythmically, prose, but they none the less correspond to the epic poetry of other peoples. The books of the prophets are miscellanies of prose and verse; and scriptural philosophy has distinctiveness largely from the way in which it poises itself evenly between the functions of poetry and prose. The only reason then for such a title as Bible Poetry is that three books of Scripture stand apart from the rest of the Old Testament in not falling under its divisions of history, prophecy, and wisdom. The three are the Book of Psalms, the work traditionally known as the Lamentations of Jeremiah, and the single relic of sacred love poetry that has come down to us as Solomon's Song. There is, however, no other point in common between the three except that they are poetry.

> Richard G. Moulton. *The Modern Reader's Bible* (New York, Macmillan, 1907), pp. 1430–31.

The interplay of biblical prose and poetry is one of the most vexing questions to Old Testament investigators. The two literary forms interweave in almost all parts of biblical composition, particularly in the prophetical books. It has been difficult to set the limits to poetry, while recent students in biblical prose have complicated the problem still more by designating the apparently prosaic narrative portions as poetry. Several investigators have escaped the issue by accepting the overlapping of Hebrew verse and prose as a standard biblical practice. [Richard G.] Moulton speaks of a middle region wherein poetry, distinguished by high parallelism, meets and interlocks with prose; the effect is a great stylistic gain in a combination of "the delight of freedom which is the spirit of prose with a sense of rhythm, which is the foundation of verse." George Adam Smith advocates the same principle, and quotes Professor [George] Saintsbury to prove the beauty of "the double appeal of poetry and rhetoric, the magical order of poetry, and the magical apparent freedom of rhetoric."

It is unsatisfactory, however, to adopt these general conclusions without a knowledge of their full implications. Is there a twilight zone wherein poetry and prose form a *mélange*? If so, where does poetry proper end, where does prose proper end, and what is the result of their blending? These questions can be answered in some measure only by a reëxamination of the exact data present in the books of the Bible. For this purpose, the book of Amos has been chosen. It might perhaps be better to look into the didactic, the proverbial poetry, or into an epic, the Book of Job, or into the Psalms. For the literary psychology of these works is relatively simple, whereas in the prophets countless problems of vague and apparently insoluble character arise. But research in the book of Amos will at least have the merit of grappling with a double problem: first, the interrelation between prose and poetry in Hebrew literature as a whole, and second, their interplay under the influence of the unique forces of prophecy.

The method of study into the prose, the poetry, and the *mélange* of both in Amos will proceed from the known to the unknown. The cases of indubitable prose in Amos will first be stated; the instances of clear poetry next; the third category will comprise the delicate shades of intermixture, and an attempt will be made to extract therefrom general conclusions on the process of interplay. . . .

The following conclusions with respect to the two problems referred to above can thus be drawn:

Sheer prose in Amos is very rare, the only two pieces which maintain it over any stretch being the superscription and a doubtful narrative portion.

Genuine parallelistic stichoi predominate, being found to the extent of nearly five-sixths of the instances. Between these two poles there are many grades of poetry verging into prose by ascending degrees. The so-called synthetic couplets contain clear stichoi in a rhythmical, symmetrical, but non-correspondent relationship. Doubtful synthetic couplets embrace those in a rhythmical arrangement wherein the text is doubtful, and at times the degree of unity of thought between the two stichoi is weak. Several special forms, relative, conjunctival, and quotational, fall within this category; they are undoubtedly poetical but have lost their parallelism.

The twilight zone between prose and poetry contains various shades of parallelism and non-parallelism. Traditional conventional phrases are grouped in rhythmical couplets wherein synonymity is lacking; simile couplets are employed, headed in one stichos by the conjunction "just as," wherein a prosaic style is noticeable; a mixture of prose and parallelistic poetry is found in rare instances. Finally close to prose, is a *saj'* form which either occurs without synonymity but with a certain rhythmical balance; or, as in the Arabic, is marked by synonymity and fairly close correspondence of terms. All these lines are long; some are a form and an outgrowth of alternate parallelism. These are fruitful examples for an investigation into the rhythmical principles back of Hebrew poetry and prose. It would seem also from the synonymous and correspondent character of the *saj'* illustrations that parallelism marks not merely the terse bona fide poetry, but also the near-prose of Hebrew.

Louis I. Newman and William Popper. *Studies in Biblical Parallelism* (Berkeley, University of California Press, 1918), pp. 80–81, 206

The Hebrew literary artist had his prose and he had his poetry; he was a refined and creative artist in both and each was quite distinct from the other. Further, his range in prose was wider than in song; in prose he could put before us real persons who were not himself but who are as real as any in Homer or Shakespeare. He created Abraham; he created Jonah; and these are individual persons. What, then, is the essential difference between Hebrew prose and Hebrew poetry? It is emotion and the emotion always goes with song. The sequence appears to be this: The Hebrew artist can tell a story straight and clear in prose; his brain is cold; he can think about his creation and develop it and shape it. It may be a creation of pathos or of terror, of repentance or of joy, but, so long as it is not the poet's pathos, repentance, terror, joy, he creates in prose and his creation is not himself. But should his brain be fired by the situation in which his character is and his own emotion roused; should he feel this situation as his own; then the thread of narrative breaks; he bursts into song; he and his character melt together and for that moment he can render only himself, how he felt and reacted to it all. It may be that after his outburst he will recover his self-possession and resume his narrative, but it will be in prose. . . .

In all Semitic song, which means all Semitic poetry, narrative is impossible. This does not mean that Semitic narrative cannot be artistic; the stories in the Old Testament are handled with consummate art. In truth, in Hebrew prose there is more art in the narrower sense of conscious handling and development of form than in Hebrew poetry, for the emotion of the poet—always a singer—prevents such calm elaboration.

Duncan B. MacDonald. *The Hebrew Literary Genius* (Princeton, N.J., Princeton University Press, 1933), pp. 21–22

In the beginning there really was no difference between poetry and prose in the beginning of writing in the beginning of talking in the beginning of hearing anything or about anything. How could there be how could there have been since the name of anything was then as important as anything that could be said about anything. Once more I tell you that the Old Testament did this thing there was not really any difference between prose and poetry then, they felt what they were and they felt what they saw and they knew how they knew and anything they had to say came as it had to come to do what it had to do. Really can you say that there was any difference between prose and poetry then. No not at all. Not then.

Gertrude Stein. *Narration: Four Lectures* (Chicago, University of Chicago Press, 1935), p. 27

Like all literature, the literature of the Bible divides into two major types: (1) poetry, speech and writing in metaphorical language, ordered by fixed rules of artistic meter and rhythm; (2) prose, speech and writing in plain and free language that is not subject to rules of artistic rhythm. In the literature of the Bible, however, even less than in other literature, there is no absolute dichotomy between these two types. Rapture and emotion, which are the source of poetic rhythm, can arise in prose discourse, too, and then even prose tends to ascend to and approach the form of poetry. The language of such sublime prose is elevated above the plain language of normal discourse and becomes metaphorical and imagistic like the language of poetry. The construction of an utterance of such prose becomes more ordered in the arrangement of its parts. The parts of the utterance are made short, and they are joined one to the other according to a certain rhythm, according to a certain flow of movement in meter, something like the peculiar rhythm of poetry. We call such prose "rhythmic prose" or "measured prose."

Measured prose constitutes almost the majority of biblical prose. Examples of it are found abundantly in all the books of the Bible. For example:

> Why are you enraged, and why has your face fallen? For if you do well, honor; but if you do not do well, sin crouches at the door, and toward you will be his desire, but you will rule over him (Gen. 4:6–7).

> If you will regard, regard the affliction of your maidservant, and pay mind to me and not neglect your maidservant, and give to your maidservant seed of men, then I will give him to the Lord all the days of his life, and a razor will not go up onto his head (I Sam. 1:11).

> Seraphim stand above him, six wings to each one, with two will one cover one's face, and with two will one cover one's legs, and with two will one fly (Isa. 6:2).

> It was, when the days of banquet came to a close, Job sent (word to his children) and sanctified them, he got up early in the morning, and he offered offerings for all of them, for Job thought, perhaps my children have sinned, and cursed [lit., blessed] God in their heart; so would Job do every year (Job 1:5).

The reason for this ceremonial rhythm in Biblical prose lies mainly in the spirit of holiness and the sublimity that permeate the words of the Bible, flowing from a perpetual sense of God's presence and of his providence over all human activity. Rhythmic construction conforms well to the peculiar style of ancient Hebrew (and ancient Semitic in general) and to its syntactic features. The sentence in ancient Hebrew is very concise, and the parts of an utterance are joined one to the other through a juncture of stitching and continuity by means of the connective *waw*, and not by a juncture of subordination by means of prepositions and conjunctions, as in [modern] Hebrew and other languages.

M. H. Segal. *Mevo' hammiqra'*. Vol. I (Jerusalem, Kiryat Sepher, 1967), pp. 35–36†

The Bible generally makes a very clear distinction between poetry and prose. Accordingly, the rapid reader grows accustomed to the features that characterize biblical poetry, having a sense of them even when he cannot define them. Examination enables us to attain precise definitions of the substantive and stylistic features of this poetry (poetry in the sense of elevated speech . . .). Indeed, the substantive character of the poetry of the Bible is best given a negative definition: This poetry never narrates. Its two preeminent domains are the expression of religious feelings (the Psalms) and the expression of wisdom ideas (Proverbs, Job). Blessings and curses, laments and love songs (Song of Songs) are considered the domain of poetry. Most prophetic oracles are formulated in poetic language, but not all of them (the speeches of Deuteronomy are formulated in a highly developed rhetorical prose). The absence of narrative poetry (epic) is especially evident in those poetic chapters in which there is a description of events (the Song at the Sea [Exod. 15]; the Song of Deborah [Judg. 5]; Ps. 78, 105, 106, 114). The description highlights the significance of the events, their religious and emotional value, it praises and it derogates, but it does not narrate the action in sequence, how what happened happened. The description nearest to a poetic narrative is the admonition against the wiles of the adulterous woman (Prov. 7), yet even it is subordinated to the didactic-wisdom framework. . . .

Biblical poetry is rich in figurative language (similes, metaphors, poetic symbols) and tends toward hyperbole ("I soak my couch with my tears"; Ps. 6:7)—in contrast to biblical prose, which is restricted for the most part to descriptions and expressions of feeling. Also, a rather large number of words, common in poetry but not in prose, endows the poetry with its stylistic singularity (*dagan, tirosh weyitshar* ["grain, wine, and oil"]; *'enosh* ["man"]; *gever* ["man"] [in prose only in contrast to woman, in poetry in the sense of *'ish, ben-'adam* ("man")]; *'orah* ["path"], *dor-wador* [= *'olam* ("eternity")]; *shahat* ["pit"]; *shehaqim* ["sky"]; and more). Similarly, you find a few grammatical forms whose usage is distinctively poetic, such as *'alei-deshe'* (instead of *'al haddeshe'* ["on the grass"]; Deut. 32:2); *zevahemo* [for *zivhehem* "their sacrifices"] (Deut. 32:38). It is likely that the usage of such forms derives from the needs of the meter . . .; in any case it is clear that parallelism . . . led to a swelling of the poetic lexicon, as it obliges the poets to utilize linguistic substitutions to a large degree. This need also influenced the shaping of poetic tropes, the crystallization of word pairs in particular. By way of example, the words *mishpat* ["justice"] and *tsedaqa* ["righteousness"] routinely occur in conjunction or in parallelism with each other. Parallelism is the most outstanding stylistic phenomenon in Biblical poetry, and it requires separate discussion.

Israel Yeivin. *'Entsiqlopedya miqra'it*. Vol. VII. Ed. by Benjamin Mazar et al. (Jerusalem, Bialik Institute, 1976), cols. 638–39†

The regularity perceivable in some parts of the Bible ought not automatically to be identified as poetic. For in using this term, biblical critics have unconsciously assumed something about the Bible (and, more recently, about parallelism) that, on inspection, will simply not hold true. There is in the Bible no regularizing of a consistency comparable to those familiar to us from Western poetics. Parallelism, or even seconding, is slightly less than consistent: it is a frequent, but not infallibly present (or absent) form of heightening adaptable to a wide variety of genres. The equation parallelism = poetry has led critics both to overlook parallelism in "unpoetic" places—in laws, cultic procedures, and so forth, and especially in *single lines* that come to punctuate, emphasize, or sum up less formally organized discourse; and, on the other hand, to attribute to biblical parallelism a consistency it lacks. . . .

If one puts aside the notions of biblical poetry and prose and tries to look afresh at different parts of the Bible to see what it is about them that distinguishes one from another, it will soon be apparent that there are not two modes of utterance, but many different elements which elevate style and provide for formality and strictness of organization. Consistently binary sentences, an obvious regard for terseness, and a high degree of semantic parallelism characterize some sections; less consistent (and less consistently semantic) parallelism is found in other parts; some narrative sections (as we have seen above) are basically built of short, simple clauses but lack correspondences between them; still others show little regularity in clause length and sentence structure. This represents a continuum of organization or formality, with parallelism of different intensity and consistency characterizing a great span of texts.

It may strike the reader as perverse to refuse simply to call the relative concentration of heightening factors "poetry" and their relative absence "prose." But the burden of proof falls on the other side. For the distinction between "poetry" and "prose" is, as noted, not native to the texts; it is a Hellenistic imposition based, at least originally, on the faulty notion that parts of the Bible were metrical (indeed, written in Greek-style hexameter and trimeter!). Although this original basis now seems absurd, the idea it supported has remained; and, like so many Hellenisms—for example, the equation of Hebrew *torah* ["teaching"] with Greek *nomos* ["law"]—it is only approximately true. To see biblical style through the split lens of prose or poetry is to distort the view; then even an awareness of parallelism will not much improve things, for it too will be distorted in the process. . . .

Of course, there is a case to be made for the use of the term "poetry" in regard to some parts of the Bible. It has, as noted, an approximate validity, and is sanctioned by a centuries-old tradition. But it is not a perfect fit; and since ancient Israel seems to have gotten along without any corresponding term, it might be better for modern critics to enclose the phrase "biblical poetry," at least mentally, in quotation marks. Indeed, as far as the study of biblical style is concerned, it might well have been better if Robert Lowth had chosen differently and declared *parallelismus membrorum* [parallelism of clauses] to be (as in Greek) a feature of prose style, that is, claimed (as some of his Jewish predecessors had) that poetry in ancient Hebrew simply does not exist. For he then would have been left free to observe different levels and intensities of parallel structure, and observe it not just where he felt "poetry" ought to be found, but throughout the Bible. And it would then have been clear that this biblical "prose," that is, "common speech on its best behavior," consists not (as in English) in the judicious arrangement of long and short sentences, the employment of familiar motifs of subordination, and so forth, but in variations on an ideal form _____/_____ //, variations whose formality, whose "structuredness," increases with the intensity of the correspondence established between the clauses. Although the term "prose" has its own disadvantages, its use would have at least clarified this one main point: passages are not either written "in parallelism" or "not in parallelism," but they are elevated with respect to the frequency and intensity of this idealized norm.

James L. Kugel. The Idea of Biblical Poetry (New Haven, Yale University Press, 1981), pp. 70, 85–87

There are several interdependent markers for poetry and prose—or rather the poetic and prosaic ends of the continuum—all of which indicate the presence, to a greater or lesser extent, of the poetic function, and the orientation towards a particular mode of reality. They are best listed summarily, so as not to isolate them from each other:

i. The sense of time in the work. Prose presupposes sequential time, e.g., history, or law, which is potential history; poetry concerns timelessness, time as recurrent pattern and stillness, in which past and future are present through dream and recollection.

ii. Prose preserves an often ironic objective distance between the writer, his audience, and his subject-matter. For example, the biblical narrator presents events as they happened, events that do not ostensibly concern him, to us who are inconceivably distant; in appearance at least, the events speak for themselves. In poetry, there is a communion between the singer and the audience, what happens is experienced timelessly, in the words of the song. It is more personal than prose, expressing the feelings and sensations of the poet (e.g. in the Psalms, or through his personae in the Song of Songs), and inviting their sympathetic adoption by the audience. Then, in determining the nature of what we are reading, we look to (a) how it establishes its sense of time, and (b) the dramatic frame of reference.

iii. Prose accordingly represents everyday life, activities, and speech: the life of sequential time and the subjective ego, differentiated from others in a common consciousness, the life which is regulated by law and from which narrative emerges; poetry is the language of liminal situations, of Job amid dust and ashes, or the enclosed garden of lovers, and, in particular, of ritual speech, when the boundaries of the ego are blurred, and which mediate between life and death, the ordinary and the sacred, timelessness and time. Thus we must also look to the *context*.

iv. Prose perceives the world through relations of contiguity, temporal and spatial, i.e. metonymy; poetry expresses it metaphorically, through relations of likeness and difference, and ultimately seeks the unity of phenomena, e.g. the recurrence of identical moments, the song of all the creatures.

Francis Landy. Journal for the Study of the Old Testament. Feb., 1984, pp. 71–72

PROSODY

Where is [Biblical Hebrew's] pre-eminence? Other languages surpass it in songs metrically constructed and arranged for tunes.

. . . The Rabbi [answers]: It is obvious that a tune is independent of the metre, or of the lesser or greater number of syllables. The verso *hodu la'donai ki ṭov* ["Praise the Lord for he is good"; Ps. 136:1] can, therefore, be sung to the same tune as *le'osei nifla'ot gedolot levaddo* ["To the one who alone does great wonders", ibid.: 4]. This is the rule in sentences in which the tune must follow the grammatical construction. Rhymed poems, however, which are recited, and in which a good metre is noticeable, are neglected for something higher and more useful. [c. 1135]

> Judah Halevi. *Kitab al Khazari*. Ed. and tr. by Hartwig Hirschfeld (New York, Bernard G. Richards, 1927), p. 125

Although many attempts have been made, without success, to restore the Hebrew metre, which is denied by some learned men to exist in the sacred scriptures, there can be little doubt that the writers of those scriptures possessed a prosody, and were well acquainted with the canons of versification. The peculiar artifices which they employed to impart beauty, and add force to their compositions, were so consonant to the laws of verse, that we cannot disassociate them, without immediately destroying the symmetry of the passages in which they are found. The acrostic, or alphabetical form, of some of the Psalms, and of the chapters of the Lamentations of Jeremiah, except the last, show, beyond a doubt, that the Hebrew poets possessed a system of versification. These poems, among which I may mention the twenty-fifth, the thirty-fourth, the hundred and eleventh, the hundred and twelfth, the hundred and nineteenth, and the hundred and forty-fifth Psalms, clearly, to my apprehension, establish the fact, that the Hebrews were acquainted with the laws of metre. This, I think, will be admitted, if we consider the peculiarly artificial form of these poems, and of some others less perfectly acrostic, but nevertheless of the same character, in which only every stanza is distinguished by its initial letter; whereas, in the first two psalms above named, every line is so distinguished. The structure of the alphabetical poems is as follows. They consist of the same number of periods as the Hebrew alphabet, namely, twenty-two, every period forming a short stanza, the sense being completed in each period. Every line of the stanza commences with its initial letter, each consecutive stanza following the order of the Hebrew alphabet; and although, as [Johann David] Michaelis truly remarks, these poems, generally, are very much beneath the sublimity of the great mass of Hebrew poetry, they nevertheless, more than any portion of it, serve to indicate the existence of Hebrew verse.

> John Hobart Caunter. *The Poetry of the Pentateuch*. Vol. I (London, E. Churton, 1839), pp. 24–25

It is easy to see how question and answer, strophe and antistrophe, are simply a development and division out of the crowd with one voice, as in the Greek chorus. So, too, in an Assyrian hymn:—

> Who is sublime in the skies?
> Thou alone, thou art sublime.
> Who is sublime upon earth?
> Thou alone, thou art sublime.

The Hebrew psalms show very clearly a more or less artistic use of the refrain sung under congregational and therefore to some extent communal conditions. These communal conditions can be guessed in their older and simpler form from such an account as is given of David and his dancing before the ark when he "and all the house of Israel brought up the ark of the Lord with shouting and with the sound of the trumpet": the personal song detached itself from the rhythmic shouts of the dancing or marching multitude precisely as the song of the wife and sister over their dead came out clearer and clearer from the wailings of the clan. So, if D. H. Müller [19th-century orientalist] be right, following in the path marked by [Bishop] Lowth, the form of Hebrew prophecy was at first choral, then was divided into strophe and antistrophe, yielding in time to an impressioned solo of the prophet himself. In any case, this single prophet, in historical perspective, lapses into the throng, into those "prophetic hordes" which [the German Old Testament scholar Karl] Budde compares with modern Dervishes, "raving bands" now forgotten or dimly seen in the background of a stage where noble individuals like Amos, still in close touch with the people, play the chief part, and hold the conspicuous place. As Amos and his brother prophets yield to the later guild whose prophecies were written, so one goes behind Amos to the "bands," to communal prophecy, to the repeated shouts and choral exhortation, and so to the festal horde of all early religious rites. The backward course would be from a prophecy written to be read, to the chanted blessing or imprecation of the seer; thence to a singing and shouting band under the leadership of one man, with constant refrain; and at last to the shouting and dancing of purely communal excitement, the real chorus. Moses and the children of Israel "sang a song unto the Lord, saying, I will sing unto the Lord. . . . And Miriam the prophetess . . . took a timbrel in her hand, and all the women went out after her with timbrels and with dances. And Miriam *answered* them, "Sing ye to the Lord." Here is certainly no premeditated verse; and it must be borne in mind that refrains, except where they have a sacred tradition behind them and are kept up by the priests, as in the Arval "minutes," easily drop from the record. Oral tradition, on the other hand, is fain to hold fast to all these vain repetitions; they are the salt of the thing. Now and then an unmistakable refrain is preserved. "And it came to pass as they came, when David returned from the slaughter of the Phillistines, that the women came out of all the cities of Israel, *singing and dancing*, to meet King Saul, with timbrels, with joy, and with instruments of music. *And the women sang one to another in their play*, and said:—'Saul hath slain his thousands, /

And David his tens of thousands.'" [I Sam. 18:6–7] That women in all nations and at certain stages of culture make songs of triumph like this, as they dance and sing, is known to the most careless reader; one or two chorals, strangely similar to these songs of the Hebrew women, may be noted from mediaeval Europe. Now it is the singing of Gothic songs of welcome by those maidens who come from their village, as the women of Israel from their cities, to meet and greet Attila, dancing as they sing. So the daughter of Jephtha greeted her sire with the singing and dancing maidens; and so in Cashmere a stranger is still met by the women and girls of a village, who form a half circle at the first house where he comes, join their arms, and sing eulogies of him, dancing to the tune of the verse. Malays and even Africans do the same.

Francis B. Gummere. The Beginnings of Poetry (New York, Macmillan, 1901), pp. 261–64

The main forms of Hebrew poetry are two—parallelism and rhythm, to which, as a third and occasional form, we may add strophe. Rhyme, so common in many languages, and a constant and necessary form of all strictly metrical poetry in Arabic, as well as a characteristic of that other type of composition in Arabic known as *saj'* ("rhymed prose"), is in Hebrew, as in Assyrian, merely occasional. Curiously enough it is conspicuous in one of the earliest existing fragments of Hebrew poetry, the song of Lamech (Gen. 4:23, 24), and yet it never developed into a form of Hebrew poetry till poetry of the Old Testament, or parallelistic, type had long become extinct, and there came, under the influence of the Moslem culture and Arabic poetry, a renascence of Hebrew poetry in the Middle Ages.

Of the two main forms of Hebrew poetry, parallelism and rhythm, parallelism is most intimately associated with the sense, and can and should be represented in translation. In its broader aspects and general differences of types it was analysed once for all by [Bishop] Lowth: but a more accurate and detailed measurement of parallelism is required. Such a more exact measurement of parallelism enables us more readily to classify actual differences in different poems and different writers; and in particular to disentangle the very different types of incomplete parallelisms and merely parallelistic distichs grouped by Lowth under the single term "synthetic parallelism." A study, more especially of the different incomplete parallelisms, also affords an opportunity of watching the intimate connexion between parallelism and at least a certain approximation to rhythm.

Merely judged from the standpoint of parallelism, rhythms fall into the two broad classes of balancing and echoing rhythms. Further metrical analysis is in detail frequently most uncertain: but while recognising this uncertainty, it is important, in order to avoid confusion, to adopt a method of measurement that is capable of giving us a clear and sufficient nomenclature. This is to be found in defining lines or distichs by the number of the stressed syllables in them. The exact number of unstressed syllables that may accompany a stressed syllable may be uncertain, but is certainly not unlimited.

A single rhythm need not be maintained throughout a poem, though there were probably limits to the degree of mixture that was tolerated. But in particular the elegy, though it commonly consisted of 3:2 distichs, was not limited to these: it certainly admitted along with these in the same poem 2:2. Mere change from a longer to a shorter distich of the same class, or even occasionally from a balancing to an echoing rhythm, is no conclusive evidence, and in many poems (for poems differ in the degree to which they are regular) is scarcely even a ground for suspecting corruption of text or change of source. On the other hand, a change in the dominant rhythm should raise a question whether or not a new poem has begun.

Finally the question remains whether, though parallelism in Hebrew seems commonly to have concurred with certain rhythmical forms, it may not in some cases, as in the Arabic *saj'*, have been used in a freer style more closely allied to ordinary prose.

George B. Gray. *The Forms of Hebrew Poetry* (London, Hodder & Stoughton, 1915), pp. 236–39

In theory one distinguishes five basic rhythms as one considers in analysis their number (isosyllabic or arithmetic), their duration (prosodic or quantitative rhythm), their pitch (rhythm of isolated languages of the Far East), their timbre (rhyme, assonance), and finally their intensity (tonic rhythm). More or less associated in the various poetic forms, one or the other predominates according to the peculiar nature of each idiom and the will of the poet. Some believe they have recovered in Hebrew poetry an isosyllabic rhythm, others a prosodic rhythm; but today there is nearly unanimous agreement in acknowledging that the fundamental rhythm of Hebrew poetry is a tonic rhythm determined by accent of intensity (ictus, arsis, *Hebung* [stress]); as it is the same in Assyro-Babylonian poetry and Ugaritic (Syro-Phoenician) poetry, one can say that such a rhythm is that of ancient Semitic poetry. This rhythm is, moreover, natural and universally more widespread than the rhythm of timbre (rhyme) with which it is often associated, seldom, however, in Israel.

It comprises two types, of the same nature: binary rhythm (cf. heartbeat, marching) and ternary rhythm (three phases of respiration). Binary rhythm seems to predominate in Mesopotamia (the poems of *Gilgamesh, Enuma Elish, Agushaya*, hymns to Ishtar, etc.) and in Egypt, while the ternary rhythm preponderates in the Ugaritic poems; both cadences are frequently attested in the Bible, but the second is much more utilized, above all in the didactic poetry of the *mashal* [proverb]; this fact, just as the constant law of *parallelismus membrorum*, attests to the kinship of the Syro-Phoenician and Israelite literatures, incidentally, if obviously. The ternary rhythm, as is known, is the most common in Greco-Latin poetry; the iambic trimeter, customary in Greek tragedy and reproducing the normal flow of conversation, can turn up in this cadence, while the hexameter, the meter of the epic of sacred humns from Homer to Vergil, corresponds to a certain extent to ternary Hebrew verse (3 + 3 accents), as Josephus (*Antiquae Judaicarum* II, 16; cf. IV, 8, 44) already said with respect to the song of Moses.

R. Tournay. *Revue Biblique.* July, 1946, pp. 349–51†

It is well known that the rejection of Greek lyric poetry in *Paradise Regain'd* (IV 331ff.) is not without precedent either in [John] Milton's own works or in earlier literature. There is, however, one aspect of the rejection which seems not to be generally understood; and here we may find a clue to the verse of the chorus in *Samson Agonistes*.

It will be remembered that Christ finds "All our Law and Story strew'd / With Hymns, our Psalms with artful terms inscrib'd" (IV. 334–35); he describes the Greek poetry as derivative from the Hebrew, and "unworthy to compare / With *Sion's* songs, to all true taste excelling, / Where God is prais'd aright, and Godlike men" (IV. 346–48). Milton refers to the passages in the Old Testament which were commonly, though not universally, supposed to have been written in verse, like Job, the Psalms, certain portions of Genesis, Deuteronomy, Isaiah and Jeremiah. The main interest was in Job and the Psalms, which latter were, as [Philip] Sidney said, "Fully written in meeter as all learned Hebricians agree, although the rules be not fully found" [*Defence of Poetry*. Vol. I. Ed. by Gregory Smith (1904), p. 155]. This opinion was often repeated and occasionally contested. But on one point all were agreed, that the Psalms were exceptionally rich in the figures of the poetic. It was sometimes suggested that the Psalter contained all the figures and tropes, but in any case it was not disputed that it was in this, as in all other respects, superior to pagan poetry, and specifically to Pindar's, with which it was most often compared. . . .

Samson Agonistes is of course Greek in structure, and Milton in his Epistle takes pains to harmonize this with the divine nature of his theme. But he disclaims any design to reproduce the characteristic structure of the Greek chorus. . . . Milton . . . tells us nothing whatsoever about the system of his choral verse except that it is not divided as the Greek tragedians divided theirs.

It has, I think, been generally assumed that he was imitating Greek measures in the choruses. . . . Instead of imitation Greek choruses he writes passages made up of lines various and irregular in length, exceedingly free in accent, and occasionally rhyming. And this was the practice also of the Psalmist and the author of Job, as some critics read them. Job, in particular, was obviously much in Milton's mind in his later years.

It is not a far step from *Paradise Regain'd* to the rejection of the Greek choral ode; Milton must have had Sophocles and especially Pindar in mind when he wrote the passage in *Paradise Regain'd*. . . . It is not unreasonable to propose that when, in his later poem, he had to write for a chorus he decided to provide it with non-Parnassian imitations of "*Sion's* songs, to all true tastes excelling."

Frank Kermode. Durham University Journal. Mar.,
1953, pp. 59–61

If serious study is required for grasping the correct rhythm of a psalm or a prophet's oration, an even greater effort must be made in the case of a narrative or a legal text. Even the legal style, which to us is the most prosaic of all prose, is in the Bible subject to rhythmical articulation. One takes, for example, the first strictly legal text found in the Pentateuch, Exodus 21, the old collection of *Mishpatim* (Laws). Its first section deals with manservants and maidservants.

If thou buy a Hebrew servant / six years shall he serve
and in the seventh—he shall go out free for nothing.
If he come in by himself, / he shall go out by himself,
but if he were a husband to a wife, / then shall his wife go out with him.

It is evident that the two main principles of Hebrew prosody—parallelism of meaning and an equal number of accentuations in the two parts of a sentence—are present in this ancient law. Only the arrangement is somewhat different, the basic rhythm being three stresses in each hemistich—if this word is permissible in speaking of a legal text—modified by interspersed parts with only two stresses. In the Hebrew original these rhythmic cadences are, of course, even more clearly audible.

S. D. Goitein. Judaism. Winter, 1954, p. 70

The good poets who employ free verse usually have a fundamental rhythmic unit in each poem, too, or vary the meter in each part in accordance with the content of the change in emotion (it is typical for "free verse" poems to be long; so, too, a long poem written in free verse or in blank eleven-syllable lines is more acceptable than one written in actual eight-line strophes). In other cases they seek special effects of rhythmic expansion and constriction, or these effects are imposed upon them by the development of concrete emotion.

In the case of Isaiah, we are confronted with long poems, composed of fragments that indicate changes of theme or aspect or emotion. We also encounter a poetic diction and a frequent use of parallelism in all its forms, which orients us toward poetic reading, that is to say, which invites us to attend to the rhythm as well.

On the other hand, the data for analysis do now allow us to obtain a uniform rhythm in every poem or section. For this reason it is not unjustified to call free verse "analogical."

Luis Alonso-Schökel. Estudios de poética hebrea
(Barcelona, Juan Flors, 1963), pp. 162–63†

Though including writings which range nearly over a millennium, the Bible has been viewed by later ages as primarily a unified work with basically a common language. Whatever may have been the developments in phonetics and prosody during the time of its creation, the Bible for post-biblical readers was the canonized text with its system of stresses, intonation marks, and vocalization. . . .

Parallelism. The foremost principle dominating biblical poetry is parallelism. Usually two versets (sometimes three or even four) are parallel to each other in one or several aspects. The parallelism may be either complete or partial; either of the verset as a whole or of each word in it: of words in the same order or reversed. It may be a parallelism of semantic, syntactic, prosodic, morphological, or sound elements, or of a combination of such elements. In most cases there is an overlapping of several such heterogeneous parallelisms with a mutual reinforcement so that no single element—meaning, syntax, or stress—may be considered as completely dominant or as purely concomitant. The parts of the parallelism may be equal or unequal in their size or form: they may be related to each other in a variety of ways: synonymous, antithetic, hierarchic, belonging to a category of some kind, etc. The principles of the parallelism used may change from verse to verse. The basis of this type of rhythm may be described as semantic-syntactic-accentual. It is basically a free rhythm, i.e., a rhythm based on a cluster of changing principles. Its freedom, however, is clearly confined within the limits of its poetics. The following is an example of a rather ordered type:

> *ha'azinu hashamayim wa'adabbera / wetishma' ha'arets 'imrei fi*
> *ya'arof kammaṭar liqhi / tizzal kaṭṭal 'imrati*
> *kis'irim 'alei deshe' / wekhirvivim 'alei 'esev*

Give ear, O, ye heavens, and I will speak;
And hear, O earth, the words of my mouth.
My doctrine shall drop as the rain.
My speech shall distil as the dew.
As the small rain upon the tender herb,
And as the showers upon the grass (Deut. 32:1–4).

There are 3:3 stresses in the first two pairs of versets, and 2:2 stresses in the last pair. But syntactically the last two pairs are linked. The words *ha'azinu* ("give ear"), and *wetishma'* ("hear") are synonymous in meaning though not in morphology; "I will speak" and "the words of my mouth" are not synonyms, but their meanings are parallel. "Heavens" and "earth" are parallel by opposition. "Rain" and "dew" both express fruition by water, but one is strong and the other is subtle, these are two poles of one scale. There is also a concatenation of the three parts: versets 3 and 4 unfold the theme of the first pair ("the words of my mouth"); versets 5 and 6 develop the images of 3 and 4. But the versets of the last pair are parallel only to one member of the previous pair ("the rain" or "the dew").

The parallelism of meaning in the last four versets is chiastic: the water is strong (3)—weak (4)—weak (5)—strong (6). In the last pair *deshe'* and *'esev* are on one level, but *se'irim* and *revivim*, though morphologically alike, are quite different in degree. Some additional devices of rhythm and sound reinforce the effect of this passage.

Rhythm. If the equivalent meaning or syntactic pattern of parallel versets draws the reader's attention to the parallelism and its reinforcing quality, it is the rhythmical structure proper which embodies it. The major rhythmic element is stress. The rhythm is accentual, but the number of stresses in each verset is not necessarily fixed or permanent. There may be an exact repetition: 3:3 stresses, or a freer relationship: 3:4, as well as changing numbers throughout the poem. The specific numerical relationship is however important. The numbers are quite often equal or similar. Moreover, whenever there is freedom it is confined within fixed boundaries. Each verset is usually a phrase, a basic syntactic and logical unit, consisting of 2, 3, or 4 stressed words. The smallness and compactness of the verset lends each stress conspicuous force. The condensed, laconic nature of biblical Hebrew also contributes to the prominence of each word within the line, the more so when it is reinforced by the parallel verset. The versets are static, independent units, well balanced against each other. This is supported by the nature of biblical syntax which favors parataxis to the subordination of clauses and phrases.

Is stress the only sound element determining biblical rhythm? For many generations scholars have argued over the "secrets" of biblical prosody: there have been attempts to correct or rewrite the text so that it might conform with pseudo-classic ideas of rhythm which require strict numbers of some kind: regularized "feet," equalized hemistichs, or stanzas of recurring numbers of lines. Such attempts seem pointless today since no exact regularity of any kind has been found and since rhythm need not be based on strict numerical regularity. Considering the rhythm to be based on free variation, it is clear, however, that stress is not enough to describe the effects of biblical rhythm. The number of unstressed syllables between two stressed ones, though not fixed in the sense of modern accentual-syllabic versification, is certainly limited: by rule no two stresses are permitted to follow each other, on the other hand long words have secondary stresses. Thus each stress dominates a group of 2, 3, or 4 syllables; there are 2, 3, or 4 such groups in a verset; and 2, 3, or 4 parallel versets in a sentence. It is a three-stage hierarchy of simple, indivisible, though flexible groups. Within this free framework there are clearly functional specific patterns, such as the so-called "rhythm of elegy" based on an opposition of 3:2 stresses. The rhythm of major stresses is so strong that sometimes it may be the only supporter of the parallelism of two versets, without any actual repetition of meaning or syntax.

Sound. Within this framework of rhythmical parallelism there is a whole gamut of sound repetition and sound patterns, freely distributed, but clearly embellishing the text. Whatever the origins of Hebrew rhyme and puns or sound patterns in later poetry, the later poets were able to draw on a variety of such devices in the Bible. There is: (1) simple alliteration: *hod wehadar, hen wahesed*; (2) a chain of one repeated sound: *TSaddiq miTSara nehelaTS* (Prov. 11:8); (3) a repetition of the same root which is syntactically justified: *' ahuda na lakhem hida* ("I will riddle you a riddle," Judg. 14:12), *huda hidatekha wenishma'enna* ("riddle your riddle and we will hear," *ibid.* 14:13); (4) puns on similar sounding roots: *pahad-pahat-pah; 'ish-'esh-'eshet; 'al taharosh 'al re'akha ra'a* (Prov. 3:29): (5) root rhyming *bavel-balal* (cf. Gen. 11:9), *tsedaqa-tse'aqa* (cf. Isa. 5:7); (6) occasional rhymes in modern sense *yenah-shulhanah* (cf. Prov. 9:2), *tsemah-qemah* (cf. Hos. 8:9), etc.

Rhyme is sometimes obviously linked to the parallel structure, e.g.,

> *pen titten la' aherim hodekha / ushenotekha le' akhzari*
> *pen yisbe' u zarim kohekha / wa'atsavekha bevet nokhri*

Lest thou give thy vigor unto others,
And thy years unto the cruel;
Lest strangers be filled with thy strength,
And thy labors be in the house of an alien; (Prov. 5:9–10).

The two sentences are similar in rhythm (3:2 stresses) and are linked by an anaphora, as well as by parallel syntax, meaning, morphology, and rhyme. Though the symmetry is pervasive and multiple, it is however neither regular nor permanent: the first versets of each line are parallel in meaning as a whole but not in each word; *'aherim* ("others") and *zarim* ("strangers") are parallel in morphology and rhyme but not in their syntactical function; *ushenotekha* ("thy years") and *wa'atsavekha* ("thy labors") are not parallel in the same sense as *'aherim* ("others") and *zarim* ("strangers"); *'akhzari* ("the cruel") and *bet nokhri* ("the house of an alien") are not synonymous in the language but become so when enforced by this context. In the same way all parallel words rhyme with each other, except for the second word. This is an extreme example of order; usually the patterns are less symmetrical and the sentence that follows may not have any of the above devices.

Benjamin Hrushovski. *Encyclopedia Judaica.* Vol. XIII
(Jerusalem, Keter, 1971), cols. 1200–1202

It is doubtful that there is any human culture in which poetry is not practiced, but precisely for that reason it is diverse, and it is difficult to advance a comprehensive theoretical definition for it. In dealing with the poetry of any particular culture one generally does not even need a definition since a description of the conventions of the poetic tradition at hand suffices. For the important matter of meter . . . one may rely on an explicit "theory of poetry" (prosody) in that tradition, or on the living practice of declaiming poems, or on both. With respect to biblical poetry, however, this is not the case. If its creators followed a set of rules, they did not transmit them to their successors, and our information about the pronunciation of ancient Hebrew . . . is not sufficient to base conjectures upon it. With no alternative, those who deal with biblical poetry have to use hypothesis and comparison with other poetic traditions. Indeed, only what is common to poetic traditions in general and the theoretical understanding that can be gained from them generally can serve as a tool for deciphering the perplexities of biblical poetry. . . .

Poetry is speech arranged according to a conventional sound pattern in order to express certain ideas considered appropriate for it in that culture. Frequently a certain style utilizing rare words, fixed tropes, and figurative language (similes and the like) functions in poetry. The sound pattern in the speech is often accompanied by music. Poetry has been found to have three criteria: With regard to content and style it is elevated speech (poetry); with regard to sound it is rhythmic speech (verse); and in its attachment to music it is song. . . . There are cultures in which each of these criteria may be—in certain compositions—highly pronounced at the expense of the others, but with respect to Israelite culture in antiquity it is doubtful that this was so. . . .

What we find with certainty in the Bible is that for every chapter or passage we identify as possessing poetic features with respect to content and style, we have only a vague sense of their meter. A little more accurate examination will show that such chapters and passages are easily divided according to their content into short utterances (sentences or quasi-sentences from a syntactic standpoint) resembling each other in length; and since this resemblance in the length of utterances is greater than in prose, it stands to reason that the poetic *versets* are identical with the poetic utterances and that there is a special concern to separate versets on an ideational basis. Because of this we are able to identify versets in biblical poetry without difficulty. Evidence for this are the poems designated with the alphabet at the head of their versets (Ps. 25; 34; 119; 145). Because the verset is in and of itself a rhythmic element . . . this phenomenon provides us with an initial understanding, albeit very imprecise, of biblical meter.

The versets for the most part divide easily into partial utterances called *stichs*. The length of a normal stich is three words; hence we find in a typical verset about six words, though there are versets of three stichs; and there are stichs of two words, or four words, and even of five words. We find evidence for the fact that the biblical authors were aware of the stich as a poetic unit in Psalms 111 and 112, in which the alphabet is designated at the head of the stichs, and in Psalm 136, in which the recurring stich "For his-grace is-forever" follows every normal stich. . . .

All languages are wont to stress one syllable in every word or in every small group of connected words; in longer words, sometimes two syllables are stressed. Thus in a stich of four words, for example, four stresses are heard:

sús werokhevó ramá vayyám (Exod. 15:1).

Particles (such as *'et, 'al, min, lo'*) and short nouns in construct and the like may be stressed or unstressed. It is therefore possible to declaim them thus:

lehaggíd ki-yashár YHẂH / tsurí welo' -'awláta bó (Ps. 92:16)

or thus:

lehaggíd kí yashár YHẂH / tsurí weló' 'awláta bó.

These features of "natural" rhythm enable us to declaim biblical poetry such that a fairly clear meter is heard. We accent the stressed syllables (according to our own pronunciation) and take the liberty of stressing or not stressing short words so that a meter as unified as possible obtains in the poetic passage before us.

Israel Yeivin. *'Entsiqlopedya miqra'it*. Vol. VII. Ed. by Benjamin Mazar et al. (Jerusalem, Bialik Institute, 1976), cols. 637, 639–40†

My conclusion has been that the ancient Canaanite and Hebrew poets were not counting syllables, at least in the pattern familiar in other oral, syllabic verse. It must be emphasized, moreover, that the oral formulae of Ugaritic and early Hebrew meter are binary, not chronemic as in Greek epic verse. These are constructed in pairs: word, phrase, and colon pairs, including paired epithets and proper names, complementing grammatical parallelism at every level.

It has been my practice for many years, therefore, to use a notation *l(ongum)* and *b(reve)* to label respectively the long colon and the short colon fundamental to Hebrew verse, a notation which leaves open the question of auditory (stress/quantitative) rhythm. Often it is useful to note the syllable count in verse as an indication of its levels of balance in a bicolon or tricolon, or in a couplet or triplet of more complex structure, but such counts imply in my analysis no theory of chronemic meter.

In archaic poetry the standard verse forms are the *l:l* and *l:l:l*. In lyric poetry one often finds b:b::b:b, or better 2(b:b), and b:b::b:b::b:b, i.e., 3 (b:b). The simple verse b:b exists but is rare. In verse composed of b units, parallelism is ordinarily between two bicola forming a couplet (b:b // b:b), but parallelism also appears not infrequently between the cola (b//b), which, along with the regularity of the caesural pause, confirms the analysis that the unit is a short colon.

In such early poems as the Song of the Sea and the Lament of David, one finds the combination of these verse forms, often referred to as "mixed meter," usually in sequences of couplets and triplets, e.g., 2(b:b)—*l:l*—3(b:b)—*l:l:l*, etc. (Cross [*Canaanite Myth and Hebrew Epic*, 1973], p. 126).

The complex verse form found *inter alia* in Lamentations 1 and the Psalm of Jonah—[Karl] Budde's "Qinah meter"—was first analyzed in stress notation as 3:2; alternately it has been described as 5:5. Each description has merit, each defects. The dominant structure I shall argue is *l:b::l:b* (using our notation) in which grammatical and semantic binarism is chiefly between corresponding bicola. However, "internal" parallelism between the "mixed" (long and short) cola of the individual bicolon is not infrequent, especially in older, orally-composed verse of this type. While *l:b::l:b* is the most frequent verse pattern, there are also variant patterns: *l:b::b:l*, b:*l::l:b*, etc. In the older examples of this complex verse the variant patterns are used more widely than in later verse, and with greater effect.

Frank Moore Cross. *The Word of the Lord Shall Go Forth*. Ed. by Carol L. Meyers and M. O'Connor (Philadelphia, American Schools of Oriental Research, 1983), pp. 132–33

RHYME

For the sake of showing you that rhyme had its conception and birth in sacredness, I here set before you these verses: *halo' hu' 'avikha qanekha / hu' 'asekha waykhonenekha* ["Is (God) not your father, your creator? (Did) he (not) make you and establish you?"] (Deut. 32:6); *lule' harashtem be'eglati / lo' metsatem hidati* ["Had you not ploughed with my heifer, you would not have gotten my riddle"] (Judg. 14:18); *kemohem yihyu 'oseihem / kol 'asher boteah bahem* ["Like them will their makers be, whoever trusts in them"] (Ps. 115:8); *ta'ama ki tov sahrah / lo' yikhbe valayla nerah* ["She tastes how good are her wares, her lamp does not go out at night"] (Prov. 31:18); *shetei mayim mibborekha / wenozelim mittokh be'erekha* ["Drink water from your cistern, and running-water from out of your well"] (Prov. 5:15); *nenatteqa 'et moseroteimo / wenashlikha mimmennu 'avoteimo* ["Let us cut off their bonds, and let us throw off from us their cords"] (Ps. 2:3); and there are many (others) like these. [1602]

> Samuel Archivolti. *Sefer 'arugat habbosem* (Amsterdam, Solomon Props, 1730), p. 102b†

The eurhythm of Hebrew poetry could now be enhanced by the correspondence of the rhythmic chiming together of the stichs strengthened by the choice of assonance. Thus would the use of rhyme come to originate in Hebrew poetry.

Now cases of alliteration and assonance . . . do turn up in the poetic parts of the Old Testament. Analogous to the above-mentioned *me* di*m*on *m*ale'u da*m* etc. (Isa. 15:9a; 24:4a, 12, 22a) is *yir'u rabbim weyira'u* etc. (Ps. 40:4; 52:8; 18:8). But who would therefore ascribe "stave-rhyme" to ancient Hebrew poetry? Moreover, we do encounter in the poetic sections of the Old Testament many assonances in the final syllables of corresponding stichs, as in *qoli // 'imrati* etc. (Gen. 4:23; Judg. 14:18b; I Sam. 18:7; Ps. 6:2; 8:5). In examples, such as the ones under consideration in Genesis 4:23 etc., someone might want to find at least what the French call *"rime suffisante"* [sufficient rhyme] . . . as in *soupir // désir*. . . . Owing to its being commonplace, such a resemblance in sound can hardly be perceived by the ear (cf. *leminéhu // leminéhu* etc., Gen. 1:12, etc.). Thus where assonance is really intended, as in *nesuy // kesuy* (Ps. 32:1), which is expressly designed as such, it does not stand at the end of corresponding stichs. At any rate, in the end in no poem do alliteration or assonance appear through all the stichs. If the assonances adduced above may be considered as rhyme, then one may ascribe to ancient Hebrew poetry at the most such sporadic rhymes, like those, for example, that occur in Shakespeare (Hamlet: *rise // eyes* at the conclusion of I.2; *thing // king* at the conclusion of Act II; *me // see* in the third act at the end of Ophelia's speech; etc.).

> Eduard König. *Stilistik, Rhetorik, Poetik in Bezug auf die biblische Literatur komparativisch* (Leipzig, Dieterich'sche Verlagsbuchhandlung Theodor Weicher, 1900), pp. 355–56†

Rhyme appears at a number of points in Ugaritic and early Hebrew poetry. Rhyme does not usually seem to be the product of a conscious effort or intent. This would be too easy in a language with case endings such as Ugaritic, or a language with as many repetitions of common final sounds as has Hebrew. Rhyme in these languages is rather a specialized type of *assonance*. Assonance is thus the actual operative factor in the composition of poetry which happens to rhyme, and rhyme is merely a sub-category of assonance. This is suggested by the observation that the vast majority of Hebrew and Ugaritic poems exhibit no rhyme patterns whatever, although assonance of various types is widespread. It is further confirmed by the fact that nearly all occurrences of rhyme in Hebrew and Ugaritic are manifested in parts rather than the whole of the poems in question. The student must deal therefore with the full range of assonance: vocalic or consonantal repetitions, paronomasia, *figura etymologica*, alliteration, rhyme, etc., all of which occur to a remarkable degree. Any key to how the poetry itself was originally composed may give the analyst more information upon which to base his decisions as to form, stichometry, and meter.

> Douglas K. Stuart. *Studies in Early Hebrew Meter*
> (Missoula, Mont., Scholars Press, 1976), pp. 19–20

REPETITION

As it is said [in Esth. 7:5]: "King Ahasueras said, he said to Esther the Queen." And as it is said [in Neh. 4:17]: "I, and my brothers, and my servants, and the men of the guard who follow me, we do not remove our clothes." Such repetitions occur only when there are at least two words intervening between the two utterances, one of which is the repetitive utterance. [10th c.]

> Saadiah Gaon. *Perushei Rav Saʿadya Gaʾon livreishit.*
> Ed. and tr. by Moshe Zucker (New York, Jewish Theo-
> logical Seminary of America, 1984), p. 192†

There are in the Torah propositions that are stated in multiple language, whereby words are reiterated and reduplicated. . . . And these are the propositions stated in multiple language of reiterated words, reduplicated in their substance . . . : "And you found his heart trustworthy, and you made a covenant with him, giving the land of the Canaanite, the Hittite, the Amorite, the Perizzite, the Jebusite, and the Girgashite, giving to his descendants" (Neh. 9:8). The lawgiver reiterated "giving" twice although once would have been enough. . . . Similarly, "Which I give to them, to the Israelites" (Josh. 1:2); it would have been enough [to say only] "to them" or "to the Israelites." Similarly, "It will be, the nation or kingdom that will not serve him, Nebuchadnezzar king of Babylon" (Jer. 27:5); it would have been enough [to say only] "him" or "Nebuchadnezzar." . . . Similarly, "The Israelites did all that the Lord commanded Moses they so did" (Exod. 39:32). The beginning of the verse and its end are the same proposition, and it would have been enough with one of them. Similarly, "The Israelites did so, and they sent them outside the camp as the Lord spoke to Moses so the Israelites did" (Num. 5:4). Here, too, he reiterated the proposition twice. . . . Similarly, "Thus shall you say to this people who have spoken to you saying, 'Your father made our yoke heavy, so you alleviate it for us,' thus shall you say to them" (I Kgs. 12:10). He reiterates, "Thus shall you say" although he had preceded it at the beginning. . . . "The king of Egypt said to the Hebrew midwives . . . he said, 'When you assist the birth . . .'" (Exod. 1:15–16). He reiterates "He said," . . . Similarly, "The three older sons of Jesse went, they went after Saul" (I Sam. 17:13). It would have been enough with ". . . went" or "they went." Similarly, "The king pitied Mephibosheth son of Jonathan son of Saul on account of the oath of the Lord which was between them, between David and Jonathan son of Saul" (II Sam. 21:7). Here, too, the proposition has been reduplicated, but there is a reason for the reduplication of something that was sworn to both of them. [10th c.]

Menahem ibn Saruq. *Maḥberet Menaḥem*. Ed. by Zvi Filipowski (London, Ḥevrat Meʿorrerei Yeshenim, 1854), pp. 70–71†

(1) Reduplication is the repeating one further time of some particular word, whether because of anger or of pity.

(2) Because of anger, for example: For Ephraim hath multiplied altars to sin, yea, altars have been unto him to sin [Hos. 8:11]. Similarly: Give them, O Lord, whatsoever Thou wilt give; give them a miscarrying womb, etc. [9:14]. Again: Ho, thy plagues, O death! Ho, thy destruction, O netherworld! [13:14]. So also in Micah: Thou shalt sow, but shalt not reap; thou shalt tread the olives, but shalt not anoint thee with oil [Mic. 6:15]. And in Nahum: Thou also shalt be drunken, thou shalt swoon; thou also shalt seek a refuge because of the enemy [Nah. 3:11]. Again, in Ezekiel: . . . nor be dismayed at their looks, for they are a rebellious house; and thou shalt speak My words unto them, whether they will hear or whether they will forbear; for they are most rebellious [Ezek. 2:6–7]. And again, in Isaiah: According to their deeds, accordingly He will repay, fury to his adversaries, recompense to His enemies; to the islands He will repay recompense [Isa. 59:18].

(3) An example of the second kind of Reduplication—when it is caused by pity—is found in Hosea: Ephraim, like as I have seen Tyre, is planted in a pleasant place; but Ephraim shall bring forth his children to the slayer [Hos. 9:13]. Also in Hosea: How shall I give thee up, Ephraim, surrender thee, Israel: How shall I make thee as Admah, set thee as Zeboim? My heart is turned within Me, etc. [11:8]. So, too, in Micah: For her wound is incurable, for it is come even unto Judah, etc. [Mic. 1:9]. Further, in Jeremiah: Therefore my heart moaneth for Moab like pipes, and my heart moaneth like pipes for the men of Kir-heres [Jer. 48:36]; Therefore will it wail for Moab, yea, I will cry out for all Moab [48:31]. [1475]

Messer David ben Judah Leon. *The Book of the Honeycomb's Flow*. Ed. and trans. by Isaac Rabinowitz (Ithaca, N.Y., Cornell University Press, 1983), pp. 479, 481

It is true that the style of the Bible is often marked by brevity and compactness. A great deal is often said in remarkably few words. But the Bible is a very emphatic book. Its aim is to impress upon the hearer or reader the great importance of the themes of which it treats. The most natural way of securing emphasis in a narrative is by amplification or reiteration. Consequently the Biblical style is often decidedly diffuse and characterized by elaborateness of detail and by repetition. A few examples will suffice to illustrate these important features and the way in which they have been made use of by the advocates of this theory. . . .

[Gen. 24] is markedly characterized by that tendency to reiteration which has been referred to above. How the servant recognized Rebekah as the divine choice for Isaac is told in prospect (vv. 12–14), in actuality (vv. 15–20), and in retrospect (vv. 42–48). There is both sameness and variety in the three accounts. . . . Especially interesting is the account of Rebekah's departure (vv. 59–61). It consists of a number of sentences of varying length, loosely connected by "and," and reads as follows:

> 59 And they sent away Rebekah their sister, and her nurse, and Abraham's servant, and his men.
>
> 60 And they blessed Rebekah, and they said unto her, Thou art our sister, be thou *the mother of* thousands of ten thousands, and let thy seed possess the gate of those which hate them.
>
> 61 And Rebekah arose, and her damsels, and they rode upon the camels, and followed the man: and the servant took Rebekah, and went.

These three verses describe the departure of Rebekah from her home to go to the far country to be the wife of Abraham's son. It is an event of great interest and emotional appeal; and the historian lingers over it as if he would make us see it from every angle. He describes it from three points of view; the family, Rebekah herself, and Abraham's servant.

Oswald T. Allis. The Five Books of Moses (Philadelphia, Presbyterian and Reformed Publishing, 1943), pp. 95, 102–3

Repetition plays a diverse role in the Old Testament. It serves, for one thing, to center the thought, to rescue it from disparateness and diffuseness, to focus the richness of varied predication upon the poet's controlling concern. The synthetic character of biblical mentality, its sense for totality, is as apparent in Israel's rhetoric as in her psychology. Repetition serves, too, to give continuity to the writer's thought; the repeated word or phrase is often strategically located, thus providing a clue to the movement and stress of the poem. Sometimes the repeated word or line indicates the structure of the poem, pointing to the separate divisions; at other times it may guide us in determining the extent of the literary unit. Our commentaries contain numerous instances where words and phrases have been deleted as mere repetition. It is a highly precarious procedure, one which violates the character of biblical writing, both prose and poetry, and is refuted quite decisively by the other extant literatures of the Near East, above all, perhaps, by the Ugaritic epics, which cast a strong light on the method and mentality of ancient Semitic thinking and literary composition. Finally, repetition provides us with an open avenue to the character of biblical thinking.

This iterative propensity of ancient Israel extends beyond its expression in poetry. In narrative, the literary genre most characteristic of her life and thought, repetition appears as a major stylistic feature. In such accounts, for example, as the wooing of Rebecca, or the Elijah stories, it is used with a high degree of artistic skill, both because of its great variety and because of its power to relate speaker and hearer in the immediacy and concreteness of dialog or to bring them into participation with common words. It is an eloquent witness to the literary genius of ancient Israel that this constant resort to iterative discourse so seldom palls or wearies the reader. . . .

The roots of repetition lie deeply embedded in the language and literature of Israel. An examination of the various modes of reduplication in Hebrew syntax or of the repetition of single words in elemental contexts of unreflected speech will reveal very clearly how the primitive spirit of the language continues to be preserved and lends to it an intensity, a spontaneity and freshness, a directness and immediacy which would be difficult to achieve in any other fashion. Thus in such stems as the $P^{e^c}al^cal$, *Pilpel*, and *Hithpalpel* the verb is given a special energy or movement. The verb *phr*, e.g., in the $P^{e^c}al^cal$ may describe the palpitation of the heart or "to go about quickly" or the *Pilpel glgl* from the root *gll* meaning "to roll."

A word is frequently repeated to express urgency as in the Song of Deborah, the great classic of the iterative style, *ʿuri ʿuri*:

Awake, awake, Deborah! / Awake, awake, utter a song! (Judg. 5:12)

To this is to be compared the similarly passionate outcry in Second Isaiah:

Awake, awake, put on thy strength, / O arm of Yahweh;
Awake as in primeval days, / the generations long ago.
(Isa. 51:9; cf. 52:1) . . .

[As] to the relation of repetition to the literary forms of the Old Testament, if we were to include within our inquiry words, phrases, and sentences which are synonymous, the evidence for the relationship would be very impressive indeed. But we restrict ourselves almost exclusively to repetition in the narrower sense. A good example, though not necessarily the most felicitous, is the acrostic poem as it is found in the Book of Lamentations. The alphabetic arrangement of the successive verses would naturally encourage repetition, but the phenomenon penetrates much more deeply. And here we are confronted with a characteristic of Hebrew literature in general: wherever the writer shows any inclination to employ the iterative style he does so in a variety of ways, i.e., he uses repetition as a creative literary device. This is especially true of Lamentations where the repetitions are abundant and varied. . . .

What is notable about this ancient poetry is that such an artificial contrivance does not stand in the way of producing literature of a high order, in which the emotions find full expression and the language bodies forth the intensity and passion of the poet.

The Old Testament provides a number of instances where the verbal structure of a poem is completely conditioned by repetition. Most notable, of course, are Jotham's fable and Amos' oracles against the foreign nations, but Job's great apologia, and many of the passages in Ezekiel, illustrate the same phenomenon.

James Muilenburg. *Vetus Testamentum, Supplement* 1, 1953, pp. 99–103

We find frequent repetition of an individual word, be it a noun, a verb, or another word, in large measure in the Bible. For the most part, repeated words occur in exclamations or out of excitement, as in: "Holy, holy, holy!" (Isa. 6:3); "Ah, Uriel, Uriel!" (Isa. 29:1); "O land, land, land! Hear the word of the Lord" (Jer. 22:29); "My bowels, my bowels, I writhe" (Jer. 4:19); "My eye, my eye flows down water" (Lam. 1:16); "Fallen, fallen is Babylon!" (Isa. 21:9); "For my sake, for my sake will I act" (Isa. 48:11); "In pieces, in pieces bring it out!" (Ezek. 24:6); "Ruin, ruin, ruin will I make it!" (Ezek. 21:32).

Or in petition: "My God, my God! Why have you abandoned me?" (Ps. 22:2); "Be gracious, be gracious to me, O my companions!" (Job 19:21); "Turn back, turn back, O Shulamite! Turn back, turn back that we may envision you" (Song 7:1).

Or in severe orders: "Aside, aside, go out from there!" (Isa. 52:11); "Raze, raze! To its foundations" (Ps. 137:7); "Stand, stand!" (Nah. 2:9).

Or in encouraging commands: "Comfort, comfort my people!" (Isa. 40:1); "Arise, arise, wear strength" (Isa. 51:9); "Awaken, awaken, O Jerusalem!" (Isa. 51:17); "Clear, clear, make way!" (Isa. 57:14); "Pass, pass through the gates, make way for the people, clear, clear the path" (Isa. 62:10).

Or in self-encouragement: "Arise, arise, Deborah! Arise, arise, utter a song!" (Judg. 5:12). . . .

And it is a noteworthy and characteristic fact that following a successive repetition, sometimes the repeated word is repeated again in the next utterance, as in:

> *Arise, arise*, wear strength, O arm of the Lord!
> *Arise* as in former days (Isa. 51:9).

> *I, I* am the Lord, and beside me there is no savior,
> *I* have foretold, and I have saved (Isa. 43:11).

> *I, I* am he, and there is no God with me,
> *I* cause to die and to live (Deut. 32:39). . . .

In several verses in the first part of the Book of Isaiah there is a special way of treating successive repetitions—it is to produce one after the other words from the same root and *with the same meaning* in a more or less large number, such as:

> He shall kindle a kindling like a kindling of fire (10:16).

> The treacherous have acted treacherously,
> And treachery—the treacherous have acted treacherously (24:16).

> Like the strike of him who struck him have they struck him?
> Like the killing of those he killed has he been killed? (27:7) . . .

And only once does such a repetition occur in Jeremiah:

> Runner to meet runner runs,
> And reporter to meet reporter, to report (51:31).

This repetition is filled with life and movement as it depicts those hurrying to bring news to the King of Babylonia of the capture of his city, and in it we feel the prophet's happiness at this downfall.

David Yellin. *Ketavim nivharim.* Vol. II (Jerusalem, David Yellin Jubilee Committee, 1959), pp. 28–30, 33–34†

There is a significant difference between a more or less exact repetition in the framework of a certain discourse of a particular speaker and the relations of repetition in the framework of a structure that combines several discourses of one speaker or, more generally, of several different speakers. Even a repetition within the framework of one discourse is apt, of course, to serve different goals. In modern literature, poetry in particular, the evolution of such a complex through a sequence of text is frequently embedded in a contextual heap or even in a drastic transmutation of meanings and their activization and/or resolution of ambiguity (see Sternberg [*Ha-sifrut*. April, 1976], especially pp. 97ff.). In biblical narrative such repetitive phenomena frequently fulfill a function of emphasis and reinforcing speech, too. Judah, for example, opens and closes his refusal to go down to Egypt without Benjamin by quoting the words of the Egyptian man: "You will not see my face without your brother with you" (Gen. 43:3, 5); this manner of expression underscores the finality of his intention. And a similar situational justification for repetition is even apt to appear in instances in which the speaker uses not the very same words but different synonymous variations of the same thing: Pharaoh, promising the world to the House of Jacob ("And I shall give you the bounty of the land of Egypt, and you will eat the fat of the land [. . .] for the bounty of all the land of Egypt is yours"; Gen. 45:18–20); or Ruth, repeating her decision five times to cling to her mother-in-law ("Do not entreat me to abandon following you. For where you go, I shall go, and where you lodge, I shall lodge. Your people is my people, and your God my God. Where you die, I shall die, and there will I be buried. Thus may the Lord do to me, and thus may he add, if death separates me and you"; Ruth 1:16–17). Internal repetition of this type has, therefore, an interesting variety of manifestations and functions. Exact repetition of a component in the framework of different speech-acts, however, even of the same speaker, is in one sense more complex from the start, being embedded in the opposition of two different speech contexts. Even so, the informational redundancy is more striking to the eye and the puzzlement in the parallelism between the utterances more poignant. Here, for example, the situational justification for the preceding instance—that is, the explanation for the repetition in terms of the speaker's desired calculation to achieve a certain effect in his listener (emphasis, for example) or in terms of verbal mimesis ("That's how people speak when they're excited")—is pushed to the side. If so, how and why do discourses and different speakers say "the same thing"?

The answer to this question changes from context to context—for example, in accordance with the composition of the repetition structure. In a "prospect→ action" combination exact repetition is apt to serve as an indirect means of delineating the one who issues the command or the one who executes the command or the relations between them. One of the effective ways of dramatizing the righteousness of Noah, the man righteous and perfect in his generation, is that up to the moment of the Flood, we had no idea why it was he who "found favor in the eyes of the Lord" [Gen. 6:8], a phrase that directs the reader to pit the words of the Lord to him before the Flood against the action that he takes pursuant to them. Pursuant to the command "Enter the ark, you and your sons and your wife and the wives of your sons with you," we hear, "Noah entered the ark, and his sons and his wife and the wives of his sons with him" (Gen. 6:18; 7:7): We get the impression that Noah followed the word of the Lord so much that despite the fact that in the meantime he received a more general guideline ("Enter the ark, you and all your household"; 7:1) that allows him some room for independent judgment, he takes pains even to bring his family into the ark in the same specific (and nonrandom) order that was indicated by the language of the original command. Exact repetition achieves a different effect with alternate expositions of the same complex of components, when the purveyor of the prospect and the executor of the command are one. Here informational redundancy and semantic correspondence are justified in terms of shedding light not on the executor of the command and his relation to the one issuing it, but on the action itself, especially on the power of that which generated it. The most impressive example of this in the Bible, and in all literature, appears in the opening of the Creation account: "God said 'Let there be light' and there was light" [Gen. 1:3]. There is no need of explanatory exegesis from the narrator to elevate the greatness of the executor and the perfection of his success, of the sort "And the Lord took account of Sarah as he had promised, and the Lord did for Sarah just as he stated" (Gen. 21:1). The laconicism of the command's formulation and the description of the execution (which says "God needs to make no effort or elaborate speech in order to generate such a revolution"), the textual proximity of the two components ("the command materializes then and there") above and beyond the perfect identity between them, identity of allusive language on top of surface identity ("every jot and tittle of the command materialized")—in these is packed the power of the effect, which aroused the professional excitement of the sophisticated rhetorician Longinus as early as the first century of our era.

Meir Sternberg. *Ha-sifrut.* Oct., 1977, p. 121†

[Repetitions] are a frequently used device of the Old Testament narrators, and they are almost always handled with some freedom. Repetitive situations of various kinds are common enough in the events told in any story: messages are passed from one person to another, instructions are first given and then executed, some actions are done over and over again. The storyteller can either use such situations to make patterns of sound and structure, or avoid the emergence of such patterns by various means. The procedure adopted is very much a matter of tradition or convention in any given manner or school of the storytelling craft. Scholars frequently point out that verbatim repetitions of words and phrases, and of lengthy passages, are characteristic of the more ancient and primitive forms of narrative, such as epic poems, or folk tales. This might be due to the circumstances that oral composition and transmission are greatly helped by regularly repeated elements; furthermore, as I have already pointed out, such elements make a story which is listened to sound better. The earlier and more primitive literatures are nearer to the oral origins of all storytelling, while highly sophisticated genres, such as classical Latin historiography or nineteenth-century novels, are typically written compositions, and consequently avoid repetitions.

All this might seem to lead to the conclusion that the narrative manner of the Bible is relatively close to ancient and primitive conventions, though—since its repetitions are not quite regular—one step higher on the evolutionary scale; or that these texts, though written, reflect some earlier orally composed and transmitted poems and stories. The various pieces of Old Testament prose could then be classified as more or less "ancient," or "advanced." To the present writer such theories seem too simplistic to be indulged in without danger. There is only one aesthetically relevant point in all this: the freedom of the Biblical storyteller to choose his treatment of repetitive situations. It is tantamount to the freedom to choose his style. Repetitive stories have clear structures, but are somewhat formal and stiff; they can be likened to pictures and photographs which look nice or beautiful because they are obviously well composed. Stories which avoid repetition are less clear in structure but also less constrained; they are rather like pictures in which the composition is neither prominent nor important, being subordinated to colour, texture, representation, or some other pictorial quality. There are, of course, endless combinations, variations and degrees of these two principles in painting (and photography). Narrative allows the same richness of variety in this respect. . . .

The patterning by repetition seems to me to function as the main anti-mimetic quality in Old-Testament stories; and the tension between these two purely aesthetic aims—mimesis versus pattern—might possibly provide a key to a deeper analysis of their artistic conventions.

Jacob Licht. Storytelling in the Bible (Jerusalem, Magnes Press, 1978), pp. 62–64

In poetry recited to a living audience a great deal of repetition is needed that a reader does not need. The Old English poem *Beowulf* contains a long recapitulation of a previous narrative, because it is close to and reflecting the conventions of oral literature. In Shakespeare, too, near the end of a play we sometimes have a summarizing speech of a kind that a theater audience would find helpful. Then again, music, which also addresses a listening audience, is capable of a degree of repetition that a reader would find intolerable. . . .

There is one curious episode in the Bible that illustrates this point. In Exodus 25ff. God gives detailed instructions for constructing the ark of the covenant and similar sacred objects, and a craftsman named Bezaleel is appointed for the task. In ordinary written prose we should expect one sentence saying that Bezaleel made all these things as he was commanded to do. We actually get, in Exodus 36ff., a repetition of each detail, with "and thou shalt make" transposed to "and he made." Such repetition is primarily to impress the reader with the importance of what is being done, but the conventions employed are close to those of oral literature.

Northrop Frye. The Great Code (New York, Harcourt Brace Jovanovich, 1982), p. 214

Equally important to the oral nature of the text are the repetitions that occur throughout. As [Everett] Fox explains in his introduction [to *In the Beginning*, 1983], such repetitions have been ignored in most other translations, which have been more concerned with providing the smoothest reading of the verse or chapter at hand. [Martin] Buber and [Franz] Rosenzweig, on the other hand, were deeply aware of the function of repetition as a unifying agent drawing themes and motifs together through the use of sound. Buber called this the "leading-word style," often utilized in poetry and popular song but absent from modern narrative forms. This is well exemplified in Fox's version of Genesis 17:23–27:

> Avraham took Yishmael his son and all those
>   born in his house and all those bought with his money,
> all the males among Avraham's household people,
> and circumcised the flesh of their foreskins on that very day,
> as God had spoken to him.
> Avraham was ninety-nine years old when he
>   had the flesh of his foreskin circumcised,
> and Yishmael his son was thirteen years old
>   when he had the flesh of his foreskin circumcised.
> On that very day

> were circumcised Avraham and Yishmael his son,
> and all his household people, whether house-
>   born or money-bought from a foreigner,
>   were circumcised with him.

The carefully balanced and spaced, rhythmical repetition of "circumcised" and "Yishmael his son" carries us into an auditory experience of drama and ceremony, awe and communion. There is a nonliterary roughness to this text, which awakens in us an ancient recognition of a different kind of truth.

Eduardo Rauch. Parabola. Jan., 1984, p. 100

RHETORIC

Here, perhaps, some one inquires whether the authors whose divinely-inspired writings constitute the canon, which carries with it a most wholesome authority, are to be considered wise only, or eloquent as well. A question which to me, and to those who think with me, is very easily settled. For where I understand these writers, it seems to me not only that nothing can be wiser, but also that nothing can be more eloquent. And I venture to affirm that all who truly understand what these writers say, perceive at the same time that it could not have been properly said in any other way. For as there is a kind of eloquence that is more becoming in youth, and a kind that is more becoming in old age, and nothing can be called eloquence if it be not suitable to the person of the speaker, so there is a kind of eloquence that is becoming in men who justly claim the highest authority, and who are evidently inspired of God. With this eloquence they spoke; no other would have been suitable for them; and this itself would be unsuitable in any other, for it is in keeping with their character, while it mounts as far above that of others (not from empty inflation, but from solid merit) as it seems to fall below them. Where, however, I do not understand these writers, though their eloquence is then less apparent, I have no doubt but that it is of the same kind as that I do understand. The very obscurity, too, of these divine and wholesome words was a necessary element in eloquence of a kind that was designed to profit our understandings, not only by the discovery of truth, but also by the exercise of their powers.

I could, however, if I had time, show those men who cry up their own form of language as superior to that of our authors (not because of its majesty, but because of its inflation), that all those powers and beauties of eloquence which they make their boast, are to be found in the sacred writings which God in His goodness has provided to mould our characters, and to guide us from this world of wickedness to the blessed world above. But it is not the qualities which these writers have in common with the heathen orators and poets that give me such unspeakable delight in their eloquence; I am more struck with admiration at the way in which, by an eloquence peculiarly their own, they so use this eloquence of ours that it is not conspicuous either by its presence or its absence: for it did not become them either to condemn it or to make an ostentatious display of it; and if they had shunned it, they would have done the former; if they had made it prominent, they might have appeared to be doing the latter. [397–428]

> Saint Augustine. *On Christian Doctrine*. Book IV, ch. 6. In *Nicene and Post-Nicene Fathers*. Ed. by Philip Schaff (Buffalo, Christian Literature Co., 1887), p. 577

[On the rhetoric of Judah's speech in Genesis 44:] "Then Judah approached . . ." [Gen. 44:18]. It is written [in Prov. 20:5], "Wisdom in the heart of a man is deep water, and a man of intelligence will draw it up." Judah's speech is analogous to a deep well full of cool water. But though its waters are cool and fine, no creature was able to drink from it. A man came and tied rope to rope and cord to cord, and by pull after pull he drew up from it and drank. Then everyone would draw up from it and drink. So, too, Judah did not budge from addressing Joseph word after word until he moved his heart. [6th c.]

> *Bereishit Rabbah*, section 93:4 (Vilna, Romm, 1909), p. 344†

An example of the several divisions of the discourse is afforded by Judah's address to Joseph (Gen. 44:18–44:34) in the Weekly Lection *Wayyiggash* [Then Judah came near, etc.: Gen. 44:18–47:27]. For the whole of the first verse— Then Judah came near unto him, and said: "Oh my lord, let thy servant, I pray thee, speak a word in my Lord's ears, and let not thine anger burn against thy servant; for thou art even as Pharaoh" [44:18]—constitutes the Introduction. As we see, the three conditions of the Introduction are met in it: first, to render the hearer well disposed—this is achieved partly by Judah's submissiveness before Joseph, and his entreaty: "Oh my lord," and "let not thine anger burn against thy servant," and partly by his words: "for thou art even as Pharaoh," words in which he has so highly praised Joseph as to make him of equal degree with the king. Secondly and thirdly, Judah makes Joseph attentive and receptive by saying "let thy servant, I pray thee, speak a word," for the Statement of Facts here requires that the hearer be simultaneously attentive and receptive, as will be clear: Beginning with the words "My lord asked his servants," etc. [44:19], all this, as far as "ye will bring down my gray hairs with sorrow to the grave" [44:29], is the Statement which Judah gives of the facts involved in this case. His saying, "And it shall be, when I come to thy servant our father, and the lad is not with us; seeing that his soul is bound up with the lad's soul; it will come to pass, when he seeth that the lad is not with us, that he will die" [44:30–31] forms a Partition, for in this the point of their disagreement is clearly brought out—the disagreement, that is, on the point of leaving Benjamin behind. It was as though Judah had said: "It is obvious to us that Jacob will die if he should not see the lad; hence to leave

him behind is something which we must not do"; but he did not say this openly
because he was speaking with humility and tact, like a servant before a king.
From these verses, also, may be understood the point wherein the brothers
agreed with Joseph—the coming of Benjamin thither; it was as though Judah had
said: "We have agreed to part of what you wish, the coming of Benjamin into
Egypt; what remains in dispute is the question of leaving him behind, for to this,
indeed, we will not agree." This was the actual Partition, but it is only hinted at
here for the reason already explained. He next says: "and thy servants will bring
down the grey hairs of thy servant our father with sorrow to the grave" [44:31];
and this is the Proof. It was as though he had said: "What proves that we ought
not agree with you in this is, that if we should so act, great punishment would
overtake us [II Kings 7:9], for we would thereby have brought about the death of
our father 'in sorrow to the grave'—a criminal deed" [Job 31:28]. Judah's words
"For thy servant became surety for the lad" [Gen. 44:32] form the Refutation.
For it was possible that Joseph would say, "Why do you alone multiply exceeding proud talk [I Sam. 2:3], while your brothers refrain?" but Judah refuted this
by saying that he had become surety for Benjamin and that it was quite proper for
him to make a greater effort than his brothers to restore the lad to his father. The
statement "For thy servant became surety" would not make good sense alongside
what had previously been stated unless we say that, as explained, it had previously been hinted that they would neither leave nor abandon Benjamin. Thereafter Judah said: "let thy servant, I pray thee, abide instead of the lad . . . for how
shall I go up to my father if the lad be not with me?" etc. [44:33–34]. This is the
Conclusion, when, in a short statement, Judah summed up what he had previously said. Thus, within the whole of this discourse, we have an Introduction, a
Statement of Facts, a Partition, the Proof, the Refutation, and a Conclusion.
[1475]

Messer David ben Judah Leon. *The Book of the Honey-*
comb's Flow. Ed. and tr. by Isaac Rabinowitz (Ithaca,
N.Y., Cornell University Press, 1983), pp. 57, 59

We may yet further consider, That as so many Passages of Scripture accus'd of
not appearing Eloquent to *European* Judges, it might be justly represented, That
the Eastern Eloquence differs widely from the Western. In those purer Climates,
where Learning, that is here but a Denizon, was a Native; the most cherish'd and
admir'd Composures of their Wits, if judg'd by Western Rules of Oratory, will
be judg'd Destitute of it. Their Dark and Involv'd Sentences, their Figurative and
Parabolical Discourses; their Abrupt and Maimed Way of expressing themselves
which often leaves much place to Guesses at the Sense; and their neglect of connecting Transitions, which often leaves us at a losse for the Method and Coherence of what they Write; are Qualities, that our Rhetoricians do not more generally Dislike, than their Practice: there being, perhaps little lesse Disparity in our
Opinions than in our Wayes of Writing, for their Pens (as if it were a Presage of
the different Changes the Jews and Greeks have made in point of Religion) move

from the Right hand towards the left. . . . The Scripture Style then, though it were not Eloquent Now, may have excellently suited the Genius of Those Times its Several Books were written in; and have been very proper for those People it was Primarily design'd to Work upon. . . .

Some famous Writers have Challeng'd *Demosthenes* and *Cicero*, to compare with the Prophet Isaiah; in whom they had not only Admir'd that Lofty Strain which Artists have term'd the Sublime Character, but even that Harmonious disposition and Sound of Words, (I mean in their Original) which the French prettily call, *La cadence des Periodes*.

> Robert Boyle. *Some Considerations Touching the Style of the Holy Scriptures* (London, printed for Henry Herringman, 1661), pp. 158–59, 164–65, 173–74

There are two sorts of eloquence, the one indeed scarce deserves the name of it, which consists chiefly in laboured and polished periods, an over-curious and artificial arrangement of figures, tinsell'd over with a gaudy embellishment of words, which glitter, but convey little or no light to the understanding.—This kind of writing is for the most part much affected and admired by the people of weak judgment and vicious taste, but is a piece of affectation and formality the sacred writers are utter strangers to. It is a vain and boyish eloquence; and as it has always been esteemed below the great geniuses of all ages, so much more so, with respect to those writers who were actuated by the spirit of infinite wisdom, and therefore wrote with that force and majesty with which never man writ.— The other sort of eloquence is quite the reverse to this, and which may be said to be the true characteristic of the holy Scriptures; where the excellence does not arise from a laboured and far-fetched elocution, but from a surprising mixture of simplicity and majesty, which is a double character, so difficult to be united, that it is seldom to be met with in compositions merely human.—We see nothing in holy writ of affectation and superfluous ornament.—As the infinite wise Being has condescended to stoop to our language, thereby to convey to us the light of revelation, so has he been pleased graciously to accommodate it to us with the most natural and graceful plainness it would admit of.—Now, it is observable that the most excellent profane authors, whether Greek or Latin, lose most of their graces whenever we find them literally translated.—Homer's famed representation of Jupiter, in his first book;—his cried-up description of a tempest;— his relation of Neptune's shaking the earth, and opening it to its center;—his description of Pallas's horses; with numbers of other long-since admired passages,—flag, and almost vanish away, in the vulgar Latin translation.

Let any one but take the pains to read the common Latin interpretation of Virgil, Theocritus, or even of Pindar, and one may venture to affirm he will be able to trace out but few remains of the graces which charmed him so much in the original.—The natural conclusion from hence is, that in the classical authors, the expression, the sweetness of the numbers, occasioned by a musical placing of words, constitute a great part of their beauties;—whereas, in the Sacred Writings, they consist more in the greatness of the things themselves, than in the words and expressions.—The ideas and conceptions are so great and lofty in their own nature, that they necessarily appear magnificent in the most artless dress.—Look but into the Bible, and we see them shine through the most simple and literal translations.—That glorious description which Moses gives of the creation of the heavens and the earth, which Longinus, the best critic the eastern world ever produced, was so justly taken with, has not lost the least whit of its intrinsic worth; and though it has undergone so many translations, yet triumphs over all, and breaks forth with as much force and vehemence as in the original.—Of this stamp are numbers of passages throughout the Scriptures;—instance, that celebrated description of a tempest in the hundred and seventh psalm; those beautiful reflections of holy Job, upon the shortness of life, and instability of human affairs, so judiciously appointed by our church in her office for the burial of the dead;—that lively description of a horse of war, in the thirty-ninth chapter of Job, in which, from the 19th to the 26th verse, there is scarce a word which does not merit a particular explication to display the beauties of.—I might add to these, those tender and pathetic expostulations with the children of Israel, which run throughout all the prophets, which the most uncritical reader can scarce help being affected with. (Sermon 27) [1760]

> Laurence Sterne. *The Sermons of Mr. Yorick.* Vol. VI.
> (London, Printed for W. Strahan and T. Cadell, 1784),
> pp. 108–14

The Hebrews were great orators. Their very poets were orators, for most of their poets were prophets, and when they rose to real heights of eloquence their sermons were poems. Even their drama, if we can call it that, was a series of great orations; some of those in Job perhaps the greatest ever uttered. Job is principally a series of fifteen speeches, all poetry. But the Hebrews used prose, too, in their appeals, speeches and exhortations, and the bulk of Deuteronomy is a great speech, an hour and a quarter long. The Hebrews were so fond of oratory that they cast their entire law in the form of speeches, uttered by God to Moses, or by Moses to the people, the priests, or the elders. Being an ancient people, their whole literary expression was dominated and colored by the spoken word. And their vivid imaginations, dramatic sense, and depth of feeling gave their eloquence an emotional quality that has never been surpassed. . . .

One of the most moving speeches in all literature is the plea addressed by Judah to Joseph to let Benjamin return with his brothers to their father Jacob. . . . With it should be read chapter 45, which contains Joseph's answer. Together they make one of the great dramatic scenes in literature, as Joseph makes himself known to his brothers. Hebrew eloquence breaks like a flood, however, in The Book of Deuteronomy. The great feature of it is the address of Moses to the People as they stand at last, after forty years of wandering, on the borders of the Promised Land. . . . The poet-orators of Judaism . . . the prophets . . . were beyond question the great contribution of the ancient Hebrew genius to the thought of mankind. It is enough to observe that the literary categories familiar to us from Greek and Latin models do not retain their definite characters when we enter the realm of Hebrew literature. Sermons may be poems, laws may be orations, and philosophies orations and poems at the same time. Only an occasional paragraph of prose can be found among the utterances of Amos, Hosea, and Isaiah . . . though not even one, in the work of their peasant contemporary Micah.

> Edgar J. Goodspeed. *How to Read the Bible* (Philadelphia, Winston, 1946), pp. 24–25, 27

One of the devices of biblical rhetoric is massing, that is, the rhetorician amasses words upon words, be they nouns, verbs, or adjectives, to augment the effect that he intends to make on his readers.

The principal basis of the Bible's rhetoric is parallelism, that is, doubling each utterance using other words, and then not a doubling of the utterance in its entirety but only in a part of it; and not only doubling it, but tripling it and quadrupling it, and sometimes even more than this when it puts a spirit of rapture in the mouth of the speaker.

In parallelism we sometimes find threefold and fourfold duplication, as in:

> Let my lesson distill like rain, / Let my utterance drip like dew,
> Like droplets on verdure, / And like spray on grass (Deut. 32:2).

Or:

> Riders of tawny she-asses, / Sitters on riding-blankets,
> And walkers on the road—/ Cry out! (Judg. 5:10)

And even in short utterances:

> And she struck Sisera, / Crashed his head,
> And bashed, / And pierced his temple (Judg. 5:26).

The use of this device, however, is much rarer than reproducing the clauses of a sentence a number of times.

In the first chapter of Isaiah we find different types of massing:

Massing of nouns: Injury, and wound, and festering sore (6). Offerings of rams, and fat of grazers, and blood of bullocks, and sheep, and goats (11).

Massing of a noun with its modifier: Sinful nation, people laden with crime, brood of evildoers, corrupt sons . . . (4).

Massing of verbs: They were not healed, and they were not treated, and they were not softened with oil (6); Wash, be cleansed, remove . . . cease doing evil, learn doing good, seek justice, relieve the oppressed, do justice to the orphan, take the case of the widow (16–17). . . .

Verbs will sometimes occur alone, indicating the excitement of the speaker, and sometimes they will occur accompanied by other words. . . .

In examples in which the *verbs* occur *alone* we see the interesting fact that after the occurrence of a few verbs alone, the last verb occurs accompanied by certain words that complement it; that is, the stormy spirit of the speaker wanes with the first words, and afterwards the quiet, which allows the words to continue. Here are a few examples:

> I shall pursue, I shall overtake, I shall divide spoil, my desire will be filled, I shall bare my sword, my hand will dispossess them (Exod. 15:9).

> He encircled it, he examined it, he formed it as the pupil of his eye (Deut. 32:10).

> I have told, and I have saved, and I have announced, and there is no alien among you (Isa. 43:12). . . .

In most examples of verbs together with nouns we find them as imperatives, in the form of commands given in a surging of the heart.

"The land quakes; the heaven, too, rains; the clouds, too, rain down water; the mountains melt from before the Lord" (Judg.5:4–5). The utterances increase in size.

> David Yellin. *Ketavim nivharim*. Vol. II (Jerusalem, David Yellin Jubilee Committee, 1959), pp. 135–36, 138–39†

HYPERBOLE

In one of the compositions I wrote before this one I already spoke on the subject of exaggeration and hyperbole, of that which leaves what is naturally possible and enters what is naturally precluded. There are examples of such items in the books of prophecy. The nature of language may sometimes demand that we rise above the ordinary and speak of things that are impossible, even though we would not authenticate them if we examined them carefully. . . . Our early sages of blessed memory call such things "overblown language."

In the Holy Books we find: "cities large and fortified to the sky" [Deut. 9:1]; "to our eyes we seemed like grasshoppers"—which is only hyperbole—"and so we seemed to their eyes"—which is a plain lie, for only the exalted God knows the hidden things [Num. 13:33]; "the mountains will move and the hills will topple"—he means that even were the mountains and hills to cease to be, [God's] love will not depart from you [Isa. 54:10]. Another item in the category of exaggeration is the verse "Though the sky like smoke would dissipate" [Isa. 51:6]. . . . Even the following verse belongs to the category of exaggeration: "All the host of heaven will molder" [Isa. 34:4]. This alludes to the passing on of the kingdoms, using the host of heaven as a metaphor for the overturning of empires. To the category of hyperbole belong: "the mountains will be soaked by their blood" [Isa. 34:3]; "and their dust will be drenched with fat" [ibid.:7]; "for a stone from the wall will cry out" [Hab. 2:11]; "[the behemoth] thinks of iron as straw" [Job 41:19]; and many similar examples that cannot be cited here. But the verse "I soak my bed with my tears" [Ps. 6:7] does not belong to this category because it has a literal interpretation. [The Psalmist] wants to say that his tears were running, for water does not destroy quickly as fire does.

And of the fine expressions in the category of hyperbole is the verse "and the rock would pour out streams of oil for me" [Job 29:6]; the text delves into describing [Job's erstwhile] happiness and gives a wonderful image of a man whose luck is with him. To this category also belongs, in my opinion, the verse "My honor was renewed to me, and my bow was transformed in my hand" [Job 29:20]. Most interpreters are of the opinion that it means his bow became strong and fair, so that after each shot it would be like new, as it was in the beginning, as though no one had shot with it. However, this interpretation is unsatisfactory. The correct explication is that this is an exaggeration in describing [his] happiness. The text says that the dry wood of which the bow was made would regenerate in his hand. . . . He describes his happiness, saying that even the dry wood would blossom in his hand by virtue of his righteousness. [ca. 1135]

> Moses ibn Ezra. *Shirat Yisra'el*. Tr. from the Arabic by Ben-Zion Halper (Leipzig, Abraham Joseph Stybel Publishing, 1924), pp. 185–87†

Hyperbole, as a literary figure, is an intentional exaggeration, by which a speaker obviously overstates his case and yet carries greater conviction. The hearer is aware of the exaggeration, but provided it be conveyed in a novel or striking manner, he is impressed in spite of himself. . . . Outside the sphere of humor hyperboles are the peculiar property of orators. The most picturesque piece of oratory in the Bible is that of Hushai the Archite, by which he induced Absalom not to pursue David. As the orator warms to his theme, he exaggerates more and more:

> Thou knowest thy father and his men, that [. . .] they be chafed in their minds, as a bear robbed of her whelps in the field. . . . When some of them (Absalom's men) be fallen . . . whosoever heareth it, will say, "There is a slaughter among the people that follow Absalom." And even he that is valiant, whose heart is as the heart of a lion, shall *utterly melt*. . . . But I counsel that all Israel be gathered together unto thee . . . *as the sand that is by the sea for multitude*, and that thou go to battle in thine own person. So shall we come upon him in some place where he shall be found, and will *light upon him, as the dew falleth on the ground*, and of him and of all the men that are with him we will *not leave so much as one*. Moreover, if he be gotten into a city, then shall all Israel *bring ropes to that city, and we will draw it into the river, until there be not one small stone found there*." [II Sam. 17:8–13]

There is a real crescendo of boasting here, it will be noticed, culminating in the absurd threat at the end.

Other hyperboles of a similar type are those used by Moses threatening Pharaoh:

> "Against any of the children of Israel *shall not a dog move his tongue*," [Exod. 11:7]

or addressing the rebellious Israelites themselves:

> "As for them that are left of you, I will send a faintness into their heart in the lands of their enemies, and *the sound of a driven leaf shall chase them*." [Lev. 26:36]

Another is put into the mouth of the Assyrian:

> "With the sole of my feet *will I dry up all the rivers of Egypt*," [Isa. 37:25]

referring to the multitude of his army, for whose drink, as some interpret it, the water of the Nile would not suffice.

Another type of hyperbole merges in personification:

> "*The sun and moon stood still* [. . .] at the light of thine arrows." [Hab. 3:11]

This is much more vivid and striking than if the prophet had said, that the sun and moon were eclipsed by God's lightnings.

Percy C. Sands. *Literary Genius of the Old Testament* (Oxford, Clarendon Press, 1926), pp. 59–60

Rhyme. *See* Prosody: Rhyme

Rhythm. *See* Prosody

SOUND

The fiery energy of Hebrew is often felt to be gained at the expense of beauty. The profusion of compressed consonants, sibilants and gutturals even conveys to Western ears an unpleasing impression of piercing intensity and harshness. But the sharper sibilants are mainly expressive of keen emotions of grief or triumph, and are thus in artistic harmony with the passionate genius of the language, while the purity with which the gutturals are breathed from the open throat tones down the harshness that might otherwise be felt. Hebrew has its full share, too, of the more liquid consonants, with a variety of vowel tones ranging from the rich broad *â* to the light *shᵉwa*, yielding the possibility of a manifold interplay of sounds. The strength of the double letters, with the normal alternations of vowel and consonant, give the language also something of the tuneful flexibility of Arabic or Italian. The Hebrew poets were fully aware of the musical potentialities of their speech, and sensitive to the magical effects produced by harmonies of sound. The musical quality of Hebrew may be appreciated even by the Western student who listens sympathetically to the rendering of the Sabbath service in the Synagogues especially of the Spanish Jews. And the poetry of the Old Testament shows harmonious effects of surprising power. The reproduction of the furious gallop of the strong ones "by the waters of Megiddo," or the crashing of the fatal blow on Sisera, in the sounding notes of Deborah's great battle-hymn (Judg. 5:22, 26), the unmistakable suggestions of the "surging of the peoples, that surge like the surging of the seas," and the "rushing of nations, that rush like the rushing of mighty waters" (Isa. 17:12ff.), and Nahum's brilliant picture of the flashing and raging of the war-chariots at the assault of Nineveh (Nah. 2:3ff.), rank among the finest verbal effects in literature. But even apart from such obvious efforts of art, and the simpler musical charms produced by alliteration and assonance, the Hebrew poets display a true power in the wedding of sounds to tones of feeling. Many of the Psalms are real studies in harmony. The first, for example, opens with a play of sibilants gliding into easy liquids and labials, as the Psalmist passes from the dark and dangerous paths of the wicked to contemplate the joyous fortunes of the good. With verse 4 the duller sounds predominate, the tone only rising in sympathy with the expression of sure confidence in verse 6. The second Psalm offers a yet more remarkable example of tonal harmony. The tumultuous gathering of the nations is depicted in a series of rushing *sh*, *r*, and *m* sounds, supported mainly by heavy vowels. As the enemy take counsel together against the Almighty, the tone rises almost to a shriek through a succession of compressed consonants, *s, ts*, and *ḥ*, mingled with the sharper vowels *i, e*, and short *a*. In verse 3 the breaking of the chains is distinctly audible in the snapping notes of the verb *nᵉnattᵉqa*. The subsequent transition from the calm majesty in which the Almighty sits enthroned in heaven to His outbreak of stormy indignation against the wicked is equally well reflected in the sound of the verses. In contrast with the rage and tumult of this Psalm, the eighth offers a good example of the feeling of repose and confidence suggested by the quieter tones of speech, while through the pastoral beauty of the twenty-third an unmistakable effect is produced by the gently rustling *sh* sounds and the murmuring *ms*. The same aesthetic pleasure is gained from a study of the finer passages of the Song of Songs and Job. In the glad Spring-song (Song 2:8ff.) the vowels and consonants seem to dance in harmony with the rhythm. The changing moods of Job are likewise reflected in the sounds. Thus the general tone of the picture of Sheol (3:13ff.) is grave and dull, the radiant vision of Job's past happiness (ch. 29) is pitched on a high, clear key, while the majesty of the Divine utterance is sustained by a rich variety of verbal harmonies.

Alex R. Gordon. *The Poets of the Old Testament* (New York and London, Hodder and Stoughton, 1912), pp. 5–8

By means of assonance, or the repetition and stressing of vowel sounds, some of the subtler effects of Hebrew verse are secured. The Hebrew poets were fond of mingling the liquids and softer radicals and of the use of the double consonant, which produces effects difficult to register in translation. The Song of Samson is a good case:

> With the jawbone of an ass
> Have I massed a mass;
> With the jawbone of an ass
> Have I slain a thousand.   [Judg. 15:16]

Here is an example of the imitation of one and another kind of noise by the spoken word, called *onomatopoeia* in rhetoric:

> Then thudded the hoofs of the horses,
> Off gallopped, off gallopped his chargers.
> Curse ye, curse ye Meroz!
> Curse ye, curse ye her townsfolk.   [Judg. 5:22–23]

A most effective instance of how the spoken word may be made to chime in with the thought is the remarkable little poem at the close of chapter 17 in Isaiah. The prophet is comparing the noisy clamor of the approaching army to the booming and dashing of waves on a rock-bound coast and the ease of its victory to the blowing of the chaff from the hillside threshing-floor by a whirlwind:

> Woe, the booming of the peoples, the multitudes!
> As the booming of the seas are they booming.
> And the crashing of the nations,
> As the crashing of mighty waters they crash:
> But Yahweh rebuketh him
> And he chides him and he fleeth afar,
> Like the chaff on the mountains by the wind,
> And the whirling dust before the whirlwind.

Byron's famous "Destruction of Sennecherib" lacks the vividness of Isaiah's briefer description, but it is interesting to compare the two.

Arthur J. Culler. Creative Religious Literature (New York, Macmillan, 1930), pp. 133–34

In looking at the O[ld] T[estament] it should be asked: which sounds did the poetic language of Hebrew contain? How were they articulated by the prophets, for example? The answer can be gotten only from literary texts. After a careful analysis I must conclude, as it was to be expected, that the prophets were in general extremely sensitive to sound-pattern, and that this sensibility was enhanced by traditions of the "trade."

A few examples:

Alliterative hendiadys: *shamir washayit* ["briers and thorns"; Isa. 5:6], *ta'aniya wa'aniya* ["heaviness and sorrow"; Isa. 29:2].

Alliterative word-pairs or parallel words: *shim'u shamayim* ["Hear, O heaven"; Isa. 1:2], *hoy goy* ["Ah, nation"; Isa. 1:4], *'am 'amora* ["People of Gomorrah"; Isa. 1:10].

Entire parallel sentences, held together by alliteration or rhyme (Isa. 40:9): *'al har gavoah 'ali lakh / harimi vakkoah qolekh* [To the high mountain go up / Strongly raise up your voice].

Concatenation of sound (Isa. 9:2):

> *hirbita haggila* [sic!]
> *higdalta hassimḥa*
> *samehu lefanekha*
> *kesimḥat beqatsir*
> *ka'asher*

[You have multiplied the jubilation / you have enlarged the rejoicing / they rejoice before you / as in rejoicing at the harvest / just like]

Sound-chiasm (Isa. 40:4): *'aqov mishor* [crooked straight]; *rekhasim biq'a* [mountain-tops valley].

Sound pattern through reiteration of a vowel (Isa. 1:21): *'ekha hayeta lezona qirya ne'emana* [How she has become a harlot, the faithful city!]; through reiteration of long vowels (Isa. 57:19): *shālōm shālōm lerāḥōq welaqārōv* [Peace, peace to far and to near!]; through reiteration of consonants and vowels (Isa. 8:15): *wekhashelu . . . wenafelu wenishberu wenoqeshu wenilkedu* [They will stumble . . . they will fall, they will be broken, they will be snared, they will be captured]; through reiteration of doubled consonants (Isa. 6:4): *wayyanu'u 'ammot hassippim miqqol haqqore' wehabbayit yimmale'* [The door jambs shook at the sound of the caller, and the temple filled (with smoke)].

A pattern through a leading-sound [*Leitklang*], perhaps through the *m* in descriptions of the sea (Isa. 11:9): *kammayim layyam mekhassim* [as water covers the sea]; through root-consonants as leading-sounds, as in the first part of the song of Mount Zion (Isa. 2 and Mic. 4), which is dominated by the sounds *n-h-r-y-l* (*nhr* = to flow, *ylk* = to go).

These examples are selected from richer material. Unfortunately we are apt not to find such patterns very impressive. As moderns we are used to reading softly poetry that is intended to reverberate and resound. Moreover, this sort of observation is scarcely cultivated in biblical scholarship.

Luis Alonso-Schökel. Vetus Testamentum Supplement
7, 1959, pp. 155–56†

A sound figure that attracts attention to one or more words in a phrase disturbs the tenor established by the syntax. The juxtaposition of like words, guided by the principle of arrangement, superimposes on the sense resulting from the syntactic structure nuances and meanings indicating another sense. In the Hebrew language, the selection of words based on sound arrangement thereby facilitates the expression of characteristic traits of this language, namely the effort toward totality and movement. In Hebrew, the repetition of groups of like sounds serves to center thought on an important point, to reveal in it diverse nuances, to focus the wealth and variety of a discourse, to prolong the thought of the author.

As has been already observed, one of the effects of the combination of two words chosen by dint of their likeness in sound is *emphasis*, which attracts the attention of the hearer-reader. The second word adduced often alludes to the meaning of the first word: It sometimes enriches it with new nuances, at other times it prolongs it, redoubles it, and gives the phrase the aspect of a meaningful tension. The effect of emphasis is nearly always concomitant with expressions that hold the pairs of like words centered on the same concept; for example, the pleonastic *welekh-lekha*, "and go forth" ([Gen.] 22:2; 26:29; 33:13); the expression *hafar be'er*, "to dig a well" ([Gen.] 26:15), which compares to a *figura etymologica*; the synonymous verbs *wayyifru wayyirbu*, "they were fruitful and grew very numerous" ([Gen.] 47:27).

The movement of sound elements to the interior of a phrase *extends* the semantic content of a concept or an expression in a direction that is not indicated by the sense of the phrase. For example, the phrase "he who spills the blood of man for (this) man will his blood be spilled" ([Gen.] 9:6) is more suggestive in Hebrew, where the words *shofekh dam ha'adam ba'adam damo yishafekh* displays in chiastic fashion two sound groups, SH-P-KH and DAM, which comprise the theme of the phrase "spilled blood." The word *dam* ["blood"], for its part, evokes the word *'adam* ["man"], which, juxtaposed with *dam*, develops the central theme in two syntactically parallel phrases: "the spilled blood of the man—the blood spilled for this man." The sound process *dam→ 'adam* conveys a development following the content: "The spilled blood of a man" will be followed by "the blood spilled for this man."

Andrzej Strus. *Biblica*. 60, 1, 1979, pp. 15–16†

STANZA

When we pass on to the highest unit of the stanza, it would appear that the stricter metrical prosody inspired by Classical literature, and the metrical system founded upon clause parallelism [as in biblical poetry], to a large extent coalesce. In modern English the more familiar conception of stanzas is that of uniform stanzas, uniform for a whole poem or large section of a poem. To this both Classical and Biblical verse add the further conception of stanzas running in pairs, strophe and antistrophe: the two strophes of a pair agree minutely in rhythm, but the rhythm may altogether change between one pair of strophes and another. The mutual relation of stanzas admits a large variety of elaborations.

Antistrophic stanzas may be alternating, or interlacing, or united by the beautiful effect of introversion; they may have introductions and conclusions, and be varied by epodes or odd stanzas. Stanzas otherwise uniform may be varied by regular duplications, by augmenting and diminution. There are the general effects of suspension and interruption; particular figures like the envelope figure, particular devices such as the refrain. This is not the place to discuss these in detail; it is enough to recognize the principle that in verse, as in other music, the ideal is to attain the highest elasticity of treatment without losing the rhythmic step.

> Richard G. Moulton. *The Modern Study of Literature* (Chicago, University of Chicago Press, 1915), pp. 476–77

The poetry of Second Isaiah and large part of the Psalter is rapturous, with spontaneous outbursts. However in Hebrew poetry there are elements of unity, with what we may call a rhetorical basis. For a time the singer sings to one theme, and this, as often appears in a stichos or couplet, with thought presented in appositional, oppositional, or progressive form. This unity persists until the poet's mind shifts to another field, perhaps only another phase of his subject. It is not surprising then to discover that we may mark out sections that have their internal unity, and yet withal relate to their neighbors with something like balanced equivalence. This does not mean a necessary equality of stanzas, but there appear to be approximations to such an ordering of the poesy, of which the writer may have been unconscious, but which arose involuntarily from the balance of the composition. As with the initial unity of a couplet or so, so there developed parallel unity, intellectual and poetical, in the successive steps of the composition. Hebrew verse exhibits in known literature, so the writer thinks, the initial and original steps towards something approximating equal stanza-formations, yet never with precise rule. It approaches the later ballad development of poetry, although there a musical tune is in control, as was not the case with Hebrew poesy.

The following is a study of the subject on basis of the Psalter. The book is a collection of what became synagogal hymns, and for many Christian groups their sole hymnal. But its origins are most diverse, ranging from the outbursts of saints and self-confessed sinners, of hearts that discovered the glory of God in history and in nature (as in Pss. 8, 104), all the way to public prayers and hymns in the temple courts and synagogues, and so the collection is well representative of the people's ancient poetry.

In part the liturgical note *selah* correctly marks stanza-divisions, at times it has evidently been misplaced. Especially is to be noted the excellent work done for the English reader by the Jewish Version (Philadelphia, 1917) in distinguishing stanzas by spacing, in this ignoring the *selah*, where its placing is not germane. The distinctions there indicated by unprejudiced editors support the present writer's contention.

> James A. Montgomery. *Journal of Biblical Literature*. Sept., 1945, pp. 380–81

By dint of a general law of aesthetics and harmonious balance, often reinforced by cultic or liturgical exigencies, the verses of Semitic poems tend to group themselves in strophes, each strophe normally corresponding to one principal idea (logical division, based on meaning). Already in Mesopotamia one observes a certain number of poems manifestly composed of strophes, distinguished in the script, as the verses are, too; there are strophes of four, ten, eleven, etc., lines. The "canticle" . . . may call for an antiphonal response. . . . It is also possible to distinguish strophes in the poems of Ras Shamra; but these are actually pericopes or "tirades" analogous to those in our *chansons de geste*.

A considerable advance in this was achieved by the Israelite poets. As was to be expected, the more ordinary strophe consisted in grouping two bicolon verses, joined by meaning, to form a distich "couplet" (or quatrain of four hemistichs), as already in the old satiric *mashal* about Siḥon (Num. 21:27f.). There is also frequently a grouping of three verses, a triad, a tristich (or a six-line stanza of six hemistichs). This strophe is more amply suitable particularly for didactic snippets or for slight notions than for longer extended units (so in the Psalms of Asaph, Job, etc.). The tercet or tricolon (three hemistichs in ternary, more rarely binary, rhythm) appears exceptional in isolation, the third member being nothing but a variant; but it can be encountered in series (so in Pss. 24:7–10; 60:8–11; 77:17–20; 93; 100; and 138). In the case of binary rhythm, more rapid than the others, there may be a strophe of two (Pss. 4, 110, etc.), three (Ps. 45, etc.), four (Pss. 68:8f.; 29; 86; etc.), or even six stichs (Pss. 46, 74), each stich-bicolon comprising four stresses with or without a median caesura (cf. the rhythm of the classic alexandrine). This is besides the binary rhythm, which seems to prefer more delicate combinations, such as one finds in Exod. 15:1–18; II Sam. 1:19f.; and Ps. 137:1–6.

It has been noted for a long time that strophes may group themselves for meaning in twos, more rarely in threes, so as to form "stanzas." Nothing is more natural; but their delimitation is often hazardous, whereas ordinarily a poem does not allow more than one type of strophe. One may note that a triad can introduce a string of couplets, and that the body of the poem is often announced by *ki* ["for"], right after the introduction. The refrains and certain repetitions (response, inclusion, concatenation) are the best criteria. *Selah*, often set off, ordinarily represents a strophic division, sometimes an important one, that being its precise signification. But it would be presumptuous to subject to a procrustean bed certain poems, resistant to any strophic arrangement and disconcerting to the wrong-headed western spirit of symmetry. We should respect the supple fantasy of the ancient Semitic genius. We should avoid above all applying to it the literary forms, drawn, for example, from the Greek world.

R. Tournay. *Revue biblique*. July, 1946, pp. 355–57†

The basic criterion for strophic division, as the pioneer Friedrich B. Köster over a century ago maintained, is that of divisions of the sense, logical thought divisions, including such phenomena as the apparent turning point of the whole poem, the synthesis or antithesis of thoughts. Here, it must be admitted, is where the inevitable element of subjectivity enters in, for frequently exactly this thought division depends upon interpretation. Just what the poet meant and how he expressed it are so closely interwoven that no strophic investigator can claim absolute assurance. Firsthand empirical investigation is the task of all who are concerned with making the meaning of Hebrew poetry clear today. . . .

What, then, are the minimum areas of agreement concerning strophic structure upon which further studies may proceed? First of all, it is clear that basic to Hebrew poetry is not simply the distich (more rarely tristich) line with its internal parallelism. From the writer's investigations into the Psalms it would appear that in as large a proportion as 70 to 75 per cent of Hebrew poetry there is to be found the couplet, the simple strophic unit formed by the conjunction of two normally distich (or bicola) lines, and in perhaps 30 per cent of the poems—sometimes in the same poems where couplets are found—there appears the next larger unit, the triad, composed of three normally distich lines. . . .

Granted the existence and relative frequency of couplets and triads as the basic strophic forms, some further questions arise: First, are there other types of such simple strophes? Yes, apparently there are at least two such, and probably more: (1) There is a form of strophe in which an added stichos or overhanging half-line appears at the end of each couplet or triad as a sort of refrain summing up the thought of the strophe and carrying forward the general logical development of the poem. Examples are found in Psalms 5 and 29. (2) In some cases there seem to appear units consisting of four lines, or perhaps rarely six lines each. In such a four-line unit, which might be termed a quatrain, chiastic structure or envelope parallelism may be found, as in Psalms 28 and 40. In such a six-line strophe as in Psalm 19 the catalogue of ideas all similar in nature constitutes a kind of bulk which precludes any smaller strophic division.

The second question: What of the organization of the simple couplet or triad strophes into larger units which may be called stanzas? Although stanzas may not occur as frequently as might be expected, there are two common types: (1) In poems composed of couplets (such as Psalms 18, 28, 39, and 40; probably in Ps. 23; and possibly in Ps. 16, 17, and 26) the combination of two couplets into a quatrain is found. Occasionally one finds a stanza of three couplets (as in Ps. 19 and 27) or of five couplets (as in Ps. 38). While there may be stanzas composed of three, four, five, or more couplets, it seems likely that the simple quatrain appears most frequently. (2) Similarly in poems composed of triads there may be combinations into stanzas of two, three, four, or perhaps rarely more triads. Psalm 22 and probably Psalm 35 contain stanzas composed of four such strophes. In addition there are obvious variations of these stanza patterns, as in Psalms 20 and 21 where the psalm is composed of stanzas made up of two or three couplets plus an additional line at the end, or in Psalm 33 which, unless textual corruption gives a false impression, is apparently composed of stanzas made up of a triad, three couplets, and a concluding line.

Charles F. Kraft. In *A Stubborn Faith*. Ed. by Edward
C. Hobbs (Dallas, Southern Methodist University Press,
1956), pp. 65–66, 71–72

STYLE

For this is especially the cause why, with the wise and the learned, and the princes of this world, the sacred Scriptures are without credit, because the prophets spoke in common and simple language, as though they spoke to the people. And therefore they are despised by those who are willing to hear or read nothing except that which is polished and eloquent; nor is anything able to remain fixed in their minds, except that which charms their ears by a more soothing sound. But those things which appear humble are considered anile [old womanish], foolish, and common. So entirely do they regard nothing as true, except that which is pleasant to the ear; nothing as credible, except that which can excite pleasure: no one estimates a subject by its truth, but by its embellishment. Therefore they do not believe the sacred writings, because they are without any pretence. [ca. 300]

> Lucius Caecilius Firmianus Lactantius. In *The Anti-Nicene Fathers*. Vol. VII. Ed. by Alexander Roberts and James Donaldson. Rev. by A. Cleveland Coxe (New York, Scribner's, 1913), p. 136

Rabbi Aḥa said: The conversation of patriarchs' servants is favored [by the Pentateuch] more than the laws of their sons. The passage about [Abraham's servant] Eliezer [in Gen. 24] is two or three columns long, narrated and then repeated, while the law that a reptile's blood does not defile as its flesh does is derived only from a superfluous word! . . . "And water to wash his feet and the feet of the men who were with him" [Gen. 24:32]. Rabbi Aḥa said: The washing of the feet of the patriarchs' servants is favored [by the Pentateuch] more than the laws of their sons, for [the Pentateuch] sees a need to write even of the washing of feet! Yet the law that a reptile's blood does not defile as its flesh does is derived only from a superfluous word! [6th c.]

> *Bereishit Rabbah*, section 60:8 (Vilna, Romm, 1909), p. 240†

Know that in all twenty-four books [of the Hebrew Bible] where the text states something and later repeats it you will find that the text abbreviates its wording, either in the first instance or in the second instance. If it abbreviated in the first instance, it returns and informs you in the second instance what it omitted in the first, as in [Judg. 13:5], where the text initially abbreviated the angel's words and did not say "[for a Nazirite of God will the boy be] from the womb to the day of his death," but when the woman recounts to her husband Manoah what the angel had said to her, she says to him, "Thus he said to me: 'for a Nazirite of God will the boy be from the womb to the day of his death'" [Judg. 13:7]. And sometimes the text enlarges at first, as in [Judg. 13:12], where Manoah says: "What will be the boy's regimen and activity?" But the text later abbreviates when it does not write in the angel's reply [Judg. 13:13–14] what his activity would be. Rather, you learn by yourself that the angel did not fail to reply to all that Manoah asked him. And so the text says with Moses, "And you all approached me and said, 'Let us send out men ahead of us'" (Deut. 1:22), but we have not found where they said that to him. Rather, you learn by yourself that they said this to him, but because Moses will eventually reproach them for this thing and will say it later, the text abbreviated initially; and so it is in many passages. [early 12th c.]

Joseph Kara. *Perushei Rabbi Yosef Kara' linvi'im ri'shonim*. Ed. by Shimon Eppenstein (Jerusalem, Makor, 1972), p. 42†

There are those who interpret [Gen. 1:1] to mean "In the beginning God created the heaven and the earth." It is impossible to say this, however, for the water preceded, as it is written "the wind of God was hovering over the face of the water" [v. 2]. . . . And he who interprets . . . "The beginning of God's creating the heaven and the earth," that is to say, before God created the heaven and the earth there was wild and waste and darkness over the face of the deep and the wind of God hovering over the face of the water, so that the water was created first— this, too, is nonsense, for it was not necessary to write "and the earth was wild and waste." Seeing as the earth was not yet created, it was not yet appropriate to call it "earth" prior to the forming of the water, since the water preceded. Nevertheless, this is the actual sense according to biblical style, which routinely anticipates and explains a thing that is necessary only for a thing that is mentioned further on in another passage. It is written "Shem, Ham, and Japheth" and also "and Ham is the ancestor of Canaan" [Gen. 9:18] only because it is written further on "Cursed is Canaan" [v. 25]. If it had not been first explained who Canaan was, we would not know why Noah denounced him. "[Reuben] lay with Bilhah, his father's concubine, and Israel [his father] heard" [Gen. 35:22]. Why is it written here "and Israel heard"? In fact, it is not written here that Jacob [Israel] spoke anything at all to Reuben. Rather, because in his dying hour Jacob said: "Unstable as water, you shall excel no more, for you [Reuben] went up into the bed of your father, then you violated the couch into which you went up" [Gen. 49:4], therefore, the text anticipates with "and Israel heard," so that you are not surprised when you see that Jacob reproved Reuben for this in his final days. And so it is in many passages. . . . There was a wind blowing over the face of the water. And the wind is necessary for that which is written further on, "God said, 'Let the water be gathered under the heaven into one place,'" etc. [Gen. 1:9], for it was by means of the wind that the water was gathered, as in the splitting of the Reed Sea when the dry land appeared: "The Lord pushed the sea with a fierce east wind all night long, and he made the sea into dry land, and the water was split" [Exod. 14:21]. [12th c.]

Samuel ben Meir. *Perush hattora*. Ed. by David Rosín (Breslau, Solomon Sattlander, 1882), pp. 3–5†

It seems to me that this episode [of getting water from the rock in Num. 20] is the same as the one in [Exod. 17] where it is written: "You shall strike the rock (and water) will come forth" [v. 7]. But there [in Exod.] the text relates how the Holy One supported Israel with manna and quail [Exod. 16] and water in the wilderness; then afterward each episode is written in its own place. You should know that these two are the same episode, for there it is written: "He called the name of this place Massah and Meribah" [Exod. 17:7], and in [Deut. 33] it says of this episode that the Holy One recounts Moses and Aaron, "whom you tried at Massah, with whom you contended at the waters of Meribah" [v. 8]. Accordingly, they are one episode, for it has even written here "They are the waters of the contention [*merivah*] of the Wilderness of Zin" [Num. 27:14], and it also writes "They journeyed . . . from the Wilderness of Sin" [in Exod. 17:1] when the Holy One told Moses to strike the rock. And so it is in many passages, where words are measured in one place and expanded in another place, for example, the passage about the spies. For it is written in Deuteronomy [1:22] that the Israelites said, "Let us send out men [i.e., spies]," but in [Num. 13] it does not say this expressly. And so in many passages. [12th c.]

> Joseph Bekhor Shor. *Perush 'al hattora*. Ed. by Ḥayyim Y. Isser (Jerusalem, no publisher indicated, 1956), pp. 98–99†

The Grand Style is practised as follows: if we adopt for it words that are the most elegant possible, whether literal or figurative; if we introduce elevated statements in any Amplification and in any Appeal to Pity; and if it is composed of Figures of Thought or of Diction which have grandeur. Most of Isaiah's discourses and certain of Ezekiel's descriptions illustrate this Style; for example: Hear, O heavens, and give ear, O earth, for the Lord hath spoken: Children I have reared, and brought up, and they have rebelled against Me. The ox knoweth his owner, etc. . . . Ah sinful nation, a people laden with iniquity, a seed of evildoers, children that deal corruptly; they have forsaken the Lord, they have condemned the Holy One of Israel, they are turned away backward. On what part will ye be yet stricken, seeing ye stray away more and more? and indeed the entire passage [Isa. 1:2–5 ff.]. This is the Grand Style because these are words of the utmost elegance; moreover, in this passage are found some Figures of the sort called for in the Grand Style, such as Apostrophe, Refining, and others; and it contains sublime ideas derived from the topic of Amplification, for Amplification is notably in evidence here. So too in the Grand Style: "Who is this that cometh from Edom, with crimsoned garments from Bozrah? This that is glorious in his apparel, stately in the greatness of his strength?"—"I that speak in victory, mighty to save."—"Wherefore is Thine apparel red, and Thy garments like his that treadeth in the winevat?" and the entire passage [63:1–2 ff.]. And again, the following: I gave access to them that asked not for Me, I was at hand to them that sought Me not; I said: "Behold Me, behold Me," unto a nation that was not called by My name. I have spread out My hands all the day unto a rebellious people, and the rest [65:1–2 ff.], for in this speech amplification, sublimity, and the Figures of Speech demanded by the Grand Style are present in marked amount.

In Ezekiel, similarly, the prophecy against Tyre and her king [26:2–28:19], the section beginning ". . . cause Jerusalem to know her abominations" [16:2]; and many others are also in Grand Style.

We practise the Middle Style if we abate somewhat the elegance and sublimity of the Grand Style, yet do not approximate the familiarity of the Simple Style. For example: Thus saith the Lord: "Moreover I will take, even I, of the lofty top of the cedar, and will set it; I will crop off from the topmost of its young twigs a tender one, and I will plant it upon a high mountain and eminent; in the mountain of the height of Israel will I plant it," and so throughout the passage [Ezek. 17:22–23 ff.]. Again: "Now, thou, son of man, wilt thou judge, wilt thou judge the bloody city? Then cause her to know all her abominations. And thou shalt say: Thus saith the Lord: O city that sheddest blood in the midst of her," etc. [22:2–3]. Also: "Son of man, there were two women, the daughters of one mother; and they committed harlotries in Egypt; they committed harlotries in their youth; there were their bosoms pressed, and there their virgin breasts were bruised. And the names of them were Oholah," etc. [23:2–4].

To practise the Simple Style is to speak in the fashion of the generality of the populace, in language familiar to them, as in the Book of Jeremiah's account of the episode of Gedaliah the son of Ahikam [40:6–41:18], and the account of the destruction of the Temple [52:12–23]; and as in the Book of Joshua, Samuel, and Kings, which for the most part do not transcend the ordinary usage and narrative manner customary with the generality of men. . . .

The Middle Style is faulty when the words and sentences are improperly arranged, so that the audience has difficulty in understanding. Thus, if instead of saying:

> How do the beasts groan! / The herds of cattle are perplexed,
> Because they have no pasture; / Yea, the flocks of sheep are made
>   desolate [Joel 1:18],

one should say:

> How groan the beasts! / Of cattle are perplexed the herds,
> Because pasture have they not, / The flocks, yea, are made deso-
>   late, of sheep,

this is expressed in faulty Middle Style. They call this Drifting Incoherence, because it is like a melted thing that has lost its shape, and which, since it is not at rest, nobody can properly grasp it. Such incoherence cannot possibly compel the hearer's attention. [1475]

Messer David ben Judah Leon. *The Book of the Honeycomb's Flow*. Ed. and trans. by Isaac Rabinowitz (Ithaca, N.Y., Cornell University Press, 1983), pp. 147, 149, 151, 153

There is a certain Coldness and Indifference in the Phrases of our *European* Languages, when they are compared with the Oriental Forms of Speech; and it happens very luckily, that the *Hebrew* Idioms run into the *English* Tongue with a particular Grace and Beauty. Our Language has received innumerable Elegancies and Improvements, from that Infusion of *Hebraisms*, which are derived to it out of the Poetical Passages in Holy Writ. They give a Force and Energy to our Expressions, warm and animate our Language, and convey our Thoughts in more ardent and intense Phrases, than any that are to be met with in our own Tongue. There is something so pathetick in this kind of Diction, that it often sets the Mind in a Flame, and makes our Hearts burn within us. How cold and dead does a Prayer appear, that is composed in the most Elegant and Polite Forms of Speech, which are natural to our Tongue, when it is not heightened by that Solemnity of Phrase, which may be drawn from the Sacred Writings. It has been said by some of the Ancients, that if the Gods were to talk with Men, they would certainly speak in *Plato*'s Stile; but I think we may say, with Justice, that when Mortals converse with their Creator, they cannot do it in so proper a Stile as in that of the Holy Scriptures.

If any one wou'd judge of the Beauties of Poetry that are to be met with in the Divine Writings, and examine how kindly the *Hebrew* Manners of Speech mix and incorporate with the *English* Language: after having perused the Book of Psalms, let him read a literal Translation of *Horace* or *Pindar*. He will find in these two last such an Absurdity and Confusion of Stile with such a Comparative Poverty of Imagination, as will make him very sensible of what I have been here advancing.

Joseph Addison. *The Spectator*. Vol. VI, No. 405 (London, Printed for S. Buckley and J. Tonson, 1713), pp. 53–54

The Hebrew poets frequently express a sentiment with the utmost brevity and simplicity, illustrated by no circumstances, adorned with no epithets (which in truth they seldom use); they afterwards call in the aid of ornament; they repeat, they vary, they amplify the same sentiment; and adding one or more sentences which run parallel to each other, they express the same or a similar, and often a contrary sentiment in nearly the same form of words. Of these three modes of ornament at least they make the most frequent use, namely, the amplification of the same ideas, the accumulation of others, and the opposition or antithesis of such as are contrary to each other; they dispose the corresponding sentences in regular distichs adapted to each other, and of an equal length, in which, for the most part, things answer to things, and words to words, as the Son of Sirach says of the works of God, "two and two, one against the other [Ecclus. 33:15]." These forms again are diversified by notes of admiration, comparison, negation, and more particularly interrogation, whence a singular degree of force and elevation is frequently added to the composition.

Each language possesses a peculiar genius and character, on which depend the principles of the versification, and in a great measure the style or colour of the poetic diction. In Hebrew the frequent or rather perpetual splendour of the sentences, and the accurate recurrence of the clauses, seem absolutely necessary to distinguish the verse: so that what in any other language would appear a superfluous and tiresome repetition, in this cannot be omitted without injury to the poetry. This excellence therefore the sententious style possesses in the Hebrew poetry, that it necessarily prevents a prosaic mode of expression, and always reduces a composition to a kind of metrical form. For, as Cicero remarks, "in certain forms of expression there exists such a degree of conciseness, that a sort of metrical arrangement follows of course. For when words or sentences directly correspond, or when contraries are opposed exactly to each other, or even when words of a similar sound run parallel, the composition will in general have a metrical cadence." (Orator.) It possesses, however, great force in other respects, and produces several great and remarkable beauties of composition. For, as the sacred poems derive from this source a great part of their elegance, harmony, and splendour, so they are not unfrequently indebted to it for their sublimity and strength. Frequent and laconic sentences render the composition remarkably concise, harmonious, and animated; the brevity itself imparts to it additional strength, and being contracted within a narrower space, it has a more energetic and pointed effect. [1753]

> Robert Lowth. *Lectures on the Sacred Poetry of the Hebrews.* Vol. I. Tr. from the Latin by G. Gregory (London, Printed for J. Johnson, 1787), pp. 100–102

I have been reading in the Old Testament again. What a glorious Book! For me, even more remarkable than the content is this presentation in which the word is, as it were, a product of nature—like a tree, like a flower, like the sea, like the stars, like man himself. It sprouts, it flows, it sparkles, it smiles—one does not know how, one does not know why, one finds everything entirely natural. That is truly the Word of God and not like other books that bear witness only to the human mind. In Homer—the other great book—the presentation is a product of art, and even though the substance, just as in the Bible, is always seized from reality, it nevertheless comes out in the form of a poetic image, recast, as it were, in the crucible of the human spirit. It is purified by a spiritual-mental process that we call art. In the Bible there is indeed no trace of art; the style here is that used in a memorandum book in which absolute spirit, as if without any individual human assistance, has entered the day's events with the same fidelity with which we write our laundry list. No judgment whatsoever can be pronounced upon this style; we can only observe its effect on our hearts and minds; and the Greek grammarians must have gotten into no little embarrassment when they were obliged to define many a striking beauty in the Bible according to traditional concepts of art. Longinus [1st-c. Greek critic] speaks of loftiness. More recent aesthetes speak of naïveté. Alas, as we have said, all criteria of judgment are lacking here. . . . The Bible is the Word of God.

Only in a single author do I find something that calls to mind that direct style of the Bible. That author is Shakespeare. In his writing too, the word sometimes stands out with that awful nakedness that terrifies and deeply shakes us; in the works of Shakespeare we see at times the very embodiment of truth without the garb of art. However, that occurs only in single moments: The genius of art, perhaps sensing its powerlessness, for a few moments relinquished its function to nature, and subsequently asserts all the more jealously its power in the graphic representation and ingenious nexus of the drama. Shakespeare is simultaneously Jew and Greek, or rather, both elements, spirit and art, have interpenetrated in him, made their peace with one another, and developed into a higher totality. [Letter to Ludwig Börne, July 29, 1830]

> Heinrich Heine. *Sämtliche Werke*. Vol. VII. Ed. by Ernst Elster (Leipzig and Vienna, Bibliographisches Institut, 1890), pp. 52–53†

Quite unique is the intercalated episode, the negotiations of Abraham with God regarding Sodom, which may almost be called a didactic composition [Gen. 18]. It is written to treat a religious problem which agitated the time of the author, and which occurred to him in connexion with the story of Sodom. These narrators have a quite remarkable fondness for long speeches, so great as to lead them to subordinate the action to the speeches. The most marked instance is the meeting of Abraham with Abimelech, chapter 20. Here, quite in opposition to the regular rule of ancient style, the events are not told in the order in which they occurred, but a series of occurrences are suppressed at the beginning in order to bring them in later in the succeeding speeches. Thus the narrator has attempted to make the speeches more interesting even at the expense of the incidents to be narrated.

It is also a favorite device to put substance into the speeches by having what has already been reported repeated by one of the personages of the story (43:13, 21, 30ff.; 43:3, 7, 20f.; 44:19ff.). The rule of style in such repetition of speech is, contrary to the method of Homer, to vary them somewhat the second time. This preference for longer speeches is, as we clearly perceive, a secondary phenomenon in Hebrew style, the mark of a later period. We observe this in the fact that the very pieces which we recognise from other considerations as the latest developments of the legend or as intercalations (13:14–17; 16:9f.; 18:17–19, 23–33) are the ones which contain these speeches.

We may find this delight in discursiveness in other species of Hebrew literature also. The brief, condensed style of Amos is followed by the discursive style of a Jeremiah, and the same relation exists between the laconic sentences of the Book of the Covenant and the long-winded expositions of Deuteronomy, between the brief apothegms which constitute the heart of the Book of Proverbs and the extended speeches which were afterwards added by way of introduction, between the oldest folk-songs, which often contain but a single line each, and the long poems of art poetry.

> Hermann Gunkel. *The Legends of Genesis*. Tr. by W. H. Carruth (Chicago, Open Court, 1901), pp. 84–85

It is difficult to object when we are told—as we very frequently are told—that there are two super-eminent works of literature in English—the Bible and

Shakespeare; but I always feel uneasy when I hear it. I suspect that the man who says so does not appreciate Shakespeare as he ought; and that he is not being quite honest about the Bible. The reason why it is difficult to object is that there is a sense in which it is true that the style of the Bible is splendid. The vocabulary on which the translators drew is singularly pure; purer than Shakespeare's vocabulary, by far. But the strength of a vocabulary does not really lie in its purity—and purity is in itself a very arbitrary conception when applied to language—but in its adaptability as an instrument. Think what you could do with Shakespeare's vocabulary as compared with what you could do with the vocabulary of the Bible: no comparison is possible. I can conceive no modern emotion or thought—except perhaps some of the more Hegelian metaphysics—that could not be adequately and superabundantly expressed in Shakespeare's vocabulary: there are very few that would not be mutilated out of all recognition if they had to pass through the language of the Bible.

And, when we consider style in the larger sense, it seems to me scarcely an exaggeration to say that the style of one half of the English Bible is atrocious. A great part of the historical books of the Old Testament, the gospels in the New, are examples of all that writing should not be; and nothing the translators might have done would have altered this. On the other hand, though the translation of Job that we have is a superb piece of poetry, I am convinced that it is finer in the Hebrew original.

John Middleton Murry. *The Problem of Style* (London, Humphrey Milford, Oxford University Press, 1922), pp. 134–35

The Bible avoids long explanatory phrases, unnecessary adverbs and adjectives. Its style seems to be based chiefly upon nouns and verbs, the nouns for the picture and the verb for the action. Even in English and other modern languages, where the translation requires the addition of many words and which therefore is always an expansion of the terser Hebrew style, even there the succession of nouns and verbs and the swift sequence of images makes the Bible style move on rapidly without lagging. For example, Jacob's sons ask permission to take young Benjamin with them down to Egypt. Jacob resists their request. He recalls his old sorrow at the loss of his son Joseph and he fears that a similar loss will befall him with Benjamin. Then he would have no children left from his beloved wife Rachel. And if this would occur, life would lose all its joy for him. He would age rapidly and die. All this he expresses in the following, swift succession of phrases: "My son shall not go down with you; for his brother is dead and he only is left; if harm befall him by the way in which you go, then will ye bring down my gray hairs with sorrow to the grave." (Gen. 42:38.)

The Prophet Isaiah desires to enumerate the evils which exist in his beloved city of Jerusalem, how violence has taken the place of peacefulness, how the nobility has lost its sense of high station and responsibility and how justice is neglected and the judges are corrupt. He states all this in a dynamic succession of sharp, short phrases, giving the picture in a minimum of words.

How is the faithful city / Become a harlot!
She that was full of justice, / Righteousness lodged in her,
But now murderers.
Thy silver is become dross, / Thy wine mixed with water.
Thy princes are rebellious, / And companions of thieves;
Everyone loveth bribes, / And followeth after rewards;
They judge not the fatherless, / Neither doth the cause of the
    widow come unto them. (1:21–23.)

The Prophet Amos, desiring to indicate that God's mandate to the prophet is one that cannot be ignored, that it startles the sleeping heart to alert attention, says it in this succession of phrases: "The lion hath roared, who will not fear? The Lord God hath spoken, who can but prophesy?" (3:8.)

Thus do the phrases in the Bible move swiftly. The style does not halt nor get lost in the swamps of verbiage. One phrase follows another quickly, and in each phrase the verb and the noun are prominent. The Book of Leviticus describes the reward that will come to the people of Israel for obedience to God's commandments. The reward is given as a happy, prosperous agricultural life in which one harvest is no sooner over than the next harvest begins. The land will have prosperity and security. Note the unbroken movement of the succession of phrases in this passage from Leviticus:

If ye walk in My statutes and keep My commandments, and do them, then will I give your rains in their season and the land shall yield her produce and the trees of the field shall yield their fruit. Your threshing shall reach unto the vintage and the vintage shall reach unto the sowing time. Ye shall eat your bread until you have enough, and dwell in your land safely. I will give peace in the land and ye shall lie down and none shall make you afraid. (26:3–6.)

The Hebrew originals in all these quotations have half as many separate words as do the modern translations, and yet even the translations reveal the ceaseless, forward motion characteristic of the dynamic Biblical style.

Solomon B. Freehof. *Preface to Scripture* (Cincinnati, Union of American Hebrew Congregations, 1950), pt. 1, pp. 83–85

I will discuss this term ["fraught with background"] in some detail, lest it be misunderstood. I said above that the Homeric style was "of the foreground" because, despite much going back and forth, it yet causes what is momentarily being narrated to give the impression that it is the only present, pure and without perspective. A consideration of the Elohistic text teaches us that our term is capable of a broader and deeper application. It shows that even the separate personages can be represented as possessing "background"; God is always so represented in the Bible, for he is not comprehensible in his presence, as is Zeus; it is always only "something" of him that appears, he always extends into depths. But even the human beings in the Biblical stories have greater depths of time, fate, and consciousness than do the human beings in Homer; although they are nearly always caught up in an event engaging all their faculties, they are not so entirely immersed in its present that they do not remain continually conscious of what has happened to them earlier and elsewhere; their thoughts and feelings have more layers, are more entangled. Abraham's actions are explained not only by what is happening to him at the moment, nor yet only by his character (as Achilles' actions by his courage and his pride, and Odysseus' by his versatility and foresightedness), but by his previous history; he remembers, he is constantly conscious of, what God has promised him and what God has already accomplished for him—his soul is torn between desperate rebellion and hopeful expectation; his silent obedience is multilayered, has background. Such a problematic psychological situation as this is impossible for any of the Homeric heroes, whose destiny is clearly defined and who wake every morning as if it were the first day of their lives: their emotions, though strong, are simple and find expression instantly.

How fraught with background, in comparison, are characters like Saul and David! How entangled and stratified are such human relations as those between David and Absalom, between David and Joab! Any such "background" quality of the psychological situation as that which the story of Absalom's death and its sequel (II Sam. 18 and 19, by the so-called Jahvist) rather suggests than expresses, is unthinkable in Homer. Here we are confronted not merely with the psychological processes of characters whose depth of background is veritably abysmal, but with a purely geographical background too. For David is absent from the battlefield; but the influence of his will and his feelings continues to operate, they affect even Joab in his rebellion and disregard for the consequences of his actions; in the magnificent scene with the two messengers, both the physical and psychological background is fully manifest, though the latter is never expressed. With this, compare, for example, how Achilles, who sends Patroclus first to scout and then into battle, loses almost all "presentness" so long as he is not physically present. But the most important thing is the "multilayeredness" of the individual character; this is hardly to be met with in Homer, or at most in the form of a conscious hesitation between two possible courses of action; otherwise, in Homer, the complexity of the psychological life is shown only in the succession and alternation of emotions; whereas the Jewish writers are able to express the simultaneous existence of various layers of consciousness and the conflict between them.

Erich Auerbach. Mimesis. Tr. by Willard Trask (Princeton, N.J., Princeton University Press, 1953), pp. 12–13

Biblical style is conditioned by the resources of Hebrew, one of the Semitic languages, which are: A. Eastern: Assyro-Babylonian; B. Western: (*a*) Northwestern: Aramaic and Hebrew; (*b*) Southwestern: Arabic and Ethiopic.

The Hebrew alphabet comprises twenty-two letters representing consonants (no vowels were written before the seventh century of our era). Some letters have two sounds as *th* in *thin* and *this*, or *s*, in *son, rose, mansion*, and *measure*. In contrast with English, in which sounds are articulated between the tongue and the lips, often scarcely opening the lips, ancient Hebrew was rich in sounds articulated within the throat, and it retained a Bedouin virility marked by sharp staccato tones, vigorous doubled consonants (such as persist in Italian but are lost in English), and deep-throated, rasping, guttural sounds.

The vocabulary of Hebrew is concrete and vivid. Words still paint a picture, ideas are often expressed by objects. Thus "my horn" means "my power"; "lip of Canaan" means the Hebrew language; religion is called "the fear of God" and morality "turning away from evil." Common actions are described visually: "he opened his mouth and spoke"; "he lifted his eyes and looked"; "he put forth his hand and took." Adjectives are rare: "a man of God" means "a holy man"; "a hill son of oil" is a fertile hill.

The English speech has been enriched by concrete expressions borrowed from the Hebrew: "to lick the dust," "the sweat of thy face," "to heap coals of fire," "a land flowing with milk and honey," "the stars in their courses," "a broken reed," "hewers of wood and drawers of water," "the wife of thy bosom."

In classical Hebrew sentence follows sentence with impressive uniformity: "My beloved had a vineyard on a very fruitfull hill; and he digged it, and cleared it of stones, and planted it with the choicest vine, and he built a tower in the midst of it, and also hewed a vat therein" [Isa. 5:1–2]. Even political oratory, perhaps the most verbose literary genre, is direct and simple in ancient Israel. Elaborate oratory appears first in Deuteronomy. How unsuited Hebrew was for complicated sentences may be seen in the ambitious but deplorable attempt of the author of Proverbs 2 to construct a colossal sentence in the Greek manner. The brilliant allegory of senility in Ecclesiastes 12:1–7 is only in appearance a single long sentence; in reality it is a series of vignettes. Metaphors are characteristic of Hebrew literature at its best. . . .

The Hebrew Scriptures do not lack classical examples of unadorned straightforward prose, lapidary in its conciseness, sublime in its simplicity. " 'Let there be light!' And there was light"; "Ye shall be as gods, knowing good and evil"; "For dust thou art, and unto the dust thou shalt return"; "Eye for eye, tooth for tooth"; "Thou are the man!"

The superb literary qualities of such simple words may be appreciated by contrasting the lucid directness of "Thou shalt love thy neighbor as thyself" (Lev. 19:18) with A. P. Herbert's rendition into what he calls "Jungle English" (in his book *What a Word!*): "In connection with my co-citizens, a general standard of mutual good will and reciprocal non-aggression is obviously incumbent upon me."

Some Biblical writers have made excellent use of irony (I Sam. 26:15; Am. 4:4f; Job 26:2–4) and sarcasm, as in two fables (Judg. 9:7–21 and II Kgs. 14:9), and in Elijah's words on Carmel (I Kgs. 18:27). The Book of Proverbs, with refreshing humor, recognizes that the most vexing type of wife is a garrulous shrew, while the most irritating type of husband is the indolent sluggard.

In addition to the concreteness, vividness, fancifulness, sublimity, sarcasm, and humor, many other moods of Hebrew style could be mentioned: pathos (Am. 5:2), exultation (Exod. 15:21), dejection (Job 3), indignation (Hos. 2:2–12), invective (Am. 4:1), grief (II Sam. 18:33), tenderness (Jer. 2:2), faith (Ps. 23).

Robert H. Pfeiffer. The Books of the Old Testament
(New York, Harper, 1957), pp. 3–5.

The rule of that biblical style that can now be formulated—that behind grammatical incongruity there is apt to lie hidden an incongruity in perspective—capitalizes upon deviations and fluctuations of the narration not only in grammatical structure (especially the transition from active to passive, and vice versa) but also in grammatical person/number (the transition from singular to plural, and vice versa):

(76)   [. . .] Pharaoh told them his dream, and there is no one to solve them for Pharaoh. (Gen. 41:8)

(77)   Egypt chased [plural] after them, and they reached [plural] them, encamped by the sea [. . .] And Pharaoh drew near, and the children of Israel raised their eyes, and behold: Egypt is traveling [singular] after them. They were very frightened, and the children of Israel cried out to the Lord. (Exod. 14:9–11)

(78)   David said to him [to the Egyptian servant]: "Will you bring me down to this troop?" He said . . . "I will bring you down to this troop." He brought him down, and behold: they are sprawling over the face of the ground, eating and drinking and celebrating with all the great loot that they had taken from the land of the Philistines and from the land of Judah. (I Sam. 30:15–16)

If it is "his dream" [76], why does "them" follow? If it is "they chased" [77], why "is traveling?" If it is "this troop" [78], why "they are sprawling [. . .] eating and drinking and celebrating?" As in interchanges between passive and active . . . each of the variations is in and of itself normal. What is puzzling is the lack of consistency, or even (in the opening example) in the very contradiction in the transition back and forth from one to the other. It is this puzzlement that impels the reader not to rest content with what is said explicitly and directs him to try to reorganize the text such that the lack of consistency will clear the way for a coherent reading. In fact, in the three instances not only does the prodding, driving force of the split in grammatical categorization become clear; it also becomes clear that the coherence that best dispels and supplants it is coherence in perspective: the fluctuation from one grammatical form to another alludes to and parallels a more comprehensive fluctuation—from one position of point of view to its counterpart—which is always bound up in covert penetration [into the characters' psyches].

I have already dealt with the first instance in an analysis of Pharaoh's dream in its entirety:

> The possibility of perspectival-interpretive split among the Egyptians is suggested. When we encounter the puzzling phenomenon of grammatical incongruity between "his dream" (in the singular) and "them" (in the plural), in the first stage we discriminate that "his dream" is the object of the king's report ("he told"), while "them" is the object of the attempt of the magicians to interpret ("there is no one to solve"). And in the second stage we justify the puzzling phenomenon—and also the very failure of the magicians, or at least their failure in Pharaoh's view—in terms of an implicit difference between Pharaoh's perception (one dream) and the magicians' perception (two dreams). (Sternberg. *Ha-sifrut.* [Oct. 1977], 126). . . .

First, this three-way comparison lays bare an array of means for focusing and highlighting grammatical incongruity. In Pharaoh's dream, the effect of transition is especially sharp, on account of the textual juxtaposition and syntactic parallelism of the opposed formations, and on account of their semantic distance: one dream and several dreams are things so well distinguished in reality that their identity departs from mere inconsistency in the direction of actual contradiction. By contrast, "troop" and "Egyptians," too, are collective nouns, and as such they may (certainly in the language of the Bible) be predicated and inflected in the singular or plural form. Because the two number forms merge into one grammatical category, fluctuation from one to the other is liable to miss the reader's eye or be dismissed as a stylistic variation alone. Hence the multiplication of compositional "compensations" for the lack of logical contradiction.

Meir Sternberg. *Ha-sifrut.* July, 1983, pp. 126–27†

THEMES AND MOTIFS

According to the measure a man metes out, such a measure is meted out to him. . . . Samson went after his eyes, therefore the Philistines gouged out his eyes, as it is said, "The Philistines seized him and they gouged out his eyes" [Judg. 16:21]. Absalom was conceited about his hair; therefore, he hung by his hair [II Sam. 18:9–10]. And because he came into [i.e., cohabited with] ten of his father's concubines, therefore were ten lances put against him, as it is said, "Ten men, weapon-bearers of Joab, surrounded him" [II Sam. 18:15]. And because he stole three hearts—the heart of his father, the heart of the court, and the heart of Israel—as it is said, "Absalom stole the heart of the men of Israel" [II Sam. 15:6]—therefore were three darts shot into him, as it is said, "(Joab) took three darts in his hand, and he shot them into Absalom's heart" [II Sam. 18:14].

And so it is with respect to benefit. Miriam waited for Moses one hour, as it is written, "His sister stood up at a distance" [Exod. 2:4]—therefore did Israel delay for her seven days in the wilderness, as it is said, "The people did not travel until Miriam was gathered back" [Num. 12:15]. Joseph had the merit of burying his father, and there is none greater than he among his brothers, as it is written, "Joseph went up to bury his father . . . and he brought up with him a chariot and drivers, too" [Gen. 50:7, 9]. Whom do we have greater than Joseph, to whom none other than Moses attended? Moses had the merit of [conveying] Joseph's bones, and there is none in Israel greater than he, as it is said, "Moses took the bones of Joseph with him" [Exod. 13:19]. Who is greater than Moses, to whom none other than God attended, as it is said, "(The Lord) buried (Moses) in the vale" [Deut. 34:6]. [ca. 200]

Mishnah. Tractate *Sotah.* 1:7–9†

Longing for the past, for the "olden times," which in the mind of man are always "better than these times," induces poets to compose special songs to describe the old times in all their glory; and such do we find as complete chapters in the Book of Psalms. Most of them speak of and describe at length the period of the nation's formation: its toil in Egypt and its liberation. As an opening, there appear in brief the events of the nation's ancestors, and in closing the events of the people in the wilderness before entering the Land [of Israel], as well as certain facts from the time of its settlement in it. . . . ([Pss.] 78, 105, 106, 135, 136). The style is generally *prosaic in a poetic form* of verses and parallel lines. . . .

Psalm 136, intended to be sung by a chorus, is a kind of easy journey over the great events that the people experienced. . . .

Apart from these complete chapters, we find here and there ancient memories that appear incidentally, as in Hosea (12:4): "in the womb he grasped his brother's heel." Isaiah (51:2) recalls "Abraham your father" and "Sarah your progenitress" and the Lord's blessing to him, and in another chapter (63:11–13) he recalls: "He who drew out his people [= God] . . . who brought them up from the sea . . . who placed in its midst his holy spirit . . . who split the water before them . . . who led them through the deep like a horse in the wilderness." And in the same chapter ([v.] 16) he recalls Abraham and Israel. And in Ezekiel (28) is a recollection of the Garden of Eden, and in chapter 16 a recollection of Sodom, its daughter-cities, and their crimes. Ezekiel, too, recalls (33:24) Abraham, when he says: "Abraham was (only) one, and he possessed the land," and similarly (14:20) Noah, Daniel, and Job, the pious men.

The principal memories, however, which appear incidentally and in large measure, are memories of *the splitting of the Reed Sea* and *the journey in the wilderness*, as in Isaiah (11:15–16): "The Lord will destroy the tongue of Egypt . . . and smite it . . . and lead dry-shod, and there will be a highway . . . as there was for Israel when it went up from the land of Egypt"; and similarly (51:10): "Are you not the one that dried up Sea, waters of the great Ocean, that made the depths of the sea into a path for the redeemed to cross"; and similarly (63:11–18): "He recalled the olden times, drawing out his people; where is he who took them up from the sea," etc. Or in Psalms (66:5–6): "Come and see the actions of God . . . He turned the sea to dry-land," etc. Or (114:3): "The sea saw, and the Jordan fled—it ran backwards," etc. Or a detailed description of the splitting of the Reed Sea (77:17–21): "They saw you, did the waters, O God, they saw you, the waters whirled," etc. . . .

But principally what is recalled is the general aspect of the Israelites' dwelling in the wilderness forty years. Sometimes the nation is described as a lover following her sweetheart even into most dangerous places, as in the words of Jeremiah (2:2): "I recall of you the faithfulness of your youth, your love as a bride, your going after me in the wilderness, in a land not sown." And sometimes they recall God's love for his people and his compassion for them when they followed in a desolate wilderness, as in (Jer. 2:6): "They did not say, 'Where is the Lord . . . who led us in the wilderness, in a land of desert and pits . . . in a land no man has crossed . . . ?'"; or (Hosea 9:10): "Like grapes in the wilderness did I find Israel," etc.; or (ibid. 13:5): "I knew you in the wilderness, in a land of great drought."

David Yellin. *Ketavim nivḥarim.* Vol. II (Jerusalem, David Yellin Jubilee Committee, 1959), pp. 25–26†

The themes of the Bible are simple and primary. Life is reduced to a few basic activities—fighting, farming, a strong sexual urge, and intermittent worship. With these must be associated death, friendship, and politics, the last being commonly without morals. From the quantitative point of view, three central subjects emerge, are endlessly iterated, and amount sometimes to monotony and sometimes to sublimity. This threefold theme is the interest of God in man, the wrath of God, and the weakness or rather the wickedness of humanity. The instinct that leads fundamentalists to regard the Bible as an inerrable message from heaven is in a literary point of view so far justified that the nature of God is central to the collection. The development, attributes, desires, frustrations, and penitence of deity are everywhere foremost and overshadow the actions of men.

This elemental quality in the themes of the Bible is at once ground and occasion of a life and outlook quite as primary as and often more primitive than that in Homer or the Greek tragic poets. We confront basic virtues and primitive vices. Men are brave, potent, loyal, faithful, devout; they are fearless or frightened; they are cunning, sensual, idolatrous, cruel, hypocritical. Women group themselves into elemental categories—harlots like Rahab, heroines like Judith, housewives like Sarah, Ruth, Rebecca. . . . The world these persons inhabit is stripped and elemental—sea, desert, the stars, the wind, storm, sun, clouds and moon, seedtime and harvest, prosperity and adversity, famine and plenty. In the third chapter of Ecclesiastes we learn that to every thing there is a season and a time to every purpose. Then follow twenty-eight such times in balanced pairs which reduce human life to its elements; as, for example, a time to seek and a time to lose; a time to keep, and a time to cast away.

Howard Mumford Jones. *Five Essays on the Bible* (New York, American Council of Learned Societies, 1960), pp. 52–53.

The predominant aspects of *midbār* wilderness in the Bible give additional evidence to the unfamiliarity with and the loathing of the "desert" which were typical of the ancient Israelite. It is the attitude of the city-dweller, the farmer, the semisedentary shepherd, even of the ass-nomad, who may traverse the desert on beaten tracks, but who would not voluntarily venture into its depth. This attitude is exceedingly different from that of the true camel-nomad, the Bedouin, to whom the desert is home.

The connotation of *midbār* as a barren, awe-inspiring, howling wilderness is intimately related to yet another category of a rather specific brand of "reality." There are to be found in the Bible some residues of a mythical conception of "wilderness," which is much more fully developed in ancient Semitic mythology and also in post-Biblical midrashic literature. . . .

As in reality, the desert also can equal "refuge": "Flee, save yourselves," is the prophet's advice to the Moabites. "Be like a wild ass in the desert" (Jer. 48:6). And the Psalmist "would wander afar . . . would lodge in the wilderness" to find shelter from his enemies, who are likened to "the raging wind and tempest" (Ps. 55:7–8).

This fact gives rise to an incipient positive image which is derived from "wilderness language": namely, the employment of "desert" as a figure for "retreat," as in Jeremiah's famous lament: "O that I had in the desert a wayfarer's lodging place, that I might leave my people and go away from them" (Jer. 9:1). This theme was not further developed in Biblical literature. Even in the Jeremiah passage the "positive" aspect is subsidiary. The prophet is not drawn into the desert, as it were, to meditate there and come face to face with his God. He does not seek communion with the Deity, but rather he longs to dissociate himself from his contemporaries.

So far we have dealt with perspectives of *midbār* in its over-all spatial–geophysical connotation. We can now turn to what we termed its "temporal–historical" connotation.

In a rather large number of its occurrences in Biblical literature *midbār* serves as a designation of the clearly circumscribed period which followed upon the Exodus and preceded the Conquest of Canaan. This period roughly falls into two unequal stretches of time. The one, spanning the first two years, includes the events from the Crossing of the Red Sea to the Sinai theophany, and to what immediately follows upon it. The other extends from that point, when Israel is encamped in the Pa'ran desert to the war against the Midianites, which is the last skirmish against desert people, and after which Israel enters the territories of the Transjordanian states. This period encompasses most of the remaining thirty-eight years. These are the years of the desert trek proper, the wanderings which were imposed upon Israel as a divine punishment for their sins and for their doubting God's power to lead them safely into the Promised Land of Canaan (Deut. 2:14–16). . . .

We now have to consider the "desert motif" in conjunction with other Biblical motifs. This is especially important in view of the twofold significance which we discerned in the account of the desert trek. The figurative employment of the trek traditions mirrors the two diverging phases in the Yahweh-Israel relationship which characterize the period of the desert wanderings. The one or the other, the "Divine grace" or the "Israel's sin and punishment" aspect, can be stressed. The re-enforcement of the one or the other is achieved by infusing into the "trek motif" new images and motifs which are anchored in *midbār* language in the wider sense of the word.

Thus we find in Jeremiah 2:6 a fusion of the historical "trek theme," as an expression of God's benevolence and guidance, with the partly mythical "wilderness-desolation" theme: "They did not say, 'where is the Lord who brought us up from the land of Egypt, who led us in the wilderness,'" and then in a new vein: ". . . in a land of deserts and pits, in a land of drought and deep darkness, in a land that none passes through, where no man dwells?"

Again in Psalm 78:52 the notion of Divine protection, inherent in the trek motif, is combined with the shepherd image, which has no roots in the historical account, but is derived from the "drift" context: "Then he led forth his people like sheep, and guided them in the wilderness like a flock."

> Shemaryahu Talmon. In *Biblical Motifs*. Ed. by Alexander Altmann (Cambridge, Mass., Harvard University Press, 1966), pp. 42–43, 45–46, 49–50

Beside the motif of many-branched love, which is popular in folk literature, there is in the stories of the Bible the motif of the blessing of children and its opposite: barrenness. Love, even when it is integrated into a biblical narrative, as in "Jacob loved Rachel," is not presented as a concern in and of itself—the text speaks of it only for the needs of the succeeding development. Not flowers but fruits are the Bible's axis of interest. The quintessence of the bond between a man and a woman is the continuation of the chain of life, the continuation of the generations; it is from this standpoint that it is told about in the Bible, and it is according to this standpoint that the fate of a woman is weighed.

The barren woman is the most deprived of women, for the major blessing of life and to a not insignificant degree the major reason for living are taken away from her, just as Rachel said to Jacob: "Give me sons, and if no, I die" [Gen. 30:1]—which is to say: Though I be walking in the land of the living, I am dead, for without sons my life cannot be called life. Nonetheless, there are several levels to the pain of barrenness. The severity of the pain decreases when the man and the woman are equal partners in it, which is not so in those families where the husband has reached fatherhood with another woman and the pain of barrenness weighs down with all its severity on only one of his wives. And what's more, the sorrow of the childless woman is even greater when the same fortune that turns away from her shines on her rival, so that the latter has many children and the former's deprivation is constantly underscored by the abundant satisfaction of the latter. With such pain had Rachel been tried in the house of Jacob, and from her mouth escaped the sharp utterance cited above.

Sevenfold was Hannah, the wife of Elkanah, afflicted, so that Peninah her rival was blessed beside her with sons and daughters, whose mere existence daily accented her barrenness. . . .

Yet Elkanah's loved wife was Hannah, not Peninah. And it was an apparent insult upon injury when Elkanah said to Hannah: "Am I not better to you than ten sons?" [I Sam. 1:8]. But the vacuum in her life was not filled by her husband's love, just as Jacob's love did not assuage Rachel. What good is love when the heart is set on motherhood! It does happen that the blessing of sons can compensate for an absence of love, for thus is it written: "The Lord saw that Leah was hated, so he opened her womb" [Gen. 29:31]. But it is not in the power of love to fill a lack of children. . . .

Four women in the Bible preceded Hannah in being barren—three of the matriarchs and after them the wife of Manoah. Yet the story of Hannah is the apotheosis of the motif of barrenness in the Bible. In this story the pangs of barrenness and the joy of the barren woman's visitation come to a blending. As much as her affliction at the beginning deepened, so did her relief climb afterward. And not only this. The story of Hannah is not blended in the sense that its beginning is a superabundance of grief and anxiety and its end is consolation and contentment, but rather in the sense that its beginning and end become for her a plowing and a harvest. Of all the biblical women who were tried by barrenness and were later visited, only Hannah, the last in the line of these women, raises herself from the trial of her life, acquires spiritual greatness, rises to the heights of prayer, looks out and sees with an eagle eye the wheel of fortune of Providence. And she outdid these women by bringing her son to Shiloh, for there was in this act a sort of maternal sacrifice, and this sacrifice of hers furnished the people of Israel with Samuel the prophet.

All five of the barren women that the Bible tells about—Sarah, Rebekah, Rachel, the wife of Manoah, and Hannah—had great sons, to wit: Isaac, Jacob, Joseph, Samson, Samuel. And is it a mere coincidence that the mothers of these great personages had their beginning in barrenness? No, it is hard to believe that the Bible would randomly string instances together; rather, it makes sense today that a kind of orderliness inheres in it. Precisely because these five women were destined to give birth to chosen sons did the birth come only after a protracted barrenness. It is as though routine biology could not pack enough power to bring the man of stature into the world, and additional power of a different type was required. So long as this addition does not come, the potential motherhood is of the type "she had difficulty [in her giving birth]" [Gen. 35:16]. However, as opposed to this, the chosen son offers appropriate recompense to the mother for the preceding pain.

Avraham Kariv. *Shiv'at 'ammudei hattenakh* (Tel Aviv,
Am Oved, 1968), pp. 126–27, 129–30†

As a humble shepherd of his father-in-law's flock Moses has reached the station most opposed to what he was and what he will be. How important persons rose unexpectedly from lowly beginnings, thus showing the working of Providence in human affairs, is a favorite biblical theme. Two other men who were "taken from following the flock" to greatness are the first literary prophet, Amos (Am. 7:15) and the ideal king, David. A dramatic representation of David's ascent, skipping (for the sake of contrast) all intermediate stages, is Psalm 78:70–72: "He chose David his servant / and took him from the sheepfolds; / From tending suckling ewes he brought him / to shepherd Jacob, his people, Israel, his inheritance. / With upright heart he tended them, / and guided them with skilful hand."

The figures of this passage illustrate the poetic fitness of the shepherd's office as a preparation for leadership. Both divine and human chiefs were regularly figured as shepherds of their people in the ancient Near East, and the people as flocks. Moses himself uses the figure in Numbers 27:17, "Let not the people of the Lord be like a flock that has no shepherd."

Moshe Greenberg. *Understanding Exodus* (New York,
Behrman House, 1969), pp. 67–68

[A] second motif to claim our attention is that of a hero helpless before a woman's wiles. Also a favorite topic of Israelite narrative art, this motif consists of: (1) a woman's feigned friendship or love; (2) a hero's submission to the woman's advances; (3) flirtatious teasing and tearful imploring; (4) a woman's victory over the hero. Elements of this powerful interplay of forces occur in the stories about Jael, Esther and Judith.

In the account of Deborah and Barak's victory over Jabin and Sisera, preserved in both a prose and a poetic version, Sisera sought refuge from Jael, the wife of Heber the Kenite. Clan loyalty weighed more heavily in her thoughts than the obligation to protect a guest in her tent. Feigning friendship, she offered him sustenance and safe lodging. Sisera submitted to her, and slept peacefully until she drove a tent peg into his skull (Judg. 4–5).

One of the scenes recorded in the Book of Esther contains this motif of an endangered hero in distorted form. Esther pretended to take special delight in Haman, the archenemy of the Jews, and invited him to a banquet on two successive nights. On the occasion of the second banquet the king offered her anything she wanted up to half the kingdom, as he had done the first night. Whereupon Esther identified Haman as her foe and sealed his fate.

The Book of Judith also makes use of the motif of an endangered hero in a woman's clutches. The beautiful widow abandoned her beseiged town in search of excitement, so it seemed. Her journey took her to the camp of Holofernes, the general of the Assyrian army, who fell victim to her charm. Judith offered him her "love" and Holofernes submitted to her. When the occasion arose, she cut off his head and took it with her to show her people that all danger had passed.

The fullest account of this motif occurs in the Samson saga. Besides the feigned love, the hero's submission, and the woman's victory it makes use of an element of suspense missing from the other stories. Here Samson teased Delilah, as it were, playing with fire until inevitably its flame devoured him. Such teasing does not occur in the other three accounts, unless Esther's treatment of Haman falls into this category. If so, the narrator has transformed that particular component of the motif completely, for here the woman teases the powerful hero.

The Samson narrative employs the motif twice, although this double usage required considerable alteration in the constituent parts. The description of his relationship with the beautiful Timnite varies the motif at one decisive stage— the destruction of the hero. In keeping with the narrator's fondness for suspense, the story anticipates a subsequent encounter with a dangerous woman. Hence this brief episode with the Timnite woman describes proffered love to the hero, submission to the woman, vexatious imploring on her part to discover something of value, and the loss of a great treasure, the wife.

James L. Crenshaw. *Samson* (Atlanta, John Knox Press, 1978), pp. 43–44

For this essay I have chosen "deception" as the point of reference. There are some eighteen instances within the story [of King David]; the number itself indicates the importance. However, this motif is not unique to this narrative. S. Thompson devotes a whole section to deception in his *Motif-Index of Folk Literature*. Further there are many instances throughout the Old Testament. The Jacob cycle is an especially fine example: the wily mother dresses the younger son in sheepskins to steal the birthright; then Jacob wakes up in his marriage bed only to find he is with the wrong woman; with his wands Jacob turns a bad business deal with Laban to his favor and makes a surreptitious get-away. Finally Rachel escapes death by pleading a lady's indisposition. This series of deceits has many functions. They reveal characters, add humor, create suspense, resolve conflicts and show that the Lord will have his way, one way or the other.

The use of deception in the "Succession Narrative" has similar functions, but many of the devices have much darker motives, with death as their final outcome. Although deception in this story is often treachery, the author shows that device can serve good as well as evil, for this long court narrative is in some sense, a study of deception. Furthermore this factor is organized to produce a configuration of plot which is played out five times in the course of the story with new situations and new characters.

Though deception becomes a theme in its own right, it is also a function of the larger theme of fidelity and infidelity which in the ancient Near Eastern world defines especially the relationship between the king and his men. Though this relationship was supported by economic and military forces, we find in the "Succession Narrative" relationships which transcend any material or self-serving motive. The faithfulness of Uriah, Ittai, Hushai, Barzillai and the tragic Joab reveal an abandonment of personal security in the service of their king. Thus the opening story of Mephibosheth in chapter 9 and that of Hanun in chapter 10 [of II Sam.] are not superfluous events; rather they serve to establish this theme. The story of Hanun opens with David's words: "I will deal loyally with Hanun the son of Nahash, as his father dealt loyally with me" (10:2). Hanun, however, because of bad counsel believes himself deceived by David and suffers the tragic consequences for his refusal to deal loyally. This story draws together the themes of deception, counsel, faithfulness and death which recur over and over throughout the whole.

Harry Hagan. Biblica. 60, no. 3, 1979, pp. 302–3

WORDPLAY

This term ["paronomasia"] refers to words that resemble one another but whose meanings are different. Logicians call them "resemblance." This usage is favored by most linguists because it is a type of rhetorical elegance. In the Holy Scriptures there are many examples, such as "In Beth-le-afrah cover yourself with dust [*'afar*]" [Mic. 1:10]; "the houses of Akhziv are a wadi [*'akhzav*]" [ibid.: 14]; "a dispossessor [*yoresh*] will I bring to you, O dweller of Mareshah" [ibid.:15]; "Now scourge yourself [*hitgodedi*], O daughter Gedud" [Mic. 4:14]; "while in the valley (*shifla*) the city sinks [*shafel*]" [Isa. 32:19]; "and Eqron will be uprooted [*te'aqer*]" [Zeph. 2:4]; "in Heshbon they planned [*hashevu*] against it evil" [Jer. 48:2]; "Tyre [*Tsor*] has built a fortress [*matsor*] for himself" [Zech. 9:3]; "O Madmen [a place name], you too be still [*tiddomi*]" [Jer. 48:2].

There is yet another type of wordplay, as in "For they are more numerous [*rabbu*] than locusts [*'arbeh*]" [Jer. 46:23]; "my kidneys [*kilyotay*] perish [*kalu*]" [Job 19:27]; "but he who befriends [*ro'eh*] fools will suffer ill [*yeroa'*]" [Prov. 13:20]; "You have not bought [*qanita*] for me with silver a reed [*qaneh*]" [Isa. 43:24]; "May God enlarge [*yaft*] Jafeth [*yefet*]" [Gen. 9:27]; "and you will be noted [*wenifqadta*] when your (empty) seat will be noted [*yippaqed*]" [I Sam. 20:18]; "of my wandering [*nodi*] you have taken account; place my tears in your waterskin [*nodekha*]" [Ps. 56:9]. [ca. 1135]

Moses ibn Ezra. Shirat Yisra'el. Tr. from Arabic by
Ben-Zion Halper (Leipzig, Abraham Joseph Stybel Publishing, 1924), p. 169†

In strictly lyrical poetry, *paronomasia* would be quite out of place; for the object of a lyric is not to produce surprise, it lives and moves alone in its own joyous or sad feelings. Only when rhetoric finds a place by the side of poetry, in the drama, *e.g.* may this artifice be employed with effect, as Canticles and Job show. It may also produce an agreeable effect in connexion with the incisiveness of a proverb. But the paronomasia is most natural to the prophetic style, it being the imitation or copy of public discourse; and there is no discourse of any length in which this artifice does not suddenly appear with its rapid and effective incisiveness, surprising and enchaining the hearers. It occurs even in discourse which is of the nature of a lamentation (Joel 1:15; Isa. 15 sq.). But the greatest prophets in all cases make use of it only when it is fitting, when the thought itself irresistibly leads to it, and it is able, with one blow, to finish off a complete and lengthy exposition. Isaiah may be referred to as a model in this respect also; whilst the prophet (Isa. 15 sq.), although for us he is ancient, is the first who observes far less moderation and calculation of effect in the employment of this artifice; which is still more the case with his successors Micah and several other later writers, who employ it in long series without a break, and thereby weaken, in fact, the effect. The plays upon names of places could be most easily continued in a longer series, as if to enliven somewhat such a dry list of names (Am. 5:5; Isa. 15 sq.; 10:29–31; Mic. 1; Zeph. 2:4–6). But since paronomasia is in all cases so characteristic a mark of the genuine form and life of prophetic discourse, it follows, as a matter of course, that it ought to be expressed in the translation with as much ease and naturalness as is possible. [1840]

Georg H. A. von Ewald. *Commentary on the Prophets of the Old Testament.* Vol. I. Tr. by J. Frederick Smith (London, Williams and Norgate, 1875), pp. 69–70

Paronomasia in the Old Testament is, like all other embellishments of speech, an element of higher style, that is, of the poetical and prophetical diction. In the historical books, except in the poetical passages embodied in them and the plays on the etymology of proper names, cases in which it occurs are few and far between. It is everywhere merely a casual, not an organic, element of diction. Hebrew poetical style hardly differs from the rhetorical; both have in common all the peculiarities which distinguish them from the lower style. But their purpose and effect may vary with the diction. What the poet uses merely as an ornament, the orator may employ as an instrument. This applies even to the "parallelismus membrorum" [parallelism of the clauses], the fundamental law of elevated style. In the poetical books, the requirements of the rhythm often give rise to the unfolding of the thought in the parallelism, while in the prophets, the development of a thought in all its aspects is the main object of the parallelism. Similar is the use of paronomasia. In the poetical books, it may contribute to rhythm or euphony, or be used as a mere embellishment; in the prophets, it serves more serious ends. The prophets use it especially in vivid and impassioned passages, in which the whirl of similar sound is meant to reflect the inner excitement and impress their hearer with the certainty and magnitude of an event or threatened calamity, as in *pahad wafahat wafah ʿalekha yoshev haʾarets*, fear, and a pit, and a snare upon thee, inhabitant of the land (Isa. 24:17); *yom tsarah umetsuqah yom shoʾah umeshoʾ ah . . . yom ʿanan waʿarafel*, a day of distress and anguish, a day of desolation and devastation, a day of clouds and darkness (Zeph. 1:15); depicting in conjunction with onomatopoeia: *buqah umevuqah umevullaqah*, empty, void and waste (is the land; Nah. 2:11); *yom mehumah umevusah umevukhah*, a day of trouble, and of tramping down, and of perplexity (Isa. 22:5; cf. Isa. 24:3; Ps. 46:4; Isa. 17:12; Ezek. 7:11).

Plays upon words are especially frequent in the prophets. As an element of the daily speech, with their biting, ironical, or sarcastic force, they are best suited to the prophetic sermons, which adhere closely to the living speech and aim to reach the mind and conscience of the hearer, and to bring home to him directly and vividly a truth or a fact. Next to the prophetic speech and the rhetorical passages in Job, plays upon words are most frequently found in the Proverbs, which are in general much dependent for their force and effect upon felicitous and pointed expression, while in the Psalms only a few are found, chiefly such as by frequent use have become set phrases, as *shuv shevit* ["to restore a captivity"] (Ps. 126:1, 4); *yareʾ* ["to fear"] and *raʾah* ["to see"] (Zech. 9:5).

Immanuel M. Casanowicz. *Paronomasia in the Old Testament* (Boston, J. S. Cushing, 1894), pp. 41–42

The use in literary discourse and poetry of words resembling one another in whole or in part is a phenomenon existing in most languages, and its origin is evidently even earlier than regular literature. The poet or bard captivates not only by the content of his words, but also by their form, i.e., by beauty of expression. Not only on the hearts of his audience does he try to work, but also on their ears, the mediators between the utterance of his mouth and their hearts. . . .

This phenomenon, which is found in the classical and modern European languages to a limited degree, is one of the special treasures of the oriental languages, which use this device for beautifying and ornamenting poetry. Accordingly, its use in the poetic books of the Bible, too, is great, and it will be considered to beautify the poetry only where it does not detract from the *content* or from the flight of the imagination.

This device was already known to our ancestors, who designated it by the term "language falling on language" [wordplay].

Wordplay, i.e., similarity in the sound of letters with a *difference* in meaning, we already find in the blessing by Noah of his sons, in his saying: *yaft ʾelohim leyafet* ["May God expand Japheth"] (Gen. 9:27), and in the cry of Samson: *bilhi hahamor hamor hamoratayim* ["With the jawbone of an ass, mass upon masses!"] (Judg. 15:16); and even in completely prosaic discourse on legal matters: *weshillah ʾet beʿiro uviʿer bisde ʾaher* ["He released his herd, and it pastured in another's field"] (Exod. 22:4). Similarly with partial resemblance: *kaqqash niddaf qashto* ["Like swept straw (he has rendered) his bow"] (Isa. 41:2); *me dimon male'u dam* ["The waters of Dimon will fill with blood"] (Isa. 15:9); *wayyakkum wayyakketum* ["They smote them and they discomfited them"] (Num. 14:45).

By means of complete and partial resemblance of the letters of which the words are composed there is also a device of using one or more letters in consecutive words without its being felt that there is before us a play on words.

Such a usage, which is found to a large degree in well-known sections of the books of Isaiah and Psalms in particular, occurs for the most part in whole verses, groups of verses, and sometimes even in whole chapters, and in reading them we feel that declaiming them emphasizes a letter that is continually repeated, articulates it with special accentuation, and that it dominates these verses. Thus we find in Isaiah (23:3 [. . .]) in the description of the downfall of Tyre:

> *uvemayin Rabbim zeRaᶜ shiḥoR / qetsiR ye'oR tevu'atah / watehi seḥaR goyim*

> [And on the Great Sea the seed of Shihor, / the harvest of the Nile—its produce, / and it became the trade of nations. . . .]

And in the marvelous opening of the vision of Nahum, describing the appearance of the Lord, the sounds of various letters pass one after the other (1:2–8):

> *beSufa uviSᶜaRa daRko . . . / goᶜeR BaYYam waYYaBBeshehu / wekhol HanneHaRot HeḥeRiv / 'uMLaL bashan wekhaRMeL . . . / haRim Raᶜashu mimmennu / wehaGGevaᶜot hitmoGaGu . . . / wehaTSurim nitteTSu mimmennu.*

> [In the wind and the storm is his route . . . / He rebukes the sea and dries it up, / and all the rivers he dehydrates. / Withered are Bashan and Carmel . . . / The mountains quake before him, / and the hills melt . . . / And the rocks shatter before him.]

The quaking of such mountains is felt in the emphasis on the resonant letter *r* [resh], the melting of the hills in the highlighting of the soft letter *g* [*gimel*], and the disintegration of the rocks by redoubling the letter *ts* [tsade].

David Yellin. *Ḥiqrei miqra'* . Vol. I (Jerusalem, J. H. Kosovsky, 1927), pp. 83–86†

Wordplay is frequently deployed between two juxtaposed stories. Every careful reader will take note of the folk etymology that holds together the words *miggen* ["he delivered"] (Gen. 14:20) and *magen* ["shield"] (Gen. 15:1). There victory delivers . . . enemies into Abram's hand; here following the victory a deep fear overcomes him, as becomes clear, and God promises to shield him. But there is another passage that has received very little attention. In the fourth, middle revelation [to Abraham] . . . we find (Gen. 15:13) for the first time in the book the word-stem ᶜ-n-h (meaning oppression), which is used of the acts of the Egyptians against the Israelites: "They will serve them, and [the Egyptians] will oppress them." And here in the next chapter, which relates the flight of Hagar the Egyptian, it recurs three times, 16:6, 9, and 11; and it does not return into use hereafter until chapter 29. Can it really be an accident that it is here spoken of an "Egyptian bondswoman" (16:1, and again 3) who "submits to oppression" and that the account of her doings closes with the word "Egypt" (21:21)? Or do we have here perhaps a classic realization of [the saying] that the acts of the patriarchs [presage] the events of the nation? In fact, the Hagar narrative is of the same type as that of Jacob's deception of his brother. In terms of the teleology of the Book of Genesis Sarah behaves according to objective justice, since Ishmael will perforce be removed from the legacy of the promise and God himself places his approval on her actions (21:12). Nevertheless, according to the religious truth of the Bible, she fails to defend her fellow human being before God, and she does not endeavor to requite human crime with divine justice; she commits a crime despite all this. The judgment of this action is like the judgment of Jacob's action. It would be irregular to decree this judgment explicitly, for both theological and narrative reasons. But from what is embedded in the words of the story you learn much. This Egyptian bondswoman is the first human to whom an angel of God appears and speaks. It indicates the intervention of God, which sometimes takes on a personal form. In three verses, one after the other, the words "An angel of God said to her" occur and are repeated in order to inform you that an august event is happening. [The appearance of the angel] is not, however, from heaven, as in the second Hagar episode, the episode in which the lad Ishmael is cast down to death; nor is it like the following story in the next chapter about the lad Isaac, who is tied up for death. Rather the angel stands opposite her on the ground and speaks to her equal to equal. Indeed, his words of assurance are extraordinary. We have been told in what has preceded that Sarah the mistress "oppressed" her bondswoman when she was "in her hand" (three times the text repeats for us the word "mistress" and six times the word "bondswoman"). And behold the angel now calls to Hagar: "Turn back to your mistress and submit to oppression under her hand." Inasmuch as he is the one who came down from heaven to this oppressed creature, he has the right to speak thus, not preaching in a spirit of servility. His true rationale emerges from the final recurrence of the word-stem '-n-h ["oppress"]: "For the Lord has heard your oppression." As a human being is placed in trouble noiselessly, can the "oppression" be heard? In fact, God can hear it. And at once the angel . . . tells her why she should submit to oppression under his mistress's hands: She is about to give birth to a son of her own heart, a wild bedouin, a bowman, who will dash across the wilderness from end to end, his agile arms plundering the produce of the settlers, and so "over the face of all his brothers," one after the other, "will he dwell." In fact, at the close of the account of Ishmael, which is the end of the Abraham narrative, by means of a wordplay the text emphasizes that this promise was fulfilled: "Over the face of all his brothers he fell" (25:18). The leading word "to hear" intermeshes the two Hagar stories (compare 21:17); but the leading word "to see" intermeshes the episode of Hagar's flight and the succeeding revelation to Abraham, the covenant revelation (17:1). The maidservant to whom the angel had spoken incognito calls to God himself by the name that arises out of her trial: "God who sees me." She explains the name in her question of surprise: "Have I indeed seen / behind him who sees me?" Like Moses in turn in the crevice of the rock (Exod. 33:22ff.) she "sees" the "hind part" of God (compare Gen. 16:13, *'aḥarei,* and Exod. 33:23, *'aḥorei*): his relation to the world of human beings, his mercy, which constrains his judgments (Exod. 34:6ff.). She sees that God sees her. No human can see anything greater than this. "Therefore he called the well"—the leading word, "well," also intermeshes the two Hagar stories—"Well of the Living One who Sees Me" (the well of the living God who sees me) [16:14]. The God who elects Israel justifies Sarah; but the living God Who Sees Me does not spurn Hagar.

> Martin Buber. *Darko shel miqra'* (Jerusalem, Bialik Institute, 1964), pp. 295–97†

The prophets of Israel, as ancient Israelite narrators generally . . . loved the kind of word-play which juxtaposes the same or similar words in such a way as to produce irony. Many instances of the ironic repetition of images, discussed above, involve paronomasia, which takes a number of forms.

(1) Reversal of ordinary or accepted meaning: Day of YHWH (Am. 5:18, 20); *heroes* of wine-drinking / *men strong* at mixing drinks (Isa. 5:22); glory (Isa. 10:2); stronghold of Pharaoh / shelter in Egypt's shadow (Isa. 30:1–3); Ariel (Isa. 29:1–2).

(2) Juxtaposition of the same word or homonyms: devisers of iniquity (*hosheᵉve 'awon*) / see how I am about to devise evil (*hinᵉni hoshev . . . ra'ah*) (Mic. 2:1,3) . . . ; turned away backwards (*nazoru 'aḥor*) / wounds not pressed (*lo' zoru*) / aliens (*zarim*) (Isa. 1:4, 6, 7); joiners of house to house / many houses desolate (Isa. 5:8, 9); Daughter Zion left (*notᵉrah bat tsiyyon*) / left us (*hotir lanu*) a small remnant (Isa. 1:8, 9); city where David encamped / I will encamp against you round about (Isa. 29:1, 3).

(3) Similar to juxtaposition of the same word, we find juxtaposition of the same root to bring about ironic effect: head of the nations (*re'shit haggoyyim*) / finest of ointments (*re'shit shᵉmanim*) / at the head of the exiles (*bᵉrosh golim*) (Am. 6:1, 6, 7); portion of my people (*heleq 'ammi*) / he divides our fields (*sadenu yᵉhalleq*) (Mic. 2:4).

> James G. Williams. *Semeia.* No. 8, 1977, pp. 63–64

Part 3
THE TEXTS

ABRAHAM

The cycle of stories about Abraham is of considerable importance from a number of points of view. It is a model example of the story-cycles of the Bible. It is easily seen that individual chapters, and even parts of chapters, are of the nature of separate stories (the repetition of certain themes shows that various traditional versions of tales about Abraham have left their traces in this cycle), but at the same time it is clear that the various tales are combined into a single whole by a common line of development. The stories are assembled for the purpose of composing a kind of comprehensive biography of Abraham, which results in the Abraham cycle being one of the broadest and most all-inclusive in the Bible. It is not two or three events that we have here, but the account of a life; the narrative pace becomes slower, and the author finds time to illuminate Abraham's character from all sides. At the same time, this is not a complete biography. Because of his specific aim, the narrator tells us nothing of Abraham's life before he receives the command to make his way to the Land of Israel. We have many stories about Abraham, and each one has its own special significance, for Abraham is the Father of his People, and there is no subject more attractive to the imagination of the people than the life of its father. There were always numerous folktales about martial heroes like Samson and miracle-workers like Elijah, but the favorite subject was the lives of Patriarchs, and especially the first of them, Abraham. It may be assumed that these stories in particular were especially significant, and therefore drew the author to combine them into a unit and thereby make their meaning clearer. In this case the author-compiler is like an interpreter of the spirit of the people. The story-cycle about the Father of the People will present us with a model figure, and at the same time will attach to this figure a series of ideas and ideals. His characteristics and the way they are combined personify an outlook on life; his actions and his reactions to the reality in which he lives assume a great symbolic significance. . . .

   In the tales of Abraham the character and what is personified in it are the essential, for Abraham's life-work is his life itself and the values that are active in it. Outstanding features of the tales of Abraham are a human character and a system of ideas, and the two are inseparably intertwined: the ideas acquire their force by being crystallized in a living personality, and the personality becomes incomparably more significant through the fact that it is the first focal point at which the history of Israel and world history meet. What is extraordinary in the stories about Abraham is that this infinite significance does not remove his character from the sphere of the simply human. Closely connected, perhaps, with this is the fact that in the Abraham story-cycle the human dimension is always accompanied by the divine dimension; which means not only that in the story of Abraham's life we must always pay attention to both his relationship to God and his relationship with man, but that the entire course of his life is at the same time simply human and determined by the hand of God. Not only does Abraham from time to time stand face to face with God, but God always accompanies Abraham throughout his path, protects him, and instructs him as to what he is to do with his life. And not only are these two dimensions not incompatible; they complement each other.

Zvi Adar. *The Biblical Narrative* (Jerusalem, Department of Education and Culture, World Zionist Organization, 1959), pp. 100–103.

The Abraham material is largely a series of vignettes, a character sketch of the highest artistry about a respected, noble gentleman; the prevailing tone is that of dignity. Abraham comes to Canaan but he does not take possession of it; he builds altars, but he does not offer regular sacrifices. He is neither a beggar nor a pauper; he is able to protect his land from the eastern kings; he is faithful to Yahweh. A touch of real genius is to be found in Abraham's abstaining from bargaining with Efron, the Hittite, over the price of a burial plot for Sarah, and his subsequent bargaining with the deity over Sodom. Notice that it is characteristic of Hebrew writing to present abstraction through the narration of concrete incidents; the saving idea of the power of the righteous is recorded as incident, not as a direct doctrine. In the Abraham material, the Biblical author ignores the recurrent theme of the pre-exilic prophets that the origin of the Hebrews was in the Wilderness; conceivably, his literary concerns forced him into a new perspective. His writing at a time when the Judaeans returned from the Babylonian exile prompted him into an incipient anachronism; he has Abraham born in Chaldea so as to leave it, just as the returning exiles had also left it.

Abraham is portrayed on a double level: he is the putative historic ancestor of the people, and he is also the exemplar for his people late in their history. The author writes as he does, not because he is ignorant of the past, but because he knows so much. He knows the Wilderness tradition, he knows the Exodus tradition, he knows of the monarchy and he knows the prophets and he knows of psalmists; he knows of the destruction of the northern kingdom and he knows of the Babylonian exile. Virtually all of these matters are present as nuances in the Abraham material. The author also knows that the neighboring peoples speak kindred languages and have kindred ceremonies. He must account for the similarity and, hence, Abraham is the father of many peoples, including those born to him by Keturah, the least-known woman in Scripture.

The account of the binding of Isaac is surely the high point in the series of vignettes. Whatever else the other incidents contribute to the portrait of Abraham, it is the binding of Isaac that clarifies his character, in the literary sense.

The laconic statement in Genesis 11:30, "Sarai was barren; she had no child," is not just a statement of fact; it is no less than a motif which shapes the writing of the Abraham material. It lends profundity to ensuing materials. Without it, Genesis 15 would make little sense, and the pathos of Genesis 22 would almost disappear. The viewpoint of the rabbis that there is no pleonasm in Scripture is, *mutatis mutandis*, a valid principle of literary understanding. So bare is Hebrew narration that what is included necessarily has significance for an understanding of the esthetics of prose narratives. The barrenness of Sarah is an invitation to the reader to share in Abraham's emotions as the narrative unfolds. It comes so early in the account because it is so important in a literary sense.

Samuel Sandmel. *Judaism.* Fall, 1973, pp. 464–65

The Abraham saga gives a new form to the travelogue of the ancient world. The dark father, who obeys a call, is not merely in search of better pastures but he is seen to move under divine inspiration. The story moves on the level of thumbnail sketches. The pilgrim's task remains obscure, his movements defy plotting, and the obstacles in his way evoke no heroic action but rather an almost passive acceptance of facts. The economy of the narrative militates against detailed description and full portrayal. Despite the anecdotal humour surrounding the birth of Isaac both Abraham and Sarah dwell in a solitude which the reader shares. The intensity of the clipped style dominates the form and reaches its climax in Genesis 22. The so-called sacrifice of Isaac can be understood as a reflection of the conflict between the generations, cultures, and even sexes. But this is to miss the true polemic, which concerns faith and obedience. The heart of the story is in a way its emptiness: the narrator has eschewed the pagan themes of the gods' loathing of men, man's usurpation of divinity, the earth's craving for blood, the slaughter of the child, the mother's protestation, the need for vengeance. There is a great silence in this story and no orgiastic climax. The substitution of the intended sacrifice by a ram caught in the thicket stands as the classical anti-climax. Abraham is not allowed to become a tragic hero.

The narrator blends several levels of narrative. He records as if he had been present, though the story clearly demonstrates that no one could have been present. He gives the word of dialogue in direct speech, as if he had been there to overhear them. He implies a divine presence, either by suggestion or bold citation, such as "God said." The narrative, therefore, moves on the secular level of observable events with dimensions of spiritual worth which cannot be measured. Thus the idyll of Genesis 24, in which Eliezer obtains Rebekah as Isaac's future wife, is a broadly conceived romance, which allows the transcendental element only to be apprehended in the leisurely progress of the meeting at the well. Gone is the clipped style and with it the sense of drama. Instead the form of the narrative favours the apprehension of detail. Yet the increasing material of human vignettes does not lessen the religious feeling of the whole. Even the later stories about Isaac, which concern themselves with domestic cares and wells, never lose the feeling of a divine Presence.

Ulrich Simon. *Story and Faith in the Biblical Narrative*
(London, SPCK, 1975), pp. 15–16

If we were to chart the events that have occurred in the human world in [Gen. 12–20], we would become aware of destinies moving in inverse proportion to what seemed their possibilities. For Abraham, the barrenness of Sarah is soon to be converted into fruitfulness, the land that was occupied and unfertile at the first will become an everlasting possession for his descendants, flowing with milk and honey. For those in the fertile Jordan valley and the civilized cities, however, come death and destruction—the Lord "overthrew those cities, and all the valley, and all the inhabitants of the cities, and what grew on the ground." The interlacing of fruitfulness with barrenness, possession with desolation, runs through the entire narrative. The word "interlacing" suggests the simultaneity of what seems to us, and to those in the narrative, to be opposites. Inherent in what those in Abraham's world seem to value most is its opposite. That is why the line from Keats' "Ode to Melancholy," indeed perhaps the entire poem, contains insights not unrelated to the Abraham legend—"Pleasure turning to poison while the bee-mouth sips." The promised land, for which Abram leaves his country, his kindred, and his father's house is barren and occupied; the beautiful woman whom Pharaoh brings into his house causes him to be afflicted with great plagues; the well watered valley chosen by Lot is filled with sinners and fought over by kings; his secure and fertile land is the site of his capture; Sarah's generous decision to give Hagar to Abram as wife causes her anger and pain; Hagar's obedience to her mistress leads to her being driven into the wilderness; the pleasure the men of Sodom seek in surrounding Lot's house and assaulting its entrance makes them blind; the little city Lot bargains for fills him with fear; the secure cave he moves to arouses the perverse scheme of his daughters. Each seemingly attractive opportunity also contains within it barrenness, pain, destruction, perversion.

As these human events and choices interlace, suggesting to us the difficulty of seeing clearly the precariousness of human existence, the Lord and Abraham, initially separated by the differences between divine and human perceptions and concerns, move into closer—almost too close—harmony and congruity. The movement of human history involving pleasure and pain impinges on Abraham less and less in the narrative. His detachment from the events around him—a psychological, not a real detachment—is suggested by the narrative's placement of the Lord's promises to him. He is promised descendants and land after the narrative informs us that Sarai is barren shortly before we learn of the famine; the promise is repeated and expanded after the destruction of Sodom and Gomorrah is foreshadowed and before the battle of the four against the five kings; he is promised a son and told of his descendants' oppression after he rejects the king of Sodom's offer and before Sarai drives Hagar into the wilderness; the covenant is made with him after Hagar is saved by the Lord and before the destruction of Sodom and Gomorrah. The distance between these future-oriented and incrementally specified promises and the depressing, at times catastrophic, events that surround them in the narrative and with which Abraham lives, gradually moves Abraham out of time, enabling us to interpret figuratively the significance of his look down toward Sodom and Gomorrah, watching the smoke of the land rise like the smoke of a furnace.

As Lot loses his possessions in nearly every sense of that word, Abraham gains self-possession, equanimity. As Lot and those from his city pervert the meaning of fruitfulness, Abraham receives fruitfulness as a gift. As Pharaoh and Lot and the king of Sodom place value on beauty in its physical and material manifestations, Abraham in chapter 18 demonstrates the beauty of service and simplicity, running from his tent door to greet his visitors, hastening to his tent to tell Sarah to "make ready quickly three measures of fine meal, knead it, and make cakes," selecting a calf, tender and good, standing silently by while his guests eat under a tree. Lot, we recall, serves his guests unleavened bread.

Abraham is not the same man in chapter 20 when he introduces Sarah as his sister to Abimelech as he was when he made the same introduction to Pharaoh in chapter 12. His knowledge of his destiny is obviously greater, but more important, he has discovered—and the narrative has identified for us—the denotations of a beauty, possession, and fruitfulness, which narrow the gap between a Lord who has a design for history and the individuals who must retain their independence as they fulfill it, between human possibilities and human limitations. Abraham's understanding prepares him well for the test in which he is asked to sacrifice his son, his only son, whom he loves.

Kenneth R. R. Gros Louis. In *Literary Interpretations of Biblical Narratives.* Vol. II. Ed. by idem with James S. Ackerman (Nashville, Abingdon Press, 1982), pp. 68–70

THE BINDING OF ISAAC

The tragic hero does at last get to the end of the story. Iphigenia bows to her father's resolution, she herself makes the infinite movement of resignation, and now they are on good terms with one another. She can understand Agamemnon because his undertaking expresses the universal. If on the other hand Agamemnon were to say to her, "In spite of the fact that the deity demands thee as a sacrifice, it might yet be possible that he did not demand it—by virtue viz. of the absurd," he would that very instant become unintelligible to Iphigenia. If he could say this by virtue of human calculation, Iphigenia would surely understand him, but from that it would follow that Agamemnon had not made the infinite movement of resignation, and so he is not a hero, and so the utterance of the seer is a sea-captain's tale and the whole occurrence a vaudeville.

Abraham did not speak. Only one word of his has been preserved, the only reply to Isaac, which also is sufficient proof that he had not spoken previously. Isaac asks Abraham where the lamb is for the burnt offering. "And Abraham said, God will provide Himself the lamb for the burnt offering, my son."

This last word of Abraham I shall consider a little more closely. If there were not this word, the whole event would have lacked something; if it were to another effect, everything perhaps would be resolved into confusion.

I have often reflected upon the question whether a tragic hero, be the culmination of his tragedy a suffering or an action, ought to have a last rejoinder. In my opinion it depends upon the life-sphere to which he belongs, whether his life has intellectual significance, whether his suffering or his action stands in relation to spirit. . . .

Before I go on to consider Abraham's last word more closely I would call attention to the difficulty Abraham had in saying anything at all. The distress and anguish in the paradox consisted (as was set forth above) in silence—Abraham cannot speak. So in view of this fact it is a contradiction to require him to speak, unless one would have him out of the paradox again, in such a sense that at the last moment he suspends it, whereby he ceases to be Abraham and annuls all that went before. So then if Abraham at the last moment were to say to Isaac, "To thee it applies," this would only have been a weakness. For if he could speak at all, he ought to have spoken long before, and the weakness in this case would consist in the fact that he did not possess the maturity of spirit and the concentration to think in advance the whole pain but had thrust something away from him, so that the actual pain contained a plus over and above the thought pain. Moreover, by such a speech he would fall out of the rôle of the paradox, and if he really wanted to speak to Isaac, he must transform his situation into a temptation (Anfechtung), for otherwise he could say nothing, and if he were to do that, then he is not even so much as a tragic hero.

However, a last word of Abraham has been preserved, and in so far as I can understand the paradox I can also apprehend the total presence of Abraham in this word. First and foremost, he does not say anything, and it is in this form he says what he has to say. His reply to Isaac has the form of irony, for it always is irony when I say something and do not say anything. Isaac interrogates Abraham on the supposition that Abraham knows. So then if Abraham were to have replied, "I know nothing," he would have uttered an untruth. He cannot say anything, for what he knows he cannot say. So he replies, "God will provide Himself the lamb for the burnt offering, my son." Here the double movement in Abraham's soul is evident, as it was described in the foregoing discussion. If Abraham had merely renounced his claim to Isaac and had done no more, he would in this last word be saying an untruth, for he knows that God demands Isaac as a sacrifice, and he knows that he himself at that instant precisely is ready to sacrifice him. We see then that after making this movement he made every instant the next movement, the movement of faith by virtue of the absurd. Because of this he utters no falsehood, for in virtue of the absurd it is of course possible that God could do something entirely different. Hence he is speaking no untruth, but neither is he saying anything, for he speaks a foreign language. This becomes still more evident when we consider that it was Abraham himself who must perform the sacrifice of Isaac. Had the task been a different one, had the Lord commanded Abraham to bring Isaac out to Mount Moriah and then would Himself have Isaac struck by lightning and in this way receive him as a sacrifice, then, taking his words in a plain sense, Abraham might have been right in speaking enigmatically as he did, for he could not himself know what would occur. But in the way the task was prescribed to Abraham he himself had to act, and at the decisive moment he must know what he himself would do, he must know that Isaac will be sacrificed. In case he did not know this definitely, then he has not made the infinite movement of resignation, then, though his word is not indeed an untruth, he is very far from being Abraham, he has less significance than the tragic hero, yea, he is an irresolute man who is unable to resolve either on one thing or another, and for this reason will always be uttering riddles. But such a hesitator is a sheer parody of a knight of faith.

Here again it appears that one may have an understanding of Abraham, but can understand him only in the same way as one understands the paradox. For my part I can in a way understand Abraham, but at the same time I apprehend that I have not the courage to speak, and still less to act as he did—but by this I do not by any means intend to say that what he did was insignificant, for on the contrary it is the one only marvel. [1843]

Søren Kierkegaard. *Fear and Trembling.* Tr. by Walter Lowrie (Garden City, N.Y., Doubleday, 1954), pp. 124–25, 127–29

God gives his command, and the story itself begins: everyone knows it; it unrolls with no episodes in a few independent sentences whose syntactical connection is of the most rudimentary sort. In this atmosphere it is unthinkable that an implement, a landscape through which the travelers passed, the serving-men, or the ass, should be described, that their origin or descent or material or appearance or usefulness should be set forth in terms of praise; they do not even admit an adjective; they are serving-men, ass, wood, and knife, and nothing else, without an epithet; they are there to serve the end which God has commanded; what in other respects they were, are, or will be, remains in darkness. A journey is made, because God has designated the place where the sacrifice is to be performed; but we are told nothing about the journey except that it took three days, and even that we are told in a mysterious way: Abraham and his followers rose "early in the morning" and "went unto" the place of which God had told him; on the third day he lifted up his eyes and saw the place from afar. That gesture is the only gesture, is indeed the only occurrence during the whole journey, of which we are told; and though its motivation lies in the fact that the place is elevated, its uniqueness still heightens the impression that the journey took place through a vacuum; it is as if, while he traveled on, Abraham had looked neither to the right nor to the left, had suppressed any sign of life in his followers and himself save only their footfalls.

Thus the journey is like a silent progress through the indeterminate and the contingent, a holding of the breath, a process which has no present, which is inserted, like a blank duration, between what has passed and what lies ahead, and which yet is measured: three days! Three such days positively demand the symbolic interpretation which they later received. They began "early in the morning." But at what time on the third day did Abraham lift up his eyes and see his goal? The text says nothing on the subject. Obviously not "late in the evening," for it seems that there was still time enough to climb the mountain and make the sacrifice. So "early in the morning" is given, not as an indication of time, but for the sake of its ethical significance; it is intended to express the resolution, the promptness, the punctual obedience of the sorely tried Abraham. Bitter to him is the early morning in which he saddles his ass, calls his serving-men and his son Isaac, and sets out; but he obeys, he walks on until the third day, then lifts up his eyes and sees the place. Whence he comes, we do not know, but the goal is clearly stated: Jeruel in the land of Moriah. . . .

What place this is meant to indicate is not clear—"Moriah" especially may be a later correction of some other word. But in any case the goal was given, and in any case it is a matter of some sacred spot which was to receive a particular consecration by being connected with Abraham's sacrifice. Just as little as "early in the morning" serves as a temporal indication does "Jeruel in the land of Moriah" serve as a geographical indication; and in both cases alike, the complementary indication is not given, for we know as little of the hour at which Abraham lifted up his eyes as we do of the place from which he set forth—Jeruel is significant not so much as the goal of an earthly journey, in its geographical relation to other places, as through its special election, through its relation to God, who designated it as the scene of the act, and therefore it must be named.

In the narrative itself, a third chief character appears: Isaac. While God and Abraham, the serving-men, the ass, and the implements are simply named, without mention of any qualities or any other sort of definition, Isaac once receives an appositive; God says, "Take Isaac, thine only son, whom thou lovest." But this is not a characterization of Isaac as a person, apart from his relation to his father and apart from the story; he may be handsome or ugly, intelligent or stupid, tall or short, pleasant or unpleasant—we are not told. Only what we need to know about him as a personage in the action, here and now, is illuminated, so that it may become apparent how terrible Abraham's temptation is, and that God is fully aware of it. By this example of the contrary, we see the significance of the descriptive adjectives and digressions of the Homeric poems; with their indications of the earlier and as it were absolute existence of the persons described, they prevent the reader from concentrating exclusively on a present crisis; even when the most terrible things are occurring, they prevent the establishment of an overwhelming suspense. But here, in the story of Abraham's sacrifice, the overwhelming suspense is present; what Schiller makes the goal of the tragic poet—to rob us of our emotional freedom, to turn our intellectual and spiritual powers

(Schiller says "our activity") in one direction, to concentrate them there—
is effected in this Biblical narrative, which certainly deserves the epithet epic.

We find the same contrast if we compare the two uses of direct discourse.
The personages speak in the Bible story too; but their speech does not serve, as
does speech in Homer, to manifest, to externalize thoughts—on the contrary, it
serves to indicate thoughts which remain unexpressed. God gives his command
in direct discourse, but he leaves his motives and his purpose unexpressed; Abraham, receiving the command, says nothing and does what he has been told to do.
The conversation between Abraham and Isaac on the way to the place of sacrifice
is only an interruption of the heavy silence and makes it all the more burdensome. The two of them, Isaac carrying the wood and Abraham with fire and a
knife, "went together." Hesitantly, Isaac ventures to ask about the ram, and
Abraham gives the well-known answer. Then the text repeats: "So they went
both of them together." Everything remains unexpressed.

It would be difficult, then, to imagine styles more contrasted than those of
these two equally ancient and equally epic texts. On the one hand, externalized,
uniformly illuminated phenomena, at a definite time and in a definite place, connected together without lacunae in a perpetual foreground; thoughts and feeling
completely expressed; events taking place in leisurely fashion and with very little
of suspense. On the other hand, the externalization of only so much of the phenomena as is necessary for the purpose of the narrative, all else left in obscurity;
the decisive points of the narrative alone are emphasized, what lies between is
nonexistent; time and place are undefined and call for interpretation; thoughts
and feeling remain unexpressed, are only suggested by the silence and the fragmentary speeches; the whole, permeated with the most unrelieved suspense and
directed toward a single goal (and to that extent far more of a unity), remains
mysterious and "fraught with background" [*see also* Style].

Erich Auerbach. Mimesis. Tr. by Willard Trask (Prince-
ton, N.J., Princeton University Press, 1953), pp. 9–12

God, testing Abraham, orders him to sacrifice Isaac. When they are going up together to the mountaintop, the boy speaks up: "My father!" "Here am I, my son."
"We've got the wood and the fire, but where is the lamb for the offering?" The
father is obliged to reply, "God, my son, will provide the lamb." These strokes
of human feeling, of insight, are so trenchant and so authentic, and they so surely
awake a response in all kinds and conditions of people, that there are moments
when the gods and heroes of the so much more expertly handled, the so much
more sophisticated Homeric poems seem less real than the nomads of Genesis
when the finger of the unknown scribe, tracing the ancient story, flashes across
the page the verses that make them live. This finger also makes the contact, momentous in its day and place, between God and the humblest life, and the God of
the patriarchal chronicle is a much more attractive deity than the God of the Garden of Eden, the Flood and the Tower of Babel. The mind that created Hagar,
dying of thirst with her baby, had also to create the God who would pity them

and allow them their role in the world. The composer of the conversation between Abraham and Isaac on their way to the sacrifice could not admit of a God who would compel His chosen agent to go through with this cruel ordeal. In these fumbling and awkward old stories, we can see man becoming aware of the conscience that begins to dignify him, that seems to tower above him.

Edmund Wilson. New Yorker. May 15, 1954, pp. 140,
143

It is a literary masterpiece, ironic in its disparity between intensity of emotion and paucity of words. There is no analysis of the psychological states of father and son, but only the agonizing pathos inferred in the terse conversation between them. In monumental starkness, the form perfectly masters and expresses the spirit. Equally it is a religious highpoint. . . . The outcome of the story gives a most emphatic rejection of child sacrifice while it respects and retains the intention of sacrifice: the giving of everything to God. Elohim accepts the intention in place of the act.

The story is redolent with the life of faith and devotion, with the conflict of interests inherent in two great loves, the most powerful that move the human race: love of family and love of God. It is not unduly subjective to see in this tale a parable of God's continual testing of his people to discover if they will live by faith. There is a terrifying irrevocability about the binding of the boy to the altar; Abraham has chosen his course, bitter as it is, and he will not renege.

Norman K. Gottwald. A Light to the Nations: An Introduction to the Old Testament (New York, Harper, 1959), p. 253

The story of the binding of Isaac may be examined in different ways, leading to the discovery of various levels of meaning. This multiplicity of meanings and approaches, which is an unmistakable sign of great literature, leads us beyond mere folklore and popular story-telling.

Since the content of the story is startling and gripping, perhaps we had better pause at the outset and look at the way it is told, how the narrator expresses what he has to say. Here the Biblical narrator has to tell us at the same time of a shocking act and of unique spiritual reactions. As a test, God commands Abraham to offer his son as a sacrifice after Abraham has longed for this son for many years, and Abraham prepares himself to do so; God stops him at the last moment when he has proved the greatness of his faith and sends him a ram as a sacrifice in place of the son. The story has no value unless it makes us understand the feelings of Abraham as he responds to the injunction and takes steps to carry it out—but is it really possible to express the feelings of a father who is about to sacrifice his son? On the other hand, we must not become too deeply involved in the expression of these feelings; after all it is not they that come first but the compliance with the command. Hence in emphasizing the purpose of the story the narrator cannot help hinting at these feelings, but at the same time he cannot linger over them too much. The problem is solved through the specific genius of the Biblical story, which tells us of inward feelings through the channel of the actions and the plot, and hints at the internal through the external, so that the reader shall find his way from the external to the internal. The Biblical story, the folktale, is a story of action; but it is also more than this, for every detail of the plot and every word of the story hint at the spiritual life of its heroes; at the same time, the Biblical story never deals with the life of the spirit directly, but conveys it through its expression in action. This characteristic of the Biblical story is particularly outstanding in the story of the binding of Isaac, because here it has a special function: it is only through hints at Abraham's feelings that the meaning of his act becomes clearer, but the consciousness that he must do the deed makes him suppress his feelings. The complex of emotions does not prevent the execution of the act. Hence we can see that Abraham is a typical Biblical hero. . . .

The narrator looks on Abraham's action as a perfect deed, because it is a perfect example of the highest value in the Bible: faith. The outlook of the story is thus identical with the outlook of the entire Bible, placing faith above and beyond everything else. Through anxiety the narrator presents to us the true greatness of man—the greatness that lies in humility, in submission, in faith, in compliance with God's word.

> Zvi Adar. *The Biblical Narrative* (Jerusalem, Department of Education and Culture, World Zionist Organization, 1959), pp. 39–40, 45

Puns penetrate the narrative from beginning to end. Since the father becomes an enemy to his son, the unexpected allusion to enemies *('oyebaw)* in the repetition of the promise recalls the frequent references to a father *('ab, 'abi, 'abiw)*. Other similarities are probably intentional too: *hanna'ar* [the lad] and *sha'ar* [gate]; *sham* [there], *shem* [name], *hashshamayim* [the heavens]; *bᵉni* [my son], *bᵉno* [his son], *binᵉka* [your son], *wayyiben* [and he built]; *shᵉbu* [stay], *wᵉnashubah* [and we shall return], *yesheb* [he dwelt]; and *'aḥar* [behind], *ne'ᵉḥaz* [caught]. The name that Abraham gives to the holy place enshrouds at least four puns (*yir'eh* [he will see], *yera'eh* [he was seen], *yᵉre'* [one who fears], *wayyar'* [and he saw]).

The story is rich in anticipation. The mountain is called the place that God will make known, or simply "there." The lamb caught in a thicket is foreshadowed long before, and Abraham's return to his lads is specifically promised. In each instance the actual realization brings a surprise. The place of the dreadful act becomes a scene of divine mercy, the lamb is providentially supplied by a satisfied deity, and the lone appearance of Abraham eclipses any anticipation that both father and son will return. The birth of so many surprises prepares the way for the last one, God's cancellation of the original mandate.

The story makes use of an economy of words. Amidst such "background," redundancy rarely appears. Exceptions are the following: *and he said* (vv. 2, 7), *and lo* (v. 13), *whisper of the Lord* (v. 16), *and Abraham* (v. 7), or *his father*

(v. 7). Restraint characterizes the narrative. Here one encounters fragmentary speeches, silence, reticence. God always recedes into the depths, without explaining the reason for the test. Abraham's earlier boldness in arguing with God (Gen. 18) produces no protest here, not even a clenched fist or bitten lip. Isaac conceals his awful suspicion; no word is spoken of the effect on his life. Has he lost faith in God and in his father? No explanation for the angel's cancellation of the divine decree is given, and no mention of Sarah's response to the good news that her son is alive and well. Most astonishingly, we do not hear a word of rejoicing when the ordeal is ended by an urgent command: "Do not stretch forth your hand against the lad, nor do anything to him."

Formulaic expressions enrich the vocabulary of the narrative. "The short and simple sentence, 'And the two of them walked on together' (8) covers what is perhaps the most poignant and eloquent silence in all literature" [E. A. Speiser. *Genesis* (Anchor Bible, 1964, p. 165)].

James L. Crenshaw. *Soundings.* Summer, 1975, pp. 251–52

As a literary composition, this tale—known as the *Akeda*—is unmatched in Scripture. Austere and powerful, its every word reverberates into infinity, evoking suspense and drama, uncovering a whole mood based on a before and continuing into an after, culminating in a climax which endows its characters with another dimension. They are human—and more: forceful and real despite the metaphysical implications. At every step, their condition remains relevant and of burning gravity. . . .

Throughout the centuries, hundreds of volumes have been written on the *Akeda,* a term recalling the fact that Isaac was *bound* to the altar, and mistakenly translated as "sacrifice" of Isaac. . . .

The Biblical narrative is of exemplary purity of line, sobriety and terseness. Not one superfluous word, not one useless gesture. The imagery is striking, the language austere, the dialogue so incisive, it leaves one with a knot in one's throat: ". . . And, some time afterward, God put Abraham to the test. He said to him: Abraham. And he answered: Here I am. And He said: Take your son, your favored one, Isaac, whom you love, and go to the land of Moriah and offer him there as a burnt offering on one of the heights which I will point out to you" [Gen. 22:1–2].

Elie Wiesel. *Messengers of God* (New York, Random House, 1976), pp. 70, 76, 80

The main message of the story is spelled out in the divine speech at the end (vv. 12b and 16–18). Its tensions and tenor, however, are conveyed—for the reasons given—by its action only. Neither can this action be made too involved, for it must retain its character of a simple carrying out of God's command. The technical problem facing the author was to construct an action sufficiently interesting to carry his message, and yet simple enough to fit it. To achieve this he resolved the action into small elements, which allow step-by-step representation. To make these small steps tangible for the telling, he uses a few elementary props: the ass, the servants, the wood, the fire, the knife. These make it possible to spin a little yarn about the preparations: how "Abraham got up early and saddled his ass and took with him two of his servants and Isaac his son, and split the wood for sacrifice" (v. 3), before actually starting on the journey. Then, as he sees the place of the sacrifice from a distance, he leaves the servants behind with the ass, addressing to them a little speech. That the servants were left behind may be significant, but surely cannot be regarded as a decisive event. It is rather a device which breaks the journey into two stages and thus creates some apparent development in the action. A similar device is employed as Abraham and Isaac set out on the last stage of the journey; for wood, fire and knife are mentioned by the narrator to provide a subject for the dialogue between son and father: "Here are the fire and the wood" etc. (vv. 6–7).

The action is not merely broken up into steps. Each step is told slowly, in considerable detail, and several sentences are long, carefully built up by balanced clauses. It is the slow-telling technique discussed above, handled with virtuosity. It flowers exactly where the story reaches its climax: "So they arrived at the place which God had told him. And Abraham built there the altar and laid out the wood, and he bound Isaac his son and put him on the altar on top of the wood. And Abraham stretched out his hand and took up the knife to slaughter his son" (vv. 9–10). This is virtual slow motion, used to force the reader's attention to the horror of the fact, while avoiding the slightest, even indirect, word of comment or emotional reaction.

The same sort of thing can be observed elsewhere in the story. The cumulative effect of this careful writing is a fine, controlled flow of narrative, which contributes much to the undoubted aesthetic success of the story.

Jacob Licht. *Storytelling in the Bible* (Jerusalem, Magnes Press, 1978), pp. 118–20

The biblical narrative reveals little about the emotional state of its participants; there are, however, a number of stylistic devices which serve to enhance characterization. The use of apposition, in a progression from the general to the specific, indicates the enormity of the sacrifice asked of Abraham: "Take your son, your only one, the one you love, Isaac." Each reference further emphasizes Abraham's special attachment to his son. The description of the journey as lasting three days accentuates the agony of Abraham's trial. The account of Abraham's leaving his servants behind emphasizes the loneliness of the trial. The fact that Isaac is made to carry the firewood for his own slaughter heightens the irony of the situation. The phrase "And the two of them went together" summarizes the event succinctly, just as the brief dialogue immediately preceding underscores the major issues. The question "Where is the lamb for the sacrifice?" reveals Isaac's concern, while Abraham's ambiguous answer, "God will see to it," indicates a moral dilemma facing Abraham which is not fully evoked in the biblical text: is it Abraham's belief that God will provide a substitute for Isaac, or does this statement indicate that Abraham is transferring responsibility to God's domain? The simple rhetorical device of repetition when the angel calls for Abraham to stop the sacrifice communicates urgency to the reader. The biblical narrative is thus rendered tersely; the reader participates in the experience by raising basic questions for which no answers are given.

> Edna Amir Coffin. In *The Bible and Its Traditions*. Ed. by Michael P. O'Connor and David N. Freedman. Special issue of *Michigan Quarterly Review*. Summer, 1983, pp. 430–31

Absalom. *See* David: Absalom

Adjuration of Heaven and Earth. *See* Moses: Adjuration of Heaven and Earth

AMOS

I see, then, that I must say something about the eloquence of the prophets also, where many things are concealed under a metaphysical style, which the more completely they seem buried under figures of speech, give the greater pleasure when brought to light. In this place, however, it is my duty to select a passage of such a kind that I shall not be compelled to explain the matter, but only to commend the style. And I shall do so, quoting principally from the book of that prophet who says that he was a shepherd or herdsman, and was called by God from that occupation, and sent to prophesy to the people of God [Am. 1:1; 7:14]. . . .

When, then, this rustic or *quondam* rustic prophet, was denouncing the godless, the proud, the luxurious, and therefore the most neglectful of brotherly love, he called aloud, saying: "Woe to you who are at ease in Zion . . ." [Am. 6: 1–6 (tr. of St. Jerome's Latin version)]. . . . Suppose those men who, assuming to be themselves learned and eloquent, despise our prophets as untaught and unskillful of speech, had been obliged to deliver a message like this, and to men like these, would they have chosen to express themselves in any respect differently—those of them, at least, who would have shrunk from raving like madmen?

For what is there that sober ears could wish changed in this speech? In the first place, the invective itself; with what vehemence it throws itself upon the drowsy senses to startle them into wakefulness: "Woe to you who are at ease in Zion, and trust in the mountains of Samaria, who are heads and chiefs of the people, entering with pomp into the house of Israel!" Next, that he may use the fa-

vors of God, who has bestowed upon them ample territory, to show their ingratitude in trusting to the mountain of Samaria, where idols were worshipped: "Pass
ye unto Calneh," he says, "and see; and from thence go ye to Hamath the great;
then go down to Gath of the Philistines, and to all the best kingdoms of these: is
their border greater than your border?" At the same time also that these things are
spoken of, the style is adorned with names of places as with lamps, such as
"Zion," "Samaria," "Calneh," "Hamath the great," and "Gath of the Philistines."
Then the words joined to these places are most appropriately varied: "ye are at
ease," "ye trust," "pass on," "go," "descend".

And then the future captivity under an oppressive king is announced as approaching, when it is added: "Ye that are set apart for the day of evil, and come
near to the seat of oppression." Then are subjoined the evils of luxury: "ye that
lie upon beds of ivory, and stretch yourselves upon couches; that eat the lamb
from the flock, and the calves out of the midst of the herd." These six clauses
form three periods of two members each. For he does not say: "Ye who are set
apart for the day of evil, who come near to the seat of oppression, who sleep
upon beds of ivory, who stretch yourselves upon couches, who eat the lamb from
the flock, and calves out of the herd." If he had so expressed it, this would have
had its beauty: six separate clauses running on, the same pronoun being repeated
each time, and each clause finished by a single effort of the speaker's voice. But
it is more beautiful as it is, the clauses being joined in pairs under the same pronoun, and forming three sentences, one referring to the prophecy of the captivity:
"Ye that are set apart for the day of evil, and come near the seat of oppression";
the second to lasciviousness: "ye that lie upon beds of ivory, and stretch yourselves upon couches"; the third to gluttony: "who eat the lamb from the flock and
the calves out of the midst of the herd." So that it is at the discretion of the
speaker whether he finish each clause separately and make six altogether, or
whether he suspend his voice at the first, the third, and the fifth, and by joining
the second to the first, the fourth to the third, and the sixth to the fifth, make
three most elegant periods of two members each: one describing the imminent
catastrophe; another the lascivious couch; and the third, the luxurious table.

Next he reproaches them with their luxury in seeking pleasure for the sense
of hearing. And here, when he had said, "Ye who chant to the sound of the viol,"
seeing that wise men may practise music wisely, he, with wonderful skill of
speech, checks the flow of his invective, and not now speaking to, but of, these
men, and to show us that we must distinguish the music of the wise from the music of the voluptuary, he does not say, "Ye who chant to the sound of the viol,
and think that ye have instruments of music like David"; but he first addresses to
themselves what it is right the voluptuaries should hear, "Ye who chant to the
sound of the viol"; and then, turning to others, he intimates that these men have
not even skill in their art: "they thought that they had instruments of music like
David; drinking wine in bowls, and anointing themselves with the costliest oint-
ment." These three clauses are best pronounced when the voice is suspended on
the first two members of the period, and comes to a pause on the third.

But now as to the sentence which follows all these: "and they were not grieved for the affliction of Joseph." Whether this be pronounced continuously as one clause, or whether with more elegance we hold the words, "and they were not grieved," suspended on the voice, and then add, "for the affliction of Joseph," so as to make a period of two members; in any case, it is a touch of marvellous beauty not to say, "and they were not grieved for the affliction of their brother"; but to put Joseph for brother, so as to indicate brothers in general by the proper name of him who stands out illustrious from among his brethren, both in regard to the injuries he suffered and the good return he made. And, indeed, I do not know whether this figure of speech, by which Joseph is put for brothers in general, is one of those laid down in that art which I learnt and used to teach. But how beautiful it is, and how it comes home to the intelligent reader, it is useless to tell any one who does not himself feel it. [397–428]

> Saint Augustine. *On Christian Doctrine*, Book IV, ch. 7. In *Nicene and Post-Nicene Fathers*. Ed. by Philip Schaff (Buffalo, N.Y., Christian Literature Co., 1887), pp. 579–81

The speeches of Amos and those of his successors combine the eloquence and comprehensibility of prose with the metre and the rhythm of poetry. Metaphors and imagery lend additional solemnity to their diction. It is therefore difficult to decide whether these utterances should be classed as prose or as poetry. In place of a more suitable description, they may be designated as beautifully formed poetic eloquence. The orations of Amos, however, did not fail to betray his station. He used similes taken from his shepherd life. They showed that, while tending his flocks, he often listened to the roaring of the lion, and studied the stars in his night-watches. But these peculiarities only lent a special charm to his speeches. [1853]

> Heinrich Graetz. *History of the Jews*. Vol. I. Tr. by Bella Löwy (Philadelphia, Jewish Publication Society of America, 1891), pp. 235–36

His language, with three or four insignificant exceptions, is pure, his style classical and refined. His literary power is shown in the regularity of structure, which often characterizes his periods, as 1:3–2:6, 4:6–11 (the five-fold refrain), and the visions (7:1, 4, 7; 8:1); in the fine climax 3:3–8; in the balanced clauses, the well-chosen images, the effective contrasts, in such passages as 3:15, 5:2, 21–24; 6:11, 8:10, 9:2–4: as well as in the ease with which he evidently writes, and the skill with which . . . his theme is introduced and developed. Anything of the nature of roughness or rusticity is wholly absent from his writings. His regular, flowing sentences form a remarkable contrast with the short, abrupt clauses which Hosea loves. It is true, in the command of grand and picturesque imagery he is not the equal of Isaiah; nevertheless his thought is often finely expressed (1:2, 5:24, 8:8, 9:5f.); and if, as compared with other prophets, images derived from rural life somewhat preponderate, they are always applied by him aptly (e.g. 3:4, 8; 5:8, 16, 17, 19; 9:9), and never strike the reader as occurring too frequently, or out of place.

Samuel R. Driver. *An Introduction to the Literature of the Old Testament.* 10th ed., rev. and enl. (New York, Scribner's, 1903), pp. 317–18

(1) The regular and simple structure of the book . . . exhibits at once Amos's style of thought. What could be more natural and easy than the series of oracles, the series of sermons, and the series of visions? It is unfortunate that some recent critics seem as blind to the simplicity of Amos's style of expression as were the older critics to its refined nature.

(2) This regularity, or orderliness, exhibits itself in detail in the repetition of the same formulas *for three transgressions, yea for four,* etc., in the opening chapters (or, to put it otherwise, in the orderly arrangement of the nations); in the use of the refrain, *but ye did not return,* etc., in the poem describing Israel's past chastisements (4:4–13); in the entire form of the first three visions (7:1–9); in the almost artificial symmetry of form seen in the accusation (7:10–14) and the reply (7:14–17); in the series of illustrations employed with such effect in 3:3ff.; in the structure, in general, of the several pieces. . . . There is here the skill, not only of the poet and the speaker, but also of the teacher. Every poem in the book is a notable example of this same direct, straightforward orderliness of thought.

(3) The imagery of Amos, like that of Isaiah, is worthy of special study. Tradition has probably been wrong in emphasizing too strongly the prevailingly shepherd-characteristics . . . which mark the figures employed by Amos. But no one will deny that he is especially fond of drawing his language from *nature.* . . .

(4) Other features of Amos's style, which may only be mentioned, are (a) its originality . . . ; (b) its maturity . . . ; (c) its artistic character, which is seen not only in strophes with refrains, but in the entire strophic structure of the various pieces, together with the measure and parallelism.

William R. Harper. Introduction to *A Critical and Exegetical Commentary on Amos and Hosea* (Edinburgh, T. & T. Clark, 1905), pp. cxxxviii–cxl

The record of his preaching is no elegantly turned essay on conduct, but the outpouring of a heart aflame with indignation at social injustice. In this lies the secret of Amos's astonishing literary style. Nothing could at first glance seem more amazing than the breadth of human interest, embracing both acute observation and wide historical knowledge, shown by this illiterate oriental farmer.

Nor is the herdsman of Tekoa unskilled in literary composition. Like Coleridge's Ancient Mariner, this ancient farmer had strange powers of speech. The orations that compose the book are written in rugged, generally pure, Hebrew; and the thought is expressed in the parallelism and accentual rhythm of Hebrew poetry. In few ancient books is the effect of the spoken word more exactly reproduced. To read the book is to feed the illusion that one is listening to impassioned oratory. Though probably the material of the prophecy is shortened from its originally spoken form, it retains all the effect of pointed and dramatic delivery, with that lyrical fervor which lends a special charm to the highest Hebrew oratory. The resemblance of the opening address with its symmetry of structure, its recurrent phrases, and its balanced clauses, to Mark Anthony's speech in Shakespeare's *Julius Caesar* is greater than any actual oration in classical or modern history.

Edward C. Baldwin. *The Prophets* (New York, Thomas Nelson, 1927), pp. 50–51

His greatness as a religious thinker and reformer is matched by his extraordinary ability as a writer. With the exception of Isaiah at his best, none of the Hebrew prophets equals the purity of his language and the classical simplicity of his style. Whether his book consists of a single address or parts of several addresses, it is one of the best arranged of prophetic books. Far from being untutored, Amos gives evidence of consciously using rhetorical devices, as in the series of oracles against foreign nations all of which are cast in the same mold (1–2), and in a similar series of literary units such as the three "Hear this word" (3:1; 4:1; 5:1), the three "Woes" (5:7, 18; 6:1), later imitated by Isaiah, and the five refrains, "Yet have ye not returned to me, saith the Lord" (4:6, 8, 9, 10, 11).

Amos is particularly apt in the use of imagery, usually taken from his own experiences in the wilderness of Tekoa: the dangers from lions, bears, and snakes (3:4, 8, 12; 5:19); the snares by which birds are caught (3:5); the fishhooks (4:2); the wagon loaded with sheaves (2:13); the locusts eating the new grass (7:1f.) lend a picturesque rural background to his words. Lacking the Aristotelian terms "cause and effect," Amos succeeds in showing, by a series of images leading up to a climax, that every effect has a cause, and vice versa (3:3–6, 8). A shrewd observer of life, Amos has portrayed most vividly the opulent life of the lords and ladies of the Northern Kingdom (6:4–6; cf. 3:12, 15; 4:1; 5:11; 8:4–6) and their gay and riotous celebration of religious festivities (2:7–8; 4:4f.; 5:21–23).

The little elegy in 5:2, so tragic in its simplicity, reveals Amos in a new light: no longer the stern prosecutor of his people—with a Bedouin's richness of vocabulary, shrewd common sense, and flaming passion—he sits overcome by grief, and in a quieter mood weeps over the inevitable doom of the Virgin of Israel.

Robert H. Pfeiffer. *Introduction to the Old Testament* (New York, Harper, 1941), pp. 583–84

The tone of Amos (except for the closing verses, which many believe are an addition) is unrelentingly severe, an expression of shocked surprise and unrelieved outrage. The indictment is directed primarily, indeed almost totally, at the highly placed and the wealthy. Amos is beyond the stage of exhortatory warning in some hope of reform; rather, he views the evil so to have accumulated that he speaks not of what may come about but of what he believes is already on the way. His figures of speech exhibit poetic contrasts, either in irony or in contempt. Moreover, passage after passage utilizes synonyms and synonymous expressions, underlining the depth of his scorn: "I hate, I *despise* your festivals; a refuge will evade the swift; the mighty hero will not replenish his strength; the swift runner will not escape, nor will the warrior on his horse; the valorous among the great heroes will flee naked on the day which will come" (2:4–16). Poetic contrast is employed recurrently:

> In all the streets there will be mourning,
> In all the wide places people will say, "Alas."
> They will summon men from the farm to mourning,
> And professional mourners to a [genuine] lament. (5:16)

Since we are told in the text that Amos was a shepherd and a tender of sycamore fruit, we have reason to wonder at the literary skill in the measured verse and high poetry of his expression. Granted that the gift of eloquence is not limited to the educated, what is significant in Amos is the poetic elegance of his eloquence. We cannot explain this.

We must also wonder at the Hebrew mind. Why did the Hebrews preserve, and even cherish, this impressive record of unsavory actions and attitudes? Why should they not, in understandable national pride, have suppressed and destroyed it? Why did they keep alive this indictment of their infamy? We cannot readily explain this; we can only observe that they felt no shame in the shameful record of their past, and, far from concealing it, they glorified the literature which portrayed their shortcomings.

Samuel Sandmel. *The Enjoyment of Scripture* (New York, Oxford University Press, 1972), pp. 247–48

BABEL, TOWER OF

By the name "leading word" we indicate a word or word-stem that recurs in a very significant way within a text, a sequence of texts, or a cycle of texts. By tracing these recurrences, a common significance to the texts can be decoded, clarified, or, in any event, revealed with greater elegance. This recurrence, as has been said, need not entail precisely the same word; rather, the word-stem may recur with some variation in form. Indeed, it is the very variation of the words that frequently intensifies the overall dynamic of the repetition. I call it dynamic because between the combinations of sound that interrelate in this fashion there develops a kind of motion, so to speak. He who compares the entire text perceives waves running back and forth. A measured repetition reflecting the internal rhythm of the text—pivoting on it, if you like—is in general the strongest means of conveying meaning without articulating it. Whether we are dealing with wordplay in the strict sense—which appears within a single syntactic context—or whether we also include under this rubric assonance and alliteration, or whether we are thinking of wordplay at a distance—in which the operation is not in juxtaposed verses but across a wider span of text—in any case, there is in addition to its aesthetic value—which we recognize in classic examples of alliteration in ancient odes—also a special expressive value, which is unique. This value is special in that the intended significance is not expressed by way of a didactic addition; it does not destroy or damage the pure structure of the narrative. . . .

By its very nature, the leading word figures not only in such passages as the Joseph narratives or the greater part of the Book of Exodus, where the episodes follow each other in an inevitable series. It figures even more where a solitary episode is rounded out or self-contained, as in the first thirty-eight chapters of Genesis and the narrative chapters of Numbers. . . .

The Bible comes to narrate how the earth was broken up following the Flood and how "the coastlands of the nations were dispersed," "each man according to his language" (Gen. 10:5; 25:32). This was the period in human history of which the poet sings (Deut. 32:8) when the Most High then divided up humankind. How did the event occur?

This brief narrative [Gen. 11:1–9] is arranged in two halves (vv. 1–4, 5–9): the action by mankind, the counteraction by God. Seven leading words interconnect the two actions: "all the earth," "language," "come, let us," "build," "city and tower" (by the end of the episode only the tower remains), "name," and the verbal stem p-w-ts "disperse."

"All the earth"—so the story opens. In the end is a threefold repetition, almost a rhyme, of the same language, except that there its meaning is not what it is here. At the outset ["the earth"] refers to the people of the entire earth, people still united. But in the end it refers to the face of the earth as it is, with people scattered and dispersed over it according to their languages. This second meaning emerges already at the close of the first half of the narrative, closing as it opened with "all the earth." We shall remark on this parallelism below.

This unified population has "one language." In the first half [of the episode] this expression is found only once; but in the second half—which relates the confounding, destroying power of an avenging God operating directly in the domain of language itself—the word occurs three times in the speech of God and an additional time in the summation presented at the end. The earth, the people of the earth, the fate of the nations of the earth are the axis of this narrative. But language is the domain in which what happens happens.

It is the arrogance of "all the earth" that brings on the catastrophe that befalls it. Over against the arrogant movement from below is the august movement from above. "Come, let us," they cry as they bake bricks; "come, let us," as they build a city with a tower "whose top is in the heaven." Nonetheless, he who descends "to see the city and the tower which the humans had made" opens with the very same call to action. The response of God—a voice from heaven. He answers man in human manner, but not in the self-exalting manner of man. You might say that this "Come, let us" of God's has an ironic tone. But it is presented within a series of linguistic parallels between the human action and the divine counter-action, all of which are ironic.

The two final leading words enunciate the motive for the human action: "Let us make a *name* for ourselves / lest we become *dispersed* over the face of all the earth." "Name" in biblical language specifically denotes the strength of a man that endures for generations after he dies.

Now out of this action there irrupts a name: the quintessential name of the rebel against God, named for the confounding, the confusion of tongues, Babylonia ["babble"]. And those who met there, who enjoyed the unity of mankind, joined forces to build a center reaching the heaven to prevent their being scattered. But it turned out that for what they had done "The Lord dispersed them over the face of all the earth." Thus do the subversive acts of man lead to their subversion.

Now the seven connections of the leading words manifest for us the link between the uprising and its resolution in the opening of national history.

> Martin Buber. *Darko shel miqra'* (Jerusalem, Bialik Institute, 1964), pp. 284–87†

Not only does the narrator treat time in an interesting way, by putting the episode of Babel's rise and fall in a primeval time which is, in terms of the history of salvation, the porch to history proper, but it is also interesting to see how he treats space. In this too, he works with precision. Describing the space for his readers with simple means, he manages to express himself plastically, to a high degree. First he makes us witnesses of a somewhat vague ("in the east," yes, but where exactly?) and somewhat aimless movement, the *nāsaʿ* in the narrow sense, which is typical of nomadic mobility. More or less accidentally the people seem to arrive at Sinear. Once they are there, there is a maximum of directedness, of concentration at one point, the city. From there a spatial revolution arises all at once: up, to the heavens, by means of a tower. The horizontal plane is not enough for the men, they want to open up a new dimension. That is their hubris, and it is precisely this vertical action which provokes vertical repression. Like a flash of lightning from a clear sky God hits back into the depth, sharply and unexpectedly. This one flash of vertical action has immense consequences for the horizontal plane, like a stone which hits a smooth water-surface. The people are scattered into all directions; nothing is left to them but the horizontal plane. After the maximum concentration maximum "decentration" sets in; after the feverish massing of energy the (comparative) calm and purposelessness of the dispersion returns. Therewith the story has been framed and is complete.

> J. P. Fokkelman. *Narrative Art in Genesis* (Assen/Amsterdam, Van Gorcum, 1975), p. 44

The Tower of Babel episode can thus be diagrammed as a symmetrical composition. . . .

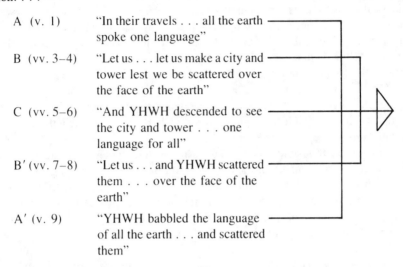

A (v. 1)   "In their travels . . . all the earth spoke one language"

B (vv. 3–4)   "Let us . . . let us make a city and tower lest we be scattered over the face of the earth"

C (vv. 5–6)   "And YHWH descended to see the city and tower . . . one language for all"

B' (vv. 7–8)   "Let us . . . and YHWH scattered them . . . over the face of the earth"

A' (v. 9)   "YHWH babbled the language of all the earth . . . and scattered them"

The thrust of the episode is captured in its formal structure. The text begins neutrally, as a statement of fact, and closes with an explanation of the origin of linguistic and geographical diversity. Between these two poles is the action: man schemes with man as the action builds from earth to heaven; God responds, confers with his pantheon, and the action shifts back to the earth. At the outset, men talk to each other in one language; and at the end, no one understands his neighbor. In the opening geographical statement there is migration, settlement and common speech. The final notice is marked by a violent spatial dispersion correlated with the fracture of language and communication. The vessels of speech and space are shattered by human action. The text makes us painfully aware that speech binds lives and loosens them, builds society and isolates persons, and is both the crown and disgrace of our human existence.

The Tower of Babel episode is linked to the preceding narratives of the primeval cycle in several ways. First is the geographic setting: the "Tower" episode uses the geographical term *qedem,* "east," in its brief introduction. The descent of man "eastward" into history is once again signalized, as with Adam and Eve, and Cain.

The challenging act of mankind in Genesis 11:1–9 is to build a tower, a staged "mountain" "with its top in the heavens." In the beginning God placed Adam on a cosmic mountain, a world center of holiness and order. After the Flood, Noah, the new Adam, is given the blessings of a regenerated mankind on a mountain. Now man builds his own mountain, his monument of power and creaturely overreaching. In ancient Mesopotamia, temple towers called ziggurats and often described as having their "top in heaven" were symbolic of cosmic mountains and used as holy shrines. Here the allusion to the building of such tower-mountains is used ironically, in a Mesopotamian setting, to express a deep ambivalence towards the works and achievements of civilization unmindful of its human limits. It also suggests a profound realization of the energies and will to self-deification which build culture ("city and tower"). A striking parallelism thus emerges between this episode on the aggressive motivations which underlie the tasks of culture and the earlier descriptions of Cain's descendants, who develop cities and art.

In fact, the achievements of culture are portrayed with sarcasm. Through their small deeds, brick by brick, men build a tower to the heavens so as to "make for ourselves a name." In the renewed world of labor and death and consciousness, man works to make a name for himself. Why? Only one answer seems plausible in this context and against the broader background of the cycle. Just as Adam left Eden without immortality, and just as the intercourse between the gods and women reintroduced immortality as a possibility (the results of the union were "men of name"!), so here the works of civilization are mocked as the way to find immortality. To make a "name" for oneself in the city (11:4) is man's doomed attempt to achieve symbolic immortality "east of Eden." This is the same lesson which Gilgamesh learned after his failed quest for eternal life, though the "Gilgamesh" narrator conveys this lesson in tones less sarcastic and more resigned.

The human drive for social achievement is thus, from the perspective of Genesis 11:1–9, the drive to build a bulwark of "works" against the fear of death and dispersion. The resultant divine punishment, which counteracts this focused energy (cf. Gen. 3), reinforces the overall teaching of the primeval cycle: that man must learn his limits; that the unchecked expression of the drive for life is ultimately counterproductive and results in death, destruction, and isolation.

The irony of mankind's attempt to "make a name," to overreach itself and immortalize its achievements, is reinforced by the tightly coiled acoustical sound track of the text, which plays back the initial achievements as failures. Mankind goes eastward to build "there" *(sham)* a tower to the "heavens" *(sham-ayim)*, and so make a "name" *(shem)* for itself. It was "there" *(sham)* that human language was confounded, and it was "from there" *(mi-sham)* that mankind was scattered over the broad earth. In fact, the reversal of destiny in this paradigmatic presentation is signaled not only by these wordplays, but also by the symmetrical repetition of its many other words and word plays (cf. the diagram). Indeed, the very bricks *(li-be-na)* out of which the tower of human pretension is constructed are themselves symbolically deconstructed and reversed when God babbles *(na-bi-la)* the language of "all the earth" (v. 1) and scatters the builders "over all the earth" (v. 9).

Michael Fishbane. *Text and Texture* (New York, Schocken, 1979), pp. 36–38

Here, I feel, may be seen the difference between the biblical episode of the Tower of Babel and the myth of Prometheus to which it has often been compared. In both narratives, indeed, we are present at the birth of man's inventive powers and their opposition by the divine power. But Prometheus is an individual who discovers and makes use of the inner potential of his human genius, while Nimrod and his associates comprise a society which seeks its norms externally, in the inertia of matter which it takes as a model. Prometheus creates a value out of the humanity of his Self, whereas the generation of Babel finds the supreme human value in the uniformity of the thing. The enterprise of Prometheus is a revolt; that of Babel, a pact with rebellious matter. The revolt of Prometheus springs from his own initiatives; that of Babel, from the resistance of the physical world in which it had enclosed itself. Prometheus launches his revolt as an altruistic gesture; the men of Babel entrench themselves in the insulation of their unfeeling egotism. It sufficed for God to break this insulation—like a strong draft bursting into a hothouse—for the word of the outside kingdoms to confuse the system and put it out of order. No word, henceforth, was any longer intelligible, for, in the face of an impersonalized humanity, man arose once more in all his inalienable otherness. The confusion of the tongues had reopened the word to diversified meanings: the word had detached itself from the thing.

As yet, however, it had still not found a point of support and renewal in man himself. God had intervened at Babel only in expectation of a Prometheus ready to reinvent a *davar* [multiple meaning: fact, object, word, event, revelation, etc.] which would be entirely human. There were two simultaneous reasons for this expectation: because the *davar*, although it also signified the thing, was not identified with it entirely, and because the *davar*, although it knew itself to be connected with God, had relinquished nothing of its human origins. A free *davar* —that is what God awaited after having liberated the *safah*. A *davar* set free by man from within and not by God from without—that was the task for which a Prometheus had to arise who would create that *davar* in an act of absolute human liberty.

> André Néher. *The Exile of the Word*. Tr. from the French by David Maisel (Philadelphia, Jewish Publication Society of America, 1981), pp. 110–11

BALAAM

From a man of such imagination we should expect effusions of a bold and elevated character, and such they are. They possess the highest dignity, brevity, animation and copiousness of imagery. There is little in the later Prophets, and nothing in the discourses of Moses, that equals them in this respect. They stand somewhere in the same rank with the Book of Job, and the narrative, by which they are introduced, with all these dreams and visions, with the fearful climax of warnings, the various high places with seven altars upon each—all this is so simple, told with such emphasis and symmetry of parts, that we seem to be brought, by a kind of magic ladder, to that for which such preparation is made. [1783]

> Johann Gottfried von Herder. *The Spirit of Hebrew Poetry*. Vol. II. Tr. from the German by James Marsh (Burlington, Vt., Edward Smith, 1833), p. 174

From the view which has been already taken of Balaam's prophecies, I think it must be clear that they are among the finest specimens of poetry with which the Bible—that sacred depository of the sublimest efforts of human intellect, operating under the immediate influence of inspiration—is so abundantly enriched. These sacred poems, rising, as they do, out of the comparative darkness of a primitive age, when literature may be truly said to have had neither name nor existence, have been declared, by the unanimous voice of commentators, to exhibit the highest attributes by which such compositions are distinguished. They are pre-eminently elevated, filling the mind with the most delightful impressions, and the ear with the most exquisite harmony, which latter quality is even retained in the simple but energetic translation authorized by the Church of England. They differ, however, essentially in their poetical character from any similar writings of Moses; and this circumstance is the strongest internal evidence of their authenticity. It shows them to have been emanations from a mind of totally different temperament, though, poetically considered, of similar organization, at least so far as it was under the direct influence of inspiration. The manner pursued in them is manifestly not identical with that of the Hebrew lawgiver; and this gives them a high specific value, as original compositions of a primitive age, which has left to posterity few records of its rude but masculine genius. The style in these noble productions has more refinement than that of Moses, but less vigour—more eloquence, but less simplicity—more grace, but less grandeur—more variety, but less condensation. It is more artificial and redundant, but less comprehensive and exact—more glowingly picturesque, but less severely graphic; and yet it possesses, in a very high degree, some of the qualities by which the style of Moses is especially distinguished. There are passages in which the condensation is singularly close; and I know of nothing, even among the Hebrew writings, which at times exhibits such a fund of meaning in so few words.

> John Hobart Caunter. *The Poetry of the Pentateuch*. Vol. II (London, E. Churton, 1839), pp. 1–3

There is in the Old Testament no verse epic, but there is one of mingled prose and verse which is of matchless beauty—the story of Balaam. The three chapters, Num., chs. 22–24, are a literary gem unsurpassed in the correctness and finish of both prose and poetry. They form a little book by themselves, and in a literary study may properly be so considered. The Balaam story is more elaborately told, and more richly adorned with poetry, than any other of the Bible stories. At the same time, we must observe that the structure is eminently that of folklore, with its numeric system of three and seven. The purpose of the book is very striking; for at that early period its meaning is the thoroughly modern idea of the unity of all mankind; only it is based, not on anthropology, but on God as its basis and Israel the unifying element, as was promised to Abraham: "In thee shall all families of the earth be blest."

Balaam himself is a grandly drawn figure, and not at all the vulgar deceiver that nearly all expositors make him out to be. . . .

The story, in its mechanical structure and frequent repetitions, gives evidence that this epic writer took it very much as he found it in the folklore which always lies at the foundation of epic. The twice-repeated embassies of Balak, king of Moab; the answers of Balaam, as much alike as the progress of ideas admits; the threefold warning as he set out; even the medium by which one warning came— the ass—all have the freshness and feeling of genuine folklore. But the character of Balaam here drawn is not traditional. The figure before us is the creation of the epic writer, and an accurate reflection of the national spirit in some period of Israel's prosperity. Such a picture of a prophet out of Israel shows a universality to which only the greatest of Israel's prophets ever attained.

Louise S. Houghton. Hebrew Life and Thought (Chicago, University of Chicago Press, 1906), pp. 106–9

The people in the Bible are not doubting, conflicted people. Yes and No do not struggle within them, the bow of their heart is bent toward a specific direction. Balaam is the only one who is caught in an internal standoff between the entice-ments of Balak and his own recoiling from his foul mission. Why is it specifi-cally Balaam who of the mighty ancients is the weak one? Because the man Ba-laam is cut from two elements: He belongs to that low sphere of lusting for silver and gold and for honor, and also to the high sphere of inspiration from Above. The lowly element in him draws him after Balak, and the high element makes him recoil from him.

It is not the Bible's way to relate what goes on inwardly in the heart of man, only what is dressed in words and deeds. With respect to words, Balaam faces only the divine sphere, and so it is with respect to his deeds. So how is it that Ba-laam is shown caught between attraction and repulsion? He is indeed shown on the road with only his ass and his machinations. There things go on that are in part the issue, in part the progenitor of his internal battle. . . .

The poor ass, innocent of any intention! The "mischief" is hers, but the stir-ring is Balaam's. It is he who unwittingly steers her into the field, it is he who presses his foot into her on one side, she pressing his foot on the other, it is he who weighs down upon her until she collapses beneath him. Why all of this? Be-cause there are moments in which it came over him that the entire matter did not sit well, when in the hidden reaches of his heart he regretted setting forth on this perverse journey. It is known that there are unconscious acts, a hidden intention secreted within them. Balaam misdirected his ass's steps, but it seems to him that she is mischievous toward him. His heart strikes him, and he strikes the ass. And lo, the voice of his conscience speaks to him from out of the throat of the ass: "These blows, what are they for? Is it normal for this poor beast to be contrary? This is nothing but . . ." [Num. 22:28, 30]. And like Lot, he is suddenly distracted and sees in front of him an angel, sword in hand! Now he knows the soul of his animal: An angel from heaven has blocked her way. For the actual ass, which carries him to the site of Balak's mission, embodies the lowly element, the bestial within him, and the envisioned angel embodies the higher element, the one that repels him. Not by way of symbol is this scene depicted, but by things as they are. Balaam really hears the voice of the ass and really sees the angel, for he is a man of visions, with a hero's sensibility; voices and apparitions come to him; they are the clothing of that which happens deep within him. These are not wonders, they are the feelings of a man endowed with peculiar talents.

> Avraham Kariv. *Shiv'at 'ammudei hattenakh* (Tel Aviv, Am Oved, 1968), pp. 50–51†

In the sixth and fifth centuries [B.C.E.], at the end of the First Temple period and the beginning of the Second Temple, there blossomed in Israel speculative literature that concerned itself with problems of prophecy. This literature is evident in the paradigm about Micaiah son of Imlah (I Kgs. 22:1–28) and in the parables about the man of God from Judah (I Kgs. 12:33–13:32) and about Jonah (Book of Jonah). The stories were meant to answer such questions as the legitimate source of inspiration in prophecy (the word of the Lord versus the spirit of the Lord), the status of the prophet vis-à-vis his God and the obligations that ensue from it, and problems of the fulfillment of the word of the Lord once it has been proclaimed and has influenced the people to change its ways. The story of [Balaam's] ass belongs to this literature, for it, too, in its own way, deals with one of the major prophetic questions: Can there be prophecy in foreign nations? Ancient Israelite tradition saw no difficulty in this. In contrast, in later stages of the religion prophecy was considered as a special grace from the Lord that was given only to Israel, and any possibility of revelation to members of foreign nations was thereby negated. The burlesque about Balaam was therefore meant to neutralize the view that he is a prophet . . . ; the neutralization was expressed through illustration, how all the qualities of prophecy were missing from Balaam when he encountered the angel on the road. Thus did the prophetic speculation seek to be rid of the oppressive memory of the pagan prophet!

The relation of the episode of the ass to the speculative-prophetic literature is also evident in several features common to all these stories. The motif of the animal that is better than the human is one such feature. The ass is superior to Balaam in her ability to see the angel, in that she rescues him from the danger toward which he was pressing, and because she chastens him with words when he chastens her with a stick. In the story in I Kings 13, too, the lion is superior to the man of God; it performed its mission and killed the rebellious prophet; yet against its nature it "did not eat . . . the carcass and did not maul the ass" (v. 28). So, too, the big fish in the Book of Jonah obeyed the Lord's command better than the prophet and spewed Jonah onto the dry land. Common, too, is the element of the miracle that is not performed by the prophet, as is conventional in the prophetic *legenda* [stories about venerated individuals], but that is performed *on* him, that is, the prophet is made a witness to it or suffers its consequences. The Lord opens the mouth of the ass to speak into Balaam's ears; he sends a lion to kill the man of God without preying upon him and his ass; and he brings a storm upon Jonah, assigns a large fish to him, brings him out onto the dry land, and makes a gourd grow above his head overnight. In addition, common to the episode of the ass and to the story of Jonah is the element of toying with the prophet. The prophet is dumbfounded by what happens and becomes angry and chagrined "unto death." So is Jonah, who does not grasp the meaning of the gourd episode, and so is Balaam, who does not comprehend the behavior of his ass; yet it is self-evident that the special purpose of the ass episode exacerbates the element of sarcasm in it. These lines of resemblance prove, even more than the general thematic, that these three stories—the episode of [Balaam's] ass, the story of the man of God, and the story of Jonah—are close with respect to the time or place of their composition.

> Alexander Rofé. *Sefer bilʿam* (Jerusalem, Simor, 1979), pp. 52–54†

It is particularly the structure of parallel actions in the Balaam story that demonstrates how, in contrast to the complaints of Voltaire and others, the Bible's polemic monotheism can produce high comedy. Balaam goes riding off on his ass to answer Balak's invitation. In the familiar folktale pattern, there are three occurrences of the same incident, the ass shying away from the sword-brandishing angel Balaam cannot see, each time with a more discomfiting effect on her rider: first he is carried into a field, then he is squeezed against a fence, and finally the ass simply lies down under him. When he begins to beat her furiously for the third time, the Lord "opens up her mouth" (elsewhere Balaam repeatedly insists that he can speak only "what the Lord puts in my mouth"), and she complains "What have I done to you that you should have beaten me these three times?" (Num. 22:28). The author, one notes, makes a point of calling our attention to the three times, for the number will be important in the second half of the story. Balaam in his wrath hardly seems to notice the miraculous gift of speech but responds as though he were accustomed to having daily domestic wrangles with his asses (Num. 22:29): "You have humiliated me! If I had a sword in my hand, I would kill you." (The Midrash *BeMidbar Rabbah*, 20:21, shrewdly notes the irony of Balaam's wanting a sword to kill an ass when he has set out to destroy a whole nation with his words alone.) Meanwhile, of course, the unseen angel has been standing by, sword in hand. Only when God chooses finally to reveal to Balaam the armed angel standing in the way does the irate seer repent for ill-treating the innocent creature.

It seems fairly clear that the ass in this episode plays the role of Balaam—beholding divine visions with eyes unveiled—to Balaam's Balak. The parallel between the two halves of the story is emphasized by the fact that in Balaam's prophecies there are again three symmetrically arranged occurrences of the same incident, each time with greater discomfit to Balak. In Balaam's prophetic imagery, first Israel is spread out like dust, then crouched like a lion, and finally rises like a star, so that the Moabite king, waiting for a first-class imprecation, is progressively reduced to impotent fury, quite in the manner of Balaam's blind rage against the wayward ass.

Now, a sequence of repeated actions in such a folktale pattern is of course a mechanical thing, and part of the genius of the biblical author here is to realize, three millennia before Bergson's formulation of the principle, that the mechanical in human affairs is a primary source of comedy. Balak's and Balaam's repetitions are much more elaborate than those of Balaam with the ass: each of the three times, Balaam instructs Balak to build seven altars and to sacrifice on them seven oxen and seven sheep, as the distraught king trundles him around from one lofty lookout point to the next; each time, the painstaking preparations result only in heightened frustration for Balak. Paganism, with its notion that divine powers can be manipulated by a caste of professionals through a set of carefully prescribed procedures, is trapped in the reflexes of a mechanistic world-view while from the biblical perspective reality is in fact controlled by the will of an omnipotent God beyond all human manipulation. The contrast between these two conflicting conceptions of reality is brilliantly brought forth in the story's artful pattern of repetitions. In each repeated instance, the Moabite king and his hired prophet go through identical preparations, and each time Balaam speaks in soaring verse—the words God has put in his mouth—which constitutes a crescendo repetition of powerful vision in counterpoint to the mechanical repetition of their futile human actions. The harmony of theological argument and narrative art in the whole story is beautifully complete.

Robert Alter. The Art of Biblical Narrative (New York, Basic Books, 1981), pp. 105–7

Binding of Isaac. See Abraham: Binding of Isaac

Burning Bush. See Exodus: Burning Bush

CREATION

Passages which represent divinity as genuinely unsoiled and great and pure . . . The lawgiver of the Jews, no ordinary man—for he understood and expressed God's power in accordance with its worth—writes at the beginning of his *Laws:* "God said—now what?—'Let there be light,' and there was light; 'Let there be earth,' and there was earth." [1st c.?]

"Longinus" on Sublimity. Tr. by D. A. Russel (Oxford, Clarendon Press, 1965), pp. 11–12

And God said—LET THERE BE LIGHT, AND THERE WAS LIGHT. It is one of the shortest passages in the whole Bible, exhibiting, at the same time, the noblest image, with magnificence and simplicity; and, indeed, the best moderns have copied and imitated, at whatever distance, the graces of the scriptures. Those authors relate actions which are to excite instantaneous admiration, by a single line, and very frequently by a single expression. . . .

The creation of the world depended only upon one word of the Deity; and Moses hath described it in a sentence. Language could not have been more compressed; meaning could not have been more comprehensive. . . .

If Milton's genius could not master it, how vain to look for any thing equivalent in Cowley or Pope. It is altogether *inimitable* and *incomparable,* being infinitely sublime and sacred in itself, and expressed in words exactly suitable. The sentence consists wholly of monosyllables, and those short, smooth, and, as it were, insisting upon a rapid pronunciation. The celerity of the words, assist in, and echo to, the command they convey.

Let there be light—Can anything flow faster or with more facility from the lip? And there was light. If the reader can manage his articulation, the image, the tone, and every thing else, will correspond. . . .

The greatest epic poets amongst the *ancients,* Homer and Virgil, have been complimented on the conciseness of *their* exordiums; but neither the Iliad or the Aeneid, reach the various excellencies which are *compressed* without being crowded, in the first chapter of Genesis.

> Samuel J. Pratt. *The Sublime and Beautiful of Scripture*
> (New York, Printed by Tiebout & O'Brien, 1795), pp.
> 8–12, 18–19

The spirit of poetry, therefore, was first exhibited in a dictionary of significant names, and expressions full of imagery and of feeling, and I know of no poetry in the world, in which this origin is exhibited in greater purity than in this. The first specimen, which presents itself in it [Gen. 1], is a series of pictures exhibiting a view of the universe, and arranged in accordance with the dictates of human feeling. Light is the first uttered word of the Creator, and the instrument of Divine efficiency in the sensitive human soul. By means of this the creation is unfolded and expanded. The heavens and the earth, night and day, the diurnal and nocturnal luminaries, creatures in the sea and on the land, are measured and estimated with reference to the human eye, to the wants, and the powers of feeling and of arrangement peculiar to man. The wheel of creation revolves with a circumference embracing all that his eye can reach, and stands still in himself as the centre of the circle, the visible God of this lower world. In giving names to all, and ordering all from the impulse of his own inward feeling, and with reference to himself, he becomes an imitator of the Divinity, a second Creator, a true *poietes,* a creative poet. [1783]

> Johann Gottfried von Herder. *The Spirit of Hebrew Poetry*. Vol. II. Tr. from the German by James Marsh
> (Burlington, Vt., Edward Smith, 1833), p. 7

The account of the Creation which this passage contains is found, upon examination, to be arranged with the most minute parallelism of matter and form. Not only are the six days furnished with opening and closing formulae which correspond, but the whole divides into two symmetrical halves of three days and three days, and each day of the first three is exactly parallel with the corresponding day of the second half. A table will illustrate the structure.

And God said—
    [Creation of Light]
And there was evening and there was morning, one day.

And God said—
    [Creation of the Firmament dividing waters from waters]
And there was evening and there was morning, a second day.

    And God said—
       [Creation of Land]
    And God said—
       [Creation of Vegetation, climax of inanimate nature]
And there was evening and there was morning, a third day.

And God said—
    [Creation of Lights]
And there was evening and there was morning, a fourth day.

And God said—
    [Creation of Life in the Firmament and in the Waters]
And there was evening and there was morning, a fifth day.

    And God said—
       [Creation of Life on Land]
    And God said—
       [Creation of Man, climax of animate nature]
And there was evening and there was morning, the sixth day.

When this structure and the fulness of its parallelism is grasped, it will appear reasonable that it should be urged as one argument in favour of understanding the chapter to be, not a narration of incidents in their order of succession, but a logical classification of the elements of the universe, with the emphatic assertion of Divine creation in reference to each.

Richard G. Moulton. *The Literary Study of the Bible.* Rev. and partly rewritten (Boston, Heath, 1899), pp. 67–68

The purpose of the . . . [Creation story] is to teach us that the whole world and all that it contains were created by the word of the One God, according to His will, which operates without restraint. It is thus opposed to the concepts current among the peoples of the ancient East who were Israel's neighbours; and in some respects it is also in conflict with certain ideas that had already found their way into the ranks of our people. The language, however, is tranquil, undisturbed by polemic or dispute; the controversial note is heard indirectly, as it were, through the deliberate, quiet utterances of Scripture, which sets the opposing views at nought by silence or by subtle hint.

All kinds of wondrous stories about the creation of the world were widespread throughout the lands of the East, and many of them assumed a literary form in epic poems or other compositions. . . .

Among the Israelites, too, there existed, prior to the Biblical account, narrative poems about the creation and the beginning of the world's history. Although these poems have not come down to us, having perished in the course of time, evidence of their existence is to be found both in this section and in other parts of Scripture. . . . Allusions to the creation-story that are unrelated to our section are found, for instance, in Job 38:4–7:

> Where were you when I laid the foundation of the earth?
> Tell me, if you have understanding.
> Who determined its measurements—surely you know!
> Or who stretched the line upon it?
> On what were its bases sunk, or who laid its cornerstone,
> When the morning stars sang together, and all the sons of God
>   shouted for joy?

There is a clear indication here of a tradition concerning the creation of the earth on a bright morning, whilst the stars and God's angels sang a paean. Undoubtedly, the author of the book of Job did not fabricate these details. Nor did he invent such concepts or terms as *lay the foundations, measurements, line, bases, cornerstone*.

Similarly, we read in Isaiah 40:12, 21–22:

> Who has measured the waters in the hollow of his hand and
>   marked off the heavens with a span,
> enclosed the dust of the earth in a measure and weighed the
>   mountains in scales and the hills in a balance? . . .
> Have you not known? Have you not heard?
> Has it not been told you from the beginning?
> Have you not understood from the foundations of the earth?
> It is He who sits above the circle of the earth,
> and its inhabitants are like grasshoppers;
> who stretches out the heavens like a curtain,
> and spreads them like a tent to dwell in.

The two passages probably derive from a common poetic source. . . .

As far as our own section is concerned, a poetic construction like . . . *hayᵉtō 'erets* ['beasts of the earth'] (1:24) next to the corresponding prose form . . . *hayyat hā'ārets* (1:25, 30); or verses with poetic rhythm like 1:27:

> So God created man in His own image,
> in the image of God He created him;
> male and female He created them.

and a number of other poetic features, which we shall discuss in the course of our exposition, also point to a poetic tradition among the Israelites anterior to the Book of Genesis. The metre of the verse, *So God created man . . .*—tetrameter—, which is also found in other verses of our section, is the most usual in the epic poetry of the Eastern peoples of antiquity, and was probably employed to a large extent in the epic poetry of Israel, too. There is no necessity to assume that the Torah took these verses verbatim from an earlier epic poem. Admittedly this is possible; but it is simpler to suppose that wherever, in the course of the Biblical story, which is mainly in prose, the special importance of the subject led to an exaltation of style approaching the level of poetry, the thought took on of its own accord, as it were, an aspect conforming to the traditional pattern of narrative poetry—an aspect, at all events, that was in keeping with ancient poetic tradition. . . .

The structure of our section is based on a system of numerical harmony. Not only is the number *seven* fundamental to its main theme, but it also serves to determine many of its details. Both to the Israelites and to the Gentiles, in the East and also in the West—but especially in the East—it was the number of *perfection* and the basis of ordered arrangement; and particular importance attached to it in the symbolism of numbers. The work of the Creator, which is marked by absolute perfection and flawless systematic orderliness, is distributed over seven days: six days of labour and a seventh day set aside for the enjoyment of the completed task. . . . Possibly the Torah perceives in the importance attributed to the number seven by non-Israelites a kind of indistinct echo of the story of creation.

It is worth noting in this connection that in the case of actions lasting the above-mentioned length of time, it was customary to divide the six days of labour into three pairs, and to relate the story somewhat as follows: on the first day and on the second such-and-such a work was done; so, too, on the third day and on the fourth that work was done; likewise on the fifth day and on the sixth the same work was done. Thereafter, when the work had been completed on the sixth day, came the seventh day, a day of conclusion and change of situation. . . . In our section the division of the days is, as we shall see later, rather different, to wit, two series of three days each. But the prevailing pattern is implicit in the rabbinic saying: "It (the Sabbath day) has no partner: there is the first of the Sabbath [i.e. week], the second of the Sabbath; the third, the fourth, the fifth, the eve of the Sabbath; but the Sabbath itself remains unpaired" (Bereshith Rabba, 11:8 . . .). [1944]

Umberto Cassuto. *A Commentary on the Book of Genesis.* Part 1. Tr. from the Hebrew by I. Abrahams (Jerusalem, Magnes Pr., 1961), pp. 7–13

The Book of Genesis opens with verses which suggest the murmurings of the primeval waters and their hushed sounds. *"bereshit bara' 'elohim 'et hashamayim ve-'et ha-'arets ve-ha-'arets hayeta tohu va-bohu ve-ḥoshek 'al pene tehom ve-ruaḥ 'elohim meraḥefet 'al pene ha-mayim."* The repeated *m*, *r*, and *sh* sounds suggest a forest or a body of water, with the waves lapping the surface in the darkness. All this is of course quite lacking in the more prosaic, though beautiful translation of the King James Version, "In the beginning God created the heaven and the earth. And the earth was without form and void; and darkness *was* upon the face of the deep. And the spirit of God moved upon the face of the waters." The combination *"ruaḥ . . . meraḥefet"* is doubtless deliberate, so to speak; it gives a deep sense of the brooding of the Divine Spirit amidst the eternal silence of the beginning of things. The story continues, in Hebrew, *"vayo'mer 'elohim"* ("and God said") *"yehi 'or"* ("Let there be light"). The suddenness with which the brief sounds *"yehi 'or"* burst upon us after the long introduction is clearly intended to suggest the suddenness with which the Voice of God broke upon the primeval stillness.

The English, "Let there be light," seems to reverberate through the empty spaces, like the loud voice of a master, walking into a dark room, shocked by the darkness. The Hebrew words may be said either loudly or quietly; in either case their force derives from their economy of sound. The Master is not interested in commanding or in being obeyed; He is concerned with the light, and wants it produced with the least possible effort on His part. He claps His hands, as it were, and His will is done.

Louis Finkelstein. In *Symbols and Society*. Ed. by Lyman Bryson et al. (New York, Harper, 1955), pp. 418–19

As with other texts of origin, Genesis 1:1–2:4a is a product of language in its creative vitality. Man must surely have intuited and experienced very early the magical power of words to create reality and control imagination. . . .

[The] narrative does not speak of origins and creations that occurred "once upon a time," but of *the* Creation that occurred "Once, at the beginning of time." This prologue takes the reader out of his own time and into the primordial time that precedes all human and cultural experience. Indeed, it so effectively transports him into the temporal-literary framework of the text that any question as to just how the narrator could know what occurred "at the beginning" is raised only belatedly. Only after the reading experience does the reader sense that perhaps this text is but a literary-theological response to the mystery of origins.

Both the reading experience of Genesis 1:1–2:4a and its content, its silences and speeches, are controlled by the narrator: the breaking of the initial, primordial silence by speech ("At the beginning"); the interruptions or linkages of the various speeches by silences; the closing of the text in its entirety into the silence of completed action. The narrator also determines the fundamental framework of the text, from the initial, forward-looking "At the beginning of Elohim's creation of heaven and earth," to the concluding and reflective "This is the account of the heaven and the earth, at the time of their creation."

The narrator, moreover, fills in the spaces between the various speeches of God. He provides both introductions to God's words ("Elohim said") and reports of the divine attitude ("And Elohim saw that it was good"). He reports the acts of creation ("Elohim said: Let there be . . ." "There was," "Elohim created," or "And it was so") and provides the transitions from day to day ("There was setting; there was dawning . . .").

The voice of the narrator is indeed a dominating presence, disclosing background, introducing action, summarizing action, and providing for continuity. But in another sense the narrator's presence is more modest, merely providing the narrative thread which laces the speeches of Elohim. While the words of the narrator are creative in the sense that they shape the literary form and style of this text, the words of God are creative in a more fundamental sense. God's speaking and creating are one and indissoluble. His words create and order the heaven and the earth; they give a syntax to the formless and the void, they transform the primordial, undifferentiated unity into order and classification.

The prosaic, reflective discourse of the human speaker ("there was") counterpoints the commanding tones ("Let there be") of the divine speeches, as well as the force expressed in naming the things of creation ("Day!" "Heaven!" "Earth!"). Indeed, the speeches of Elohim would be overpowering without the calming and alternating rhythm of the human speeches which precede, intervene between, and follow them.

It is precisely through this divine-human counterpoint that two dramatic aspects of Genesis 1:1–2:4a emerge. First is the action-result sequence whereby the daily "creations" are brought into existence by speeches of action ("Let there be") and of result ("And there was"). The second aspect consists of the almost stereotyped repetition of key words (e.g., "created," "saw," "separated," "good"), which allows the reader to focus fully on the uniqueness of each day and its events. The concluding daily refrain ("There was setting; there was dawning: day x") at once sums up what has passed and anticipates what is to follow.

The text thus provides a reflection of an orderly, harmonious creation. The alternation of the narrator's voice with divine speech, of description with prescription, serves to present "the creation" as a dispassionate recitation recurrently punctuated with vital divine energy. The text shifts rhythmically between actions and results which utilize the same words ("separate" . . . "call" . . . "see" . . . "make") and sequences. Its economy of vocabulary and technique produces a dictum of controlled energy and force.

Michael Fishbane. *Text and Texture* (New York, Schocken, 1979), pp. 3, 6–8

DANIEL

As the book was intended to consist of partly narrative and partly prophetic matter, it could not from the very first admit of any strict artistic unity . . . the instruction by means of simple narration breaks up of itself into a loosely connected series of separate pieces; in a similar way the fundamental matter of the prophetic element also is broken up into the various outward divisions of time and inward moods of spirit in which it dawned more and more perfectly and distinctly upon the mind of Daniel; and instead of comprehending all that has to be said regarding the future in one single, complex, but rigidly connected whole, which is supposed to have presented itself from one definite situation to the spiritual eye and ear of Daniel . . . everything prophetic is brought forward more and more completely in one book in a series of pieces in accordance with the requirements of clearness or certainty. Small pictures of limited range, but the delineation of each executed with all the greater distinctness, animation, and richness of colour, must be thus produced both in the narrative and in the prophetic portions of the book. We may say, therefore, that the author intended to draw a series of separate scenes as with the strong strokes of frescoes, on the one side for the purposes of instruction by history, on the other for warning and encouragement by prophecy. And in this respect all the separate pieces of the book show great excellence: indeed, it may be said that the same literary art as applied to prophecy which we found used by Hosea . . . is again met with here in an entirely new form of development. In this style of literary painting there lies also a peculiar charm. Every piece thus supplies a picture which can be looked at with satisfaction, in the contemplation of which it is possible to get completely absorbed. But how does this charm increase when the fundamental thought is seen to come out in each successive piece afresh in another manner and at the same time more and more fully and distinctly. [1840]

Georg H. A. von Ewald. *Commentary on the Prophets of the Old Testament.* Vol. V. Tr. by J. Frederick Smith (London, Williams and Norgate, 1881), pp. 177–78

Such is this extraordinary book—a strange mixture of the sublime and the commonplace, the outcome of intellectual abasement and of the most profound moral movement that the world has ever seen. It puts those rhetoricians who at a glance set a well-written phrase above an ill-written one, completely at fault.

The Book of Daniel is the best example we have of the alternation there is in the history of man between intellect and morality. Compared with Isaiah, the Book of Daniel shows complete literary falling off. Its language is detestable— flat, prolix, incorrect, and sometimes untranslatable; and yet Jewish thought has made in these few ill-written pages marvellous progress: it has passed beyond its first stage, which is simply monotheistic, to its Messianic stage, in which it has charmed all mankind by the offer of infinite hope. All things are born out of corruption. The decay of one thing is the beginning of another. The literary weakness of a work is no reason why it may not have a foremost part to play in the history of mankind. . . .

In reading we put up with enigmas that need reflection, with elaborated riddles, in which ideas are forced together without any thought of coherence. In Daniel this fault is carried to an extreme: a horn speaks, and has eyes. There is nothing artistic in the composition of these puzzles, which serve to express the writer's thought. There is everywhere incongruity, the very opposite of the Greek laws of harmony. That sense of the divinity revealed in the human form set forth in Greek sculpture is completely wanting. The fanatical author of these visions has but one thing in view—to stamp his thought in by rude force; to make a powerful impression upon the reader. In this he has succeeded; and no doubt he was a witness of the extraordinary impression produced by his work.

Ernest Renan. *History of the People of Israel*. Vol. IV
(Boston, Roberts Brothers, 1896), pp. 306–8

The author of Daniel is far more notable for his religious zeal than for his literary art. Even the best parts of his book (chs. 2–7), which he wrote in Aramaic, are not to be classed with earlier (Ruth, Jon., Tob.) and later (Jud., Esth., Sus.) Hebrew short stories. In comparison with these, Daniel's style is crude, the plots are elementary, and the happy endings are produced less subtly and more artificially by an abrupt intervention of the *deus ex machina*. The six Aramaic chapters are arranged somewhat mechanically in pairs within pairs, like three concentric Chinese spheres: 2 and 7, 3 and 6, 4 and 5, dealing respectively with the passing of the four pagan empires and the advent of the Jewish one, with the miraculous deliverance of the martyrs, and with the divine humiliation of arrogant tyrants. In spite of the notable variation of the details, the recurrence of the same themes produces a certain monotony which would have been avoided by a writer of greater talent and imagination. The individual stories are separate, self-contained entities, without mutual connections. This abruptness, to a lesser degree, may be noted occasionally within the single episodes and gives to the collection an anecdotic character, depriving it of that organic unity, that dramatic concatenation of events which is one of the outstanding literary qualities of the Joseph stories in J and E—a masterpiece which our author emulated without remotely equaling.

Like the author of the Priestly Code and the Chronicler, our writer is a theorist rather than a brilliant storyteller. All three use narrative material merely to substantiate dogma and to provide legal precedents. Being uninterested in the tales per se, they fail to visualize scenes and persons, and lack the skill needed to create the illusion of reality: their characters are shadowy types, their scenery is mere stage setting. In Daniel, for instance, it is impossible to imagine the form of the fiery furnace (3:19–26) and of the den of lions (6:16f., 23f. [H. 6:17f., 24f.]), or to conceive even vaguely the appearance of the fourth beast (7:7f.).

This sense of unreality is increased by implausible exaggerations which are not charmingly naïve, like those of fairy tales, but conventional and stilted, like those of P and the Chronicler, being dictated by dogma and, in Daniel, also by symbolism. . . .

The author's mind was fascinated by the colossal, and appropriately he had, like the little horn, "a mouth speaking great things" (7:8). There is something baroque in his style, particularly in the speeches, which are usually pompously grandiloquent. Hyperbolically, the greatness of pagan kings is said to reach unto heaven and their dominion to the ends of the earth (4:22 [H. 4:19]). . . .

Except for the prolix and resounding speeches and royal decrees in the book, the style is generally concise and abrupt, often factual and unadorned like that of the Priestly Code. In contrast with the great prophets of earlier times, the writer seldom uses similes. His comparisons are obvious and usually derived from other writings: for example, the chaff (2:35; cf. Hos. 13:3; Ps. 1:4). . . . At times, with extreme conciseness, the author uses the *comparatio compendiaria* in which a part is likened to a whole, as "his heart was made like [the heart of] the beasts" (5:21): see 1:10; 4:16, 33 (H. 4:13, 30). . . .

Despite its stylistic blemishes, the Book of Daniel is a great literary monument, the first real apocalypse and the classic example of this literary genre. The numerous Jewish and Christian imitations are evidence of the importance of our book in the history of literature. The stress on the colossal, the grotesque, the imaginary, as well as the mechanical structure, pomposity, and aridity of the style may not be pleasing to our modern literary taste. Nevertheless, the author achieved occasionally dramatic power (3:17 f.; 4:29–31 [H. 4:26–28]; 5:29f.) and epic grandeur (7). The present writer would consider the vision of the four beasts and of the heavenly assizes (ch. 7) as the outstanding creation of our author: the contrast between the horrible chaotic monsters and the luminous heavenly scene dominated by the dignified "ancient of days" and the "one like unto a son of man" arriving on the clouds of heaven, is depicted magnificently, with admirable restraint and noble simplicity. The abysmal chasm separating mankind's "storm and stress" on this earth and its Utopic deams of "peace on earth, good will toward men" has hardly ever been visualized more dramatically.

Robert H. Pfeiffer. Introduction to the Old Testament
(New York, Harper, 1941), pp. 770–72

The events of the episodic Daniel are among the most famous in the Bible: the three holy children in the fiery furnace, the handwriting on the wall, and the lion's den. The visions with which these adventures are interwoven are calculated to drive home, in terms of allegory, the points the narratives make in terms of action.

Aesthetically, however, Daniel with its mixture of separate adventures and vision is what would be called today a confusion of genres or kinds. It is a confusion that did not trouble the creator of the book if he was one man rather than several. His edifying intent was single; he employed whatever artistic forms came to hand. Perhaps because of the absence of such edifying intent three other episodes in the Daniel cycle are found only in the Apocrypha. In the Bel and the Dragon stories and in The History of Susannah, Daniel appears not as a seer and a defier of pagan authority but in the role of a clever secular man who by his own wit sets matters to rights. His cross-examination of the elders in the Susannah story, his trap for the priests in the Bel and the Dragon tales may entertain; but they are beside the instructive point of the Daniel narratives contained in the Old Testament proper.

Harold H. Watts. *The Modern Reader's Guide to the Bible*. Rev. ed. (New York, Harper, 1959), pp. 167–68

Like the other Old Testament narratives, the story of Daniel (Dan. 1–6) is firmly established in a historical setting. The events that are narrated occur during the exile of Judah after the nation had been carried into captivity by the Babylonians.

The plot of the story is not structured as a single climax but as a series of ordeals. Each chapter is a separate action, as follows: the testing of the four Hebrew youths, Daniel's interpretation of Nebuchadnezzar's dream, the fiery furnace ordeal, Nebuchadnezzar's account of his fall and restoration, Belshazzar's feast, and the ordeal of Daniel in the lions' den. The conflicts in this plot occur both on an individual and on a national level. On the individual level, Daniel, the protagonist, encounters a number of antagonists, including kings, a pagan life style, the threat of losing his Jewish identity, jealous colleagues, and hungry lions. But Daniel's personal conflicts occur in a broader context of international conflict between the Jewish nation, with a strong religious identity, and the Babylonians, with an equally strong pagan orientation.

A characteristic feature of the style is the elaborate repetition of phrases and speeches. In fact, the story of Daniel has a style that is more clearly reminiscent of oral epic than any other Old Testament narrative.

There are several important dimensions to Daniel's heroism. As a hero, Daniel, whose name means either "God is judge" or "God is my judge," is wholly idealized. As in the story of Joseph the narrator selects details that idealize the hero and describe him in superlatives. In effect, such literature holds up a model of virtue as a goal toward which the reader can aim. Daniel is a nationalistic hero, as evidenced, for example, when he refuses to compromise on the question of the ceremonial laws regarding the preparation of food, something that set the Jewish nation apart from other nations. Daniel is also a hero of ability and integrity. He is valedictorian of his class, admired and befriended by one pagan king after another despite his strong religious convictions. Above all, Daniel is depicted as a religious hero. His life revolves around God. His religious intensity is what impresses the pagans around him, some of whom speak of "the God of Daniel." He is preeminently the man of God who does not allow his high position in society to lead him to compromise his faith.

There are some noteworthy features of the "world" of the story. It is a supernatural world in which there is constant acknowledgment of the existence of a spiritual world and frequent interpenetration of the supernatural world into the visible order of reality. The atmosphere is oriental, full of spiritual awareness. All of this produces a sense of mystery. There are many dreams, mysterious and having great importance in the lives of people. There are many astrologers and interpreters of dreams around the court.

The world of the story is, secondly, a political world. The courts of great and powerful rulers form the setting for the action. The personal story of Daniel takes place against a background of rising and falling kings. Dreams usually have a political significance in the story. The hero himself is a statesman—an adviser to rulers.

Finally, the world of the story is a world in which God is sovereign. Repeatedly God is shown to be the one who is in control of events on earth and in the lives of individuals. He is the still point of stability in a world of change, and He is the only one who can reveal the truth in a world replete with mystery.

> Leland Ryken. *The Literature of the Bible* (Grand Rapids, Mich., Zondervan, 1974), pp. 67–68

The late Charles Laughton included in his selection of readings from world literature, on a gramophone record, the story of Shadrach, Meshach and Abed-Nego (Daniel, ch. 3), who refused to worship Nebuchadnezzar's idol and were thrown into the fire from which they escaped unharmed. The story is impressive enough, though somewhat crude; it lacks depth and subtlety, the plot is very plain and the style is solemn, clumsily ornate and stiff. Charles Laughton could have certainly found a better story in the Old Testament, yet the excellence of his choice becomes apparent as soon as one hears his voice reading the text. He obviously did not choose this story from purely literary grounds, but rather because he knew that one can make it sound magnificent.

This effect is entirely due to two formal features of the text, which are brought forward by reading aloud: a good prose rhythm (which cannot be discussed in this context), and a wealth of sonorous repeated phrases. I shall list only the more prominent ones. There is a long list of dignitaries bearing impressive titles in verse 2, repeated immediately in verse 3. Then there are the "peoples nations and tongues" in verses 4, 7 and 29. The burning fiery furnace is heard roaring eight times (vv. 6, 11, 15, 17, 20, 21, 23, 26). Even more impressive is the king's command that "all who shall hear the sound of the cornet, flute, harp, sackbut, psaltery and all kinds of music" must "fall down and worship the golden image" made by the king. The longish sentence appears four times (vv. 5, 7, 10, 15), conveying to our ear the noise and pomp of the king's idolatry. All these sounds, charged with significance, are heard again and again as one listens to the story. Its aesthetic effect depends on them almost entirely.

> Jacob Licht. *Storytelling in the Bible* (Jerusalem, Magnes Press, 1978), pp. 51–52

Although the Book of Daniel lacks the type of linguistic correspondence displayed by the Joseph story and the Book of Esther, it bears general similarities in settings and events. Like the stories of Joseph, and of Mordecai and Esther, Daniel 2–6 is set at the court of a foreign king. All three narratives display some concern for the details of court life (cf. Gen. 47:13–26; Esth. 1:3, 6–10, 14; 2:12–15; Dan. 2:2, 27; 3:2–4, 10; 5:2–7). As in the Joseph story and the Book of Esther, banquets occur in Daniel 2–6 as characteristic court events. Of particular interest is the banquet of Daniel 5:2–3, which suggests the king's actions to be influenced by his consumption of wine. We are reminded here of the royal banquet described in Esther 1.

In the Joseph story and in the Book of Esther, a concern with the details of court life serves as a literary device, lending an air of verisimilitude to the stories. A similar judgment may be rendered with respect to the setting of Daniel 2–6. The settings of the three narratives also suggest that Jews can attain success at the court of a foreign king. Like the story of Joseph and the Book of Esther, Daniel 2–6 lacks any hostility toward the foreign monarch.

Daniel and his companions, like Esther and to some extent Joseph, undergo elaborate preparation prior to meeting the king (Dan. 1; cf. Gen. 41:14; Esth. 2:8–15). Esther and Daniel find favor with those in charge of their training, due in part to their physical attractiveness (Esth. 2:7–17; Dan. 1:4; cf. Gen. 39:6b).

Parallels also exist between the figures of Joseph, Daniel and Mordecai. Mordecai and Daniel are portrayed as members of the community of Jews exiled from Jerusalem by Nebuchadnezzar (Esth. 2:5–6; Dan. 1:1–5; 5:13). In all three cases, the "ethnic" identities of the heroes contribute to the development and movement of plot.

The three narratives portray the dangers which confront the heroes as a result of their positions at court. The protagonists, however, successfully overcome these dangers and are placed in positions of even greater authority. In each story, the king's disturbed sleep leads to personal recognition of the respective heroes (cf. Gen. 41; Esth. 6; Dan. 2), and their rewards include new clothing and jewelry (Gen. 41:42; Esth. 6:8–11; Dan. 5:29; cf. Esth. 8:2). The change in heroes' personal fortunes anticipates and extends beyond them personally, resulting in either the deliverance of the people of Israel, or the praise and acknowledgement of its God.

The Joseph story and the Books of Esther and Daniel do not share any dominant motifs, although Dan. 6:1–28 raises the question of obedience to the king's irrevocable law. On the other hand, the stories share some formulaic motifs, e.g., the king's disturbed sleep and the manner in which service to the king is rewarded.

Like the stories of Joseph and Esther, Daniel 2–6 displays no hostility to the foreign king. To the contrary, Daniel and his companions overcome the dangers that confront them and prosper at the foreign court. These facts suggest the possibility of a shared theme among the stories, viz., that of a dual loyalty. The piety of Daniel and his companions often contributes to their adversity. Yet the tales clearly indicate that the heroes' eventual success in overcoming danger is due, in fact, to their tenacious loyalty to Yahweh. A dual allegiance to God and to king is not only possible in Daniel 2–6, it is in some ways demanded. It is because of the wisdom and skills given by Yahweh that Daniel can serve his king so ably. Daniel 2–6 points to a particular ordering of priorities such that loyalty to Yahweh leads to the greatest possible service to one's king.

Inherent in this similarity of theme, however, is the greatest difference between the Joseph and Esther stories and Daniel 2–6. The latter constantly stresses Yahweh's sovereignty. The primary concern of the Book of Daniel as a whole, in fact, is to demonstrate that "God is sovereign over history and is guiding it towards an end determined by himself" [Norman Porteus. *Daniel* (1965), p. 18]. This emphasis is conspicuously lacking in the Book of Esther and appears greatly restricted in the Joseph story. Despite their general similarities in settings and events, the theocentric focus of Daniel 2–6 sets it apart from the Joseph story and the Book of Esther.

> Sandra B. Berg. *The Book of Esther* (Missoula, Mont., Scholars Press, 1979), pp. 143–45

DAVID

As the Compositions of David are of the Lyric kind, there is a greater variety of style and manner in his works, than in those of the other two [Job and Isaiah]. The manner in which, considered merely as a Poet, David chiefly excels, is the pleasing, the soft, and the tender. In his Psalms, there are many lofty and sublime passages; but, in strength of description, he yields to Job; in sublimity, he yields to Isaiah. It is a sort of temperate grandeur, for which David is chiefly distinguished; and to this he always soon returns, when, upon some occasions, he rises above it. The Psalms in which he touches us most are those in which he describes the happiness of the righteous, or the goodness of God; expresses the tender breathings of a devout mind, or sends up moving and affectionate supplications to Heaven.

> Hugh Blair. *Lectures on Rhetoric and Belles Lettres.* Vol. III. 2d ed., corr. (London, Printed for W. Strahan, T. Cadell, 1785), p. 197.

The sense of a strong visual imagination pervades the writing, and an intensity that makes the scenes stand out like pictures. Tamar, bowed and with her hand laid on her head, the figure of mourning, Shimei on the hillside cursing and throwing stones, Mephibosheth, untended and with his feet unbound, greeting David on his return, Joab's pursuit of Amasa: described not as an old and garrulous man would remember them, with wealth of irrelevant description, but with the artist's eye for the telling detail. All the characterization is developed in action. Two of the most striking examples of real literary skill are the speeches of the woman of Tekoa and of Hushai the Archite. Both speeches are meant to deceive, and the author has shown their speciousness in their unnecessary length and flowery language. Figures of speech are comparatively rare in Hebrew prose, and especially simile, which is more complex than the metaphor which comes naturally to the Oriental. In both of these passages, however, the speaker uses simile, homely simile which would be natural to the characters: "as water spilt on the ground, which cannot be gathered up again" [II Sam. 14:14]; "as a bear robbed of her whelps in the field" [II Sam. 17:8]; "we will light upon him as the dew falleth on the ground" [II Sam. 17:12]. As a result of this literary device a smooth persuasiveness is given to the arguments suggesting the insincerity of the speakers. To my mind these two speeches show clearly the conscious artistry of the writer.

> Brooke Peters Church. *The Golden Years: The Old Testament Narrative as Literature* (New York, Rinehart, 1947), pp. 29–30

Now turn to the account of David's flight from Jerusalem and Absalom's rebellion and see its character as a whole and whether I am not right in saying that it is one of the great pieces of the world's literature. I suppose I ought to say that no one can taste the full flavour of it without reading it in the original. In a measure this is true. The stuff is written in classical Hebrew and the writer knows how to use his own tongue. The phrases are pithy, compact, with every word telling. But Hebrew, because of its natural picturesqueness and its want of subordinate sentences, translates better than most languages.

The man, for example, had an eye which could see and a pen which could report the thing he saw. He can etch a character in a few sentences and leave it without any need for underlining or multiplying remarks. We know Absalom in a moment, when we see him at the gate of Jerusalem and watch him drawing the decent countrymen who are returning disappointed from court, because David in his weary old age is not exercising his function as judge. "Lo, thy matters are good and right," he says to the worthy man already flattered by the king's son taking him by the sleeve, "but there is no one to put thy cause through. If only I had the power as I have the will, there would be fewer wronged men like you today in Israel." Give me the job, in fact, and you will see the millennium. It is the perennial demagogue.

He could describe a man too; and describe him as he ought to be, by the thing he does in the hour which demands him. David is sunk in the harem, under the spell of Bathsheba. The moment the rebellion breaks under Absalom, he starts awake. And when the situation seems desperate, everything rallies behind him. He steps naturally and inevitably into the front; and all the little shady people, who have been swarming into prominence, take at once the second place. Joab, with his clever trick of left hand stabbing disappears and with a few swift, unhesitating decisions, David orders his war, breathes courage into his broken ranks, knows what must be done. Everything owns its master and falls into line at once.

> Adam C. Welch. *Kings and Prophets of Israel*. Ed. by Norman W. Porteous (London, Lutterworth Press, 1952), pp. 100–101

It is clear that a large part of the life of David as given in the Bible contains history and not legend. In Absalom's rebellion, for example, or in the scenes from David's last days, the contradictions and crossing of motives both in individuals and in the general action have become so concrete that it is impossible to doubt the historicity of the information conveyed. Now the men who composed the historical parts are often the same who edited the older legends too; their peculiar religious concept of man in history, which we have attempted to describe above, in no way led them to a legendary simplification of events; and so it is only natural that, in the legendary passages of the Old Testament, historical structure is frequently discernible—of course, not in the sense that the traditions are examined as to their credibility according to the methods of scientific criticism; but simply to the extent that the tendency to a smoothing down and harmonizing of events, to a simplification of motives, to a static definition of characters which avoids conflict, vacillation, and development, such as are natural to legendary structure, does not predominate in the Old Testament world of legend. Abraham, Jacob, or even Moses produces a more concrete, direct, and historical impression than the figures of the Homeric world—not because they are better described in terms of sense (the contrary is the case) but because the confused, contradictory multiplicity of events, the psychological and factual cross-purposes, which true history reveals, have not disappeared in the representation but still remain clearly perceptible. In the stories of David, the legendary, which only later scientific criticism makes recognizable as such, imperceptibly passes into the historical; and even in the legendary, the problem of the classification and interpretation of human history is already passionately apprehended—a problem which later shatters the framework of historical composition and completely overruns it with prophecy; thus the Old Testament, in so far as it is concerned with human events, ranges through all three domains: legend, historical reporting, and interpretative historical theology.

> Erich Auerbach. *Mimesis*. Tr. by Willard Trask (Princeton, N.J., Princeton University Press, 1953), pp. 20–21

David as portrayed in the Succession Narrative is the most fully delineated of all the characters in the Old Testament. The real greatness of this psychological study is measured by the fact that even so, he remains for the reader an essentially elusive personality. This is not due to any vagueness or inconsistency on the part of the author. On the contrary, it is the very richness and variety of his literary creation which raises the figure of David to a stature comparable with the great tragic heroes of literature. The character is drawn so close to life that we find it impossible to understand him fully, because he has the complexity of a real person. It is this enigmatic manner of his portrayal which has occasioned the expression of so many different views concerning the meaning and purpose of the Succession Narrative. In incident after incident we see more than one possible explanation of David's conduct. Was he really magnanimous to Meribbaal (II Sam. 9:1–13), or was he merely being prudent in arranging to have him under his eye? And what of his piety? When he accepted the death of his child with the words "But now he is dead; why should I fast? Can I bring him back again? I shall go to him, but he will not return to me" (12:23); when he sent the Ark back to Jerusalem with the words, "Behold, here I am, let him do to me what seems good to him" (15:26); when he prevented Abishai from killing Shimei, saying, "If he is cursing because Yahweh has said to him, 'Curse David,' who then shall say, 'Why have you done so?'" (16:10)—was this genuine piety, or was it a calculated attempt to impress his followers? Are these further examples of David's well known cunning, such as he revealed when he sent Hushai back to Jerusalem to "defeat the counsel of Ahithophel"? Here surely the author has deliberately left his readers in doubt.

Not only David's clemency and piety but even his greatness is similarly left an open question. David was, in the end, successful—though he had more than once come close to total failure—in the achievement of his political and military aims. He left behind him a strong kingdom and an assured succession. We are allowed to see some of the factors which contributed to this success: David's personal charm and his ability to command complete loyalty (especially in Joab, Ittai, Hushai); his craftiness, especially when hard pressed; his personal courage, as when he wanted to take the field in person against Absalom; his tactical skill and ability to come to a swift decision, as when he temporarily abandoned Jerusalem to Absalom. Yet over and over again, as king and statesman, he shows the most absurd ineptitude: though accustomed to the role of judge, he is unable to distinguish between a true and a fictitious story whether it is Nathan (II Sam. 12:1–6) or the wise woman of Tekoa (14:1–11) who tells it; he is totally blind to the fact that Absalom is steadily undermining his position; he is incapable of seeing, until it is rudely pointed out to him by Joab (19:1–8) that his uncontrolled grief over the death of Absalom will have such a demoralizing effect on the troops who have just risked their lives to defend them against Absalom that he is throwing away everything which he has just regained. And it can hardly be accidental that it is only when he is old and feeble and a mere puppet in the hands of others that the succession to the throne can be settled by others who see, as he had never been able to do, the dangers into which the State has been thrown by his refusal to name a successor. So the author leaves us with yet another enigma: was it real greatness, or was it luck, together with the possession of loyal subordinates, which preserved David's kingdom and secured the all-important succession to the throne? It is significant that Joab, in the plainest speech in the book, emphasizes that David owes his life to his subordinates, and even comes close to suggesting that he owed his kingdom to them from the start (19:7).

It is in his portrayal of David's faults that the author comes closest to giving us an unambiguous picture. David's relations with his children provided an unusually good opportunity for a psychological study. The author never states baldly that the tragedies of Amnon, Absalom and Adonijah were due to David's own weaknesses, but he suggests it quite unmistakably in two ways: by portraying the sons as having inherited the weaknesses of their father and by describing in detail, quite objectively, the relations between David and Absalom.

Roger N. Whybray. *The Succession Narrative* (London, SCM, 1968), pp. 35–37

Structurally the story of [David and the Kingdom] is simple: David gains the throne (it is given to him); it is taken away from him, but restored (though somewhat uneasily); and finally he himself gives it away, or, as the event may alternatively be interpreted, it is again, but now successfully, taken from him. The story is about a person, David, and in the final analysis its major impact is in terms of David the man, not David as a cipher for some particular political philosophy or institution. . . . Nevertheless, it is also about a kingdom, Israel: it is formally structured around certain political events (accession, rebellion, succession), while political categories such as the relation between king and subject play a significant role in the telling of the story.

And it is about giving and grasping. This is the catalyst or source of dynamic in the plot. Through it the narrator weaves a subtle correlation between the private and public life of King David, so that curiously the Bathsheba episode dominates the central political events of rebellion and coup that follow it. The king who is content to be given the kingdom (II Sam. 2–4) nevertheless seizes with violence the woman of his desire. The theme of seizure then erupts in the rape of Tamar, the taking of Amnon's life and (in political form) the major incident of the rebellion of Absalom. With the loss of his throne we see again momentarily the radical, magnanimous David who will allow the matter of the kingdom to rest in the hands of others. His fortunes improve and he is restored, but the restoration is marked by compromise. The end of the episode has a falling tone again. The final segment (I Kgs. 1–2) shows the death of the king in the context of the norms of political life. The theme of grasping is predominant and is expressed in terms of David as well as of others (notably Solomon). The kingdom is finally taken from him. Ironically the agent of seizure is Bathsheba, the benefactor her son.

The author, through the texture of his prose, through the significant juxtaposition or paralleling of events, speeches, and characters, and in some cases through the presentation of crucial incidents on a purely inferential basis, is continually exploring the range of perspectives open to the participants in and the interpreters of the situations that constitute the stuff of his story. We find in the narrative no simple *tendenz* or moralizing but rather a picture of the rich variety of life that is often comic and ironic in its contrasting perspectives and conflicting norms. Not that the author is amoral or immoral; but his judgement is tempered by his sense of the intricacy and ambivalence of the situations that confront his characters. He has a powerful, yet sympathetic, sense of the frailty of man, and this, I believe, sums up his treatment of David, the "hero" of the story. However bleak the final scenes of the narrative, however biting the irony of some of the earlier scenes (especially the Bathsheba episode) it remains the case that David is the one truly engaging character in the story. However momentarily, he confronts us with a manner of action that breaks out of the mundane.

To characterize such a vision as essentially propagandist or didactic is odd, to say the least. This is the work of no pamphleteer nor teacher: the vision is artistic, the author, above all, a fine teller of tales.

David M. Gunn. *Semeia*. 3, 1975, pp. 35–36

The large cycle of stories about David, which is surely one of the most stunning imaginative achievements of ancient literature, provides an instructive central instance of the intertwining of history and fiction. This narrative, though it may have certain folkloric embellishments (such as David's victory over Goliath), is based on firm historical facts, as modern research has tended to confirm: there really was a David who fought a civil war against the house of Saul, achieved undisputed sovereignty over the twelve tribes, conquered Jerusalem, founded a dynasty, created a small empire, and was succeeded by his son Solomon. Beyond these broad outlines, it is quite possible that many of the narrated details about David, including matters bearing on the complications of his conjugal life and his relations with his children, may have been reported on good authority.

Nevertheless, these stories are not, strictly speaking, historiography, but rather the imaginative reenactment of history by a gifted writer who organizes his materials along certain thematic biases and according to his own remarkable intuition of the psychology of the characters. He feels entirely free, one should remember, to invent interior monologue for his characters; to ascribe feeling, intention, or motive to them when he chooses; to supply verbatim dialogue (and he is one of literature's masters of dialogue) for occasions when no one but the actors themselves could have had knowledge of exactly what was said. The author of the David stories stands in basically the same relation to Israelite history as Shakespeare stands to English history in his history plays. Shakespeare was obviously not free to have Henry V lose the battle of Agincourt, or to allow someone else to lead the English forces there, but, working from the hints of historical tradition, he could invent a kind of *Bildungsroman* for the young Prince Hal; surround him with invented characters that would serve as foils, mirrors, obstacles, aids in his development; create a language and a psychology for the king which are the writer's own achievement, making out of the stuff of history a powerful projection of human possibility. That is essentially what the author of the David cycle does for David, Saul, Abner, Joab, Jonathan, Absalom, Michal, Abigail, and a host of other characters.

One memorable illustration among many of this transmutation of history into fiction is David's great confrontation with Saul at the cave in the wilderness of Ein Gedi (I Sam. 24). The manic king, one recalls, while in pursuit of the young David, has gone into a cave to relieve himself, where by chance David and his men have taken refuge. David sneaks up to Saul and cuts off a corner of his robe. Then he is smitten with remorse for having perpetrated this symbolic mutilation on the anointed king, and he sternly holds his men in check while the unwitting Saul walks off from the cave unharmed. Once the king is at a distance, David follows him out of the cave. Holding the excised corner of the robe, he hails Saul and shouts out to his erstwhile pursuer one of his most remarkable speeches, in which he expresses fealty and reverence to the Lord's anointed one, disavows any evil intention toward him (with the corner of the robe as evidence of what he could have done but did not do), and proclaims his own humble status: "After whom did the king of Israel set out?" he says in verse-like symmetry, "After whom are you chasing? After a dead dog, after a single flea?" (I Sam. 24:15).

At the end of this relatively lengthy speech, the narrator holds us in suspense for still another moment by choosing to preface Saul's response with a chain of introductory phrases: "And it came to pass when David finished speaking these words, that Saul said"—and then what he says has a breathtaking brevity after David's stream of words, and constitutes one of those astonishing reversals that make the rendering of character in these stories so arresting: "'Is it your voice, David, my son?' and Saul raised his voice and wept" (I Sam. 24:17). The point is not merely that the author has made up dialogue to which he could have had no "documentary" access; Thucydides, after all, does that as a stylized technique of representing the various positions maintained by different historical personages. In the biblical story the invented dialogue is an expression of the author's imaginative grasp of his protagonists as distinctive moral and psychological figures, of their emotion-fraught human intercourse dramatically conceived; and what that entire process of imagination essentially means is the creation of fictional character.

> Robert Alter. *The Art of Biblical Narrative* (New York, Basic Books, 1981), pp. 35–37

The author of the Davidic biography, a circumstantial character history that makes [the ancient Roman biographer] Suetonius' *Tiberius* look like a comic book, takes his reader through David's development from shepherd to therapon to exiled mercenary to statesman to leader to victor to ruler. He traces the growth of a personal lust, an independence of the law, that results in murder and adultery; he imputes to it David's Lear-like status, and the tragedy of the old man to hold his own either politically or in bed.

This historian twice raises the issue of contradictory testimony in his account. In the first instance, after Absalom has murdered his half-brother, Amnon, the report reaches David that "Absalom has smitten all the king's sons; not one of them is left." David panics. But Jonadab ben-Shima, the king's cousin, dismisses the rumor, noting that Absalom had had it in for Amnon, and for Amnon alone, ever since Amnon raped Absalom's full-sister, Tamar. Shortly thereafter, Jonadab's deduction is corroborated by the sight of David's other sons fleeing toward the capital (II Sam. 13:28–36). Here, special knowledge (Jonadab's and David's) leads to a critical stance toward an exaggerated claim. The evidence in currency is tested against the background of the parties involved.

> Baruch Halpern. In *The Poet and the Historians: Essays in Literary and Historical Biblical Criticism*. Ed. by Richard Elliott Friedman (Chico, Cal., Scholars Press, 1983), pp. 44–45

ABSALOM

The story of Absalom is a splendid example of a complete and absolute whole in a broad and comprehensive framework. Every word in each verse is fully significant, and the same is true of each sentence in every picture, each picture in every scene, each scene in every episode, and each episode in the entire drama. We speak of scenes, in the language of drama, because the drama is an excellent example of a broad whole that depicts a complete world. In the drama there is a beginning, a middle and an end. There is development, complication and denouement, there are primary and secondary heroes, and they are all involved in a central plot and an important series of events. From these points of view, Absalom's revolt is a true drama. Its unity is clearly shown by its structure, by its division into acts, scenes and pictures, in the transitions between one camp and the other in order to show the development of the action from all points of view, and in the inverse parallelism between the end of the drama and its beginning. Its dramatic quality lies in its clear and surprising action: in spite of its carefully calculated structure the flow of the action is not held up for a moment, and even if you can guess the general course of the plot from the first chapter, from time to time something new and unexpected arises.

Organic unity, dramatic structure, dramatic quality—these are not enough when you come to examine the greatness and the quality of the story of Absalom's revolt or of the long Biblical story in general. Its main greatness lies not in the portrayal of a world, but in what that world contains, in the nature of the events and the nature of the people, in the conception of man, society and history that is latent in it.

> Zvi Adar. *The Biblical Narrative* (Jerusalem, Department of Education and Culture, World Zionist Organization, 1959), pp. 186–87

A skilful narrator can add to the impact of his story by sometimes giving the reader this better knowledge and sometimes denying it. . . . Some examples can be mentioned briefly here without any claim to full description of their effects. . . .

At [II Sam.] 13:24–27 the reader knows what Absalom's real intentions are, while the king does not. The king's words at verse 25 ("in order not to be a burden to you") acquire an ironic ambiguity: the surface meaning refers to the expense Absalom would incur in providing a feast for the king and his court, but in a deeper sense the king's presence would indeed be a burden for Absalom, for it would make the planned murder of Amnon very difficult, if not impossible.

All through 14:4–12 the reader knows more than the king. Besides contributing suspense to the narrative (when will the king realize what is afoot?), this situation wins the reader's sympathy for David who is shown acting in all sincerity as the ideal king, willing to have justice done to a defenceless widow.

At 14:28–33, on the other hand, the reader is not given more knowledge than the personages but is obliged to read between the lines as best he can. The narrator gives him no help to understand the short reconciliation scene of verse 33, and the reader's feeling of insecurity suggests that this verse cannot be the end of the story.

The reader's better knowledge during Hushai's dealings with Absalom in Jerusalem (16:16–17:14) adds considerably to the impact of this pericope. Irony and double meanings abound. Hushai's acclamation "Long live the king" (16:16) refers on the surface to Absalom, but the reader knows that it is David's life that depends on the outcome of Hushai's mission; Absalom accepts Hushai's affirmation of life, and thereby enters on the path that leads to his own death. Then Absalom's rhetorical question, "Is this your loyalty to your friend?" (16:17) is meant as the statement "You have shown no loyalty to your friend," but for the knowledgeable reader the statement is another one: "This *is* Hushai's loyalty to his friend." Double senses return in Hushai's words at 17:7. Ahitophel's counsel is indeed "not good"—for David and his men it would be disastrous. Then Hushai addresses Absalom: "You know your father and his men . . ." (v. 8); but Absalom does not know them, for if he did he would have accepted Ahitophel's advice (17:1–3) without further ado. Hushai characterizes David and his men as "warriors and in bitter mood" (*marei nefesh*, 17:8), but the reader knows that they are exhausted and in need of refreshment (*wayyinnafesh sham*, 16:14). David is lying in ambush "even now" (*hinne ʿatta* 17:9), says Hushai; but the reader knows that David is waiting in a vulnerable position on the near side of the Jordan (16:14). The double sense to *tova* "good," already met in verse 7, reappears in verse 14a: Hushai's advice is indeed better—for David, not for Absalom.

In brief, then, the narrator can give the reader better knowledge than one or more of the personages, or he can make the reader learn the story as an observer beside the personages. . . . It is contextual analysis that will determine the narrative effects of these various situations as they occur.

Charles Conroy. *Absalom! Absalom!* (Rome, Biblical Institute Press, 1978), pp. 113–14

Examining Absalom's uprising story in the light of Aristotle's *Poetics*, we discover that it contains all the vital elements which constitute a tragedy in the literary sense of the word.

The character of the protagonist, namely Absalom, fits perfectly Aristotle's demands for a proper delineation of the tragic hero. We find that Absalom is neither wicked nor base. His lot is fatally reversed from a high state of a successful and widely appreciated prince to the low predicament of a hated and pursued foe. This reversal occurs to Absalom due to his tragic errors, which cause him to suffer undeserved affliction. Absalom's tragic errors are of two kinds: those which involve horrible deeds and therefore are morally reprehensible in spite of their reasonable motivations, and those which are morally good, but practically most fatal to him. Among the first kind of errors we can include Absalom's murder of Amnon and his planned revolt against David. Of the other kind, the most significant and consequential tragic error was his rejection of Ahitophel's practical advice in favour of Hushai's impractical but morally sound advice.

These tragic errors of Absalom's choices reflect a human predicament very effectively. One can find himself in the awkward position where a morally sound choice is not really practical, while the practical choice cannot morally be justified. Yet he has to make his choices and act accordingly. We would not necessarily regard him as a villain.

From this point of view it becomes very clear that the popular picture of Absalom as a villain is very far from the truth. We should rather view him as a fellow human moved by forces and events beyond his control.

This is what Aristotle means when he says that the tragic hero should be as human as anyone else.

Sarah Halperin. *Dor le Dor*. Fall 1982, pp. 13–14

NATHAN'S PARABLE

By viewing David in terms of energy we discover a precise and subtle balance in the text. David passes *two* verdicts, verse 5d ("The man that hath done this thing shall surely die.") and verse 6a ("And he shall restore the lamb fourfold."). The former corresponds with his last and worst crime, the murder of Uriah, and therefore it precedes the other (psycho)logically. The latter corresponds with 11:2–4, 27, the adultery and the marriage with Bathsheba. David may suppress whatever he wishes, but his conscience and sub-conscious preserve the connection between his two crimes and his excitability as judge and even make this relationship apparent to the discrete observer. For this reason we are no longer surprised to hear David's motivation for passing verdict in two parts. First, he employs fairly general terms such as "thing" and "did" (v. 6b); then, he renders an excellent portrayal of the rich man's mentality in 6c, "he had no pity," again a nice projection of himself and evidence of the infallible self-knowledge carried deep within Man's sub-conscious.

With one tug Nathan removes the veil. With twice two syllables, *'attā hā'īsh,* "thou art the man," Nathan holds the mirror up to David's face. This shocking confrontation causes David to discover, at his own expense, that life without death is impossible. Like the rich man, David finds himself in the realm of the dead souls where possession and material things are important and reification is the unspoken law. He can only return to the land of the living, there where the poor in spirit experience mutual love and understanding, by passing through the narrow gateway of death. David is, as we would say in plain English, "scared to death." The deeper sense of this expression receives the impression of the king's seal in the form of an oath. His own judicial verdict obliges David to meet death face to face.

Nathan shows the monarch how wickedly he has acted, and David cannot flee this truth which implies the death of a very strong ego. Thus the most difficult hour in David's life commences in 12:7. "To suffer one's death and to be reborn is not easy." Only when the whole truth has been allowed to resound (12:7–12) and David has fully acknowledged it with the words "I have sinned against the Lord" (v. 13b) can the supreme judge rescind (v. 13de) and replace (v. 14b) the death sentence.

Through David's real position we arrive at *the second level* where 12:1–4 suddenly becomes a parable which refers to the triangle of David-Bathsheba-Uriah. The first level is that of the communication Nathan-David as a report of a theft (N-D, only during the narrated time of 12:1–6!); the second level at which David only arrives in 12:7, taking up a position different to ours but analogous to it, is that of story-listener (S-L) or text-reader. The transference of meaning takes place through two aspects.

Aspect A, parallel to the narrated time of verses 1–6, has already been discussed for the most part in terms of David's inner world. It discloses the connection between the parable and reality, especially via four elements:

	rich	-	David	
	poor	-	Uriah	
N-D	lamb	-	Bathsheba	S-L
	herds	-	harem	

Because a parable is not a comparison, we need not look fanatically for a counterpart in David's reality to each of its elements. The text itself, however, does offer two more stimulating allusions. Corresponding to the lamb-Bathsheba analogy is the lamb's being "as a daughter" for the poor man; the Hebrew *bat* reminds us of Bathsheba. In the nuclear line 3c, we see her/the lamb eating/drinking/sleeping, concrete representations for intimacy and safety. And it is this intimacy and safety which her husband Uriah had denied himself when David had offered him taking leave in an effort to conceal the fruit of his adultery. In 11:11d, Uriah refuses "to eat, drink, and sleep with my wife" (N.B. on the basis of loyalty to sovereign and fatherland!). Afterwards, David still tries yet again to arrange this '*kl*/*shth*/*shkb* (11:13b) by one last, miserable trick, "eating/drinking/making drunk." Functioning as an allusion on the second level, the parable's pivot discloses how David's egoism is the *coup-de-grâce* for the *Ich und Du* [I and Thou] of Uriah-Bathsheba.

Aspect B. It is not difficult to reprehend this David. It is tempting to elevate oneself by being indignant about so much evil, but then one is doing the same thing as David in regard to the rich man. Nathan takes a different approach. Before confronting David with his dark side (12:7sqq.), he lets him see his good side. Although it is a considerable switch, the David of 12:5 is congenial. Although his reaction may be somewhat exaggerated, its basis is real and sound. The parable makes a strong appeal to his feeling of righteousness, and this feeling appears to be alive and well. Hereby David as a whole comes into motion.

J. P. Fokkelman. *Narrative Art and Poetry in the Books of Samuel*. Vol. I: *King David* (Assen, Netherlands, Van Gorcum, 1981), pp. 11–19

At its most basic level Nathan's story depends on the antithetical parallel established in the first line: rich man/poor man. Verses 2–3 elaborate the contrast by specifying the particular content of the contrast. (1) The rich man had very many flocks and herds. (2) The poor man had *nothing* except one little ewe which he had bought. The contrast emphasizes the position of the poor man by piling up descriptions of his lamb in human terms. The poor man raised her; the verb, *way^ehayyeha*, has a wide range of meaning, but it can clearly connote personal, human nurture (cf. Ezek. 16:6). The lamb grew up with the poor man and his sons, pointing here to the intimacy of the human relationship. The lamb is not of the barnyard nor even a pet, but is one with his children. The verb, *wattigdal*, clearly carries such personal, human connotations (cf. Gen. 21:8, 20; Exod. 2:10f.; Judg. 13:24; I Sam. 2:21, 26; I Kgs. 12:8, 10; II Kgs. 4:18; Ezek. 16:7). To eat food of the family and to drink from the cup are acts of hospitality for visitors, not for pets or barnyard residents (Gen. 18:5; Judg. 19:5f.; I Sam. 28:22). And the final designation of the lamb's relationship (*uvheqo tishkav*) is patently a description of human relationship. It can refer to a sexual (Gen. 16:5; II Sam. 12:8; I Kgs. 1:2), but it can also refer to a parent-child relationship (cf. Num. 11:12; Ruth 4:16; I Kgs. 3:20; 17:19). These descriptions of the familial relationships set up the final simile: "She was like a daughter to him."

The contrast sets up the situation described in verse 4. One might normally expect, under such circumstances, that the rich man would take an animal from his own abundant flocks or herds and prepare the feast for the visitor. But verse 4 notes explicitly that he "was unwilling to take one from his own." Rather, he took the poor man's one lamb, the member of his family, and prepared it as the entree for his guest. And with that tragic note, the story comes to an end.

The structure of this story does not build on an arc of tension from an initial complication to a resolution. It does not highlight a virtue in the poor man nor even by structural design a vice in the rich man. Rather, the dominant structural feature is the contrast. And the center of the contrast is the lamb, an active member of the poor man's family and a passive victim of the rich man's hospitality. It makes no difference for the structure of the story to observe that an ancient principle of social order relative to the responsibilities of the host permitted appropriation of an animal from a neighbor with the recognition that the host would pay the owner an appropriate fee. Nor does it clarify the story to suggest that the issue at stake is theft since the rich man obviously stole the lamb of the poor man and the story makes no reference to payment. The focus of the structure falls on the contrast, with the lamb functioning as the crux that marks the situation as a tragedy.

George W. Coats. *Interpretation.* Oct., 1981, pp. 371–72

DAVID AND BATHSHEBA

The first verse of [II Sam.] chapter 11, which is the exposition of this story from the personal life of David, apparently serves as a mere informative exposition, reporting, with no ulterior motives, only the necessary background data, such as the time of the event, the war being waged at the time, the locations of the story's protagonists. This innocent and uncalculating information, however, warrants —from the standpoint of what is implicit in it—further examination, for already within it is revealed the beginning of the ironic perspective [of the narrative].

In the opening verse are two main parts, which are blatantly asymmetrical:

[1] It was at the turn of the year, at the time when kings go out,
David sent Joab and his servants with him, and all Israel,
and they destroyed the Ammonites and laid siege to Rabbah.
[2] And David stays in Jerusalem. . . .

In a sentence in which a short sentence-part follows an especially long sentence-part and in which the parts are equivalent from any standpoint (as in the verse before us), the reader tends to prolong his reading of the shorter part with the aim of making it equivalent (at least from the standpoint of the reader's feeling) to the reading time of the longer part. Therefore, whereas the first, longer part of verse 1 [. . .] is gulped down quickly, the shorter part is "dilated," which brings about a lingering on each individual word and an emphasis of this part, as though meaningful pauses were created between the words: "*And David // stays // in Jerusalem.*" By means of this directed lingering, secondary, connotative meanings are activated, and attention is aroused about additional aspects of "And David stays in Jerusalem," additional to the aspect of dry information about the geographic whereabouts of the king.

These aspects of the opening sentence direct the reader to set up the king *staying in his house* in opposition to *all the others,* who were sent by him *to war.* . . . The specification "Joab and his servants with him, and all Israel" for a moment creates the impression that in Jerusalem there remained no one but David himself, and the verbs "and they destroyed," "and they laid siege" build a drastic contrast to "stays." This is an apt introduction to a story one of whose central ironies is what the king does in his city while the nation is at war in the field . . . [ellipsis in original]. . . .

The ironic direction that was defined at the opening of the narrative will be developed through its course. The narrator exploits well the simultaneous event, the war. The war episode is not transmitted together with the story of David and Bathsheba just because it occurred *in the same period* (even though this is one of the realistic reasons for its being brought in). It is not tied to the story of David and Bathsheba in the area of verisimilar connections (or patterns) only (in this area it is relevant to the story because it makes possible David's meeting Bathsheba, who stayed alone in the city, and the murder of Uriah), but it *also* builds literary connections, connections of parallelism, by serving as an ironic spotlight illuminating what happens in the city. This function of the war episode guides the distribution of materials in the text. The story opens with an announcement of the war. Its second part (in chapter 12) concludes with a description of *the victory*—and thus the story of the war serves as a framework for the personal story. The situation of the victory story has not been guided by chronological considerations. *Preceding it* a chain of events is narrated: the birth, the death of the child, the second pregnancy of Bathsheba, and the birth of Solomon. The victory certainly occurred before this chain of events from the personal life of the king came to its conclusion, for the siege of Rabbah did not last for nearly two years! However, the chapter's montage principle has been guided by structural-thematic considerations, and the narrator seeks to relate the victory only after *he has concluded* the entire personal story. He goes backward from a chronological standpoint, then, and adduces matters that will be more meaningful if they are told at this point . . . (12:26–31).

Presenting the victory story specifically at the end enables the narrator not to cut into the narrative continuity (which is important to him) of the second part of the personal story. The *victory story* is not requisite for the story of David and Bathsheba to be able to take place (in contrast to the fact of the war's existence). However, relating this episode in the framework of the context of the story of David and Bathsheba makes it more than a chronicle per se; the war story turns into an indirect formative device of the story of David and Bathsheba itself. The fact that the narrative does not dwell on the description of the conquest itself but rather on relating the minor side of it—the apparent conquest by David—begs for interpretation. In fact, the details that are narrated concerning the victory story build up an ironic analogy to the personal episode: The king stayed in Jerusalem, others waged his war, and he wins the fruits of someone else's victory and names the city for himself—this is an apt final correspondence of ironic illumination of the narrative about the king *who wins someone else's wife* and "whose name is called by his." *See also* Narrator: Informational Gaps and Redundancy.

Menakhem Perry and Meir Sternberg. Ha-sifrut. Summer, 1968, pp. 267–69†

The critical exegete approaching an ancient work must make a conscious and systematic effort to free himself to a high degree from his own literary assumptions and aesthetic precepts, so that he may interpret the work itself and decide between alternative interpretations in accord with the standards inherent in it. Indeed, [Menakhem Perry and Meir Sternberg, *Ha-sifrut*, Summer 1968, pp. 263–92] properly admit that the interpretive process must be directed and limited, inter alia, by "the conceptual mindset that the work's generic character arouses in the reader" (p. 269, and see especially note 5). In spite of this, in actuality they have not considered at all the literary genre to which the "story" under discussion [David and Bathsheba] belongs and what its affiliations entail. It is more or less agreed among Bible scholars that the episode of David and Bathsheba (II Sam. 11–12) is an integral part of a long historiographic composition (II Sam. 9–20 + I Kgs. 1) whose theme is: who of David's sons will succeed to his throne? That is to say, the story of adultery and murder was occasioned to serve as a key to understanding the chain of sordid and bloody events that beset the royal house, just as the episode of confession and repentance serves as the beginning of the resolution to the riddle of the succession to the throne by the son of Bathsheba. The author's identity is not known to us, but from his realistic writing style and precise factual knowledge about the anguish of the king and the clandestine affairs of his court we may conclude that he was an eyewitness to the events he described. This intimate acquaintance with David's personality did not upset the marvelous balance between complete admiration for the greatness of his protagonist, deep penetration into the polar components of his psyche, and a ripe understanding of their dynamic interaction. This combination of intimacy and distance, homage and criticism, endowed his story with its historical credibility, psychological authenticity, and literary charm. It seems that this combination was made possible by dint of an Archimedean point that provided the narrator with his theological perception of human action and fate in relation to the providence of God and the rightness of his judgment. The participation of the reader in this manner of seeing is what endows the historical narrative with its moral significance and its religious power. The narrator's goal was, then, to describe events, explain their connections, and to draw a lesson from their course.

He produced a historiographic composition that is narrative (from the point of view of form) and didactic (from the point of view of aim).

I do not mean to claim that it is impossible to attribute to such a historiographer ironic naïveté and sophisticated ambiguity. It is possible but very far from likely. To the contrary, the mark of a historiographer is that he strives to enhance—not to undermine—his credibility as a narrator, just as his distinctively causal viewpoint reflects an attempt at a rational connection of events. And his clearly didactic aim leaves no room for intentional obfuscation. One who means to show that transgression leads to transgression, to warn that sin begets punishment, and to confirm that repentance earns forgiveness, does not on the moral plane, speak with marbles in his mouth. Furthermore, a writer who attributes to God's intervention both the exposure of a well-concealed crime and punishment and forgiveness in a balanced combination is not likely to need Nathan the prophet to hide behind and use as a mouthpiece. Rather, the silences of the narrator and the many gaps he opened demand a different interpretation from the one presented to us [by Perry and Sternberg].

Grave psychological and literary dangers lurk, of course, at the door of the didactic story. To guard against oversimplification and flat moralizing, biblical narrative periodically monitors itself from passing judgment on its protagonists' behavior and from articulating its lessons. It is this extreme restriction on explicit moral and religious pronouncements that gave rise to the famous question concerning the justification for including the historical, narrative Genesis in the book destined to serve as Torah (commentary of Rashi to Gen. 1:1 [in which Genesis is explained as the introduction to the laws of the Pentateuch in order to justify God's taking the Land of Canaan away from its inhabitants and giving it to the Israelites]). But concealing the didactic character of biblical narrative was destined only to strengthen its influence. The purpose of silence on the main theme is not the creation of irony but objectification: we draw the lesson directly from the related facts instead of getting it prepared and preformulated, relying on the authority of the narrator. In all this our story does not deviate one bit from the true form of biblical narrative, and there is, therefore, no way to propose a specific solution to this all-encompassing problem.

Uriel Simon. Ha-sifrut. Aug., 1970, p. 606†

II Samuel 11, the story of David's adultery with Bathsheba, is the first of several chapters dealing with the personal and domestic life of the hero. . . .

David is not the only hero of ancient literature who is diverted from his pursuits by sexual relations with a beautiful woman. Odysseus, whose fidelity to home and wife is unquestioned, has sexual relations with both Calypso and Circe. Unlike David, however, he is not morally reprehensible within the logic of the story because his relations are involuntary relations with goddesses, whose advances he could not disregard without harm. His sexual infidelity to his wife is not even considered objectionable by the narrator or his wife Penelope. In this regard the real contrast between the stories of Odysseus and David is not between the two heroes, but rather between the conceptions of deity that emerge from the two stories. In the biblical account, the holy God is displeased with the sin of adultery, as evidenced by the narrator's statement that "the thing that David had done displeased the Lord" (II Sam. 11:27). The underlying principle is clear: adultery is horrible because it is a perversion of something God-ordained and sacred, namely, faithful wedded love. The stories in classical mythology that depict gods and goddesses (such as Calypso and Circe in *The Odyssey*) engaging in promiscuous sexual relations with each other and with humans reflect a low view of the gods, who are made in man's image, and a low view of the sanctity of wedded love, the perversion of which is not notable because the thing itself is not regarded highly in the first place.

The contrast between David and Aeneas is also instructive. The relationship between Aeneas and Dido constitutes a diversion from the hero's duty to found the Roman Empire. It is an act that displeases Jupiter, and in this it resembles the story of David. But why does it displease Jupiter? It displeases him because the love affair diverts Aeneas from his political task. By contrast, God is displeased with David because he has committed an immoral act of sin—a violation of God's moral law. Similarly, the essential nature of Aeneas' sin is that he has allowed passion to conquer his reason, while David's act is disobedience to a personal, holy God. The resolution of Aeneas' sin lies simply in his allowing the light of reason to dispel the dark passions that have momentarily gained control of his sense of duty. David's restoration, however, involves his coming to terms with the past act. He cannot simply walk away from the act by a resolve to reform. His sin needs forgiveness from a holy and forgiving God, as is made particularly clear in Psalm 51, written on the occasion of David's sin with Bathsheba.

Leland Ryken. *The Literature of the Bible* (Grand Rapids, Mich., Zondervan, 1974), pp. 62–63

The scene begins (II Sam. 11:2ff.) with David walking about on the roof of the palace, from where he "sees" a woman bathing. He sees nothing but her beauty—no moral prohibitions against taking her, nor her conjugal relationship to one of his own soldiers who is fighting one of his wars. Afterward, Bathsheba sends word that she is pregnant and David immediately sends for Uriah, her husband. The narrative gives no details about his facial expression or his reaction or what he is scheming. The ellipsis respects the integrity of the character's mind and indicates where the narrator cannot or wishes not to look. David's motives are perhaps too horrible to view or too opaque to comprehend.

The narrative presents David's reaction to bad news elliptically twice more. Uriah arrives and is sent home presumably so he can have intercourse with his wife. He refuses, however, because the Israelite soldier is under oath to refrain from intercourse while the army is in the field. The narrative reports, "David heard that Uriah had not gone home, and said to him . . ."—stripping away all but the most essential action to focus on David's maniacal fixation with his immediate problem. Nothing else exists for him (and the narration) but its resolution. This time David gets Uriah drunk in an attempt to make him forget his oath. When the ploy fails, he immediately writes a letter for Uriah to take back to his commander, Joab, ordering the latter to arrange Uriah's death in battle. The haste with which David arrives at the new strategy indicates that now, for him, removing the stigma of his adultery is purely a tactical problem. He plots murder as dispassionately as he tempts Uriah to go to his marriage bed. The story's even narrative hand stresses the terrible evenness of David's fixation.

Uriah's innocent blindness counterpoints David's myopia; Uriah is unaware of the plots against him, unbendingly following his soldier's code of duty—even delivering his own death sentence. But another character in the story recognizes, better than David, his characteristic tendency to fix his mind this way. When Nathan comes to admonish David for his crime, he tells David a parable about a rich man, with many sheep, who steals the beloved lamb of a poor man who has only one. David becomes so absorbed in the story that he misses the obvious parallel. He has what could almost be called an ideal reader's reaction, crying out in anger at the villain's deed: "As the Lord lives, the man who did this deserves to die. He shall pay for the lamb four times over because he has done this and shown no pity." Nathan then says to David, "You are the man." [II Sam. 12:5–7] He knows, as Joab knows, that David must be approached indirectly. His intense singularity of perception must be allowed to release itself before David can hear what a calmer eye can see.

Jan Wojcik. In *The David Myth in Western Literature*. Ed. by Raymond-Jean Frontain and Jan Wojcik (West Lafayette, Ind., Purdue University Press, 1980), pp. 17–18

DAVID AND GOLIATH

A performance, written with the greatest art, and managed with the most masterly judgment . . . This Goliah of Gath reminds one of Homer's Ajax, and, indeed, the process of the engagement between the giant and David, is, in many particulars, like the ceremony of the single combat of Telamon and Hector.

The above description of Goliah's person, and warlike preparations, are more military and formidable than the hero of Homer. . . . His moving with majestic pace to combat, is less terrific than Goliah's triumphant march in the full view of the astonished Philistines. There seems also less propriety in Hector's *pause of fear*, than in the inapprehensive and intrepid conduct of David, who though not so practised like Hector, was, nevertheless, uniformly brave and heroic to the very heart, without ever finding that heroism suspended, even at the presence of Goliah.

Samuel J. Pratt. *The Sublime and Beautiful of Scripture*
(New York, Printed by Tiebout & O'Brien, 1795), pp.
159, 171–73

The story of David and Goliath (I Sam. 17) is a favorite with children, and no wonder—its appeal is to the most naive and least sophisticated of literary tastes. It has all the ingredients of a good story. There is vivid conflict, involving the pagan bully against the children of God, in a war setting. The single combat simply heightens the sense of conflict by concentrating it in a single event. The conflict is between obvious right and obvious wrong, making it compelling. From the point of view of David and the narrator, the issue at stake is nothing less than "that all the earth may know that there is a God in Israel" (v. 46). The struggle between two competing sets of values is made even clearer when David says to the giant, "You come to me with a sword and with a spear and with a javelin; but I come to you in the name of the Lord of hosts, . . . whom you have defied" (v. 45). The story also possesses a villain—a giant, no less, who evokes instinctive feelings of horror and moral revulsion when he defies the armies of God. The narrative features a boy hero, a homespun underdog who does in the proud enemy of God. It appeals to the romantic strain in us—to our instinct for wish fulfillment, even though we realize that life is tragic as well as comic. There is concreteness of presentation; we can hear the giant defying Israel and see David picking up five smooth stones and visualize him running to meet Goliath. Finally, the story displays a firm sense of structure. The storyteller does not clutter the narrative with too many details. He begins with an exposition of background information, conveys a sense of rising action, constructs his story around a single climax, and, once the climax has been reached, quickly brings the story to a conclusion.

Leland Ryken. *The Literature of the Bible* (Grand Rapids, Mich., Zondervan, 1974), p. 61

An analysis of the Biblical story of David and Goliath (I Sam. 17) in ethnopoetic terms is presented here. This is a first attempt to analyse a Biblical story in these terms, with all the limitations entailed in such an attempt. Not being a Biblical scholar, but a folklorist, I am the more aware of these limitations.

We will examine the story from the following aspects: (a) narrative syntax: texture, plot structure, formulaic number; (b) narrative semantics: repertoire of the contentual terms (anthropomorphic, zoomorphic, and object-like), and the dimensions of time and space.

On the basis of our examination of these aspects, we will try to determine whether or not to consider our text as stemming from oral literature, and if so, to which genre does it belong; and further, how does this fact contribute to our understanding of the Biblical text. Two genres of oral literature may serve as models for our story: the heroic fairy tale and the romantic epic. . . .

In the *heroic fairy tale*, the hero enters the marvelous world and wins the marvelous king's daughter after carrying out various tasks. Among the more prominent tasks is that of defeating a monster, which is a rival suitor who tries to win the king's daughter for himself. . . .

The *romantic epic* is a sub-genre of that epic which is current in the narrating community. It can be a historic or a national epic (the national epic is on a higher level of symbolization than the historic epic; it does not tell of concrete historical characters and events. Examples of national epic: Russian epic songs). The romantic epic tells (a) of a hero who wins a bride after carrying out certain tasks, or (b) of a pair of lovers, or a married couple, who are separated by hostile forces (natural or supernatural) and who struggle to reunite. The plot structure of the romantic epic is similar to that of the heroic fairy tale as sketched by [Vladimir] Propp. Supernatural elements penetrate easily into this sub-genre. During his struggles and adventures, the hero can leave the realm of this world and enter various kinds of supernatural worlds, while supernatural powers may interfere between him and his bride. . . .

A comparison of the qualities of our story . . . with those listed under "romantic epic" . . . identifies our story with this genre of epic (sub-genre 'a': hero wins hand of princess), and not with the heroic fairy tale. While Propp's model of the fairy tale serves well for an analysis of the text, the latter can also be analyzed by means of the models prepared especially for analysis of the epic ([Aleksandr Pavlovich] Skaftymov's model), something which cannot be said of the heroic fairy tale. The semantic elements leave no doubt that our text belongs to the romantic epic genre.

Let us review again, in brief, the qualities of our story:

characters:

All the characters are human, of realistic dimensions; "our" characters are also historical and more detailed.

hero:

Hero starts out weak, young; he is drawn by independent motives when he announces his wish "to take away the reproach from Israel" and to restore the honor of "the armies of the living God".

objects:

All the objects are natural. The weapons of both heroes are exceptional: Goliath's weapons are larger than the usual, while David's are smaller than the usual and are not appropriate—or so it seems—to the situation, but they have no supernatural components.

animals:

All the animals are natural, and function as requisites, or as proof in an argument. They do not aid the narrative characters.

dimension of time:

> The narrative takes place entirely within natural time, in the historical frame-
> work of the battle between the Israelite tribes and the Philistines, and during
> the lifetimes of its central personages: David and Saul.

dimension of space:

> The story takes place within the realm of "our country"—Judah, in well-
> specified places. There are no supernatural elements in this space.

In conclusion: Our text is a short, prose record of an ethnopoetic epic work
(real or imitated) which was possibly composed in verse form; its genre is the romantic epic of type "a," a sub-genre of the historic epic.

Heda Jason. <i>Biblica</i>. 60, No. 1, 1979, pp. 36, 62,
65–66

"The Philistine of Gath, Goliath by name, came up out of the ranks of the Philistines, and spoke the same words as before. And David heard" ([I Sam.] 17:23).
In contrast to Saul and all Israel who heard and "were dismayed and greatly
afraid," no mention is made of David's reaction to what he has heard. This is a
striking example of the "there, but not here" effect of Old Testament narrative.
The precision and detail of the previous section (17:11) draws attention to the
lack of such information in the present section (17:23). The lack of comment on
David's reaction also marks a change in the mode of narration since there will
now be room to wonder what is happening, what is being said.

> All the men of Israel, when they saw the man, fled from him, and
> were much afraid. And the men of Israel said, "Have you seen
> this man who has come up? Surely he has come up to defy Israel."
> (17:24–25)

Verse 24 reintroduces the theme of appearance and perception and relates it to
the theme of speech and hearing. The imbrication of the themes is marked by the
syntax and terminology of verses 23–25. Verses 23–25 move from David's
talking to the appearance of Goliath who speaks and whom David hears. The
men of Israel then see Goliath and flee. Verse 25 joins the two themes as the men
ask about "seeing" the man who has come up to challenge them in a "speech."

All the men of Israel see Goliath, flee, and are very much afraid. The army
reacts with fear to both hearing and seeing Goliath. Saul has dropped from the
narrative; of him it has only been said that he reacts in fear to hearing Goliath's
challenge. Now a function of the description of Goliath in verses 4–7 can be discerned. Goliath, as described, is seen by the army, and by most commentators,
as a formidable warrior who is "perfectly terrifying in his sheer, malevolent
power" . . . and who is dressed in "frightening array" . . . .

But is this the only way to perceive him? Could not he also be seen as a big man encumbered by heavy armor with little range in combat and vulnerable to an attack launched from a distance? His coat of mail weighs 125 or more pounds, he has no bow and arrows, and his shield is carried before him by another, "and his shield-bearer went before him." And, regardless of the reader's view of Goliath, could not this be David's perception of him? The view would be in accord with his determination to fight the Philistine. The remainder of the story does not contradict the assumption; on the other hand, neither does it confirm it as the only possible interpretation. The text never speaks of David seeing Goliath, although it does present Goliath's perception of him: "And when the Philistine looked, and saw David, he disdained him; for he was but a youth, ruddy and comely in appearance" (17:42). The presence of the comment emphasizes the lack of any mention of David's view of Goliath.

The description of Goliath introduces an indeterminate aspect into the narrative through its literal and precise details. They are definite; it is their significance for the narrative, the perception of them by a character or reader, that is equivocal. By playing upon the reciprocity of detail and equivocation, the narrative remains undecidable. With one hand it offers answers to the questions that it raises, but it has already taken them back with the other hand.

> Peter D. Miscall. *The Workings of Old Testament Narrative* (Chico, Cal., Philadelphia, Scholars/Fortress, 1983), pp. 59–61.

DAVID'S LAMENT FOR SAUL AND JONATHAN

Saul is honoured with a particular panegyric, because he had enriched his people, and contributed to the general felicity and splendour of the state. This passage, by the way, is most exquisite composition; the women of Israel are most happily introduced, and the subject of the encomium is admirably adapted to the female characters ("Ye daughters of Israel weep over Saul," &c. II Sam. 1:24). Jonathan is at last celebrated in a distinct eulogium, which is beautifully pathetic, is animated with all the fervour, and sweetened with all the tenderness of friendship. . . .

There appears to be something singular in the versification of this Elegy, and a very free use of different metres. It neither consists altogether of the long verses, nor yet of the short ones (which are the most usual in the poetry of the Hebrews); but rather of a very artful and happy mixture of both, so that the concise and pointed parallelism serves to correct the languor and diffuseness of the elegiac verse: and this form of versification takes place also in some of the Psalms. Certainly there is a great appearance of art and design in this nice and poetical conformation of the periods: and that no grace or elegance should be wanting to this poem, it is no less remarkable for the general beauty, splendour, and perspicuity of the style. [1753]

> Robert Lowth. *Lectures on the Sacred Poetry of the Hebrews*. Vol. II. Tr. from the Latin by G. Gregory (London, Printed for J. Johnson, 1787). pp. 156–59

The only general remark necessary about the two Dirges [on Abner and on Saul and Jonathan]—the sole specimens of their class among our poems—is that neither breathes the name of God nor hope of another life. In the Dirge on Saul and Jonathan this is most impressive. For there we find a keen relish of life and a most passionate lasting of love, an appreciation of the virtues of the dead and a magnanimous forgiveness of the injuries which one of them had wrought—every instinct proper at the thought of the great dead except the instinct of hope. It may be said, of course, that in the abandonment of grief—grief which is nobly and splendidly passionate in the Dirge on Saul and Jonathan—God and the life to come are naturally forgotten. Yet the silence of these dirges is also the silence of all the narratives and poems through which we have passed; and but illustrates that weird absence of hope which is characteristic of the pagan Arabs and of early Israel even in their mourning for virtuous and beloved men. . . .

The Dirge on Saul and Jonathan, chapter 1:17–27, which is taken from the Book of Yashar, may have suffered like the Song of Deborah from a long oral tradition; or the irregularities of the metre may be original and due to the strong, sobbing passion of the poet. The lines are mainly of 4 stresses each, and here and there a shorter follows a longer as in the true Kinah [lament] rhythm. Neglecting the parallelism, some print lines of as many as 5 and even 7 stresses and so make six quatrains with a couplet to open and a couplet to close the series.

> George A. Smith. *The Early Poetry of Israel in Its Physical and Social Origins* (London, Oxford University Press, 1912), pp. 96–97

It may be the gracefulness of the poet by which David has captured our hearts. While we were still children we were shaken to the depths of our hearts by his lament over Saul and Jonathan when the news of their fall on the mountains of Gilboa reached him. And if nothing had reached us but these lines of lamentation, we would say: It is none other than the heart of a very great poet who has uttered them.

The words of the lament are few, but every inflection in them is filled with the essence of heart and the essence of grace, like a sublime poem. It was not without reason that these marvelous lines have been engraved in the hearts of all the generations and have been memorized as the most elevated expression of "Those beloved and pleasant in their lives, in their deaths not parted"—the grief of a very dear comrade and the eternal tenderness that his loss has left behind him. And how simple are the words in which the heart pours out its deep pain:

> I am in sorrow over you, Jonathan my brother,
> you were so pleasing to me!
> Your love for me was more wonderful
> than the love of women [II Sam. 1:26].

Or the call to mourning to the nation bereft of its king and hero:

> Daughters of Israel, wail for Saul,
> who would dress you in scarlet with ornaments,
> who would put gold ornaments on your dresses! [1:24]

And in the finale the eternal image:

> Mountains of Gilboa!
> Let there be no dew and no rain upon you and fields of offerings
> for there was the shield of heroes loathed! [1:21]

And the repeating howl:

> How the mighty have fallen! [1:19, etc.]

From a heart full of tears and exultation have these lines spurted, lines in which is vouchsafed, as a model, "the gold ornaments" of ancient Hebrew poetry, of the ancient Hebrew tongue.

> Jacob Fichman. *'Arugot* (Jerusalem, Bialik Institute, 1954), pp. 259–60†

When David hears that Saul and Jonathan are dead, he sings a lament that haunts men's memories to this day and stands among the world's great poems. In theme, design, imagery, it is a masterwork which even in translation has an astonishing power to move the heart. . . . Carrying a double theme of sorrow—national and personal—the poem begins with Israel's grief, mentions a song of women, tells the fierce bravery of Saul and Jonathan, speaks of another song of women, and ends with David's personal grief.

The structure is both concentric and progressing: centered in the middle three sections by the theme of bravery symbolized in shield and bow and sword, in eagle and lion; concerned in second and penultimate divisions with songs—warning Israel to keep the disaster secret lest the daughters of the Philistine sing triumph songs, and then inviting Israel's daughters to sing their lament; framed at beginning and end by images of the mountains of death where sorrow took its rise.

The movement progresses, because it first tells of national grief for the beauty of heroes fallen upon the mountains; it then looks to the enemy who killed them; renews their praises; turns toward home where the women of Israel are reminded of Saul's favors, and ends, not with national, but with personal grief. The images symbolize masculine courage in weapons and fierce beasts, but also softer feminine beauty in such phrases as daughters, dew and rain upon the mountains, scarlet and gold and jewels.

These two poles of masculine strength and feminine loveliness are brought together at the end where the fierce warrior, Jonathan, is "beloved and lovely," and his friendship "wonderful, passing the love of women." Finally, the movement of the poem is carried along by the refrain which gathers meaning as it goes because it is shaped by incremental repetition. At first the poem merely says, "How are the mighty fallen!" Then it adds a phrase: "How are the mighty fallen in the midst of battle!" And finally it tells how even their weapons are ruined: "How are the mighty fallen, and the weapons of war perished!"

> Laurentia Digges. *Adam's Haunted Sons* (New York, Macmillan 1966), pp. 249–51

DEBORAH, SONG OF

The first sentences exhibit a striking picture of maternal solicitude, both in words and actions; and of a mind suspended and agitated between hope and fear:

> Through the window she looked and cried out,
> The mother of Sisera, through the lattice:
> Wherefore is his chariot so long in coming?
> Wherefore linger the wheels of his chariot? [Judg. 5:28]

Immediately, impatient of his [Sisera's] delay, she anticipates the consolations of her friends, and her mind being somewhat elevated, she boasts with all the levity of a fond female. . . .

Let us now observe, how well adapted every sentiment, every word is to the character of the speaker. She takes no account of the slaughter of the enemy, of the valour and conduct of the conqueror, of the multitude of the captives, but "burns with a female thirst of prey and spoils." Nothing is omitted, which is calculated to attract and engage the passions of a vain and trifling woman, slaves, gold, and rich apparel. Nor is she satisfied with the bare enumeration of them; she repeats, she amplifies, she heightens every circumstance; she seems to have the very plunder in her immediate possession; she pauses and contemplates every particular:

> Have they not found?—Have they not divided the spoil?
> To every man a damsel, yea a damsel or two?
> To Sisera a spoil of divers colours?
> A spoil of needlework of divers colours,
> A spoil for the neck of divers colours of needlework on either side [5:30].

To add to the beauty of this passage, there is also an uncommon neatness in the versification, great force, accuracy, and perspicuity in the diction, the utmost elegance in the repetitions, which, notwithstanding their apparent redundancy, are conducted with the most perfect brevity. In the end, the fatal disappointment of female hope and credulity, tacitly insinuated by the sudden and unexpected apostrophe, "So let all thine enemies perish, O JEHOVAH!" [v. 31] is expressed more forcibly by this very silence of the person who was just speaking, than it could possibly have been by all the powers of language. [1753]

> Robert Lowth. *Lectures on the Sacred Poetry of the Hebrews*. Vol. I. Tr. from the Latin by G. Gregory (London, Printed for J. Johnson, 1787), pp. 291–94

In the greatest war-song of any age or nation—the exultation of Deborah over Sisera's complete defeat, and subsequent assassination by the hand of Jael, the wife of Heber the Kenite—no doubt personal revenge might seem to blaze high above Deborah's faith in her nation and her God, as the kindling or exciting spiritual principle which brings the scene in such marvellous vividness before her eyes. But though this feeling may add perhaps some of the fire to the later part of the poem, it is clear that her faith in the national unity, and God, as the source of the national unity, was the great, binding thought of the whole. The song dwells, first, with the most intense bitterness on the decay of patriotism in the tribes that did not combine against the common foe. . . .

And the transition by which she passes to her fierce exultation over Sisera's terrible fate shows distinctly what was the main thought in her mind. "There was peace," we are told, between the king of Hazor, whose forces Sisera commanded, and Heber the Kenite; the latter was only distantly akin to the people of Israel; the help of his tribe was not expected; and yet, though the aid of many true Israelites was wanting, from *his* house came the blow, treacherous though it was, which rid the nation of the dreaded and hated enemy. . . .

The exultation with which the poet dwells on the treachery of the act, on the helpless prostration of the great captain's corpse before a mere woman's knees; the terrible minuteness with which she gloats over the raised expectations of the mother of the murdered soldier; the picture of the "wise ladies" in attendance suggesting triumphant reasons for the delay, and of the anxious eagerness with which she even suggested these reasons to herself—no doubt indicate fierce personal as well as fierce patriotic triumph. But the whole tenor of this grand poem and the conclusion, "So let all thy enemies perish, O Lord: but let them that love thee be as the sun when he goes forth in his might," at all events prove that the personal hatred was so closely bound up with the representative feelings of the writer as a judge of Israel, and with her trust in the Lord of Hosts, that the latter lent a kind of halo to the unscrupulous ferocity of the former.

> Richard M. Hutton. *Essays Theological and Literary*. Vol. II. 2d ed. rev. & enl. (London, Macmillan, 1880), pp. 215–17

The Song of Deborah, the only political poem of larger range in the Old Testament, is, from a purely aesthetic point of view, a masterpiece. Whether sometimes the characteristics of great events are emphasized in terse phrases, whether again the synonyms are heaped in luxuriant diffuseness, and a very small scene is transfused with a dazzling light, or whether the grim discords of revenge resound, we always feel the same admiration for the passion and power of this God-gifted poet. The defects of the composition should, of course, not be glossed over. The fusion of the particular episodes into a living organism has not yet been achieved. In the epic descriptions we have attempts at an epic, but the Israelites lacked the inclination and probably the gift for its completion. Still, the pictures arranged in a loosely ordered series produce a uniform and powerful overall effect whose majestic impression is inescapable. From a moral point of view, one may object here or there, but when, as in this case, religion and patriotism are so closely united, we cannot ever apply the standard of common morality. Untroubled by reflection, young Israel traced the living breath of God in the storm wind that swept over the battlefield and saw in the destruction of its enemies the action of Yahweh. What moves the poet is expressed in his artistic vision and the classic style, but it is also a living religious experience.

> Hugo Gressmann. *Die Anfänge Israels* (Göttingen,
> Vandenhoeck & Ruprecht, 1914), pp. 192–93†

This song may seem to us disjointed, but it was not, is not so in reality. The links are unexpressed in the written words but they would be rendered by the voice and the dramatic gestures of the singer. And even in the words we can see a certain stately progress, broken by outbursts of emotion, by sharp addresses of praise and scorn and by still more sharply contrasted pictures. And the culminating contrast that closes it all is of high art, the contrast between Jael in her tent and the mother of Sisera in her palace.

> Duncan B. MacDonald. *The Hebrew Literary Genius*
> (Princeton, N.J., Princeton University Press, 1933),
> p. 18

The Song of Deborah is almost universally regarded as a genuine historical song, that is to say a spontaneous poetical outbreak of the heart of man, who having taken part in a mighty historical event is now impelled to master it in rhythmical form, to grasp, to express, to transmit it. It has been rightly said of the songs of the Afghans in their revolt against England a hundred years ago, contemporaneous songs in many respects similar to, although much inferior to the Song of Deborah, that they are a cry of history itself. The singer of the Song of Deborah is not only near the event, but stands in the midst of the actual occurrence; he calls to the actors, stirring them up and encouraging them, he blesses and curses not on account of something previously done, but in the midst of the tempest of events not yet subsided. His heavily galloping rhythm he feels as a pacing in the midst of the event; the singing *nephesh,* the breath-soul, rises and falls heavily, like the step of the heavily armed man. So we are to understand that much discussed cry (v. 21) uttered the moment enthusiasm threatens to stop the singer's breath: "Tread forth, my soul, with strength." This historical song is a religious song. Here they praise and glorify a god for victory. This type of religious poetry we know from Akkadian literature. . . . But the Song of Deborah is different from all the religious songs of victory I know in the literature of the world. Its character is apparent as soon as we look at it: a special poetic means here serves an utterly religious purpose. This means is repetition.

The Song of Deborah, though early, is nevertheless a song of masterful formation. The strongest of its forms is the refrain. And this form obviously is not first created because of aesthetic motives and later appointed to serve religious purposes as well but, so far as we can judge, it was born of religion. It is known that many early lyric forms spring from a magical aim such as used to set up against the hard, unbound, demonic element, one that was bound and binding: the secret of the likeness appears as something that silences and subdues. The class of Biblical forms especially noteworthy, the repetitive forms—alliteration, assonance, paronomasia, key words, key sentences, refrain etc.—has the particular purpose of emphasizing the most important aspect of the religious message, to point again and again at the fundamental idea or ideas of the belief round which the rest are grouped, and which the recipient of the message is requested to perceive as such with concentrated intention. A good example of this is to be found in the refrains of the Song of Deborah.

> Martin Buber. *The Prophetic Faith*. Tr. from Hebrew by Carlyle Witton-Davies (New York, Harper 1949), pp. 8–9

So we come to the high point of the action: the mighty clash of two armies, nine hundred chariots, horses, ten thousand Israelite soldiers. One expects here what one is accustomed to in the *Iliad,* for the reader has been gradually filled with suspense. False expectation: the magnificent battle is dispatched with a single verb, *wayyahom,* "to muddle." The partisan of Homer shakes his head as he finds, to his disappointment: Yes, this Hebrew storyteller has spirited away the combat with a *deus ex machina*.

Homeric standards, however, are not appropriate here. The climax consists of (1) an oracle: a promise, "he will be delivered" in the future; (2) an oracle: "today, he is delivered" in the present; (3) fulfillment: Yahweh himself acts, he triumphs unobstructed. We have here no battle description because the power of God is all-surpassing. Theologically, a single action-word suffices to counter "Sisera and *all* his chariots and *all* his troops." For the believing Israelite the action here reaches its peak. And yet, from a purely narrational viewpoint, one must admit that ancient Hebrew narrative art was not developed enough to describe a battle. Lyric can impressionistically project single images, as, for example, the Song of Deborah does the galloping flight of the princes in the celebrated verse [Judg.] 5:22 "Then clattered the horses' hooves, the dash-dashing of his stallions"; or the stunning description in Nahum 3:1–3.

If the fighting does not emerge vividly the defeat does: Sisera must abandon his chariot and flee "on foot." The Israelites are climbing uphill on foot, the field commander of the enemy is fleeing on foot.

Now the action can pass on to the second act, and here the storyteller shows himself to be a master. Until now, the action had two strands, Barak and Sisera, which have finally met, indeed intertwined; now it is necessary for the two strands to separate, to pursue each other; yet it is also necessary for their simultaneity to find expression. All that is accomplished by a simple touch:

> Sisera climbs out of his chariot, flees on foot,
> (meanwhile) Barak pursues chariots and soldiers, until many fall,
> (meanwhile) Sisera flees on foot to Jael's tent. . . .

Luis Alonso-Schökel. *Biblica*. 42, No. 2, 1961, pp. 162–63†

As a song of exultant patriotism and of praise to Israel's God, it presents seven swift scenes of a mighty contest in which stars and rivers fight beside human warriors. Each scene flames to a dramatic climax of its own; the whole forms a wonderful unity built concentrically, with three scenes of preparation, then the call and response of the tribes at the center in scene four, and the battle with its results in the last three pictures.

An introduction announces the theme of praise, then the pictures flash in vivid life before the viewer who sees: 1) the Lord in majesty; 2) Israel in desolation; 3) her leaders oblivious of danger; 4) the tribes called to war, with those who come and those who delay; 5) the clash of battle joined; 6) Jael, instrument of rescue; 7) Sisera's mother, image of desolation. . . .

One of the main artistic principles of the poem has been contrast. The power of Yahweh in his storms and the helplessness of Israel in desolation; the poverty of a land where caravans cannot come, and the luxury of the leaders with their white asses and saddlecloths; the zeal of some tribes and the apathy of others— each balances the other. This stately progress is broken by bursts of emotion, exhortations to action, sharp addresses of praise and scorn, and sharply contrasted pictures. Two of these appear in the concluding sections.

Here at the end the poem moves from armies of nameless men to two individualized women: Jael in her tent, and the mother of Sisera in her palace. Gestures may have introduced the new theme, for it comes with sudden words:

> Most blessed of women be Jael . . .
> of tent-dwelling women most blessed.
> He asked water and she gave him milk,
> she brought him curds in a lordly bowl.

[Judg. 5:24–25]

The irony is terrible when the ruthless Jael offers milk, the food of children, to the enemy. With a leap from the hospitable matron to the fierce avenger, the poem exults in her need: ". . . He sank, he fell, he lay still at her feet."

But sudden as shifting of torchlight comes the last picture—of Sisera's mother, who does not know her son is dead. The song makes good use of the ironic situation, as this nameless woman watches for her son who will not return. . . . Here is economy and understatement like that of the English ballads with their tragic burdens.

> Laurentia Digges. *Adam's Haunted Sons* (New York,
> Macmillan, 1966), pp. 183–84, 186–87

An analysis of the many techniques of poetic style in evidence in the ode reveals a poem that is artfully composed and skillfully interwoven, that possesses an amazing ability to capture and direct the imagination of the audience. For example, the writer of Judges 5 has given unity and form to the ode through a number of motifs, among which are: the cosmic power of Yahweh, before whom the order of the world is shaken, and before whom the enemy is annihilated; the watery chaos, which threatens Israel, but yet under Yahweh's control sweeps away the enemy; the hammering hooves, which express the Canaanite loss, and as a consequence will not sound in the courtyard to relieve the anxious mother; the desperate flight of Sisera, which contrasts so strikingly with the victory procession fantasized by his ladies; and the focus on women, which contrasts the daring Jael with the shaken and self-deluding Canaanite ladies. While these motifs are prominently employed in the various scenes of the ode, they are not overtly and directly linked, nor are the consequences of their interplay explicitly enunciated. The poet's style is rather to express his message subtly, to provide hints that cleverly and effectively focus the audience's attention. To enhance his indirect style, the poet has relied heavily on literary devices such as: repetition; allusion; onomatopoeia; vowel and consonant patterns; abrupt transitions; varying rhythmic patterns; anticipation; and the element of surprise. The cumulative effect of these devices is to make the poet's message clear, even though that clarity comes to focus more in the mind of the audience than in the ode itself. That is to say: the poet's style is paratactic.

> Alan J. Hauser. *Journal of Biblical Literature*. March,
> 1980, pp. 40–41

Decalogue. *See* Exodus: Ten Commandments

Deluge. *See* Flood

Deutero-Isaiah. *See* Isaiah II

DEUTERONOMY

Drama and oratory have entered into complete fusion in the great Book of Deuteronomy. This presents itself as the farewell of Moses to Israel: in the main it is a series of orations, while the fifteen chapters containing the Book of the Cove-

nant make a document read as appendix to one of the orations. The whole sup-
poses an underlying dramatic situation, which has fascinated the minds of literary readers—the situation of Moses as the one man who realizes the Promised
Land, and yet the one man of all present on the occasion who is never to enter it.
In this situation we follow, first, an oration in which Moses announces the secret
of his own deposition; then, the oration on the delivery of the Book of the Covenant to the Levites and Elders who are to succeed him. A third oration connects
itself with a rehearsal of the dread ceremonial of the Blessing and the Curse, and
is the masterpiece of all literature for the rhetoric of denunciation. A fourth oration culminates in the retirement of Moses and the installation of Joshua. With a
change natural in Hebrew literature, oratory gives place to song. The finale presents the passing away of the hero, scattering blessings as he goes, and rising to
his old physical vigor as his parting words glorify the mission of Israel for all
time. The briefest narrative—like an extended stage direction—tells of the retirement into solitude and death. A great dramatic movement binds all parts of
the book into a unity, while oratorical monologue has taken the place of dramatic
dialogue.

> Richard G. Moulton. *The Modern Study of Literature*
> (Chicago, University of Chicago Press, 1915), pp.
> 47–48

In its language and style, Deuteronomy is fully as influential in the literary history of Israel as it is in thought. Very rarely will anyone familiar with the flavor
of Israel's earlier prose and with Deuteronomy be in any doubt as to whether a
piece of Hebrew narrative antedates or follows the publication of Deuteronomy
in 621 B.C. The imaginary addresses of Deuteronomy are singularly different in
style from the actual addresses of Amos and Isaiah or any other of Israel's great
public speakers. Deuteronomy has its own glories of style, but they are not those
of Israel's oratory. Compare, for example, the burning utterances of Amos, in
his fourth address (Am. 5:1–9) with the words ascribed to Moses contemplating
the immediate passage of the Jordan (Deut. 8:1–10). In contrast, Deuteronomy
is leisurely and quiet; a solemn earnestness and a certain formal dignity make its
quality.

This is perhaps even more noticeable in one of the noblest passages of the
book (Deut. 6:4–19), compared by way of contrast, with the great arraignment
of Isaiah I (1:1–9). It will be recalled that this chapter of Isaiah was counted a
perfect example of the prophetic type of speech with its rapid succession of apostrophe, mandatory address, tender appeal, and glorious promise, and its wealth
of figurative language. It has, too, its own dignity and rolling phrases, but its
wave crests are lashed into white foam, very different from the dead-swell of
Deuteronomy's deep sea.

In contrast with the simple, direct, story-telling style of Israel's earlier prose
writers, Deuteronomy at times suggests the finished style of the Greek writers
who were trained in the rules of expression. Prose has become almost a con-

scious art; henceforth we may not expect to find the charming, naive narratives that were written from the days of Solomon to those of Jeroboam II. With the coming of great generalizations into thought, spontaneous emotion must be checked by the cold grasp of reflection, and poetic interest in the vicissitudes of individual heroes must give place to the recording and interpreting of national movements.

Henry T. Fowler. *A History of the Literature of Ancient Israel* (New York, Macmillan, 1927), pp. 184–89

Other and more elaborate styles of prose appeared in Israel, of which the most original and powerful is that of the Book of Deuteronomy, a style of mysterious source but of immediate and prolonged influence on the national literature. The rhythm is unlike the rhythm of any other prose in the Old Testament. It may have been the invention of one man; but so haunting and infectious is its music that it was caught up by a school or schools of writers and developed and even exaggerated (as textual criticism has shown) to an extent which indeed its peculiar cumulative structure provoked. Deuteronomy retells the earlier history of Israel and, under the influence of the great prophets, re-enforces the ancient truths and laws of the national religion with a fresh original rhetoric, inspired by an imagination more full of colour and by a warmer zeal than those of the earlier Hebrew histories and codes. It is lavish in resonant words and phrases, and in musical repetitions; urgent and expansive, yet frequently falling back from its urgency in order to explain, qualify, or refine. The music of its phrasing overcomes all feeling of redundancy. As I have said elsewhere, "Deuteronomy is like a flowing tide upon a very broad beach, the long parallel waves dashing, withdrawing and dashing again."

George A. Smith. In *The Legacy of Israel*. Ed. by Edwyn R. Bevan and Charles Singer (Oxford, England, Clarendon Press, 1927), p. 17

The solemn majesty of Deuteronomy with its concluding pathos forms a supremely fitting ending to the Torah. Too often its literary values of which the final editors had a keen sense are ignored in the maze of surrounding scholarship. The ideas expressed in one form of art have perhaps never been more adequately translated into another form than in the case of Michelangelo's "Moses." The grandeur of the figure, its exorable sternness, its infinite sadness, its amazing strength match the character of the great Lawgiver set forth in the last book of the Torah.

John R. Macarthur. *Biblical Literature and Its Backgrounds* (New York, Appleton, 1936), p. 127

In the Book of Deuteronomy the author has drawn the character Moses giving his people a father's rebuke, acting bitter and gracious: "You know that it is not for your righteousness that the Lord your God is giving you this good land to possess—for you are a stubborn-necked people . . . for you have been rebelling against the Lord from the day I knew you" [9:5–6]. He tested them—not one thing of all they did to anger him on the route on which he guided them did he forget; but he also recalls, recalls their devotion—for "only on account of your ancestors has the Lord desired to love you and has chosen their seed after them from all the peoples" [10:15]. In this "stubborn-necked people" he recognizes also the delightful boy of God, whom he reproves and whom he loves. And how wonderful are the short verses in which the Promised Land glows in a glorious light, a humble light, with an outer radiance and with an inner radiance: "And the land to which you are crossing over to possess is a land of mountains and valleys, from the rain of whose sky you will drink water—a land which the Lord your God perpetually seeks, the eyes of the Lord your God are on it from the beginning of the year until the end of the year" [11:11]! Is any landscape imprinted more permanently on the heart than these simple and sublime intimations of grace?

But the charm of the book (also the charm of the editor who knew how to combine the sections so perfectly) is in that a rhythmic unity is implanted in it—a rhythmic unity that turns to exultation. Sweetness of reminiscence and bitterness of rebuke, law and justice, words of confession and words of promise and assurance—a special tenderness bathes it all. The voice is watered by strength and compassion, the reprimand of a cruel heart and a loving heart rising like the crest of one continuous wave, growing even mightier, without abatement. Like matching lines of verse do song and prose emerge here—and who can discriminate here between song and prose? Is there not in any complete verse, be its subject the most "prosaic," the absoluteness of perfect poetry? The Bible proves this to a degree that could not be more convincing. Whatever is given complete expression—that is poetry.

Indeed there is something clear and soulfully melodious here, of which there is no example in biblical prose. It seems that here the early Hebrew genius reached its peak of expressiveness. Here it recognized itself and sang itself in one lapse of self-consciousness. . . .

As in any book having a strong rhythm the repetitions are swallowed, each additional stress freshening the preceding utterance, and each repeating paragraph adding taste. "For the Lord your God is bringing you to a good land, a land of waterways and springs coming out of valley and mountain" [8:7]. Time after time you hear the ringing of the water, which was endless magic to a people wandering in the wilderness, so again: "A land of wheat and barley and vine and date and pomegranate, a land of olive oil and honey" [8:8]—another world, new, blessed by God and a source of blessing to the people who would deserve it.

In small chapters is the law of Israel concentrated, the Torah of Israel that crystallized, the illuminating Torah of man. In words brief and eternal: "Now, Israel, what does the Lord your God ask of you but that you revere the Lord your God [10:12] . . . who does justice to the orphan and widow and loves the alien, giving him food and raiment; so you shall love the alien . . ." [10:18–19]. Thus is intimated here Israelite humanism beside zealous religious fanaticism. Love of God and fear of God, flowing from an exalted religious recognition—coupled here in one concept: Adherence to God is like adherence to the highest perfection in the world. . . .

Out of the bitter experience of the past or out of a desire to admonish, to caution the people, the composer reveals here with deep cruelty the abysses to come. In the rebuke as in the assurance is the warm, clear, loving tone of the book played. Here the poetry of admonition turns into a vision of terror. The passage about exile is underscored as a tragic fate, which only the nation, by fortifying and elevating itself, can annul and thereby redeem itself.

In the grandeur of the poem *Ha'azinu* ["Give ear"—ch. 32], where something lapidary is stamped on the solid prophetic verse, and in the Blessing of Moses [ch. 33], where a primitive light and primitive allusions envelop the whole, the book of wonders is closed—a sort of great synopsis of the legislation of the Torah and the poetry of the Torah together.

Happy is he who absorbed this refreshment in his youth!

Jacob Fichman. *'Arugot* (Jerusalem, Bialik Institute, 1954), pp. 248–51†

The author of Deuteronomy has endowed the book with the typical features of an oration. The rhetorical technique is here fully developed. As is expected of a good orator the author directs his message to the heart and emotions of his audience, enlivening and variegating the ancient traditions by retelling them in such a manner as to capture and maintain the interest of his listeners. The ancient traditions make no reference, for example, to the apparel of the desert generation or to the physical adversities of the journey; the author of Deuteronomy, on the other hand, to achieve the desired effect, adds with rhetoric colouring: "Your clothing did not wear out . . . upon you, and your foot did not swell, these forty years" (Deut. 8:4; cf. 29:4). In order to impress upon his listeners the greatness of the manna miracle, he adds: "And he fed you with the manna, which you did not know, nor did your fathers know" (8:3); and he does the same whenever he wishes to stress whatever was exceptional in the event (13:7; 28:36). He brings out vividly the contrast between the desert and the good land promised to the Israelites. The desert in which Israel wandered is described in exceptionally strong tones: "a great and terrible wilderness, with its fiery serpents and scorpions, thirsty ground . . . where there was no water . . ." (8:15). Against this he juxtaposes the goodness of the land Israel is to inhabit: "For the Lord your God is bringing you unto a good land of brooks of water, of fountains and springs, flowing forth in valleys and hills, a land of wheat and barley, of vines and fig-trees and pomegranates, a land of olive-trees and honey, a land in which you will eat bread without scarcity" (vv. 7–9). Though the description may be essentially correct, there is doubtless an element of exaggeration in it: it is, as S. R. Driver notes, "an eloquent and glowing description." His comparison of the land of Egypt with Palestine is fanciful and distorted. Egypt is depicted in the early Biblical sources as the choicest of countries: "Like the garden of the Lord, the land of Egypt" (Gen. 13:10); yet the author of Deuteronomy, bent on convincing his audience of the superiority of the land promised them, exaggerates its shortcomings, remarking disparagingly that the land of Israel "is not like the land of Egypt . . . where you sowed your seed and watered it with your feet, like a garden of vegetables" (11:10–12).

The deuteronomic orator often employs rhetorical phrases such as: "your eyes see," . . . "you have seen" . . . (11:7; 29:1 et al.) to implant in his listeners the feeling that they themselves have experienced the awe-inspiring events of the Exodus; and he repeats these phrases again and again as if to hypnotize his audience. The device of the rhetorical question is also used significantly and with purpose: "Did a people ever hear the voice of a god . . . ?" (4:33).

Having chosen the oration as their literary medium, the deuteronomic authors put their speeches into the mouths of kings and political leaders, who were of course accustomed to speaking before assemblies and large audiences. Indeed, the author of Deuteronomy describes Moses as speaking "unto all Israel" (Deut. 1:1; 5:1; 29:1), that is to a vast audience consisting of tribal chiefs, judges, elders, officers, men, women, children, and even alien residents (Deut. 29:9). Joshua delivers his valedictory address before the elders of the people, chieftains, judges, and officers (23:2, cf. 24:1, a verse redacted by the Deuteronomist). This emphasis on vast audiences in the oration scenes and the detailed enumeration of the various leading classes participating in them is peculiar to the book of Deuteronomy and deuteronomic literature.

> Moshe Weinfeld. *Deuteronomy and the Deuteronomic School* (Oxford, Clarendon Press, 1972), pp. 171–73

On first glance, the book of Deuteronomy seems to us like propaganda, like "socialist realism" in the pejorative sense of the term ("Quotations from Chairman Moses")—but on closer inspection, we find that it supplies the missing element in the preceding books of the Torah, and in the history that is to follow: the will to action, to historically significant change, to deeds which are simultaneously unblinkered and singleminded. The book of Deuteronomy, called by Jews of a later age, through a creative misreading of a verse, "the second Law" *(Deuteronomos* or *Mishneh ha-Torah),* is the consummate *reply* to the first four books. Only with the addition of this book do we have a complete Torah. Here we find a fully matured Moses, who, at last, can perform the task of bringing the God of Israel to a newfound maturity.

> Joel Rosenberg. *Response.* Summer, 1975, p. 89

The immediate hero of the book is Moses as the spokesman of God. The only other person who is quoted by the narrator is God. . . . Thus there are only two direct voices which the narrator asks us to attend to in the book: Moses' and God's. Deuteronomy may be described therefore as the speech of the Deuteronomic narrator in which he directly quotes only two figures in the story, predominantly Moses and sometimes God. . . .

In interpreting the book, do we understand Moses' word as subordinate to the narrator's, or is the narrator's word subordinate to that of Moses? The narrator might be said to be the main carrier of the implied author's ideological stance since he alone conveys to us Moses' conveying of the words of God that constitute most of the book. But if so, one notices that, as a vehicle for the book's ultimate semantic authority (he alone can tell us what Moses says that God says to the reader of the book), the narrator seems at great pains to impress upon his reader that it is Moses, and Moses alone, who possessed the type of reliable authority to convey accurately and authoritatively the direct words of God that form most of the book. We find ourselves in a dilemma: we are asked by the narrator to accept his assertion that "there has not arisen a prophet since in Israel like Moses, whom the Lord knew face to face . . ." (34:10), at the same time as it is only the Deuteronomic narrator who knows Moses face to face! If the path to God is through Moses, the path to Moses is through the text's narrator. Does the reader interpret the reported words of Moses by means of the reporting context: "Moses was God's greatest prophet, therefore believe *him* when he says . . ."? Or does one interpret the reporting words of the narrator by means of the reported words of Moses: "Moses said such and such, therefore believe *me,* as narrator, when I say . . ."? . . .

Although the narrator has deliberately put himself in the background and Moses in the foreground, the narrator's word, for very specific reasons, remains visibly separate on the surface of the text. Since the book's surface is constructed mostly in two voices, and since the implied author could have chosen completely to merge his narrator's voice with the voice of his hero, as seems to be the case in the Book of Qoheleth [Ecclesiastes], it is clear that Deuteronomy emphasizes, even on the phraseological plane, a distinction between the word of Moses and the word of the narrator. What are the implications of such an arrangement?

The most obvious functions of the narrator's words are that they situate the words of Moses in time and space (when, where, and in what circumstances Moses spoke the words reported by the narrator), and that they define the preeminent position Moses held as leader and legislator of his people. It is also clear that the narrator does not attempt to interpret the words of Moses to any great extent in the Book of Deuteronomy. This is to be expected since the other main section of the history, Joshua–II Kings, so clearly and so often indicates that it functions as the Deuteronomist's main interpretation of the word of Moses found in Deuteronomy. The *overt* function of the narrator's direct utterances in Deuteronomy is to represent to his readers the word of Moses as preeminent, and Moses himself as the greatest prophet in Israel's history.

On the other hand, there are clear indications, even within the brief scope of fifty-six verses, that the content and distribution of the narrator's direct utterances serve to exalt his importance as one who is as necessary to his contemporaries as Moses was to his, and to legitimize that self-serving claim by means obvious and subtle.

Robert Polzin. *Moses and the Deuteronomist* (New York, Seabury Press, 1980), pp. 26–30

ECCLESIASTES

How greatly the symbolic treatment extends the range of poetic topics may be best seen in an illustration taken from another book of the Bible. A sonnet in [ch. 12 of] Ecclesiastes, by universal confession one of the gems of poetry, is wholly constructed out of the most unpromising material; for it is a *tour-de-force* of enumeration applied to symptoms of senile decay and death. It is highly instructive, in the discussion of imagery and symbolism, to put side by side two treatments of the same theme, one by a great Elizabethan poet, the other in the oriental style of Ecclesiastes. Sackville *(Induction to the Mirror for Magistrates)* places in his underworld an image of Old Age: the necessities of the situation lead him to an extreme of imagery and other devices of realistic effect. . . . In the powerful vision of Sackville every detail paints a picture; the Biblical sonnet introduces ideas which have no visible resemblance to the spectacle of old age, and yet the comparison they call for stirs a melancholy pleasure. Light fitly symbolises the joy of mere existence: the darkening of sun and moon and stars recalls the gradual loss of pleasure in life for its own sake. Youth with its troubles and quick rallying knows only the summer showers: when the rallying power is gone, "the clouds return after the rain." The "wither'd fist still knocking at death's door" stamps the picture of the infirmity upon the imagination: the shaking hands recede into the distance when, with a whole group of like infirmities, they are represented by the elements of panic in a city—trembling keepers, strong men bowed down, grinders ceasing to work and spectators to look out of windows, while every door is made fast. Similar dim symbols just touch the loss of appetite, of sleep, of voice; the timid and uncertain gait; the sparse hairs of age, its feeble strength. The sudden bursting of the caper-berry that has been long shrivelling up marks the transition to the reality that is being symbolised:

> Man goeth to his long home,
> And the mourners go about the streets.

For the actual death that puts a period to the gradual decay other apt symbols follow: the house lamp of gold that has been secretly straining its silver chain now suddenly dropped and extinguished; the pitcher that has gone daily to the fountain, the cistern wheel that so long has mechanically turned, at last broken and useless. A long string of life's dull infirmities, from all of which realistic imagery must shrink as things unlovely, has been transformed into a thing of enduring beauty by casting over it the softening veil of symbolism.

> Richard G. Moulton. *The Literary Study of the Bible.*
> Rev. ed. (Boston, Heath, 1899), pp. 221–24

Koheleth is modern, because with great literary skill he deals with those aspects of human life which are always the same. He is almost brutally frank in holding the mirror up to life. For all that, he is neither a scoffer nor a pessimist. He loves life and has intense sympathy with the struggles and sufferings of humanity, but he smiles at the attempts of zealous reformers to change human nature or to improve a state of things, which (as he believes) follows logically from the conditions under which mankind carves out its career. . . .

Perhaps the most serious defect in the book from the point of view of literary art is the absence of any system in the development of this theme. The book is more in the nature of a series of *causeries,* passing lightly from one phase of the subject to the other without regard either to logical order or strict consistency. There is no gradual approach to a climax as there is in the unfolding of the central theme in the far more systematically constructed book of Job, with which Koheleth is allied. In Job, each aspect of the perplexing and apparently insoluble problem of the reason for unjust suffering in a world supposed to be created by a wise and just God is thoroughly exhausted before another is taken up. When we reach the end of the discussion between Job and his friends, despite the imperfect character of the last series of speeches, we feel that everything that could be brought forward has been said. Not so Koheleth, who is suggestive rather than exhaustive, lighting up his theme sporadically here and there, but not illuminating all its angles. . . .

Koheleth is not afraid of the charge of inconsistency, but he would have his answer ready, "Why not—life itself is full of inconsistencies." And so, literary artist though he is by the very simplicity and pungency of his style, he is willing to be inartistic when it comes to the unfolding of his theme. He indulges in repetitions, and jumps rapidly, without logical transition, from one aspect of his subject to the other. . . .

Koheleth reminds one most of Omar Khayyam, who represents the natural reaction against a stern Islamic environment, as Koheleth marks a reaction against the unbending ecclesiasticism and conventional piety of his Jewish surroundings. The touch of irony in Omar Khayyam's immortal quatrains is singularly like that which we encounter in Koheleth. . . . In their attitude towards life, both are free from any real bitterness. Their cynicism is without any sting, or if occasionally there is a sting it is gentle; it pricks a little but does not bite. Both are enamored of life, despite its sorrows and its imperfections. To both life means joy—joy for joy's sake, with perhaps this distinction, that Omar Khayyam has no fear of *ennui* resulting from joy, whereas Koheleth advocates as a preventive the combination of toil with joy, so that the enjoyment may be more lasting. The undertone of sadness, too, is common to both, suggested by the brevity of life and by the approach of old age, devoid of enjoyment, with the shadow of death thrown across one's path. . . . Both writers are worldly in their spirit and their outlook; and this is the severest indictment—if it be one—to be preferred against their productions. *Carpe diem* [enjoy the day]! is the motto of Koheleth and of Omar Khayyam alike. . . .

[Ernest] Renan, whose own nature found a response in Koheleth and who was fascinated by the book as everyone must be who penetrates its spirit, goes so far as to say that it is the only amiable book written by a Jew. That is hardly correct, for we have a modern analogy to Koheleth (as Renan himself suggests) in Heine, who looks upon the world in the same smiling manner. . . . [Heinrich] Heine is a nineteenth-century Koheleth; and he possesses the same irresistible charm. His pen, though trenchant, is never dipped in venom; his irony, though pointed, is tempered with pathos. Even his satire, when most biting, betrays his amiability. The analogy between the two might be carried further, for their skepticism is much of the same order: they are both "gentle cynics."

Morris Jastrow. *A Gentle Cynic* (Philadelphia, Lippincott, 1919), pp. 8–9, 124–26, 189–91, 195

The Book of Ecclesiastes is easily the greatest surviving product of Hebrew philosophic thought. Its philosophical line of connection and development is with the utilitarianism of the Book of Proverbs, which it pursues to a bitter and ironic end. But the book itself, like all Hebrew literature, is a free personal creation, including several literary elements quite disjoint from philosophic systems. . . .

It falls in the great and ever appealing literature of self-revelation and puts him beside Marcus Aurelius, Sir Thomas Browne, Pascal, and many others their like. We can see him in it clarifying himself to himself, enjoying the luxury of confession, of talking, if indirectly, about himself and enjoying, too, the creative impulse we all know about ourselves. This self-confession had occurred, again and again, in the Psalms, in a devout form addressed to Jehovah. It belongs, as we have seen, to the very kernel of the subjective Hebrew soul. But here, having no such God of comfort as would respond to confession, Ecclesiastes makes it to himself like Marcus Aurelius in his "conversations with himself." And he enjoyed making it for his own private exercise and satisfaction like Sir Thomas Browne in his *Religio Medici,* and like Sir Thomas Browne, too, Ecclesiastes had a keen enjoyment of skill in phrasing and happy expression in creative words. And of necessity he was forced to a philosophy of life and of what lies behind life, even as Pascal in his *Pensées.* All this, because it was the rendering, full and complete, of a great personality, made his a great book, a friendly, a lovable book—the only lovable book, said [Ernest] Renan, ever written by a Jew—which has caught and held the most varied minds, from St. Paul to Thackeray and Edgar Allan Poe, whether they fully understood it or not. For it is of the quality of great literature to have myriad meanings for its myriad readers. No one can exactly tell what and all Shakespeare meant; and we have to be content that what each of us finds that he implicitly meant. So with Ecclesiastes; every age has found itself in his book and yet there is no end. It is safe to say, that of the Hebrew literature that has reached us, this book is the fullest and most perfect flowering of the essential Hebrew genius in its strength and in its weakness.

Duncan B. MacDonald. *The Hebrew Literary Genius* (Princeton, N.J., Princeton University Press, 1933), pp. 197, 199

In every age, men have sought the key to the understanding of this modern classic, which accidentally happened to be written two millennia ago. There will be times when it will not suit the temper of the age, but it will never be outmoded as long as the systole and diastole of human life survives, and men fluctuate between progress and reaction, growth and decline, hope and dissilusion. . . .

Not every century can boast a work that gives perfect utterance to a universal mood. No matter how radically the conditions of existence may change, such a work remains as the supreme expression of a basic, ever-recurring pattern in the life of the human spirit. To this chosen group of masterpieces the Book of Koheleth, or "Ecclesiastes," belongs. . . .

Like other writers since, who were raised in a religious tradition from which they have broken away in whole or in part, Koheleth uses a *traditional religious vocabulary* to express his own special vision. The modern reader will think of Ernest Renan, Anatole France and George Santayana as manifesting at times a somewhat similar trait. A few examples of this tendency may be cited. Traditional morality declared that he who fulfilled God's will, would be happy. Koheleth declares that he who is happy is fulfilling God's will!

> Indeed, every man whom God has given wealth and possessions
> and granted the power to enjoy them, taking his portion, and re-
> joicing in his labor, that is the gift of God, for it is God who pro-
> vides the joy in a man's heart. (5:18) . . .

This clothing of the hedonistic principle in religious guise is not without analogy in Hebrew literature. The Book of Proverbs counsels: "Hear, my son, and be wise, / and walk in the ways of your heart." (23:19) . . .

The second unique characteristic of Koheleth's style which has not been adequately noted, with disastrous results for the understanding of the book, is *his use of proverbial quotations*. . . . Koheleth's use of this folk-material is so varied and individual that it may fairly be described as creative. It is beyond question one of the most charming features of his style. At times he cites a proverb simply because he agrees with it, and he may elaborate upon it with a characteristic comment. Thus the most confirmed cynic will agree that "Through sloth the ceiling sinks in, / And through slack hands the house leaks" (Eccl. 10:18). . . . Frequently, however, Koheleth's comment on the proverb that he quotes subtly changes the meaning of the text, shifting the ground from the realm of the matter-of-fact and the practical to the uncharted regions where speculation and scepticism have free reign. . . .

Another noteworthy device by which Koheleth expresses his divergence from commonly accepted views is the use of *contrasting proverbs*. . . . He cites a proverb expressing a widely accepted point of view and then subtly registers his disagreement, not by a lengthy argument, but by citing another utterance diametrically opposed. Where Koheleth's sympathies lie in these debates is easy to determine. In each pair of contrasting proverbs, the latter represents his standpoint. . . .

It is clear that the Book of Koheleth is not a debate, a dialogue, or a philosophical treatise. It is best described as a *cahier* or notebook, into which the author jotted down his reflections during the enforced leisure of old age. They differ in mood, in style, and in length. At times when he grows impassioned, he develops a subtle inner rhythm, as in the majestic opening section of Chapter 1. At others, the rhythm is much more pronounced, as in the unforgettable "Allegory of Old Age" in Chapter 12. Generally, however, his medium is prose.

It is possible that these brief essays were collected and edited by Koheleth himself, since the book opens and closes with the theme, "Vanity of vanities, all is vanity," and the first and last sections are the most eloquent and moving of all. Very often, the end of a section can be recognized by Koheleth's reverting, after a discussion of his subject, whether it be wealth, wisdom or corruption, to one of his two fundamental themes—the tragedy of man's ignorance of ultimate truth, and his God-given duty to achieve happiness.

The author's fascinating personality is thus reflected in a style rich in nuance and eloquent in its reticence.

Robert Gordis. *The Wisdom of Ecclesiastes* (New York,
Behrman, 1945), pp. v, 1, 30–33, 35, 37

Next to Job, whose voice rises as though from ancient depths, Ecclesiastes is a thoroughly modern work. In this book the beginning of a new expression, a new culture is inaugurated. Its style is burnished differently, sharpened differently. Here it is told of the tribulations of the wealthy life, of unbroken thirst, of the disappointments that come not because of disaster and poverty but precisely with wealth, with satiety; and with all the wealth, the heart remains hungry, impoverished, and empty. Thus, here there is no outburst, as in Job, but rather a transparent poison, dripping slowly, stirring up as well as calming down.

Yet it cannot be said that the book is written out of skeptical complacency. The pace is restrained, the breathing is restrained. But from the curt, aphoristic speech striving to summarize all the conclusions in a poignant, concentrated saying—to grasp the pillars of existence at one verse-end—the book suddenly passes into a huge storminess resembling a wind rushing from hidden places, and again from the storm, deadening the heart to a silent protest. No more is this the prophetic ax that "fell heavy." This was the new pace, attesting to a deep, philosophical awareness, if not to a philosophical complacency, a stoic perfection. Cool, contemplative, alien to the spirit of Israel even in tired, sere times.

Jacob Fichman. *'Arugot* (Jerusalem, Bialik Institute,
1954), p. 291†

Is Ecclesiastes prose or verse? It would be hard to say. The first two Chapters are, I suppose, prose, but prose which has taken on an extra suggestiveness and emotional stress. At the same time, the patterning has the minimum of formality.

The parallelsim gives us the energy of poetry without its formal discipline. The idea rather than the form is supreme. Indeed, the formal distinction between prose and poetry determined by the practical object of the former as against the aesthetic values of the latter are foreign to the Hebrew spirit. If we were to consider the type of moral philosophy (signified by the Hebrew term *Hokhmah*) which the book seeks to inculcate we would notice likewise that it takes in rational expediency, but also wonder, awe, and devotion. This itself tends to demand an appropriately rich and flexible style which shall have the extra weight of poetical expression in reserve. Koheleth has something of the irony and disillusionment of the Stoic-Cynic diatribes, as well as something of their dialectical manner, but unlike the Stoics (and unlike Bacon) the Jewish sage can drop his irony and detachment and give rein to a more personal and emotional impulse. The self-sufficiency of the Stoic philosopher is finally lacking:

> Be not rash with thy mouth, and let not thine heart be hasty to utter any thing before God: for God is in heaven, and thou upon earth: therefore let thy words be few. (5:2.)

And then one remembers the grave elegiac poetry of the last Chapter on the approach of old age and death, compared to the onset of the wet season in the Land of Israel:

> Remember now thy Creator in the days of thy youth, while the evil days come not, nor the years draw nigh, when thou shalt say, I have no pleasure in them. While the sun, or the light, or the moon, or the stars, be not darkened, nor the clouds return after the rain. [12:1–2]

Without the formalities of verse, this is surely deeply imagined poetry; but it is flexible enough to alternate with a kind of dry prose, detached, ironical, even humorous, as when the Preacher, after having "set in order many proverbs," wryly warns his disciples that "of making books there is no end; and much study is a weariness of the flesh." [12:12]

Harold Fisch. Jerusalem and Albion (New York, Schocken, 1964), pp. 44–45

Ecclesiastes might well be the most misunderstood book in the Bible. Most commentators have found the theme of the book to be inconsistent with the rest of biblical teaching. How such a view of the book arose is baffling. It is no exaggeration to say that this book espouses the most basic theme of biblical literature —that life lived by purely earthly or human values, without faith in God and supernatural values, is meaningless and futile. The key term in the book is the phrase "under the sun." This phrase, or its equivalent "under the heaven," occurs thirty times in the book and denotes that which is only earthly. To be "under the sun" is to be earth-bound, cut off from the supernatural order.

In developing his theme, the writer has chosen a common literary device. He demonstrates at length the inadequacy of any world view other than a theocentric one, and he combines with this demonstration an affirmation of an alternate world view. This means that the individual passages must be placed carefully in their contexts. If we read every passage as being equally indicative of the writer's settled philosophic position, we are left with a meaningless collection of contradictory statements, for it is indisputable that the views of some passages contradict those of others. Actually the contradiction is part of a meaningful pattern in which the writer's negative comments are understood to be the conclusions that emerge when he limits his gaze to the earthly scene. When the narrator voices despair over the futility of life under the sun, he is not affirming this as his final answer to life's existence.

The matter of the theme of Ecclesiastes is closely tied to the question of the work's structure. Typical statements about the structure of the book are that it "is without formal structure" or is "a miscellany of wisdom literature" or "a miscellaneous collection of proverbs." In fact, however, Ecclesiastes is one of the most rigidly structured books in the Bible. The principle of organization is dialectical, that is, based on a conflict between opposites. Passages of negation and affirmation follow each other from the beginning of the work to the end. The narrative conflict underlying the dialectical structure is the contrast between a God-centered world view and all the other world views. . . .

In addition to giving his work a dialectical structure, the author has seized upon one of the oldest of all literary devices, the quest motif. He pictures himself as a wise man in search of the good life. His approach to the quest is partly narrative, in which he describes his quest as a series of actions, and partly lyric, in which he praises the good life and dispraises the varieties of inadequate world views.

The book does not have a chronological or narrative unity. It does have unity of other kinds, however. Both the quest motif and the dialectical juxtaposition of positive and negative passages provide unity, as does the stylistic device of antithesis. The recurrence of stock words and phrases is perhaps the most discernible element of unity. The phrases "under the sun," "eat and drink," "vanity of vanities," "this also is vanity" recur, giving a unity of poetic texture.

Two features of the imagery of the book are worthy of note. For one thing, the imagery of the book does much to give it an elemental quality. There are constant references to the sun, to eating and drinking, to the cycles of nature, to death, and to God. A second feature of the imagery is its comprehensiveness. The narrator mentions virtually all of the activities of men. There are references to the city, cultivated fields, gardens, the temple, a house, a bedchamber, courts of justice, seats of power, and battle. The preacher is concerned with all of the main areas of life—wealth, power, religion, social relationships, work, and pleasure.

Leland Ryken. *The Literature of the Bible* (Grand Rapids, Mich., Zondervan, 1974), pp. 250–52

EDEN, GARDEN OF

The story of the Garden of Eden is one of the most beautiful, not only in the Bible, but in all literature, and has deservedly come to be regarded as one of the world's immortal classics. Its story is told simply and directly. The several incidents are clearly and concisely pictured. The climax is dramatic, when the guilty pair, conscious of their sin, must come forth from their hiding-place at God's call, and by excusing themselves with a half lie, incriminate themselves irrefutably.

Despite its simplicity and brevity, the portrayal of character is delicate and effective. The serpent, cunning and evil-minded, purposely overstates God's command and asks, "Hath God said: Ye shall not eat of any tree in the garden?" And the woman, guileless and unsuspecting, falls into the trap, and even enlarges upon God's actual words, "Of the fruit of the trees of the garden we may eat; but of the fruit of the tree which is in the midst of the garden, God hath said: Ye shall not eat of it, neither shall ye touch it, lest ye die." And when she has, so naturally and humanly, let herself be enticed by the alluring beauty of the tree and the seeming benefits which it might confer, and has eaten, her first thought is of her husband; "and she gave also unto her husband with her, and he did eat." And finally, when directly charged by God with their sin, each seeks to shift the responsibility; the man puts the blame partly upon the woman and partly upon God Himself, for having made her, and the woman in turn shifts the blame to the serpent. Touches so delicate reveal the master's hand.

The story shows remarkable power of condensation and suggestion. The one sentence, "And they were both naked, the man and his wife, and were not ashamed", pictures their state of pristine innocence far more effectively than any detailed explanation. Similarly, after both have eaten of the forbidden fruit, and both they and the reader of the story are anxiously awaiting the results, the few words, "And the eyes of them both were opened, and they knew" . . . what did they know; what was this strange and wonderful knowledge which came from eating the forbidden fruit? . . . "they knew that they were naked," are powerfully suggestive.

> Julian Morgenstern. *The Book of Genesis*. 2d ed. (New York, Schocken, 1965), pp. 45–46

The action of Genesis 2 begins with God's placing man in the earthly paradise. Verse 8 tells us simply, "And the Lord God planted a garden in Eden, in the east; and there he put the man whom he had formed." These words capture in eloquent simplicity a phenomenon that has seized the human imagination and consciousness through the centuries. It can be called the paradisal ideal, and it is an archetypal human longing. . . .

Descriptions of the earthly paradise in literature have always had certain conventions. The place of perfection is always remembered as a garden. As such, it has been a place of profuse vegetation and fragrance. Verse 9 of Genesis 2 briefly attributes sensuous richness and pleasure to the Garden of Eden when it states that "out of the ground the Lord God made to grow every tree that is pleasant to the sight and good for food." It is important to note the way in which a description such as this arouses our own picture of paradise without imposing its own detailed conception upon us.

Paradise has archetypally been a realm removed from ordinary existence and impossible to return to in the flesh. It is a condition always placed somewhere and sometime outside normal human experience. The remoteness of the Garden of Eden in the Genesis account is evident in the fact that although it is given a geographic location ("Eden" means a definite geographic area), it has never been precisely located. Verses 10 to 14 capture the paradoxical nature of paradise as being both real and inaccessible. These verses seem to place paradise in an identifiable geographic locale, but for us even this precise localization has been lost. Why the remoteness? we might ask. According to early Genesis, paradise is remote from our experience because it was lost. Since paradise is presented as being both real and lost, it combines the themes of yearning and nonpossession, or desire and inaccessibility.

Paradise has been conventionally described as both a place and a way of life. As a way of life it is a place of rest, pleasure, contentment, virtue, beauty, closeness to nature, youthfulness, harmony, and freedom. Because of the extreme brevity of the story told in Genesis 2, these motifs are left largely undeveloped. Once again the reader is left to imagine the details of the paradisal way of life.

Paradise has ordinarily been characterized by an absence of civilization, and it has that identity in early Genesis. Virtue is displayed negatively, as the absence of ordinary fallen human experience. Since the life described is one of natural simplicity, there is an almost total lack of the complex social roles that we experience. The self-enclosed nature of the garden makes its existence one in which the ordinary actions of men are absent. It is a world that existed before men sailed the seas or built cities.

The paradise of Genesis 2 is conventional in all these ways. There are a few additional traits peculiar to the Hebraic version of the paradisal garden. In the biblical account, it is made clear that the garden was planted by God. This implies two important principles: nature is God's art, manifesting His creative craftsmanship, and nature is God's provision for His creatures, especially man. A second major distinction of the biblical description of paradise is that, in contrast to pagan myths, it was not a place of inviolable retirement but was from the beginning a place of trial. This means that the Garden of Eden is depicted as a place and condition of perfection, but with a potential for change.

When God put man into the Garden of Eden, He established some basic conditions of reality. The fact that He put man "in the garden of Eden to till it and keep it" (Gen. 2:15) shows that work was part of God's ideal for people and that life in paradise was not idle but purposeful. God also placed within the garden a prohibited tree (vv. 16–17), the fruit of which could not be eaten without penalty of death. The forbidden tree is important for several reasons. It is evidence of God's provision for man because it provided man the opportunity to demonstrate his love and gratitude to God in action as well as word. It also shows that the universe God created is a law-bound universe that operates according to moral and spiritual laws as well as physical laws. Finally, the forbidden tree establishes the conditional nature of prelapsarian perfection and makes moral choice an essential part of human existence.

Leland Ryken. *The Literature of the Bible* (Grand Rapids, Mich., Zondervan, 1974), pp. 37–39

The action of Genesis 2:4b–3:24 unfolds in a series of seven scenes distinguished from one another principally by shifts in *dramatis personae* and changes in literary form.

(1) 2:4b–17: a predominantly narrative section whose only active figure is Yahweh God. Man is present in a completely passive role.

(2) 2:18–25: a second predominantly narrative section wherein the active role of Yahweh God is supplemented by subordinate activity on man's part. Woman and the animals appear as passive figures.

(3) 3:1–5: a dialogue between the snake and the woman.

(4) 3:6–8: a narrative with two characters, the woman and the man.

(5) 3:9–13: a dialogue involving Yahweh God, the man, and the woman.

(6) 3:14–19: a monologue of Yahweh God; the snake, the woman, and the man are present as passive figures.

(7) 3:22–24: a predominantly narrative section whose only active figure is Yahweh God. The man is present in a completely passive role. . . .

The basic structural principle of the Eden account is the concentric arrangement of its scenes. The pattern involves *dramatis personae,* themes, and in some cases, internal structural elements of each scene. Scene 4 is the climax and turning point of the narrative. . . .

Scene 1

narrative
Yahweh God, the man
from *'adamah* [ground] to garden
vocabulary

Scene 7

narrative
Yahweh God, the man
from garden to *'adamah*
vocabulary

Scene 2

narrative
Yahweh God, man, woman, animals
relationships among the creatures
2:24–25 [etiology]

Scene 6

monologue
Yahweh God, man, woman, snake
relationships among the creatures
3:20–21 [etiology]

Scene 3

dialogue
the snake, the woman
eating from the tree
three statements

Scene 5

dialogue
Yahweh God, the man, the woman
eating from the tree
three questions-and-answers

Scene 4

narrative
the woman and her husband
eating from the tree
concentric structure of scene . . . .

The movement within the garden relates the story to the literary topos of the "quest for the center." The symbolism of "the center" is a mythological universal: it is the locus of "absolute reality, sacred power, and immortality" [Mircea Eliade, *Patterns in Comparative Religion* (1958), p. 380]. This holds true of the center of the garden of Eden as well. But in almost every other particular the Eden account is a systematic reversal of the "quest for the center," calculated to produce a contrary literary effect.

In the standard myths, supernatural powers hostile to man surround the center with obstacles and guardian monsters to thwart his access—the quest is for heroes only. In Genesis, Yahweh God's goodwill and concern are evident throughout the account. The divine prohibition is for man's own protection. There is no obstacle beyond this prohibition, and no guardian but man himself. The attainment of the center requires neither endurance nor courage; all man need do is betray the divine trust. Thus the grandeur of the heroic achievement is transformed into the sordidness of a sin of disloyalty.

The reversal carries through into the effect the tale has on its hearer. A hero epitomizes what is best in man, and the hearer naturally identifies with him. The hearer shares vicariously the hero's quest, his victory, his glory. The resultant sense of ennoblement awakens in the hearer a desire to imitate in his own life the admirable qualities exemplified by the hero. In the Eden account, the hearer identifies with the *'adam* "Man" as prototype and ancestor of the race. He thus becomes inextricably enmeshed in the man's sin and shares his sense of shame. This awakens in him the desire to disassociate himself from the sinful characteristics he sees at work in the man, and to seek to remove them from his own life.

Jerome T. Walsh. *Journal of Biblical Literature*. June, 1977, pp. 161, 169–70, 173

No story seems more directional than the Garden story (Gen. 2–3). It traces, among other things, the origin of death, of procreation, of cultivation, of social discord, of human knowledge, of guilt, punishment and suffering. These changes are shown as something unprecedented and irreversible. If any tale could symbolize the flow of time, or, indeed, could epitomize that distinctly temporal art, the art of narrative, it would seem to be this one. Yet the very telescoping of the Garden story's manifold cultural concerns into so compact a form suggests a subtler and more complex discourse, less temporal and less narrative in character, for which the purported time-scheme of the story serves as a kind of armature. Perhaps the encapsulation of these "non-narrative" concerns into a simple fable, convenient for repetition and folk transmission, is itself a more remarkable labor than its reverse, the unfolding of the non-narrative discourse through exegesis and analysis, but it is possible to show that such discourse is already in the text, and not merely a construction of postbiblical commentary. . . .

Let us begin by noting that certain elements of the Garden story present themselves more immediately and explicitly to the reader's attention as "non-narrative" elements: pauses in the story's action for the sake of thematic enhancement or amplification. Namings and etiological statements are the most obvious of such pauses, although in some sense it is possible to say that *all* elements of the story have a "non-narrative" dimension, as we shall see more fully later on, and in any case, quite a number of alleged traditional elements of the story have been adjudged "extraneous" or "supplementary" by commentators. I shall try to restrict myself here to those that appear distinct *formally*, rather than merely by virtue of motivic content.

I shall provisionally distinguish three main types of departure from narrative action. The first is best represented by the parenthetic description in 2:10–14 of the "four rivers" that emerge from the Garden to water the four major regions of the world. This idiosyncratic item of geographical lore can be regarded as a more or less autonomous motif within the story, in the sense that no other aspects of the story (other than the overall implicit equation of the Garden with a cosmological "center") are hinged upon its information, and we may, for present purposes at least (without discounting the importance of the cosmological theme to the story's meaning), regard 2:10–14 as part of the main stock of narrative, and its role in the unfolding of the story's "microredactional" structure as subordinate to that of the narrative segment in which it occurs. (One should, as well, regard the etiologically-weighted divine pronouncements in 3:14–19a as a departure of this type: important to the unfolding of the story's symbolism from the standpoint of motivic content, but structurally subordinate to the narrative segment in which it occurs, although later it will be necessary to specify the function of this departure more explicitly.)

The second and third types of digression, on the other hand, namings (2:23, 3:20) and explicit (not implicit) etiological statements (2:24, 3:19b) *are* significant structuring elements, first, by virtue of their occurrence as doublets, second, because of their placement. The ancestor of humanity is portrayed naming his female companion twice, first *'ishah* ("woman"), secondly *hawwah* ("Eve," or possibly "Life-giver"), with the story's main action intervening between the two namings. The etiological statements likewise occur twice, once just after the first naming, once just before the second.

The resultant "microredactional" picture of Gen. 2–3 (implicit etiologies are spelled out as such) is as follows:

Narrative (2:4–22): Creation of man, garden, beasts, woman (2:5 and 18–22 are laden with implicit etiologies: origin of rain and tilling; origin of animal names, of woman from man's rib, of human society).

Naming (2:23): Man calls his companion "woman" ('ishah) and himself "man" ('ish).

Etiology (2:24): "Therefore does a man leave his father and his mother, and cling together with his wo-man, and the two of them become one flesh."

Narrative (2:25–3:19a): The temptation, transgression and punishment (14–19a laden with implicit etiologies: origin of snake's posture, of enmity between snake and man; of woman's pain in childbearing, of her passion for and dependence on her male companion; of hard labor, tilling, breadmaking and, above all, of death and burial).

Etiology (3:19b): "For dust thou art, and to dust thou shalt return."

Naming (3:20): Man ('adam) calls his companion "Eve" (hawwah).

Narrative (3:21–24): God clothes human pair, expels them from garden (3:21 is an implicit etiology: origin of hide-clothes—cf. 3:7b: origin of plant fiber clothes). Birth of a child (4:1) completes one generation.

This the reader will readily recognize to be palistrophic (or, more commonly, chiastic):

Narrative
   Naming
      Etiology
         Narrative
      Etiology
   Naming
Narrative

The story's broadest form-critical subdivisions thus manifest a quite orderly symmetrical arrangement. Moreover, in its palistrophic formation, the resultant structure bears strong resemblance to the redactional arrangement Fishbane showed operating between stories in the Jacob cycle, thus further justifying a characterization of it as "microredactional." We should be aware, as well, that this analysis does not interfere with any of the hypotheses proposed regarding prior literary and/or additional preliterary sources: the segments here designated "narrative" could still reflect composite segments of narrative or traditionary units, such as those suggested at the beginning of this essay. The division of elements I have proposed, however, makes clearer that at least some of the inherited elements of the story are intended to exhibit parallel relationships—something we would not see as clearly if we treated all of these elements as equivalent in weight or function. The author's task seems not merely to have been to weave a connected narrative from available traditions, but to combine traditions into a conceptual framework.

Joel W. Rosenberg. Prooftexts. May, 1981, pp. 1, 5–7

EHUD

It is told in terse reportorial style, with no attempt at artistry or dramatic contrast. No necessary detail is omitted, nor is an unnecessary detail included. From the vividness of the description it might be suspected that the author of the crime and the story were identical. That Ehud was left-handed and that Eglon was fat were facts perhaps available to any storyteller; but that the fat closed up about the sword, and that the blade was inserted so far that it came out behind, were details that might have been inferred from the premises, but sound more like the testimony of an eye-witness. For the description is active, not passive, as it would have been, had the report been made by those who found the corpse. In any case, it is a noteworthy example of visual description, though the details are too unsavory to make it pleasant reading.

Brooke Peters Church. The Israel Saga (New York,
Macmillan, 1932), pp. 217–18

The narrator indicates [Ehud's] hand with ironic emphasis. This hand determines the objective action, and at the same time its linguistic designation becomes a stylistic protagonist—I mean, it becomes the object of wordplays and repetitions; "hand" is a leading-word of the narrative. The man is a "right-hander" (Benjaminite-Southerner), and still he is a "left-hander": *ben hayyemini 'ish 'iṭṭer yad yemino* [lit., "son of the Right (South), man lame in his right hand"]. Through this *hand* the Israelites deliver the tyrant their tribute: *beyado* ["with his hand"]. The narrator expresses the three words "to deliver," "hand," and "gift" with a smile.

How the tribute was collected and of what gifts it consisted does not interest the narrator, for he is thinking of another gift. Thus he shows us in detail how the protagonist obtains a double-edged dagger "a yard long," how he "girds" it "under the robe, at his right hip" (the wrong place). The narrator, who finds no time to describe the gifts, who suppresses all the preparations for the embassy, has the time and the inclination to enumerate precise details when they serve the ends of the action and extend the action. Here the reader may anticipate something, even though he does not yet know it. Anticipation without knowing extends the narrative.

The king has not been presented to us yet. Only as Ehud—and with him the narrator—arrives, does he step onto the stage. He steps onto it carnally: "Eglon was terribly fat." If the name *'eglon* actually evoked in the audience the two ideas of "cattle" and "to be round," then this introduction of the king is simultaneously precious and malicious. The king is a fat, round head of cattle. Here it becomes no longer amusing but ridiculous, and the [word] *me'od* ["very much"] marks a pause.

The next verse serves as a connector: it condenses two events in a single, stylistically well-formed parallelism. . . . The rhythm is 4 + 4 (*wayyehi* is an anacrusis), the word *minha* ["tribute"] is a rhyme, and with the repetition of this word the gifts are once and for all dispensed with. The first half denotes the transmission of tribute with the periphrastic usage *ka' asher killa lehaqriv* ["when he had finished presenting"], the second half, *wayyeshallah 'et ha'am* ["he released the people"], stands ellipitcally for Ehud's and his people's return to the "idols," where he dismisses them and comes back alone. . . .

With this we reach a high point. Now the narrator describes precisely, in detail, swiftly. There is hardly any speaking. Twice Ehud announces his message, first as a "secret," then more precisely as an "oracle." The first time the king orders religious silence (*has* ["hush"]) and the courtiers vanish. The second time he stands up. Speaking is a pretense for action: Ehud does not announce the oracle; the king speaks only one syllable, and this requires silence. The king makes but a single gesture, and now Ehud acts.

Protagonist and antagonist are alone in the royal chamber. The king stands before God; he has left the royal throne. Now they act man to man. This action, calculated in every respect, is depicted with masterly technique.

One could call the technique "Homeric," were it not universal. The action is broken down into discrete movements, each movement delineated precisely, comprising a swiftly unfolding series. Physicality and plasticity make it all palpable—left hand, right thigh, belly, fat. The tempo prevents an impression of morose brutality. The rhythm of 4 + 4 + 2 with a threefold rhyme, accelerates the tempo:

wayyishlah	*'ehud*	*'et yad*	*semolo*	
[he extended	Ehud	hand	his left]	
wayyiqqah	*'et haherev*	*me'al*	*yerekh*	*yemino*
[he took	the sword	from	thigh	his right]
			wayyitqa'eha	*bevitno*
			[he plunged it into his belly]	

Then the rhythm returns to 4 + 4 + 4, with the rhyme still only at the end:

wayyavo'	*gam hannitsav*	*'ahar*	*hallahav*
[it went in	even the handle	after	the blade]
wayyisgor	*hahelev*	*be'ad*	*hallahav*

[it closed   the fat   over   the blade]
ki lo'   *shalaf*   *haḥerev*   *mibbiṭno*
[for he did not draw out the sword from his belly]

Important, too, are the effects of sound. . . .

That is the foreground of the description. It is palpable, physical, swift; nicely shaped through rhythm and sound-effects. From here it is not far to fore-grounding, which [Erich] Auerbach has ascertained in Homer. But we should look more deeply. We should not be intoxicated by the melody line and miss the chords. Thus if a leading-word is more than a common word, the repetition (of it) in a prominent place creates associations, which make out of the whole a pro-portioned structure. The riches and the rounding, which this stylistic device lend to a short narrative, a good reciter can fully bring out.

> Luis Alonso-Schökel. *Biblica.* 42 No. 2, 1961, pp. 149–52†

I do not hesitate to label the story of Ehud a very coarse one; I am not sure that the ancient Hebrews thought it so. I think, rather, that they saw rich humor in the manner in which Eglon is deceived. I think that to them it was very funny that Ehud is able to plunge not only the sword, but also the hilt, into the fatty belly of the king, and let the abdominal fluids ooze out. I think they found it very funny that the servants of Eglon, wondering why the interview with Ehud stretched out, attribute to Eglon a prolonged visit to what the British, in a euphemism, call the cloakroom. As far as brevity is concerned, the account of Ehud is scarcely a half-page. The description of him is limited entirely to the information that he is left-handed. Again the account moves quickly from beginning through climax to end.

> Samuel Sandmel. *Judaism.* Fall, 1973, p. 459

The scene [of Ehud's confrontation with Eglon] closes with a reversal of the opening movement: Ehud goes out, closing and locking the doors and Eglon's servants go in. That movement gives to the scene a slapstick tone: "Murderer and body guards cross paths in the space of one verse, at which the narrator again laughs" ([Luis] Alonso-Schökel. [*Biblica.* 1961, p. 153]). When the servants find the doors locked, they say: "He [Eglon] is only relieving himself in the closet of the cool chamber" ([Judg.] 3:24). Irony is added to the coarse humor, for the reader knows that the king is indeed lying there with feces running out. After waiting for some time, the servants act. In the technical language of film, three "close-ups" are shot in rapid succession: they take the key, open the door, and then the camera turns upon the king fallen on the floor, dead. Playful irony shifts once again to gruesome death, giving to the whole scene a macabre effect.

> Leonard L. Thompson. *Introducing Biblical Literature* (Englewood Cliffs, N.J., Prentice-Hall, 1978), pp. 31–32

The phraseological composition of the story reveals it to be concerned with the difficulty with which the word of God is interpreted. There are only five reported utterances in the story, and all but the last have to do with the unexpected and ambiguous nature of the word of God. After Ehud, the left-handed one, had fashioned his two-edged sword, he approached Eglon and says, "My lord king, I have a word for you in private" (3:19). We already know that this "word" is Ehud's hidden, two-edged sword, so that Eglon's response, "Silence!" (3:19), is ironic, since he unknowingly characterizes this secret word as one which will not be heard, but somehow felt. Then, alone with Eglon in his private chambers, Ehud reveals the *source* of his silent word: "I have a word from God for you" (3:20). Ehud then thrusts this two-edged word of God deep within Eglon's belly, locks the doors of the chamber from without, and flees. When Eglon's servants come, they find the doors locked, and say, "Surely (*'akh*) he is relieving himself in the closet of his summer place." The contrast between the certainty with which they utter their interpretation of the situation (*'akh*) and the obvious error of their judgment is underlined and symbolized in the story by the image of the locked doors. Only after they were "ashamed to delay any longer" do the servants open these doors and discover what the word of God here signifies—not Eglon's relief but Israel's release. Only with the final utterance of the story, Ehud's command to the Israelites "Follow me, for the LORD has delivered your enemy the Moabite into your hands" (3:28), do we encounter reported speech that can be termed a "correct" interpretation of a situation. Ten thousand Moabites are killed, Moab becomes subject to Israel, and there is peace in the land for eighty years.

There are also some illuminating temporal shifts in the story. When Ehud approaches Eglon in his summer place, the narrative shifts to a more deeply synchronic point of view emphasizing the perspective of the participants: "He [Eglon] was sitting (*yoshev*) in the roof chamber" (3:20). But after the word God was announced, Eglon rose from his throne as if to foreshadow that this word of God signified the end of his rule. Then, after the murder, a second shift to a more synchronic viewpoint emphasizes the central image of the locked doors: "the doors being locked (*dal^etot* [. . .] *n^ec^ulot*)" (3:24). Finally, a series of three synchronic verb-forms describe from within, as it were, the gap between the servants' interpretation of the situation and the true state of affairs, and positions the cause of this distance between them, so that the sequencing of the narrative mirrors its semantic content:

error:	"Surely he is relieving himself (*'akh mesikh hu'*)" (3:24)
cause of error:	". . . and behold there was no one to open the doors . . . (*w^ehinne 'enennu pote^ah*)" (3:25a)
true state of affairs:	"there was their master lying on the floor dead (*nofel . . . met*)" (3:25b) . . .

When we turn to the spatial composition of the story, we are immediately hindered by certain semantic ambiguities that seem to be a built-in feature of the narrative. Where in fact is the summer palace of Eglon? Is it in Israel or Moab?

The story is deliberately vague on this point. . . .

It is almost as if the spatial ambiguity of the story serves a deeper ideological purpose. It is all the same, whether the assassination at the summer palalce took place in Moab or in Israel, and one's suspicions about this are heightened by the contrast between this glaring ambiguity and the overwhelmingly specific emphasis of the rest of the narrative. The story begins with Moab invading the land of Israel, with God's permission—a fact immediately complicated by the reader's recollection of Israel's original by-passing of Moab during the journey toward the Jordan (Deut. 2–3). Surely Israel's plight is now the result of their continual sinning; but we have no information about the relation of Moab's sudden ill fortune and *their* standing with Yahweh. If they also were presently at odds with Yahweh for some reason, then the story is about the fluctuating fortunes of two nations, both of whom deserve punishment. On the other hand, if Moab is to be considered an innocent party in the story, simply a tool of Yahweh, then we have a story about Moab's undeserved loss of their king and ten thousand soldiers. We have therefore the impression that *retribution* is really not what is at stake here in the story, but rather the inability of man always to predict his destiny, whatever may be his current relationsip with the LORD. What is important here is on the one hand the ever present condemnation of Israel's apostasy, and on the other hand the paradoxical fact that subjugation or deliverance equally may be Israel's experience during their continued apostasy.

Robert Polzin. Moses and the Deuteronomist (New
York, Seabury Press, 1980), pp. 157–59

The courtiers' erroneous assumption that their bulky monarch is taking his leisurely time over the chamber pot is a touch of scatological humor at the expense of both king and followers, while it implicates them in the satiric portrayal of the king's credulity. This last effect is heightened by the presentation of their direct speech at the end of verse 24, and the switch of the narrative to their point of view in verses 23 and 24. Let me retranslate these clauses literally to reproduce the immediate effect of seeing the scene through their eyes that one experiences in the Hebrew: "The courtiers came and saw, look, the doors of the upper chamber are locked. . . . They waited a long time and, look, he's not opening the doors of the upper chamber, and they took the keys and opened them, and, look, their lord is sprawled on the floor, dead." The syntax of the concluding clause nicely follows the rapid stages of their perception as at last they are disabused of their illusion: first they see their king prostrate, and then they realize, climactically, that he is dead. An enemy's obtuseness is always an inviting target for satire in time of war, but here the exposure of Moabite stupidity has a double thematic function: to show the blundering helplessness of the pagan oppressor when faced with a liberator raised up by the all-knowing God of Israel, and to demonstrate how these gullible Moabites, deprived of a leader, are bound to be inept in the war that immediately ensues.

In fact, great numbers of the Moabites are slaughtered at the fords of the Jordan, the location of the debacle perhaps suggesting that they allowed themselves to be drawn into an actual ambush, or at any rate, that they foolishly rushed into places where the entrenched Israelites could hold them at a terrific strategic disadvantage. Ehud's assassination of Eglon, then, is not only connected causally with the subsequent Moabite defeat but it is also a kind of emblematic prefiguration of it. The link between the regicide and the war of liberation is reinforced by two punning verbal clues. Ehud thrusts *(tq')* the dagger into Eglon's belly (v. 21), and as soon as he makes good his escape (v. 27), he blasts the ram's horn —the same verb, *tq'*—to rally his troops. The Israelites kill 10,000 Moabites, "everyone a lusty man and a brave man" (v. 29), but the word for "lusty," *shamen,* also means "fat," so the Moabites are "laid low [or subjugated] under the hand of Israel" (v. 30) in a neat parallel to the fate of their fat master under the swift left hand of Ehud. In all this, as I have said, it is quite possible that the writer faithfully represents the historical data without addition or substantive embellishment. The organization of the narrative, however, its lexical and syntactic choices, its small shifts in point of view, its brief but strategic uses of dialogue, produce an imaginative reenactment of the historical event, conferring upon it a strong attitudinal definition and discovering in it a pattern of meaning. It is perhaps less historicized fiction than fictionalized history—history in which the feeling and the meaning of events are concretely realized through the technical resources of prose fiction.

Robert Alter. *The Art of Biblical Narrative* (New York, Basic Books, 1981), pp. 39–41

ELIJAH

The most dramatic story of all is that of Elijah. Lively and vigorous dialogue, sudden entrances and exits, the clash of strong wills, scenes and characters that inspire fear and pity, rapid action, climax, victory and defeat, all these are of the drama, and all these will be found in the story of Elijah.

The personality of this prophet is generally admitted to be the most dramatic in the Old Testament. His entrance into the history is sudden, and the obscurity of his private life only enhances the glamour of his public appearances. These are rare and only occasioned by some sin of exceptional magnitude committed by the reigning house. He comes to denounce, and he departs on each occasion as abruptly as he came.

Elijah's will clashes with Jezebel's as they fight for the conscience of Ahab. The dramatic scenes are numerous, the meeting, after the famine, between Elijah and Ahab, arranged through Obadiah, the trial of fire on Mount Carmel, the announcement of the rain, the revelation to Elijah in the desert, the call of Elisha, and the ascension of Elijah. Notice how the coming of the rain is announced. The employment of the boy as messenger keeps up the suspense, and the reader uses the boy's eyes, and the cloud is described in direct speech. It is the same dramatic use of an additional actor as the use of a watchman in the stories of Jehu and of the death of Absalom. The scene on Mount Carmel is the terrible climax, but the action moves rapidly, and failure follows on the heels of triumph.

Everything Elijah does is dramatic. In calling Elisha to be prophet, he casts his mantle over him, as he follows the plough, and leaves him without a word. His action in II Kings 1 is like the rest. The final scene is a worthy close to the drama. Elijah impresses us so powerfully that one feels that artistic propriety, if nothing else, demands that he should not die like common men, but make a more dramatic exit. When he goes round to confirm the schools of prophets, to which he acted no doubt as an Archbishop to his clergy, the end is duly led up to by prophecies. "Knowest thou that the Lord will take away thy master from thy head to-day." And Elisha replied, "Yea, I know it; hold ye your peace." [II Kgs. 2:3] A new interest is given by the doubt whether Elisha will fully succeed to Elijah's powers. Elisha's great outcry closes the drama, "My father, my father, the chariots of Israel and the horsemen thereof." And he saw him no more.

Percy C. Sands. Literary Genius of the Old Testament
(Oxford, Clarendon Press, 1924), pp. 36–37, 40

The author seems to have been a man of rare spiritual insight and power, able to grasp the inner significance of Elijah's teaching. The story has lived for its spiritual quality quite as much as for its human interest, and stands out in high relief from its context. The style is not as smooth and flowing as in the life of David; there is a quality of rugged strength about it that is perfectly suited to the subject, and suggestive of Elijah's character and career. Throughout the narrative there is an absence of personal description of the prophet that seems intentional; apparently it was not Elijah as a man that interested the author, but Elijah as the man of God. The tales were chosen from this standpoint, and the personality they reveal is austere, remote, forbidding, even in his most human moment of despair on Horeb.

The author of the Elijah sequence was a preacher, a philosopher, a poet, and above all, an artist. He was not merely a national but a world dreamer, who saw the wide issues of life and approached universal problems with the impersonality of the seer. With the vision and creative vitality of genius, he infused life and power into a shabby fanatic who came from nowhere and disappeared as mysteriously as he appeared. With great restraint and an amazing economy of means, which suggest the artist's conscious pruning and elimination, he built up an epic structure.

Brooke Peters Church. The Israel Saga (New York,
Macmillan, 1932), pp. 276, 279.

The stories about Elijah (I [Kgs.] 17–19; 21) date from about 800 B.C. Like the early stories concerning Jeroboam I, Ahab, Jehu, and Joash, they are masterpieces from the best period of North Israelitic prose literature. The author of the

Elijah stories has full command of the resources of Hebrew style, and with simple means obtains brilliant effects. He thus conveys to the reader a vivid picture of the misery and suffering caused by a three-year famine, not by describing the people starving and by depicting gruesome scenes like that of II [Kgs.] 6:25–30, but indirectly. Elijah is fed miraculously by the ravens (I [Kgs.] 17:2–7), through the inexhaustible earthen jar of meal and cruse of oil belonging to the widow at Zarephath (17:8–16), and by an angel (19:5–8); Ahab himself and his major-domo, Obadiah, go through the land looking for pasturage to keep the horses and mules alive (18:3–6).

The author is particularly effective in dialogues (18:7–15, 17f.; 21:2f., 5–7) and in the description of scenes, whether charmingly simple (19:19–21), intensely dramatic (18:20–40), or even spiritually infused with the divine presence (19:9–14). His apposite use of irony and sacasm is unexcelled (18:27). But his greatest achievement is the living portrait of the gigantic figure of Elijah, a second Moses . . . with moments of heroic grandeur, as on Carmel (18:36–40), followed by moods of abject fear and utmost despair (19:2–10).

The similarity between the Elijah cycle and the political stories from the history of Israel's kings . . . is confined to literary excellence. Their authorship and character are wholly different. The political stories present the point of view of the court and nobility, and are the work of able historians; the Elijah stories reflect a plebian viewpoint (notably I [Kgs.] 21) and, originating on the lips of the common people, were redacted by an admirer of the prophet endowed with great literary talent. The first are factual and objective, the second legendary. In these stories, Elijah does not appear as a mere "man subject to like passions as we are," according to the prosiac characterization of [St.] James (5:17), but as a superman of heroic stature, contemplated by a reverent popular imagination through the haze of legend, the only champion of the God of Israel defying in solitary grandeur Ahab's displeasure and Jezebel's fury. . . .

The stories of Elijah are incomplete—the original beginning and end are lost—but, as in an ancient Greek torso, what remains seems somehow to have taken on the virtue of what is lost. The beginning of 17:1, by its very abruptness and suddenness, achieves an artistic effect and instantly conveys an impression of the swift, unpredictable appearances and disappearances of the prophet.

Robert H. Pfeiffer. *Introduction to the Old Testament*
(New York, Harper, 1941), pp. 403–5

In chapters 18 and 19 of I Kings, the account of the crisis on Mount Carmel and its sequel, the "second" revelation on Mount Sinai, we find the central, climactic events in Elijah's battle against Ba'l. The two chapters are marked strongly by traits of oral composition, and in their present form are little shaped by the Deuteronomistic historian. These chapters share with the Elijah cycle as a whole the shaping of Elijah into the figure of the new Moses. Elijah's translation to heaven in Transjordan opposite Jericho is strongly reminiscent of Moses' death. The dramatic parting of the river Jordan by Elijah, like the splitting of the river in the

Gilgal cult, carries the symbolism of the splitting of the sea by Moses. Elisha plays the minister of Elijah (I Kgs. 17:21) as Joshua is minister (*meshārēt*) to Moses, succeeds him, and crosses Jordan on dry ground in the path of Joshua.

More important for our purposes are the parallels in the episodes at Carmel and Sinai. At Carmel the events are shaped into the pattern of covenant making. As Moses built an altar at Sinai and set up twelve stones for the twelve tribes (Exod. 24:4), and Joshua erected the twelve stones at Gilgal in the Gilgal covenant festival (Josh. 4:3), so Elijah built an altar of twelve stones "according to the number of the tribes" of Israel (I Kgs. 17:31). Similarly we find the covenant-motif "cleansing from alien gods" in the Carmel episode, beginning in Elijah's words, "How long will you straddle either side? If Yahweh be God follow him, and if Ba'l, follow him." [I Kgs. 18:21], and ending in Elijah's command to slay the prophets of Ba'l [I Kgs. 18:40]. While this motif is more familiar from Joshua's speech in Joshua 24, it is found also at Sinai in the aftermath of the affair of the golden bull. Moses said, "Whoever is on the side of Yahweh, [rally] to me" [Exod. 32:26]. Moses then led the Levites in a slaughter of the devotees of the bull.

Parallels between Moses and Elijah in the episode at Sinai in I Kings 19 are even more striking. In the present form of the Sinai traditions, Moses returned into the mount for a second sojourn, following the slaughter of the apostates. Probably we have to do here with a doublet in the Epic tradition. At all events, Elijah's sojourn in Sinai is parallel to this second sojourn, immediately following the slaughter of the prophets of Ba'l. In fear, rage, and dispair, Elijah fled, and under divine guidance and care was led to Sinai. The account of the sojourn in the mount in I Kings 19:9–14 shows direct dependence on the archaic lore of Exodus 33:17–23; 34:6–8. Elijah "came thence to *the* cave," that is, the "hole in the rock" [I Kgs. 19:9a parallel to Exod. 33:12f.] where Moses had been hidden. Not only did Elijah return to the holy mountain; he returned to the very site of Yahweh's supreme revelation to Moses, the theophany in which Yahweh passed by Moses in the cave, reciting his own names in Moses' hearing, and, granting Moses his request, permitted him, a mortal, a glimpse of the back of his "Glory." From the point of view of the traditionist who composed the pericope in Exodus 33:12–23, Yahweh's "passing" and Moses' glimpse of his back represented the ultimate approach of the godhead to Israel, the definitive revelation. The narrative in I Kings 18 and 19 has prepared us for a repetition of this theophany, the most audacious parallelism between Moses and Elijah.

> Frank M. Cross. *Canaanite Myth and Hebrew Epic* (Cambridge, Mass., Harvard University Press, 1973), pp. 191–93

The main goal of the author of the story of Elijah's battle against Baal worship is to perpetuate the impression and the influence of the episode of the drought and the test on Carmel as everlasting evidence of the nothingness of Baal and the exclusive divinity of the Lord. As far as we can tell, the struggle with Baal worship is not for him a legacy from the past but rather an actual concern in which Elijah the prophet takes a part by means of his story. To this end the author makes felt the awesomeness of the famine in Sarephath and in Samaria, describes at great length the conditions of the test on Carmel and the fullness of effort of the two contending sides, and emphasizes the magnitude of the reaction of all present to the falling of the Lord's fire on his altar. Yet, because in spite of all this Baal worship continued in Israel, the main theme of the story is not *victory* (which was temporary) but *miracle* (whose force is enduring). "All the people's " falling prostrate, the cry " The Lord is God," and the seizure of the Baal prophets at the command of the Lord's prophet are presented as testimony to the authenticity and power of the miracle, a miracle that the succeeding generations could ignore only at their peril. Their response to what happened on Carmel depends to a decisive degree on the story's power to bring the past to life in so authentic a form that the feet of the reader, too, stand on the heights of Carmel on that great day, and his mouth too cries, "The Lord is God!" This could not have been achieved without construing the character of the prophet as the man who did battle against the Baal prophets in his zeal for the Lord and who earned for Israel the miracle of the fire and the blessing of rain out of his love for his people. [Gerhard] von Rad is correct in saying that "the subject of the Elijah stories is basically not the prophet himself, but Jahweh" ([*Old Testament Theology*. Tr. by D. M. G. Stalker, 1965, Vol. II, p. 24]), for the personality and actions of the prophet come to provide the signs and miracles with a surfeit of reality by force of anchoring them in historical circumstances and human realia.

There is, then, no place for the common problem: What (connection) is there between the Carmel narrative and the miracle stories in chapter 17, which all happened on the private level and make no mention of Baal worship? The claim that the episode of the drought and test is understandable even without the background of Elijah's events at Wadi Kerith and Sarephath only seems to be well-founded. For such an understanding can only be incomplete, because the analogy between the private and public events is what imbues the latter with the prophet's personality, providing them with biographical depth and comparative continuity. It emerged from our close reading of chapter 18 that the key to putting Obadiah, Ahab, and Israel through tests lies in putting the widow through the test, for both Obadiah's recoil from the prophet as the one who brings disaster and Ahab's hostility to him as the "ruiner of Israel" were set up by the confrontation between the prophet and the widow. This analogical connection is valid because it holds not only for the reader but also for the protagonist of the story. After all, the prophet's actions in chapter 17 not only illuminate his actions on Carmel; they actually set them up. Elijah's success in reviving the widow's son serves to make him understand the expressions of suspicion and hostility from those to whom he is bringing the blessing of rain. The one who responded with flour and oil at Sarephath will respond with fire and rain on Carmel; and the one who stretched over the boy and prevailed over death, will bend over the ground of Carmel and will hasten the end of the drought; the one who brought the Sidonian woman who was about to throw him out of her house to declare "The Lord has spoken truth through your mouth" will bring the Israelites who refrained from saying a word to him to cry out: "The Lord is God, the Lord is God."

Uriel Simon. 'Iyyunei miqra' ufarshanut. Ed. by M. Goshen-Gottstein and U. Simon (Ramat Gan, Israel, Bar Ilan University, 1980), pp. 115–16†

An excellent example of a carefully woven literary tissue is the group of tales about Elijah in I Kings 17–19. Although several other Elijah stories lie close by (I Kgs. 21; II Kgs. 1–2), this group is set off by the deuteronomic material in I Kings 16 and an unrelated war story in I Kings 20. Moreover, only I Kings 17–19 within the Elijah cycle has as its central theme the battle for the establishment of the exclusive worship of Yahweh in Israel against the forces of Baal. Thus its placement and theme justify the consideration of it as a separable literary composition. Of course, many of its episodes may originally have circulated independently; the signs of multiple authorship and redaction are clear. Yet, at the same time, the narrative as a whole has been carefully shaped both thematically and structurally.

Thematically, the narrative operates on two levels. On one level, it presents the sacred biography of the prophet Elijah from his first appearance in Israel until the appointment of his successor. In three parts, corresponding basically to the present chapter divisions, the narrative charts the coming of age of Elijah, his public life, and his resignation from office. On another level, the life of Elijah serves as a context for the struggle between Yahweh and the forces of Baal in Israel. Implicit in the first part, Yahweh's defeat of Baal becomes explicit in the public arena in the contest on Mount Carmel. And the third part points to the final victory of Yahweh in the future.

Structurally, the artistry of the narrative may be seen from two perspectives. On the one hand, the episodes are arranged in a logical linear progression. Although they may originally have functioned in other contexts, they have been creatively integrated into this narrative and subordinated to its theme and purpose. Through the repetition of key-words and motifs, the discrete episodes become scenes in an ordered drama. On the other hand, each of the three chapters displays the same sequence of elements. This parallel development creates a set of correspondences cutting across the three chapters and reinforcing the unity of the whole. Parallel episodes build upon each other and thus generate a cumulative logic subliminally undergirding the narrative . . . .

The subordination of individual episodes, some of which may have circulated independently, into the present narrative context has created a whole greater than the sum of its parts. To excise verses or scenes as "secondary" may (or may not!) help to recover the original text but destroys the art of the received text. For the individual scenes derive their full meaning from the context into which they have been placed. To be sure, the history of interpretation, both ancient and modern, has focused on certain episodes apart from their contexts.

Thus the contest on Carmel and the theophany at Horeb have frequently been seen as individual classic expressions of the power of the God of Israel. Yet, however stunning these scenes are in isolation, their meaning is truncated when they are lifted from the narrative contexts into which the biblical author has placed them. Their placement within the narrative as a whole determines the perspective in which the author meant them to be viewed.

Elijah's great triumph on Mount Carmel, for instance, is brought into new focus by Jezebel's revenge. However decisive the victory might have seemed as Elijah races ahead of Ahab to Jezreel, he runs directly into Jezebel who is still in control. In light of Yahweh's directives to Elijah on Horeb, the fire on Carmel is seen to be but the beginning in a battle against Baal which must continue. Similarly, the placement of the sublime account of the "still small voice," a masterpiece of biblical expression, after the Carmel scene gives it a special dimension. The author thus creates the most dramatic of contrasts between the silence of Baal and the voice of Yahweh which is beyond not within the elements of nature that Baal was believed to control.

Robert L. Cohn. Journal of Biblical Literature. Sept. 1982, pp. 333–34, 349–50

ELISHA

[With] Elisha we seem to see a change of another kind affecting prophecy. Prophetic action will naturally include miracle, but we now begin to find the miraculous part of it becoming an interest in itself. The "sign of the prophet" is at first the symbolic act—tearing of robe or rending of altar—which serves merely as text for the prophetic message. But gradually it comes to be the wonder-working act which draws attention for its own sake: the cycle of Elisha stories reads for the most part as a succession of mystic wonders, much like the cycle of Samson with its feats of physical strength: wonders of axe heads swimming, a cruse of oil multiplying, children cursed and destroyed by bears, leprosy healed or returning at the prophet's word. There appears a decadence, not in prophecy itself, but in the attitude of the public mind to prophecy; the wonder of the sign becomes to the onlooking people more than the moral truth which that sign is to convey.

Richard G. Moulton. The Modern Reader's Bible (New York, Macmillan, 1907), p. 1380

From the literary standpoint the story of Elisha is weak. It is a shadowy imitation of the history of Elijah, in some cases so palpable an imitation as to make it seem incredible that a writer could have copied so naïvely. It is very fragmentary, quite lacking in the unity and purpose of the earlier story, and sounds more like a collection of short anecdotes than a connected narrative. Almost every miracle that Elijah worked is repeated in some form by Elisha. Elijah healed the widow's son, Elisha the Shunamite woman's; Elijah performed the miracle of the cruse of oil, Elisha filled the jars of the prophet's wife; Elijah brought rain in time of drought, and Elisha with slight variation did likewise. Finally, when Elisha is dying, Joash at his bedside uses the same words that Elisha uttered when Elijah was translated, "My father, my father, the chariot of Israel and the horsemen thereof!" [II Kgs. 2:12]

A comparison between the two histories brings out in clear relief the difference between the artist and the craftsman, a distinction that is repeatedly apparent in Hebrew literature, where it can always be used to separate the lasting from the ephemeral. . . . The author of the Elisha sequence had none of . . . [Elijah's] creative ability, and his stories, except for the Naaman-Gehazi episode, which is clever though superficial, were mere shadows of his predecessor's, and so could leave no impress on time. The stories are diffuse, disconnected and chatty; the conception of deity petty and revengeful; the appeal personal and ephemeral. There is no basic structure, no building up to a climax. In their time they may have been of value, but when that time was passed they ceased to appeal to a wider public.

Brooke Peters Church. *The Israel Saga* (New York, Macmillan, 1932), pp. 278–79

Elisha in many respects looks like a double of Elijah, and some scholars have urged that the two cycles refer to a single prophet. Similar experiences are attributed to each (the revival of the widow's son, the parting of the Jordan with a mantle, and the calling down of punitive fire), and it is not beyond possibility that in instances the action of one has been credited by tradition to the other. But on the whole Elisha emerges as a prophet with a character all his own. The primary distinction is that Elijah was a solitary champion of Yahweh, while Elisha was at the head of bands of prophets. . . .

The miraculous element in the Elisha cycle is extensive and as fantastic as the Old Testament affords. Miracle in the Old Testament is generally in the service of moral and religious purpose; the intrinsic meaning of the miracle is in its witness to God's purpose with his people. . . . But in the Elisha stories miracle is adventitious. It is used to enhance the skill and cunning of Elisha. We rather feel ourselves in the midst of a medieval saint's company. In fact, Elisha is the only figure in the Old Testament of whom miracles are related mainly to enhance the man; of all others, the miracle is the action of God—as often amazing to the Hebrew leaders as to the people. . . .

Of particular beauty is the account of the Syrian Naaman who humbled himself in search of an Israelite prophet to cure his dread leprosy and who was not disdained for being a foreigner. . . . The narrative stands also as one of the classic rebukes of venality.

Norman K. Gottwald. *A Light to the Nations: An Introduction to the Old Testament* (New York, Harper 1959), pp. 263–64

Elisha, it seems to me, is much less interesting as a character, not only because he is less mysterious than Elijah or because he spends most of his time at home giving directions to others, but because he has so few recognizably mortal characteristics. That he is usually the offstage prompter is evident from the narrative. In the moments which *do* reveal certain aspects of Elisha, it seems to me something important is missing. When he goes with Elijah to receive his mantle, Elijah three times tells him to stay put because the Lord has directed Elijah only to Bethel, Jericho, and the Jordan. Each time Elisha insists, "As the LORD lives, and as you yourself live, I will not leave you" (II Kgs. 2:6b). We get a sense of the firmness of Elisha. He is not going to take any orders from Elijah, and he is not prepared to go into sentimental mourning over Elijah's departure. He will remain with him to the end. When they get to the river, Elijah says," Ask what I shall do for you, before I am taken from you." And Elisha responds, "Let me inherit a double share of your spirit." Elijah rightly points out, "You have asked a hard thing" (vv. 9b–10a). It is not a humble request that Elisha makes, although not in context a proud one; but it indicates again his firmness, his certainty of what he is about to do. . . . After he hears that the king [of Israel] has rent his clothes, he sends him a message, "Why have you rent your clothes? Let him come now to me, that he may know that there is a prophet in Israel" (5:8). We are struck by, "Let him come now to me." Elisha is not going to go out for anyone except his Lord. When he is offered a reward by Naaman after he has cured him, Elisha refuses it: "As the LORD lives, whom I serve, I will receive none" (5:16b). Naaman urges him to take it, but Elisha continues to refuse. He expects no reward. He knows what he has to do, he has his assignment, his mission, and he is going to carry it out. He is completely committed—it is not a time for prizes, for compromises, for making accommodations. When he hears that his servant Gehazi has deceitfully taken the reward for himself, he criticizes and punishes him—"Was it a time to accept money and garments, olive orchards, and vineyards, sheep and oxen, menservants and maidservants? Therefore the leprosy of Naaman shall cleave to you, and to your descendants forever" (5:26b–27a). There is not much sympathy for others in Elisha, in part because of his enormous confidence, sense of authority and of mission. But he is wise. He tells the king of Israel, after the enemy has been defeated, "You shall not slay them. . . . Set bread and water before them, that they may eat and drink and go to their master" (6:20–22). Elisha is not excessive in his zeal, and he understands the need not to torture further or to kill a captured enemy force. All these episodes—and there are others— suggest what I believe is missing in the character of Elisha. He is certainly confident, self-assured, firm, and very impressive as a leader. But he never doubts, never questions; he is never rebuked; he never seems to have any awareness of his own position, any consciousness of the fact that he is isolated in the state; he never considers the possibility that he could be wrong. Elisha can instruct us, but we have difficulty arousing any feeling for him.

Kenneth R. R. Gros Louis. In *Literary Interpretations of Biblical Narratives* Ed. by Kenneth R. R. Gros Louis et al. (Nashville, Abingdon Press, 1974), pp. 184–86

ESTHER

The contrasted characters—the sensual monarch, the unscrupulous minister, the proud Puritan, the brave woman, brave with true womanly courage—are drawn in few lines, but with marvellous skill. The plot, with its play of character against character, its rapidity of movement, its dramatic incident, its plotting and counter-plotting, shows the highest constructive skill; and the moral inspiration of the story, inciting to hate of the sensuality of Xerxes and the crafty malice of Haman, to admiration for the courage of Mordecai, and a love that is more than admiration for the womanly bearing of the queen, is all the greater because the narrator does not formulate it; and the story is all the more religious in its spirit because it is so wholly free from the phraseology of religion in its language.

> Lyman Abbott. *The Life and Literature of the Ancient Hebrews* (Boston, Houghton Mifflin, 1902), p. 191

To many critics, moreover, the narrative as a whole seems to read as a romance rather than as a history: the incidents at each stage seem laid so as to prepare for the next, which duly follows without hitch or interruption. It is true, certainly, that considerable art is shown in the composition of the book. Mordecai and Haman stand in manifest contrast to each other; the two edicts and the circumstances of their promulgation (3:12–15; 8:10–17) are similarly contrasted; the climax of difficulty and danger for the Jews is reached, from which, by an unexpected turn of events, they are suddenly released; the double banquet (5:4–8; 7:1) allows scope in the interval for the contrasted pictures, first of Haman's exultation (5:9–14), then of his vexation (6:11–13)—a prelude and omen of the greater humiliation that is to follow (ch. 7). Fact, however, is proverbially sometimes stranger than fiction: so that it is somewhat precarious to build a far-reaching argument upon appearances of this nature. At the same time, it must be allowed that incidents thus mutually related are *accumulated* in Esther; and they, at least, authorize the inference that, whatever materials the narrator may have had at his disposal, he has elaborated them with the conscious design of exhibiting vividly the dramatic contrasts which they suggested to him.

> Samuel R. Driver. *An Introduction to the Literature of the Old Testament*. 10th ed., rev. and enl. (New York, Scribner's, 1903), pp. 482–83

We are dealing in the first instance with *fairy-tale motifs*. Primitive narrative is more childlike than the stricter "history" that arose only in later cultural development; primitive narrative arranges life according to its poetic needs, and with uninhibited credulity considers many things possible that certainly do not occur in prosaic reality. Hence it is in keeping with the oldest narrative style that the queen's banquet takes place three times; here the author surely does not consider the fact that it is particularly advisable at court to make the most of the one favorable all-too-fleeting hour. For the childlike mode of thinking it seems quite reasonable that the state itself guarantees men their domestic right against women's attempts at rebellion—whereby, of course, the wish is probably father to the thought. And how appealing is the idea of an unknown young girl's being raised to the throne and in that way being able to become a rescuing angel for her people, although real kings do not usually marry unknown maidens. And likewise, Mordecai must immediately become "the second" in the realm: In folkloristic style the hero finally becomes king (how many fairy tales end in this way!); but, to be sure, in the Persian realm this will not do at all for a Jew, and so one probably has to be satisfied with his having the position of first minister.

More frequent by far than such childishnesses, however, and by far less harmless, are the exaggerations that the book contains. A series of these originate in the sense of admiration that the grandeur and might of the empire inspire. The king in his lavishly munificent mood must straightway be prepared to make a present of "half of the kingdom," for otherwise he is no real king! The festival for his coronation must last one hundred eighty days; after all, it is a regal festival! And the maidens must take a whole year to get themselves ready for him; that is what is seemly for those who are to please the sovereign of the world! In wretched reality even the ruler of a great realm has only many— perhaps even very many—maidens in his harem; but here *all* the beautiful virgins are brought before him. And how rich is such a king who has at his disposal the treasures of the entire world: he makes a present of ten thousand talents as if they were nothing at all! In this way, too, does one picture in the most luminous colors the magnificence he offers his guests or the splendors bestowed upon his favorites. With awe and wonder one gazes upon the court etiquette that surrounds him; but one pictures it as so strict that even the queen, if she is not summoned, has no means of approaching him without endangering her life. It is whispered about that even the autocrat secretly lets himself be guided by his wife and his minister, that he makes decisions about matters that are little known to him and thereby calmly glosses over the life and death of his subjects. However, to allow himself to be so quickly influenced as to enact such bloody decrees—as is here the case—would in real life indicate a foolish imprudence and at the same time a terrible cruelty. Consequently even Haman is all too swiftly condemned and executed, and Mordecai is all too rapidly raised up; in real life both events would of course not take place quite so quickly. The Persian realm is indeed large, and the Persian chancellery must write in many kinds of languages and scripts; but that the realm is so extensive that it takes its messengers, traveling with the utmost speed from the capital city, nine months to reach the frontier provinces is surely greatly exaggerated. Likewise exaggerated is the assertion that the Persian state scribes make use of as many languages and scripts as there are regions and peoples.

Hermann Gunkel. Esther (Tübingen, J. C. B. Mohr,
1916), pp. 50–51†

Whoever wrote it was a master in the art of omitting nonessentials and of concentrating attention upon what really counted. He knew how to grip his reader's at-

tention at the start, how to mass or distribute his details in harmony with his main design, and how to make each part of the narrative contribute its quota to the larger or superintending purpose. I do not forget the story of Joseph, the idyllic charm of Ruth, or the fragments of vivid epics found in Judges. But Esther, more than any of these, seems to me a sort of anticipation of an art that is to-day considered almost distinctively American—I mean the art of the modern short story.
. . .

One of the distinctive excellencies of the story lies in the handling of the background and in making it subserve the underlying purpose of the narrative. You remember that Shakespeare begins *Macbeth* with the appearance of the witches who chant

Fair is foul and foul is fair.

This is one of the great keynote scenes in modern literature. Fair things were in fact to prove foul, and foul things fair; friends were to appear as enemies and enemies were to be disguised as friends. The entire play pivots around this chant of the witches. With equal art Esther begins with Persian bigness that was not greatness and pits consistently against it Jewish greatness that was not bigness. The Persian king ruled over one hundred and twenty-seven provinces; the Persian banquet lasted one hundred and eighty days and was topped off by a luncheon of seven days; the gallows prepared for Mordecai was eighty-three feet high; the money to be wrested from the Jews was eighteen million dollars. Against this background we see only a captive Jewish orphan, named Esther, and her cousin, named Mordecai. "Little is big and big is little" is the unsung refrain that binds together the diverse incidents of the story as the witches' words bind together the diverse incidents of Shakespeare's play.

But the characters are to me more interesting than the plot. The author of the story had not only an unerring feeling for background and incident but an equally sure eye for character traits. Each character is portrayed from within. A few deft strokes and the controlling motives stand clearly limned. In no other book of the Bible is there a more effective use of conversation, the direct words being given wherever vividness is desired. Ahasuerus, Memucan, Haman, Mordecai, and Esther all speak in the first person and all speak self-revealingly. This use of direct discourse is peculiarly a mark of the modern short story and is thus another link binding the technique of Esther to our own times. To feel the superiority of the direct form of statement here employed, recast some of the conversations and note the loss in force and appeal. Instead of "Who knoweth whether thou art come to the kingdom for such a time as this?" suppose the form had been: "Mordecai asked Esther if she was acquainted with any one who knew whether she was come to the kingdom for such a time as that." The skeleton remains, but the life has gone.

As in Genesis, so in Esther, each character is a type but also an individual. The two terms are often confused. The writer of Esther, like Shakespeare, probably had no conscious thought of the distinction here made between the individual and the type; but both wrote from life and in life the distinction is writ large upon every page.

Charles Alphonso Smith. *Keynote Studies in Keynote Books of the Bible* (New York, Fleming H. Revell, 1919), pp. 60, 63–64, 70–71

The outstanding feature of the book is its strong nationalistic spirit. It breathes the air of Ezra and Nehemiah with their intolerance of mixed marriages, whereas the Book of Ruth, which glorifies the marriage between a Jew and a Moabitess, might be regarded as a counterblast to this extremism. Throughout the story of Esther there is a strong current of artificiality. Poetic justice makes a strong appeal to everyone, but its appearance in real life is generally rare. In the structure of the story in the Book of Esther, poetic justice may be almost said to run riot. Haman had the right to demand reverence from Mordecai, but eventually it is Haman who has to do reverence to Mordecai. Haman prepared a gallows for Mordecai. Instead he is hanged on it himself. Haman had a ring given him by the king when he was promoted to the chief place next to the king. The ring and the position went to Mordecai. Haman had a fine house and possessions; these went to Esther. Haman and those who plotted with him the destruction of the Jews perished. The Jews, throughout the far-flung Persian empire, instead of being massacred on the day appointed, massacred their adversaries. The turning of the tables in every case is perfect. In fact, it is too perfect. There are no loose ends where one would expect and would, under the circumstances, value loose ends. We know that often the wish is father to the thought. In the Book of Esther the wish is parent to a great many thoughts.

Edward Robertson. *John Rylands Library Bulletin.* Dec., 1944, pp. 473–74

The narrative art of the Scroll of Esther cannot be compared with the modest, quiet, subdued tone of the classic stories of the Torah, the Prophets, or the Scroll of Ruth. It more properly belongs to the genre of the apocryphal books, such as the Book of Judith. Whereas biblical narrative is like the "land flowing with milk and honey" [Exod. 3:8]—wholesome, healthy, nourishing the soul—the narrative art of the Scroll of Esther bears the scent of a banquet of wine—pungent and irritating. Indeed, by dint of its pungency, tension, and provocativeness, the Scroll of Esther stands in contrast to the entire Bible. This fact finds its explanation in the circumstances and milieu out of which this Purim proclamation stemmed. It is these we must examine if we are to understand the nature of the Scroll of Esther. . . .

We do not find in the Scroll of Esther the scent of Israelite soil that pervades all the other narratives of the Bible. Here the milieu is entirely alien. The concerns that are described are foreign. The axis on which everything turns is the king. "The king": This is the word that is imprinted in the ears of all those who hear the Scroll. This is no wonder in a state dominated by a despot, the words of whose mouth determine life and death. Even so, if we compare, say, the words of Nehemiah, who also was a high official in the court of the king of Persia, we see that Nehemiah never forgets for a moment that "this man"—thus he refers to the king—is nothing but an instrument in the hands of God. In this Purim proclamation of the courtier Mordecai, however, it seems that the narrator's interest is devoted entirely to the concerns of the king and the glory of his court. How does the book's decisive scene, the account of Haman's fall, end? Not with a word of thanks to the saving God, not with an outburst of joy at the rescue of the people, but rather: "And the king's wrath subsided." As though all our anxiety were over whether the king's diabetes would get worse were he, heaven forbid, to get a little angry!

The entire book continues in this fashion. The elegant description of the banquet at the beginning of the book is unnecessary for the action itself, but in order to show the honored wealth of the king and the splendid glory of his grandeur, the writer depicts for us, just as in a Persian epic, the walkways of variegated stones in the king's garden, the purple drapery spread over the heads of the guests, and the one-of-a-kind [drinking] vesssels. . . . The narrator himself very much enjoyed his description because the court, with all its excesses and splendor, is the very world in which he lived. . . .

It is of interest to compare the Scroll of Esther with the story of Joseph. There, too, one of the Hebrews was made viceroy in an alien land. The greatness of Joseph [like that of Mordecai] is told with delight, but the Torah passes over this lightly and briefly. The main point is not the glorification of Joseph's prestige, but rather the human background, what happens between Joseph and his brothers. It is characteristic of the Scroll of Esther that every single personage is called by name, even those who have no importance, such as the king's seven wise men, Bigtan and Teresh, Shashgaz, and Hegai. Yet in the story of Joseph, even the butler, a decisive character in the narrative, is not designated by a name. The difference is understandable: a courtier is familiar with and concerned about the personages of the court, his colleagues. The Torah, however, comes to tell us only those matters that have a lesson in them. In the Joseph story we learn about Egyptian manners only what is necessary for the essence of the narrative. But the Scroll [of Esther] is so dedicated to describing the alien milieu that today it is considered to be one of the most faithful depictions of conditions in the Persian empire. In short, the Scroll of Esther is a diaspora book, written in the diaspora, for the diaspora, from the perspective of the diaspora. . . .

The narrative art of the Scroll of Esther is nothing but a mirror of life in the Persian court. Just as court life is full of suspense, rises and falls, shocks and revolutions, so is the narrative itself. . . . In general, the narrator is an artist of contrasts. At the moment that the banquet's happiness reaches its apex, it is turned into sorrow—with the fall of Vashti. . . . Just as we rejoice and are happy over Esther the Jewess becoming queen of Persia, Haman is elevated to power and orders the destruction of all the Jews. And so on. . . .

There is another important quality that is learned in the court of the king: the quality of restraint. Haman restrains himself when he sees Mordecai, Esther restrains herself twice when she approaches the king, and so does the narrator restrain himself by bringing us to our destination, not directly, but in a roundabout way and through delays. Esther did not become queen at once; we first have to go through the preparations in the harem with her. She is not ready immediately to act for her people. We learn of her hesitations and her refusals, and even after her consent we [i.e., the Jews] must fast for three days before the decisive step is taken. . . . The decisive step is not taken at the moment we expect it. Preceding it is a long sequence of unanticipated developments.

I find an even finer restraint in that the writer does not mention the name of God even once. There can be no doubt that he did this intentionally. The narrative, whose major subject is the persecution of the Jewish people on account of their religion, is entirely sacred and a religious narrative. If in spite of this the writer refrains from mentioning God's name even in a place where normal Hebrew idiom would require it, it is clear that we have here the modesty and humility of someone who does not want to resemble the holy writings that preceded him.

Shelomo Dov Goitein. '*Omanut hassippur bammiqra*'
(Jerusalem, The Jewish Agency, 1957), pp. 66–72†

We now can turn to an analysis of the central characters in our story. The couple-arrangement as outlined above by itself indicates the "type" approach of the author. One observes a marked homogeneity between the components of each pair. In all three cases the couple provides for a double representation of their inherent characteristics. True, there are some differences in the weight apportioned to the individual components. Vashti and Zeresh merely bring into better relief the distinct features portrayed in their respective partners. In the Mordecai-Esther combination the relationship is reversed. Esther plays the major role. But thus the equilibrium of the triangle is maintained. The typological factor is further underlined by the lack of depth in the portrayal of the heroes which becomes even more obvious in the bare delineation of the minor figures, e.g. Ahasuerus' courtiers, Esther's maids or Haman's sons. In contrast to the biblical historical narrative, as best seen in the David-stories, the heroes of the Esther-narrative do not undergo any meaningful development. The situations change—the dramatis personae remain static in character.

Rather than ascribe this one-dimensional depiction of the main figures to the inadequate literary skill of the writer, as [Hermann] Gunkel asserts with regard to the introductory part of the narrative, we tend to derive it from the moralizing tenor of the story. The author is not interested in the dramatis personae on their own account, but in the values, virtues and vices which they represent. In fact the glossing over of strictly individual traits enhances the general applicability of the moral illustrated and is perfectly in tune with wisdom narration.

In essence the three couples exemplify the traditional wisdom-triangle: the powerful, but witless dupe—the righteous wise—the conniving schemer.

The "witless dupe" obviously is represented by Ahasuerus. One has often remarked on the unbelievable stupidity displayed by the king throughout our story.
It is generally agreed that the portrayal of Ahasuerus, whom rabbinic tradition
aptly styled *t-p-sh* ["foolish"], cannot reflect historical reality. In a masterly re-
count Gunkel brings to the foreground the prevailing features in the description
of Ahasuerus and concludes that it was the author's intention to paint "*das Bild
eines persischen Herrschers, wie ihn sich die Untertanen vorstellen*" [the picture
of a Persian ruler as his subjects imagine him (Hermann Gunkel. *Esther*. Tübingen, J. C. B. Mohr, 1916, p. 64)]. This statement is somewhat misleading. In
the last analysis the Persian setting is of secondary importance. Ahasuerus is the
personification of the traditional "witless king" out of the book of the wise. This
figure has no intrinsic relations to Persian royalty, but rather is an "ideal" type
which was conceived by an eclectic process of abstraction and simplification
within a circumscribed literary tradition. This is the immature and gullible king
of the pitiable land with which Qoheleth commiserates (Eccl. 10:16; cp. Is. 3:4).

Wisdom teaching considers lack of wit not a regrettable inborne deficiency,
but a punishable defect. The power of perception can be improved by proper
training. Whosoever neglected to be adequately educated must pay for his negligence. One can learn to size up a situation and to make the best of it. Therefore,
defeat is anathema, even if incurred in the pursuance of lofty principles. There is
no room for the idealistic dreamer in the world of wisdom. Voluntary suffering,
when it can be averted, becries the fool. For these reasons the author of Esther
has not a word of pity, not to mention admiration, for Vashti who forfeited a
kingdom for mere sentiments of propriety. Such behavior can be attributed only
to sheer foolhardiness which makes Vashti a suitable companion for Ahasuerus.

Ahasuerus is so easily deceived that his weakness becomes the source of his
courtiers' corruption: When a ruler hearkeneth to falsehood, all his servants are
(become) wicked (Prov. 29:12). Unaware of his folly he waxes conceited, irrita-
ble and unpredictable. Sitting at table with him is a precarious affair since nobody can foresee his actions. Rulers like him the sage had in mind when he advises: When thou sittest to eat with a ruler, consider well what is before thee
(ibid. 23:1). And things will happen. The king's anger easily flares up and then
woe to the man who caused it (Prov. 20:2). His reactions are swift, uncontem-
plated and therefore soon regretted. The sequence of emotions which recurrently
is attributed to Ahasuerus is a stereotype in wisdom literature: his anger is kindled (Esth. 1:12, cp. 7:4), he acts with inane haste (ibid. 5:19–21), e.g. condemning a villain for a crime he had not committed (ibid. 7:9), and regrets his
deeds once he returns to his senses (ibid. 2:1).

In the same fashion the Assyrian king Esarhaddon, enraged by the accusations of Nadin, orders the execution of the faithful Ahiqar without even stopping
to contemplate the matter, just as his father Sennacherib had acted in his time on
a different occasion. . . .

Neither Sennacherib, Esarhaddon or Ahasuerus intentionally do evil. Their
behaviour rather is immature. They can be led to acknowledge their mistakes, or

at least to reconsider their hasty decisions. Thus Ahiqar and Esther are able to prevent harm by speaking the right words at the appropriate time. This goes to prove that though "a king's rage is like the angel of death, a wise man will pacify him" (Prov. 16:14).

Shemaryahu Talmon. *Vetus Testamentum*. 13, 1963, pp. 440–43

Even though the style of Esther is admittedly "awkward and laboured," . . . the story is nonetheless told in a clear and interesting way. Since the author was writing a historical novel and could have far greater freedom with his sources than, say, the authors of Genesis who had to operate within well-established traditions, he had virtually a free hand in structuring his plot. For example, the story of Vashti was probably an unrelated harem tale which the author adopted (and adapted) because, in addition to explaining how and why Xerxes deposed his first queen and began looking for another, it also provides a colorful and interesting introduction to Xerxes and his court. . . . The author is free enough to make even Zeresh, the wife of Mordecai's sworn enemy, the spokesman for his own Jewish ethnic pride (6:13).

The plot is skillfully constructed, with due attention given to increasing suspense and the reader's interest. For example, Esther, under pain of death, goes unsummoned to the king (4:11–5:2); on two separate occasions she *refuses* to state her petition to the king in spite of his promise to grant her any request (5: 4, 8); and the king asks Haman how he should honor the very man Haman plans to hang the next day (5:14, 6:6).

The author is especially interested and effective in his use of irony. For example, Vashti was deposed for being disobedient once (1:17–19)—Esther was disobedient twice and yet was rewarded (5:1–2, 8); Haman obeyed the king's command, humiliating though it was (6:11–12)—Mordecai deliberately disobeyed a royal command, yet was handsomely rewarded (3:2, 8:1–2); the city wept while the king and Haman drank (3:15); Haman, thinking that he was prescribing royal honors for himself was actually prescribing them for Mordecai, his bitter enemy (6:6–9); Haman was hanged on the gallows which he had intended for Mordecai (7:9–10).

While chapters 1–2 and 8–10 are reportial or descriptive in character, chapters 3–7 are quite dramatic, in part because of the author's effective use of irony (see above) and direct address (see 3:3, 8–9, 11; 4:11, 13–14, 16; 5:3–5, 6–8, 12–14; 6:3–11, 13; 7:2–6, 8–10).

There are very few really puzzling passages in the book, in part because the author, or an early glossator, explains many of the foreign words and practices. . . . Repetition, *the* characteristic literary weakness of the book, is also one of its strengths: this very frequent repetition in the form of identical or synonymous words, phrases, and even entire sentences makes for greater clarity. . . . The Greek translator of Esther was a sophisticated stylist who so disapproved of these redundancies and repetitions that he deliberately omitted them.

Carey A. Moore. *Esther, The Anchor Bible*. Vol. 7B (Garden City, N.Y., Doubleday, 1971), pp. lv–lvi

Esther is in many ways like Judith. The story is about a beautiful Jewish woman who uses her charms on a heathen king in order to save her people from destruction. The story is better told than the first half of Judith but less well than the second. In character it is, briefly, more sophisticated and less pious than Judith. Its greater sophistication is shown, for example, in the presence of what pretend to be historical documents (in chs. 13–16—only found in the Greek additions); in the sustained irony of the king's treatment of the villain Haman (chs. 7 and 8); and in the enjoyment of the sexual aspects of the story (e.g. 7:8, 2:12–14). Its lesser piety is shown, for example, in the lack of conviction in prayers (e.g. 14:18; the prayers, too, are found only in the Greek additions); in the reluctance of the heroine Esther to help her people in the hour of need (4:11); and in the replacement of religious by nationalistic feeling.

> J. C. Dancy. *The Shorter Books of the Apocrypha* (Cambridge, England, Cambridge University Press, 1972), p. 131

The outstanding literary characteristic of the author of Esther is his interest in the swift flow of the action. He, therefore, strips the plot of all nonessentials, concentrating on events rather than on motivations, on incidents rather than on descriptions of character. Thus, he does not inform us as to the reasons for the king's two banquets, or Vashti's disobedience, or the grounds for Bigthan and Teresh's conspiracy. We are not told why Mordecai instructs Esther not to reveal her origin, nor why he himself refuses to bow down to Haman.

Because of the same over-riding consideration, the author does not concern himself with filling in the background against which the incidents take place. The structure of government and administration in Persia, the relations subsisting between the Jews and the general population, the religious practices and ethnic customs of the people—all these are passed over in silence, so as not to impede the swift pace of the narrative.

It is, therefore, necessary for the reader to be on the alert for hints that shed light on various aspects of the book. A meticulous examination of the text can disclose significant insights into such subjects as the social stratification in Persia, the official position of Mordecai, and the terms of the edict issued after Haman's downfall, in addition to various other aspects of the book.

> Robert Gordis. *Journal of Biblical Literature*. March, 1976, p. 45

EXODUS

Genesis is a great artistic whole; Exodus consists of a chaotic débris of brilliant fragments of historical romances. Egypt for the Hebrews, as for the old Greeks, was the land of marvels. It lay at the end of an easy caravan journey from

Palestine, but its people were essentially as queer to the Hebrews as they were to Herodotus. Things went there, and people did them, in a different way. The natural phenomena even were very different. Amos had seen the inundation of the Nile and it was for him a picture of the quivering of the soil in an earthquake (8:8). Signs and wonders, then, were fully in place in such a land. And it was with signs and wonders that Jehovah had brought His people up out of Egypt. But the narrative which tells this is jumbled, broken, repeated, to the despair of commentators. Yet there survive brilliant pictures in it: Moses holding out his rod against the sky; a glittering net of hail and lightning flashes. . . .

Such pictures show the work, surviving in scraps, of a conscious, descriptive artist. But the confusion is there, too. What lies behind this confusion? We may conjecture a combination of historical romances. . . . The present hypothesis is that we must posit such a group of early Hebrew romances as lying behind the stories of the Exodus and the desert wanderings. This would explain the often picturesque phrases and elaborate detail; the very popular heaping up of wonders; the confusions and repetitions. It enables us to retain the broad historical event, guaranteed again and again by the Hebrew tradition; the outstanding historical figures; the essential reality of the spiritual fact. The imagination of the people, working on the known marvels of Egypt, would furnish the wild tangle of the rest.

> Duncan B. MacDonald. *The Hebrew Literary Genius*
> (Princeton, N.J., Princeton University Press, 1933),
> pp. 135–36

Superb is the ending of Exodus. The glory of God fills the newly finished Tabernacle and his Chosen People march on guided by the Pillar of Cloud by day and by the Pillar of Fire by night. The book as a whole, even though the movement is retarded by legal codes and by building specifications, has an onward and inevitable sweep. A magnificent panorama it is, bringing forward the narrative of the chosen people to their wanderings in the wilderness. . . . Whether the Exodus took place under Mineptah about 1220 B.C., or under Ahmosi I in 1580 B.C., or, as some destructive critics would have us believe, never took place at all, is not of interest from the literary standpoint. The Book of Exodus remains the world's great epic of Deliverance, the epic of the most remarkable and most influential people of which history has record, and this deliverance has so stamped itself on the mind of that people that after well nigh three thousand years it still forms the theme of their most solemn annual festival.

> John R. Macarthur. *Biblical Literature and Its Backgrounds* (New York, Appleton, 1936), p. 115

The prose of the book varies in accordance with its subject matter, which, as we have seen, consists of narratives, laws, and architectural descriptions. The law is set down, considering its age, in a fixed and fully developed legal terminology, clear and succinct, rarely resorting to roundabout phrases or falling into redundancy. The salient point of law or rule is put in an opening sentence with corollaries, exceptions and extenuating circumstance following in parallel or semi-dependent clauses. The phrasing of some of the laws is so taut and compressed that it hits us with the force with which David's pebble discomfitted Goliath. Only in one instance, in that of the *lex talionis*, is the full impact of its energetic, pithy brevity felt in translation. But even in this instance, the Hebrew *shen tahat shen* (tooth for tooth), *ayin tahat ayin* (eye for eye), is the more terse and explosive. Elsewhere renditions give us the content of the law but in no way approximate the inimitable brevity of its form. Compare, by way of illustration, the Hebrew with the King James Version in the following three statements:

makkeh 'ish va-met mot yumat.	He that smiteth a man, so that he die, shall surely be put to death. [21:12]
Ve-gonev 'ish u-me-kharo ve-nimtsa veyado mot yumat.	And he that stealeth a man and selleth him, or if he be found in his hand, he shall surely be put to death. [21:16]
'elohim lo tekallel ve-nasi be'amkha lo ta'or.	Thou shalt not revile God, nor curse a ruler of thy people. [22:28]

In the last example the reader will have recognized the familiar Biblical parallelism, the distinguishing feature of Hebrew poetry.

The construction of the tabernacle and its furniture and the manufacture of the priests' garments are described in language that is equally precise, concise and refined. The narrator goes about his task with consummate skill as if he were himself the artist, designer and craftsman, and had himself conceived and executed the whole pattern. First he assembles in five brief verses all the necessary material, the bright metals, the fine fabrics, the dyed skins, the polished wood, the pure oil, the sweet spices, the fragrant incense, and the resplendent stones. Next, while our dazzled eyes are still fixed on the precious stuffs, he tells us in less than a score of rapid syllables, in a stich whose last two words delicately balance its first, that it will be employed in the making of God's sanctuary. A final prefatory sentence emphasizes the thought that the pattern of the work was designed by God Himself. In the center of that design, as we proceed with the description, stands the tabernacle like the shaft of a seven-branched candelabra. Preceding it are to be found accounts of the ark, the table of the shewbread, and the menorah, and following it those of the altar, court, and priests' garments. Whether this arrangement has any symbolical or theological significance is a matter of conjecture. It may be that in giving the tabernacle its central position, the author meant to indicate a distinction between the objects that were to converge more immediately on the Deity and the others which were to be more in use by man. It may also be that he had no other purpose in mind than to relieve the monotony of impression by means of the symmetry of form. If he did not altogether succeed and is at times tedious, the fault lies in the technical nature of the subject and the fidelity with which he adheres to it and not in his lack of skill

as a writer. He made every stroke of his pencil count, fitting accessory and unavoidable details into a minimum of words as neatly as Bezalel did the onyx or
carbuncle into its ouch or setting. No matter how intricate an operation might be,
his account of it is as brief as it is lucid. Whether he casts rings of gold, or measures the length, breadth and height of a piece of acacia-wood, or models the
contours of the ark, or folds a canvas, or puts a clasp into a loop, or arrays Aaron
with his gorgeous long and flowing robe and leads him into the sanctuary, his
trail dragging slowly along to the cadence of its jingling bells, he remains the
master throughout. If nothing else the frequency with which prophets and psalmists adopted his imagery bears witness to the felicity of his delineations.

But unencumbered and meticulous as is the style of its legal and descriptive
portions, the grand simplicity and beauty of the prose of Exodus were reserved
for the narratives. It is in them that we find the same enduring aesthetic qualities
that we have observed in Genesis. Not that the two are altogether alike. They
could no more be that than are *Paradise Lost* and *Paradise Regained*. For they
differ in so many respects: in background, in *mis en scène*, in dramatis personae
and in the drift of the narration. The subject matter of Genesis is undefined and
uncommon and, one might say, is no longer to recur. "There can never be,"
wrote [William] Hazlitt, "another Jacob's dream. Since that time the heavens
have gone farther off, and grown astronomical." There will certainly not be
again another Creation or any of the things related in the first eleven chapters of
the book, nor will it be treated with the freshness, simplicity, and naiveté it is
there dealt with. There the author reverently drew aside for a fleeting moment the
curtain which forever conceals the mystery of cosmic and human beginnings.
Fortunately he possessed the genius and faith to clothe the awful majesty his
eyes beheld in the sublimity of the Hebrew idiom. Here no such opportunity presented itself. Even the vision of the burning bush and the Sinaitic theophany, of
which as we shall soon see the author took full advantage, are echoes of Creation
and previous revelations. It is the God of the Fathers calling, upon whom Moses
had enduringly meditated and of whom even the people had vague recollections.
In Genesis, if we may so put it, we come upon the artist when he first conceives
the image in his mind, in Exodus we watch him transfer it to the canvas.

Solomon Goldman. *From Slavery to Freedom* (New
York, Abelard Schuman, 1958), pp. 27–29

The opening chapters of Exodus, through their reverberating language and thematic motifs, contain echoes of the entire book of Genesis. Similarly, the following chapters of Exodus pick up the reverberations of the language and themes of
these first two chapters, now enhanced with new content and meaning. A dominant theme which we have noted throughout this story, broken only by the final
three verses, is the behind-the-scenes activity of God. This contrasts sharply with
the description of divine intervention beginning in Exodus 3 and building to a climax in Chapters 15 and 19. In Exodus 3:7, which further develops the new form
of divine activity begun in 2:23–25, God states: "I have seen the affliction of my

people . . . and have heard their cry. . . . I know their sufferings, and I have come down to deliver them . . . and to bring them up." The key word in this series is *yarad* "come down," which, as in the Tower of Babel story and elsewhere, heralds the mighty acts of God. Though mentioned explicitly only in connection with the midwives, the presence and activity of God are clearly perceived in the events surrounding Moses' birth. But what accounts for the silent, hidden characteristic of the Deity in this part of the narrative? I would propose that part of the answer lies in Genesis 46:3–4, where God says to Jacob, "Do not be afraid to go down to Egypt; for I will there make of you a great nation. I will go down with you to Egypt, and I will also bring you up." The key word in this series is again *yarad* "go down." Here the word is not heralding a mighty act of God; it is akin, I would suggest, to the archetypal theme of the descent into the underworld.

> James S. Ackerman. In Kenneth R. R. Gros Louis. *Literary Interpretations of Biblical Narratives* (Nashville, Abingdon Press, 1974), pp. 115–16

The story of the exodus from Egypt to Canaan meets the test of long narrative. The story is nationalistic in emphasis, recording the formation of Israel as a nation and depicting the decisive event in the early history of the nation. A great deal of the story is devoted to describing the values and doctrine that can be said to sum up the Hebrew spirit. The story is set in history and is filled with historical allusions. It is unified partly by a normative hero and partly by the quest for the promised land. The Epic of the Exodus displays a strong didactic impulse, and the presence of divine beings is pervasive. The only major way in which the Epic of the Exodus fails to meet the definition of epic is in the area of stylistics. There is virtually a total absence of the high style typical of epic. Instead of poetry there is prose. There is little pleonasm, little use of epithets or epic formulae.

Of all the famous epics, *the Aeneid* of Virgil is the clearest parallel to the Epic of the Exodus. Both epics tell about the formation of an empire and are a call to its readers to contemplate the early history of their nation. Both are quest stories in which a group of people travel from one geographic area to another in order to establish a stable nation in a promised land. Both stories are unified around a hero who is a leader of people and who embodies the normative values of the story. Both epics are religious epics, filled with references to the proper worship of deity. Both epics embody and praise the virtues accepted as being normative in the society from which the epics arose.

The parallels between the Epic of the Exodus and other epics should not be allowed to obscure the important way in which the biblical epic differs from traditional epic. Conventional epic is humanistic in the sense that it exists to praise and glorify a human hero. The conventional epic hero is godlike in his accomplishments; indeed, he may even be of divine parentage, as Aeneas is. Heroes like Aeneas or Achilles or Beowulf merit praise by virtue of their own superhuman deeds. Traditional epics focus on human endeavor and show man accomplishing heroic feats. Their stories are essentially stories of human merit. . . .

It is at once apparent that the Epic of the Exodus is, like Milton's epics, an anti-epic. Everywhere we find the traditional epic values inverted. For the praise of men, the writer has substituted the glory of God. Instead of depicting human strength, this epic depicts human frailty and sinfulness. Instead of a story in which a human warrior leads his nation to victory through superhuman feats on the battlefield, this narrative attributes the mighty acts of deliverance to God. Indeed, the human warriors are usually passive spectators of the mighty acts of God. Instead of a human leader who depends on his own qualities of greatness, the storyteller here depicts a reluctant leader who is unsure of his own claims to leadership, inarticulate, of obscure origin, and meek. Instead of exalting the nation about whom the epic is written, this epic continually stresses the imperfections of the Israelites—their rebelliousness, their lack of faith, their tendency to complain. Whereas the traditional epic stresses physical warfare, the Epic of the Exodus places even more emphasis on spiritual conflict. Moral rebellion against God frequently replaces the conventional theme of armed conflict between nations. The usual epic formulae and virtues are attributed to God rather than to a human hero. . . . Whatever glory there is in the epic belongs to God, who repeatedly contends with human sinfulness and leads the Israelites to Canaan in spite of themselves. This anti-epic theme reaches its culmination in the song that Moses sings shortly before his death (Deut. 32), a song that praises God's faithfulness and dispraises Israel's waywardness. The song has the whole weight of the previous story behind it and is the logical terminus of the anti-epic motif in the Epic of the Exodus.

Leland Ryken. The Literature of the Bible (Grand Rapids, Mich., Zondervan, 1974), pp. 81–83, 85

Chapters 1–2 are also important thematically. The outwitting of Pharaoh by the Hebrew midwives and by Moses' sister foreshadows the climactic events of the story (as does Moses' murder of the Egyptian) and serves to orient us to the literary world we are entering, analogous to the way "once upon a time" introduces us to a fairy tale world. We learn right away that this story belongs to the genre of folk story in which clever stratagems by the oppressed enable them to triumph over the superior but unjust forces of the wicked. And these anticipations of later events help us to sort out our allegiances and prepare us emotionally for the denouement. We know who is going to win and even how they are going to win. We also know whom we want to win: stories with clear-cut moral themes tend to arouse clear-cut emotions, a strong sympathy for the weaker party and an intense antipathy toward the stronger. It is crucial that we do not in any way sympathize with Pharaoh, so pains are taken to present him in an uncomplimentary light from the very beginning. . . .

A reticent hero is a typical convention of this type of folk story. He adds a welcome but quite tolerable tension to the story. Might Moses fail? Surely not

. . . but maybe. Aaron enters as reinforcement. He too performs a stereotyped role: the hero's sidekick. But Aaron is never well integrated into the story, and just as well could be edited out. Once Moses has returned to Egypt and has met Aaron, we are prepared for the confrontation with Pharaoh. . . .

Returning now to the definition of comedy as a story in which the hero is finally incorporated into the society to which he properly belongs, we recognize that Exodus 1–15 is a comedy. It has two heroes. The visible, immediate hero is Moses. The story begins with his estrangement from his kinsmen at birth and moves through his return to his people and final acceptance by them as leader. The invisible, ultimate hero is Yahweh. The story begins with estrangement, both physical (Yahweh is in Midian and his people in Egypt) and social/religious (Pharaoh is their king whereas Yahweh should be), and ends with reunion. The means by which the two heroes are integrated with their proper societies is the agon, or contest, between Moses and Pharaoh. As often in comedy at its best, this integration represents the establishment of a new community, a socially free and morally just one, which replaces an old, unjust one. As also often in comedy, the birth of the new society is marked by some festive celebration which ends the story or play (Exod. 15).

In most comedies there is a blocking agent, an *alazon*, an impostor, who obstructs the hero's path to the land of the free and home of the brave. Pharaoh, of course, is this agent. He must either be incorporated into the new society or cast out from it, in which case he becomes a *pharmakos*, or scapegoat. Because comedy as a genre tends toward the happiest possible ending, in many comedies the blocking agent is incorporated into the new society. Such is not the case in Exodus, where Pharaoh and his army are destroyed. Exodus is like most comedies, however, in that the force which brings about the overthrow of the *alazon* comes from beyond the human world, from Fate, or Chance, or the gods.

David Robertson. *The Old Testament and the Literary Critic* (Philadelphia, Fortress Press, 1977), pp. 19–20, 25–26

THE BURNING BUSH

The section which deals with the Revelation at the Burning Bush cannot be regarded as a compilation from varying sources and documents. All that is needed is to remove a few additions, and there appears before us a homogeneous picture; any apparent contradiction can be accounted for by the fact that the text has not been fully understood. The style and composition of this section show that it is the fruit of a highly cultivated dialectic and narrative art; but certain of the essential elements of which it is composed bear the stamp of early tradition.

Moses, tending the flocks of his father-in-law, leads them out of the accustomed steppe on one occasion; just as we hear of the Bedouins of the same district moving with their flocks into the hills, where the animals find pastures that are still green. There Moses suddenly finds himself at the "Mountain of God," Mount Horeb or Sinai. "Mountain of God" (or "of gods") had been its name since time untold, presumably because mysterious phenomena, either of volcanic or other character, take place on it and local tradition therefore claims that divine beings reside there. Here Moses sees the "burning bush." Just as the mountain is described as "*the* mountain of God," that is, the mountain known as "a god-mountain," so is the bush described as "*the* thornbush," that is, the specific bush which is known to grow upon Sinai. The name *seneh*, which is peculiar to it (no other kind of bush is called so) echoes the name of the mountain, which is omitted of set purpose at this point. The word *seneh* repeated three times in the same sentence suggests the name Sinai, that is used only when the nation reaches the mountain in order to receive the revelation. . . .

After the God tells his chosen one who he is, he reveals the cause and purpose of the message with which he wishes to entrust him. The sentence with which this partial address begins, and that with which it ends, balance one another like the members of a building, through the two key-words *ammi*, my people, and *Mitsraim*, Egypt. These are repeated in both, and denote the subject and the aim of the act: "I have indeed seen the sufferings of my people who are in Egypt" [Exod. 3:7, 10]. To attribute the two sentences, as is so often done, to different sources, constitutes a misunderstanding of the entire form and sense of the speech. With this repeated "my people" at the commencement and close of the passage, YHVH recognizes Israel in a fashion more powerful and unequivocal than would have been possible by any other verbal means. To be sure, he has not yet designated himself their God. He will become the God of Israel as a people solely through the revelation to the people; now he wishes to be known only as the God of their forefathers, to whom he had once promised the land whither he would lead Israel. But since he so stresses the naming of Israel as his people, he shows that the bond uniting them had been established of old. No new, no alien god talks in such a way. This likewise indicates the hopelessness of the attempt sometimes made to attribute this first speech, which refers to the patriarchs, to some later stratum of the text. Try to insert at this point the phrase assumed to have been in the original, namely "I am the god," i.e. "I am the god of this mountain," and the message, flaming with historical revelation and historical faith, shrinks, one might well say, to a private remark which conveys nothing.

And now begins the great duologue in which the God commands and the man resists. As we have it before us, it is clearly disfigured by supplements, inserted by editors, which should not be considered as sections of a source. To begin with, something is introduced between the two first objections of the resisting man, namely his inadequacy and his inability to tell the people what they would demand to hear of the name and hence of the character of the God, on the one hand; and the final passage which returns once again to his inadequacy, on the other. In the interpolated passage Moses asks how he can demonstrate the reliability of his message to the people and is instructed to perform wonders. Here later narrative motifs are introduced in evidence, largely in order to link the story of the revelation with that of the negotiations with Pharaoh; but by this both sections are impaired. The style differs here from that in the undoubtedly genuine parts of the narrative of the burning bush; it is more loose, more expansive, more wordy. Here necessity does not hold sway as it does there; the purposeful repetitions are replaced by casual ones; and finally a rhetorical note is to be heard. The hard rhythm has become a thin absence of rhythm, the firm composition has become negligent; even the structure of the sentences is careless. The contents do not resemble those of the genuine parts; questions and answers move at a lower level. In the genuine part every reply gives some essential information as to the will and work of the God; but here there is, so to speak, a technical atmosphere. [1946]

Martin Buber. Moses (New York, Harper, 1958), pp. 39, 45–46

The theophany of the burning bush depicts in dramatic imagery the growth of the superego along the lines of ethical monotheism. The taming of the instincts, the process of sublimation, the re-direction of psychic energy to moral and religious purposes, are symbolically portrayed, as Moses endeavors in truly heroic yet significantly human fashion, to identify with the God of Israel and the superego demands He represents.

The mechanisms of defense employed in the narrative make him as human in a psychological sense as he has been through the ages on a more intuitive level. As with all biblical heroes, Moses did not have greatness thrust upon him—he achieved it. In his situation, particularly, the imperfections common to man, are clearly attributed to him. Thus, the human tendency to deify "the great father" is guarded against.

Dorothy F. Zeligs. Moses: A Psychodynamic Study (New York, Human Sciences Press, 1985), pp. 77–78

THE TEN COMMANDMENTS

There is nothing ornate, circuitous, diffuse, or remote about them. The shortest of them, come upon us precipitately, like a rapid series of explosions. At first we barely distinguish them one from another. What re-echoes in our whole being is a resounding monosyllable, the Hebrew *lo* or the three English monosyllables "you shall not." The longest commandments are so phrased that the explanatory and completive matter can be peeled off without disturbing the essence or meaning, the intent or purpose of the law. "You shall not carve an image for yourself" is perfect and entire, and wanting in nothing. It excludes all images, anything resembling the likeness of anything else. Again a Hebrew monosyllable—*lekha* ["for yourself"]—speaks volumes. Make not an image, it says, to be in anyway related to you or a part of you, to be anything more than the inanimate and inert thing that it is. The additional matter, except for the threat and promise, does not carry us beyond this. . . .

The directness and familiarity of the language of the Decalogue [are strik-ing]. From the first to the last commandment it is the singular "thine, thine, thou, thou." It is God speaking directly to every man, pointing, as it were, His finger at him, impressing him with his worth, with his responsibility for action and that of his community. In the circumstances the individual is lifted out of the crowd, out of automatism, indifference, neutrality, and apathy. . . .

No less advantageous and effective than the directness and familiarity of the language of the Decalogue, has been its elasticity. Generally speaking this qual-ity is common to the whole Hebrew Bible. Almost all of its pages abound, as it were, in illustrative fragments, symbolic torsos, the unfinished, the suggestive, and the evocative. So it is not surprising that the words before us, which more than any were believed to be God's, should be elastic, easily capable of receiving and holding in their conciseness the richest and most elaborate codes, the product of a civilization far more advanced than that in which the Decalogue came into being.

However, far more than mnemonic devices, brevity, terseness, directness, and elasticity, it was intrinsic value that gained for the Decalogue universal rec-ognition and acceptance. Age after age this miniature code, presented in the Bi-ble much more as a thunderous overture to the rules and laws of the covenant be-tween God and Israel than as a system of law in itself, has been acclaimed as the foundation-stone of civilization, the anchor of associative living, a comprehen-sive summation of the fundamental duties of a human being toward God and his neighbor, laying down the basic articles of religion—the sovereignty and spiri-tuality of God, and asserting the claims of morality in the sphere of human relations—home, occupation, society, and, though addressed to one people, far from national narrowness. Its very words, its Thou shalt and Thou shalt not, have come to symbolize faithfulness, virtue, uprightness, moral rectitude, scrupulous-ness, good behavior, and goodheartedness. They have come to be employed as synonyms for temperance, continence, self-restraint, and self-discipline. They have been accepted as directives to men how best to live among themselves and up to God.

Solomon Goldman. From Slavery to Freedom (New York, Abelard Schuman, 1958), pp. 613–15

The Ten Commandments are replete with such elements of artistic form as or-dered recurrence, variation, balance, pattern, contrast, and centrality. Recur-rence according to a discernible order is evident in the series of ten main com-mandments, each phrased as a command and eight of the ten beginning with the repeated formula, "You shall not." Variation is played off against this recurrence by the interspersing of long and short commands (1 is short, 2 is long, 3 is short, 4 is long, 5–9 are short, 10 is long). Balance is present by virtue of the fact that there are four commands dealing with man's relationship to God and six dealing with man's relationship to his fellow man. Pattern can be seen in the way in which the negative and positive statements unfold in an A-B-A sequence (1 to 3 are negative, 4 and 5 are positive, 6 to 10 are negative). The fact that there is a total of ten commandments conveys a sense of completeness. Contrast is also present, since for each command there is an implied contrast between the pattern of conduct described in the command and its opposite. Each command sets up the possibility for choice between two ways of life. The Decalogue employs the artistic device of centrality, much as a painting does, with the concept of law the focal point around which the individual parts are arranged.

There are several important themes in the Decalogue as a whole. One of these is the sovereignty of God. God is the one who gives the laws and who speaks all of the words. The commandments bear the imprint of God's moral character and are a concrete expression of what He is like. The Ten Commandments are presented as a summary of God's will for human life, and they accordingly begin with a call to God-centered living.

A second overriding theme is the moral responsibility of man. The Decalogue is a call to righteous living before both God and society. It is a testimony to the fact that man, in the biblical view, is a moral creature. The Decalogue, moreover, sets up the unavoidable state of human life—a choice between good and evil, which is at the same time a choice for or against God. It is a variation of the great theme of the Bible—the spiritual warfare between darkness and light.

A third theme is what I shall call the beauty of order. The Ten Commandments affirm that life, as it was meant to be lived, is a law-bound life. There are certain spiritual and moral rules inherent in the universe, just as there are physical laws. Personal and social freedom are gained only as man recognizes the moral order that exists and is violated with such miserable results. The very form of the Decalogue, with its clear design and firm sense of structure, embodies the concept of order.

> Leland Ryken. *The Literature of the Bible* (Grand Rapids, Mich., Zondervan, 1974), p. 89.

EZEKIEL

Ezekiel is much inferior to Jeremiah in elegance; in sublimity he is not even excelled by Isaiah: but his sublimity is of a totally different kind. He is deep, vehement, tragical; the only sensation he affects to excite is the terrible: his sentiments are elevated, fervid, full of fire, indignant; his imagery is crowded, magnificent, terrific, sometimes almost to disgust; the language is pompous, solemn, austere, rough, and at times unpolished: he employs frequent repetitions, not for the sake of grace or elegance, but from the vehemence of passion and indignation. Whatever subject he treats of, that he sedulously pursues, from that he rarely departs, but cleaves as it were to it; whence the connexion is in general evident and well preserved. In many respects he is perhaps excelled by the other prophets; but in that species of composition to which he seems by nature adapted, the forcible, the impetuous, the great and solemn, not one of the sacred writers is superior to him. His diction is sufficiently perspicuous, all his obscurity consists in the nature of the subject. . . . The greater part of Ezekiel, towards the middle of the book especially, is poetical, whether we regard the matter or the diction. [1753]

> Robert Lowth. *Lectures on the Sacred Poetry of the Hebrews.* Vol. II. Tr. from the Latin by G. Gregory (London, Printed for J. Johnson, 1787), pp. 89–95

Ezekiel is the wild soothsayer: a genius of the cavern, whose thought is best expressed by a beast-like growling. But listen. This savage makes a prophecy to the world—the prophecy of progress. Nothing more astonishing. Ah! Isaiah overthrows? Very well! Ezekiel will reconstruct. Isaiah refuses civilization; Ezekiel accepts, but transforms it. Nature and humanity blend together in that softened howl which Ezekiel utters. The conception of duty is in Job; in Aeschylus, the conception of right. Ezekiel introduces the resultant third conception—the human race ameliorated, the future more and more emancipated. It is man's consolation that the future is to be a sunrise instead of a sunset. Time presents works for time to come; work, then, and hope! Such is Ezekiel's cry. . . .

This man, this being, this figure, this swine-prophet, is sublime. And the transfiguration that he announces, he proves. How? By transfiguring himself. From this horrible and defiled mouth there issues splendid poetry. Never has grander language been spoken, never more extraordinary. "I saw visions of God. A whirlwind came out of the North, and a great cloud, and a fire infolding itself." . . . And again: "There was a plain and dry bones, and I said, 'Bones, rise up'; and when I beheld, lo! the sinews and the flesh came up upon them, and the skin covered them above; but there was no breath in them. And I cried, 'Come from the four winds, O breath, and breathe upon these slain that they may live!'" [37:2, 7, 8–9] [1864]

> Victor Hugo. *William Shakespeare.* Tr. by Melville B. Anderson (Chicago, McClurg, 1887), pp. 49–51.

Of all the prophets he is the most Eastern. All the prophets speak in figures; Ezekiel in hardly anything else but figures. All the prophets are abrupt, sudden, dramatic in transition; Ezekiel hardly has transitions. He does not proceed by pedestrian steps; he flies, he baffles, he eludes—you see him only, as it were, when he alights from his brusque flights. He leaps from jag to jag of precipitous utterance, and leaves the reader to bridge the connexions. He speaks forked lightnings. All the prophets are often obscure by consequence of this Hebraic abruptness; Ezekiel is yet more obscure. All the prophets are at times obscure with intention, Ezekiel is habitually obscure with intention. Parable is the common counter of his speech. . . .

But try a little to see like an Eastern; overcome your most Saxon hatred of parable, and you shall find compensation; majesty in the parables, boldness in the imagery. You shall find that impressive review of the iniquities of Israel and Judah, under the figure of the two harlots, with its grand brutalities. For a hirsute power of denunciation, a terrible minatory plainness from which our modernity recoils, are among this prophet's marked characteristics. He has not the lofty and most moving pathos of Jeremiah, nor the lyric sublimity of Isaiah; in spite of his lavish use of figure, he is less lyric than either of these, has more of the character of harangue. But he has full grandeur. Yea, one passage is also powerfully lyric. It is that most imaginative, solemn, and majestic denunciation of Egypt, who is bidden to join the mighty nations perished in their glory, that shall welcome him to their abode in the earth.

The famous and indecipherable vision of the cherubim, for those who are not repelled by the peculiar forms of Hebrew symbolism, has a strange sublimity of conception. To us, at least, it is tremendous: but it must be read in a receptive mood. A certain mystic and inscrutable beauty is a frequent character of Ezekiel, with his tendency towards symbolic vision. Such is the lament over Tyre, which foreshadows the character of the Apocalypse. . . . To him, indeed, everything comes by way of vision and concrete sign. Such is that bold (and for once readily comprehensible) image of the dry bones.

In fine, this is a poet without the softer graces; rugged, eloquent, Hebraic to a degree, with his sharp transitions, his crowding imagery; yet affording, also, passages of direct and pregnant common sense, akin to his uncompromising plainness of invective; pre-eminently a visionary, who sees all things through the *eye*, and with the frequent grandeurs of the born visionary; yet, in his style, lacking somewhat the lyric form and the lyric wing.

Francis Thompson. *The Academy*. Jan. 29, 1898, pp. 115–16

Even in unambiguously prosaic discourses in [Ezekiel] one senses a rhythmic elevation, a prosodic pattern in the expression of his thought, but on the whole he was a man of prosaic rhetoric, and it is a very significant fact that he almost always expressly states in his literary writings where he strikes up a song. Perhaps we may gather from Ezekiel 33:32 that he actually excited the rapture of the people of his colony with such songs, especially when their content turned against the enemies of Judah. And it is understandably so, for the songs that have been transmitted in his book manifest even today—although its text has for the most part been transmitted in an extremely deplorable condition—a still noteworthy poetic art; although they are not a little remote in their overall character, they approach those of Isaiah, even Jeremiah.

J. W. Rothstein. *Hebräische Poesie* (Leipzig, J. C. Hinrichs, 1914), p. 48†

As regards its structure, the Book of Ezekiel, though its general movement is lucid enough, betrays to some extent the naïveté of an author to whom the art of literary invention is new. It should be noted that his seems to have been one of the earliest books to adopt the written as distinguished from the oral type, and his sense of organism is naturally somewhat undeveloped. He has not yet worked out the idea of a logically interrelated structure, wherein part rises out of part and makes for consecution and climax. The framework of the book, if such it can be called, is like that of a diarist or journalist; the happening in time seeming to have a greater logical value in his mind than it has in the coordination of ideas. . . .

The style of the book, while vigorous and vivid, shows similar marks of a literary art not quite subdued to a limpid repose and naturalness. The staring effects of style with which the work abounds—visions, symbolic figures, parables, acted prophecies—seem to a degree self-conscious and elaborated. In the descriptive passages, too, the choice of details is rather accumulative than selective, as if the author had not mastered the art of making a little description go a good way. One can feel this everywhere in the symbol (for example, 3:1–3; 47:1–12), imagery (for example, 17:1–10), and acted prophecy (for example, 4:1–8) with which his work is alive.

The most salient trait of Ezekiel's style, perhaps, is his extraordinary realistic and visualizing sense. Every idea seems to stand out in concrete form and measure and color, as if the matter-of-fact observer were usurping the idealizing consciousness of the poet. This visualizing power may be felt in such passages as his celebrated vision of the appearance of the "likeness of the glory of Jehovah" (1:4–28), described thus in periphrastic terms which virtually evade the actual *sight* of God; his realistic vision of the charnel valley (37:1–15); and in the architectural details of the projected new temple (40–42), in which last the poet yields place to the artisan. In several cases his intense realization of things has the effect of clairvoyance (for example, 8:3–18; cf. 21:21–22) or telepathy (24:2). No other prophet has this power in such degree. It is as if, after all the dim ways through which Jehovah had led his people, the prophet felt himself walking almost in the blaze of fulfillment (cf. 12:21–24), and as if his style gathered realism from it.

John F. Genung. *A Guidebook to the Biblical Literature* (Boston, Ginn, 1919), pp. 260–62

The style of Ezekiel reflects the paradoxical contrasts of his personality. His moods are nearly as varied and contradictory as those of Dante, whose writings range from a dialectic discussion of abstract political and theological problems to the love poetry of the *Vita Nuova*; and within *The Divine Comedy* from sordid reality to visionary perfection, from abstruse scholastic and scientific discussions to the passionate drama of Francesca. Both Ezekiel and Dante sought escape from the abuses, iniquities, and tragedies of reality to a world created by their imagination.

The contrast between the vivid poetry and the dull prose of Ezekiel is even more striking than in Jeremiah. In Jeremiah, and probably in Ezekiel, some of the most dreary and repetitious prose sections were penned by a secretary or by later redactors.

Significantly, the poetic sections of Ezekiel's book are almost all allegorical: the wild vine (15), the ungrateful bride (16), the vulture, the cedar, and the vine (17), the lioness, her whelps, and the uprooted vine (19), the sword (21), the two unchaste sisters (23), the rusty caldron (24:3–14), the ship Tyre and the downfall of the prince of Tyre (28), the Egyptian crocodile (29; 32), the lofty pine (31). It is not surprising that the prophet's hearers complained that he was obscure and said, "Is he not a speaker in parables?" Sensitive to this criticism, Ezekiel took pains to explain most of his parables when he prepared them for publication.

From the literary point of view, Ezekiel's allegories are descriptive rather than dramatic, fantastic rather than realistic. Usually they consist of the portrayal of an animal, plant, or thing, and picture its destruction. It is only in the allegories of the foundling girl, reared by Jehovah to become his bride (16), and in the story of the two sisters who became harlots (23) that we find the germs of a dramatic development. The most distinguished and really great poetry, free from exaggerations and distasteful imagery, is that of the allegories of the whelps (19) and of the ship Tyre (27). Here we have Ezekiel the poet at his best, writing with unusual clarity and simplicity, and withal with impressiveness and force. His pictures here are vivid and natural; in fact the details of the ship Tyre are so true to life that Ezekiel 27, together with the *Odyssey* and Acts 27, is one of the most important literary sources for our knowledge about ancient navigation.

The prose style of Ezekiel at his best is lucid and adequate, but lacks distinction; at its worst it is pedantic, monotonous, and repetitious. Ezekiel is essentially visual, excelling in descriptions of real or imaginary scences; however, he lacks restraint, is prone to emphasize technical details, and has more phantasy than creative imagination. As an orator he probably failed dismally. His discourse on personal responsibility (18) shows a keen mind and a noble conscience, but no rhetorical skill or stirring eloquence. His best description in prose is that of the bones coming to life (37), his most involved is that of the divine chariot (1).

The diction of Ezekiel is postclassical. His Hebrew is tinged with new words and expressions; his vocabulary shows the influence of Aramaic. Despite his limitations as a speaker and as a writer, despite his eccentricities, his daydreaming, his fanatical zeal and dogmatic tone, Ezekiel wrote a book destined to exercise an incalculable influence on the history of his people.

Robert H. Pfeiffer. The Books of the Old Testament
(New York, Harper, 1957), pp. 286–87

[Besides the inaugural vision], the other great vision of the book is the justly famous Valley of Dry Bones. It is less abstruse than the call vision and has a plainer purport. Yet the same qualities of Ezekiel's mind show through the symbolism: a fierce concentration, a grotesque baroque distortion of reality, a stripping away of nonessentials, a stark coming to grips with the uncompromisingly true. We feel the otherworldly realism that peers from an El Greco painting or soars through a Franck symphony. Men do not hesitate long before Ezekiel: either they are repelled by his austerity and oddity or else they grasp at once how grandly he encompassed the supreme realities. Not accidentally have Negro spirituals chosen as their subjects the visions of the prophet: "'Zekiel saw de wheels, way up in de middle ob de air!" and "Dem bones, dem bones, dem dry bones!" They exert a fascination upon the folk mind. The essential idea of national restoration Ezekiel shared with Isaiah and Jeremiah but he had to express it in his peculiar way. What more telling means of picturing the prostrate hopes of Israel in exile than a desert landscape of parched bones, and "they were very dry"! What more thrilling manner for expressing the doubt and hesitation of even the finest leaders of Israel than the repartee of Yahweh, "Son of man, can these bones live?" [37:3] and the reply of Ezekiel, "O, Lord God thou knowest"! Prophesying to the bones, he sees them reconnected before his eyes and clothed with sinews—but still they do not live. Then he prophesies to the four winds and the breath (or wind) falls upon the corpses and they live and stand as a great army. "Son of man, these bones are the whole house of Israel." Only a divine tour de force could bring Israel out of the grave of exile and Ezekiel knew it. The aesthetic shock of Ezekiel's bold and jabbing style, like gobs of pigment smeared on canvas, suits the uproar of his time and the sharp simplicities that could alone console a mind like his.

> Norman K. Gottwald. *A Light to the Nations: An Introduction to the Old Testament* (New York, Harper, 1959), p. 389

Ezekiel's role [in ch. 37] is not messenger but *spectator*. Ezekiel is observing an event in which he is forcibly placed. Within that event he is indeed given a message to deliver (vv. 12–14), but that message is only part of the experience, and it will not be delivered until some time after the visionary experience. Here, as in chapters 8–11, the oracle is formally a narration of a visionary event. The prophet simply tells what he saw and heard. He is neutral insofar as he does not openly involve his own ego in the message. Ezekiel is an essentially passive spectator. It is true that he speaks the words that bring about the rising of the bones, but his part in the event is similar to that of a spectator invited up from the audience to "help" a stage magician by waving a wand over the magician's hat. Ezekiel carefully maintains a distance between himself and the events he saw.

By choosing this stance the rhetor steps into the audience, as it were, and aligns himself with them. He makes no explicit claims about the vision's plausibility. He does not request that the audience accept what he saw and certainly does not argue for the truth of his vision. Such a request would invite refusal, and such an argument would invite refutation. In effect the prophet says, "Here is what I saw. I too was surprised. Now believe it or not." This stance gives an impression of objectivity. More important, by taking the point-of-view of an audience the rhetor makes his audience's point-of-view congruent with his own. The audience looks over the rhetor's shoulder and watches the event unfold from the same angle of vision. Alignment of perspective encourages alignment of belief.

The most important rhetorical strategy of this vision is its central image. An image is a concentrated representation of reality. It makes the diffuse and abstract concrete and immediate. The most powerful images are foreign to our everyday experience. Images that conform to everyday experience have didactic value. They are useful in reinforcing accepted truths and in helping the auditor assimilate ideas that are complex or abstract. Strange, shocking, and bizarre images on the other hand are needed when one seeks to break down old frameworks of perception and to create new ones. They offer a way of transmitting the rhetor's fundamental perceptions of reality even when these perceptions are not amenable to rational exposition. Such images may attack our normal system of expectations in order to replace it with a new one.

Ezekiel does not merely predict the resurrection of the nation, for then all hope would rest on his listeners' confidence in his accuracy as forecaster, and there are more powerful forces working against hope. He is certainly not just relying on argumentation, for rational argumentation could hardly create belief in the absurd. Ezekiel's primary strategy is boldly to affirm the absurd. He does so by implanting within his auditors an image that will restructure their view of reality. He will seek to make them expect the unexpectable. What they are to expect is the resurrection of the "dead," i.e., exiled, nation and its return to its land. To achieve this (and not to teach the doctrine of individual resurrection) Ezekiel uses the image of the revival of bleached-out bones, the last remnants of rotted corpses.

Let us look carefully at the image and how it unfolds. The image is first of all dynamic, not static. The image is a configuration of a *process*. The process is movement from death to life. It is portrayed as movement from chaos to order, like the movement of the creation story. The scattered bones gather themselves together, sinews bind them together, flesh grows and skin covers it and thus binds it to sinew and bone. Then they are given the breath of life (which comes in from the four directions, thus reinforcing the centripetal movement of the overall imagery), and they finally stand up—not as separate individuals, but as a great army, an organized unit. The memorability of this image is increased by the double relation of the event, first as command (4–6), then as narration (7–10). Details are sparse, because it is a process the auditors are to picture and remember, and each step must be precise and distinct, with no unnecessary elaboration that might transfer attention from the process to the pictorial details of the envisioned objects.

The dramatic movement of the visionary event is carefully modulated to create suspense and intensify the imagery's impression. The dramatic movement unfolds through the dialogue between the first persona, Ezekiel, and the second persona, God, which is encompassed in the voice of the first. . . .

God does not make the bones rise immediately. He announces what will happen and then makes us wait for it to happen. To increase the suspense and draw the audience closer, he invites the spectator to participate. God orders Ezekiel to pronounce the "magic" words. (In this detail too there is a message, though it is kept carefully in the background: Prophets will be God's agents in the national resurrection when it comes.) Ezekiel just says that he prophesied as ordered (v. 7a) and does not quote his own words. He thus carefully keeps his own role in proper perspective. He is passive and not really affecting the outcome. . . .

God's success goes beyond what was predicted. The scattered bones not only come to life, they rise as an army. They are organized and they have power.

Michael V. Fox. *Hebrew Union College Annual.* 51, 1980, pp. 9–11

THE FLOOD

In the history of world literature, heroic poetry—or the epos, to call it by its Greek name—preceded narrative prose; and apparently there is reason to believe that the latter (in which, for instance, the vast majority of the sections of Genesis and many other sections of the Torah are written) first came into being as a sequel to, and development of, epic poetry, which, both in its Eastern and Western forms, evinces a great love of repetition, due to the very nature of the epos, which was originally intended to be heard and not read. . . . Many and varied are the circumstances that conduce to reiteration in heroic poetry, and all of them are represented in the books of the Bible. . . . Here it will suffice to indicate that one of the most common instances is that in which a poem tells of the giving of an order and afterwards of its execution. The poet then begins by stating: So-and-so commanded so-and-so and said to him, Do this and this and this. After citing the words of the one who gives the command, he continues: And so-and-so did that and that and that. All the details of the action are reiterated in the very words used by the poet when quoting the injunction.

On the other hand, narrative prose is not so fond of verbal repetitions, for it was meant to be read rather than heard, and the reader, unlike the listener, has no predilection for what he already knows by heart. On the contrary, reiteration, in the *ipsissima verba* [the very same words], may at times be burdensome to him. Consequently, prose is inclined, when reverting to a given subject, to modify the expressions, or to shorten them, or to change their order. This is what happens in the narrative prose of the Pentateuch. However, abridgement and variation are not possible in every instance. For example, when the topic is essentially technical, as in the sections dealing with the work of the Tabernacle (Exod. 25–31, 35–40), it is impossible to abbreviate or to vary the text. Then verbal repetitions occur as in epic poetry. First it is related that the Lord commanded Moses to make the Tabernacle and all its appurtenances and explained to him all the details of the work, and then we are told that Moses carried out the task, and the particulars are restated in full. Complete sections recur in identical form, with one change: in place of verbs in the imperative, like *make* etc., we find verbs of implementation, *made* etc. But when the subject is not primarily technical as in the case of the construction of the Tabernacle, and hence does not require meticulous exactitude of detail, the repetitions in prose are not word-for-word restatements.

In the section of the Flood, which is mainly concerned with the narration of events, and in which technical matters, like the particulars of the building of the ark, do not predominate, the Torah uses chiefly the method of abridgement. After stating that God commanded Noah: "Make yourself an ark of gopher wood; rooms make in the ark, and cover it inside and out with pitch," etc., the execution of the command is not narrated in the same words. If it were an epic poem that we had before us here, or if the details of the construction of the ark were the main theme of our section, it would subsequently have been written: So Noah made for himself an ark of gopher wood; he made rooms in the ark, and covered it inside and out with pitch, etc. But since this is not consonant with prose style and there was no specific need for it, the Torah did not reiterate the words of the Divine command, and was content to state with extreme brevity (6:22): "And Noah did this; according to all that God commanded him, so did he."

The position is different, however, in this, the fourth paragraph. Here we have a mighty and amazing spectacle: the tremendous, endless procession of all the creatures streaming from all parts of the earth to Noah's abode in order to find shelter with him in the ark. This time a brief and anaemic expression, such as "And Noah did this; according to all that God commanded him," or the like, would have been inadequate; a detailed description was necessary. Hence the matters on which Noah was previously instructed are repeated here, and this reiteration presents us, as it were, with a magnificent and graphic picture of that wondrous scene, the mass pilgrimage from all parts of the world to the one place that promised salvation to every species of creature. But it is not an exact verbal and mechanical repetition as it might have been in epic poetry; there are variations that give greater vividness to the entire account and heighten its effect, but in general the phrases of the Divine commands are reiterated and this conforms basically to the age-old literary tradition. [1949]

Umberto Cassuto. *A Commentary on the Book of Genesis.* Part II. Tr. by Israel Abrahams (Jerusalem, Magnes Press, 1964), pp. 79–81

The foregoing study of the biblical Deluge story leaves no room for doubting the direct connection between it and the Mesopotamian tradition. Yet a closer look at the two and a careful understanding of the purposes of the Bible leave us with quite a different impression. The Hebrew version is an expression of the biblical polemic against paganism. This assault is carried on, not on the level of dialectics, but indirectly and inferentially. Through an inspired process of selection, revision and addition, whether deliberate or intuitive, the original material has been so thoroughly reshaped as to become an entirely new and original creation purged of its polytheistic dross. What in the Mesopotamian tradition was apparently of local importance became in the Bible a major event of cosmic significance. What there is largely casual and contingent has become here causal and determinative. Like the Creation narrative, that of Noah and the Flood has been made into a vehicle for the expression of some of the most profound biblical teachings, an instrument for the communication of universal moral truths, the medium through which God makes known what He demands of man.

Nahum M. Sarna. *Understanding Genesis* (New York, Melton Research Center, 1966), p. 59

The repetition of lists in the flood pericope recalls the long repetitions in classical epic poetry, Homer and the Aeneid, but also Ugaritic epics. And it recalls the immediate repetition of strophes in Sumerian hymns. However these are verbatim repetitions, and the purpose seems to be somehow connected with oral recitation, where the aspect of memory is all important, and where repetition of considerable units, even several times over, creates, not only an emphasis, but also a pleasure of familiarity in repetition. This pleasure may, with many reservations, be compared to the pleasure of singing a chorus again and again, with verse in between, e.g., "It ain't gonna rain no more no more," or even "Old MacDonald had a farm." The priestly repetition of the list frustrates any hope of familiarity —no one could hope to join in, the second time round! It is a repetition which unites, orders, and structures the pericope. Its essence is variety within the system. . . .

As ch[apter] 9 must be considered a theological conclusion, corresponding to the introduction in 6:11–13, 8:15–19 must be considered the third large section of the pericope. It contains the list of the saved twice, presented in perfectly parallel form, in a command-fulfillment structure. Thus the priestly writer has created a most ritual exit, in the most structured and symmetrical unit of the pericope. After the rather bombastic rhetoric of the flood description of the previous section, these legal lists, and this highly artificial, disciplined, ritualistic style, provide an introduction to the divine proclamation of ch[apter] 9, which may be compared to the building of the tent and its equipment as introduction for the descent of God's glory upon Israel in Lev[iticus] 9.

Sean E. McEvenue. *The Narrative Style of the Priestly Writer* (Rome, Biblical Institute Press, 1971), pp. 50, 66

One mark of the coherence of the flood narrative is to be found in its literary structure. The tale is cast in the form of an extended palistrophe, that is a structure that turns back on itself. In a palistrophe the first item matches the final item, the second item matches the penultimate item, and so on. The second half of the story is thus a mirror image of the first. This kind of literary structure has been discovered in other parts of Genesis, but nowhere else is it developed on such a large scale. This may be partly due to the fact that a flood narrative is peculiarly suited to this literary form.

Gen. 6:10 to 9:19 appears to be a palistrophe containing 31 items. It begins and ends with a reference to Noah. Then Noah's sons are named and so on. Particularly striking are the references to days (lines H, I, L, O). The periods of time form a symmetrical pattern, 7, 7, 40, 150, 150, 40, 7, 7. The turning point of the narrative is found in 8:1 "God remembered Noah."

Genesis 6:10-9:19

A	Noah (6:10a)
B	Shem, Ham and Japheth (10b)
C	Ark to be built (14–16)
D	Flood announced (17)
E	Covenant with Noah (18–20)
F	Food in the ark (21)
G	Command to enter ark (7:1–3)
H	7 days waiting for flood (4–5)
I	7 days waiting for flood (7–10)
J	Entry to ark (11–15)
K	Yahweh shuts Noah in (16)
L	40 days flood (17a)
M	Waters increase (17b–18)
N	Mountains covered (19–20)
O	150 days waters prevail ([21]–24)
P	GOD REMEMBERS NOAH (8:1)
O'	150 days waters abate (3)
N'	Mountain tops visible (4–5)
M'	Waters abate (5)
L'	40 days (end of) (6a)
K'	Noah opens window of ark (6b)
J'	Raven and dove leave ark (7–9)
I'	7 days waiting for waters to subside (10–11)
H'	7 days waiting for waters to subside (12–13)
G'	Command to leave ark (15–17[22])
F'	Food outside ark (9:1–4)
E'	Covenant with all flesh (8–10)
D'	No flood in future (11–17)
C'	Ark (18a)
B'	Shem, Ham and Japheth (18b)
A'	Noah (19)

This is a palistrophe on a grand scale. Up to a point it is not surprising to find one in the flood story. After all, a palistrophic literary structure closely resembles the real-life situation. Noah enters the ark with the animals, and then later they leave it. The waters rise and then fall. In other words the story naturally falls into two halves which ought to resemble each other to some extent. The surface structure of the narrative mirrors the deep structure of the event being described.

What then is the function of the palistrophe? Firstly, it gives literary expression to the character of the flood event. The rise and fall of the waters is mirrored in the rise and fall of the key words in its description. Secondly, it draws attention to the real turning point in the saga: 8:1, "And God remembered Noah." From that moment the waters start to decline and the earth to dry out. It was God's intervention that was decisive in saving Noah, and the literary structure highlights this fact. This large-scale palistrophe co-exists alongside the smaller literary and syntactic patterns in these chapters noted by other scholars. Similar phenomena are observable in Genesis 1 and 17. Artists must necessarily be concerned as much with the details of a work as with the overall effect.

Gordon T. Wenham. *Vetus Testamentum.* July, 1978, pp. 337–40

Following man's infractions and misdemeanors, God's wrath breaks forth and the cosmos is destroyed. The Flood is described as a reversal of the creation itself: "both the springs of the mighty deep [*tehom*, cf. Gen. 1:2] and the sluices of heaven were opened" (7:11). This anticreation imagery of the destruction is confirmed by the language used of the restoration, which is presented as a *new creation*. The description of the re-creation begins in Genesis 8:1–3, which describes how the wind of Elohim blew over the earth and stopped up the waters of the deep (cf. Gen. 1:2):

> And Elohim remembered Noah, and all the creatures and animals which were with him in the ark. And *Elohim brought a wind over the earth*, so that the waters abated. Thus the springs of the *deep [tehom]* and the sluices of the heavens were stopped up; and rain was withheld in the heavens. The waters began to recede from the earth, until they were diminished after 150 days.

This depiction recalls the biblical and ancient Near Eastern imagery of the primordial combat with the sea monster, noted in chapter 1 (cf. Psalms 74:12–15; 89:10–12; 104:6–10; 148:6). The imagery used here portrays Elohim's vigorous control over the forces of the world, which can be ordered or unleashed at His will. It is thus fitting that the sign of the covenant in Genesis 9, after the reordering of the watery chaos, is the bow—an ancient weapon of divine combat. The Bible often presents God's intervention in history to defeat Israel's enemies with the imagery of bows, arrows, and nets (note especially Habakkuk 3:9ff.). Similar weapons were also employed by Marduk in his cosmogonic battle against Tiamat. The combat bow in Genesis 9, however, is hung in the heavens

—a sign of divine promise and resignation. The world will no longer be destroyed because of man's evil actions. Primordial fears are put to rest.

The "recreation" motif begun in 8:1–3 concludes with the renewal of mankind on a mountain (8:4) and recapitulates in 9:1–2, 6–7 the language of Genesis 1:26ff.:

> And Elohim blessed Noah and his sons, and said to them: "Be fruitful and multiply and fill the earth; and may your lordship and power rule the creatures of the earth, the birds of the heavens; and all that swarms on the earth and swims in the sea I have given to you . . . for man was created in the image of God. But be fruitful and multiply, swarm on the earth, and increase thereon."

Noah is thus portrayed as a new Adam in a renewed creation. The hopes of comfort and consolation anticipated in 5:29 are now consummated.

> Michael Fishbane. *Text and Texture* (New York, Schocken, 1979), pp. 33–34

GENESIS

No History in the World can be more justly wrote than the Book of Genesis. The Description of Hagar and her son Ishmael, is one of the most moving Pictures of Distress imaginable . . . How concisely, how emphatically is Jacob's Love for Rachel compriz'd in one Verse [Gen. 29:20]. *And* Jacob *served seven years for* Rachel, and *they seemed unto him but a few Days, for the Love He had unto her*. There is more of Nature, of Expressiveness, of Affection in that simple Passage, than in all the motley Descriptions of *French* or *Italian* Romance. The whole Passion of Love is crowded into a few Words.

The Beauty of such Passages as These, where the Affections are to be describ'd, and made (as it were) visible to Us, does not consist in a Flourish of Words, or Pomp of Diction, not in the *ambitiosa ornamenta* of Rhetorick, but in a natural and easy Display of tender Sentiments, and in opening those Softnesses which are supposed to arise in the Bosoms of the Persons introduced. For this purpose nothing is more effectual, than a decent Simplicity of Language.

> John Husbands. *A Miscellany of Poems by Several Hands* (Oxford, J. Husbands, 1731), sigs. h1ᵛ, h3ʳ–h3ᵛ

Our Book of Genesis stands in the whole Old Testament by itself. It produces on us the effect of a single, great work of genius, complete and rounded and contrasting sharply with the chaotically jumbled stories of its professed continuation, Exodus. In the beginning of Exodus there are the materials of good stories, but they are far from being well told; they have not passed through the brain of a real story-teller. And Genesis stands thus apart not only in the literature of the Hebrews but in the entire literature of the world. It is safe to say that there is no other book which combines as it does a philosophical study of the fundamental institutes of human life, a psychological study of a family of marked characteristics, developing into a people equally marked, and a political and economic study of that people over against the rest of the world, personified in the great figure of an adventurer of their race; the whole told in clear, objective stories which can be the delight of children, yet with a depth of sheer thought behind them which has stirred and led the thinking of the world more deeply than have the speculations of Plato. . . . a single, unified, great literary phenomenon postulating a great literary creator. As to who he was we have absolutely no clue; as to when he lived we can only make guesses. But as to his greatness as artist and philosopher there can be no shadow of doubt; nor as to the depth of his influence on the thinking of the world from Ecclesiastes to our own day. He is the greatest Unknown of Hebrew literature, which has so many unknown or only partially revealed figures.

> Duncan B. MacDonald. *The Hebrew Literary Genius*
> (Princeton, N.J., Princeton University Press, 1933),
> pp. 96–97

In my dispute with the Documentary Hypothesis I would not maintain that the author of the Torah spun the entire work purely out of himself or that he made use of no sources. The Torah itself refers once to an older source. But it is impossible to distinguish the sources and tributaries of the great stream. . . . And the "redactor" is none other than the author himself. Genesis is a unified work, designed, thought out, and worked out in a single spirit.

> Benno Jacob. *Das erste Buch der Tora: Genesis* (Berlin,
> Schocken, 1934), p. 10†

Shall we insist that there is no epic in the Bible? If we disregard for the moment the question of form, what does Genesis offer? We have, in the first place, the national sweep which we required of an epic, the formation of a nation and its ideals. We even have the long genealogies with individuals representing tribes and tribal movements exactly as in the second *Iliad*, and stories of the patriarchs derived from older cycles exactly as are the stories of Homeric heroes. In the second place, we have, very definitely, an adequation of the nation to an environment potentially hostile. The Hebrews, gradually separated from the rest of the human stock, are made at home in a hard world dominated by human enemies and controlled by an exacting deity. And is not the effect upon the reader, at least the reader who lends himself to the book, to give him a vicarious adequation to his world? Some of us who are anemic or whose viscera sag, who punch time-clocks and answer bells, get a momentary feeling of human dignity from reading of the pride of Achilles; and some of us from reading that we are part of a divine plan under Providence.

Such an epic is true, and its truth bears no relation to the truth or falsity of the details which make it up. The moon is a satellite of the earth; the moon is queen of heaven; these statements offer a contradiction only to the smallest mind. The one truth in no way vitiates the other. We *need* not regard Genesis as a fable to see in it an epic of this sort. And if we may look upon Genesis as a sort of epic, then it is certainly of the genuine and profound sort which offer a way of life. But I should insist also that Genesis is to the highest degree philosophical. Composed, as it well may be, of the various materials of which the higher critics have so long told us: scraps of ancient poetry, legends of the patriarchs, myths of foreign derivation, bits of tribal history—with what purposeful wisdom, with what mature and civilized direction the final author shaped and informed the whole! The misconception, widely prevalent, that the Hebrews were not a philosophical people arose out of the simplicity of those who took the too obvious course of seeking Hebrew philosophy in the socalled "Wisdom Books" of the Bible, in the pigeonhole, so to speak, labelled "Wisdom." . . .

We are not in the habit of looking to Genesis for the most effective biblical examples of conscious literary art. It is, in fact, difficult for any modern reader to look at Genesis except through spectacles that have been tinted purple and amber by the centuries during which this book has occupied its central position as a focus of pious regard, or of scorn. It is therefore refreshing to get the clear-eyed view of a pagan literary critic who looks upon it steadily and with the same focus which he employs for Aeschylus or Homer. If that excellent literary critic sometimes called Dionysus and sometimes Longinus did live, as modern scholars incline to believe, in the time of Augustus, the quotation from Genesis in his treatise "On the Sublime" is the earliest indubitable citation from the Bible in a secular author. [*See also* Creation]

Moses Hadas. *Menorah Journal*. Jan.–Mar., 1938,
pp. 19–21

The prose of Genesis is singularly noble and profoundly tinged with emotion. The form rises to the content, and the majesty of the one inspires the sublimity of the other. The style is firm, concise, and free from the slightest shadow of rhetoric and artifice. The enduring aesthetic qualities of the book that have seized upon the mind of untold generations are its incisive, unforgettable expressions, its plastic and at the same time transcendent images, its seductive, almost aching naturalness, its vivid portrayal of character, and its uncanny skill in storytelling.

Probably the most oft-quoted sayings in conversation as well as in literature have come from Genesis. Simple, pithy and sparkling, unpretentious, as it were, careless of effect, their artless poignancy takes a strong and lasting hold on the memory. . . . "Let there be light." "In the image of God created He him." "It is not good that the man should be alone." "Bone of my bones, flesh of my flesh."

"The woman whom Thou gavest me." "In the sweat of thy face shalt thou eat bread." "Dust thou art, and unto dust shalt thou return." "The voice of thy brother's blood cries unto me." "Am I my brother's keeper?"

The images in Genesis are vivid, picturesque, forceful, authentic, and withal suggestive, detaching themselves from their incarnation in the twinkling of an eye, and turning to feelings or ideas. Invariably derived from cognate and homogeneous subjects, or borrowed from the most obvious and familiar objects, they are never forced or farfetched. At times they reach like silent shadows over the landscape, and at others they burst out in a violent blaze of fury. As a figure of speech there is perhaps nothing comparable to that of the spirit of God brooding over the fathomless abyss. It is awful in apprehension and rivets the heart and mind in reverential silence. . . .

These memorable phrases and images are organically connected with the naturalness that pervades the whole of Genesis, which describes to the word the life without and within. It makes no attempt to disguise or embellish the homely realism and concreteness of the environment, but presents nature and man in the raw. Some of its scenes are primal, tumultuous, and pitiful; others pastoral, sequestered, and dignified. . . .

The portrayal of character corresponds to the naturalness of the background. The people throughout the book are normal and familiar, such as we are accustomed to meet in our day-to-day intercourse with our fellow men. The things that happen to them, on the whole, are neither unusual nor miraculous, and no black magic upsets or degrades the orderliness of their lives. They are not depicted, as is often the case in the epics, as fantastic supermen, or as gods in disguise, or as knights bent on chivalry, or paladins on some incredible adventure. They are shown to be, beginning with the first man, consistently human in every respect. . . . It is therefore the more remarkable that, despite their nearness and familiarity, Adam and all the other characters in Genesis should at the same time also stand out as marked individuals. For though they are lifelike, alive, and normal, they are not the conventional or average human types. They eat, sleep, shepherd the flock, till the soil, make love, and generally pursue the interests common to all men. But there is something more to them than that. They are stirred by the deeper issues and profounder feelings of life. The routine occupations of today cannot hold the whole of them; they carry in their heart a message for the future, and represent in their being something greater than themselves—faith, people, mankind.

The character that illustrates best the coalescence of these divergent aspects of personality and that is perhaps more skillfully limned than any of the others in Genesis is Abraham. He was so marvelously executed that he could strike Nietzsche as being nearer to us than any of the heroes of the ancient Greeks, [Johann Gottfried von] Herder, as the most august figure of antiquity, and Max Mueller, as second only to Jesus in the whole history of the world. He was, Charles Kingsley said, "a prince in manners and a prince in heart." We are struck dumb at the self-assurance with which he calls upon God to be just. . . .

The same harmonious and masterly combination of the universal, particular, and symbolic is present, to speak briefly and summarily, in the easily-ruffled and quick-tempered Sarah, submitting patiently and heroically to her husband's trials, cherishing his faith and hopes; in the pampered, self-indulgent, meek, and gentle Isaac, calm and confident in the face of death; in the radiant, fascinating, kind, and courteous Rebekah, resolutely outwitting and casting aside her older son because the oracle had favored the younger; in the crafty and contriving Jacob thirsting for God's promise; in the "bluff and honest" Esau taken up completely with the present moment; and in the vain and vaunting Joseph, victorious in temptation, and trial and foreshadowing the destiny of a people.

Solomon Goldman. *In the Beginning* (New York, Harper, 1949), pp. 103–7

The opening of Genesis is wonderful: the spirit of God in the darkness that hovers or broods on the waters, the sudden decree of light, the teeming of earth, sea and sky. The story of the Garden of Eden and the episode of Cain and Abel are imperfectly disengaged from some very ancient matrix of folklore, and parts of them are blotted in obscurity. . . . What we do find in the story of Adam and his family are those living and salient traits—the relations of Adam and Eve, the sullen personality of Cain—that give these fragmentary legends a human truth and have caused them to haunt our imaginations; and you have, also, the earliest examples of that specialty of the Jewish genius—the development of the moral consciousness, of man's relations with God. This dawning of the moral sense brings with it, for Adam and Eve, an immediate awareness of their animal nature and the impulse to clothe themselves. . . .

The wonder is, with all this untidiness, these absurdities and incongruities [in some of the stories in Genesis], that the dialogue should be so telling, the situations presented with so sure a stroke, that the personalities of the principal characters should remain so convincing and so interesting. Abraham, Jacob and Joseph are created as living figures in a way that makes relatively unimportant the imprecisions of the different versions; it is even perhaps true that their outlines are thrown into a kind of relief by the factual uncertainty of the legend. . . . [Also the] strokes of human feeling, of insight, are so trenchant and so authentic, and they so surely awake a response in all kinds and conditions of people, that there are moments when the gods and heroes of the so much more expertly handled, the so much more sophisticated Homeric poems seem less real than the nomads of Genesis when the finger of the unknown scribe, tracing the ancient story, flashes across the page the verses that make them live.

Edmund Wilson. *New Yorker*. May 15, 1954, pp. 135 –36, 138, 140

In my mind, despite anomalies and contradictions, Genesis is crystal clear. The first account of creation was recognized as majestic in the Hellenistic world almost 2,000 years ago. An issue of tone arises in the so-called J account. With what misguided solemnity it is usually read! The verve and dash and humor with which it is written completely escape the modern reader. Traditional exegesis —sometimes Jewish, sometimes Christian—contributes its own distortion. Christians should be alert at this point to my Jewish prejudice; we Jews have never interpreted the Eden story as the fall of man. We have normally attributed that to Genesis 6. We also do not make it quite as resounding a fall! On the other hand, Jewish exegesis has had its own excesses, too, and I would judge that the virtues and trespasses of both sides of exegesis weigh pretty much the same number of pounds. The Eden story is meant to be witty, witty in the same way that Jonah is witty. It begins with a pun, that the serpent was *arum* and Adam and Eve were *arom*, "wise" and "naked." Fun is poked at them on the supposition that one can become wise by eating a piece of fruit. They eat the fruit—how wondrously in the account they pass the buck!—but the sum total of their wisdom is that they are naked, so that they sew fig leaves for themselves and in the next chapter, God graciously sews leather garments for them.

The story of primeval man is wondrously arranged; of course, some editor could not resist his anti-Canaanite sentiment to the point that he has disrupted the story of Noah and his three sons by introducing confusion as to whether the second son is Ham or Canaan. Again, the author need not have postponed to the age of Noah the division of humanity into the residents respectively of Asia (Shem), Africa (Ham), and the Mediterranean Isles (Japheth). The author, though, knew of the tradition of a flood, a universal flood; he uses it, and it is after the flood that humanity becomes divided into its three continents as at Babel—again a humorous matter meant seriously! Then comes the origin of the Hebrews.

Samuel Sandmel. Judaism. Fall, 1973, pp. 463–64

The text that the literary critic will find most interesting to study is the book as a whole. Because of the principle of synecdoche texts gain richness and complexity from having diverse, not easily assimilable, parts set in relation to one another. To dissect Genesis into J, E, and P and study these separately defies no sacred tenet of literary criticism; it is just less challenging and less exciting. Whatever the text, once it is chosen it is considered as if it were written by one author. If the entire book of Genesis is the text, then the fact that it was put together out of originally separate strands, if indeed it was, or that it went through several recensions, is of ancillary importance. And certainly an attempt to solve structural or conceptual difficulties by relegating parts of the text to later redactors is a way of avoiding the interpretive enterprise. A thoroughgoing interpretation involves a consideration of all parts of the text, not only on their own but also in relation to each other. The meaning of the Joseph story (Gen. 37, 39–50), for example, depends as much on its relationship with the Abraham and Isaac stories (Gen. 12–36), the primeval history (Gen. 1–11) and Tamar's outwitting of Judah (Gen. 38) as it does on its own internal structure and language. To understand the Joseph story as a microcosm mirroring by its form and content the macrocosm not only of the book of Genesis but also of the entire Bible is the goal of literary interpretation.

David Robertson. *The Old Testament and the Literary Critic* (Philadelphia, Fortress Press, 1977), pp. 6–7

The text of Genesis seems to speak with many voices. For a book whose basic arrangement is chronological, tracing the history of a single family, it exhibits a good deal of discontinuity on the surface. Here time flows uniformly, there taking startling jumps; fragments are followed by more or less full-blown tales; genres alternate, from mythic to genealogical to folkloristic. In addition, scholars often portray Genesis as a collection of historically diverse materials that were compiled by scribes for whom deviating from received tradition was anathema. Hence the repetitions, the inconsistencies, and the irregular pacing.

Is Genesis then at best a collection of stories related to the origins of Israel, with most of its seams showing? That hardly seems likely. If one approaches the book with an open mind, alert to its structure, without making assumptions beforehand, there is a scheme that begins to emerge. Whatever the compositional history of Genesis may have been—and it certainly appears to have been a complex one—we have before us the product of a rather single-minded consciousness. Using the Buber-Rosenzweig method of focusing on repeating words and key themes as the text presents them, it is possible to make some careful generalizations about the book's organization and to speculate on its overall intent.

On its most obvious level Genesis is a book about origins. It seeks to link the origin of the people of Israel with that of the world, relating in the process how various human characteristics and institutions arose.

On the surface this parallels much of ancient literature and folklore. All peoples are interested in their own beginnings, picturing them in a way which validates their present existence. Genesis, however, is different in that like the rest of the Torah, it downplays the heroic element of the people's origins and in its place stresses God's role in them. Moreover the one great omission—the origin of God—establishes from the beginning a unique basis for a tribal chronicle. From Genesis and subsequent books we learn primarily about God's relationship to the people and what he expects of them; almost everything else is subordinated to this purpose.

Preliminarily one can speak of at least seven major themes whose recurrence establishes their importance in the book:

1. *Origins:* Of the world, of humanity, and of the people of Israel.
2. *Order/Meaning in History:* By means of stylized or patterned chronology—reliance on certain round numbers such as 3, 7, and 40—it is suggested that human events are not random but somehow planned.
3. *Blessing:* From creation onward God bestows blessings on his creatures in general and on the fathers and mothers of Israel in particular.

4. *Covenant:* God concludes agreements with human beings.
5. *God Punishes Evildoing:* God is provoked to anger not by his capricious-
   ness but by human failure to uphold justice and morality.
6. *Sibling Conflict, with the Younger Usually Emerging the Victor:* The order of nature (primacy of the firstborn) is overturned, demonstrating that
   God, not nature, is the ruling principle in human affairs.
7. *Testing:* God tests those who are to carry forth his mission; the result is
   the development of moral character.

Superseding these important themes, which occur throughout the Bible in
various forms, is the dominant one of *continuity*, represented by the unifying
word in Genesis *toledot* ("begettings"). The word appears eleven times, often accompanied by long genealogical lists. The names may deflect attention from
what is central to Genesis. The major thrust of the book would seem to be toward
human fecundity, following the early divine command to "bear fruit and be
many" (1:28), and pointing toward the eventual fecundity of the people of Israel
(which will only be realized in the book of Exodus). Such an emphasis seems appropriate in a book about origins.

Ironically, however, the undercurrent in Genesis points not to life and its
continuation, but rather to its threatened extinction. In story after story the protagonist, his people, and occasionally the entire world are threatened. In at least
one case (Avraham) a perfectly legal and natural solution is found—the birth of
Yishmael as his heir—only to be rejected by God in favor of a more difficult
one: a son born to an elderly woman.

It is clear that the stress on continuity and discontinuity has one purpose: to
make clear that God is in control of history. Human fertility and continuity in
history come not from magical rites or from the arbitrary decisions of the gods,
but from a God who bases his rule on justice. Nature disappears as a ruling factor
in human affairs, replaced by a principle of morality which is unshakable precisely because it comes from a God who is beyond the rules of nature.

But the result is a book which abounds in tension. From the beginnings of human history (ch. 4) we encounter contradictions and opposites, whether on a
small scale (fertility and barrenness) or a large one (promise and delayed fulfillment). Nowhere is this so clear as in the dramatic high point of the book, Genesis
22. As Avraham stands with knife upraised, the entire enterprise of Genesis
hangs in the balance. But the entire book is replete with such tensions and con-
tinuity-threatening situations. There are barren wives, brothers vowing to kill
brothers, cities and even a world being destroyed by an angry God. The main
characters of Genesis thus emerge as survivors, above all else. Noah sets the pattern, but he is merely the first, and too passive an example. The Patriarchs must
brave hostile foreigners, bitter intrafamily struggles, and long wanderings before
they can find peace.

While by the end of the book many of the tensions have been resolved, one
conspicuously has not: God's promise of the land of Canaan. As the book ends,

"in Egypt," we are left to ponder how this God, who keeps his promises to "those who love him" (Exod. 20:6), will bring the people back to their land—a land inhabited by someone else and in which the Children of Israel own only a burial site. Yet despite the tension, we may assume from the experiences of the Patriarchs that God will indeed "take account of" the Israelites (50:24), that he will take whatever ill has been planned against them and "plan-it-over for good" (50:20).

> Everett Fox. *In the Beginning* (New York, Schocken, 1983), pp. xxxiii–xxxv

Disparate elements are somehow juxtaposed, in art or life or both, creating a kind of dissonance, and an artist comes along who resolves that dissonance through the creation of a new form. . . . Something similar might be said . . . of that eclectic "Redactor" of Genesis, for that matter, who pressed the folk and priestly voice of his tribe into a contiguous relationship so profound that I myself am still affected by it, 20-some centuries later.

> Robert Coover. *The New York Times Book Review*. March 18, 1984, p. 38

HANNAH

Even though the subject of the story is the birth of Samuel, its main emphasis is not on Samuel or his birth, but on Hannah, who bore him. This is the source of the independence of the story, and it is the starting point of its special character: the story is based on a folkloristic and mythological theme, but by a fundamental transformation of this theme it transfers the accent to the human element. The transition from the birth of the hero to the woman who bears him is a transition to the human, and Hannah is an outstanding example of humanity. The answer to the question: What is the subject of the chapter?—is: The birth of Samuel. But the answer to the question: Who is the hero of the chapter?—is: Hannah. The genius of the Biblical tale is shown here in this diversion of the emphasis from the birth of Samuel to Hannah, from the superhuman hero to the heroine whose entire heroism consists in her humanity.

After the appearance of Elkanah in the first verse, the narrator presents his wives in the second verse, and in the simplest possible words gives the basic fact that determines Hannah's fate: "And Peninnah had children but Hannah had no children" [I Sam. 1:2]. . . .

And here there arises an interesting question of character: How can a refined woman like Hannah mitigate her bitterness? This Hannah does by her prayer to God. From a dramatic point of view, this prayer is the climax of the action, and it can be followed only by a gradual denouement, but its interest from the point of view of the character of the central figure is even greater than its significance for the plot, for there can be no better evidence of the refinement of Hannah's nature. Hannah does not reply to Peninnah or complain to Elkanah; instead she goes aside in God's sanctuary and pours out her soul to the Almighty. In this story, more perhaps than in any other Biblical tale, we feel the significance of prayer. Hannah's prayer in chapter 2 is a hymn of thanksgiving for happiness and salvation, but in chapter 1 her prayer arises from her need and the unhappy life for which she seeks a remedy. The narrator tells us not only of the emotional source of the prayer and the need which it meets, but also of its effect and the action that follows it: "So the woman went her way, and did eat, and her countenance was no more sad" (18); after the prayer coming from the depths the one who prays feels that he is answered; the prayer redeems Hannah from her bitterness of soul and purifies her.

> Zvi Adar. *The Biblical Narrative* (Jerusalem, Department of Education and Culture, World Zionist Organization, 1959), pp. 21, 24–25

[Hannah's] first prayer, the prayer from out of the straits [cf. Ps. 118:5], she prayed with no words at all, and yet she brought her mute supplication to the ear of the One on High—and the text relates *how* she prayed. Now, as her prayer breaks out from expansive grace, her locked heart and her locked mouth open, and the text relates *what* she prayed. The greatness of the "how" is transformed into the greatness of the "what."

Hannah opens with the double exchange that has taken place in her life. The inner exchange: Her heart, a well of grief, is filled with elation: "My heart is elated!" [I Sam. 2:1]. And the outer exchange: She, the insulted and degraded, how she is elevated before her detractors: "My honor has grown high!" [loc. cit.]

Her heart was only elated, it did not become high, while her honor grew high but her spirit did not. No wreath of triumph reaches the goal on its own, no merit stands up on its own; rather: "My heart is elated through the Lord, my honor has grown high through the Lord." Not only that, but she sees herself as merely an illustration of the deeds of the Master of deeds, and out of this she embarks from the circle of the private domain to the public places of the human world. The thanksgiving prayer in her mouth for the exchange of one extreme for the other that took place in her life becomes a paean of wonder to the One who makes exchanges without limit.

> Avraham Kariv. *Shiv'at 'ammudei hattenakh* (Tel Aviv, Am Oved, 1968), p. 129†

The overall form which the Song [of Hannah] takes is difficult to define in any final way because the Song seems to lie somewhere between a hymn and a song of thanksgiving. That it may partake of both is not surprising; [the German biblical scholar Claus] Westermann has pointed out that psalms often combine a report of

God's deeds (as in songs of thanksgiving) with description of his greatness and glory (the hymns). Such a phenomenon is to be found in the passage before us. Like the typical hymn, the Song of Hannah has three sections: the introduction, body, and conclusion. Typically the introduction is a call to praise of God, but here joy of the worshipper is expressed instead. The body of the hymn most often states the reason for praise, as is done in verses 4–8 of the present work. The conclusion repeats the summons to praise in most hymns, whereas the focus in the last strophe of this Song is a climactic prayer that Yahweh may bless his anointed one. The hymn expresses thanksgiving to Yahweh as one would expect in a song of thanksgiving but the references remain surprisingly general. Typically one difference between a song of thanksgiving and a hymn is that the former cites specific items for which one is thankful. The present hymn does not do this but also spends much time in describing the nature of God. Yet, of course, its overall mood is that of thankfulness.

The closest parallel to the Song of Hannah is Psalm 75 which has elements of the song of thanksgiving in it but is most appropriately viewed as a cult liturgy. The psalm begins with reference to prior testimony in the cult concerning the history of God's deeds among them. Then the psalmist proceeds to contrast the sorry fate of those who would oppose God (vv. 2–8) with the blessings visited upon the faithful. This motif of contrast is but one of the clear parallels between Psalm 75 and the Song of Hannah. Another motif in common is that of warning. The psalmist warns against arrogance (v. 4) as does the author of I Samuel 2. Much of the imagery is identical: God makes firm the pillars of the earth (v. 3b; cf. I Sam. 2:8c); he breaks off the horns of the wicked, but exalts the horns of the faithful (v. 10; cf. I Sam. 2:1, 10c).

A. David Ritterspach. In *Rhetorical Criticism*. Ed. by J. J. Jackson and M. Kessler (Pittsburgh, Pickwick Press, 1974), p. 72

The author succeeds in communicating to the reader the feeling that the rather humdrum events of the tale are important; not because Samuel is going to be born as an answer to Hannah's prayer, but rather because her quiet despair and her sorely tested human dignity are presented as subjects significant in their own right. It is somewhat difficult to see how the mood of the tale is built up until one realizes that there are several apparently irrelevant descriptive details in it, such as the portions distributed by Elkanah to his family (4b–5), or Eli's chair by the doorpost (v. 9). These bits of mise en scène deepen the mimetic value and suggest the emotional atmosphere of the piece. Nevertheless, they are not quite sufficient as an explanation of the tale's effect. The decisive technical means employed is rather a kind of "epic breadth" which compels the reader to notice the mood of the story. It is produced by the long, slightly stilted speeches, and—quite generally—by longish slightly tautological sentences, such as: "He had two wives, the name of the one was Hannah and the name of the other was Penninah, and Penninah had children, but Hannah had no children" (v. 2). The

whole story is told in such longish carefully balanced—and occasionally tautological—sentences. They are not as repetitive and long-winded as the kind used
in the story of the Flood; consequently there is no solemnity in the effect, which
is restricted to an even flow of the narrative and an almost uniform slow tempo of
the telling, which does not change much as the story passes from straight narrative to scene. The device employed to produce the special effect of quiet sadness
is thus revealed, in the last analysis, as a very slight, almost imperceptible manipulation of the telling time.

Jacob Licht. *Storytelling in the Bible* (Jerusalem, Magnes Press, 1978), p. 115

This entire interweaving of exposition, narration proper, and dialogue is executed within a frame of expectations set up by the annunciation type-scene, and
the role of that particular convention ought to be mentioned in order to round out
our sense of the artistry of the episode. The very use of the convention, of
course, points to a weighty role in history for the child who is to be born, since
only for such portentous figures is this sort of divine intervention in the natural
order of conception required. . . . Now, the crucial central motif in the annunciation type-scene is the barren wife's being vouchsafed an oracle, a prophecy from
a man of God, or a promise from an angel, that she will be granted a son, sometimes with an explicit indication of the son's destiny, often with the invocation of
the formula, "At this season next year, you will be embracing a son."

What is interesting about Hannah's annunciation, when it is compared with
other occurrences of this particular type-scene, is the odd obliquity of the promise. We hear the words of Hannah's prayer but no immediate response from God.
The barren mother's bitterness is given unusual prominence in this version—
perhaps, one might conjecture, because it is a thematically apt introduction to the
birth of a lonely leader whose ultimate authority the people will finally circum-
vent to establish the monarchy against which he warns.

The particular form taken here by the annunciation is virtually ironic. Eli the
priest, who at first grossly misconstrued what Hannah was doing, prays for or
perhaps promises the fulfillment of her prayer, and whatever his purpose, it appears to be sufficient to make Hannah feel reconciled with her present condition.
If his statement is meant as a consoling prediction, he is a singularly ignorant
conduit of divine intentions, for Hannah has not even told him what it was she
was praying for, only that she was pleading to God in great anguish. The effect
of all this is to subvert the priest's role as intercessor. The generalized peti-
tion/prediction he pronounces to her is really superfluous, for it is her specifically worded heartfelt supplication for a son that God answers through the fact of
conception. Compared to the angels and men of God who deliver the good news
in other annunciation type-scenes, the priest here plays a peripheral and perhaps
slightly foolish role. This oblique undermining of Eli's authority is of course essentially relevant to the story of Samuel: the house of Eli will be cut off, his iniq-
uitous sons will be replaced in the sanctuary by Samuel himself, and it will be

Samuel, not his master Eli, who will hear the voice of God distinctly addressing him in the sanctuary. The idea of revelation, in other words, is paramount to the story of Samuel, whose authority will derive neither from cultic function, like the priests before him, nor from military power, like the judges before him and the kings after him, but from prophetic experience, from an immediate, morally directive call from God. For this exemplary figure of prophetic leadership, Hannah's silent, private prayer and the obtuseness of the well-meaning priest who superfluously offers himself as intercessor between her and God provide just the right kind of annunciation.

Robert Alter. *The Art of Biblical Narrative* (New York, Basic Books, 1981), pp. 85–86

HOSEA

Hosea has a rich and vivid imagination, while his style is full, brief and sententious. And notwithstanding several strong figures, which simply testify to the poetic boldness and originality as well as the simple straightforwardness of those times, he manifests great tenderness and warmth of language. His poetry is everywhere purely original (with the exception of a few manifest reminiscences from Amos 4:3; 8:14), full of force of thought and beauty of treatment. Hence much is here flung off with wonderful ease, which was subsequently taken up by others and expanded in various forms. Yet in his style the soft and the flowing prevails, and then again the violently strained and abrupt, whilst the overwhelming sorrow causes much to be rather indicated than completed. Upon his entire language also there lies the oppression of that age and of his heart heavily laden therewith; there is no previous prophet so elegiac as Hosea; that ancient section Isaiah chapters 15–16 is alone comparable to it, and is generally very similar. In fact, this prophet, who possesses genuine poetic spirit and power, and whose thoughts follow in great and beautiful proportions, is urged to speak really by sorrow; a divine amazement, anger and sorrow give him words, which roll on in exhaustless stream, yet always beautiful, soft and tender, all aglow with the warmth of the poet-heart. . . .

On close examination we discover, that the book is a whole beautifully executed in complete accordance with a definite artistic plan. . . . [1840]

Georg H. A. von Ewald. *Commentary on the Prophets of the Old Testament*. Vol. II. Tr. by J. Frederick Smith (London, Williams and Norgate, 1876), pp. 218–19, 222

As a man and as an author Hosea stands in many ways in striking contrast with the great Judaean Amos. He is tenderer, more sensitive, and also more gifted in mind than the herdsman of Thekoa. He was controlled by his feelings more than by strong will; and therefore he was inclined to find guidance and support in the reason and in knowledge, like many a man whose nature has a peculiarly large share of emotion. Hosea practises his poetic art with more conscious purpose than does Amos, and perhaps he was a more "cultured" man. But he does not write so vividly, nor so surely striking the point, as does the other. He is just as eager a reformer; but he has a somewhat narrower spirit. . . . Hosea is certainly, like Amos, one of the truly great poets of Israel. Many a tender lyric, many a moving song, and many splendid pictures hold fast the soul of any reader who knows how to lift his thoughts over into the strange world of this Prophet.

> Bernhard Duhm. *The Twelve Prophets*. Authorised tr. by Archibald Duff (London, Adam and Charles Black, 1912), pp. 30–31, 33

The Book of Hosea . . . is one of the most complete, the most unified in the Bible. Even with all the many corruptions that befell it, its language is simple, clear, and concise. Not only the complete book, or a complete verse, but every individual link comprises a sharp, poignant ideational unit. An artful charm is added when a speech unit is cut loose and does not follow up the preceding one, when it is not laden with rhetorical descriptiveness, when it is not at all dryly prosaic.

It is a complete, characteristic prophetic work; the seal of organic unity is stamped upon it—a tier of bricks from which it is hard to extract even one.

Nevertheless, Hosea, like most of the prophets, was a man of riddles; even in this little book not everything is of a piece.

While the first chapter is written in allusive language, relating shocking things about the prophet and his family life, it is perfectly clear that an editor's hand touched the book and, as is the custom of editors, filled in what was missing in the original. This editor was, apparently, no streetsweeper, and the first chapter, to which he added, is nicely styled; but from the whole story there rises a scent of legend, and this Gomer, daughter of Diblaim, about whom are related things that would be unseemly for a daughter of Israel like Sarah— . . . it is very doubtful that she is a "historical personality." The names "Not-My-People," "Not-Loved" were invented by the clever editor on the basis of Hosea's descriptive style (ch. 2): "In place of it being said of you, 'You are not my people,' it will be said of you 'Children of the living God.'" The story in chapter 3, too ("The Lord said to me again: Go, love a woman who loves evil and is adulterous"), which gives the impression of an actual event, proves that the first story is founded in the imagination. There was no need at all to double the domestic tragedy, and the word "again" does not mean a review of what had been.

> Jacob Fichman. *'Arugot* (Jerusalem, Bialik Institute, 1954), pp. 245–46†

Hosea's book is not an easy one to read, largely because of its swift changes of mood in which threatening gives way to hope, curses to blessings, disgust and hatred to love. In order to read it intelligently and, therefore, to understand its author, one should be aware of its three parts: the first, a biographical and auto-biographical account of Hosea's marriage, given in chapters 1 to 3; the second, a series of addresses, probably, in the form we now have them, much mutilated from a lost original (if there were, indeed, a complete original) and given in chapters 4 to 11; and, lastly, a final chapter, 14, in which Hosea expresses both hope and expectation of the return of Israel to God and of her reinstatement as His people.

Mary Ellen Chase. *The Prophets for the Common Reader* (New York, W. W. Norton, 1963), p. 82

No student of the Bible can fail to be shaken by the pathos and rage of the prophecies of Hosea, who drew much of his imagery and religious insights from his picture of a tragic experience of marital love.

In Hosea's chastisement, the totality of Israel—what the rabbis call *knesset Israel*—is represented by the mother-wife figure, while the individuals of Israel are designated as the children. The mother has been seeking false and foreign lovers, but in the end she will say: "I will go and return to my first husband; for then it was better with me than now [2:9]." Here, God is openly and forthrightly—unabashedly anthropomorphically—represented as Israel's husband . . . .

It is significant that Hosea's imagery added nothing to what is already *implied* in the Decalogue. Harlotry meant to him principally religious infidelity, idolatry, worship of strange gods. The greatness of his message thus lies not in the originality of its concepts, but in their direct and poetic formulation. Hosea's poetic power lay not only in his raging passion against the infidelity of Israel, but in his promise of restitution in the same figure of speech: "And I will *betroth* thee unto Me forever, yea, I will *betroth* thee unto Me in righteousness and in justice, in loyalty and in *love*. And I will *betroth* thee unto Me in faithfulness; and thou shalt know the Lord [2:21–22]."

Gerson D. Cohen. In *The Samuel Friedland Lectures 1960–66* (New York, Jewish Theological Seminary of America, 1966), pp. 9–10

Hosea's message is different from that of his contemporaries Isaiah, Micah, or Amos in respect of form. Instead of short, clearly-contoured units easily detachable from one another, what are most prominent in Hosea are larger entities with a relatively uniform subject-matter. The messenger formula is certainly still found, but with Hosea the process of combining short sayings into larger units seems to have gone on side by side with the permanent establishment (perhaps in writing) of the component parts of the tradition. On the other hand, the borrowing from non-religious literary categories which is so marked a feature of Amos or Isaiah is almost completely absent in Hosea. The result of these factors is to give Hosea's way of speaking, taken as a whole, a much greater uniformity. Using his diction to draw conclusions about his person, we are given the impression that Hosea was a man of extremely strong feelings. His preaching, more than that of any other prophet, is governed by personal emotions, by love, anger, disappoint-ment, and even by the ambivalence between two opposite sentiments. Since the prophet lends this emotional ardour to the words of God himself—or, to put it better, since Yahweh catches the prophet up into his emotions—in Hosea the di-vine word receives a glow and a fervour the intensity of which is characteristic of the message of this prophet alone.

> Gerhard von Rad. *The Message of the Prophets*. Tr. by D. M. G. Stalker (New York, Harper & Row, 1972), p. 111

Isaac, Binding of. *See* Abraham: Binding of Isaac

ISAIAH I

Isaiah, the first of the prophets, both in order and dignity, abounds in such transcendant excellencies, that he may be properly said to afford the most perfect model of the prophetic poetry. He is at once elegant and sublime, forcible and or-namented; he unites energy with copiousness, and dignity with variety. In his sentiments there is uncommon elevation and majesty; in his imagery the utmost propriety, elegance, dignity, and diversity; in his language uncommon beauty and energy; and, notwithstanding the obscurity of his subjects, a surprising de-gree of clearness and simplicity. To these we may add, there is such sweetness in the poetical composition of his sentences, whether it proceed from art or genius, that if the Hebrew poetry at present is possessed of any remains of its native grace and harmony, we shall chiefly find them in the writings of Isaiah. . . . [1753]

> Robert Lowth. *Lectures on the Sacred Poetry of the He-brews*. Vol. II. Tr. from the Latin by G. Gregory (Lon-don, Printed for J. Johnson, 1787), pp. 84–85

Isaiah is, without exception, the most sublime of all Poets. This is abundantly visible in our Translation; and, what is a material circumstance, none of the Books of Scripture appear to have been more happily translated than the Writings of this Prophet. Majesty is his reigning character; a majesty more commanding, and more uniformly supported, than is to be found among the rest of the Old Tes-tament Poets. He possesses, indeed, a dignity and grandeur, both in his concep-tions and expressions, which is altogether unparalleled, and peculiar to himself. There is more clearness and order, too, and a more visible distribution of parts, in his Book, than in any other of the Prophetical Writings.

> Hugh Blair. *Lectures on Rhetoric and Belles Lettres*. Vol. III. 2d ed., corr. (London, Printed for W. Strahan, T. Cadell, 1785), p. 198

We have still to seek for a definition of poetry. The writings of Plato, and Bishop Taylor, and the "Theoria Sacra" of Burnet, furnish undeniable proofs that poetry of the highest kind may exist without metre, and even without the contra-distinguishing objects of a poem. The first chapter of Isaiah (indeed a very large portion of the whole book) is poetry in the most emphatic sense; yet it would be not less irrational than strange to assert, that pleasure, and not truth, was the immediate object of the prophet. In short, whatever *specific* import we attach to the word, poetry, there will be found involved in it, as a necessary consequence, that a poem of any length neither can be, or ought to be, all poetry. Yet if an harmonious whole is to be produced, the remaining parts must be preserved *in keeping* with the poetry; and this can be no otherwise effected than by such a studied selection and artificial arrangement, as will partake of *one*, though not a *peculiar* property of poetry. And this again can be no other than the property of exciting a more continuous and equal attention than the language of prose aims at, whether colloquial or written.

> Samuel Taylor Coleridge. *Biographia Literaria* Vol. II
> (London, Rest Fenner, 1817), p. 11

Another, Isaiah, seems placed above humanity, and resembles a rumbling of continual thunder. He is the great reproacher. His style, a kind of nocturnal cloud, is lighted up with images which suddenly empurple all the depths of his obscure thought, and make us exclaim, "It lightens!" Isaiah engages in battle, hand to hand, with the evil which, in civilization, makes its appearance before the good. . . . He stands upon the threshold of civilization, and he refuses to enter. He is a kind of mouthpiece of the desert speaking to the multitudes, and demanding, in the name of the sands, the brambles, and the winds, the sites of the cities. . . .

Those things with which Isaiah reproached his time—idolatry, debauchery, war, prostitution, ignorance—still exist. Isaiah is the undying contemporary of the vices that make themselves servants, and of the crimes that make themselves kings. [1864]

> Victor Hugo. *William Shakespeare*. Tr. by Melville B.
> Anderson (Chicago, McClurg, 1887), pp. 48–49

He sounds the whole gamut of human emotion, from the terror and anguish caused by the capture of Babylon to the burst of exultation from the inhabitant of Zion upon the overthrow of Sennacherib's host. . . .

Witness the fulness of his vocabulary, the logical arrangement of his matter, the rich variety of his style, the loftiness of his tone. Prose and verse are alike facile to his speech. He can sing with the lyric poets; observe the two psalms in chapter 12, and the song of the vineyard in chapter 5. Often again we find an epic quality in his oracles; that against Tyre, for example, and those against the Syro-Ephraimite league, and the burden of the valley of vision. Still more marked is the presence of the dramatic element; beginning at the moment of his first entrance, when like the Greek chorus he calls upon heaven and earth to witness the ingratitude of Israel; clearly manifest in the watchman of chapter 21, who brings tidings from Babylon and answers the call from Edom; specially prominent at the close of chapter 10, when the terrible Assyrian speeds from point to point till at Nob he shakes his hand at the mount of the daughter of Zion; and at this crisis . . . the divine actor steps upon the stage and Lebanon falls by a mighty one.

The vast reach of Isaiah's thought appears . . . in his familiarity with Nature, and with the geography, history, and contemporary politics of his own and other nations; and also in his penetration into all spheres of human life, intellectual, emotional, and moral.

> Wm. H. Cobb. In *The Bible as Literature*, by Richard G. Moulton et al. (New York, Crowell, 1896), pp. 150–51

Isaiah's poetical genius is superb. His characteristics are grandeur and beauty of conception, wealth of imagination, vividness of illustration, compressed energy and splendour of diction. These characteristics, as is natural, frequently accompany each other; and passages which exemplify one will be found to exemplify another. . . . The blissful future which he foresees, when the troubles of the present are past, he delineates in colours of surpassing purity and beauty; with mingled wonder and delight we read, and read again, those marvellous pictures of serenity and peace, which are the creations of his inspired imagination (2:2–4; 4:2–6; 9:1–7; 11:1–10; 16:4b–5; 29:18ff.; 30:21–26; 32:1–8, 15–18; 33:5f., 20ff.). The brilliancy and power of Isaiah's genius appear further in the sudden contrasts, and pointed antitheses and retorts, in which he delights; as 8:22–9:1; 17:14; 29:5; 31:4f.; 1:3, 10. . . .

Isaiah's literary style shows similar characteristics. It is chaste and dignified: the language is choice, but devoid of all artificiality or stiffness; every sentence is compact and forcible; the rhythm is stately; the periods are finely rounded (e.g. 2:12ff.; 5:26ff.; 11:1–9). Isaiah indulges occasionally—in the manner of his people—in tone-painting (17:12f.; 28:7f.,16; 29:6), and sometimes enforces his meaning by an effective assonance (5:7; 10:16; 17:1,2; 22:5; 29:2,9; 30:16; 32:7, 19), but never to excess, or as a meretricious ornament. His style is never diffuse: even his longest discourses are not monotonous or prolix; he knows how to treat his subject fruitfully, and, as he moves along, to bring before his reader new and varied aspects of it: thus he seizes a number of salient points and presents each singly in a vivid picture (5:8ff.; 7:18ff.; 9:8ff.; 19:16ff.). Isaiah has the true classical sense of *peras* [restraint, balance]; his prophecies always form artistic wholes, adequate to the effect intended, and having no feature overdrawn. He, moreover, possesses a rare power of adapting his language to the occasion, and of bringing home to his hearers what he would have them understand: thus, with a few sentences, he can shatter the fairest idols, or dissipate the fondest illusions (1:2, 3, 4); 2:6ff.; 3:14f.; 5:8ff.; 22:1ff.; 22:15ff. . . . or win his hearer's attention by the delicate irony of a parable (5:1ff.), or by the stimulus of a significant name (8:1, 19:18, 30:7), or enable them to gaze with him upon the majesty of the Divine Glory (6:1ff.) or to wander in imagination (11:1ff., and elsewhere) over the transformed earth of the Messianic future. And he can always point the truth which he desires to impress by some apt figure or illustration: for instance, the scene of desperation in 3:6f., or 8:21f., the proverb in 9:10, the child in 10:19 (cf. 11:6), the suggestive similes in 17:5, 6, the uneasy couch 28:20, the disappointing dream 29:8, the subtle flaw, spreading insidiously through a wall, 30:13f. No prophet has Isaiah's power either of conception or of expression; none has the same command of noble thoughts, or can present them in the same noble and attractive language.

> Samuel R. Driver. *An Introduction to the Literature of the Old Testament.* 10th ed., rev. and enl. (New York, Scribner's, 1903), pp. 227–29

The passages that may with certainty be attributed to him possess a distinctive style. What Matthew Arnold says of Homer's style would apply equally well to Isaiah's, for it has the qualities of plainness of thought, plainness of style, noble-ness, and rapidity, which Arnold attributes to the Greek. It is an oratorical style full of pith and pungency. Perhaps its most striking peculiarity is its compres-sion, which, however, does not result in obscurity. Much of the effect of this is of course lost in the translation which fails to reproduce, for example, in 29:16 the terse vigor of the Hebrew, where the one word *haphkekem* represents five words in the English, "Ye turn things upside down." Similarly the English trans-lation fails to reproduce the assonances which are another noticeable feature of Isaiah's style. In 5:7, a passage in which the prophet assumes the role of a min-strel, and tries to enlist attention by the lively measures of a love song, he ends with two couplets intended to point the moral in a way that would be emphatic and easily remembered:

> He looked for justice (*mishpāt*), but behold bloodshed (*mispāh*);
> For righteousness (*tsĕdāqāh*), but behold a cry (*tseʿāqāh*).

These plays upon words, though a rather marked feature of Isaiah's style, are really used sparingly, and never without telling oratorical effect. They certainly do not sound playful. Even the occasional flashes of humor in Isaiah's oracles produce no effect of playfulness. A good example is to be found in the seventh chapter (v. 20). Ahaz in opposition to Isaiah's advice had hired at great expense the king of Assyria to defend him against the kings of Syria and Israel. This Isa-iah satirically refers to as the hiring of a foreign razor, and adds threateningly:

> In that day will Yahveh shave with a razor that is hired in the
> parts beyond the River, even with the king of Assyria, the head
> and the hair of the feet; and it shall also consume the beard.

The meaning, of course, is "You may hire the razor, but God will give you a close shave from head to foot, even cutting off the beard"—which to an ancient oriental meant a degradation complete and shameful.

> Edward C. Baldwin. *The Prophets* (New York, Thomas Nelson, 1927), pp. 75–76

Let us look at a few passages in order to gain some idea of the poetic power of the prophets. Take first the famous passage of Isaiah, in which he describes the approach of dread Assyria. Summoned by Jahveh Himself—a thought both sublime and terrible to the Israelite of that time—Assyria advances from the end of the earth, marching with unresting haste. No obstacle, such as usually delays an army's advance, stops its course. With his terrible war-cry, like the roar of a lion making his adversary quake, he springs upon Israel, and then stands shrieking over his prey. An obscure image, borrowed from the ancient Creation-myth, concludes the dreadful description—darkness covers heaven and earth, and through the darkness sounds the roar of the enemy, like the roaring of the raging sea. Primeval chaos—darkness and great waters—again prevails; the last fight and end of the old Germanic gods, as we should say, has come:

> He raises a banner for the people from afar
>> and hisses it on from the end of the earth:
>>> it comes hasting on, at full speed!
> No stumbler, no tired man amongst them!
>> It needs neither slumber nor sleep!
> The girdle of its loins is not loosed,
>> the thong of its shoes is not broken.
> Its arrows remain sharp,
>> its bows are all bent.
> The hoofs of its steeds
>> are like to the flint,
>>> its wheels like the storm.
> It raises a roar like the lion,
>> it roars like the young lion and howls,
> and seizes the prey and bears it away
>> and there is none who can save.
> It howls over it
>> on that day
>>> like sea roaring.
> If one looks to the earth—distressful darkness,
>> and the light grew dark in the clouds. [5:26–30]

Among all the battle scenes which the Assyrians and Egyptians have left us, there is not one that can compare in vivid grandeur with this Old Testament picture.

Take another passage of the same prophet, describing the end of the Assyrian dominion and the coming of the Messiah. In a time of misery, due to foreign oppression, the prophet sees his people walking in "the land of darkness," that is, in the land where the sun is unknown—a legendary idea that also appears elsewhere. But he also sees the hour of deliverance, when the sheen of the glorious light pierces into this awesome land. That will be a day of rejoicing, of rejoicing like that of the harvest-time, or like that of the people dividing the booty brought home at the end of a war. What means this light? Why this joy? The prophet explains it in a parable. Up till now Israel was like a beast of burden, sighing under the heavy oppression of Assyria; now Jahveh has broken the yoke and destroyed the oppressor's rods. Then a new image rises before the prophet's eye: the enemy's army is destroyed; the battlefield is strewn with the weapons of the enemy, cast away in his sudden flight. These are all gathered into a great heap, and what till now was Israel's terror is burned in the fire—the war boots in which the enemy had once marched with the noise of thunder, and the martial cloaks stained with the blood of the slain. Then the prophet's eye passes from the deliverance to the deliverer. A new ruler appears in Israel, a mysterious child, bearing on his shoulder the rod of a prince. And by means of a series of Divine names the prophet announces what the characteristics of this new ruler will be. Wise in counsel, never at a loss, he will be "wonderful," and in his strength he will be like to a god. Like a father he will guard his people for ever and give them the peace they long for. Thus on David's ancient throne—for the Wonderful One is of David's line—there will arise the dominion of righteousness and peace for ever. But all this is due to the "zeal" of Jahveh Zebaoth, who will not allow His people to be robbed or harmed by the heathen.

> The people, who are walking in darkness,
>   saw a great light:
> Those who dwelt in the dark land,
>   Glory shines upon them!
> Thou bringest great rejoicing   and great exultation
>   they rejoice before thee   as with harvest joy,
>   as men rejoice,   when they divide the spoil.
> For the yoke of his burden,   the staff of his neck
>   hast thou as on Midian's day   broken!
> For every war boot that strode along noisily,
>   Every robe, stained with blood,
> they were burned,   they were food for the fire!
>   For a scion has arisen for us,
>   a son given to us,
>   who bears on his shoulder dominion,
>   and his name is:
> Marvel in counsel,   a God of a hero,
>   Father for ever,   prince of peace.
> Great is righteousness   and peace without end
>   on David's seat   and in his realm:
> he bases it firmly
>   on justice and righteousness
>   from henceforth for ever!
> Jahveh Zebaoth's   zeal accomplishes it! [9:1–6]

No one who looks fairly at such pictures can ever lose the impression made by these strong colours. Surely it is high time that men should awake from their neglect of the prophetical writings.

Hermann Gunkel. *What Remains of the Old Testament, and Other Essays*. Tr. from the German by A. K. Dallas (New York, Macmillan, 1928), pp. 21–25

The outstanding quality of Isaiah I's style is its sublimity, which ranks with that of Aeschylus and of Milton. His imagination is superb: his diction opulent. Figures of the utmost boldness and loftiness crowd one another. In this respect he forms a marked contrast to Ezekiel and Jeremiah whose figures are often homely and commonplace. Even those which Isaiah draws from the country life of Palestine have a characteristic force and vividness. Not only was he a poet of the highest order, but he shows in his compact well-rounded sentences and brilliantly effective discourses the marks of the supreme orator.

The translators of Isaiah in the Authorised Version have given the English-speaking world some most magnificent passages of prose and free verse. Its rhythmical quality is attested by the way in which hundreds of the lines have been set to music by Handel in his "Messiah." An unusually large number of expressions from Isaiah have passed into the language, being used many times by those who have no idea of their origin. The book abounds, too, in noble longer passages.

John R. Macarthur. *Biblical Literature and Its Backgrounds* (New York, Appleton, 1936), p. 241

For Isaiah the vision of his calling [ch. 6] was a profound experience; later he gave this experience linguistic shape. One can and should read the text not without trepidation. Yet the sound pattern is to be noted: the numerous consonants in the description of the seraphim, the long vowels of the hymn, the intensification of consonants in the description of the shaking of the temple, the stammering in monosyllabic words having many i-vowels (*'oy li ki nidmeiti ki 'ish* ["Woe to me, for I am finished, for a man . . ."; Isa. 6:5]).

Another observation, however, is more important. Although Hebrew prosody as a rule prefers two-part constructions (gemination, hendiadys, parallelism), here several times we come across three-part constructions in the text: three pairs of wings, three [exclamations of] *qadosh* ["holy!"], *ki* three times in the prophet's first discourse, three actions of the seraph, three propositions in his discourse, three components in Yahweh's discourse (eyes, ears, heart), threefold devastation (city, houses, fields). The basis for this fact lies, as was said, not in Hebraic practice; nor in the poet—for elsewhere he prefers concise language; nor in chance—for Isaiah does not write at random. The high incidence of three-part constructions is probably to be explained by a crucial element that the poet brought to his vision as the experience itself, that being the threefold *Qadosh* ["Holy, holy, holy"]. This threefold scansion becomes basic and evokes rhetorical powers: the prophet remains polarized in the departure [from convention] of creating the threefold scheme and uses it against the traditional and characteristic style.

It does not matter whether the explanation presented here is absolutely correct as such. What is crucial is that an explanation of this kind can and must be sought. People who are themselves creatively gifted might take the polarization of consciousness described above as self-understood. He who would thus interpret a work of art would perhaps want to discuss an explanation of this kind but would not in principle reject it.

In Isaiah 30:9ff. we observe a rare phenomenon, which I—with Dámaso Alonso—would call a "successive forking": an element is developed into two elements, the second element of which is developed into two elements, and so forth.

> *'am meri hu' banim kehashim*
>> *banim lo' 'avu shemoa' torat YHWH*
>> *'asher ' ameru laro'im lo' tir'u*
>>> *welahozim lo' tehezu lanu nekhohot*
>>>> *dabberu lanu halaqot hazu mahatalot*

> [*A rebellious people* it is, deceitful *sons,*
>> *sons* that desire not to hear the Lord's instruction,
>> which *says* to the prophets "Do not prophesy"
>> and to the *visionaries* "Have no *visions* of reproval *for us*,"
>>> speak *to us* pleasantries,
>>>> *envision* playfulness.]

In normal parallelism of members the second element answers to the entire first element, a third new element follows, and the fourth element is again an echo of the third. The thought strides forth as with two legs. In our case the last part of the first proposition releases an echo, the latter part of which releases a new echo, the latter part of which releases a new echo, and so forth. The stylistic operation no longer resembles a marching with two legs but a shadow, which lengthens toward evening.

Luis Alonso-Schökel. *Vetus Testamentum, Supplement* 7, 1979, pp. 157–59†

Isaiah [chapter] 1 is an example of a vivid text, rich in vocabulary with a diction conveying an illusion of emotional depth. The description of the disaster, verses 5–7, is not a conventional description, and the vocabulary is rare. Thus, the combination: *kol-ro'sh loholi w*^e*khol-levav dawway* is uncommon: the pair *ro' shlevav* is irregular. Similarly, the combination *makkah t*^e*riyyah* is unique but the relation between *petsa' w*^e*habburah* is found elsewhere (Prov. 20:30). There is, therefore, a tendency to avoid the narrow use of a traditional formula. Stylistically, the prophetic text is a mixture of two elements: the traditional element presents Isaiah as a child of his literary tradition while the innovative element portrays his deliberate attempt to break the literary tradition. This literary relationship between the old and the new requires clarification. First, even in the modern period, which is distinguished by its literary individual creativity, it is impossible to create entirely new ways of expression; to do so can ruin in advance any channel of communication with the audience. Second, an effective appeal to the audience can be achieved only when the author or speaker somehow breaks the tradition at certain points. Then his message is understood; he is not entirely disconnected from the code of communication, but, on the other hand, his style does not follow the routine; he requires concentrated attention from his audience. Isaiah, by using the traditional code, *ro'sh holi* and *levav dawway*, on the one hand, but the pair *ro'sh-levav*, on the other, as well as the conventional code *makkah + petsa' wᵉhabburah* together with the uncommon combination *makkah ṭriyyah*, still follows a certain communicative code but avoids the cliché. It is obvious that Isaiah 1 is a dynamic text which reflects a deliberate attempt to communicate effectively with the audience. This is done through a careful selection of vocabulary as well as the devices of repetition, synonyms; and in verse 8, for instance, the deliberate attempt to communicate with the audience is revealed through the device of "dwelling" on the subject reflected by the series of three metaphors, two of which are just repetition. In short, the prophetic text cannot be taken as a brief communication constructed in fixed formalistic style. The prophetic speech is a vivid text, which must be studied on the basis of its dynamic nature.

It is obvious that Isaiah's intention in verses 5–8 is to "dwell" on the subject in order to achieve a certain pragmatic goal. Verses 5–8 are not separated from verses 4 + 9. Structural discourse analysis indicates that the subject of verses 5–8 is referred to in verse 4 while the particle *lule* in verse 9 connects the verse with the previous ones as a condition. . . . Since verse 9 indicates that the people no longer live under immediate military threat, we must conclude that the detailed description of the "almost" catastrophe is actually a tool used by Isaiah in order to illustrate a point: the people are sinners (v. 4) and God saves them (v. 9). What is the relationship between the sin, the catastrophe, and God's saving act? The text of verses 4–9 does not provide a clear answer to this question. And, above all, there is a tension between the detailed description of the disaster and the indication of the sin with no specific detail. . . .

The speaker portrays his audience's suffering not as an act of sympathy but in order to indicate the cause. He does this, however, in a two fold way. On the one hand, Isaiah establishes a connection between suffering and punishment, but, on the other, he depicts the past events in a lively way, thus creating an emotional impact. The function of emotion in an argumentative discourse is important since it influences in a way which cannot be achieved by purely reasonable argument. In our case, Isaiah creates the feeling of fear and, at the same time, its opposite: confidence. That is to say, the prophet revives the emotions of the fear of an invasion, but points further to God the saviour, thus establishing the people's notion of dependence on God; a notion which could be released as a consequence of the people's complaint.

Yehoshua Gitay. *Vetus Testamentum*. 33, 1983, pp. 213–15, 218–19

The prophetic figurations are to a considerable degree a kind of deceptive rhetoric. Contrast Isaiah's call, in chapter 6 of his book, to the call of Moses, upon whose authority supposedly it is founded. Moses attempts to evade the call, but Isaiah volunteers, saying: "Here am I; send me." Moses asks Yahweh to name Himself, that he, Moses, may declare Who sent him when he descends into Egypt to speak to his fellow Jews. Isaiah does not even know what he is being called upon to do or to say. The legacy of J declares itself only in the frightening irony of Yahweh's injunctions to Isaiah:

> Go, and tell this people:
> Hear ye indeed, but understand not;
> And see ye indeed, but perceive not.
> Make the heart of this people fat,
> And make their ears heavy,
> And shut their eyes;
> Lest they, seeing with their eyes,
> And hearing with their ears,
> And understanding with their heart,
> Return, and be healed. [vv. 9–10]

Isaiah's irony, like J's, involves the clash of incommensurate orders of reality, the clash of Yahweh and his people—always a clash, rhetorically speaking, despite the promise of every covenant. But Isaiah's irony swerves away from J's into an irony less uncanny to us. J is never bitter; indeed, like Homer, J is sublimely beyond bitterness. Isaiah, strong poet though he be, falls into bitterness *in order to get started*. His bitterness is the cost of his call, or as we would say, the sign of his originality. It *individualizes* Isaiah, by making him memorable at the very start of his prophetic mission. J's Moses is genuinely bewildered that he, a man anything but eloquent, should have been chosen. Isaiah is a knowing latecomer, and he tropes his own conscious eloquence through the image of the glowing stone with which one of the seraphim touches his, the prophet's, mouth. That glowing stone upon the lips is as much Isaiah's mark for his own originality as the transparent eyeball was [Ralph Waldo] Emerson's, or the Holy Spirit brooding over the vast abyss to make it pregnant was Milton's. J as narrator of the tales of Jacob or of the Exodus feels no need for self-dramatization, though I hear his personal sign in the extraordinary tribute he pays Wrestling Jacob: "The sun rose upon him as he passed Penuel, limping on his hip" [Gen. 32:32]. But Isaiah, like all of the writing prophets, and like the Milton of the invocations, cannot get started without dramatizing himself.

Harold Bloom. *Raritan*. Winter, 1984, pp. 16–17

ISAIAH II

Force is the predominant feature of [the first] Isaiah's oratory; persuasion sits upon the lips of the prophet who here speaks [Isaiah II]; the music of his eloquence, as it rolls magnificently along, thrills and captivates the soul of its hearer. So, again, if the most conspicuous characteristic of [the first] Isaiah's imagination be *grandeur*, that of the prophet to whom we are here listening is *pathos*. The storms, the inundations, the sudden catastrophes, which Isaiah [I] loves to depict, are scarcely to be found in this prophecy. The author's imagery is drawn by preference from a different region of nature altogether, viz. from the animate world, in particular from the sphere of *human emotion*. It is largely the figures drawn from the latter which impart to his prophecy its peculiar pathos and warmth (see 49:15, 18; 61:10b, 62:5, 66:13). His fondness for such figures is, however, most evident in the numerous examples of *personification* which his prophecy contains. Since Amos (5:2) it became habitual with the prophets to personify a city or community as a *maiden*, especially where it was desired to represent it as vividly conscious of some keen emotion. This figure is applied in these chapters [40–66] with remarkable independence and originality. Zion is represented as a bride, a mother, a widow, i.e. under just those relations of life in which the deepest feelings of humanity come into play; and the personification is continued sometimes through a long series of verses. Nor is this all. The prophet personifies *nature*: he bids heaven and earth shout at the restoration of God's people (44:23; 49:13; cf. 52:9; 55:12); he hears in imagination the voices of invisible beings sounding across the desert (40:3, 6; 57:14); he peoples Jerusalem with ideal watchmen (52:8) and guardians (62:6). Akin to these personifications is the *dramatic* character of the representation, which also prevails to a remarkable extent in the prophecy: see 40:3ff.; 49:1ff.; 50:4–9; 53:1ff.; 58:3a; 61:10f.; 63:1–6.

> Samuel R. Driver. *Introduction to the Literature of the Old Testament*. 10th ed., rev. and enl. (New York, Scribner's, 1903), pp. 241–42

The very fact that his name is lost seems symbolic of the relative unimportance of specific facts in his writing. His message is a message of comfort and of spiritual uplifting. His people are hopelessly subdued and political action has no meaning for them or for him. We know from his prophecy that Judah is captive in Babylon; but his prophecies contain almost no description of the condition under which the people lived; and the promises of comfort to them are vaguely large and figurative. The promises of unalloyed bliss in the later chapters of the book made to the people apparently after the return to Jerusalem, when their miserable state must have been a bitter contrast to their jubilant hopes, seem to be heightened almost in proportion to their present despair. . . .

On the other hand no portion of the literature of the Old Testament is more individual in style and thought or more gloriously uplifting in expression than the oracles of this great prophet of the Exile. He rises to a new level of faith with the indomitable buoyancy which was the genius of Israel at each crisis of its religion. The ancestral idea that Jehovah would protect them in all events against the gods of the heathen was finally shattered; but this new seer boldly declares that Jehovah is the God of the whole earth: "Have ye not known? have yet not heard? hath it not been told you from the beginning? have ye not understood from the foundations of the earth? It is he that sitteth upon the circle of the earth, and the inhabitants thereof are as grasshoppers; that stretcheth out the heavens as a curtain, and spreadeth them out as a tent to dwell in" [Isa. 40:21–22]. . . . This trimphant exultation in the omnipotent power of Jehovah is the keynote of his message.

Nevertheless this characteristic and jubilant elevation only emphasizes the disturbance of the equilibrium which we found in Amos and Isaiah. The Isaiah of the Exile is not a statesman charged with the responsibility for the political actions of his nation. He bears a message of comfort and of hope; but he proclaims a future whose details are not unveiled. Isaiah always had his feeling in firm control; and though it rise to white heat, it only gives the words of his oracle a stronger motion without changing their character. The Isaiah of the Exile in contrast is carried away into lyrical utterances which almost become pure rhapsody: "Sing, O heavens; and be joyful, O earth; and break forth into singing, O mountains: for the Lord hath comforted his people, and will have mercy upon his afflicted" [Isa. 49:13].

Such passages are wholly different from the grave and terse utterances of Isaiah [I] and his stern consciousness of fact. By the side of the prophet of the exile, Isaiah [I] seems more austere and more remote, a figure isolated in antiquity: and beside Isaiah the prophet of the Exile seems carried away by emotion and imagination, and uncontrolled by the stern sense of fact.

> J. H. Gardiner. *The Bible as English Literature* (New York, Scribner's, 1906), pp. 239–42

The greatest poet in the Bible. He is a new appearance there, not like anyone before him. He himself was perfectly aware that it was so; he realized that what he said was new. Over and over he repeats the word joyfully: "New things do I declare—Sing unto the Lord a new song—New heavens and a new earth" [42:9]. . . .

Indeed, his newness, the difference between him and the prophets before him, is startling. They thunder of God's vengeance; he sings of God's kindness. They see the world a place of black evil; he sees it full of gladness, the waste places breaking forth into joy. They look at mankind and find only cruelty and treachery and vileness; he looks at God, as infinite in mercy as in power. . . .

In the first Isaiah the phrase oftenest repeated is, Woe unto them. So begin God's terrible threats to the wicked. Essentially, He says to them only, "Fear me." "Fear and the pit are upon thee, O inhabitant of the earth" [24:17]. In the second Isaiah the words perpetually repeated are, "Fear not," and, extraordinarily, God, the awful God, is the reason why there is nothing to fear. His own words are: "Fear not, for I am with thee"; "For I the Lord thy God will hold thy right hand saying, Fear not. Thou shalt know that I the Lord am thy saviour" [41:10, 13; 49:26]. These would have been strange statements to Amos. But this new message which was to blot out the remembrance of the past had never been heard before in all the world; even Hosea had caught only part of it. The God of fear, the nameless poet declared, was ended. The Ancient of days, whose terror had darkened all the ages, had gone, and, in the poet's radiant vision, he would never return.

Edith Hamilton. *Spokesmen for God* (New York, Norton, 1949), pp. 223–24

Poet and prophet meet in Second Isaiah. It is difficult to say whether he is more the one than the other; the distinction would not have occurred to him. He is both poet and prophet, and both in a pre-eminent degree. But he is so much the poet, so much a master in the art of poetic composition, that one can never be unaware of his literary genius. He is the proclaimer of the Word of God as the other prophets were. But he transfigures the prophetic forms into great artistic compositions. The elevation and urgency of his prophetic mood are matched by forms of expression commensurate with the thoughts which surged through his soul. He has been frequently accused of exaggeration and excess. But it must be remembered that he writes as an Oriental. Moreover, the significance of the events he proclaims justifies his use of superlatives. For his thought is always of God and of his imminent coming in world history, and his remarkable capacity for participation in the event that had been disclosed to him in the heavenly councils taxed all his powers of thought and feeling.

The intensity of the prophet's thought and feeling is expressed in many ways. He lifts his voice in exulting triumph as he sees the approach of Israel's conquering Lord. He breaks into ecstatic hymns again and again as the event takes place before his enraptured eyes (cf. 42:10–13; 44:23; 45:8; 49:13). The theme of redemption almost invariably stirs him to songs of praise. He who calls upon Israel to sing is himself Israel's most exultant singer (52:7–12; 54:1–10). The contemplation of creation, as of redemption, kindles in him the impulse to praise and glorify God. When he lowers his eyes from his vision to the actual conditions among his people, he is stirred to words of vehement judgment. Yet his compassion creates some of the most moving lines in the whole of scripture (43:1–4; 44:21–22; 48:18–19; 49:14–16; 54:6–8). In the confession of 50:4–9 and 53:1–9 he portrays a figure of inexpressible poignancy. He who sings the hymn of redemption, calling upon heavens and earth, the mountains and the deserts, to join in the great chorus, knows the depth of grief and alienation. Above all, his lyrical gifts are always undergirded by a profundity of religious faith and a self-identification with his time which give them the power they have. . . .

The poet is a master of form, but he is never bound to any single type.

> Hear, you deaf;
> and look, you blind, that you may see!

> Who is blind but my servant,
>> or deaf as my messenger whom I send?
> Who is blind as my dedicated one,
>> or blind as the servant of the LORD? (42:18–19)

The parallelism of members, the variety of grammatical constructions, the repetitions, the climax, the rhetorical devices of exclamation and question—all serve to produce a superb effect upon the reader. . . .

We stand in these poems on the verge of an eschatological drama in which creation, history, and redemption constitute the central themes. Each of these great themes is presented in dramatic ways. God is the central figure from beginning to end; Israel's life and destiny are dynamically involved in the events by which he manifests himself; crucial episodes such as the floodwaters of the time of Noah, the call of Abraham, the exodus from Egypt, the desert wandering, the covenant with David, are recalled and related to the vast pattern of the divine purpose. The purpose of God is a dominant motif in the poems, and they all lie under the tensions of its imminent fulfillment. . . .

It is worth noting, too, that this dramatic style pervades every poem, the so-called servant songs (42:1–4; 49:1–6; 50:4–9; 52:13–53:12) as well as the others. Yet nowhere do we have anything approximating a drama; all the materials are here except the architectonics of the drama itself. The scope of the poet's perspective, the literary forms and types, the imminence of a great divine event, decisive and redemptive, make these poems the supreme achievement of the Hebrew mind in history. . . .

The author was a great prophet, perhaps the greatest of all the prophets, certainly in the range of his vision, his grasp of the great tradition, and the exulting passion of his faith. He was a poet of remarkable lyrical gifts, a master of literary form, and a singer given to joy and praise. He was a man of a sympathy so inward and stirring that it extended itself to the whole realm of nature—heavens and earth, mountain, sea, and desert—to all things animate and inanimate, to mother and wife, to children, and to animals. When he says of the Lord's coming that all flesh shall see his glory, it is no empty phrase. He scales the heights of ecstatic praise and descends the abyss of darkest grief. He knows the Oriental capacity for scorn and contempt; at times his anger seems beyond restraint. But in reality it is not so. His compassion triumphs. His invectives are overcome by oracles of grace and promise. He is Israel's profoundest thinker. The drive of his enthusiasm and ardor tends to obscure this, but it is significant that his feeling always matches the content of his thought. Martin Buber calls him "the originator of a theology of world-history" [*The Prophetic Faith*, 1949, p. 208], and this is in reality the case.

> James Muilenburg. *The Interpreter's Bible*. Vol. V
> (Nashville, Abingdon Press, 1956), pp. 386–88, 398

Deutero-Isaiah is the greatest poet among the prophets of Israel. Isolated Psalms may rival or excel his average but only the book of Job presents so consistently elevated a style. He was a lyricist, gifted with capacities for stirring and expressing the deepest emotions of his people. No small part of the spell he casts over the minds of men is his rare union of beauty and truth, the soaring phrase that lifts the torpid soul. At the same time he addresses himself realistically to the plight of the exiles and the frustration of Jewish religion. His poetry is rhetorically ornamental, but its object is this earth and God's triumph through Israel to all the world.

From his pen pours a flood of imagery, a surging tide of emotion unparalleled in the Old Testament; his intensity and ecstasy never flag. His imagery displays a special fondness for human emotions, as he carries anthropomorphism to its Old Testament pinnacle. Yahweh is conceived as a travailing woman (42:14), a solicitous mother (49:14–15); Israel is God's servant, recalcitrant and yet his one hope for the world (42:18–25; 43:8–10). The style is punctuated with all the arts of Hebrew literature: the rhetorical question, the heaping up of verbs, the short direct quotation, repetition of key words, profusion of imperatives, participial hymn style. He lays claim to the rich variety of types of speech, some drawn from the prophetic tradition: vision and audition narratives (40:3–5, 6–8), oracles of salvation (40:1–2; 43:1–7), invectives (48:1–11), admonitions (51:1–8), theophanies of self-affirmation (43:11–13). Others are gathered from wider poetic usage, some cultic in nature: laments (53:1–9), mocking songs (47), and hymns (40:12–26); judicial proceedings or lawsuits (41:1, 21–22); and heraldic messages (40:9–11).

The limits of the strophes and the nature of the types are nebulous, mainly because the prophet transmuted everything he appropriated and combined the forms with sovereign independence. His creative genius breaks and fuses the forms in strange configurations shaped by the torrent of his message. Form criticism is mainly helpful in showing some of the sources of his literary material, but these sources no more account for Deutero-Isaiah's artistry than the separate legends of Genesis explain the Yahwist's skill.

The rhetorical intensity of the work corresponds to the scope of the prophet's theme. Unlike any prophet before him, Deutero-Isaiah takes the whole of God's action in history as his province ("the former things . . . and the new thing(s)," 43:18; 46:9; 48:6). His historical sweep encompasses the nations and the special tradition of Israel from Noah to the Exile. He knew JE uncommonly well. The prophetic convictions have been thoroughly mastered: sin and redemption, covenant and grace—to which he adds his own themes of witness and praise, sacrifice and redemption through suffering. One meets the substance of Amos and Hosea, Jeremiah and Ezekiel on every page, even to their images and vocabulary. When one encounters such monumental cohesiveness in a Hebrew prophet the temptation is to look for the structure or plan of his work. Many have insisted that the only coherence is the ecstatic style, that actually the work is an assemblage of poetic fragments. [Robert H.] Pfeiffer speaks of "an incoherent succession of ecstatic shouts," [Ludwig] Koehler of the pouring out of "a whirlpool of thoughts, a deluge of declarations." More recent interpreters have stressed the organic unity of chapters 40–55 and have even traced the development of the basic themes from the announcement of comfort for the restored city of Jerusalem to the revelation that the victory of God among the nations is to be achieved by Israel's suffering. Wisdom resides in both positions. The unity that exists is at best circuitous. The major themes have a vast sprawling, cyclical character. They appear and reappear in ever-shifting contexts. The musical compositions that come to mind when reading Second Isaiah are the fugue and the cyclical symphony in which themes recur at random, often transfigured. The book does not have the thread of plot to hold the epic poetry together and yet it is vaster in conception than the fleeting moods of lyric poetry. The orderliness of the thinker struggles to hold the caprice of the poet in check.

> Norman K. Gottwald. *A Light to the Nations: An Introduction to the Old Testament* (New York, Harper, 1959), pp. 402–3

Deutero-Isaiah was the most enthusiastic of the prophets. He had wonderful truths to proclaim, but he never attempted to convince men by the force of his logic alone; he placed himself on the highest level and by the contagious power of his enthusiasm and of his own profound belief he tried to inspire them with new hope and courage, with new loyalty and trust. How well he knew the human heart! How he touched every chord by the music of his words! He carried the people away by his own enthusiasm to see his vision and to hope with him. He had passages of exquisite beauty; as with the touch of a mother's tenderest caress he comforted, as seldom a man has comforted, for he was one of the greatest comforters of the race. No preacher could excel him in the moving power of his appeal, "Ho, every one that thirsts, come ye to the waters" (55:1–3); no saint could surpass him in his certitude,

> For the mountains may depart,
>   and the hills may be removed;
> But My lovingkindness shall not depart from thee,
>   neither shall My covenant of peace be removed,
>   says Yahweh, that has mercy upon thee. (Isa. 54:10)

This prophet wrote only in poetry. That is why some critics cannot regard 44:9–20, in which the folly of idolatry is ridiculed with biting irony, as coming from him, for it is entirely in prose. . . . [It] is not a serious argument, for Isaiah 40–55 is not a single poem but a collection of poems, and there is no reason to expect a close connection between them and the adjoining passages. Indeed, the understanding of the book is deepened and its literary attraction is enhanced, if the individual units are separated and read and enjoyed by themselves; else even this author may become monotonous, although his rhythmic language is melody to the ear. Deutero-Isaiah is surpassingly gentle when he comforts, overpowering when he describes Yahweh's omnipotence, clear and forcible when he reasons, compelling when he sets forth his hope or calls to repentance, always beautiful, never dull or commonplace. His style is so finely wrought and so clearly marked that it can never be forgotten when its peculiarities have once been perceived. Many later poets and prophets show the influence which his style had upon them.

Julius A. Bewer. *The Literature of the Old Testament.* 3rd ed., completely rev. by Emil G. Kraeling (New York, Columbia University Press, 1962), pp. 227–28

The major themes of Second Isaiah—the strong monotheism, emphasis on love, warnings to God's enemies, belief in God as creator and controller of history—are obviously not new themes in the Old Testament. Its images, like its themes, also are not new. What is new is the tone of celebration in chapters 40–55, a celebration the audience is asked to participate in. This is an account of a triumphant return, a rebirth, a renewal; it is a series of poems for an army returning from war, written to revitalize, to arouse and encourage by speaking comfortingly and confidently to a frustrated, religiously perplexed people.

The setting of the opening is perhaps God's council at which God's decision is announced:

> Comfort, comfort my people,
>   says your God.
> Speak tenderly to Jerusalem,
>   and cry to her
> that her warfare is ended,
>   that her iniquity is pardoned,
> that she has received from the LORD's hand
>   double for all her sins. (40:1–3) . . .

[Beginning with verse 12, the great poem of chapter 40] then offers a more complex statement of God's power. To this point, we have been told that the Israelites should be free of fear because the Lord is coming, that they should speak confidently to their enemies, and given one hint—that the power of God is not like earthly power, that this king is also a shepherd. Nevertheless, the Lord *is* King.

> Who has measured the waters in the hollow of his hand
>   and marked off the heavens with a span,
> enclosed the dust of the earth in a measure
>   and weighed the mountains in scales
>   and the hills in a balance? (v. 12)

Even as it describes the might of the Lord, the poem continues to work within extremes similar to those already established between God's world and man's, between a mighty king and a gentle shepherd. There is a constant expansion and contraction of the images, as if we were looking at the same subject from different ends of a telescope. We are asked to imagine all the waters of the universe—a vast image—and then told they are in the hollow of God's hand. Something enormous is compressed into something small, as if they belonged together.

From the image of God's hand, the poetry explodes out into the extreme limits of the heavens, and compresses again to a measure, in which, however, all the dust of the earth is contained. For God, the mountains are in scales, the hills in a balance. On one side, we have immense things—the waters, the heavens, the dust of the earth, mountains and hills; on the other, we have minute things—a hand, a measure, scales, and a balance. But from the perspective of this God, they are the same. . . .

The themes and images which follow in later chapters of Second Isaiah constantly echo the great poem of this chapter. In a sense the act of remembering, of recalling what has been forgotten, occurs throughout Second Isaiah in structure as well as in theme. We are asked repeatedly to recall the statement of chapter 40: that is our focal point, informing us of what we once knew, reminding us of what we have forgotten. God, we know, seeks to comfort Israel, to revive the fallen spirit of his people. A key literary question about Second Isaiah, therefore, concerns its persuasiveness. Can it rally a people? Is it successful in comforting Israel? Is it realistic in its appraisal of man's capabilities? Does it acknowledge counter-arguments? How does a poem arouse and encourage a confused nation? What themes and images does it employ which can inspire a new confidence for the future? . . .

The verbs which run through the poems—*behold, lift up, assemble, look, hear, listen, hearken*—indicate that to this point Israel has been like a blind and deaf people. The Israelites are constantly reminded that God is not only present, if it would only see and hear, but also Israel's friend—"you, Israel, my servant, Jacob, whom I have chosen, / the offspring of Abraham, my friend" (41:8). God will help Israel, we are told three times in chapter 41; he will hold Israel's hand; he will punish her enemies and lead her into a new day. The key point is that God is in control of history and that his word has promised Israel redemption and peace.

Second Isaiah not only exhorts its audience to awaken, listen, look, remember, but also describes what will happen if it does. As if to make the point more persuasive, the account of the fate of Babylon depicts what happens to those who do not believe in the Lord as creator, controller of history, and redeemer. The images and motifs which depict Babylon's destruction are the opposites of those which describe God's "new thing." For Babylon, there will be no peace, no joy, no renewal, no song, no light. Instead of soaring into the sky like eagles, Babylon will "come down and sit in the dust . . . sit on the ground without a throne" (47:1). . . .

The centrally placed chapter 47 contrasts in imagery and motif with all of the other chapters in Second Isaiah. This poem, like the poem of chapter 40, teaches and persuades through the device of contrast, this time exemplifying what befalls those who do not remember what chapter 40 contains. . . .

Chapter 55 brings together in a simple statement much of what has preceded in Second Isaiah. We have heard throughout of water springing from rocks in the desert in the wilderness. The miracles past, we are now invited, simply: "Come, buy wine and milk / without money and without price." Urged throughout to be alert, to listen and see, the Israelites are now invited quietly by God to incline their ears, "and come to me; hear, that your soul may live" (v. 3). . . . War is ended, Israel's sins are pardoned, a new historical time is about to begin.

> Seek the LORD while he may be found,
>   call upon him while he is near:
> let the wicked forsake his way,
>   and the unrighteous man his thoughts;
> let him return to the LORD, that he may have mercy on him,
>   and to our God, for he will abundantly pardon. (vv. 6–7)

In a sense, these lines summarize what Second Isaiah has asked Israel to do; but the task is quietly stated. And then we are taken back to the contrasts of chapter 40, but without the extremes of those verses; the gap between God and man is stated by God simply, in an almost fatherly way, "my thoughts are not your thoughts, / neither are your ways my ways." Instead of using the vast images which so diminished man in chapter 40, God explains, "As the heavens are higher than the earth, so are my ways higher than your ways and my thoughts than your thoughts" (v. 9). This is still a statement about the immensity of God, but man is not overwhelmed by it.

Kenneth R. R. Gros Louis. In *Literary Interpretations of Biblical Narratives* Ed. by Kenneth R. R. Gros Louis et al. (Nashville, Abingdon Press, 1974), pp. 208–9, 211–12, 215–16, 219–21, pp. 224–25

JACOB

The main root of the narratives consists of two folk-tales, both of which tell *how the precedence passed from Esau to Jacob*, i.e. they both deal with what is really one theme, although, according to one version, this took place by purchase, and, according to the other, by deception. Both are at one also in the statement that the two are brothers—an interjected introduction calls them twin brothers; also that they differ in calling and in natural gifts. *Jacob is shepherd, Esau is hunter. In all their main features the narratives are based on this difference of calling between the two.*

The first saga tells how Esau . . . makes over his birthright to Jacob for a "mess of pottage." This narrative sets in contrast types of two different occupations—a very frequent subject of folk-tale. In German folk-tale we find brought thus together farmer and woodcutter, cobbler and tailor, shepherd boy and king's daughter. It is also a familiar feature of this kind of tale that the representatives of the callings are *brothers*. "A certain man had two sons: the one was a cobbler, the other a smith." That is a typical opening of a German folk-tale. Hebrew saga knows also of two brothers—Abel, a shepherd, and Cain, a tiller of the ground. Another tradition, almost entirely lost, told of three brothers, Jabal, a shepherd, Jubal, a musician, and Tubal, a smith. That the different actors are conceived as brothers is explained by the fact that the relationship of brother is one of the simplest family relationships, just the type that primitive narrative is able to conceive and handle. The regular *motif* of such "tales of calling" is that the one claims to be superior to the other. Such stories would be told where representatives of the callings lived together and one was keen to magnify its importance and its superiority over the other. . . . Abel and Cain dispute as to whose sacrifice is to gain God's favour. Here Jacob and Esau dispute about the "birthright." This, it is to be understood, carries with it the whole inheritance left by the father and the dominion over the other. Admittedly it belongs by right to the hunter, but the shepherd has purchased it from him. Such a tale can only have arisen in a country in which shepherds and hunters dwelt together, as is still the case, for example, among the Targi in the Sahara, among the Masai, Abyssinians, etc. Those who tell each other stories of this kind are shepherds themselves, and they relate with pride and glee how the hunter, although he was the first-born and his calling was considered the superior one, had to take an inferior place behind the shepherd. . . . In its naïve way, the tale has given the historical process by which the hunter gave way before the shepherd, but it also reveals splendid powers of detailed observation. The hunter's only skill is that of knowing how to kill the animal that comes into his power. He lives, therefore, from hand to mouth. If he comes home some day empty-handed, he must just go hungry. But as long as he has something to eat to-day he does not trouble about to-morrow. "Esau ate and drank, rose up and went forth, having thrown away his birthright" [Gen. 25:34]. On the other hand, the shepherd is a man of a different type. . . . He does not kill the animals in his care, but draws daily profit from them. He has food every day, and wisely thinks not only of to-day, but also of the morrow. ·Thus Jacob the shepherd proves superior to the hunter Esau. The whole narrative is thus to be understood as a folk-tale dealing with men of different callings.

In the related narrative of *Jacob's deception* the same *motif* undergoes another twist. In this tale, the thing that belongs of right to Esau, and which Jacob desires, is the father's *blessing*. The blessing, i.e., occupies here the place held by the birthright in the other story. There is a simple philological explanation of this interchange. *Bekora*, "birthright," and *Beraka*, "blessing," have a phonetic resemblance. Such plays on words were always popular in Israel. Moreover, the blessing in question implies a precedence of the one over the other. It implies the better inheritance and dominion over the brother, i.e. in effect it amounts to the same thing as the birthright. In form, such a blessing is a magic word. When once it has been pronounced it cannot be recalled. . . .

This story [of the ruse by which Isaac is deceived] also is completely on the level of the folk-tale, where the same plot is frequently met with, how the clever but weak one outwits the strong but stupid one, and where there is a special fondness for the childish, roguish exchange of clothes. . . . As A. Thimme says in his book *Das Märchen* (p. 56): "In the tale there is no feeling of moral indignation at such roguery, because laughter over the success of the trick displaces all moral resentment."

Our tale shows representatives of two callings in conflict, and the shepherd supplants the hunter. The latter is pictured as belonging to a rough type of humanity—he is as hairy as a kid and his odour is so strong that it is even perceptible in his new clothes. On the other hand, the shepherd is more civilized. He is smooth of skin and attaches more value to personal cleanliness. The hunter roams about out of doors and is his father's favourite; but the mother loves best the quiet Jacob, who stays about the house. The hunter's venison tastes better than the tame meat provided by the shepherd, but the art of cookery is already able to conceal such differences. The hunter is a violent man—Esau means to kill his brother; but the shepherd does not deal in violence, he avoids the open crime, but he is clever and reaches his goal by trickery.

In view of all this, there can be no further doubt in any mind that the Esau stories are really examples of tales of callings, with a plot of shepherd *versus* hunter, and that the ethnological colour of the narrative was added at a later stage. In all these compositions we see the same principle at work—we are dealing with ancient folk-tales interwoven with historical reminiscences.

In the Laban stories the plot is similar. They deal with the young astute shepherd and his successful contest of wits against a man who is really his superior. It is easy to understand how the two similar cycles of stories attracted each other and were referred to the same person.

> Hermann Gunkel. *What Remains of the Old Testament, and Other Essays*. Tr. from the German by A. K. Dallas (New York, Macmillan, 1928), pp. 179–84

Jacob, or Israel, the father of the Twelve Tribes, is fully as crafty and tricky as the Homeric Odysseus, and bargains and argues and pleads with his jealous God, just as Odysseus does with Athene.

Wherein then, it may be asked, lies the greatness of this Patriarch's character? Wherein, for all the patient and humble and much-enduring men and women who have learnt by heart this tale "of our Father Jacob," is to be found the secret of the attraction that holds them? Does it not lie, as in all exciting stories from the beginning, in the protagonist's intense *awareness of his destiny*, his intense self-consciousness in everything he does, the unconquerable tenacity of his purpose? Isn't the whole secret of the Old Testament's attraction for egoists like ourselves to be found in that remark of Goethe's, "Earnestness alone makes life eternity"? The crafty, amorous, patient, unswerving, unwarlike Jacob takes his life with a gravity, with an awareness, with a sense of responsibility that is overwhelming, that is sublime, that is something before which all obstacles melt, as if by a slow, resistless magic!

Think of what the man must have felt when he awoke that morning after that tricky marriage—"*and behold it was Leah*"! But to serve another seven years for the woman he loved was as inevitable to his incorrigible tenacity as it was to steal Esau's birthright. Every sunrise that smote red into his tent found him, metaphorically speaking, wrestling with his angel, found him with his obstinate head on some sacred stone.

"How mysterious, how memorable," he is always thinking, "is this godlike spot, this godlike dawn, this godlike hour!" And with his "ladder" always ascending from time and space into the Nameless, Jacob naturally, inevitably, becomes Israel, the father of multitudes!

> John Cowper Powys. *Enjoyment of Literature* (New York, Simon & Schuster, 1938), pp. 15–16

Yet another function is known for the "leading word": whenever the text seeks to allude to the atonement of a sin without referring to the atonement explicitly. Here parallel wording comes to indicate the retributive nature of the later events in [a character's] life; one verse answers to another, and atonement covers over the guilt.

When you follow through a narrative of this kind you are like one who discovers an ancient midrash hidden in the body of the biblical text, though in your heart a doubt rises. Yet the parallels are so precise, making up a complete and tidy tissue, that you must, despite yourself, admit: The roots of the "hidden meaning" are infused in the sources of the primal shape of the tradition.

A verse like Jeremiah 9:3 suffices to inform us that even biblical man found something to be desired in the deed that Jacob did to his brother, that even biblical man found it to be a perverse deed; Hosea 12:4 can also be interpreted in this spirit. The narrative of the Book of Genesis has the essential function of explaining the evolution of the generations of Israel through a primal election, out of which stems the obligation to choose over and over, in each generation. Such a narrative presented the alienation of the firstborn as an act of divine providence, so that one could not speak of [Jacob's act] as a perverse deed. There is no place in this renowned narrative for deviant observations of this kind. Nevertheless, [biblical man] was not at liberty to deny the highest principle of the biblical theology of history, holding that divine control leaves room for the free activity of man and his responsibility for it, so that history is not a monologue of internal voices but a real dialogue. This dilemma finds a remedy in the form of the "leading word" of the Bible. This technique already seems to have operated in the very selection of traditions, even perhaps in the very formation of the tradition. That is, leading ideas here preceded their materialization as leading words.

When Esau bursts out in "a very great and bitter cry," Isaac reacts (Gen. 27:35): "Your brother has come in guile and he has taken your blessing." Esau responds: "Isn't his name called Jacob [*Ya'aqov*] and he has cheated me [*wayya-'aqveni*] now twice / My birthright [*bekhorati*] he has taken, and behold now he has taken my blessing [*birkhati*]."

Here you have four leading words: "guile," "birthright," "blessing," and "name."

In his place of exile, in which God certainly shields him but does not withhold from him mishaps, Jacob gets to see with his own eyes what guile perpetrated against a man by his own kin really is. In his words of complaint the first leading word returns. Relying on the same word stem he asks Laban (29:25): "Why have you beguiled me?" And what is Laban's response? The second leading word. The very essence of the "guile" has been that just as Jacob the younger son had disguised himself as the firstborn, so had he married by means of disguise the firstborn daughter instead of the younger one. "It is not done thus in our place," replies Laban, "to give (in marriage) the younger daughter before the firstborn one." What was there [in Jacob's theft of the blessing] the birthright [bekhorah] is here [in Laban's deception of Jacob] the firstborn daughter [bekhirah].

Time and again Laban "toyed" with Jacob (31:7), but God stood at his right hand so that in the end Jacob would leave having the upper hand. After twenty years he returns to his birthplace, having already become "two camps." He wishes to meet with Esau and beseech him. But before that he must withstand his last test, the night struggle with the "man." That struggle revolves on two things: the blessing and the name (blessing, name, name, name, name, blessing, name — that is the sequence of leading words). The blessing taken by conquest will expiate the blessing that was stolen. "I shall not release you / unless you bless me." Behold at this the man asks for (Jacob's) name. He replies: "Jacob"; and as the verse from Jeremiah proves, the biblical reader hears in this name "he-who-lies-in-ambush-at-the-heel ['eqev]." The very saying of the name embodies an admission of guilt, and it is this that the man wished to hear expressly from Jacob's mouth. Only now does he remove from himself his name, his guilt: "Your name will no longer be called Jacob"—this may be plausibly interpreted: Your name will no longer connote the ambusher at the heel—"but Israel" (he who fights for God). The good struggle atones for the bad struggle, the name that became shameful was exchanged for a holy name.

Three more times the leading word "name" returns to uncover the meaning of the episode. In any event the blessing comes, unsaid, and it seems that it is in effect no more than the wish for a blessing, but it is enough: from now on the blessing of the struggle expiates the blessing of the theft. Soon enough (35:10) God himself will articulate the renewal of the man Jacob-Israel, thus bringing it to completion. But first must come the appeasement of the brother, and this too is accomplished by the signature of the leading word, "blessing": "Take now my blessing which has been brought to you!"—thus does Jacob seek Esau's acceptingness of his gift (33:11). And when he accepts it, on the interpersonal level, too, "blessing" atones for "blessing."

Martin Buber. Darko shel miqra' (Jerusalem, Bialik Institute, 1964), pp. 290–92†

The Jacob cycle is different. While the unity of thought is not immediately apparent, the unity of narration becomes manifest at once. Hardly a single incident of the Jacob story could be told by itself and be perfectly intelligible. One event flows out of another, and in turn leads up to something else. For example, to tell the story of Jacob's winning of Rachel without having first told of Esau's hatred of Jacob and of the latter's consequent flight from home, would be tantamount to beginning a long serial story in the middle without knowing anything of the causes and events which preceded and paved the way for this episode. Or, even more indicative, the story of Jacob's final meeting and reconciliation with Esau would be absolutely unintelligible without a full knowledge of their previous relations. In other words, unlike the creation-flood and Abraham cycles of stories, we have here, in the present Biblical form, not a group of independent Jacob stories, united by a common theme, but one single Jacob story, which is a unit of narration as well as of thought.

The procedure of the compilers is easily perceived. They took the old, independent Jacob traditions, and wove them together into one complex and highly dramatic narrative. The legend of the struggles of the two brothers in the womb of their mother serves as an effective introduction or prelude to the story, in that it foreshadows dramatically the future relations of the two men. The story of the father's blessing, originally, in all likelihood, a parallel version of the birthright story, they presented as a subsequent and supplementary incident in the relations of Jacob and Esau. Thereby they heightened the dramatic effect of the situation and brought out the contrasted characters of the two men more pointedly and emphatically.

> Julian Morgenstern. *The Book of Genesis*. 2d ed. (New York, Schocken, 1965), pp. 188–89

Three issues are of primary importance in Genesis 25:19–35:22: *birth, blessing*, and *land*. These correspond, as will be recalled, to the threefold patriarchal blessing given to Abraham (12:1–3). The first of these issues is the concern for *birth*. It first surfaces with Rebekkah's barrenness, her difficult pregnancy, and the birth of Jacob and Esau; and it appears as well with Rachel, who is initially barren, and spends her early years in preoccupied agony over her failure to conceive and give birth. The second is that of *blessing*: God blesses Isaac in Philistia; Jacob steals Isaac's blessing, Isaac blesses both brothers, Jacob is blessed by a divine messenger at Penuel; and God blesses Jacob at Beth-el. The third issue in the Cycle is *land*: both Isaac and Jacob are promised and receive the land of Canaan as part of the divine promise and patriarchal inheritance.

However, it must be emphasized that none of these three factors appears independently. A series of polarities pervade the text and charge it with life force and dramatic tension. The first issue, birth, functions together with its opposite: barrenness. The contrastive pair *barrenness/fertility*, in its variety of expressions, lies at the heart of the personal anxieties of Rebekkah and Rachel, and the interpersonal tensions between Rachel and Leah. The fact that all the major women in Genesis, and many outside it, are initially barren and struggle for their matriarchal inheritance is undoubtedly a hint at the continuity of the curse of Eden. But the various tensions over childbirth also bring to expression deep anxieties over cultural continuity, and a one-dimensional perspective on the role of the female in a patriarchal world. Esau, it will be recalled, is reproached for his breach of endogamy in 26:34ff. (cf. 27:46 and 28:9), and the concern for continuity through a true line also motivates Isaac's blessing in 28:1ff. The tension is also brought to negative expression in the episode of Dinah's rape by the uncircumcised Shechemites in chapter 34.

The second issue, blessing, also functions together with its opposite. The contrastive pair *nonblessing/blessing* underpins the motivations, strife and actions of Rebekkah, Jacob, Isaac, and Esau. Indeed, the desire for blessing is a primary driving power of Genesis 25:19–35:22. Its counterpoint can also be characterized as *curse*, as the very language of the narrative indicates. After Rebekkah urges Jacob to deceive Isaac, Jacob says he fears he might receive a curse (*qelalah*) instead of the blessing (27:12). Similarly, when Isaac blesses Jacob, he says: "those who curse you will be cursed (stem: *'arar*), and those who bless you will be blessed" (27:29; cf. 12:3). It may also be noted that the issue of blessing is of interpersonal importance in Jacob's relations with Laban (30:27, 30) and Esau (33:17). The hope for a blessing and fear of a curse clearly charge the actions of this Cycle.

Land functions in this Cycle as subject of the binary pair *exile/homeland*. The actions of Genesis 25:19–35:22 can thus be viewed along a spatial axis. Jacob flees from Canaan and has an encounter with the divine at the border shrine of Beth-el (28:10ff.): he stays in Aram until Rachel gives birth, whereupon he returns and encounters the divine at the border shrines of Mahanayim and Penuel (cf. 32). The shrines mark the transition of action from sacred to profane space, and back. The promises of land inheritance in the divine blessings to Isaac (26:4, 24) and Jacob (28:13; 35:12) underscore this value of settlement on the land as a sign of divine grace and favor. Only when Jacob resettles in Canaan is his patriarchal destiny confirmed (ch. 35).

> Michael Fishbane. *Text and Texture* (New York, Schocken, 1979), pp. 60–61

A number of commentators have observed the predominance of the motif of strife in the chapters under consideration. J. P. Fokkelman shows, for example, how the rivalry in Gen. 25:27–34 deals with the *bekhora* ("birthright") and in Gen. 27:1–46 with the *berakha* ("blessing") (Fokkelman [*Narrative Art in Genesis* (Assen, 1975)]: 86–112). Two further instances of strife develop before the Esau-Jacob strife is resolved: (i) The relationship between Jacob and his uncle (and father-in-law) at Haran becomes increasingly strained so that Jacob finally takes his leave without so much as a farewell (Gen. 31:17–31). This contention ends in a pact or covenant between Laban and Jacob in Gilead (Gen. 31:43–54). (ii) The relationship between Jacob's wives becomes increasingly strained as Leah is fruitful and Rachel barren. The tension between the two sisters is a clear variation on the rivalry between Esau and Jacob. The first-born (Leah/Esau) are not favored; the younger (Rachel/Jacob), though favored, must wait for the coming of the fruits (children/flocks) which the preferred status implies. The strife between the two sisters is nowhere explicitly resolved, but finds surcease in their joint agreement to leave their father (Gen. 31:14–16).

Strife also finds expression in two passages (chs. 26 and 34) which immediately precede and follow the Esau-Jacob rivalry. In chapter 26, Isaac and the Philistines contend over material resources (notably water, but presumably also pastures for grazing); friction develops, further, over Isaac's wife. In chapter 34, the contention is between Shechemites and the sons of Jacob; the chief source of inimical relations is the rape of Dinah. In the latter instance, Jacob becomes apprehensive about how his sons' reprisal against the Shechemites will have affected his social relations with the inhabitants of the land by making him odious among them (Gen. 34:30). In chapter 26 a covenant (bĕrît) brings the contention to a conclusion (vv. 26–30); in chapter 34 a covenant is deceitfully promised and not honored by the sons of Jacob (vv. 8–25).

In sum, there can be little question that the dominant motif in Genesis 25–36 is the motif of strife.

Two fairly prominent sub-motifs which constitute an integral part of the strife motif are deceit and retribution. Instances of deception are these: Isaac of the Philistines (Gen. 26:7); Rebekah and Jacob of Isaac (Gen. 27:5–45); Laban of Jacob (Gen. 29:18–25; cf. also 31:41); Rachel of Laban (Gen. 31:19–35); and the sons of Jacob of the Shechemites (ch. 34). The motif of retribution is implicit throughout the cycle. Some form of punishment falls upon the deceitful: Isaac, who deceives the Philistines, is in turn deceived (ch. 27); Rebekah, who is the chief instigator of the deception of Isaac, is deprived of her son's presence (Gen. 27:43–45); Laban, who deceives Jacob in his promise of Rachel and in his agreement to terms of wages, is in turn deceived by his daughter and is the poorer for his deception of Jacob (Gen. 31:9, 19–35); Rachel, who deceives her father as to her possession of his household gods—or because of her possession of them!—suffers an early death (Gen. 35:16–20). . . . Jacob, after the deceit of his father, must undergo an exile of arduous labor (chs. 29–31), is plagued with a limp (Gen. 32:32 [Engl. 32:31]), and—to cite evidence from outside the cycle proper—is forced through famine to leave the promised land for Egypt (cf. Gen. 43:1; 45:6; 46:26). Finally, the two chief instigators of the deception of the Shechemites, Simeon and Levi, are cursed to be scattered (Gen. 49:5–7).

John G. Gammie. In *Encounter with the Text*. Ed. by Martin J. Buss (Philadelphia/Missoula, Mont., Fortress Press/Scholars Press, 1979), pp. 118–19

JACOB AND ESAU

The story of the struggle between Jacob and Esau (Gen. 25:19–34; 27) actually comprises a unified literary-artistic unit that may be divided into three scenes: scene 1: the birth (25:21–28); scene 2: the episode of the stew and the sale of the birthright (25:29–34); scene 3: the struggle over the blessing (27).

Even though the entire story is apparently a domain unto itself, the events in these three scenes make up a crystallized literary tissue, and because they are ordered and developed in a chronological sequence and tied together in a mutual bond, in a cause-and-effect relationship. If we make use of the literary criteria of [E. M.] Forster, we have before us a crystallized literary plot that demands of the reader not only curiosity vis-à-vis the order of the story's development per se, but also perceptiveness and memory, the ability to examine each additional fact not only in isolation but also in light of the other facts. . . . Indeed, many words and verses in this story gain a deeper significance only at the conclusion of a close reading of all three scenes because each scene in the story throws light on its companion, clarifies and elucidates elusive and obscure points in the others.

Scene 1 comprises a sort of overture to the entire story, the background or foundation for what happens. It introduces us to the basic data for the evolution of the plot. By means of the vision of the divine oracle (25:23), which stands at the center, it lays bare the situation in whose framework the contention between the two brothers evolves, until it reaches its climax in scene 3. All the details of the story evolve in graduated fashion and strive toward one goal: a basis for the superior position of Jacob in relation to his brother. The scene does not skimp on turns of phrase and artistic devices for informing us directly and indirectly of the uniqueness of the struggle, which although it erupts between just two persons is pregnant with deep, fateful significance for their descendants. Accordingly, the description of the pregnancy and the birth is full of many dramatic markings. . . .

The element of the struggle over the birthright and the inheritance also figures with the sons of Abraham, Ishmael and Isaac, except that there the struggle was conducted between two brothers who were born to different mothers—one the servant and one the lady—and the root of the struggle was the fact that there were two mothers. In the story [of Jacob and Esau] the struggle takes place between twin brothers, and its inception was in the womb of the mother: "The sons grappled within her" (25:22). The strange and unusual pregnancy of Rebekah, which is one of a kind in biblical literature, brings her to need "to inquire of the Lord" (loc. cit.). . . .

The facts that scene 1 supplies to us evolve in the course of the plot so that the range of significance of the various words and images expands. I shall indicate a few examples:

(1) In scene 1 Esau's outward appearance is described as "ruddy all over, like a hairy mantle" (25:25). The outward description of Jacob is not presented here, but from scene 3 (27:11) we learn that Jacob was "a smooth man." This outward

contrast between the hairy man and the smooth man, which is hinted to us here in a sort of aside, comprises, as is well known, a crucial factor.

(2) Scene 2 again examines the significance of the name "Edom" ["Red One"], whose basis according to scene 1 is in the fact of Esau's ruddiness, and introduces it in a new dimension—as an expression of Esau's ravenousness: "Let me gulp now from this red, red (stuff). . . . Therefore his name was called 'Edom'" (25:30). It is extended in scene 3, in Jacob's attempt to win the blessing by deceit: disguising himself as the hairy Esau.

(3) Similarly, in scene 3 are examined the etymology and significance of the name "Jacob" ["Heel-er"], which according to scene 1 derives from the fact that he came out [of the womb] "his hand holding onto the heel of Esau" (25:26). In scene 3 this name is linked to features of Jacob's cheating and deceit, as Esau experienced them: "Isn't his name truly Jacob ["Cheater"], for he has now cheated me twice" (27:36).

Reuben Ahroni. Beth Mikra. April–June, 1978, pp. 327–29†

More often, action and words combine to give a vivid portrait, as in the following scene between Jacob and Esau.

> Jacob prepared a stew; and Esau came in from the field famished. Esau said to Jacob, "Please serve me some of that red stuff for I'm famished." (Therefore they called his name Edom.) And Jacob said, "Sell me your birthright right now." And Esau said, "Look, I'm going to die. What do I need a birthright for?" And Jacob said, "Swear to me right now." So he swore to him; he sold his birthright to Jacob. So Jacob gave Esau bread and lentil stew, and he ate and drank and got up and left; Esau disdained the birthright. (Gen. 25:29–34)

Esau's speech and action mark him as a primitive person. He is concerned with immediate gratification of his physical needs and cannot think about abstract things like a birthright. He does not even know what he is eating—"that red stuff"—just that he needs to eat quickly or "I'm going to die." The verbs in verse 34 come in a stark sequence, emphasizing the simplistic nature of the man. Poor Esau is not very bright, and this both repels the reader and makes him feel sorry for Esau.

Jacob, on the other hand, is as shrewd as Esau is dull-witted. He understands his brother and can easily manipulate him. Perhaps he timed his stew to Esau's homecoming. Certainly he realized that he had Esau at a disadvantage and that he had to act quickly; the words "right now" appear in both of Jacob's lines. Esau was a man of the present moment; at that moment Esau needed the stew more than the birthright, so he sold it to Jacob.

The picture of Esau from his own words and actions is not quite the same as the narrator's evaluation of these actions. To the narrator, Esau disdained the birthright, treated it with contempt. But from Esau's point of view it is not a contemptuous or rebellious action, but one done out of ignorance and shortsightedness.

> Adele Berlin. *Poetics and Interpretation of Biblical Narrative* (Sheffield, England, Almond Press, 1983), p. 39

JACOB'S STRUGGLE WITH THE ANGEL

The sequential schema, that is, can be read in two ways: 1) Jacob himself crosses over the ford—if need be after having made several trips back and forth—and thus the combat takes place on the left bank of the flood (he is coming from the North) *after he has definitively crossed over*; in this case, *send over* is read *cross over himself*; 2) Jacob sends over but does not himself cross over; he fights on the right bank of the Jabbok *before crossing over*, in a rearguard position. Let us not look for some *true* interpretation (perhaps our very hesitation will appear ridiculous in the eyes of the exegetes); rather, let us consume two different pressures of readability: 1) if Jacob remains alone *before* crossing the Jabbok, we are led towards a "folkloric" reading of the episode, the mythical reference then being overwhelming which has it that a trial of strength (as for example with a dragon or the guardian spirit of a river) must be imposed on the hero *before* he clears the obstacle, *so that*—once victorious—he can clear it; 2) if on the contrary Jacob having crossed over (he and his tribe), he remains alone on the good side of the flood (the side of the country to which he wants to go), then the passage is without structural finality while acquiring on the other hand a religious finality: if Jacob is alone, it is no longer to settle the question of and obtain the crossing but in order that he be *marked* with solitude (the familiar *setting apart* of the one chosen by God). There is a historical circumstance which increases the undecidability of the two interpretations. Jacob's purpose is to return home, to enter the land of Canaan: given this, the crossing of the River Jordan would be easier to understand than that of the Jabbok. In short, we are confronted with the crossing of a spot that is neutral. The crossing is crucial if Jacob has to win it over the guardian of the place, indifferent if what is important is the solitude, the mark of Jacob. Perhaps we have here the tangled trace of two stories, or at least of two narrative instances: the one, more "archaic" (in the simple stylistic sense of the term), makes of the crossing itself an ordeal; the other, more "realist," gives a "geographical" air to Jacob's journey by mentioning the places he goes through (without attaching any mythical value to them).

If one carries back on to this twofold sequence the pattern of subsequent events, that is the Struggle and the Naming, the dual reading continues, coherent to the end in each of its two versions. Here again is the diagram:

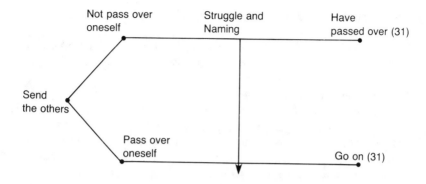

If the Struggle stands between the "not pass over" and the "have passed over" (the folklorizing, mythical reading), then the mutation of the Names corresponds to the very purpose of every etymological saga; if on the contrary the Struggle is only a stage between a position of immobility (of mediation, of election) and a movement of setting off again, then the mutation of the Name has the value of a spiritual rebirth (of "baptism"). All of which can be summarized by saying that in this first episode there is sequential readability but cultural ambiguity. No doubt the theologian would grieve at this indecision while the exegete would acknowledge it, hoping for some element of fact or argument that would enable him to put an end to it. The textual analyst, judging by my own impression savours such *friction* between two intelligibilities. [1971]

Roland Barthes. *Image/Music/Text*. Tr. by Stephen Heath (New York, Hill & Wang, 1977), pp. 129–31

Jacob's wrestling with God at the brook Jabbok (Gen. 32:22–32) is one of the great moments in world literature. The nighttime setting of the encounter (v. 22) adds to the mood of danger and urgency. By sending his family and "everything that he had" across the stream (v. 23), Jacob is reduced to essential humanity, being "left alone," as the narrator states (v. 24). This is the context of Jacob's encounter with a divine wrestler. Mystery pervades the unexplained presence and identity of a man who wrestles with Jacob until daybreak. Jacob's equally strange insistence that he will not let the stranger go unless he blesses Jacob is the type of event that calls for interpretation, in [Erich] Auerbach's terms. The request is made because the mysterious wrestler is God. Jacob's new name, Israel, means "he who strives with God" and signifies a new relationship with God. It also confirms the identity of Jacob as the one who strives. The stranger is never explicitly identified as God, but that identification is implied when Jacob names the place "Peniel," saying, "For I have seen God face to face, and yet my life is preserved" (v. 30). The rising of the sun (v. 31) is a fitting symbol for the beginning of a new era in Jacob's spiritual existence, and the limping due to the disjointed thigh (vv. 25, 31) is a permanent reminder of the significance of the event.

Leland Ryken. *The Literature of the Bible* (Grand Rapids, Mich., Zondervan, 1974), p. 56

A strange adventure, mysterious from beginning to end, breathtakingly beautiful, intense to the point of making one doubt one's senses. Who has not been fascinated by it? Philosophers and poets, rabbis and storytellers, all have yearned to shed light on the enigmatic event that took place that night, a few steps from the river Jabbok. An episode told by the Bible with customary majestic sobriety. . . . *Jacob was left alone. And a man wrestled with him until the break of dawn.* It was a silent struggle, silent and absurd. What did the stranger want? Nobody knew, not even Jacob. They wrestled until dawn, neither uttering a word. Only then did the assailant speak: *Day is breaking, let me go.* And a suddenly belligerent Jacob refused, setting conditions: *I will not let you go, unless you bless me.* . . .

A confused and confusing episode in which the protagonists bear more than one name, in which words have more than one meaning and every question brings forth another. One constantly gets the feeling of being shut out, of watching an event through an almost opaque screen. . . . We stumble on a secret even more impenetrable than that of the averted sacrifice of Isaac. There at least one felt that one understood, however superficially, why the characters acted as they did and what motivated them. Here we are left in total darkness. . . .

It is almost like a mystical poem, barely coherent, barely intelligible, not only to the reader but even to the protagonists. Why did the nocturnal visitor attack poor Jacob whose name he claimed not to know? . . .

This is one of the most enigmatic episodes in Jacob's life and even in Scripture. One that ended well for him, since it brought him a new dimension—secret and sacred—a dimension he seemed to need.

Elie Wiesel. *Messengers of God* (New York, Random House, 1976), pp. 106–7, 109–10

The impression of almost all readers is that the story is told in a deliberately, perhaps unnecessarily cryptic manner. There is an annoying ambiguity in regard to the identity of the actors in verses 25 and 26 [of Gen. 32]: "when he saw that he could not win he touched the hollow of this thigh. . . ." Only the following words ("so the hollow of Jacob's thigh became dislocated") clarifies the matter, retroactively. This situation is then repeated in verses 27 and 28: "he said . . . he said . . . he said. . . ." Only the "Jacob" of the end of verse 28 allows the reader to identify the speakers, again, in retrospect. Also troubling is the inconsequence of blessing and naming in [vv. 27–30].

These ambiguities would perhaps be insignificant, mere infelicities of narrative, if they did not accompany and exacerbate the logical inconsistencies and non-sequiturs of the plot. The story seems to have no plain, simple meaning as a story. Who was Jacob's opponent? What were his motives? Who won the struggle, Jacob or his assailant? Was the latter a man or *'elohim*, a divinity? These questions may be restated as two sets of basic oppositions: victory-defeat and human-divine. They may be compared to twin vines that in their intertwining have formed a twisted thicket to entrap the reader. They obscure the logic of the narrative. . . .

It is possible to view the enigma of the story of Jacob's wrestling bout abstractly, as a web of relationships between different kinds of structural features: the perceptual processes of isolation and integration; basic thematic oppositions; complexes of internal and external contexts. But they all fuse into a single concrete fact: the story is a non-story, a mask.

Yet, on another level, in another dimension of meaning, certain other facts leap from its words, impressing themselves on the reader's perceptions with no narrative mediation. I believe that light from this new dimension suffuses also the narrative levels, illuminating the paradoxes with a new significance.

The first such fact is Jacob's thigh. Could any Israelite have heard those words, in whatever context, without immediately grasping their national import? Israel is the people that came forth from that potent thigh, *yotse'ei yerekh ya'aqov* ["those coming out of Jacob's thigh"] (Gen. 46:26; Exod. 1:1; cf. Judg. 8:30). Touching that thigh is automatically an act of national significance. . . .

In this story the associative plane of meaning stands apart from the narrative. This may now be posited as the central literary problem: the story is written on two discrete levels: (1) a narrative level, the baffling, contradictory progression of the plot. In conformity with Saussurian linguistic terminology, it may be termed "syntagmatic." Its hero is Jacob the man, hero of the saga. (2) a level of national meaning, whose hero is Jacob the ancestor. It may be termed "associative," corresponding to the other plane of meaning in [Ferdinand] de Saussure's terminology. The relationship between these levels is the core of the story's dynamic, the ultimate source of one's feeling of paradox but also, if viewed in terms of literary strategy, the clue to comprehending the intention of that paradox.

Such a duality of levels is entirely expected. Most patriarchal narratives have a national dimension of significance. This fact was recognized by the Rabbinic principle *ma'asei 'avot simman labbanim*, "the actions recounted of the patriarchs are indicative of what would later happen to their descendants." The relationship is typological, almost magical. The building of altars, the acquisition of parcels of land, the journeys through the length and breadth of Canaan, all these foreshadow, even *effect* Israel's later occupation.

There is surely no other place in Genesis where the reader is more attuned to a resonance of past and future than Genesis 32. The situation is extreme: the eponymous ancestor of the nation is about to receive the national name: no casual matter.

Stephen A. Geller. *Journal of the Ancient Near Eastern Society.* 14, 1982, pp. 44–45, 50–51

JEREMIAH

Jeremiah, though deficient neither in elegance nor sublimity, must give place in both to Isaiah. St. Jerome seems to object against him a sort of rusticity of language, no vestige of which, I must however confess, I have been able to discover. His sentiments, it is true, are not always the most elevated, nor are his periods always neat and compact; but these are faults common to those writers, whose principal aim is to excite the gentler affections, and to call forth the tear of sympathy or sorrow. This observation is very strongly exemplified in the Lamentations, where these are the prevailing passions; it is however frequently instanced in the prophecies of this author, and most of all in the beginning of the book, which is chiefly poetical. The middle of it is almost entirely historical, the latter part, again, consisting of the six last chapters, is altogether poetical; it contains several different predictions, which are distinctly marked, and in these the prophet approaches very near the sublimity of Isaiah. On the whole, however, I can scarcely pronounce above half the book of Jeremiah to be poetical. [1753]

> Robert Lowth. *Lectures on the Sacred Poetry of the Hebrews.* Vol. II. Tr. from the Latin by G. Gregory (London, Printed for J. Johnson, 1787), pp. 87–89

In reading the Book of Jeremiah we do not get the peculiar impression of a speaker reënforced by a man of letters, as in Deuteronomy, nor the literary savor of a cultured and creative statesman, as in Isaiah. We feel rather the vehemence of the preacher and censor of morals, as he comes to close grips with the people, men of the Temple courts and city gates and public places. The impending catastrophe of national overthrow, for which his whole prophetic activity must be a deep-laid preparation, was too near and pressing to favor leisurely care for authorship. Accordingly, as a literary production the Book of Jeremiah is somewhat formless—rather an accumulation of utterances hot from their immediate occasion, or of biographical incidents preserved by a secretary, than a planned and consecutive structure. This trait was natural enough, perhaps, from the way in which the book was composed. Its substance consists of public utterances or rhapsodies which the prophet had delivered at various times and carried in mind from the beginning of his career, and then, in the fourth year of King Jehoiakim, dictated to Baruch, in the hope that with such repetition in written form they would have a better chance to effect their purpose (36:1–4; cf. vv. 17, 18). . . .

The style of the book, more especially of the parts containing the prophet's earlier rhapsodies, is tense and impassioned, well-nigh to excess; nor is it wanting in the cogency of lucid figure and telling phrase, a quality which sends his words straight to their aim, evincing not only the fervid preacher but the born master of diction. Many of the most cherished and vital passages of Scripture are his. At the same time, as one reads the book at length, one becomes aware of a certain lengthy and profuse tendency, a fault perhaps, as we see in modern times, of a dictated style. . . . For the rest, the parts of the book relating to affairs after Jehoiakim's fourth year are largely the work of Baruch the scribe, and are to great proportion in narrative prose.

It is not merely by his literary power, however, but far more by his personality, that Jeremiah has left his indelible impress on the heart of the ages. His was a personality compounded to a quite wonderful degree of tenderness and strength, and revealed through a lifelong experience truly tragic.

> John F. Genung. *A Guidebook to the Biblical Literature*
> (Boston, Ginn, 1919), pp. 229–31

> I looked to the earth—and behold a chaos
>   To the heavens—and their light was gone.
> I looked to the hills, and lo, they quivered,
>   And the mountains shook.
> I looked—and behold, no man was there,
>   And all the birds of heaven were flown.
> I looked to the cornland—and lo, a desert,
>   And all its cities were razed away. [4:23–26]

The supreme greatness of this creation cannot be disposed of by a sweep of the pen. Here we have matchless form. . . . Here we have sublimity that can find few parallels in literature. Here we have lines that Matthew Arnold would surely have styled immortal. Professor [John] Skinner entitles it "A Vision of Chaos" [*Prophecy and Religion*, 1951, p. 37]. It is certainly eschatological in meaning. The theme is one of cosmic scope, and it is couched in language of dignity and high seriousness.

> James Muilenburg. *Journal of the National Association
> of Biblical Instructors.* Vol. 1, 1933, p. 20

In literary quality his poetic oracles and "Confessions" match neither the superb style of Amos and Isaiah at their best, nor the epic brilliance of his contemporary Nahum; but all in all these poems deserve a place—perhaps near the edge—in the golden age of Hebrew literature. The emotional strain, which Jeremiah has in common with Hosea, distinguishes our prophet from the three writers just mentioned. It is only in Amos 5:2 and, to a lesser degree, in Isaiah 1:7f. that these prophets are overcome by the tender sadness and compassion so typical of Jeremiah. . . .

Compelled to live in the capital, Jeremiah longed for the countryside. His imagery, like that of Amos, is drawn from field and forest, wilderness and desert (2:6f.). But he had a stronger feeling for nature, in its charming and terrifying aspects, than the earlier prophets—a feeling that in the Old Testament is more intense only in Job, Song of Songs, and some Psalms. His famous contrast between the living waters of nature and the leaky cisterns of the city (2:13) reveals his preference for what is natural to what is artificial. . . .

The wild barren hills and ravines between Anathoth and the Dead Sea—a desolate wilderness—made an abiding impression on the prophet. He was haunted by the horrors of arid, uninhabited, gloomy wastes, by the desolation of the bare hills which he names *shefayim* (3:2, 21; 4:11; 7:29; 12:12; 14:6), a word that is characteristic of our prophet. . . .

Jeremiah excels in the description of gruesome imaginary horrors: the plight of Judah invaded by the Scythians (4:7, 13, 19–21, 23–26, 31; 5:15–17; 6:24–26; 8:15–17; 10:19f.); the terrors of darkness on "the mountains of twilight" when the way is lost (13:16); the premonition of impending calamity (12:5f.); the figure of Disaster peering from the north (6:1); Death, presented for the first time in literature as the Grim Reaper, entering through the windows or cutting down children and youths in the streets and letting their bodies lie like rows of grain stalks behind the harvester (9:17–22 [H. 9:16–21]).

Such macabre touches (cf. also the metaphor in 5:16), so revealing of the inner thoughts of the prophet, are unknown in literature before him and, except for an occasional personification of death in Job 18:13f. and 28:22, are entirely alien to the writers of the Old Testament. Equally original in the lyrics of Jeremiah is the preoccupation with mourning and funerals. . . .

Imaginary scenes filled with horror or pathos, coupled with the prophet's forebodings of ruin and moods of hopeless despair, give to his lyrics a characteristic note of intense gloom, tender melancholy, and acute mental anguish. Deeply moving are his pathetic pictures of the cessation of human activity in the midst of silence (7:34; 16:9; 25:10; 33:11), darkness (13:16; 23:12), and chaos (4:23–26).

In his ecstatic states, the future calamity becomes present and its contemplation stirs him to the depths of his being. . . . Intrusion of his own personal feelings in the proclamation of the divine message is typical of him alone among the prophets. From the literary point of view, some of the words of Jeremiah are a unique combination of denunciation and personal feelings, of sermons and lyrics; some oracles may be called, with G. Hölscher (*Die Propheten*, p. 235), "visions in lyric form."

These two elements, the objective and the subjective, are, however, separated in other utterances of Jeremiah. His moving appeal to North Israel to return to Jehovah (in 2–3) and his hopes for a future regeneration of the nation (in 30–31) are presented objectively, without any reference to his personal feelings; conversely, his "Confessions" are entirely lyrical.

In his "Confessions" Jeremiah is purely subjective, for even his dialogues with the deity are in essence dramatizations of inner struggles between opposite moods and desires, chiefly between fidelity to his arduous duties as a prophet and his personal propensity for a quiet life. In these lyrics he analyzes his states of mind and his motives. . . .

The literary importance of the "Confessions" is out of proportion to their intrinsic qualities of style, which are not outstanding. They mark the beginning of a new type of devotional—one could even say mystical—poetry, in which a human soul shaken by doubts, tormented by remorse, and distressed by anguish and fear finds peace and joy in the sense of the nearness of God. . . . Through his own inner struggles and victories, our prophet has created the language of the devout soul in the presence of its Maker.

Robert H. Pfeiffer. *Introduction to the Old Testament*
(New York, Harper, 1941), pp. 511–14

Jeremiah's descriptive talent is both concrete and poetic. Sensitive to detail, he never stops at the surface. He captures the colors of the sky at twilight, the changing light of the desert, the thirst of the earth, the savagery of man as well as the desire of God to bring His creation closer to Him. Jeremiah always finds the proper term, the precise word to describe a landscape which, to this day, one may discover when visiting Anathoth or the hills overlooking Jerusalem at dawn. He is masterful when he communicates the mood of people awaiting war while yearning for peace; he achieves a certain tone where realistic metaphors mix with breathtaking lyricism to illustrate human frailties and moral decadence.

> Even the stork in the sky knows her seasons,
> and the turtledove, swift and crane
> keep the time of their coming;
> But my people pay no heed
> to the Law of the Lord [8:7].

Elie Wiesel. *Five Biblical Portraits* (Notre Dame, Ind.,
University of Notre Dame Press, 1981), p. 107

Jeremiah being a prophet, the status of language or of the cry is at least as important as the genre concept of prayer. Formal analysis can type [Jer. 20:]7–12 as a prayer. But if there were a genre called "the cry," surely we would consider it at least as fitting. I do not mean psychologically that Jeremiah cries from the depths of his soul; I mean something like "whenever I speak, I shout" or "I cry violence and plunder." . . .

For a literary mind what is central is the relation of direct speech to indirect speech; the relation of the cry to direct address, or to Yahweh as a name; and how this kind of directness is mediated by language. The desire of immediate justification or immediate success in seeing one's accuser, of seeing oneself justified, has to pass through the mode of language and even through words which God has put into the prophet's mouth. It is not the desire only that is mediated but also the words themselves. The words which Jeremiah uses against God are God's own words which he uses against Judah in Jeremiah 2 and 3, and which the prophets elsewhere hear spoken by God. Israel has played the harlot, Israel has betrayed me, and so on. Is it this precarious conversion of God's words that we call prayer?

Certainly the prayers in the *Siddur* [Hebrew prayerbook] often petition God in God's own words. God may listen to the words that he has used. So his own words are given back and made persuasive toward him. Man's petition to God in God's own words, that precarious cry, is prayer. . . .

To me it seems to point to a radical indeterminacy: when the poet says "you have enticed me," does he mean, "you have enticed me with those very words? I believed your words and your accusations, but now I am the one betrayed." "You have overwhelmed me," but what has overwhelmed him? I would suggest that what has overwhelmed Jeremiah is not just "terror on every side" or the man of that name who put him in the stocks; rather it is what is suggested by Jeremiah 1: "and the word of the Lord came unto me, saying . . . ."

It is the *word* that comes, and it says

> Before I formed thee in the belly I knew thee and before thou camest forth out of the womb, I sanctified thee. I have appointed thee a prophet unto the nations. Then said I: "Ah, Lord God, behold I cannot speak for I am a child."

It is not only the correspondence of Jeremiah 1:4–6 but what comes later in Jeremiah 20, "Cursed be the day wherein I was born," which is important. These verses answer the question, by what is the prophet overwhelmed? He is overwhelmed, as prophets are, by the word of God. The simplest meaning of these opening verses is, "you were mine by election, I knew you by omniscience, I knew you were the man to do the job." But, "Before I formed thee in the belly I knew thee," is so radically figurative that a generic displacement occurs which goes toward a certain Christian idea without being Christian, toward "In the beginning was the Word," toward the seminal and inseminative power of the word. . . .

My mind as an interpreter—and you'll notice how long I am taking in this crossing—turns at this point, strangely enough, to [the French psychoanalyst Jacques] Lacan. "Before I formed thee in the belly I knew thee" understood in the light of "In the beginning was the Word," could be an epigraph for Lacanian psychoanalysis. Lacan's concept of the "Discourse of the Other" can be understood as restating this predetermination with which it is our fate to deal.

Although Jeremiah's "Oh, Lord God, behold I cannot speak for I am a child" could be a first refusal or a scrupulous ritual step ("Oh, I'm not worthy" or "I'm not ready"), God has taken that excuse away by saying, "I have already given you prophetic speech. My word has predetermined you." Moreover, when Jeremiah 20:7 states, "you have overwhelmed me and prevailed," it is as if God's own prophecy to the prophet were coming true. There is an internally predicted pattern to the book of life and a literary interpreter rejoices when he sees the book turning on its own axis. What is being completed is surely an inner figure of that kind.

Geoffrey Hartman. In *The Biblical Mosaic*. Ed. by Robert M. Polzin and Eugene Rothman. (Philadelphia, Fortress Press, 1982), pp. 190–93

No analysis of prophetic poetry can be adequate which does not pay some attention to that aspect of prophetic language which may be called "bawdy." Bawdy language is a characteristic element in the Bible, and the prophets, being users of strong language and graphic metaphor, use it regularly. This is especially true of Hosea, Jeremiah and in particular Ezekiel. In the cases of these prophets, the use of bawdy language arises out of the involvement of the community in the fertility cults of the local Canaanite religion. When condemning such involvement the prophets used the language appropriate to such a practice, so the terms employed are necessarily bawdy, though they may be intended as metaphors. The ambiguity of language arises here because it is the worship of false gods which is being condemned under the metaphors of adultery and whoremongering. The worship of these gods (the local numina represented manifestations of the one god Baal) may have included sexual activities, or the language describing the worship may have been derived from the breakdown of marriage (cf. Hosea's difficult marriage as a figure for the land polluted by abandoning Yahweh). In this latter case only the language is sexual; the behavior described by it is (forbidden) religious ritual devoted to the cult of Baal, a cult which appears to have been practised "upon every high hill and under every green tree" (Jer. 2:20; 3:6, 13; cf. Deut. 12:2; I Kgs. 14:23; II Kgs. 16:4; 17:10; Ezek. 6:13). The difficulty of determining whether the language is descriptive or metaphoric should not distract attention from its essential bawdiness.

As one approach to Jeremiah's poetic language, the following bawdy images from his early work may be scrutinized:

> For long ago you broke your yoke
>   and burst your bonds;
>   and you said, "I will not serve."
> Yea, upon every high hill
>   and under every green tree
>   you *bowed down (tsō'āh)* as a harlot. (2:20)

> Look at your way in the valley;
>   know what you have done—
> a restive young camel interlacing her tracks,
>   a wild ass used to the wilderness,
> in her heat sniffing the wind!
>   Who can restrain her lust?
> None who seek her need weary themselves;
>   in her month they will find her.
> Keep your feet from going unshod
>   and your throat from thirst.
> But you said, "It is hopeless,
>   for I have loved strangers,
>   and after them I will go." (2:23–25)

The images are drawn from the Canaanite cult of sacred prostitution (2:20) and from nature (2:23f.), and the prophet, using strong language which includes obscene elements, depicts the community as wild animals in the desert feverishly sniffing the wind in search of satisfaction for their lust. It is a community driven on by lust which cannot be controlled, even though advised to restrain itself (2:25). This kind of activity is described as "orgies on the mountain" (3:23), though again the language may be metaphoric and refer to crowded gatherings at the cult centres. . . .

Jeremiah's other uses of metaphors are equally impressive. The image of the choice vine degenerated into a wild one (2:21) echoes the similar use of vine imagery in Isaiah (Isa. 6), though the vine as an image of Israel is too common in the Bible for direct borrowing to be necessary. Images of the approaching army threatening the life of the community abound in the oracles and graphically illustrate the growing encirclement of the city (cf. 4:5–7, 13–17, 19–21, 29; 5:6, 15–17; 6:1–6, 22–26; 8:16; 10:17f., 22). The invitation to the community, "Run to and fro through the streets of Jerusalem, look and take note! Search her squares to see if you can find a man, one who does justice and seeks truth; that I may pardon her" (5:1), reminds the modern reader of the Greek Cynic philosopher Diogenes, whose reputation for unconventional views includes the story of his wandering about the city at midday holding up a lamp and searching for an honest man. The image of death coming up into the windows, entering the palaces and killing the children in the streets is a powerful one (9:21). Equally powerful is the way the prophet describes the coming invasion in meterological terms: "A hot wind from the bare heights in the desert toward the daughter of my people, not to winnow or cleanse, a wind too full for this comes for me" (4:11f.). An example of the way metaphor crowds on metaphor and the images change while making the same point may be seen in 4:30f.:

> And you, O desolate one,
> what do you mean that you dress in scarlet,
>> that you deck yourself with ornaments of gold,
>> that you enlarge your eyes with paint?
> In vain you beautify yourself.
>> Your lovers despise you; / they seek your life.
> For I heard a cry as of a woman in travail,
>> anguish as of one bringing forth her first child,
> the cry of the daughter of Zion gasping for breath,
>> stretching out her hands,
> "Woe is me! I am fainting before murderers."

How vivid these images are of a tart applying make-up before going out to meet her lovers, whose intentions are murderous, and a woman terrified by the experience of giving birth for the first time. The sense of doom carried by these metaphors is also conveyed by the image drawn from community reactions to a bad harvest: "The harvest is past, the summer is ended, and we are not saved" (8:20).

Robert P. Carroll. *From Chaos to Covenant: Prophecy in the Book of Jeremiah* (New York, Crossroad, 1982), pp. 61–62, 64–65

JOB

There is a passage in the book of Job amazingly sublime; and this sublimity is principally due to the terrible uncertainty of the thing described. *In thoughts from the visions of the night, when deep sleep falleth upon men, fear came upon me and trembling, which made all my bones to shake. Then a spirit passed before my face. The hair of my flesh stood up. It stood still, but I could not discern the form thereof; an image was before mine eyes; there was silence; and I heard a voice—Shall mortal man be more just than God?* [Job 4:13–17] We are first prepared with the utmost solemnity for the vision; we are first terrified, before we are let even into the obscure cause of our emotion; but when this grand cause of terror makes its appearance, what is it? it is not, wrapt up in the shades of its own incomprehensible darkness, more awful, more striking, more terrible, than the liveliest description, than the clearest painting could possibly represent it.

> Edmund Burke. *A Philosophical Enquiry into the Origin of Our Ideas of the Sublime and Beautiful.* 2d ed. (London, Printed for R. and J. Dodsley, 1759), pp. 108–9

Several Hebrew scholars are of the opinion that this book was written by Moses; here, indeed, we find the same simplicity, the same sublimity as in Genesis, and the same predilection for certain verbs and certain turns of expression. Job is the perfect type of melancholy; in the works of men we meet with traces of this sentiment; and, generally speaking, all great geniuses are pensive; but no one, not even Jeremiah, *he alone whose lamentations,* according to [Jacques Bénigne] Bossuet, *come up to his feelings,* has carried the sadness of the soul to such a pitch as the holy Arab. In vain we should attempt to account for the tears of Job, by asserting that they were excited by the sands of the desert, the solitary palm tree, the sterile mountain, and all those vast and dreary images of southern nature; in vain we should have recourse to the grave characters of the Orientals; all this would not suffice. In the melancholy of Job there is something supernatural. The individual man, however wretched, cannot draw forth such sighs from his soul. Job is the emblem of *suffering humanity,* and the inspired writer has found lamentations sufficient to express all the afflictions incident to the whole human race. [1802]

> François René de Chateaubriand. *The Beauties of Christianity.* Vol. II, Pt. 2. Tr. by Frederic Shoberl (London, Printed for Henry Colburn, 1813), pp. 197–98

Biblical critics seem agreed that our own Book of Job was written in that region of the world. I call that, apart from all theories about it, one of the grandest things ever written with pen. One feels, indeed, as if it were not Hebrew; such a noble universality, different from noble patriotism or sectarianism, reigns in it. A noble Book; all men's Book! It is our first, oldest statement of the never-ending Problem,—man's destiny, and God's ways with him here in this earth.

And all in such free flowing outlines; grand in its sincerity, in its simplicity; in its epic melody, and repose of reconcilement. There is the seeing eye, the mildly understanding heart. So *true* everyway; true eyesight and vision for all things; material things no less than spiritual: the Horse,—"hast thou clothed his neck with *thunder?*"—he "*laughs* at the shaking of the spear!" [ch. 39] Such living likenesses were never since drawn. Sublime sorrow, sublime reconciliation; oldest choral melody as of the heart of mankind;—so soft, and great; as the summer midnight, as the world with its seas and stars! There is nothing written, I think, in the Bible or out of it, of equal literary merit.

> Thomas Carlyle. *On Heroes, Hero-Worship and the Heroic in History* (London, Chapman and Hall, 1840), p. 13

This is not the voice of a man, this is the voice of a time. The expression comes from the most profound of ages. It is said that in the era in which the man expressed himself, the world was in its infancy; yet everything indicates that in this epic of the soul, in this drama of thought, in this lyric philosophy, in this elegiac moan, wisdom and melancholy are advanced in years. . . .

If any book has especially depicted the poetry of the old, of discouragement, bitterness, irony, reproach, complaint, impiety, silence, prostration, then resignation, that impotence that inevitably changes into virtue, then the consolation that by divine piety elevates the dejected spirit, that book, of course, is the book of Job, that dialogue with oneself, with one's friends, with God, that lyric Plato of the desert.

One does not know precisely in what place, or above all in what time this poem or story came forth from a man's fiber. It has been said he may have been Moses; but Moses, according to the Bible itself, was not eloquent, not a poet; he was above all a statesman, a historian, a legislator. Job has the tongue of the greatest poet who ever articulated human speech. This is eloquence and poetry cast in a single mold and indivisible from all cries of man. He recounts, he argues, he listens, he responds, he gets angry, he challenges, he apostrophizes, he inveighs, he roars, he exclaims, he sings, he weeps, he mocks, he implores, he reflects, he judges himself, he repents, he acquiesces, he reveres, he soars on the wings of his religious enthusiasm over his own pain; in the depth of his despair he justifies God against himself; he says, "Fine!" This is the Prometheus of speech, aloft in heaven crying and bleeding away in the very talons of the vulture that preys upon his heart! This is the victim turned judge by the sublime impersonality of reason, celebrating his own agony and like Brutus of the Romans sending up shoots of his song toward heaven, not as an insult but as a libation to the just God!

Job is no longer the man; he is humanity! A race that can feel, think, and express itself with this tone is truly worthy of conversing with the supernatural and of speaking with its Creator.

> Alphonse Marie Louis de Lamartine. *Cours familier de littérature*. Vol. II (Paris, published by the author, 1856), pp. 441–44†

In this strange book there is not a moment in which one does not feel vibrate the fine and delicate touches which make the grand poetic creations of Greece and of India so perfect an imitation of nature; in it entire sides of the human soul are at fault; a kind of grandiose stiffness gives to the poem a hard aspect, which resembles a tone of brass. But never has the position, so eminently poetical, of man in this world, his mysterious struggle against an inimical power which he sees not, his alternatives justified equally by submission and revolt, inspired so eloquent a plaint. The grandeur of human nature consists in a contradiction which has struck all sages and has been the fruitful mother of all elevated thought and of all noble philosophy; on the one hand, conscience declaring right and duty to be supreme realities; on the other, the experiences of every day inflicting upon these profound aspirations inexplicable contradictions. Hence that sublime lamentation which has endured since the beginning of the world, and which to the end of time shall bear towards heaven the protestations of the moral man. The poem of Job is the most sublime expression of that cry of the soul. In it blasphemy approximates the hymn, or rather is itself a hymn, since it is only an appeal to God against the lacunae which conscience finds in the work of God. The pride of the nomad, his religion, at once cold, severe, and far removed from all devotion, his haughty personality, can alone explain that singular mixture of exalted faith and of audacious obstinacy. [1859]

> Ernest Renan. *The Book of Job.* Tr. by A. F. G. and
> W. M. T. (London, W. M. Thomson, 1889), p. 40

The Book of Job evinces the consummate artistic genius that created it by reading like a transcript from life, with its struggles, its doubts, its eddying inconsistencies. The action reaches its end, not by the arrow-line of a homiletic plan, but through such gropings and stumblings, such gradual discoveries of the true way, as must content us all in this mystery-encompassed existence. . . .

[The artistic unity of the poem] centres in a *person* rather than in a system of thought or reasoning; it is Job himself, the man Job, with his bewilderment of doubt, his utter honesty with himself and the world, his outreaching faith, his loyalty through all darkness and mystery to what is Godlike, who is the solution of the Job-problem, far more truly than Job's words, or the words of Elihu, or the august address from the whirlwind. How God deals with men, and how men may interpret his dealings; why God sees fit to afflict the righteous; these are indeed important questions, and not to be ignored; but more vital still is the question what Job *is*, becomes, achieves, in the fiery trial of God's unexplained visitation. In the answer to that personal question lies the supreme answer to all the rest. It is not a mere author that we find here, but a man. And as we trace the progress of Job's soul, step by step, revealed to us through his own words and through the attacks of his friends, we shall be brought to a contemplation of greatness in life and character such as, for sublimity, it will be hard to parallel in literature, however highly we may value the divinest creations of an Aeschylus or a Milton.

> John F. Genung. *The Epic of the Inner Life, Being the
> Book of Job* (Boston, Houghton Mifflin, 1891), pp. 9,
> 17–18

There is nothing comparable with it except the *Prometheus Bound* of Aeschylus. It is eternal, illimitable; in magnitude and magnificence it is unsurpassed and unsurpassable. Its grandeur is prophetic and poetic; its scope is the relation between God and Man. It is a vast liberation, a great goal-delivery of the spirit of Man; nay, rather a great Acquittal. . . .

But to the greater number of persons the Book of Job suggests little more than the Patriarch's patience, his Comforters, and his wife's wickedness; possibly also the apparition that made Eliphaz' hair stand on end. They perceive neither its consummate art nor its transcendent importance. . . .

How much more wretched was this Semitic Prometheus than his Grecian analogue? The Fire-stealer, chained to his rock on the Caucasus, had at least the pleasure of his own unbending pride, and the knowledge of his final deliverance and the triumph of his cause; whereas, although Job is anything but *patient* . . . yet he is not unsubmissive to the divine will. He never indulges in the satisfaction of renouncing God—of treating God as his enemy; and he never but once rises to the expectation that his wrongs will be righted, and even then he thinks it will only be after his death [19:23–27]. The parallel between Prometheus and Job is, however, much more exact than is generally recognised. . . . The Chorus of sea-nymphs, for instance, is a very close counterpart to the Chorus of Job's friends; and the opening speech of Prometheus on the arrival of the Nymphs resembles that with which Job breaks the silence, in presence of his friends. . . . After the episode of Io's entrance and frenzied flight the remainder of the tragedy is occupied with the colloquy between Prometheus and Hermes, who, like the Deity in the Book of Job, is accompanied by a storm, and, in this case, an earthquake. The reproofs of Hermes, however, have no effect on Prometheus, but the Nymphs are terrified into repudiating the suffering god and all his works. This latter portion of the drama has the strongest likeness to many parts of Job. . . .

Job's refusal to please his own pride by becoming Satanic—that is, by ceasing to search for Knowledge of God or boasting that he already possesses it—is cleverly accentuated by the author of the poem; for when his wife visits him, this is the very thing which she invites him to do. Satan's suggested temptation is reproduced in her lips, the Hebrew word translated *renounce* being the same word as he had used. *Dost thou still hold fast thine integrity*? she cries; *renounce God, and die!* [2:9] This little touch, carrying on at the same time the dramatic intention, would alone prove the masterhand of a great poet.

Francis Burdett Money-Coutts. *The Poet's Charter, or the Book of Job* (London, John Lane, The Bodley Head, 1903), pp. 33, 36–37, 54–57

I think the greatest book I know on the subject [Egotism] is the book of Job. Job was a great, splendid Egoist. But whereas Hardy and the moderns end with "Let the day perish—" [Job 3:3] or more beautifully—"The waters wear the stones; thou washest away the things which grow out of the dust of the earth; thou destroyest the hope of man. Thou prevailest for ever against him, and he passeth;

thou changest his countenance, and sendest him away" [14:19–20] the real book of Job ends—"Then Job answered the Lord and said: I know that thou canst do everything, and that no thought can be withholden from thee. Who is he that hideth counsel without knowledge? Therefore have I uttered that I understand not: things too wonderful for me, which I knew not. Hear, I beseech thee, and I will speak: I will demand of thee, and declare thou unto me. I have heard of thee by the hearing of the ear, but now mine eye seeth thee. Wherefore I abhor myself, and repent in dust and ashes" [42:2–6].

If you want a story of your own soul, it is perfectly done in the book of Job—much better than in [Dostoevsky's] *Letters from the Underworld*. But the moderns today prefer to end insisting on the sad plight. It is characteristic of us that we have preserved, of a trilogy which was really Prometheus Unbound, only the Prometheus Bound and terribly suffering on the rock of his own egotism. [Letter to Gordon Campbell, Dec. 1914]

D. H. Lawrence. *The Collected Letters*. Vol. I. Ed. by Harry T. Moore (New York, Viking, 1962), p. 301

When, at the end of the poem, God enters (somewhat abruptly), is struck the sudden and splendid note which makes the thing as great as it is. All the human beings through the story, and Job especially, have been asking questions of God. A more trivial poet would have made God enter in some sense or other in order to answer the questions. By a touch truly to be called inspired, when God enters, it is to ask a number more questions on His own account. In this drama of skepticism God Himself takes up the rôle of skeptic. He does what all the great voices defending religion have always done. He does, for instance, what Socrates did. He turns rationalism against itself. He seems to say that it if comes to asking questions, He can ask some questions which will fling down and flatten out all conceivable human questioners. The poet by an exquisite intuition has made God ironically accept a kind of controversial equality with His accusers. He is willing to regard it as if it were a fair intellectual duel: "Gird up now thy loins like a man; for I will demand of thee, and answer thou me" [38:3]. The everlasting adopts an enormous and sardonic humility. He is quite willing to be prosecuted. He only asks for the right which every prosecuted person possesses; He asks to be allowed to cross-examine the witness for the prosecution. And He carries yet further the correctness of the legal parallel. For the first question, essentially speaking, which He asks of Job is the question that any criminal accused by Job would be most entitled to ask. He asks Job who he is. And Job, being a man of candid intellect, takes a little time to consider, and comes to the conclusion that he does not know.

This is the first great fact to notice about the speech of God, which is the culmination of the inquiry. It represents all human skeptics routed by a higher skepticism. It is this method, used sometimes by supreme and sometimes by mediocre minds, that has ever since been the logical weapon of the true mystic.

Socrates, as I have said, used it when he showed that if you only allowed him enough sophistry he could destroy all the sophists. . . .

This, I say, is the first fact touching the speech; the fine inspiration by which God comes in at the end, not to answer riddles, but to propound them. The other great fact which, taken together with this one, makes the whole work religious instead of merely philosophical is that the other great surprise which makes Job suddenly satisfied with the mere presentation of something impenetrable. Verbally speaking the enigmas of Jehovah seem darker and more desolate than the enigmas of Job; yet Job was comfortless before the speech of Jehovah and is comforted after it. He has been told nothing, but he feels the terrible and tingling atmosphere of something which is too good to be told. The refusal of God to explain His design is itself a burning hint of His design. The riddles of God are more satisfying than the solutions of man.

Thirdly, of course, it is one of the splendid strokes that God rebukes alike the man who accused and the men who defended Him; that He knocks down pessimists and optimists with the same hammer. And it is in connection with the mechanical and supercilious comforters of Job that there occurs the still deeper and finer inversion of which I have spoken. The mechanical optimist endeavors to justify the universe avowedly upon the ground that it is a rational and consecutive pattern. He points out that the fine thing about the world is that it can all be explained. That is the one point, if I may put it so, on which God, in return, is explicit to the point of violence. God says, in effect, that if there is one fine thing about the world, as far as men are concerned, it is that it cannot be explained. He insists on the inexplicableness of everything; "Hath the rain a father? . . . Out of whose womb came the ice?" [38:28f.]. . . .

This we may call the third point. Job puts forward a note of interrogation; God answers with a note of exclamation. Instead of proving to Job that it is an explicable world, He insists that it is a much stranger world than Job ever thought it was. Lastly, the poet has achieved in this speech, with that unconscious artistic accuracy found in so many of the simpler epics, another and much more delicate thing. Without once relaxing the rigid impenetrability of Jehovah in His deliberate declaration, he has contrived to let fall here and there in the metaphors, in the parenthetical imagery, sudden and splendid suggestions that the secret of God is a bright and not a sad one—semi-accidental suggestions, like light seen for an instant through the cracks of a closed door. . . .

The Book of Job is chiefly remarkable, as I have insisted throughout, for the fact that it does not end in a way that is conventionally satisfactory. Job is not told that his misfortunes were due to his sins or a part of any plan for his improvement. But in the prologue we see Job tormented not because he was the worst of men, but because he was the best. It is the lesson of the whole work that man is most comforted by paradoxes. Here is the very darkest and strangest of the paradoxes; and it is by all human testimony the most reassuring.

G. K. Chesterton. Introduction to *The Book of Job* (London, Palmer & Hayward, 1916), pp. xix–xxiv, xxvi–xxvii

There is a startling nearness, a painful immediacy in Job's description of suffering that can rise from no vicariousness, no sympathy, no mere force of imagination. It is the poet's soul itself that has been hurt, and that has conquered its hurt. In the traditional forms of his own literature there are utterances of complaint, of piteous prayer, of faith, of hope. But there were no traditional forms which gave voice to doubt, to accusation, to defiance. The different mood demanded a different form, and the dramatic form was ready to hand and welcome. His essay at dramatic writing could hardly have resulted in anything more successful than Job. Our poet was a hakam [sage], completely, if we may trust his text, the child of the Hebraic tradition, with its myth and magic as well as its wisdom woven into the very substance of his mind. The use of mythological material is indeed greater in Job than in any other of the wisdom books of the Bible, or in the prophets, just as it was strongly marked in the dramas of Euripides. I cannot help thinking that it is the dramatic form that makes the poet bring this material into the foreground. It is a form which causes the long and lyrical utterances of prophets and psalmists to stand out, and the disputations of the schools. The poet is much more interested, one gathers from the study of it, in precept and idea than in action; what would be central for him would thus naturally be the agon. And the other elements of the Euripidean drama would be so modified in terms of the Hebraic temperament and literary tradition, that there would be at once the form without the substantial plot-construction of that drama, and such corrections of the form as would obviously suggest themselves. The most important of these would be the modification of the function of the chorus, so that it became absolutely detached from the action and acquired completely the character of a didactically lyrical interlude in commentary. Euripides himself, no less than the generation succeeding Euripides, had made such modifications. So also the author of Job.

Thus, like the Greek tragedies, Job consists of the dramatic treatment of an ancient legend. It has a prologue which tells as swiftly and deftly as the Euripidean prologue all that precedes the opening of the action. . . .

After the prologue comes the drama itself. It is complained that nothing happens. But from the poet's point of view the dialogue is the happening; it culminates in the challenge of the justice of God. In form it has the characteristics of the Euripidean *agon*. The speeches are set, argumentative, and however tense with emotion, always within the bounds of the literary methods of the "wisdom books." . . .

Prologue, *agon*, messenger, choruses, epiphany, epilogue, they are all evident with just those differences from the Greek that may be expected from the difference in tradition and background between the two authors.

Horace M. Kallen. The Book of Job as a Greek Tragedy
(New York, Moffat, Yard, 1918), pp. 26–28, 37

Like Lucretius, Dante, and Goethe, the author of Job possessed at the same time great poetic genius and incredible erudition. His command of language and powers of expression are unmatched at his time; he used the greatest vocabulary of any Hebrew writer (being in this sense the Shakespeare of the Old Testament). He knew all there was to be known in his time, being a consummate scholar of encyclopedic knowledge, and was endowed with the power of introspection to the highest degree. He reflected profoundly and originally on the ultimate problems of theology and religion, attaining results that have hardly been surpassed. Immanuel Kant devoted a considerable portion of his monograph *On the Failure of All Philosophical Attempts in Theodicy* to an exposition of the Book of Job —and reached similar conclusions.

The style of our poet is no less original than his language and thought. Only his meter is the standard one. . . .

The style of the Book of Job is highly personal. A considerable portion of the poem was written under the spell of intense emotions. The poet seems to have placed in the mouth of Job his own feelings, doubts, and hopes (B. Duhm, *Hiob*, p. 9), thus transforming the pious and patient character of legend into a titanic challenger of the deity, passing from moods of abject despondency and hopeless pessimism to flaming indignation bordering occasionally on hysterical frenzy. With desperate tenacity Job, conscious of his innocence, clings to the remnants of his faith, which brutal reality and the cold doctrine of retribution implacably applied to his case by his friends have miserably wrecked. Occasionally a fleeting glimpse discloses to his tormented soul a vindicator in the heavens, a God of justice who will clear him of false charges (16:18–22; cf. 13:15f.; 14:13–15). In the famous passage, "I know that my redeemer liveth" (19:25–27), Job seems to be certain that God will avenge him and that he will witness (even though dead) his own vindication. . . .

These varying moods are reflected in a style rich in contrasts. Nevertheless, there are some general characteristics that may be noted in the literary art of our poet. The basic quality may be defined as the immediate actuality conveyed by his words. His vivid imagination pictures reality in its manifold variety, with little distortion or exaggeration. Only in those glimpses of the vindicator in heaven, just mentioned, does the poet set sail for alluring regions of fancy, otherwise avoiding that imaginary world of blissful illusions in which the Second Isaiah and later apocalyptic writers loved to reside. This sense of reality expresses itself, on the one hand, in admiration for the magnificence and harmony of the natural world and, on the other, in bitter disillusion with regard to the human world.

No poet in the Old Testament has a keener appreciation of nature nor a more scientific understanding of its functioning. . . .

Characteristic of our author and significant for his literary art is his interest in the habits of animals, particularly the untamed birds and beasts of the wilderness. He delights in painting vignettes of a lion's den (4:10f.; 38:39f.), of the ravens (38:41), of the mountain goats and hinds (39:1–4), of the wild asses (6:5; 39:5–8), of the wild ox (39:9–12), of the battle steed (39:19–25), of the hawk (39:26), and of the vulture (39:27–30).

The author is a master in the use of simile and metaphor. Usually he draws his comparisons from flora, fauna, and natural phenomena, but also from human activities. . . .

It is clear that the author's wonder before the magnificence of nature, which conveys but a faint idea of the power and wisdom of the Creator, contrasts with his contempt for miserable human beings, in whom God is no more interested than in wild animals. His vivid imagination personifies natural objects and phenomena, whose beauty enraptures him. With classic diction he speaks of "the eyelids of the dawn" (3:9), and of the time when "the stars of the morning sang together" (38:7). Job appeals to the earth, "O earth, cover not my blood!" (16:18); he calls the grave his father and the worms his mother and sister (17:14).

Robert H. Pfeiffer. *Introduction to the Old Testament*
(New York, Harper, 1941), pp. 687–89

When I first read it as a child, it seemed to me that the record of Job's tribulations was relieved only by a kind of gloomy and unwilling humor—a humor not intended by the author, but supplied by my own exasperation, for my childish sense of proportion and justice was at length so put upon by this dreary tidal flood of calamities that I had to laugh in protest.

But any reader of intelligence and experience who has read that great book in his mature years will realize how false such a picture is. For the Book of Job, far from being dreary, gray, and dismal, is woven entire, more than any single piece of writing I can recall, from the sensuous, flashing, infinitely various, and gloriously palpable material of great poetry; and it wears at the heart of its tremendous chant of everlasting sorrow the exulting song of everlasting joy.

It is the sense of death and loneliness, the knowledge of the brevity of his days, and the huge impending burden of his sorrow, growing always, never lessening, that makes joy glorious, tragic, and unutterably precious to a man like Job. Beauty comes and passes, is lost the moment that we touch it, can no more be stayed or held than one can stay the flowing of a river. Out of this pain of loss, this bitter ecstasy of brief having, this fatal glory of the single moment, the tragic writer will therefore make a song for joy. That, at least, he may keep and treasure always. And his song is full of grief, because he knows that joy is fleeting, gone the instant that we have it, and that is why it is so precious, gaining its full glory from the very things that limit and destroy it.

He knows that joy gains its glory out of sorrow, bitter sorrow, and man's loneliness, and that it is haunted always with the certainty of death, dark death, which stops our tongues, our eyes, our living breath, with the twin oblivions of dust and nothingness. Therefore a man like Job will make a chant for sorrow, too, but it will still be a song for joy as well, and one more strange and beautiful than any other that man has ever sung:

> Hast thou given the horse strength? hast thou clothed his neck with thunder?
> Canst thou make him afraid as a grasshopper? the glory of his nostrils is terrible.
> He paweth in the valley, and rejoiceth in his strength: he goeth on to meet the armed men.

He mocketh at fear, and is not affrighted; neither turneth he
back from the sword.

The quiver rattleth against him, the glittering spear and the
shield.

He swalloweth the ground with fierceness and rage; neither
believeth he that it is the sound of the trumpet.

He saith among the trumpets, Ha, ha; and he smelleth the battle afar off, the thunder of the captains, and the shouting.
[35:19–25]

That is joy—joy solemn and triumphant; stern, lonely, everlasting joy,
which has in it the full depth and humility of man's wonder, his sense of glory,
and his feeling of awe before the mystery of the universe. An exultant cry is torn
from our lips as we read the lines about that glorious horse, and the joy we feel is
wild and strange, lonely and dark like death, and grander than the delicate and
lovely joy that men like Herrick and Theocritus described, great poets though
they were.

> Thomas Wolfe. *The Hills Beyond* (New York, Harper,
> 1941), pp. 191–93

Job is no more than the outward occasion for an inward process of dialectic in
God. His thunderings at Job so completely miss the point that one cannot help
but see how much he is occupied with himself. The tremendous emphasis he lays
on his omnipotence and greatness makes no sense in relation to Job, who certainly needs no more convincing, but only becomes intelligible when aimed at a
listener *who doubts it*. This "doubting thought" is Satan, who after completing
his evil handiwork has returned to the paternal bosom in order to continue his
subversive activity there. Yahweh must have seen that Job's loyalty was unshakable and that Satan had lost his bet. He must also have realized that, in accepting this bet, he had done everything possible to drive his faithful servant to
disloyalty, even to the extent of perpetrating a whole series of crimes. Yet it is
not remorse and certainly not moral horror that rises to his consciousness, but an
obscure intimation of something that questions his omnipotence. He is particularly sensitive on this point, because "might" is the great argument. But omniscience knows that might excuses nothing. The said intimation refers, of course,
to the extremely uncomfortable fact that Yahweh had let himself be bamboozled
by Satan. This weakness of his does not reach full consciousness, since Satan is
treated with remarkable tolerance and consideration. Evidently Satan's intrigue
is deliberately overlooked at Job's expense.

Luckily enough, Job had noticed during this harangue that everything else
had been mentioned except his right. He has understood that it is at present impossible to argue the question of right, as it is only too obvious that Yahweh has
no interest whatever in Job's cause but is far more preoccupied with his own affairs. Satan, that is to say, has somehow to disappear, and this can best be done

by casting suspicion on Job as a man of subversive opinions. The problem is thus switched on to another track, and the episode with Satan remains unmentioned and unconscious. To the spectator it is not quite clear why Job is treated to this almighty exhibition of thunder and lightning, but the performance as such is sufficiently magnificent and impressive to convince not only a larger audience but above all Yahweh himself of his unassailable power. Whether Job realizes what violence Yahweh is doing to his own omniscience by behaving like this we do not know, but his silence and submission leave a number of possibilities open. Job has no alternative but formally to revoke his demand for justice, and he therefore answers in the words quoted at the beginning: "I lay my hand on my mouth" [40:4]. . . .

The poet of this drama showed a masterly discretion in ringing down the curtain at the very moment when his hero gave unqualified recognition to the *apophasis megale* ["the great denial"] of the Demiurge by prostrating himself at the feet of His Divine Majesty. No other impression was permitted to remain. An unusual scandal was blowing up in the realm of metaphysics, with supposedly devastating consequences, and nobody was ready with a saving formula which would rescue the monotheistic conception of God from disaster. Even in those days the critical intellect of a Greek could easily have seized on this new addition to Yahweh's biography and used it in his disfavour (as indeed happened, though very much later) so as to mete out to him the fate that had already overtaken the Greek gods. But a relativization of God was utterly unthinkable at that time, and remained so for the next two thousand years.

The unconscious mind of man sees correctly even when conscious reason is blind and impotent. The drama has been consummated for all eternity: Yahweh's dual nature has been revealed, and somebody or something has seen and registered this fact. Such a revelation, whether it reached man's consciousness or not, could not fail to have far-reaching consequences. [1952]

C. G. Jung. *Answer to Job*. Tr. by R. F. C. Hull (Princeton, N.J., Princeton University Press, 1969), pp. 16–17, 23–24

The book of Job is a rare and ingenious achievement. Its anonymous creator has fashioned a work so unique that it does not fall into any of the literary genres of antiquity or modernity. Though it partakes of the motifs and imagery of wisdom literature, it is infinitely more engaging and personal in its impact than anything written in the ancient Near East. As literature it is neither epic, drama, lyric, or didactic poetry; and yet it partakes of something of each. As religion it is unrivaled in its proclamation of "faith in spite of." The obstacles to trust in God are presented ruthlessly and incisively, and the final triumph of faith is as rugged and convincing as the hero's most savage protests. . . .

[The author's] vocabulary teems with uncommon and otherwise unknown Hebrew words. In this he was like Shakespeare, for his fertile imagination and grasp of language led him into the evocation of emotion and the unraveling of thought through novel usages and the outright coining of expressions. There is no Old Testament parallel to the distinction and grandeur of his poetry, unless it be in Deutero-Isaiah. Both have a sweeping and exalted eloquence, but whereas the prophet is ornate and visionary, the saga's style is savagely chaste and psychologically penetrating. The poet sustains his gifts through three cycles of speeches and into the whirlwind speech without abatement.

Forcefulness of thought accounts primarily for the writer's impact. In a relentless pursuit of argument through the contention of personalities, he forges a style perfectly suited to his aim. By putting the words directly in the mouths of the participants and by allowing them unmitigated expression of emotion, a quality of realism is achieved that transcends the clichés of lament and suffering from which the poet does not wholly escape. It is really this titanic eruption of intellectual power, this bold delineation of divine-human encounter at the frontier of meaningful existence, that makes the work appealing. Here are men not merely talking about religion, or playing at it, but testing the strength and relevance of the roots of moral and religious conviction. The author has more in mind than puncturing common theories about punishment and reward; he has a concept of man vis-à-vis God that must be heard in its own right.

What were the resources at the poet's disposal? There was a long tradition of Egyptian and Babylonian theodicy, of inquiry into the ways of the gods with men. We have already alluded to the Babylonian Job, probably the closest parallel to the Hebrew book. . . . Whether he knew precisely this work or not, the author of Job had imbibed a spirit that sensed the essentially irrational and inexplicable ways of the divine. Yet how immeasurably surer was his development of the theme! There is no parallel to the scope of his work, and the monotheistic base of his thinking is never for a moment qualified, even by the figure of the Satan who derives all his power from divine permission.

Job, the legendary patriarch of unexampled piety and suffering, seems to have exerted a fascination over the mind of the poet analogous to Hamlet's spell over Shakespeare or Faust's bewitchment of Goethe. The Job of legend is known from the prophet Ezekiel who, seeking to press home his pleas for individual responsibility, averred: ". . . even if these three men, Noah, Daniel, and Job, were in it [the land] they would deliver but their own lives by their righteousness" (14:14; cf. v. 20). The Daniel mentioned is hardly the young man of exilic frame, the hero of the biblical book. He is rather the ancient Daniel, righteous judge in the *Aqhat* text from Ras esh-Shamra. Noah is of course the survivor of the flood. Similarly the Job of the prologue is an ancient prototype of righteousness.

The disparity between the prose prologue and epilogue and the poetic dialogue is not merely a matter of literary form but of more fundamental considerations. In the *prologue* Job is a nomad of blameless character. His piety is epitomized in sacrifice, his suffering is a testing engendered by the Satan's doubts of his fidelity, and he submits utterly to the divine chastisement. In the *poetic dialogue*, however, Job lives a settled existence, admits to some measure of sin (though never adequate to account for his plight); of sacrifice we hear nothing

nor does the Satan or the notion of suffering as testing appear; and rather than ac-
quiesce, Job rebels and rails bitterly against God. To this may be added the more
frequent use of the name Yahweh for the deity in the prologue as against Elohim
in the poetry. The prose also has a "fresco-like" quality, reminiscent of the patriarchal legends in Genesis; whereas the poetry is imbued with psychological
introspection.

Some of these discrepancies are not insurmountable (e.g., Job was probably
a seminomad who lived in a house for part of the year and wandered with his
flocks for the remainder); but the cumulative effect of the many factors suggests
that the prologue and epilogue are traditional material, to some degree already
fixed, which the poet took as the starting place for his own work. The theory that
the prose was added to the poetry falls to the ground because the poetry is senseless without the sort of introduction that the prologue provides. In an effort to remove the stigma of manifold reward from the poet, some critics have treated the
epilogue as a later addition. Whether the Job legend was in written or oral form
when the poet received it is uncertain. The problem of bringing into accord the
prose and poetry is ultimately insoluble. Probably the popular tale about Job was
so well known to his public that the poet told it as everyone knew it and then
went on to develop his own interpretation and analysis of the great sufferer.

> Norman K. Gottwald. *A Light to the Nations: An Intro-
> duction to the Old Testament* (New York, Harper,
> 1959), pp. 472–73, 475–78

The Book of Job is different. Here, for once, the problem of evil raises doubt,
and no solution is provided. Job has been likened to a Greek Tragedy, and especially to *Prometheus Vinctus* both in form and in subject-matter. Certainly it
comes nearer to Tragedy than anything else in the Bible. Yet it is not a Tragedy.
The effect intended and produced on the reader is quite different.

The mere fact that Job is restored to prosperity in the epilogue does not matter very much, irrespective of whether we regard this as a later addition or not.
After all, the epilogue itself acknowledges that evil done cannot be undone, for it
says that Job's relations and friends "bemoaned him, and comforted him concerning all the evil that the Lord had brought upon him," and this even after God
had given him twice what he had before. The Book of Job is not a Tragedy, because the grandeur of the hero is deliberately shrunk to nothing before the sublimity of the power he has questioned. Compare Chapter 13, verses 15–16, with
Chapter 42, verse 6:

> Behold, He will slay me; I wait for Him: [or: I have no hope:]
> But I will argue my ways before Him.
> This also shall be my salvation,
> That a hypocrite cannot come before Him.

Here Job is sublime, equally matched in debate with God. But in the end, when
God has reminded him of the limitations of human understanding, he says:

> Wherefore I abhor my words, and repent,
> Seeing I am dust and ashes.

One might perhaps say that Job is still sublime if one felt that so bold a spirit could not acknowledge his nonentity without great effort. Still, the main point is that the result of Job's contest with God shows God superior in every way. . . .

Tragedy glorifies human resistance to necessity, religion praises submission. To put it crudely with [Jean] Anouilh, the tragic hero says "No" to the forces which oppose and crush him; religion commends resignation. Iphigenia tries to escape her fate; Jephthah's daughter accepts hers without question. Prometheus defies Zeus; Job lays his hand upon his mouth.

> D. D. Raphael. *The Paradox of Tragedy* (Bloomington,
> Indiana University Press, 1960), pp. 47–49, 51

The Book of Job features a dialogic structure with the addition of a frame narrative which apparently derives from an older literary stratum but which, even so, seems to have been reworked with regard to the dialogue composition.

Yet, the dialogicity here is of a special kind: It is a continuously dialectic dialogue, a dialectic often recalling the complaints and rebuttals of an actual court of law. In the center stands Job's litigation, with God as his judge. There is no apology speech here; it is more properly called a protest or objection, not actually an objection to the sentence—for Job cannot acknowledge that a sentence has in fact been meted out to him—but rather, if you like, an objection to a punishment that was not based on a sentencing. . . . Job demands what in an earthly court of law one calls "due process." Nevertheless, he knows deep down that his demand is suppressed from the start. Because of his power and might over the creatures God can adduce even the righteous man who condemns himself. "Though I am right, my mouth will condemn me" (Job 9:20). "I am condemned," cries Job, "so why do I toil for nothing?!" (9:29). He goes even further than this. In truth a human being sins by just being human, so how can he, the unfathomable One on High, depend on these sinner-humans? "I have sinned, what can I do to you, O watcher of man . . . and why should you not forgive my sins?" (7:20–21).

In wondrous fashion this complaint is already signified in the first part of the frame narrative. Here it is transmitted to us, outside the dialectic, in epic, unambiguous terms, that what Job was receiving was not punishment but a test by which God was testing "a man honest and upright, God-fearing and shunning evil" (1:8); so God himself acknowledges and says in praise (of Job). The character of the "Satan," the one who causes (people) to stumble, the one who "induces" God "to swallow (Job) gratuitously," has likely been transposed from a work of ancient folklore. Yet the version that is set before us reveals unity in the dialogic structure of the book. One unifying device is the word *ḥinnam* ["gratuitously"], serving here as a leading word, in both its usages, one denoting "without recompense" and the other denoting "without reason." The Satan asks God in their first conversation (1:9ff.): "Does Job fear God *ḥinnam* (for nothing)? Have you not protected him, his family, and all that is his?" In the second conversation this word returns, as was indicated above, in its crucial meaning. God sees what he has done to Job as an action that was done *ḥinnam* (without reason): Job did not provoke it, it was rather a test, and the test continues. The link to Job's words in this verse catch the eye: "He strikes me with a tempest, and he multiplies my wounds *ḥinnam* (for no reason)" (9:17). One of the "friends" will not admit that God would so act. Rather, it is Job who is to be blamed: If God thus punishes him, (Job) must be "injuring his brother *ḥinnam* (for no reason)" (22:6).

There is another, more characteristic leading-word network, which, though it is limited to the domain of the frame narrative and is not utilized in the dialogue composition, is clearly influenced by the dialectic in it. I am speaking of the verb "to bless" in its diametrically opposed senses, as it refers not only to receiving a blessing but also to taking leave of blessing, to make a blessing on taking leave and departing. Here the Satan says to God (1:10ff.): "You have blessed his endeavors . . . touch that which is his, and then he will surely bless [i.e., take leave of] you." Preceding these remarks is the statement of Job that he would routinely say at times when he feared that his children might sin: "They might bless [i.e., take leave of] God in their hearts" (1:5). At at the height of catastrophe his wife says to him (2:9): "Do you still cling to your piety? Bless [i.e., take leave of] God and die!" Job rejects her words as vile, and by means of the leading word this rejection interconnects linguistically with his statement that is reported just then: "The Lord has given and the Lord has taken, may the name of the Lord be blessed" (1:21). The dialogue itself, in conformity to the style of this contrastively woven book, opens with Job's first complaint in the form of a curse (3:1): He curses the day he was born. He curses the existence that was decreed for him, and he blesses the God who issued the decree. Through all his complaints and all his protests he does not cut himself off from his God. Rather, it is through his very complaints and protests that he testifies to Him who sits in secret on High. . . .

The frame narrative gives expression to information that is neither the privilege of Job nor the dialogue composition. It explains the hidden element in Job's fate as a test. As always God "tests" those human beings to whom he is close and whom he loves. The conclusion of the frame narrative attests that Job, the man of complaint and protest, withstood the test and bore witness to his God. As at the beginning (1:8; 2:3), here, too, God many times calls him "his servant" (42:7ff.), and now this epithet symbolizes an eternal mission, the mission to be a "mediator" (which is the meaning of the term "he prayed" in 42:8, 10).

> Martin Buber. *Darko shel miqra'* (Jerusalem, Bialik Institute, 1964), pp. 340–42†

Job's friends are like the liberal clergy of so short a time ago. They believe that creation is demonstrably conservative of good, that justice eventually triumphs, and the good man reaps his reward. They deny evil as such. In one way or other they argue that the evils of the world are really goods, they are privative, educative, disciplinary, deserved, misunderstood, illusory, but never gratuitous, much less malevolent. The poet underlines every speech of the "comforters" with irony like the mounting bass notes of an organ.

Job answers simply, "I have been just and harmless in heart and deed, and I have suffered harm and injustice from the course of events." Finally he swears an oath, he stakes his integrity as a person on his innocence. Then the Almighty answers as a Voice from the Whirlwind. He answers the oath, the commitment, not the arguments. He begins with a rebuke, "Who is this that darkens counsel by words without wisdom?" and ends with another, this one to Eliphaz, "My wrath is kindled against you and your friends, for you have not spoken of me what is right . . ." [42:3, 7]. The Voice from the Whirlwind says that both Job's defense of himself and his friends' defense of the Almighty are foolishness, but offers no explanation, only simply confrontation, omnipotence to contingency. The speech of the Almighty, one of the very greatest poems in all literature, is a parade of power, devoid of moral content, but intolerably charged with the *tremendum*, the awe and judgment of the utterly other.

The Voice in the Whirlwind is a person speaking to a person, and so, looking back from the point attained by the wisdom of Job, is the Voice on Sinai; the Torah is transformed from a legal document to speech, "I am the Lord thy God . . ." [Exod. 20:2]. It is remarkable that dialogue in the Bible is brief and preemptory and rare—Abraham, Amos, Moses, Isaiah, Jeremiah—less than a hundred verses altogether, of command and submission, and even dialogue between man and man is almost as scarce—until we come to Job. Suddenly dialogue is imported from the wisdom literature of the ancient Orient and placed at the center of Jewish religion.

The acceptance of the incomprehensibility of the justice of God is not a rational act, it is an act of prayer, of communion. Job's final words are a prayer of humble access, a voicing of the breakdown of logic and evaluation in an abiding state of calm ecstasy. The Book of Job makes sense only as a vehicle for contemplation, for the deepest kind of prayer, which culminates in the assumption of unlimited liability, what the Byzantines and Russians loved to call the divinization of man.

The upholder of the universe takes Job into communion with himself, with the awesomeness of infinite process. Job no longer needs vindication. The word becomes meaningless, a vanished shadow lost in the terrible illumination of a tragic sense of being, beyond the natural and temporal order altogether.

Kenneth Rexroth. *Saturday Review*. April 23, 1966,
p. 21

What appears in the Bible as the Book of Job consists of a prose prelude and a prose epilogue, with sandwiched in between them, a poetic drama in formal verse. So much is now agreed upon. What is uncertain, and not becoming any clearer, is the relation between the folk-tale frame—the narrative opening and end—and the poem. How the poem came to be so framed and when, what the frame does to it, and myriad derivative minor questions still admit of great differences of opinion. As a result the import of the book as a whole and of the poem, if it is taken separately, remains indeterminate. . . .

The prose opening and the prose end are folk tale at its highest but with a calculatedly enigmatic character for the opening, which is focused in the baffling figure of Satan (the Adversary), a figure associated with prodigious consequences for our tradition. Folk-tale opening and folk-tale end are, *as they stand*, shaped to presuppose and require some sort of colloquy between Job and his three friends (the "comforters") who come to visit him. The verse drama appears, superficially, to supply this. But just before it begins comes a brief prose transition and immediately after its close another prose transition dealing with the three friends and disposing of them. It is these two junction pieces that stick the prose tale and the verse drama together. The big problem, *What, if anything, have the tale and the poem to do with one another?* naturally turns in part on these short transitional passages. They need to be pondered in close connection with what precedes and follows them in the tale as well as with what may be thought to take place in the drama. There are also a number of breaks in the poem—matter of varying quality, some great and some mediocre, having been inserted; and there is evidence of considerable disturbance—some speeches being out of order and some probably missing.

I. A. Richards. *Beyond* (New York, Harcourt Brace Jovanovich, 1974), pp. 44–45

Few books in the Old Testament have discrepancy and contradiction so central to their make-up as the book of Job. Many scholars have solved the problems these contradictions entail by employing a process of subtraction, that is by eliminating What-Does-Not-Fit. Otto Eissfeldt summarizes very well the results of this de-husking procedure [*The Old Testament: An Introduction.* Tr. by P. R. Ackroyd, 1965, pp. 456–62]. First of all one separates the outer folktale (1:1–2:10 and 42:7–17) from the inner speeches because they offer different solutions to Job's problem: in the folktale there is an outward restoration of his fortunes by God, in the speeches an inner conquest of his sufferings by Job. Then, a majority of scholars regard Elihu as a second-class citizen of the story, inserted at a later stage, since his appearance is not anticipated nor does it have any effect on what follows. His speeches interrupt what is clearly intended as a direct movement from the speeches of Job to the speeches of God. Moreover, Elihu's view that suffering is a source of blessing contradicts God's speeches which point out that no solution to the problem of suffering is possible. The precious chaff of the wisdom poem in chapter 28 is the next to go, since it does not fit into its present context as part of Job's speeches in chapters 27–31. If Job had indeed at this point proclaimed this hymn to divine wisdom, it no longer would have been necessary for God, in chapters 38–41, to direct Job to His wisdom which surpasses all human understanding. No small number of critics also reject the speeches of God and Job's replies (38–42:6) as insertions. Finally we must not forget to mention whatever in chapters 3–27:10 and 29–31 shows *Inconsistency*, such as weak and doleful statements from the rebellious mouth of Job.

I find these and similar attempts at analysis counterproductive. Indeed, confrontation of inconsistencies appears to be as much a feature of the book's structure as of its content. Attempts to remove these inconsistencies can be characterized as academic "failure of nerve" just as the platitudes of Job's friends are a "failure of nerve" in the face of Job's problems. By removing the book's inconsistencies, some scholars have succeeded in removing its message. This chapter begins to describe how these many inconsistencies are essential to its message.

The major contradictions in the story appear to be connected with a major theme of the book: for any thinking person there is a contradiction between what he has been taught to *believe* about divine justice and what he experiences almost daily in his life. God, who is all powerful and all just, rewards with good fortune those who obey him and punishes with inexorable might those who disobey him. The good prosper and the bad suffer. So we are taught to believe. Within the Hebrew Bible this theme is not simply representative, for example, of the Deuteronomic strain in the text, although it finds a classic formulation in such sources. It pervades the Tetrateuch, the Prophets, and the wisdom literature of Israel. Personal experience, however, contradicts this article of faith. The evil prosper, the good die young and often we experience ourselves suffering unjustly without any hint of what we are suffering *for*. Innocent suffering is a fact of common experience. Now this theme of the contradiction between a man's religious beliefs about the justice of (the) god(s) and his own personal experience is not peculiar to Israel. It is well known within the wisdom literature of the Ancient Near East of which Job forms only one small example. However, the book of Job presents the problem and works toward its solution with a genius that is characteristic of that type of literature often called myth. A central concern of the book can be expressed in terms of a contradiction between what a member of society should believe and what he actually experiences. The fleshing-out of this theme in the story takes place in such an obviously inconsistent fashion that one realizes—as it were intuitively—that this clash must be essential to the story.

Robert M. Polzin. *Biblical Structuralism* (Philadelphia/Missoula, Mont., Fortress Press/Scholars Press, 1977), pp. 57–59

At the very beginning of the poetic argument in the book of Job, the great death-wish poem that takes up all of Chapter 3, we enter the world of Job's inner torment. Now these first thirty-seven lines of God's response to Job constitute a brilliantly pointed reversal, in structure, image, and theme, of that initial poem of Job's. Perhaps the best way to sense the special weight of the disputation is to observe that it is cast in the form of a clash between two modes of poetry, one kind spoken by man and, however memorable, appropriate to his creaturely condition, the other the kind of verse a poet of genius could persuasively imagine God speaking.

The poem of Chapter 3 advances through a process of focusing in and in—or to shift metaphors, a relentless drilling inward toward the unbearable core of Job's suffering, which he imagines can be blotted out by extinction alone. The external world—dawn and sunlight and starry night—exists in these lines only to be cancelled. Job's first poem is a powerful, evocative, authentic expression of man's essential, virtually ineluctable egotism: the anguished speaker has seen, so he feels, all too much, and he wants now to see nothing at all, to be enveloped in the blackness of the womb/tomb, enclosed by dark doors that will remain shut forever.

In direct contrast to all this withdrawal inward and turning out of lights, God's poem is a demonstration of the energizing power of panoramic vision. Instead of the death wish, it affirms from line to line the splendor and vastness of life, beginning with a cluster of arresting images of the world's creation and going on to God's sustaining of the world in the forces of nature and in the variety of the animal kingdom. Instead of a constant focusing inward toward darkness, this poem progresses through a grand sweeping movement that carries us over the length and breadth of the created world, from sea to sky to the unimaginable recesses where snow and winds are stored, to the lonely wastes and craggy heights where only the grass or the wildest of animals lives.

In Job's initial poem, various elements of the larger world are introduced only as reflectors or rhetorical tokens of his suffering. Here, when the world is seen through God's eyes, each item is evoked for its own sake, each existing thing having its own intrinsic and often strange beauty. In Chapter 3, Job wants to reduce time to nothing and contract space to the small dark compass of the locked womb. God's poem, by contrast, moves through aeons from creation to the inanimate forces of nature to the teeming life on earth and, spatially, in a series of metonymic links, from the uninhabited wasteland (v. 26) to the mountain habitat of the lion and the gazelle (the end of Ch. 38 and the beginning of Ch. 39) and the steppes where the wild ass roams.

This general turning of Job's first affirmation of death into an affirmation of life is minutely worked out in the language and imagery of the poem that God speaks. Job's initial poem begins by setting out the binary opposition between day and night, light and darkness, and then proceeds through an intensifying series of wishes that the light be swallowed up by darkness. By contrast, the opening verset of God's speech summons Job as someone "darkening counsel," and the emphatic and repeated play with images of light and darkness in the subsequent lines makes it clear that this initial characterization of Job is a direct critique of his first speech and all that follows from it. . . .

Perhaps the finest illustration of this nice match of meaning and imagery between the two poems is the beautiful counterbalance between the most haunting of Job's lines wishing for darkness and the most exquisite of God's lines affirming light. Job tries to conjure up an eternal starless night: "May its twilight stars go dark, / may it hope for light and find none, / may it not see the eyelids of the dawn" (3:9). God, near the beginning of His first discourse, evokes the moment when creation was completed in an image that has become justly famous in its own right but which is also, it should be observed, a counterimage to 3:9. "When the morning stars sang together, all the sons of God shouted for joy" (v. 7). That is, instead of a night with no twilight stars, with no glimmer of dawn, the morning stars of creation exult.

Robert Alter. Commentary. Jan., 1984, pp. 35–36

JOEL

Joel's oratorical power was, perhaps, even greater than that of Amos. His highly coloured description of the ravages of the locusts and the accompanying calamities is a stirring picture; the reader feels himself to be an eye-witness. The extant production of Joel's prophetic eloquence, with its rhythm and metre and even a certain strophic structure, also occupies the middle between poetry and prose. The only speech of his which has been preserved is divided into two halves; in the one half he describes the misfortunes of the nation, blames their perverted ideas, and points out wherein their conversion must consist; and in the other, he seeks to fill their hearts with a joyous hope for the future. Joel endeavoured to carry his trembling, wailing and despondent hearers, who had collected on the Temple Mount, beyond the narrow boundaries of their present sorrow to a higher view of life. He told them that God had sent the plagues as forerunners of a time full of earnestness and awe, of a day great and fearful, destined to purify them and lead to a higher moral order. The sorrows of the present would pass away and be forgotten. Then the great day of the Lord would dawn. [1853]

Heinrich Graetz. History of the Jews. Vol. I. Tr. by
Bella Löwy (Philadelphia, Jewish Publication Society of
America, 1891), pp. 238–39

The poem is a series of seven visions: the fourth or central vision makes the keystone. The first vision is a starting-point which presents the Land of Judah desolate and mourning: successive choruses of Old Men, Revelers, Priests, Husbandmen, lament particular aspects of the desolation, and then all draw together in a national picture of distress. With the second vision—higher up the ascending half of the movement—the trouble has intensified: judgment is advancing to a crisis. The sound of the trumpet seemed to announce a day of judgment; mysterious forces of destruction are advancing—

> The land is as the Garden of Eden before them,
> And behind them a desolate wilderness; [2:3]

they are now among the houses of the city, and amid rocking earthquate is heard a Voice that must be the Voice of Jehovah. Higher still in the ascending movement, the third vision commences with a great surprise: the Voice of Jehovah is a voice calling to repentance—

> Rend your hearts and not your garments [2:13]

and in the Chorus of the Whole People there is a stirring of response—

> Who knoweth whether he will not turn and repent, and leave a blessing behind him? [2:14]

The Chorus of the Whole People, led by the Priests, appeal for mercy. So we reach the keystone of the arch with the words—

> Then was the LORD jealous for his land, and had pity on his people. [2:18]

It is a transformation of the desolate scene, for what Jehovah speaks realizes itself instantly to the imagination. But the poem cannot end here. There is a further stage—beginning the descending half of the arch—a stage of sanctification poured from above upon high and low, young and old; if signs of judgment appear, it is now judgment on behalf of Judah and against the nations her foes. The descending movement brings a sixth vision—this new judgment advancing to a crisis: voices summon the nations of the earth, voices summon the heavenly hosts, to the "valley of the LORD's decision"; the prophetic spectator has a glimpse of "multitudes, multitudes in the valley of the LORD's decision" [4:14]. All is swallowed up in darkness and earthquake: these pass, and the seventh vision is of the Holy Mountain and Eternal Peace. What the arch structure has symbolized is a clear progression, bound into still clearer unity by effects of symmetry. The seventh vision of the Holy Mountain stands opposed to the opening vision of a land desolate and mourning; if the second vision is of judgment *on* Judah advancing to a crisis, the sixth vision gives us judgment *for* Judah advancing to the valley of Jehovah's decision; the third stage of repentence at the last moment is balanced by the fifth stage of an "afterward" of sanctification; and the center of the whole is turning from judgment to mercy. Structural interpretation has given us a conception as artistically beautiful as it is spiritually convincing. And there is still room for the interpretation of exegesis to deal with particular details: with the riddling suggestions of a locust plague that might possibly shadow an occasion for the poem; or with the much-discussed apostrophe to Tyre and Zidon—expanded out of proportion to its place in the scheme—and the recognized doubt whether this is a later interpolation.

Richard G. Moulton. *The Modern Study of Literature* (Chicago, University of Chicago Press, 1915), pp. 104, 106–7

In his opening verses he summons the drunkards, but that is to lend vividness to his picture of facts, because men of such habits will be the first to feel a plague of this kind. Nor does Joel yet ask his hearers what the calamity portends. At first he only demands that they shall feel it, in its uniqueness and own sheer force. Hence the style of the passage, letter for letter, is one of the heaviest in prophecy. The proportion in Hebrew of liquids to the other letters is not large; here it is smaller than ever. The explosives and dentals are numerous. There are key-words, with hard consonants and long vowels, used again and again: *Shuddad, 'avla, 'umlal, hovish.* The longer lines into which Hebrew parallelism tends to run are replaced by a rapid series of short, heavy phrases, falling like blows. Critics have called it rhetoric. But it is rhetoric of a high order and suited to the prophet's purpose. Look at 1:10: *Shuddad sadeh, 'avla, 'adama, shuddad dagan, hovish tirosh, 'umlal yitshar.* Joel loads his clauses with the most leaden letters he can find, and drops them in quick succession, repeating the same heavy word again and again, as if to stun the careless people into some sense of the bare weight of the calamity befallen them.

> George Adam Smith. *The Book of the Twelve Prophets.* New and rev. ed. Vol. II. (Garden City, N.Y., Doubleday, Doran, 1929), pp. 396–97

Now comes a graphic description of the advance of the locusts and of the awful havoc wrought by them. Travelers who have witnessed these plagues verify every point in Joel's account—the gloominess and darkness, the whirring of the wings of thousands upon thousands of the insects sounding like the crackling of fire, their onward march in regular lines, the absolute nakedness and desolation of the land over which they have passed. With it all there falls upon the beholder a sense of helplessness such as one experiences in an earthquake, the feeling of being in the grip of a power against which man is helpless. With amazing swiftness, astonishing realism, and artistic beauty, our prophet gives us the picture. It is a masterpiece of description.

The scene changes. The prophet calls the people to repentance, "Rend your hearts and not your garments, and turn unto the Lord your God; for he is gracious and merciful, slow to anger and of great kindness, and repenteth him of the evil" [2:13]. This repentance assures them of forgiveness and restoration. In superb poetry that restoration is pictured; but before it is completed, there is judgment of the nations. The poem becomes apocalyptic. The prophetic spectator sees, "Multitudes, multitudes, in the valley of decision, for the day of the Lord is near in the valley of decision. The sun and the moon shall be darkened, and the stars shall withdraw their shining" [3:14–15]. The poem ends with a beautiful picture of Jerusalem, the city of peace, upon the holy mountain. A magnificent pageant is presented by the Book of Joel.

> John R. Macarthur. *Biblical Literature and Its Backgrounds* (New York, Appleton, 1936), pp. 282–83

The central theme is the "day of Yahweh." Therefore, it is very important, in studying the rôle of imagery in this book, to determine whether the visitations of grasshoppers which Joel describes are real or whether they are figures of speech for the doom to come on the day of Yahweh. If we take the entire book into consideration, the latter view is certainly more reasonable. And this is by no means discredited by the fact that concrete and realistic language continually alternates with figurative language in this book in the traditional way. Thus, Joel can speak of the swarms of grasshoppers as "a nation powerful and without number," with "lions' teeth" (1:6), as "warriors," "soldiers," and "thieves" (2:7 ff.). But he also uses other figures to describe the visitation, especially the figure of fire, a devouring fire (1:19; 2:3); he speaks of the day of doom as "a day of darkness and gloom, / a day of clouds and thick darkness" (2:2); in 3:3f., he alludes to "portents in the heavens and on the earth, blood and fire and columns of smoke" and to how "the sun shall be turned to darkness, and the moon to blood"; and in 4:15, he tells how "the sun and the moon are darkened, / and the stars withdraw their shining," a figure which later becomes standard in apocalyptic literature. In order to depict the doom which is about to come upon the people, Joel uses the figures of the scythe which passes over the ripened harvest and of the winepress which overflows with the "blood" of grapes, that is, of the enemies. He also compares Israel with a vine and a fig tree (1:7) which are laid waste, and thus exhorts the "virgin" Israel to lament "for the bridegroom of her youth" (1:8). On the other hand, he declares (4:18) that during the coming messianic age "the mountains shall drip sweet wine, / and the hills shall flow with milk." On the whole, the imagery of Joel is strongly influenced by the Canaanite syncretistic cultic environment in which the prophet lived and which he undoubtedly opposed.

Ivan Engnell. *A Rigid Scrutiny: Critical Essays on the Old Testament.* Tr. and ed. by John T. Willis (Nashville, Vanderbilt University Press, 1969), pp. 279–80

JONAH

"Shipmates, this book, containing only four chapters—four yarns—is one of the smallest strands in the mighty cable of the Scriptures. Yet what depths of the soul does Jonah's deep sea-line sound! What a pregnant lesson to us is this prophet! What a noble thing is that canticle in the fish's belly! How billow-like and boisterously grand! We feel the floods surging over us; we sound with him to the kelpy bottom of the waters; sea-weed and all the slime of the sea is about us! But *what* is this lesson that the book of Jonah teaches? Shipmates, it is a two-stranded lesson; a lesson to us all as sinful men, and a lesson to me as a pilot of the living God. As sinful men, it is a lesson to us all, because it is a story of the sin, hardheartedness, suddenly awakened fears, the swift punishment, repentance, prayers, and finally the deliverance and joy of Jonah. As with all sinners among men, the sin of this son of Amittai was in his wilful disobedience of the command of God—never mind now what that command was, or how conveyed— which he found a hard command. But all the things that God would have us do are hard for us to do—remember that—and hence, he oftener commands us than endeavours to persuade. And if we obey God, we must disobey ourselves; and it is in this disobeying ourselves, wherein the hardness of obeying God consists."

> Herman Melville. *Moby-Dick* (New York, Harper, 1851), pp. 45–46

The Book of Jonah is generally underrated; one reason is, it is judged by commentators, who have never tried to tell an immortal story, so they underrate a man immeasurably their superior, since the able narrator is above the able commentator, and high as heaven above the conventional commentator, who is mad after types, and who follows his predecessors, who follow theirs, "ut anser trahit anserem" [like the blind (lit. goose) leading the blind].

The truth is, that "Jonah" is the most beautiful story ever written in so small a compass.

Now, in writing it is condensation that declares the master; verbosity and garrulity have their day, but only hot-pressed narratives live for ever. The Book of Jonah is in forty-eight verses, or one thousand three hundred and twenty-eight English words.

Now, take one thousand three hundred and twenty-eight words in our current narratives: how far do they carry you? . . . Even in those close models, "Robinson Crusoe," the "Vicar of Wakefield," "Candide," "Rasselas," one thousand three hundred and twenty-eight words do not carry the reader far; yet in the one thousand three hundred and twenty-eight words of Jonah you have a wealth of incident, and all the dialogue needed to carry on the grand and varied action. You have also character, not stationary, but growing just as Jonah's grew, and a plot that would bear volumes, yet worked out without haste or crudity in one thousand three hundred and twenty-eight words.

> Charles Reade. *Bible Characters* (New York, Harper, 1889), pp. 76–77

The literary merits of the story are again its simplicity of diction, its absence of superfluous detail, its rapid movement (note especially ch. 1, vv. 4–6, 15, 16), its vivid use of dialogue, but above all the dramatic way in which the characters of the persons are expressed in the action, so that the moral of the book is brought out as much by what they do, as by the gentle remonstrance of Jehovah, which itself is perfect in its brevity. In a word the literary value of the book cannot be fully appreciated apart from its artistic treatment as a parable. . . .

Note how it [Nineveh] is drawn in a couple of strokes, "that great city," "their wickedness is come up before me" [1:2], and the drama begins at once. . . . A single verse is enough to describe the storm, the next rapidly contrasts the fear and hasty action of the sailors with the negligence of Jonah. The diction of the original Hebrew is vivid, personifying the ship, "the ship *thought to be bro-ken*," i.e. "thought it would be broken." [Also] the character of the sailors as heathen is kindly and sympathetically drawn. Though less enlightened than Jo-nah, they in a sense convert him by their unselfishness and piety.

Percy C. Sands. *Literary Genius of the Old Testament*
(Oxford, Clarendon Press, 1924), pp. 41–43

The story of Jonah is . . . a short story with a moral—like the Book of Ruth, which is much less fantastic, or the stories about Daniel. Whether the hero was identified with an actual prophet living in the time of Jeroboam II, which is not to be excluded, or was a legendary character, like Daniel, is totally irrelevant to an understanding of the book. In spite of its abrupt close, as soon as the lesson has been stated, the book is a perfectly good short story—with a beginning, a mid-dle, and an end.

As with Oriental fiction in general (cf. Daniel, Tobit, the *Arabian Nights*, etc.), the supernatural is the *pièce de résistance* of the narrative. The storm at sea, the big fish, the gourd, and the worm are all explicitly said to have been di-vine miracles. Such coincidences as the cessation of the tempest when Jonah was cast overboard seldom occur in real life. A man's survival for three days in the belly of a fish, or even a whale, which is the only marine animal of sufficient size, is physiologically improbable, to say the least, even if alleged modern parallels are taken into account. The instantaneous and general conversion of Nineveh to the religion of Jehovah could not be taken seriously for a moment by historians of antiquity. They also know perfectly well that no Assyrian king was ever called "King of Nineveh" (3:6), a title no less absurd than "King of Lon-don," and that Nineveh was never "an exceeding great city of three days' jour-ney" (3:3), for the circuit of its walls in the time of Sennacherib measured about eight miles.

The author of the story utilized ancient myths and folk tales in his story of the fish. . . . Drawing his main character from II Kings 14:25, he made use of the legendary stories of Elijah and Elisha (compare, for instance, 4:3 with I Kgs. 19:4b and 4:5, 6 with I Kgs. 19:4a, 5a) in some incidents of Jonah's career. The author's views on repentance through fasting and sackcloth, followed by divine forgiveness, are obviously derived from Joel (compare 3:5 with Joel 1:13f.; 3:9 with Joel 2:14; 4:2 with Joel 2:13 [cf. Ezek. 34:6]). The strange prescription that domestic animals, as well as human beings, should fast and wear sackcloth as a sign of repentance, finds a parallel in Judith 4:10 and may be a Persian cus-tom. . . .

Out of such miscellaneous materials, the author has composed a charming story intended to teach the lesson clearly expressed at the end of the book (4:10f.; cf. 3:9f.; 4:2), namely that Jehovah's loving-kindness and compassion are not re-stricted to the Jews but extend to the heathen as well.

Robert H. Pfeiffer. *Introduction to the Old Testament*
(New York, Harper, 1941), pp. 587–88

The story is told as if these events had actually happened. However, it is written in symbolic language and all the realistic events described are symbols for the inner experiences of the hero. We find a sequence of symbols which follow one another: going into the ship, going into the ship's belly, falling asleep, being in the ocean, and being in the fish's belly. All these symbols stand for the same inner experience: for a condition of being protected and isolated, of safe withdrawal from communication with other human beings. They represent what could be represented in another symbol, the fetus in the mother's womb. Different as the ship's belly, deep sleep, the ocean, and a fish's belly are realistically, they are expressive of the same inner experience, of the blending between protection and isolation.

In the manifest story events happen in space and time: *first*, going into the ship's belly; *then*, falling asleep; *then*, being thrown into the ocean; *then*, being swallowed by the fish. One thing happens after the other and, although some events are obviously unrealistic, the story has its own logical consistency in terms of time and space. But if we understand that the writer did not intend to tell us the story of external events, but of the inner experience of a man torn between his conscience and his wish to escape from his inner voice, it becomes clear that his various actions following one after the other express the same mood in him; and that *sequence in time* is expressive of a *growing intensity* of the same feeling. In his attempt to escape from his obligation to his fellow men Jonah isolates himself more and more until, in the belly of the fish, the protective element has so given way to the imprisoning element that he can stand it no longer and is forced to pray to God to be released from where he had put himself. (This is a mechanism which we find so characteristic of neurosis. An attitude is assumed as a defense against a danger, but then it grows far beyond its original defense function and becomes a neurotic symptom from which the person tries to be relieved.) Thus Jonah's escape into protective isolation ends in the terror of being imprisoned, and he takes up his life at the point where he had tried to escape.

There is another difference between the logic of the manifest and of the latent story. In the manifest story the logical connection is one of causality of external events. Jonah wants to go overseas *because* he wants to flee from God, he falls asleep *because* he is tired, he is thrown overboard *because* he is supposed to be the reason for the storm, and he is swallowed by the fish *because* there are man-eating fish in the ocean. One event occurs because of a previous event. (The last part of the story is unrealistic but not illogical.) But in the latent story the logic is different. The various events are related to each other by their association with the same inner experience. What appears to be a causal sequence of external events stands for a connection of experiences linked with each other by their association in terms of inner events. This is as logical as the manifest story—but it is a logic of a different kind.

Erich Fromm. *The Forgotten Language* (New York, Holt, Rinehart and Winston, 1951), pp. 22–23

The very first chapter of Jonah excited our imaginations. It is in and of itself a great work of narrative art! Into fourteen verses is concentrated a story full of action that sticks in your imagination for your whole life. Every word is in place here—bright, strong, well aimed. Jonah comes, chased by the spirit of the Lord, to Jaffa; he tarries not—he finds a boat, pays the fare, and descends into it "to go toward Tarshish, from before the Lord" [1:3]. Pay heed to the brevity of the expression: "from before the Lord"! On what account or for what reason he is fleeing is never stated more explicitly. It is only suggested that his mission weighs heavily upon him. It is just that he believes that there, in Tarshish, at a distance from God, it will be alleviated. You will admit that it is no great triumph of the prophet over God that in Tarshish God's power is lessened.

The pace of the story is fast, lively, natural, as in the more elevated narratives of the Bible. Only what is essential is narrated, so only what is essential stands out. There is not a single superfluous line. Behold, God cast down a great wind into the sea, and there was a great storm, so that "the boat was reckoned to break up" [1:4]. This expression seemed to us little ones new—we had never found another like it in the Bible; and, like all linguistic novelties, it made an impression and was always retained in our memories. We remembered, too, the image of the sailors "crying out, each man to his god" [1:5], starting to cast out the vessels to lighten the ship. Jonah is the same; he sees himself guilty and ostracized before God, who pays no mind to the danger. He descends to the hold of the ship, lies down there, and slumbers, until the captain approaches him and chides him: "Why are you slumbering? Get up, call out to your God, perhaps God will consider us and we will not perish" [1:6]—harsh, embarrassing words. The captain does not know that the passenger and his God had a falling out, that he cannot come before him in prayer. But when the boatmen cast lots in order to know for whose sin the calamity has come upon them, and the lot falls on Jonah, he reveals his secret to them and says: "A Hebrew am I and the Lord God of the sky do I fear" [1:9]. Now it is expressly related that he and his God had a falling out and that he is afraid of him. The clever narrator has saved his secret for the right moment. . . .

From the point of view of narrative art, there is no doubt that the first chapter is the finest. It is thoroughly taut, like the sails of the ship into which the confused prophet descended, thoroughly dramatic, rich in action; it presents to us a company of men in the heart of the sea, all of them contemplating the danger of perishing, and yet, the danger does not extinguish the light of humanity within them. Even after Jonah himself advises them to throw him into the sea, they are reluctant, and they attempt to row to dry land without performing this awful act. And their brief prayer, "Please, O Lord, let us not perish for the life of this man and do not place upon us innocent blood, for you O Lord, whatever you desire, you do!" [1:14]—stirs the heart by its simplicity, its brevity of expression. We are once again convinced that only what is said without much verbosity makes an impression—even a prayer to God.

But what is important here is not the form but the generosity of the book's author, who sees even the pagans as human beings, as compassionate people by nature. It is no wonder that he sees even the inhabitants of Nineveh, whose "evil has arisen before the Lord" [1:2], as people who can be reformed. . . .

The Book of Jonah . . . is neither a book of prophecy nor a book of history, but rather a folktale, a kind of parable whose substance is suffused with the moral that is brought out at the end of the book.

We do well not to ignore the fact that this is not a book by Jonah but a book about Jonah. Jonah is the protagonist of the folktale but not its author. The author is endowed with a deep humanistic spirit. His perception of God and of prophecy is a great perception. There is no doubt that the great prophetic books were well known to him. And, as was said, he realized the great role of the prophet.

The book attains, as we have seen, all the great features of the stories of the Bible: The author knows what to tell, and, especially, what not to tell so as not to blur the essence. He knows how to arouse our imaginations through stylistic clues, so that we fill in what he has wisely suppressed. . . .

A pure spirit is spread over the pages of this little book. A soft breeze, blowing at sunset, stills, comforts. The dialogue between God and Jonah is wonderful. Here is intimate contact—albeit with a touch of irony—between man and his God.

> Jacob Fichman. 'Arugot (Jerusalem, Bialik Institute, 1954), pp. 267–68, 270–71†

Among the many variations of the Night Journey [archetype] in myth and folklore, one of the most forceful is the story of Jonah and the whale—perhaps because in no ancient civilization was the tension between the Tragic and Trivial planes [of life] more intensely felt than by the Hebrews. The first was represented by the endless succession of invasions and catastrophes, the exacting presence of Jehovah and of his apocalyptic prophets; the second by the rare periods of relatively normal life, which the over-strung spiritual leaders of the tribe condemned as abject. Jonah had committed no crime which would warrant his dreadful punishment; he is described as a quite ordinary and decent fellow with just a streak of normal vanity—for he is, justifiably, "very angry" when, in the end, God does not raze Nineveh as Jonah had prophesied at His bidding, and thus makes Jonah appear as an impostor or fool.

Now this very ordinary person receives at the beginning of the story God's sudden order to "go to Nineveh, that great city, and cry against it"—which is a rather tall order, for Jonah is no professional priest or prophet. It is quite understandable that he prefers to go on leading his happy and trivial life. So, instead of responding to the call from the Tragic Plane, he buys a passage on a ship to Tarshish; and he has such a clean conscience about it, that while the storm rages and the sailors cry "every man unto his god" and throw the cargo into the sea, Jonah himself is fast asleep. And therein—in his normality, complacency, in his thick-skinned triviality and refusal to face the storm, and God, and the corruption of

Nineveh; in his turning his back on the tragic essence of life—precisely therein lies his sin, which leads to the crisis, to the Night Journey in the belly of the whale, in "the belly of hell." . . .

The story sounds in fact like an allegory of a nervous breakdown and subsequent spiritual conversion. Jonah might serve as a symbol for Dimitri Karamazov, or any of the countless heroes of fiction who progress through crisis to awakening.

> Arthur Koestler. *The Act of Creation* (New York, Macmillan, 1964), pp. 360–61

The story opens on an imposing note: "Now the word of the Lord came unto Jonah the son of Amittai, saying, Arise, go to Nineveh, that great city, and cry against it; for their wickedness is come up before me."

This is the great theme of the calling. The language is noble and magnificent, and we expect the prophet's anguished recital of his unworthiness, also in moving and passionate language. Nothing of the sort. "But Jonah rose up to flee unto Tarshish," fled moreover without deigning to utter a single word. I suspect that the author is having some gentle fun here at the expense of the formula and style of prophetic literature, but the main point is that we are surprised. We are impressed from the beginning by the individuality, indeed the quirkiness of the prophet. He is *sui generis* and not without a left-handed charm.

The style remains elevated in the recounting of the embarkation of Jonah and of the Lord's sending "out a great wind into the sea" [1:4]. It is still possible at this point that we are dealing with a rather solemn "hound of heaven"–type narrative, with Jonah's flight motivated by, say, anguish. But this possibility is neatly and effectively destroyed by the prophet's unprecedented behavior during the storm. "But Jonah was gone down into the sides of the ship; and he lay, and was fast asleep" [1:5]. This supports the previous suggestion of quirkiness; Jonah appears here fully as the man who is out of step with everyone else, the man who never gets the word. He is a *shlemiel*—a born loser. . . .

Face to face with this delightful picture of Jonah snoring away amidst the terror and turmoil of the tempest, we can no longer read the account as deadly serious. Jonah is revealed as a comic character; the account, as humorous in a marvellously deadpan fashion.

This is not to say that we are not moved, and moved deeply, as we read on. The humanity of the sailors, their unwillingness to abandon Jonah even when they learn the truth about him is touching. But it is the genius of this comic artist that he can—like Chaucer and Charlie Chaplin—be simultaneously funny and moving. Humor and compassion are inextricably mixed in the conclusion of the incident: "So they took up Jonah, and cast him forth into the sea: and the sea ceased from her raging. Then the men feared the LORD exceedingly, and offered a sacrifice unto the LORD, and made vows" . . . [1:15–16].

The irony and humor lie in the fact that this maverick prophet is successful in turning men toward the Lord even when he is not trying, even when he is in fact fleeing from his commission and his God. Not only is there this striking incongruity between the intention of the prophet and his effect, but also we become aware of a certain playfulness in the nature of the Lord who has arranged affairs in so paradoxical a manner. . . .

One of the most effective of comic techniques is what might be called "capping." The artist builds his structure up to a climax of absurdity. Then, with but the slightest of pauses and with perfect timing so essential for full comic effect, he rises to a yet higher level of incongruity and surprise. This is exactly what the author of Jonah now does. We are once again surprised, when we thought that nothing could accomplish this, at the reaction of the prophet to his fantastic success. "It displeased Jonah exceedingly."

It is when we come to consider Jonah's reasons for this unexpected reaction that we reach both the comic heights of the story and its human depths. "I pray thee, O LORD, was not this my saying, when I was yet in my country? Therefore I fled before thee unto Tarshish: for I knew that thou art a gracious God, and merciful, slow to anger, and of great kindness, and repentest thee of the evil." [4:2] This statement demands close attention. I think that the commentators who emphasize Jonah's Hebraic exclusiveness or his hatred of non-Jews go badly astray. They miss the real point of the argument and also fail to see the kind of crazy logic which informs it. Here we face the theme of "reason gone mad" directly, but it is reason.

Jonah's argument goes something like this: "You gave me a commission as a denouncing prophet, calling upon me to preach destruction upon this city. But I knew, I knew from the very beginning, that you would renege. How did I know? I was absolutely convinced of your enormous mercy and your love. This being so, I realized at once that you were setting me up to be a fool and a liar. Really, Lord, you are a great trial to a man. But, you did issue the commission of destruction, and I did carry it out, although under protest. Now, the very least you can do is be faithful to your word." . . .

I am convinced that our author strikes deeper here than is generally realized. Jonah turns out not to be *shlemiel* but *mensh*—a real man. He has a kind of twisted independence of mind and a great integrity of spirit; he is well worth listening to. His root question, "Since you are a loving God, why do you pretend to be so fierce and terrible?" is not trivial. It constitutes, I think, a fundamental and legitimate criticism of ordinary prophetic modes, which are too often vulnerable to the charge of being negative, of failing to emphasize sufficiently the positive qualities of the Lord; namely, that he is a "gracious God, and merciful, slow to anger, and of great kindness." Under the guise of high comedy, the author of Jonah is insinuating important truths.

Donald F. Rauber. The Bible Today. Oct., 1970,
pp. 33–35

We should note the literary craftsmanship of the story. Its structure, careful plotting, and interwoven motifs reinforce the theme of the priority of mercy over retributive justice. The three examples of God's mercy interact. The disobedient

Jonah prays and is released from the whale. Likewise, the wicked Ninevites repent and are saved from destruction. The third instance, like the first, favors the recalcitrant Jonah, this time with shelter from the sun—even without a prayer of submission. It is also linked to the second instance, both by Jonah and by God, but with a characteristic difference, for the edification of the reader.

Unthinking and selfish, Jonah feels the same about the two episodes, linking them by expressing his feelings in identical words. His reaction both to the deliverance of Nineveh and to the destruction of the plant is, "It is better for me to die than to live." That is not God's way of connecting the two events, however. He wants Jonah to change his perspective; to think about the word "pity," to see the real connection between the two instances of it, and to answer a question. Jonah's selfish concern for his own comfort is called, perhaps with irony, "pity" for the plant. God indulgently attributes pity to Jonah as if speaking to a small child ("You're sorry you hit your baby brother; you love him, don't you?"). This same pity is just what God says he, himself, has shown to the Ninevites. . . . His final words ask Jonah the question—rhetorical to the reader, but evidently a problem to Jonah: "Should not I pity Nineveh?" The implied logic is typical of the rabbis: if pity is due the lowly plant, how much more is pity due the far more valuable and numerous inhabitants of Nineveh!

> Thayer S. Warshaw. In *Literary Interpretations of Biblical Narratives*. Ed. by Kenneth R. R. Gros Louis et al. (Nashville, Abingdon Press, 1974), pp. 194–95

The author has constructed his story in two major parts (chs. 1–2 and 3–4) which are virtually parallel detail for detail until 4:8b is reached. There is also a thematic parallelism between the major motifs, with the focus initially upon the non-Israelites (the sailors in ch. 1, the Ninevites in ch. 3), then upon Jonah (chs. 2 and 4). Thus in chapters 1–2, both the sailors and Jonah are threatened with destruction; they respond with prayer to Yahweh; Yahweh reacts to their prayers by rescuing them; and they conclude by worshiping Yahweh. In chapters 3–4, the Ninevites and Jonah are confronted by a crisis involving destruction (for Jonah the crisis is not his own destruction, but the fact that Nineveh apparently will not be destroyed!); they respond to Yahweh: the Ninevites with faith and repentance, Jonah with anger, complaint, and a request for death; this is followed by Yahweh's response: to the Ninevites by changing his mind about destroying the city, to Jonah by encouraging the prophet to change his mind about wanting the city to be destroyed. Thus, structural analysis presupposes the integral relationship of the psalm (2:2–9 [H 3–10]) to the book as a whole, contrary to the general scholarly consensus which has rather seen it as the inept interpolation of a later editor. Though the vocabulary and linguistic characteristics of the psalm indicate that the author did not compose it especially for his story, its formal, structural, and meaningful compatibility with other elements in the prose parts suggests that it could well have been the writer himself who inserted it precisely in its present position. . . .

At the end of the first half of the story, when the sailors and Jonah have been faced with similar perils, they both supplicate Yahweh, are rescued by him, and cultically respond to him in similar fashion. But in the last two chapters, the conduct of the Ninevites and Jonah is radically distinct, so that the conformity in chapters 1–2 serves to heighten and emphasize the lack of it in chapters 3–4. The most striking contrast is that Jonah, unlike the Ninevites, does not repent. Though the writer clearly wants to emphasize the limitless character of the merciful divine will to save, offered equally to non-Israelite and Israelite, he wants also to stress the link between the two parts of the human response—prayer and repentance. With respect to prayer, Jonah was on the same plane as the sailors, but with respect to repentance, his response does not match the Ninevites', and at the end he is contemplating death instead of life.

> George M. Landes. In *The Interpreter's Dictionary of the Bible*. Supplementary vol. (Nashville, Abingdon Press, 1976), pp. 489–90

The argument beneath the story is made up of three points: (a) that a prophet cannot escape his calling; (b) that God always accepts true repentance, even where it means that a genuine prophecy does not come true; and (c) that He spares His creatures for the simple reason that He likes them to exist. Each point is conveyed by an episode in the story. The first is conveyed by the episode of the futile voyage (ch. 1); the second by the account of Jonah's mission in Nineveh (ch. 3); and the third by the story of the plant (ch. 4). The three episodes combine to produce a plot, which has its turning point in the second episode, since it is Jonah's success in Nineveh that makes the tension between the prophet's integrity and God's mercy into an actual conflict. The central episode is thus structurally the main one: the conflict in it is prepared by the first episode, while the third and last episode resolves the conflict, closing the story. These considerations reveal a clearly structured plot, which produces the effect of a strongly "logical," or coherent, narrative. Additional coherence is supplied by cross-references. I have already shown, discussing repetitions, how Jonah's "cry" (the message he is told to deliver to Nineveh) is twice mentioned (1:2; 3:2) before being fully quoted the third time (3:4). This results in the repetition of the word "cry," with a few other words, and emphasizes the nexus between the very beginning of the story and its climax. Jonah also explains in the last part of the story why he fled to Tarshish (4:2) when first sent, and thus neatly ties the beginning to the end. Some readers are also impressed by the correspondence in the behaviour of the seamen and the people of Nineveh; or between the two didactic miracles of the fish and the plant.

In all these things the Book of Jonah conforms to the normal storytelling usage of the Old Testament. Its one atypical feature is the relative independence of its parts. Usually, in the Old Testament, the three "classical" components of exposition, main piece and resolution merge into a single uninterrupted narrative. In the Book of Jonah they are episodes, separated by clear breaks or pauses in the narrative flow. Each episode is formally treated as a complete story, making some (though partial) sense of its own; each deals with a clearly defined theme: each has a separate exposition (1:1–3; 3:1–3; 4:1–4) and a proper ending. The reader is made to pay equal attention to the details and features that keep the whole strongly integrated, and to the partial plots and meanings of the episodes. The story is a unity, yet loosely structured. The effect of a loose composition is intensified by the insertion of Jonah's prayer (ch. 2), an independent psalm that functions as a poetical intermezzo, enforcing a pause in the flow of the prose.

The Book of Jonah has no connection with the grand sequence of sacred history. It stands by itself. It is the single longish piece of narrative in the Old Testament that is no history at all, but fiction pure and simple. Its fondness for wonders, in the manner of folktales, is less decisive in determining its fictional character than its clear subservience to a moral. It is a story made up to convey an idea, not a piece of history told in a way that shows its significance. The narrative materials — or fictional events — are obviously chosen and arranged to express the idea; the aesthetics follow directly from the requirements of the idea. It is this freedom from the awkwardness of fact, that makes the little book a perfect example of the narrator's art, on a higher, more complex level than usual in the Old Testament.

Jacob Licht. *Storytelling in the Bible* (Jerusalem, Magnes Press, 1978), pp. 121–24

Since the Book of Jonah is premised on the solid and reassuring idea of the patience of God, one is not surprised to discover that God "stomached" Jonah's insolence and, with the aim of overtaking Jonah as he formerly overtook Moses or Jeremiah or even Cain and Adam, He sent him a messenger in the form of a tempest. Wouldn't the tempest make Jonah "cry unto his God" as the sailors all cry out, each one unto his God (Jon. 1:5)? One can see that God counted on panic and its immediate reactions to bring Jonah to his senses. Fear — raw, instinctive fear — wouldn't it bring Jonah to "turn back toward God" and renew the dialogue, if only with a cry?

But Jonah rejected the offer. In the midst of this tempest which raised a turbulent symphony all around him, he alone remained immovably silent. Like a warrior determined to stake his all, he scorned the conciliatory message which his adversary sent him and tore it into a thousand pieces. And he went a step further: having chosen silence as his weapon, he burnished it to the point of making it murderous. While the sailors were outvying one another in crying out toward heaven and were busy lightening the ship, Jonah "was gone down into the innermost parts of the ship; and he lay, and was fast asleep" (Jon. 1:5).

This "going down," observes [the Jewish religious thinker] Ernst Simon, was an accentuation of the flight. In the heart of the ship, Jonah sought the lowest point where he would be farthest from heaven and from his God. As for sleep, one should add, it was an accentuation of the silence, but a special kind of accentuation whose character it is not hard to determine. The term used in the text, *wayyeradam*, is unambiguous: it indicates the snoring drunkenness of the hobo.

. . . By sleep, or rather, by this form of sleep, Jonah entered into the realm of inert slumber. Now he was not only a man who does not speak but a being in a state of psychic and physiological hibernation. His silence now recalled that of night (it must have been dark down in the hold, and the captain must have had difficulty in distinguishing the sluggish mass hidden in an obscure corner), and it was soon to resemble that of death. For we are not surprised to learn that when he was overtaken by a second, urgent message from God—the lot which fell to him—he sought to evade this new message, and it now only remained for him to opt for suicide: "Take me up, and cast me forth into the sea" (Jon. 1:12). It is the strictly logical outcome of his previous behavior. From one stage to the next, Jonah's silence had deepened until it was identified with that of death. In his endeavor to resist God's call, in his attempt to obstruct the dialogue, Jonah used successively the most challenging forms of silence: flight, with his back to the interlocutor; the physical torpor of sluggish inertia; darkness and death.

Had the Book of Jonah ended here, at the conclusion of the first chapter, it would have been an example, unique in world literature, of the triumph of tragic absurdity. Camus might have regarded it as the supreme instance of the apotheosis of liberty through suicide. Even more than Prometheus and Sisyphus, Jonah might have represented the victorious challenger of God. For, with Prometheus and Sisyphus, life, however painful and troubling, permits the possibility of future changes; whereas with Jonah, at the moment of death, triumphant liberty reaches its goal. All is accomplished; God has been unable to vanquish the liberty of man.

> André Néher. *The Exile of the Word.* Tr. from the French by David Maisel. (Philadelphia, Jewish Publication Society of America, 1981), pp. 155–56

JOSEPH

In the history of Joseph (which certainly is told with the greatest variety of beautiful and affecting circumstances), when Joseph makes himself known, and weeps aloud upon the neck of his dear brother Benjamin, that all the house of Pharaoh heard him;—at that instant, none of his brethren are introduced as uttering aught, either to express their present joy, or palliate their former injuries to him.——On all sides, there immediately ensues a deep and solemn silence;—a silence infinitely more eloquent and expressive, than anything that could have been substituted in its place.——Had Thucydides, Herodotus, Livy, or any of the celebrated classical historians, been employed in writing this history, when they came to this point, they would, doubtless, have exhausted all their fund of eloquence in furnishing Joseph's brethren with laboured and studied harangues;

which, however fine they might have been in themselves, would nevertheless have been unnatural, and altogether improper on the occasion.—For when such a variety of contrary passions broke in upon them,—what tongue was able to utter their hurried and distracted thoughts?—When remorse, surprise, shame, joy and gratitude struggled together in their bosoms, how uneloquently would their lips have performed their duty?—how unfaithfully their tongues have spoken the language of their hearts?—In this case, silence was truly eloquent and natural, and tears expressed what oratory was incapable of. [Sermon 27]

> Laurence Sterne. The *Sermons of Mr. Yorick*. Vol. VI (London, Printed for W. Strahan and T. Cadell, 1784), pp. 117–20

[The story of Joseph (Gen. 37, 39–50)] appears to be one of the most *beautiful* and interesting narratives in the whole lettered world; nor will it, perhaps, be easy to match it, even as it now stands translated, by any composition, in any language. . . .

As a piece of writing, it possesses at one and the same time, and in the highest degree, every elegance of literature: in point of style, it is various and masterly; the images are pathetic beyond the force of encomium *to do them justice*, and the morality and virtues inculcated, are obvious, important, and domestic. Were it possible to alter, without taking from its beautiful simplicity, what a noble subject is here for an epic poem!

> Samuel J. Pratt. *The Sublime and Beautiful of Scripture* (New York, Printed by Tiebout & O'Brien, 1795), pp. 92–93

To give examples from the modern art of our upper classes of art of the second kind, good universal art or even of the art of a whole people, is yet more difficult, especially in literary art and music. If there are some works which by their inner contents might be assigned to this class (such as *Don Quixote*, Molière's comedies, *David Copperfield* and *The Pickwick Papers* by Dickens, Gogol's and Pushkin's tales, and some things of Maupassant's), these works are for the most part—from the exceptional nature of the feelings they transmit, the superfluity of special details of time and locality, and, above all, on account of the poverty of their subject matter in comparison with examples of universal ancient art (such, for instance, as the story of Joseph)—comprehensible only to people of their own circle. That Joseph's brethren, being jealous of his father's affection, sell him to the merchants; that Potiphar's wife wishes to tempt the youth; that having attained the highest station he takes pity on his brothers, including Benjamin, the favorite—these and all the rest are feelings accessible alike to a Russian peasant, a Chinese, an African, a child, or an old man, educated or uneducated; and it is all written with such restraint, is so free from any superfluous detail, that the story may be told to any circle and will be equally comprehensible and touching to everyone. But not such are the feelings of Don Quixote or of Molière's heroes (though Molière is perhaps the most universal and therefore the most excellent artist of modern times), nor of Pickwick and his friends. These feelings are not common to all men, but very exceptional; and therefore, to make them infectious, the authors have surrounded them with abundant details of time and place. And this abundance of detail makes the stories difficult of comprehension to all people not living within reach of the conditions described by the author.

The author of the novel of Joseph did not need to describe in detail, as would be done nowadays, the blood-stained coat of Joseph, the dwelling and dress of Jacob, the pose and attire of Potiphar's wife, and how, adjusting the bracelet on her left arm, she said, "Come to me," and so on, because the subject matter of feelings in this novel is so strong that all details except the most essential — such as that Joseph went out into another room to weep — are superfluous and would only hinder the transmission of feelings. And therefore this novel is accessible to all men, touches people of all nations and classes, young and old, and has lasted to our times, and will yet last for thousands of years to come. But strip the best novels of our times of their details and what will remain? [1897]

Lev Nikolaevich Tolstoy. "What Is Art?" In *The Novels, and Other Works*. Vol. XIX (New York, Scribner's, 1899), pp. 490–91

Another characteristic feature of the Joseph story is its discursiveness, which stands in notable contrast with the brevity of the older narratives. We find in it an abundance of long speeches, of soliloquies, of detailed descriptions of situations, of expositions of the thoughts of the personages. The narrator is fond of repeating in the form of a speech what he has already told. What are we to think of this "epic discursiveness"? Not as an especial characteristic of this particular narrative alone, for we find the same qualities, though less pronounced, in the stories of the wooing of Rebeccah, of Abraham at the court of Abimelech (Gen. 20), in some features of the story of Jacob (notably the meeting of Jacob and Esau); and the stories of the sacrifice of Isaac and various features of the story of Abraham and Lot also furnish parallels.

Very evidently we have to do here with a distinct art of story-telling, the development of a new taste. This new art is not satisfied, like its predecessor, with telling the legend in the briefest possible way and with suppressing so far as possible all incidental details; but it aims to make the legend richer and to develop its beauties even when they are quite incidental. It endeavors to keep situations that are felt to be attractive and interesting before the eye of the hearers as long as possible. Thus, for instance, the distress of Joseph's brethren as they stand before their brother is portrayed at length; there is evident intent to delay the narrative, so that the hearer may have time to get the full flavor of the charm of the situation. Thus Joseph is not permitted to discover himself at the very first meeting, in order that this scene may be repeated; he is made to demand that Benjamin be brought before him, because the aged Jacob hesitates a long time to obey this demand, and thus the action is retarded. Similarly in the story of the sacrifice of

Isaac, the narrative is spun out just before the appearance of God upon the scene, in order to postpone the catastrophe and intensify the interest.

The means that is applied over and over again to prolong the account is to report the same scene twice, though of course with variations. Joseph interprets dreams for Egyptian officials twice; Joseph's brethren must meet him in Egypt twice; twice he hides valuables in their grain sacks in order to embarrass them (42:25ff., 44:2ff.); twice they bargain over Joseph's cup with the steward and with Joseph himself (43:13ff., 25ff.), and so on. Sometimes, though surely less frequently, it is possible that the narrators have invented new scenes on the basis of the earlier motives, as with the last scene between Joseph and his brethren, chapter 50. . . .

The narrator of the stories of Joseph shows himself a master of the art of painting the portrait of a man by means of many small touches. Especially successful is the description of Joseph's inner vacillation at the sight of Benjamin (43:30), and the soul painting when Jacob hears that Joseph is still alive (45:26), and elsewhere. But while in these later narratives the incidental features of the old legend are still developed with greater detail, on the other hand this very fact has naturally thrown the chief features somewhat into the background and made the original point of the whole less obvious. This result has been further favored by the circumstance that the original points had in many cases ceased to be altogether clear to those of the later time. Thus in the story of Joseph the historical and aetiological elements have lost importance.

Hermann Gunkel. *The Legends of Genesis.* Tr. by
W. H. Carruth (Chicago, Open Court, 1901), pp. 82–86

The Joseph cycle is the most sophisticated and polished of the stories of Genesis. It was chiefly a product of the north, reflecting the culture and travel of cosmopolitan centers, and designed to appeal to people whose tastes were growing jaded under the weight of luxury. Confusion of sources is less apparent than in any of the other tales. At the outset there is one discrepancy, for the company to which Joseph was sold is Midianite at one point and Ishmaelite at another. But this is a minor contradiction. In general, the sequence of events is smooth and finished, and the reader is carried along by the swiftly moving narrative with unflagging interest.

Every device is used to stimulate the imagination. There is the contrast between poverty and sudden wealth, between obscurity and prominence, between weakness and power. In comparison to the other Genesis stories, more subsidiary detail and description are used, even to a faded attempt to picture a rich foreign court. Here the colors of the original description were probably more vivid, for what is left is barely an impression.

Characterization was of less importance in the Joseph than in the Jacob cycle. Joseph is described as "comely and well-favoured" and pictured as a charming boy; but when the course of events has absorbed the author's attention, his hero sinks back into a shadowy lay figure, and the human interest again centers on Jacob. The ten older brothers, except at rare moments, act as a body and are scarcely differentiated. And Benjamin, Joseph's full brother, is a mere shadow.

It is strange that Joseph should not have been more strongly colored, for the author has given a detailed physical description of him, and at the outset of the tale he promises to be a vivid figure. But Joseph's characteristics were not essential to the story. He did not create the situations, but was adapted to them. In the Jacob cycle and in the Abraham legends every anecdote was told to show the hero's reaction, for this was the primary object of the narrator. There could have been no Jacob cycle without just such a man as Jacob, but the Joseph cycle would have been quite as good a story with any lay figure. It was a tale of adventure, and events were of far more importance than characters. Furthermore, the latter phases of Joseph's life were set in an environment that was unfamiliar to the narrators and the audience. Their experience gave them no insight into the manners and mental processes of courtiers. Kings and courtiers they knew by hearsay, but these were withdrawn from the world of men and what they did and why were matters of mystery to the simple minds of the people. As a result of this provincial outlook, when Joseph became one of the great ones of the world he lost his human quality and became unreal.

The plot of the Joseph cycle seems to have been a natural growth, for it flows along with no apparent effort and one event follows another with the inevitable quality of the best fairy tales. It is probable that numerous episodes were grafted on the original nucleus of the story as it made its way down through the ages, but all signs of seams and patches are gone. For a story as elaborate as this to have reached such a finished state suggests a long period of development, and it is probable, therefore, that the origins of the Joseph cycle can be placed in very high antiquity.

> Brooke Peters Church. *The Golden Years: The Old Testament Narrative as Literature* (New York, Rinehart, 1947), pp. 72–73

We must now turn to the overarching irony of providence that provides the theme of the entire story. Modern psychologists did not invent "sibling rivalry." Jacob loves Joseph too well, a theme that we saw also behind the irony of his own career. But the father's too evident preference for the young boy quite naturally causes the other sons to hate him. All of this is succinctly put in [Genesis] 37:3–4. And on this ironic incongruity—that love should produce hate—the entire story depends.

For the desire of the brothers to rid themselves of the young pest comes both out of their own hatred for him and out of their assumption that to get rid of him will reinstate them in Jacob's affections. Their spontaneous scheme is successful—though it would appear that someone else collects the cash (v. 28). But Joseph seems able to turn all he touches to gold. His expert interpretation of dreams in prison (ch. 40) makes possible his interpretation of the Pharaoh's dream (ch. 41:1–36), and the rags-to-riches theme of his success comes to its astounding climax (vv. 37–45). That much in itself would have been enough to establish the ironic theme of the Joseph story. When, however, the storyteller weaves the family back into the story in conjunction with the famine (ch. 42:1–5), the irony deepens still further. The boy, disposed of into slavery, now can dispose of his brother's destinies. Where his own dreams brought him to grief with his brothers before, now his interpretation of others' dreams have brought him to Pharaoh's favor and therefore to his position over the brothers. Their ignorance of his identity adds to the irony hanging over their abject request to buy food (ch. 42:6–38). We have, therefore, the dramatic irony of the difference between the character's perception of his situation—that,he is dealing with an evil and tightfisted Egyptian—and the reality of the situation—that he is dealing with his little brother. But this is simply the underlying irony of the whole, which is finally explicated in two different but related ways:

> But now, do not be dismayed or displeased with yourselves, having sold me here. To maintain life, God sent me on before you. For these two years, famine has been in the land, and for five years more there will be neither plowing nor harvesting. But God sent me before you to make you a remnant in the land, and to maintain your life for great survival. So now, it was not you who sent me here but God, and he has made me like a father to Pharaoh and a lord to his whole household and a ruler in all the land of Egypt (ch. 45:5–8).

After Jacob's death, attempting to forestall any grudge Joseph might have borne them, the brothers concoct a message from Jacob requiring Joseph to forgive them for their previous misdeed. Joseph's reply is the epitome of magnanimity, and it also expressed the fundamental irony of the entire story:

> Do not be afraid. For am I in God's place? You planned evil for me; God planned it for good, in order to make sure the survival of a numerous people as on this day (ch. 50:19–20).

The ascription of ultimate causality to God caps the ironic theme of the story.
Edwin M. Good. *Irony in the Old Testament* (Philadelphia, Westminster Press, 1965), pp. 111–13

No one who reads the Joseph Story can help but be struck by the symmetry of the plot. Setting and roles appearing in the development are duplicated with subtle contrasts in the resolution. Thus Joseph and Benjamin are both "sons of old age," both fall at various times in the story into the power of their brothers, and both enjoy the protection of an elder brother. But Joseph is hated, Benjamin loved; Joseph the object of the brothers' malevolence, Benjamin the test of their reform. Again the scene in chapter 45 is at once the duplicate and the contrast to that set at Dothan in chapter 37. The last time Joseph was alone with his brothers he was a weak, powerless lad, and they tore his clothes off and threw him in a pit to die.

Now, the first time they meet with him alone since that long ago day at Dothan, the situation is completely reversed. They are the destitute, he the powerful. What is the reason for the statement in 45:1 that no one stood with Joseph when he revealed himself? To prevent the Egyptians from learning of his relationship to these Hebrews, or to prevent them seeing him emotionally upset? These answers both may be partly relevant; but it is a fact that the removal of the Egyptian servants heightens the contrast with the scene in chapter 37. The Egyptians, through whom Joseph indirectly derives his power, leave him, and the situation recalls that encounter fifteen years earlier at Dothan: Joseph is alone with his brothers. How will they treat him after all that has transpired? Realizing the mercy Joseph has shown them, and the lesson he has taught them, how will they react? The keen sensitivity of the author will allow but an understatement, beautiful in its abbreviation, poignant in its innocent expression: "but his brothers could not answer him, for they were dismayed at his presence." That is all. The reader must imagine the rest.

Pursuant to Joseph's revelation of himself the brothers hasten back to their father with the news. Had they not also been the bearers of "news about Joseph" back in chapter 37? Then they came with a blood-stained garment, now they come with carts. In both scenes Jacob is pursuaded by the evidence, and—a poignant touch—from the story itself there is no suggestion that Jacob ever learned of the fabrication of the earlier evidence.

Donald B. Redford. A Study of the Biblical Story of Joseph (Leiden, Brill, 1970), pp. 71–72

The reader is immediately struck by the craft of the Joseph narrative (Gen. 37–50). Rarely in Western literature has form been woven into content, pattern sewn into meaning, structure forged into theme with greater subtlety or success. The result is a narrative of profound paradox that first reveals then resolves itself in absolute symmetry. To look closely at the major patterns of paradox is to discover how the literal level of the narrative fully engenders the meaning and how pattern finally unravels predicament.

The structure is primarily created and controlled by (1) the three sets of dreams which become reality and give us one paradox; (2) the four sets of analogous relationships that Joseph enters into—at home, in Potiphar's household, in prison, and in Pharaoh's household—relationships that provide us with a second paradox; and (3) the variations on the "pit" episode which combine both narrative and symbolic purposes to become the central repositories of paradox as well as provide the links of concatenation through which the other elements combine into the final and deeper significance of the story.

Less central to the main narrative but no less important to its deeper meaning is the Judah/Onan/Tamar story (Gen. 38), which intrudes upon but finally does not disturb the pattern and symmetry of the Joseph narrative. This story within a story presents a paradox which mirrors those of the larger narrative and is essential to the final significance and pattern of the whole.

Another major structuring device is Joseph's clothing. His coats and cloaks operate primarily at the narrative level as symbols of his position and of transition as Joseph moves from the home of Jacob to the household of Pharaoh.

It is ultimately in the combination of these various recurring elements of the story that its meaning resides—inseparable from them and discoverable only through them. From the surface of narrative pattern emerges a deeper structure of meaning that reveals that the superficially different elements are manifestations of a single theme.

> Donald A. Seybold. In *Literary Interpretations of Biblical Narratives*. Ed. by Kenneth R. R. Gros Louis et al. (Nashville, Abingdon Press, 1974), pp. 59–60

Nothing is left out, not only in the Midrashic tales, where one is used to it, but even in Scripture, where the literary flaws of the text are surprising. The narrative is too long, too slow, too transparent, it lacks both mystery and momentum. Compared with the chapters dealing with the sacrifice of Isaac or Jacob's encounter with the angel, it seems overwritten and overstated, each episode is retold three times, reiterating obvious points. It all seems clear and simple. Too simple.

And also, not only is the cast too large, its characters all run off in different directions. We have difficulty focusing our attention on any one protagonist, any one crisis, any one conflict. So much dispersion is disconcerting. Abraham's problem was his confrontation with God; Isaac's his confrontation with his father; Jacob's his confrontation with his brother. But Joseph's? He has too many problems, involving so many people that the reader is at a loss as to which clue, which thread to follow to untangle the plot. To begin with, what is the major theme? The father's sadness? The brothers' malice? The Pharaoh's candor? The yearnings of a frustrated wife? The intrigues at the royal court? The Aristotelian rules of theater are violated; there is no unity of time, place or action. What we have is an incredible epic, unfocused, panoramic, disdainful of detail and lacking the terseness and sobriety of a work of art.

> Elie Wiesel. *Messengers of God* (New York, Random House, 1976), 143–44

Two conclusions can be formulated as the result of this structural analysis. 1) With the exception of Genesis 38 and 47:13–26, along with some secondary commentary, the Joseph story shows remarkable unity. Each of the major structural elements develops clear functional cohesion with all other parts of the whole. Following the exposition with its presentation of the principal figures and the points of tension that bring them into conflict with each other, a detailed description of the tension's scope sets the tone of the narrative. A broken family faces the tragedy of jealous hatred, violent attack, and exile for the victim from Canaan to Egypt. Then with a digression to show the rise of Joseph to power in Egypt, a second display of the story's scope of crisis puts the pressure points in the tension at the opposite poles. The two elements of complication also form a frame around the digression that integrates its motifs into the flow of the narrative as a whole. The impact of the complication elements is to project responsibility for the broken family onto no single figure, but rather to embroil all members of the family equally in a tragic struggle. The next element brings the tension to a denouement, creating the context for reconciliation when virtually no prospects for reconciliation had previously been possible. The reconciliation theme, moreover, provides the occasion for completion of a structural dialectic characteristic for the entire story: The break in the family opens with Joseph sold as victim from Canaan to Egypt. The tragedy then reaches a point of resolution when the broken family finds reconciliation in Egypt, with the entire family moved from Canaan to Egypt. The final element ties up all the lines of the narration, with the family actually transferred to Egypt. None of these elements can be dropped as duplications without seriously impairing the artistic quality of the story. Indeed, even the secondary additions to the story merge with the plan of unity in the narrative.

2) The principal structural focus of the story pinpoints the shift in setting from Jacob in Canaan to Israel in Egypt. This shift cannot be divorced from the perspective of patriarchal traditions. The promise for a great posterity lies at the basis of the procedure, at the basis of God's leadership in moving first Joseph, then Jacob to Egypt. Neither can it be divorced from the exodus traditions. In Egypt Jacob's family grows to a numerous people, only to face a Pharaoh who did not know Joseph (cf. Exod. 1:8). The story as it is now formed functions basically and substantially as a bridge between two major themes of Pentateuchal traditions. It can therefore hardly be taken as an isolated piece of narrative, inserted secondarily into its present context.

> George W. Coats. *From Canaan to Egypt* (Washington, D.C., Catholic Biblical Association of America, 1976), pp. 53–54

The Story of Joseph and his Brothers can not be rightly described as uniform in texture, though it certainly is a narrative unit composed as a whole, rather than a sequence of stories haphazardly tied together. The author evidently changes his style to suit his convenience; this observation can be made about features other than the varying degrees of coherence. Thus the introductory chapter (37) about the selling of Joseph is rather explicit in style, but restrained in the emotions shown, while the passage about the Egyptian woman is full of sound and fury (as I have tried to show in discussing "small-scale" repetitions). There are three pairs of dreams in the story; one might, indeed, argue that dreams are a deliberate and significant recurrent motif in the tale. Each pair of dreams, however, is treated differently. Joseph tells his dreams unbidden; their interpretation is given as a spontaneous angry response of his audience (Gen. 37: 6–12). The butler and the baker (ch. 40) must be persuaded to tell their dreams, their interpretation is presented as a careful professional job. In the style of this interpretation the parallelism between the two dreams is strongly underlined (see vv. 12 and 18); there is even some punning on it (see vv. 13, 19, and 20). Only Pharaoh's dreams are twice told (Gen. 41: 2–7; 17–24).

Though his style changes, the author can be shown to be constant enough in his habits. One such constant feature is his predilection for pairs. There are three pairs of dreams, the last pair is twice told. There are also two brothers, Reuben and Judah, active in the tale; two lowly stations of life which Joseph goes through in Egypt, slavery and imprisonment; two visits of the brothers to Egypt and two arguments between the brothers and their father between the visits; and some further two's. The number two as a principle of composition has the advantage of making possible several devices utilizing repetition, as discussed in a previous chapter in this study. The author prefers two's to three's, because three's make strong and possibly tedious patterns. He has, however, Joseph weeping three times (Gen. 42:24; 43:29; 45:2), because this is very convenient to show Joseph's mounting emotion.

The Joseph story is the most intricately composed, complex and relatively long unit in the Old Testament. Though highly successful it does confirm the rule that the art of storytelling in the Old Testament works best on a small scale. The interpreter may be most impressed by the various cross references and signs of careful overall composition in this tale; the author, however, did not mind breaking his tale up into manageable pieces. Even in the central part of his composition, which is strictly coherent, he has paid the greatest attention to the individual episodes and scenes. The grand effect of this tale is due to the parts, rather than to the whole.

Jacob Licht. Storytelling in the Bible (Jerusalem, Magnes Press, 1978), pp. 141–43

The preeminent instance of biblical narrative as a fictional experiment in knowledge is the story of Joseph and his brothers, for in it the central actions turn on the axis of true knowledge versus false, from the seventeen-year-old Joseph's dreams of grandeur to his climactic confrontation with his brothers in Egypt twenty-two years later. This theme of knowledge is formally enunciated through the paired key-words, *haker*, "recognize," and *yado'a*, "know," that run through the story (the French *connaître* and *savoir* may indicate the distinction between the terms better than these English equivalents). Joseph is of course the magisterial knower in this story, but at the outset even he has a lot to learn—painfully, as moral learning often occurs. In his early dreams, he as yet knows not what he knows about his own destiny, and those dreams which will prove prophetic might well seem at first the reflex of a spoiled adolescent's grandiosity, quite of a piece with his nasty habit of tale-bearing against his brothers and with his insensitivity to their feelings, obviously encouraged by his father's flagrant indulgence. The heretofore shrewd Jacob on his part is just as blind—and will remain so two decades later—as his old father Isaac was before him. He witlessly provokes the jealousy of the ten sons he had by his unloved wife Leah and by the concubines; then he allows himself to be duped about the actual fate of Joseph at least in part because of his excessive love for the boy and because of his rather melodramatic propensity to play the role of sufferer. Finally, the ten brothers are ignorant of Joseph's real nature and destiny, of the consequences of their own behavior, of the ineluctable feelings of guilt they will suffer because of their crime, and climactically, of Joseph's identity when he stands before them as viceroy of Egypt. Events, or rather events aided by Joseph's manipulation, force them to knowledge and self-knowledge, this arduous transition providing the final resolution of the whole story.

> Robert Alter. *The Art of Biblical Narrative* (New York, Basic Books, 1981), p. 159

The story of Joseph and his brothers (Gen. 37–50) poses a particular sort of challenge to the modern reader. Especially in the early episode concerning the sale of Joseph into slavery (37:18–36 with 39:1), the text becomes almost consistently inconsistent. It wavers back and forth between conflicting narrative sequences, or "versions" of the story's action. According to one version [sequence (a)], the brothers throw Joseph into the pit with the original intention of letting him die. But then, at the behest of Judah, they sell Joseph to a passing caravan of Ishmaelites, who in turn sell Joseph in Egypt. According to the second version [sequence (b)], the brothers throw Joseph in the pit, but Reuben plans to deceive the others and return Joseph surreptitiously to their father Jacob/Israel. Then, unexpectedly, a passing group of Midianite traders removes Joseph from the pit and thereby confounds Reuben.

Such narrative style, in which inconsistent lines of action are interlaced through the text, may have been both familiar and acceptable to an ancient or preliterate audience, but it has rubbed against the sensibility of modern, Western readers. . . .

Within the narrative concerning the sale of Joseph there are two narrative sequences. At points the two sequences coincide, and at points they present incompatibilities in conflict with each other. Each, alternately, reaches for the reader's acceptance. The effect may be likened to an experience such as would be produced by viewing two films, partly different and partly the same, superimposed on a single screen. Where the films are similar, a clear image would be seen as the frames from both films correspond. But where the films are divergent, the images would be confused and unintelligible; one film would obstruct the perception of the other. The chief difference between the two analogous experiences is that in viewing two superimposed films the blur is perceived immediately, while in reading two clear but contradictory narrative accounts, the "blur" is perceived upon reading the second account in trying to make sense of it in light of the preceding account.

Yet, a structure that is similar to the one that we find in the sale of Joseph episode may be found in the classic film *Rashomon* (1951), by the Japanese director Akira Kurosawa. In its core section the film presents the audience with five conflicting accounts of a crime of passion as told by five characters, three of them directly involved and two of them witnesses. The audience is never given the means by which to determine what had "objectively" occurred.

In our text, sequences (a) and (b) are conflicting or competing intelligibilities. The structure of the narrative, which juxtaposes components of sequence (a) with components of sequence (b), produces the very sense of ambiguity and conflict that is conveyed by the actions delineated within the two sequences. The two sequences are thus played off against each other in terms of narrative arrangement and action-sequence.

In sequence (a) the brothers are master of their machinations, selecting a plan for doing away with Joseph and ultimately attaining their end. In the subordinated sequence, they plan to deceive their father, and again they achieve the object of their designs. The degree of their attainment is signified in the text through the language of Jacob/Israel's reaction to seeing the bloodied robe in verse 33. He duplicates verbatim the words that Joseph's brothers had construed in order to deceive their father (v. 20): "An evil beast has eaten him."

But sequence (b) provides an antithesis to sequence (a). Reuben sways his brothers from their original scheme, planning to rescue Joseph himself and deceive the brothers. But the Midianites catch them all unawares and foil Reuben and stymie the brothers by taking Joseph. (Since the continuation of the story requires that Joseph go down to Egypt, it is necessary that the brothers succeed to some degree and that Reuben fail.)

The effect of this juxtaposition is to produce an ongoing dialectic between the machinations of the brothers and the countermeasures of Reuben. The actions of each sequence are thereby blurred in the reader's *ultimate* perception. In terms of the narrative's action, the brothers' success in achieving their end in sequence (a) is compromised and delayed by the efforts of Reuben and the surprise appearance of the Midianites in sequence (b). The only actions that appear without obfuscation are those in which both sequences converge: The brothers plan to do away with Joseph . . . Joseph is thrown into a pit . . . Joseph is taken to Egypt by passing traders (of ambiguous identity) . . . (Jacob/Israel is led to believe that Joseph was killed by a wild animal).

In the larger context of the entire Joseph story, later references in the text continue to reinforce the equivocal reading of the sale of Joseph. When Joseph is imprisoned in Egypt, he tells his fellow inmates that he was "stolen from the land of the Hebrews" (40:15), which seems to correspond to the message in 37:28 that the Midianites "pulled and raised Joseph out of the pit." But when Joseph discloses his true identity to his brothers, he announces: "I am Joseph, your brother, whom you sold to Egypt" (45:4; cf. v. 5). This seems to conform to the "allusive" reading of 37:28, in which we understand that the brothers sold Joseph to the Ishmaelites. The two sequences, when visualized, vie with each other in their respective claims to intelligibility—like the conflicting testimonies in *Rashomon* —and have the effect of blurring our image of what happened. In the end, the reader cannot be certain of what human events actually took Joseph down to Egypt.

But the story's ambiguity concerning the natural or human chain of events that led to Joseph's servitude in Egypt throws into bolder relief the actual "cause" of Joseph's fate. As Joseph himself explains to his brothers—and via the narrative to the reader—"Now it was not you who sent me here, but God" (45:8; cf. vv. 5, 7). By blurring the human factors leading to the enslavement of Joseph, the narrative sharpens our image of the divine factor in bringing it about. . . .

An equivocal reading of the sale of Joseph leads to the realization that, in the view of our narrative, it is not crucial to our understanding of the story whether the brothers sold Joseph to the Ishmaelites or the Midianites kidnapped him. It is important, rather, to perceive that the descent of Joseph to Egypt and his subsequent rise to power there reveal divine providence in history.

> Edward L. Greenstein. In *Literary Interpretations of Biblical Narratives*. Vol. II. Ed. by Kenneth R. R. Gros Louis et al. (Nashville, Abingdon Press, 1982), pp. 114, 121–23

JUDAH AND TAMAR

This story [Gen. 38] is characterized by E. A. Speiser, in his superb Genesis volume in the Anchor Bible series, as "a completely independent unit," having "no connection with the drama of Joseph, which it interrupts at the conclusion of Act I" [p. 299]. The interpolation does, of course, as Speiser and others have recognized, build a sense of suspense about the fate of Joseph and a feeling of time elapsed until Joseph shows up in Egypt, but Speiser's failure to see its intimate connections through motif and theme with the Joseph story suggests the limitations of conventional biblical scholarship even at its best. . . .

[As for] the intentionality of the analogies I have proposed between the interpolation and the frame-story, such doubts should be laid to rest by the exact recurrence at the climax of Tamar's story of the formula of recognition, *haker-na* [please recognize] and *vayaker* [recognized], used before with Jacob and his sons. The same verb, moreover, will play a crucial thematic role in the dénouement of the Joseph story when he confronts his brothers in Egypt, he recognizing them, they failing to recognize him. This precise recurrence of the verb in identical forms at the ends of Genesis 37 and 38 respectively is manifestly the result not of some automatic mechanism of interpolating traditional materials but of careful splicing of sources by a brilliant literary artist. The first use of the formula was for an act of deception; the second use is for an act of unmasking. Judah with Tamar after Judah with his brothers is an exemplary narrative instance of the deceiver deceived, and since he was the one who proposed selling Joseph into slavery instead of killing him (Gen. 37:26–27), he can easily be thought of as the leader of the brothers in the deception practiced on their father. Now he becomes their surrogate in being subject to a bizarre but peculiarly fitting principle of retaliation, taken in by a piece of attire, as his father was, learning through his own obstreperous flesh that the divinely appointed process of election cannot be thwarted by human will or social convention. In the most artful of contrivances, the narrator shows him exposed through the symbols of his legal self given in pledge for a kid (*gedi 'izim*), as before Jacob had been tricked by the garment emblematic of his love for Joseph which had been dipped in the blood of a goat (*se'ir 'izim*). Finally, when we return from Judah to the Joseph story (Gen. 39), we move in pointed contrast from a tale of exposure through sexual incontinence to a tale of seeming defeat and ultimate triumph through sexual continence — Joseph and Potiphar's wife.

> Robert Alter. *The Art of Biblical Narrative* (New York, Basic Books, 1981), pp. 3–4, 10

Not a love story like Jacob's, nor on the other hand a primitive tale of the victory of procreation over consciousness like the story of Lot, the tale of Judah and Tamar (Gen. 38) is in many ways the most complete working out of the motif of sexual mis-taking in Genesis. This story is more like the secular comic treatment of the bed trick because it takes place (unlike the Lot episode) in a detailed social setting of village and family life and (unlike the Jacob story) it carries the plot through to the all-important scene of recognition which justifies the woman.

Unlike Leah, who is passive and manipulated by Laban, Tamar is the sole arbiter of her own fate, the prime mover and protagonist of her own story. She uses her sex in a cunning way to capture for herself something wrongly denied her — the desired status of a mother. Like the heroine of a Shakespearean tragicomedy (indeed like Helena in *All's Well*) she knows how to exploit the natural weakness of her man by playing the degrading part of a loose woman at the roadside. But she turns this shameful episode of accidental sex into a serious obligation by taking pledges which eventually serve as proofs of paternity.

While our other examples of the trick give unequal weight to the various elements of the situation, the story of Judah and Tamar is worked out with grace and proportion giving each element its due. The reasons for the deception are there — Judah's failure to keep his promise to give her his third son in marriage. The scene of bargaining between harlot and client at the roadside is imagined in detail. In it the man's importunate desire is offset by the woman's logical, cunning argument that draws out of Judah the pledges (signet, bracelet and staff) that will eventually justify her. Then comes the complication of the plot when Judah cannot find the harlot again to redeem his pledge. By separating the various strands of the plot, leaving Judah shamed without his pledges and having Tamar melt back into her widowhood, the story makes possible the all-important, climactic scene of discovery and recognition.

In this scene the woman's shame only implied by Tamar's disguise as a harlot is made explicit as her pregnancy becomes public and is condemned. She is exposed and sentenced to death. Here as in countless final scenes of comedy to which indeed it is related, signs, identifying marks and objects come into play to establish names and relationships, discover the truth and solve riddles. Recognition of objects, of persons, above all of responsibility is the topic here as Judah the figure of authority and the stern judge of whoredom is confronted with the tangible evidence of his breach of promise as head of a family, his blindness as a lover and clearest of all—his fatherhood.

This is such a classic and perfect recognition scene because it does not limit itself to the mechanical discovery of identities through signs. It is a scene of true moral recognition, for in its course Judah recognizes his own guilt in his failure to provide the widow with a husband and justifies the woman whose apparent sexual sin was to be punished. So, as in comedy, at the very last moment in a scene of tense confrontation, the truth of past deeds comes into the open and an accidental wayside sexual impulse is transformed retroactively into an act of natural compensation which establishes a family.

The story's order and unity may be summed up in the way the text is arranged around the crucial terms of knowledge and recognition. When Judah goes in unto Tamar by the roadside we are told that he "knew not" that she was his daughter-in-law. Judah's ignorance is the condition for this act of apparently wild, accidental sex. In the climactic scene Judah's recognition of his pledges justifies the woman. In this way honorable recognition redeems the potential harm of the blind act of passion. Finally, in a coda, the text returns to the denial of knowledge by the roadside. "And he knew her again no more," but now in a specifically sexual sense. Just as lack of knowledge originally made sex possible so knowledge and discovery finally forbid it. Unlike the protagonists of secular comedy the partners of this story must remain separate. The happy end is children for Tamar rather than marriage. Salvation as so often in the Bible lies in the birth of sons.

Zvi Jagendorf. Prooftexts. May, 1984, pp. 190–92

Koheleth. *See* Ecclesiastes

LAMENTATIONS

The Prophet, indeed, has so copiously, so tenderly, and poetically bewailed the misfortunes of his country, that he seems completely to have fulfilled the office and duty of a mourner. In my opinion, there is not extant any poem, which displays such a happy and splendid selection of imagery in so concentrated a state. What can be more elegant and poetical, than the description of that once flourishing city, lately chief among the nations, sitting in the character of a female, solitary, afflicted, in a state of widowhood, deserted by her friends, betrayed by her dearest connections, imploring relief, and seeking consolation in vain? What a beautiful personification is that of "the ways of Sion mourning because none are come to her solemn feasts?" . . .

But to detail its beauties would be to transcribe the entire poem. I shall make but one remark relative to certain passages, and to the former part of the second alphabet [Lamentations employs for the most part an alphabetical sequence less common than the familiar one] in particular. If, in this passage, the Prophet should be thought by some to affect a style too bold and energetic for the expression of sorrow, let them only advert to the greatness of the subject, its importance, sanctity, and solemnity; and let them consider that the nature of the performance absolutely required these to be set forth in a style suitable, in some degree at least, to their inherent dignity; let them attentively consider these things, and I have no doubt, but they will readily excuse the sublimity of the Prophet. [1753]

> Robert Lowth. *Lectures on the Sacred Poetry of the Hebrews*. Vol. II. Tr. from the Latin by G. Gregory (London, Printed for J. Johnson, 1787), pp. 137–39

But the most regular and perfect Elegiac Composition in the Scripture, perhaps the whole world, is the Book, entitled the Lamentations of Jeremiah. As the Prophet mourns in that book over the destruction of the Temple, and the Holy City, and the overthrow of the whole State, he assembles all the affecting images which a subject so melancholy could suggest. The Composition is uncommonly artificial. By turns, the Prophet, and the city of Jerusalem, are introduced, as pouring forth their sorrows; and in the end, a chorus of the people send up the most earnest and plaintive supplications to God. The lines of the original too, as may, in part, appear from our translation, are longer than is usual in the other kinds of Hebrew Poetry; and the melody is rendered thereby more flowing, and better adapted to the querimonious strain of Elegy. [1783]

> Hugh Blair. *Lectures on Rhetoric and Belles Lettres*. Vol. III. 2d ed. corr. (London, W. Strahan, T. Cadell, 1785), pp. 195–96

Exquisite as is the pathos which breathes in the poetry of these dirges, they are thus, it appears, constructed with conscious art: they are not the unstudied effusions of natural emotion, they are carefully elaborated poems, in which no aspect of the common grief is unremembered, and in which every trait which might stir a chord of sorrow or regret is brought together, for the purpose of completing the picture of woe. And hence, no doubt, the acrostic form of the first four dirges. As in the case of the Psalms . . . the acrostic form is an *external* principle of arrangement, where the subject is one which does not readily admit of logical development; and hence it secures the orderly and systematic expression of the emotions with which the poet's heart is filled.

> Samuel R. Driver. *An Introduction to the Literature of the Old Testament*. 10th ed., rev. and enl. (New York, Scribner's 1903), p. 459

The book is not a unity; it does not pretend to be. It is a collection of five poems, four of them dirges in the strict sense, and the fifth a Psalm such as Israel's poets often uttered in times of distress. Each has its own literary characteristics, and internal evidence makes it practically certain that they are not all the work of a single author. They are not of equal literary merit, and they vary a good deal in the intensity of their feeling. While the first four, at any rate, may reasonably be referred to the siege of Jerusalem by Nebuchadnezzar, to the fall of the city and to its consequent desolation, we get the impression that some are nearer than others to actual disasters which they describe.

Chapters 1–4 are acrostic poems, though no two of them are exactly alike in their construction. . . .

The metre in all these is that which seems most appropriate to the dirge, i.e., 3:2 varied occasionally with 2:2. It was, in fact, in this book that a definite metre, of the kind now generally admitted first attained wide acceptance, and though earlier students recognized only the 3:2 (a theory which led to some curious results), it received the name of Qinah, or "dirge," metre. It was not till long afterwards that it was noticed in other poems which could not possibly be classed as "dirges," e.g., in Psalm 23.

The first poem gives us a picture of the desolation of Jerusalem and of her people. It opens with the characteristic Hebrew groan—How! It is not a question, it is an exclamation of suffering, and stands outside the metrical scheme of the verse. This "anacrusis" is not infrequently used by the Hebrew poets to give emotional emphasis to what follows. The first line gives the key to the whole poem; the city that was once so great and beautiful, the place that once stood so high in the esteem of the peoples, has now fallen to the depths. . . .

In spite of the somewhat artificial flavour which an acrostic inevitably produces, the language has a solemn beauty, and whether we will or no we are carried back into the actual circumstances which called the dirge forth. The poem stands high among the world's lyrics of sorrow.

Chapter 2 may well be thought to stand even higher. In form, as we have seen, it closely resembles chapter 1, differing only in the places taken by two letters of the alphabet. Like the first poem, the second is a cry of woe and desolation, but it is much nearer to the actual disaster. . . .

When we reach chapter 3, we are conscious at once of being in an entirely different atmosphere. The metre is still that of the Qinah, but this by no means compels us to regard the poem as a dirge. The use of the acrostic letter at the beginning of each of the three lines assigned to it gives an artificial air to the whole. The gloom is far from being so intense as it was in the first two chapters. . . .

With chapter 4 we are back once more in the atmosphere of 586 B.C. The poem differs from chapter 2 mainly in having a two-line instead of a three-line stanza, but in other respects the two are closely similar and may be the work of the same poet. . . .

Chapter 5 stands apart from the other four in several ways. Its metre is 3:3, not that of the Qinah, and it is not an acrostic poem. It does, however, contain 22 verses, the right number for an acrostic. . . .

The only thing [the five poems] have in common is that they are poems written in deep distress, though this is far more intense in some cases than in others. . . . The book, small as it is, remains the classic example of literary beauty rising out of the deepest suffering.

Theodore H. Robinson. The Poetry of the Old Testament
(London, Duckworth, 1947), pp. 206–16

This entire elegy—the grace of later poetry is upon it. A personal voice is felt (and not only in "I am the man . . ." [Lam. 3:1ff.]). Although it is the sorrow of the nation, and not the sorrow of the individual, there is no discriminating between them. It is a sign that the distance between the poet and the audience has been shortened. The prophet was a messenger, a voice of God. Here the speaker's own voice stands out more and more, even when he addresses the many.

There is no need to prove, especially by external signs (verses following the alphabet and more), that the hand of Jeremiah did not write these elegies, even though it is essentially his voice that emerges from them. Jeremiah—his poetry and his life—was a model for the later poet. Jeremiah is the hero of Lamentations.

Nevertheless, whereas Jeremiah too was lyrical, here there is an additional translucence: the complaint of an orphan era. It is thoroughly saturated with ancient archetypes. It no longer relies on itself alone. Here [the author uses] few primary images, such as those that grow out of nature, the land, without "surrendering the quill." And even where you find strong colorful embroidery—such as "Her officers were like stags, they found no pasture, and they went before the pursuer for lack of strength" [1:6]; "With our breath we bring forth our bread because of the sword of the wilderness" [5:9]; "Those who pursued us are swifter than eagles, they chased us over the mountains" [4:19]; "He has made me dwell in the dark places like the forever dead" [3:6]; and more and more—here the essence of the power is not in elementary graphicness but in a certain intimate sound, a certain delicacy of touch, such as: "The wind of our nostrils, the anointed of the Lord, has been captured in their nets" [4:20]; "She weeps, weeps at night, her tears on her cheeks" [1:2]; "He sits alone and still, for he has borne it upon himself" [3:28]; "I was a laughingstock among my people, their tune all the day" [3:14]; "Recall, O Lord, what has befallen us, look and see our disgrace" [5:1]. Here is both complaint and justification—complaint turned into prayer.

Jacob Fichman. 'Arugot (Jerusalem, Bialik Institute,
1954), pp. 289–90†

There can be no question about the literary excellence of these five poems. Among the collective laments of the ancient Near East they are without peer. Under the discipline of acrostic form and the chaste economy of the *Qinah* [lament]

metre, the poet has created in clearly defined strophes a sincere and powerful vehicle of expression. His wealth of imagery is ceaseless; his turn of phrase generally felicitous. The old forms of speech are employed, but under the stress of
emotion they are given unexpected depth or combined in original ways.

The question of the relation betwen the Psalter and other Biblical poetry is
not easily answered, but there is reason to believe that the Book of Lamentations,
written under the duress of the supreme historical tragedy of the Old Testament
period, initiated fresh impulses in religious poetry. . . . One finds in the laments
of later Judaism no appreciable advance on the modes of expression set down in
these exilic poems. As an embodiment of national sorrow, the literary imagery
and even the terminology of lament remained determinative of later ages.

> Norman K. Gottwald. *Studies in the Book of Lamenta-
> tions* (London, SCM, 1954, rev. 1962), pp. 112–13

If the Book of Lamentations does indeed exude a sense of primal outrage, it is
only because its authors labored and schemed to exploit in new ways the devices
of language available to them in order to mount a successful literary representation of primal outrage.

The text of Lamentations, which is in fact deeply figured and deeply troped,
instructs us in how lacking in innocence the representation of extreme events
must necessarily be. . . .

The theme of unexplained or undeserved individual suffering is dealt with in
many places in bibical literature, but nowhere, except in Daniel at the very close
of the biblical period, is the problem in the least related to the vicissitudes of history. Individual affliction may be a problem but never an historical problem. The
ordeal of Job and the persecutions of the many unnamed supplicants in Psalms
are fixed in reference to no time or place. History partakes only of the relations
between God and the people of Israel as a whole. When the people sins it is the
people as a corporate body, not selected individuals, that is punished, and it is
likewise the people as a whole that is the subject of redemptive acts.

No event was more clearly experienced and understood in this way than the
catastrophe of 587. And it is just this, the irreducibly collective nature of the
event, that posed one of the great difficulties in writing of the Destruction. It is
by individuals that pain and humiliation are experienced even if they are inflicted
on a group for group reasons, and it is only by virtue of the knowledge born of
our individual experience of these states that we are susceptible of being moved
to pity or anger. If we assume that the goal of such a work as Lamentations is to
achieve the maximum register of pain so that we might be so moved, then how
difficult must have been the task of making the ordeal of a collective entity pathetic and to do so without betraying the integrity of the collective and thereby
dissolving the fate of the nation into an anthology of separate vignettes.

The solution undertaken by the authors of Lamentations was to transfer to the
collective the attributes of individual experience and to view the nation as a
whole in the aspect of a single individual; simply put: personification. The nation

is represented as an abandoned woman or, in a more complex instance, as a persecuted man. Although this may seem like a simple move, the ways in which the personification are worked out in the text are not simple, nor are the uses to which it is put, and the fact of the necessary resort to personhood in Lamentations is the first instance and perhaps the most subtle in what amounts to a general principle in Hebrew literature of responses to catastrophe.

Jerusalem, personified as *bat tsiyon*, Fair Zion, is pictured as a once beautiful woman who was ravaged and abandoned by the enemy. Her friends betrayed her, and all her children have been torn from her and sent into exile, and she has been left utterly alone with no one to console her. Once a great beauty, bedecked with precious jewels and ornaments, she had amused herself promiscuously without giving heed to the consequences of her defilement. In a moment all her glory was dragged down and soiled. "All who honored her despise her, / For they have seen her nakedness" (1:8); once an object of admiration, now she is an outcast. Wretched and forlorn, she sits by the side of the road, sighing for the loss of her children and bewailing her afflictions.

The serviceableness of the image of Jerusalem as an abandoned fallen woman lies in the precise register of pain it articulates. An image of death would have purveyed the false comfort of finality; the dead have finished with suffering and their agony can be evoked only in retrospect. The raped and defiled woman who survives, on the other hand, is a living witness to a pain that knows no release. It is similarly the perpetualness of her situation that comes through most forcefully when Zion is pictured as a woman crying bitterly alone in the night with tears wetting her face (1:2). The cry seems to ululate permanently in the night; the tear forever falls to the cheek. It is a matter not just of lingering suffering but of continuing exposure to victimization. *'Almana*, "widow" is the term used to describe Zion in the opening verse of Lamentations, and we know that in the Ancient Near East *'almana* designated not so much a woman who has lost her husband as the social status of a woman who has no legal protector and who may thus be abused with impunity. As an imaginative invention, furthermore, the figure of the forlorn woman is precise in its correspondence to the conditions of the historical moment. Nebucadnezzar's army had dealt Jerusalem a double blow: the city was razed and its leaders were led away into exile. The figure of the grieving woman who remains forlornly in place while her sons are taken captive to a far-off land mirrors the simultaneous stasis and dispersion that were Israel's fate.

It is in the illicit aspect of womanhood that the possibilities of the figure are best exploited. Even in the anguish of her victimage Zion is not held to be entirely innocent of complicity in her fate. . . .

Now once the substance of the figure has been laid down—that is, the identifying of the personification and the thing personified—there remains to be established the mode in which we see and hear the Zion figure. There remains the question of relationship. We are shaken into an awareness of this issue when precisely in the middle of the first chapter of Lamentations a voice begins to speak in the first person. This is a moment of importance in the text. It is then we realize that until this point Zion has been described in the third person and that now she begins to speak in her own voice. At first she speaks about her treatment by God and then she appeals *to* God directly; shortly afterwards God's actions are described by an unidentified voice, which is revealed as that of the poet, who in turn addresses Zion and exhorts her to cry out to God. And so the text continues to move through a series of manipulations of speakers and addressees in which sudden shifts are announced by no explicit notation and are often discoverable from grammatical markings alone.

Who speaks to whom about whom as seen from whose point of view? It is in the play of these questions, which defines the rhetorical situation of the text, that the deepest theological business of Lamentations gets transacted. If we can state the theme of Lamentations as an exploration of the traumatized relations between Israel and God in the immediate aftermath of the Destruction, and if we pause to realize that as a poem Lamentations has as its medium dramatized speech and not theological statement, then we must appreciate the significance of the poem's rhetoric. It is through transformations of the rhetorical situation that the fundamental categories of God, Israel and adversary are brought into relationship, and thus, in this way, the drama of the covenant played out. The credibility of these rhetorical transactions, it should be kept in mind, is predicated upon the construct of individual personhood, which guarantees the possibility of a believable human speaker.

Alan Mintz. Prooftexts. Jan., 1982, pp. 1–4

MOSES

The Style of Moses is concise, nervous, simple, emphatical. The Diction of his Prose is natural and unstudied; of his Poetry strong and bold. We may apply to Moses Mr. [Joseph] Addison's Character of Livy (*Spectator*, no. 420). "He describes every Thing in so lively a manner, that his History is an admirable Picture; and touches on such proper Circumstances in every Story, that his Reader becomes a kind of Spectator, and feels himself all the Variety of Passions, which are correspondent to the several Parts of the Relation." All there is Action and Dialogue; the Historian retires out of Sight as much as possible, and the Persons themselves are introduced upon the Stage. This is that noble Way of Writing so peculiar to the Ancients. This is that noble, yet simple Manner, in which the Eastern People excel, and which appears so beautiful in the most refined of all the Greek Historians, I mean Xenophon.

John Husbands. Preface to A Miscellany of Poems by
Several Hands (Oxford, J. Husbands, 1731), sigs,
h1^r–h1^v

Heretofore I had not particularly admired the character of Moses, probably because the Hellenic spirit was predominant in me, and I could not pardon the lawgiver of the Jews for his hate of all that constitutes art. I failed to perceive that Moses, notwithstanding his enmity to art, was nevertheless himself a great artist and possessed the true artistic spirit. Only, this artistic spirit with him, as with his Egyptian countrymen, was applied to the colossal and the imperishable. But not, like the Egyptians, did he construct his works of art from bricks and granite, but he built human pyramids and carved human obelisks. He took a poor shepherd tribe and from it created a nation which should defy centuries; a great, an immortal, a consecrated race, a God-serving people, who to all other nations should be as a model and prototype: he created Israel. [1854]

> Heinrich Heine. *Prose Miscellanies*. Tr. by S. L. Fleishman (Philadelphia, Lippincott, 1876), p. 272

The essence of the Wandering in the Wilderness. A man who leads his people along this way with a shred (more is unthinkable) of consciousness of what is happening. He is on the track of Canaan all his life; it is incredible that he should see the land only when on the verge of death. This dying vision of it can only be intended to illustrate how incomplete a moment is human life, incomplete because a life like this could last forever and still be nothing but a moment. Moses fails to enter Canaan not because his life is too short but because it is a human life. This ending of the Pentateuch bears a resemblance to the final scene of [Gustave Flaubert's] *Education sentimentale*. [Oct. 19, 1921]

> Franz Kafka. *The Diaries 1914–1923*. Ed. by Max Brod (New York, Schocken, 1949), pp. 195–96

The story of the finding of the infant Moses by the daughter of the Pharaoh is as tender and moving a tale of childhood as was ever written, equaled perhaps by that of the child Samuel, but not often in later literature. The account of the call of Moses amid the awesome surroundings of the desert, where men have their visions and dream their dreams, of the burning bush, of the breaking down by the God revealed to him of every excuse for not assuming leadership—all this is work as powerful as was ever produced in the name of literary art. No less so is the sequel—the return to Egypt, the conflict with the Pharaoh, the plagues, the victory and the flight, concluding with that great ode of triumph led by Sister Miriam on the farther shore of the overwhelming sea.

> Hilary G. Richardson. *Life and The Book* (New York, Macmillan, 1929), pp. 107–8

The most stirring and dramatic part of the four books that follow this patriarchal Genesis, namely Exodus, Leviticus, Numbers, and Deuteronomy, which are by far the least inspiring and the least interesting books in the whole Bible, have to do with the extraordinary personality of Moses, furious leader and far-sighted lawgiver, who must have been a sort of inspired Hebraic Merlin with his neurotic moods of "meekness," his fits of blind wrath, his black magic, and his terrifying intimacies with Jehovah.

Certain stories we are told about Moses carry upon their face, casually though they are related, the very seal of psychological truth. Such is the story, for instance, of how Aaron and Miriam, his brother and sister, revolted against him, because he, the great eugenic medicine man, took to wife an Ethiopian woman.

But do we not get the whole secret of the magnetic ascendancy of Moses in the effect of his appeal to his divine friend against these jeering purists, this high priest and this priest-loving lady; an appeal that was so effective that the great soothsaying Miriam had to flee from the face of that Ethiopian, and from the face of the whole camp, literally sick with terror!

In this single sentence it can be seen why it is that the English, the most individualistic of all races, had until yesterday such a mania for this Hebrew book.

> And the Lord came down in the pillar of the cloud and stood in
> the door of the tabernacle, and called Aaron and Miriam and they
> both came forth. And he said, "Hear now my words: if there be a
> prophet among you I the Lord will make myself known unto him
> in a vision and will speak with him in a dream. My servant Moses
> is not so, who is faithful in my house. With him will I speak
> mouth to mouth, even apparently, and not in dark speeches; and
> the similitude of the Lord he shall behold; wherefore then were ye
> not afraid to speak against my servant Moses? [Num. 12:5–8]

From the disappearance of Moses—for none knoweth his sepulchre unto this day—to the establishment of the kingdom under Saul and David the Old Testament intensifies its awe-inspiring drama.

John Cowper Powys. Enjoyment of Literature (New York, Simon & Schuster, 1938), pp. 16–17

The chief importance of these books [Exodus, Numbers, Deuteronomy], and indeed almost their sole value as literature, lies in the story of Moses, not for the events of his life but for the character of the man. Perhaps unconsciously, perhaps by intention, this study of an individual becomes one of the definitive statements of the supreme importance of a leader in human affairs. There have been repeated attempts to prove that there never was such a person. . . . But to have invented a person as real as Moses and to have rewritten past history so completely would have required almost superhuman skill and a genius of incredible proportions on the part of the priests and prophets. . . . There is no proof that Moses did not exist, and his image is so clear and real that it seems to me more than probable that there was an actual figure to serve as the original. Whether there was or not, however, the character of Moses is of amazing vividness and truth. Ikhnaton of Egypt has been called the "first individual." Moses, who, if we grant his existence, must have lived about one hundred years later, may be called the first individual who achieved world-wide importance. . . .

Like all great reformers, great artists, great visionaries, men who have seen

God face to face, Moses was intensely lonely. Aside from Jahweh himself, he found no one with whom he could converse with understanding. He seems to have been far in advance of his time and environment, by breeding and education as well as by natural ability.

Except for an occasional phrase, such as the passage from Numbers 12 ["Now the man Moses was very meek, above all the men which were upon the face of the earth"], no effort is made at an exposition of this personality which vitalized and gave meaning and direction to the story of the deliverance and subsequent wanderings of the Hebrews. No regret is expressed for his disappointment, no excuse made for his failings. In the end Moses stands out in sharp relief as a real person, complex, made up of all the natural human elements, and supremely tragic.

> Brooke Peters Church. *The Golden Years: The Old Testament Narrative as Literature* (New York, Rinehart, 1947), pp. 79–80, 84–85

Of all the leaders of the Old Testament, there is only one whose whole life-span from birth to death is covered by the narratives. It has been pointed out that the pattern of his life corresponds almost exactly with the typical trajectory, the rise and fall, of the tragic heroes of mythology. His parents were of the principal family of the Levites, and near relatives. He was reputed to be of royal lineage, the son of Pharaoh's daughter. Pharaoh attempted to kill him at birth, but he was spirited away, and reared secretly. We know nothing of his childhood. On reaching manhood he kills an overseer who is afflicting his countrymen, and flees to Midian, where he marries the ruler's daughter. He returns to Egypt, and, as a Magus, gains magical victories over Pharaoh (the staff turned into a serpent, the leprous hand healed, the water turned to blood). He becomes a leader, ruler and law-giver, but later loses the favour of Jehovah and is removed from his leadership. He disappears mysteriously from the top of a mountain. In all this there is a close correspondence with the pattern shown by such diverse figures as Oedipus, Theseus, Romulus, King Arthur, Robin Hood. . . [p. 191].

Through so much that is tedious, repetitious, cliché-ridden, we have the impression of an immense integrity, relieved by outbursts of very human despair at Moses' terrible responsibility:

> And Moses said unto the Lord, Wherefore hast thou afflicted thy servant? and wherefore have I not found favour in thy sight, that thou layest the burden of all this people upon me? [Num. 11:11].

Rebellion, transgression, intercession, pursue their oscillating courses. Even Aaron and Miriam engage in a plot, and are confronted by Jehovah in person, and Miriam is smitten with leprosy [Num. 11:12]. Again the congregation mutiny: 'Would God that we had died in the Land of Egypt! or would God we had died in this wilderness!' [Num. 14:2]. It is not difficult to imagine the horrors of that life, the punishment of "this evil congregation" by thirst, by raids from the Amalekites and Canaanites [Num. 14:45].

Yet it is not all gloom. There are lyric fragments, such as the digging of the well:

> And from thence they went to Beer: that is the well whereof the Lord spake unto Moses, Gather the people together, and I will give them water. Then Israel sang this song, Spring up, O well; sing ye unto it: The princes digged the well, the nobles of the people digged it, by the direction of the lawgiver, with their slaves. [Num. 21:16–18].

Many dramatic incidents in the story are familiar. It is wholly human, and would become even more perspicuous and vital if it could be purged of much that we now consider irrelevant. At the end, in the mysterious death-scene on the mountain top of Pisgah that looks over Jordan to the Promised Land, we have the impression of a complex and noble figure. It is less, perhaps, the image of the stern-faced hornéd prophet of Michelangelo's vision, burdened with the Stone Tables; but rather a great and versatile leader infinitely provoked with all the problems that any leadership involves; human in his despair at the fallibility and petulance of the chosen people; unwearying in his terrible doom of incessant confrontation with God on their behalf. The patience of Job has become proverbial; it seems pale beside that of Moses [pp. 193–94].

T. R. Henn. The Bible as Literature (New York, Oxford University Press, 1970)

But the masterpiece in the Tetrateuch is the portrayal of Moses. That he almost perishes in enslavement and that his own mother is hired to be his nurse, constitute a pleasant child's tale. That he is raised in the palace, alienated from his people, prompts the double incident of his rescue of a Hebrew, and then of his repudiation by this same Hebrew, so that he must take flight to seek complete separation from his people in Midian. These matters, however, are what you might call, simply, the data. Beyond the data is the conception: When the Hebrews developed from three solitary people into the twelve sons of Jacob and then became a people, they as yet had no laws, no sacred calendar, no land of their own, and indeed, they did not even know the name of the Deity to whom they were to be loyal. What Moses does is to take a raggle-taggle, formless, shapeless people out of enslavement and refashion them into an extraordinary people. The author deals basically with three characters: Moses, the children of Israel, and the Deity. He must proceed in such a way that the children of Israel, who are protagonists, are never the heroes; the Wilderness wanderings are, on the surface, an account of the *infamous* deeds of the Hebrews.

Note what it is that Moses, the architect of the Laws, of the calendar, the rites and ceremonies, must undergo: complaints, murmurings, disaffection, yearning for the fleshpots of Egypt, the incident of the golden calf, the Rebellion of Korah and the Reubenites, the maligning of his wife by his own brother and sister. The only title that Moses bears is "man of God." Not a king, not a ruler; Scripture describes him as humility itself.

Samuel Sandmel. Judaism. Fall, 1973, p. 466

ADJURATION OF HEAVEN AND EARTH

The exordium is singularly magnificent, the plan and conduct of the poem [Deut. 32:1–43] is just, natural, and well accommodated to the subject, for it is almost in the order of an historical narration. It embraces a variety of the sublimest subjects and sentiments, it displays the truth and justice of God, his paternal love, and his unfailing tenderness to his chosen people; and on the other hand, their ungrateful and contumacious spirit. The ardour of the divine indignation, and the heavy denunciations of vengeance, are afterwards expressed in a remarkable personification, which is scarcely to be paralleled from all the choicest treasures of the Muses. The fervour of wrath is however tempered with the milder beams of lenity and mercy, and ends at last in promises and consolation. . . .

The subject and style of this poem bear so exact a resemblance to the prophetic as well as the lyric compositions of the Hebrews, that it unites all the force, energy, and boldness of the latter, with the exquisite variety and grandeur of imagery so peculiar to the former. [1753]

> Robert Lowth. *Lectures on the Sacred Poetry of the Hebrews*. Vol. II. Tr. from the Latin by G. Gregory (London, Printed for J. Johnson, 1787), pp. 256–57

The main idea of the poem is the rescue of the people by an act of grace, at a moment when ruin seemed imminent. The poem begins reproachfully; but throughout tenderness prevails above severity, and at the end the strain becomes wholly one of consolation and hope.

The Song shows great originality in form, being a presentation of prophetical thoughts in a poetical dress, which is unique in the Old Testament. . . . The theme is developed with great literary and artistic skill; the images are varied and expressive; the parallelism is usually regular, and very forcible.

> Samuel R. Driver. *An Introduction to the Literature of the Old Testament*. 10th ed. rev. and enl. (New York, Scribner's, 1903), p. 96

NAHUM

None of the minor prophets, however, seems to equal Nahum, in boldness, ardour, and sublimity. His prophecy too forms a regular and perfect poem; the exordium is not merely magnificent, it is truly majestic; the preparation for the destruction of Nineveh, and the description of the downfal [*sic*] and desolation are expressed in the most vivid colours, and are bold and luminous in the highest degree. [1753]

> Robert Lowth. *Lectures on the Sacred Poetry of the Hebrews*. Vol. II. Tr. from the Latin by G. Gregory (London, Printed for J. Johnson, 1787), p. 99

Nahum's poetry is fine. Of all the prophets he is the one who in dignity and force approaches most nearly to Isaiah. His descriptions are singularly picturesque and vivid (notice especially 2:3–5, 10; 3:2–3); his imagery is effective and striking (e.g. 2:11f.; 3:17–18); the thought is always expressed compactly; the parallelism is regular; there is no trace of that prolixity of style which becomes soon afterwards a characteristic of the prophets of the Chaldaean period.

> Samuel R. Driver. *An Introduction to the Literature of the Old Testament.* 10th ed., rev. and enl. (New York, Scribner's, 1903), p. 336

The literary form of Nahum hovers between the Doom Song and the Rhapsodic Discourse. The first two of its seven sections are discourse, with the pendulum alternation between the ideas of judgment and mercy. From the third section the doom form prevails. Messengers coming over the mountains proclaim the long expected event: brilliant lyrics picture the fall of Nineveh. Judgment threatens the great city, but finds it prepared with all its military pomp.

> The chariots rage in the streets,
>   They justle one against another in the broad ways:
> The appearance of them is like torches,
>   They run like the lightnings [2:4].

> Richard G. Moulton. *The Modern Reader's Bible* (New York, Macmillan, 1907), p. 1422

The superb strong word-pictures and the astoundingly impetuous movement place the author among the world's great literary artists. We still can see the flaming chariots with their scarlet-clad warriors: we still can hear the noise of a whip and the noise of the rattling of the wheels, and of the prancing horses, and of the jumping chariots. Brilliant pictures, replete with vivid realism, follow in quick succession—the preparations, the repulses, the flight, the spoils, the heaps of corpses. Then come taunting passages recalling Assyria's former greatness:

> Where is the dwelling of the lions,
> And the feeding place of the young lions,
> Where the lion, even the old lion, walked,
> And the lion's whelp,
> And none of them afraid? [2:11]

Then the savage interruption:

> Behold, I am against thee
> Saith the Lord of Hosts [2:13].

Down to the last, in many respects beautiful taunt, it is a continuous exultation, with immense variety in tone:

Thy shepherds slumber, O king of Assyria:
Thy nobles shall dwell in the dust:
Thy people is scattered upon the mountains,
And no man gathereth them [3:18].

There is no healing of thy bruise;
Thy wound is grievous:
All that hear the bruit of thee shall clap the hands over thee:
For upon whom hath not thy wickedness passed continually? [3:19]

Like Obadiah, Nahum is hardly to be read for spiritual edification; although even the most idealistic of peoples are prone to see in the defeat of their enemies the advancement of the cause of righteousness, and to rejoice and be glad in it. We read the little book for sheer artistic enjoyment. Nothing can deprive Nahum of his place as one of the strongest, most spirited, and vivid of poets. His work must be placed in the first rank of war poetry.

John R. Macarthur. *Biblical Literature and Its Back-grounds* (New York, Appleton, 1936), pp. 301–3

Nahum, who is numbered among the twelve minor prophets of the Old Testament, was not, in fact, a prophet at all. He was instead a great poet of war, second only to the unknown creator of the Song of Deborah. He was numbered among the prophets only because the original title of his martial song was *The Book of the Vision of Nahum, the Elkoshite*, which title with its prophetic word *vision* gave him an entirely undeserved place and recognition. Place he surely deserves and the highest of recognition, but as a poet and not as a prophet.

Nahum was a contemporary of Jeremiah . . . [he] was not only a great poet; he was a great patriot. A complete and confirmed nationalist, he hated the "bloody city" of Nineveh, "full of lies and robbery." His fury against that "well-favored harlot, the mistress of witchcrafts that selleth nations through her whoredom" [3:4], inspired his triumphant lines which together form an ode of great literary power. It is a poem of bloodshed and horror, of vengeance and destruction, with little to relieve its savagery and violence; but it must be admired for the sheer power and force of its expression and for its awful, but brilliant, imagery.

The poem is carefully formed. There are two main divisions, each consisting of three parts. The first division includes the whole of Chapter 2; the second comprises Chapter 3 to Verse 18, which closes the ode with a dirge over the fallen city. Each of the divisions deals with the same material, although the order is somewhat different: the attack on Nineveh, the crimes of the city, its capture and complete destruction.

Nahum excels in superb word-pictures and in the atmosphere of noise and tumult: the scarlet tunics of the fighting men, the flaming of the justling chariots, the noise of cracking whips and of prancing horses, the corpses piled in heaps, the shaking of the fir trees. He is masterly, too, in the haste of his lines which speed on with the speed of the battle itself. *Keep the munitions, watch the way, make thy loins strong, fortify thy power mightily.* . . . *The chariots shall rage in the streets, they shall justle one against another in the broad ways: they shall seem like torches, they shall run like the lightnings* [2:1, 4]. His figures are apt and brilliant: the strongholds of Nineveh shall be like fig trees with the first ripe and falling figs; the devouring fire shall eat like the cankerworm and the locusts; the kings and captains of Nineveh are like grasshoppers before the hot sun. Now he questions: *Where is the dwelling of the lions?* [2:11] Now he commands: *Take ye the spoil of silver, take the spoil of gold;* now he bursts into lurid prophecy: *Behold, I am against thee, saith the Lord of hosts, and I will burn her chariots in the smoke* [2:9, 13] . . . *and I will cast abominable filth upon thee, and make thee vile;* now he mocks and taunts: *Behold, thy people in the midst of thee are women!* [3:6, 13] . . . And when his fury has at last ceased with the destruction of Nineveh, we can perhaps admire most of all the quiet, almost still, lines and words of his epitaph in Verse 18:

> Thy shepherds slumber, O King of Assyria!
> Thy nobles shall dwell in the dust!
> Thy people is scattered upon the mountains,
> And no man gathereth them [3:18].

> Mary Ellen Chase. *The Bible and the Common Reader*
> Rev. ed. (New York, Macmillan, 1952), pp. 179–81

The fall of Nineveh in 612 B.C. is depicted by the prophet Nahum in one of the most spectacular—and neglected—pieces of poetry in the Old Testament. Nothing like it exists in ancient literature, or, for that matter, in modern Hebrew poetry. The poem, with its eyewitness immediacy and conciseness, its rhythmic energy and alliterative excitement, the color and savagery of its battle scenes, the great heave of sarcasm, relief, and exultation at the end, is magnificently equal to the event—the fall of Assyria, the most powerful and ruthless empire the world had yet seen. . . .

Nahum's poem on this critical juncture in history is, for the most part, devoid of theological rationalization and includes no word of compassion for the vanquished. . . . But precisely because the poem lacks an overt theological message it stands on its own as a human document and an artistic achievement. It captures a moment in Judah's history when, for the first time in decades, national independence and unity seemed within reach and Judah breathed free of the Assyrian yoke.

> David Aberbach. *The Jewish Week–American Examiner.* Jan 18, 1981, p. 31

Nathan, Parable of. *See* David: Nathan's Parable

Pentateuch. *See* Moses in this section and the Bible in Section I

PROPHETS

[Prophecy] is the highest degree and greatest perfection man can attain; it consists in the most perfect development of the imaginative faculty. Prophecy is a faculty that cannot in any way be found in a person, or acquired by man, through a culture of his mental and moral faculties; for even if these latter were as good and perfect as possible, they would be of no avail, unless they were combined with the highest natural excellence of the imaginative faculty. . . .

Part of the functions of the imaginative faculty is, as you well know, to retain impressions by the senses, to combine them, and chiefly to form images. The principal and highest function is performed when the senses are at rest and pause in their action, for then it receives, to some extent, divine inspiration in the measure as it is predisposed for this influence. This is the nature of those dreams which prove true, and also of prophecy, the difference being one of quantity, not of quality. Thus our Sages say, that dream is the sixtieth part of prophecy; and no such comparison could be made between two things of different kinds, for we cannot say the perfection of man is so many times the perfection of a horse. In *Bereshit Rabba* (sect. 17) the following saying of our Sages occurs, "Dream is the *nobelet* (the unripe fruit) of prophecy." This is an excellent comparison, for the unripe fruit (*nobelet*) is really the fruit to some extent, only it has fallen from the tree before it was fully developed and ripe. In a similar manner the action of the imaginative faculty during the sleep is the same as at the time when it receives a prophecy, only in the first case it is not fully developed, and has not yet reached its highest degree. But why need I quote the words of our Sages, when I can refer to the following passage of Scripture: "If there be among you a prophet, I, the Lord, will make myself known unto him in a vision, in a dream will I speak to him" (Num. 12:6). Here the Lord tells us what the real essence of prophecy is, that it is a perfection acquired in a dream or in a vision (the original *mar'eh* is a noun derived from the verb *ra'ah*); the imaginative faculty acquires such an efficiency in its action that it sees the thing as if it came without, and perceives it as if through the medium of bodily senses. These two modes of prophecy, vision and dream, include all its different degrees. [ca. 1190]

Moses Maimonides. *Guide for the Perplexed*. Tr. from the Arabic by M. Friedländer. 2d ed., rev. (London, Routledge & Kegan Paul, 1904), pp. 225–26

This species of [prophetic] poetry is more ornamented, more splendid, and more florid than any other. It abounds more in imagery, at least in that species of imagery which, in the parabolic style, is of common and established acceptation, and which, by means of a settled analogy always preserved, is transferred from certain and definite objects to express indefinite and general ideas. Of all the images proper to the parabolic style, it most frequently introduces those which are taken from natural objects and from sacred history: it abounds most in metaphors, allegories, comparisons, and even in copious and diffuse descriptions. It possesses all that genuine enthusiasm, which is the natural attendant on inspiration; it excels in the brightness of imagination and in clearness and energy of diction, and consequently rises to an uncommon pitch of sublimity: hence also it often is very happy in the expression and delineation of the passions, though more commonly employed in the exciting of them; this indeed is its immediate object, over this it presides as its peculiar province.

In respect to the order, disposition, and symmetry of a perfect poem of the prophetic kind, I do not know of any certain definition, which will admit of general application. Naturally free, and of too ardent a spirit to be confined by rule, it is usually guided by the nature of the subject only, and the impulse of divine inspiration. There are not wanting, it is true, instances of great elegance and perfection in these particulars. Among the shorter prophecies, I need only mention those of Balaam, each of which is possessed of a certain accuracy of arrangement and symmetry of form; they open with an elegant exordium, they proceed with a methodical continuation of the subject, and are wound up with a full and graceful conclusion. There are many similar instances in the books of the Prophets, and particularly in Isaiah, which deserve the highest commendation, and may with propriety be classed with the most perfect and regular specimens of poetry. [1753]

> Robert Lowth. *Lectures on the Sacred Poetry of the Hebrews.* Vol. II. Tr. from the Latin by G. Gregory (London, Printed for J. Johnson, 1787), pp. 68–69

The prophetic style, which, as the reproduction or copy of solemn oral discourse, must form the broad basis of a prophetic book, has a peculiar form of its own. On the one hand, it is too exalted in subject-matter and spirit to permit it to sink to the level of common prose; but, on the other hand, too essentially intended to produce immediate effect upon the affairs of life to suffer it to depart so far from these as is allowable in the case of the purely poetic style. Accordingly, it oscillates in such a manner between prose and poetry, that, in its inward aims and effort, it rises to the height of poetry, whilst in its external form it adopts freer and common habits, in order that it may produce effect more immediately upon life, and also retain the peculiar wealth and adaptiveness of oratory. The prophetic style owes its peculiar form entirely to the combination of these two instinctive aims; and its difference from the strictly poetic style is felt most perceptibly when the two styles are brought into juxtaposition, as Habakkuk 3. Prophetic discourse is always in this form; and it is observed throughout in particulars, such as the formation of words and of sentences, and the management of the various parts of each discourse. Still it is of the nature of such a hybrid style that it will rise to the height of pure poetry oftener in the case of one prophet than in the case of another. The form in which we meet with it in books is certainly essentially the same as that in which it was spoken, especially in the form of the words and the sentences, save that, when written, it received in all respects a more compact and symmetrical finish. It also became so firmly established that even writing that had had no oral origin often adopted its form, until at last, in the hands of writers who rarely or never spoke in public, it lost its fresh colour and genuine life; and, partly owing to the unwieldiness of the subject, as, e.g. in the long visions of Ezekiel, chapter 40, sq., sank more and more into prose. [1840]

Georg H. A. von Ewald. *Commentary on the Prophets of the Old Testament*. Vol. I. Tr. by J. Frederick Smith (London, Williams and Norgate, 1875), pp. 67–68

The oracles of these ancient prophets have a rugged grandeur and elevation which set them apart as almost the highest peak in all the writings of men; and the individual prophets have characteristics which can only be brought out by recognizing the period from which their utterances spring. At the same time there is no more inspiring passage in all history than the way in which the prophets of this small people, a helpless buffer state between the great empires of the Nile and the Euphrates, at each crisis in their history rose triumphant above the limitations of temporal weakness and distress. . . .

The first great prophets show the penetrating and statesmanlike understanding of fact fused by the intensity of their emotion and transfigured to words of glowing fire. Two hundred years later, in the prophets of the time of the Exile one finds the firm and earnest perception of fact on the one hand in Ezekiel, Haggai and Malachi, and on the other the soaring imagination and emotion of the Isaiah of the Exile, and the mystical visions of Zechariah; but by this time we find no example of the two forces fused into one. . . .

[The] oracles of the prophets differ from anything else in the Old Testament in the fact that the man who utters them feels that the words spring from his lips completely formed, without volition of his own. This consciousness of detachment appears strikingly in the account of how Amaziah, the priest of the sanctuary at Beth-el, tried to silence Amos . . . (Am. 7:12–15). Here Amos, unlike Isaiah and Jeremiah and most of the other prophets, seems to feel little responsibility for results: it is as if he felt his function to be fulfilled when he had thrust his message on the unwilling attention of his hearers. In the Psalms and in Job the passionate faith or distress of the individual Jew rings through the verses and imparts the note of poignant feeling which makes them kin to the whole world. In the prophets, even in the yearning love which shines through the messages of Hosea or the bitter and burning despair of Jeremiah, there are always a larger thought and a majesty which befit the words of the Lord God of Hosts.

As a result of this sense of possession by the hand of Jehovah the prophetic writings show a feeling for the proportions of things which makes them the best possible foundation for a study of modern literature. It is easy for a student of any form of art to get into the frame of mind of Walter Pater, that sublimated sentimentalist, and feel that the only effort worth a refined man's attention is to free himself from the turmoil and dust of life, and dwell in a half-ascetic, half-aesthetic Olympus of beautiful words and beautiful things. To a student of these books of the prophets such an attitude is impossible, for they continually occupy themselves with the solid realities of history and human fate. With them it is not a question of whether an individual man shall taste the last drop of sweetness or wisdom from this world's cup, or even, as with Shakespeare at his highest, of how the tangle of character and circumstance in man's fate shall work itself out into clear portrayal: the prophets are concerned with the fulfillment of the will of God, and with bringing his chosen people to a compelling sense of the righteousness that shall regenerate the world. . . .

The inmost essence of their power lies in its spiritual elevation. To these prophets, to Amos and Hosea and Isaiah, to Jeremiah, Ezekiel and the Isaiah of the Exile, to Joel and Malachi and Zechariah, with all their unknown contemporaries and coworkers, it was given to touch the realities of the world of this life with the vivifying force of the unseen. Their oracles were phrased in the words of the things which men can see and hear and feel, but they are filled with the palpable breath of the things which lie beyond our present capacities to comprehend. More than the other writings of the Old Testament they spring from what, because it is inexplicable, we call genius.

> J. H. Gardiner. *The Bible as English Literature* (New York, Scribner's, 1906), pp. 215–16, 218, 246–49

To the literary mind no part of the Old Testament is more attractive than the Books of the Prophets; they make the most unique contribution of the Bible to world literature. . . . The earlier prophets, such as Elijah, are men of action. There is no "Book of the Prophet Elijah"; men like Elijah, Elisha, Micaiah, enter into literature as heroes of stories which others narrate. But the later prophets, like Isaiah and Jeremiah, without ceasing to be men of action, are also men of letters. Ancient Israel is one of the great literary peoples of the world. In its first stages, as with other peoples, story and song predominate; when it reaches its maturity the higher literary forms develop. The prophets become lyric poets, orators, dramatists; even—to take in the special case of Ezekiel—we must add, artists. Thus for these later prophets there is a double function. To their own day and generation they, like their predecessors, are leaders of national action. But beyond this function their literary gifts have fitted them for a wider and a perpetual audience. The same spiritual message which they have from day to day fitted to passing emergencies they now, through these other literary channels, convey to the spiritual world of all time.

> Richard G. Moulton. *The Modern Reader's Bible* (New York, Macmillan, 1907), pp. 1388–89

The prophetic poet starts from no articulated scheme of philosophy, no stereotyped theology. The great Hebrew prophets deal in no proofs of the existence of God. . . . Their message is not that God exists, for no one disputes that, but that he is a God of righteousness and mercy who hates the cruelty and the license of magical nature cults. . . .

Sin, moral evil, as the source of all we suffer, righteousness and repentance as the promise of better things—these are the recurring themes of prophetic poetry. . . .

But in all this the prophets were thinkers. There is reason in their reasonings even when these go astray in their immediate application. The best commentators do not fail to emphasise the warning that prophecy of the kind we meet with in the first and greatest prophets, Hosea, Isaiah, Jeremiah, has nothing in common with the utterances of what we should call psychic mediums—diviners and necromancers. The prophets speak as men possessed, but not in the sense that their own personality is pushed aside. Their inspiration is that of their whole personality, their reason is at work on premises too manifold and profound to be brought up and defined, as science demands, without loss, without some degree of abstraction. . . . But this does not imply that they will always be able to define their thought in general terms or be able to argue logically. They will often speak in symbols, in images; for the prophet is always to a greater or less extent also a poet. All the sensuous, symbolic language of poetry can be illustrated from their writings—Allegory . . . Prophets and poets—the Hebrew writers were both, and so greatly both that our religious tradition has assigned to them a place apart.

> Herbert J. C. Grierson. *Milton and Wordsworth: Poets and Prophets* (New York, Macmillan, 1937), pp. 9, 17, 20–21, 25

Each has his special style, ranging from the thick, tenebrous utterances of Jeremiah to the sad serenity of the "Suffering Servant" passages in Isaiah. . . .

In certain books, the Old Testament prophets exhibit a kind of hallucinatory power—Nahum and Ezekiel are instances. No one can forget the vision of the whirlwind with which Ezekiel opens, nor the nightmare of destruction it is the purpose of the three chapters of Nahum to depict.

But though the prophets have their distinguishable styles, in the Old Testament they seem, if one reads them continuously, to create an atmosphere, to live in a universe of their own making, out of which a common language springs. It is true that this universe is lively with familiar images—chariots and men of war, grass that comes up and is cut down, fine linen, swords, wine, oil, corn, birds, wind, great beasts, stars, storm, and darkness, but these images are not so much the products of empirical observation as of inwardness, a brooding imagination that overcomes the visible world and sees men and events in it as moving hieroglyphs of an arcane language known or half-known to the elect only. I have spoken of the hallucinatory power of this style. I can illustrate it, I hope, by even so short a passage as this from the second chapter of Nahum:

> But Nineveh is of old like a pool of water; yet they shall flee away. Stand, stand, shall they cry; but none shall look back. Take ye the spoil of silver, take the spoil of gold; for there is none end of the store and glory out of all the pleasant furniture. She is empty, and void, and waste; and the heart melteth, and the knees

smite together, and much pain is in all loins, and the faces of them
all gather blackness.

As in William Blake, so in this passage: the hypnosis of vision is greater than the
sum of its parts and manufactures meaning in proportion as it is extended. Not
only does vision appeal to our eschatological sense, which delights in any picture
of *Götterdämmerung*, but the images in such a passage are of the stream-of-
consciousness kind. Thus the prophetical books anticipate and often surpass
much modern poetry. For example, Conrad Aiken and T. S. Eliot, heaping up
disparate, yet associated images in poems like *Senlin* or *The Waste Land*, consciously or not parallel and repeat the method of the prophets.

> Howard Mumford Jones. *Five Essays on the Bible* (New
> York, American Council of Learned Societies, 1960),
> pp. 55–56

["The highest thing in art (and the hardest), it seems to me, is to create a state of
dreamy meditation" (Gustave Flaubert, letter of August 1853)]. The very opposite applies to the words of the prophets. They suggest a disquietude sometimes
amounting to agony. Yet there are interludes when one perceives an eternity of
love hovering over moments of anguish; at the bottom there is light, fascination,
but above the whole soar thunder and lightning.

The prophet's use of emotional and imaginative language, concrete in diction, rhythmical in movement, artistic in form, marks his style as poetic. Yet it is
not the sort of poetry that takes its origin, to use Wordsworth's phrase, "from
emotion recollected in tranquility." Far from reflecting a state of inner harmony
or poise, its style is charged with agitation, anguish, and a spirit of nonaccep-
tance. The prophet's concern is not with nature but with history, and history is
devoid of poise.

Authentic utterance derives from a moment of identification of a person and a
word; its significance depends upon the urgency and magnitude of its theme. The
prophet's theme is, first of all, the very life of a whole people, and his identification lasts more than a moment. He is one not only with what he says; he is involved with his people in what his words foreshadow. This is the secret of the
prophet's style: his life and soul are at stake in what he says and in what is going
to happen to what he says. It is an involvement that echoes on. What is more,
both theme and identification are seen in three dimensions. Not only the prophet
and the people, but God Himself is involved in what the words convey.

Prophetic utterance is rarely cryptic, suspended between God and man; it is
urging, alarming, forcing onward, as if the words gushed forth from the heart of
God, seeking entrance to the heart and mind of man, carrying a summons as well
as an involvement. Grandeur, not dignity, is important. The language is luminous and explosive, firm and contingent, harsh and compassionate, a fusion of
contradictions.

The prophet seldom tells a story, but casts events. He rarely sings, but casti-
gates. He does more than translate reality into a poetic key: he is a preacher

whose purpose is not self-expression or "the purgation of emotions," but communication. His images must not shine, they must burn.

The prophet is intent on intensifying responsibility, is impatient of excuse, contemptuous of pretense and self-pity. His tone, rarely sweet or caressing, is frequently consoling and disburdening; his words are often slashing, even horrid—designed to shock rather than to edify.

The mouth of the prophet is "a sharp sword." He is "a polished arrow" taken out of the quiver of God (Isa. 49:2).

> Tremble, you women who are at ease,
> Shudder, you complacent ones;
> Strip, and make yourselves bare,
> Gird sackcloth upon your loins.
> (Isa. 32:11)

Abraham J. Heschel. *The Prophets* (Philadelphia, Jewish Publication Society of America, 1962), pp. 6–7

Like all inspired poets, the Prophets had to enlarge and modify the original ecstatic impulse into comprehensible sentences and give it a poetic form. The original word or phrase which provided this impulse underwent a rational and artistic elaboration. The less reflection and elaboration this nucleus betrays and the more tersely it expresses the immediate impact of inspiration, the nearer we are to its genesis. Indeed, we can sometimes catch the Prophet's inspiration in its crude phase prior to its elaboration.

On the whole, the inspiration of the Prophets depended on their faith, moral sense, and susceptibility to an ecstatic experience, often induced by the sight of an object and the sound of its name. It entailed rational elucidation and enlargement of the primary, embryonic oracle and its artistic shaping and improvement, although the element of poetic skill is never explicitly mentioned in the Prophets. The Divine source and force of inspiration is recognized by them, but they nevertheless retain and assert their own personality.

This belief in the Divine origin of inspiration and in the ecstatic state of mind which makes the poet responsive to it makes the Prophetic concept similar to its Platonic counterpart as presented in *Ion*. Yet the dissimilarities between the two concepts are more conspicuous and significant than the similarities. . . .

Plato's second, more appreciative view of inspiration, expounded in the *Phaedrus*, is more akin to the Prophetic concept. In both *Phaedrus* and the Prophets the inspired man is actively involving his personality when he responds to inspiration. Both the Platonic and Prophetic poets conjure up a vision of a perfect world, moral or aesthetic. Their respective sources and stimuli of inspiration are also comparable. First, a supernatural, extrasensory source which in the Bible is God and in Plato the recollection of the prenatal view of Reality; second, the external stimuli which for the Prophets create the associative, sensuous link to the subject matter of their poetry, and are objects of everyday life, like a pan, a belt, a basket of fruit, and for Plato beautiful objects.

Also, in both concepts inspiration brings about a moral, spiritual purification or ennoblement. In the Hebrew concept, however, this purification is a preparation for the inspiration proper, whereas in the *Phaedrus* it is its concomitant or result.

In both the Greek and Hebrew concepts inspiration derives from a transcendental power, and the poet's response to it is one of mad ecstasy. Yet two differences stand out. First, the conscious, "uninspired" skill which the poet needs is implied, but not mentioned in the Bible. Second, the compulsive force of the Prophet's inspiration, involving his mind and conscience, is contrary to the sterile inactivity of Plato's purely mimetic poet and much deeper, more active, and more demanding than the inspiration of his beauty-loving and philosophical poets. Inspiration in both views comes from the outside, but only in the Hebrew view is it so internalized that the poet can defy it and consciously yield to it.

These differences reflect, I think, the divergent Platonic and Hebrew notions of divinity or of the highest principle. Plato conceives of the Idea of God as the origin of real existence, as the Being which is the cause of all other beings. The highest principle is considered by him as something static, harmonious, quiescent. In contrast, in the Hebrew concept God is grasped in analogy with the highest, noblest human functions, with the functions of a conscious, ethical, dynamic personality. Moreover, Plato's attitude is that of an intellectual aesthete, the contemplative man who stands outside life and beholds it as a spectacle. The Prophet's attitude is ethico-religious; it implies a conscious and resolute choice, although it leads to submission to the ethical, universal Divine. It is for this reason that the Prophet's experience of Divine inspiration engrosses and absorbs all of his being.

> Abraham A. Avni. *Comparative Literature*. Winter, 1968, pp. 60–63

Hebrew poetry is intimately linked with prophecy which has no parallel among Eastern or Western peoples. In spite of superficial resemblances to ecstatic practices in the ancient East, it is a unique phenomenon. According to Maimonides, the great medieval sage, "It is the greatest perfection man can attain." According to the acute critic of prophecy, Sigmund Mowinckel, prophets—"the *Nevi'im* . . . were filled by divine power to raving point." Generations of scholars, Jewish sages and Church Fathers, philosophers and poets tried their intuitive and reasoning powers on the solution of the sphinxlike riddle of prophecy. But it has eluded their intellectual and spiritual grasp. At best it can be described and evaluated in subjective terms. Intensity of experience and intensity of expression are its dominant characteristics. But the great poetry of a Shakespeare and a Goethe may also boast such distinction. What makes prophets unique poets is a belief and a claim that their words are inspired by an all-seeing, all-knowing Power which transcends human wisdom: God. From that point of view prophets are poets of faith. The misnomer "prophet" which has the meaning "one who foretells" in Greek and in the languages of the West, contributed to the misunderstanding of his function. For the Hebrew equivalent of the term, *navi'*, probably means "one who is called." But whatever the nature of that divine power or ecstatic experience of the prophets, be it supranormal or a heightened form of psychic tension, the timelessness of their utterance and the universalism of their message has been noted by their admirers and detractors. Yet they never lost sight of Israel, which they wished to elevate by sheer moral power above all its neighbors. Chauvinism and universalism were intertwined in their utterance. Prophets were also builders of ideal dreamlands in verse, and they served as examples and prototypes to Sir Thomas More and Samuel Butler, Sebastian Mercier and Restif de la Bretonne, Bellamy and Orwell. They did not use the word "utopia" . . . but they said "the end of days." . . . Since they opposed the surrounding cultures and their ethical *laissez-faire* with all the great eloquence at their command, they were driven to advance the Jews to the status of a chosen people. This idea, maligned through the ages and rejected by Jewish Reform and Reconstructionism in our own times, had nothing in common with the supercilious attitude of the Greeks to other nations. It was elevated by duty to humanity and service to mankind. In spite of the great diversity of prophetic writing, the idea of service and duty gives them their unity. This idea is no stranger to the philosophical literature of the Greeks but it reached only highly cultured individuals. The prophets, who were poets and who couched their simple ideas in images and visions, had an abiding influence on their people and, through them, on the entire world. They may be said to have shaped a nation in their image—perhaps the only example of a people transformed by the magic touch of poetry.

> Eisig Silberschlag. In *The Princeton Encyclopedia of Poetry and Poetics*. Enl. edition ed. by Alex Preminger et al. (Princeton, N.J., Princeton University Press, 1974), pp. 338–39

Any reader of the Scriptures will be struck by the contrast between the terseness and rapidity of the narrative books, and the extravagantly repetitious, tirelessly metaphorical exfoliations of the prophetic books. (The comparison is not as unfair as it may seem: the prophetic books are as much concerned as the narratives with the course of events in Israelite history, past and future. In any case, one finds repetition and downright incoherence in the narratives, too, as a result of the spatchcocking together of material from the different sources.) On this subject I can perhaps best speak autobiographically or anecdotally. When I was working on my novel *The Rape of Tamar*—a fictional retelling of the story about the rape of King David's only daughter by her brother, Amnon, and the revenge subsequently taken upon him by yet another brother, Absalom—it occurred to me that every phrase, virtually every word, in the relevant chapter of II Samuel was like a seed. Dry, hard, small, compressed, apparently lifeless, it was capable of astonishing growth, if it was planted in one's mind and saturated with whatever capacity one had for imaginative response and understanding. Reading almost any of the prophetic books is an experience of a greatly different kind.

There are many concise, pregnant utterances within them: agreed. But the more one reads, the more one feels impelled to put up a defense against them—a kind of breakwater in the mind—to prevent oneself from being overwhelmed by the constant, unrelenting roar of verbiage, beating down upon the page with all the fury and ultimate monotony of waves on a beach.

The assiduity and ingenuity with which the prophets say the same things over and over again in slightly different ways produce one surprising side effect. One can get from their books a richly detailed picture of what conditions of daily life must have been like for the people of Israel during the monarchical period. The narratives tell us much; in many respects the prophets tell us even more. The persistent use they make of the most familiar objects and practices in their imagery is just one sign of their power as creative artists; especially when one thinks of the hortatory and minatory ends for which they wrote. From their books one can learn about the climate and topography of the country; about the crops people grew on their land; the clothes they wore; the herds they tended; the furniture they had in their houses; the ways in which they stored their food; the occupations they followed; the kinds of medical treatment that were available to them; and much else besides.

Samuel Johnson would not have agreed with what I have just said about the appearance of familiar objects in great poetry. He found risible and disgusting Shakespeare's phrase "the blanket of the dark," in *Macbeth*; the vulgar associations of the word "blanket" were in Dr. Johnson's view incompatible with the dignity of high tragedy. One wonders what he might have made of Isaiah's vividly metaphoric description of how little security or comfort the kingdom of Judah had gained in making an alliance with Egypt against the Assyrian invader. "For the bed is too short," he wrote, in evocation of everyone's memory of a tormented night, "to stretch oneself on it; and the covering too narrow to wrap oneself in it" (28:20).

But then, the prophets never cared about their dignity or grandeur, or the dignity and grandeur of their readers; only Yahweh's mattered to them. To illustrate the demands and admonitions of their God they were prepared not only to use the lowliest objects ("wash-pots," etc.) as metaphors in their writings; they were also ready to make, as it were, walking icons of themselves. They transformed themselves into visible personifications of the abject state and forlorn hopes of Israel. Isaiah went about barefoot and with loosened garments as a "sign and portent" of the disasters that would follow the alliance with Egypt referred to above; Jeremiah appeared with a yoke over his shoulders to show the Israelites that they had no choice but to submit to the Babylonians; Amos proclaimed his wife's infidelities as an analogue of Israel's infidelities to Yahweh; Ezekiel lay on his side for a number of days equal to the years that the people would suffer their punishment.

Synecdoche, metaphor, personification—these are terms used in rhetoric and literary criticism. Yet they can be properly invoked here to characterize not the writings of the prophets (as transcribed by them or by their disciples) but their reported actions. Nothing could illustrate better than these pieces of dramatic mimicry, these "real" yet wholly figurative actions, the ever-trembling, self-energizing *instability* of the relationship between the literal and the metaphorical in the Scriptures.

Dan Jacobson. *The Story of the Stories* (New York, Harper & Row, 1982), pp. 131–33

PROVERBS

[1] A Maxim is a short saying about the way of the world by means of which a conclusion, presently or in future applicable, is held to be self-evidently true. Thus, we have here taken "maxim" as in David's statement: "As saith the proverb of the ancients: Out of the wicked cometh forth wickedness; but my hand shall not be upon thee" [I Sam. 24:14].

[2] The whole of the Book of Proverbs is made up of this Figure. It is divisible into two classes, as there is a simple form of it, and a complex. The simple Maxim is also found in two sorts, as there is a form without reason given, and one with.

[3] Examples of the first: A divine sentence is in the lips of the king: his mouth trespasseth not in judgment [Prov. 16:10]; The Heart of the wise teacheth his mouth, and addeth learning to his lips [16:23]; A gift is as a precious stone in the eyes of him that hath it: withersoever it turneth, it prospereth [17:8]; To do righteousness and justice is more acceptable to the Lord than sacrifice [21:3]; Whoso stoppeth his ears at the cry of the poor, he also shall cry himself, but shall not be answered [21:13]. All these maxims belong to the simple class, and are without reason explicitly stated in the text.

[4] An example of the second form of simple Maxim, that with the reason given: A man of great wrath shall suffer punishment; for if it deliver him, yet will it wax again [19:19]. The intended meaning is that punishment inevitably overtakes a person of great wrath, and this forms the Maxim. The reason given is that if such wrath can sometimes deliver its possessor—by waxing great against the object of his anger: because his heart will be hot [Deut. 19:6] and make him victorious—then such wrath will each time again wax great until stern punishment comes to him at men's hands: for since wrath of this kind is a trait of which nature is intolerant, its possessor must, in the end, inevitably sustain curses, maledictions, and the incessant stroke [Isa. 14:6]. Another example: A cabal of the wicked shall drag them away—the Maxim proper—because they refuse to do justly—the reason [Prov. 21:7]. Thus again: Vexation is better than laughter, for by the sadness of the countenance the heart may be gladdened [Eccl. 7:3]; He that hath a bountiful eye shall be blessed, for he giveth of his bread to the poor [Prov. 22:9]. And again: The hunger of the labouring man laboureth for him, for

his mouth compelleth him [16:26]. In other words, a laborer's hunger labors for his need, the reason being that he could not function without laboring for his need, "for his mouth compelleth him"—that is, "his mouth" forces him to such labor because food and drink are indispensable necessities. "Compel" (*'ākhaf*) and "force" (*kāfaf*) are two separate roots that have the same meaning, as Rabbi David [Kimḥi] has said. The verse parallels All the labour of man is for his mouth [Eccl. 6:7].

[5] The complex Maxim, in its turn, is a composite of several maxims. It likewise subdivides into varieties, for there is a form without reason given, and another with reason given. Examples of the first: He that refuseth correction despiseth his own soul, but he that hearkeneth to reproof getteth understanding [Prov. 15:32]; By the blessing of the upright a city is exalted, but it is overthrown by the mouth of the wicked [11:11]: In the multitude of words there wanteth not transgression, but he that refraineth his lips is wise [10:19]; He that is greedy of gain troubleth his own house, but he that hateth gifts shall live [15:27]. Each of the foregoing examples is compounded of two maxims.

[6] An example of the form with reason given: He that committeth adultery with a woman lacketh understanding: He doeth it that would destroy his own soul; wounds and dishonour shall he get, and his reproach shall not be wiped away. After these maxims, the text gives the reason in these words: For jealousy is the rage of a man, and he will not spare in the day of vengeance [6:32–34].
[1475]

> Messer David ben Judah Leon. *The Book of the Honeycomb's Flow*. Ed. and tr. by Isaac Rabinowitz (Ithaca, N.Y., Cornell Unversity Press, 1983), pp. 437, 439, 441

Great Part of the Book of Proverbs, is only a Collection of moral Sentences, yet such a Collection as is not to be equall'd in all the Heathen World. [Solomon's] Precepts shew a deep Insight into Human Nature, and his Characteristics are drawn with the utmost Nicety. Every Figure is represented in its proper Attitude, and distinguish'd by its peculiar Habit. 'Twou'd be worth while in this View, to compare them *with* the *Characters* of Theophrastus, and his imitator Bruyere. There are also some shining Passages in the Descriptive Way. See the Description of Wisdom, chapter 3; of an Ill Woman, chapter 5; of a Sluggard, chapter 6; of a Harlot seducing a Foolish Youth, chapter 7; the Confession of *Agur*, chapter 30; *Lemuel's* Lesson, chapter 31, which concludes with the Description of a good Woman.

> John Husbands. Preface to *A Miscellany of Poems by Several Hands* (Oxford, J. Husbands, 1731), sig. K6

This work consists of two parts. The first, serving as a proem or exordium, includes the nine first chapters; and is varied, elegant, sublime, and truly poetical; the order of the subject is in general excellently preserved, and the parts are very aptly connected among themselves. It is embellished with many beautiful descriptions and personifications; the diction is polished, and abounds with all the ornaments of poetry; insomuch, that it scarcely yields in elegance and splendour to any of the sacred writings. The other part, which extends from the beginning of the tenth chapter to the end of the book, consists almost entirely of detached parables or maxims, which have but little in them of the sublime or poetical, except a certain energetic and concise turn of expression. . . .

Solomon himself, in one of his proverbs, has explained the principal excellencies of this form of composition; exhibiting at once a complete definition of a parable or proverb, and a very happy specimen of what he describes:

> Apples of gold in a net-work of silver
> Is a word seasonably spoken [Prov. 25:11].

Thus he insinuates, that grave and profound sentiments are to be set off by a smooth and well-turned phraseology, as the appearance of the most beautiful and exquisitely-coloured fruit, or the imitation of it perhaps in the most precious materials, is improved by the circumstance of shining, as through a veil, through the reticulations of a silver vessel exquisitely carved. Nay, he further intimates, that it is not only a neat turn and polished diction which must recommend them, but that truth itself acquires additional beauty, when partially discovered through the veil of elegant fiction and imagery. [1753]

Robert Lowth. *Lectures on the Sacred Poetry of the Hebrews.* Vol. II. Tr. from the Latin by G. Gregory (London, Printed for J. Johnson, 1787), pp. 164–66

Perhaps the proverbs are most characteristic when they turn upon the varying aspects of social life. Cameo pictures of social types abound. There is the prating fool, winking with his eye; the practical joker, as dangerous as an madman casting firebrands about; the talebearer, and the man who "harps upon a matter," separating chief friends; the whisperer whose words are like dainty morsels going down into the innermost parts of the belly; the backbiting tongue, drawing gloomy looks all around as surely as the north wind brings rain; the false boaster, compared to wind and clouds without rain; the haste to be rich; the liberal man that scattereth and yet increaseth, while others are withholding only to come to want; the speculator holding back his corn amid the curses of the people; the man of wandering life, like a restless bird; the unsocial man that separateth himself, foregoing wisdom for the sake of his own private desire; the cheerfulness that is a continual feast. The times of the wise men seem to have been acquainted with genteel poverty: "Better is he that is lightly esteemed, and hath a servant, / Than he that honoureth himself, and lacketh bread." . . . Some of these social sayings rest upon the curious observation of what Ben Jonson would have called humours: the humour of the buyer, saying, It is naught, and when he is gone away, boasting; the humour of the mendicant, whose fellows give him a wide berth— "his friends go far from him! / He pursueth them with words, but they are gone."

Of the same sort is the delightful picture of the parvenu at the great man's table, distracted between the dainties and awe at the presence: he is advised to keep a knife to his hungry throat. Most unexpected of all is the proverb of the inopportune man that "blesseth his friend with a loud voice, rising early in the morning:" but his blessing counts for a curse!

It is not only social types that thus appear in the sayings of the wise: social questions have their place. Proverbs are devoted to the relations of servant and master, wife and husband, parents and children. And there is the perpetual question of rich and poor. The saying that the appetite of the labouring man laboureth for him might have served Aristophanes as text for the discourse of Poverty in his *Plutus*. The wise view the rich and poor mingling in the incidents of life, and proclaim that the same Lord is maker of all. They point out that there are some compensations even for poverty: "The ransom of a man's life is his riches: / But the poor heareth no threatening." . . .

What are the methods by which these topics are treated? Without attempting minute analysis I may remark that three characteristics of gnomic method stand out. Antithesis is the very life blood of the proverb: antithesis, in the form of adversative or other contrast, belongs to the vast majority of them. "Understanding is a well-spring of life unto him that hath it: / But the correction of fools is their folly." . . .

Next in importance to antithesis, comparison is a mode of emphasis in proverbial sayings: "A rebuke entereth deeper into one that hath understanding / Than an hundred stripes into a fool." . . .

A third mode of treatment found in the proverbs is the kind of comparison called imagery. Very striking images are employed by the wise men, especially in the fourth book of Proverbs. Such is the simile of the will o' the wisp:

> The getting of treasures by a lying tongue
> Is a vapour driven to and fro;
> They that seek them seek death.

Three striking similes are massed together in a single saying, where the contentious woman is compared to continual dropping in a very rainy day; restraining her is like holding the wind, using force is like fighting slippery oil.

The reader of Proverbs must be on his guard against a first impression of commonplaceness. Proverbs have a prerogative to be commonplace; their mission is to voice the most widely diffused experience. And there is no literary function higher than that of giving point to what is ordinary, and rescuing a truth from the obscurity of obviousness. No impression is left on the mind by the dry statement that the behaviour of a pair of lovers is irreducible to principle. But Agur can strike a spark . . . :

> There be three things which are too wonderful for me,
> Yea, four which I know not:
> The way of an eagle in the air:

The way of a serpent upon a rock;
The way of a ship in the midst of the sea;
And the way of a man with a maid.

> Richard G. Moulton. *The Modern Reader's Bible* (New York, Macmillan, 1907), pp. 1453–56

What progress there is in the substance of the Book of Proverbs is to be traced rather in its manner than in its matter. The items of the matter are like so many casual remarks or *obiter dicta*,—each proverb being complete in itself, deriving no support or suggestion from the one before, making no preparation for the one succeeding. Nor do the supposedly later compilations reveal an appreciable advance in reflection or spiritual discovery. So far as the movement of subject matter is concerned the book may be regarded as a body of static Wisdom, every utterance of it a truth to itself. In the manner, however, that is to say, in the structure and style of the individual proverb, there is traceable a movement, a development, which may be briefly described as the *mashal* ["proverb"] working itself free.

What is meant by this may be noted by any reader who follows the text with due attention to style, beginning of course at chapter 10, where the older Solomonic proverbs begin. As a preliminary, however, it is to be remembered that the unit of expression adopted by the Solomonic sages was the parallelistic couplet, the native art-form of Hebrew poetry; which unit they proceeded to develop, according to their idea of making its expression at once lucid and cryptic, into a couplet containing the maximum of suggestion, condensation, and epigrammatic point. The result, as compared with the ordinary Hebrew parallelism, was somewhat analogous to the so-called heroic couplet of Pope and Dryden as compared with the more steady flow of descriptive or dramatic blank verse. So by their skillful cultivation the *mashal* couplet became the artistic vehicle of the crisp, pointed, thought-provoking pronouncement desired in the conversion of a run-wild popular saying into a refined literary form. They had sought their material in the homely thought of the common people, such as expresses itself in maxims, and their treatment of these maxims was like turning a rustic remark into verse, with the added endeavor to make the verse itself an adage.

With this refinement of the form goes refinement of the thought. As soon as it steps beyond the homely folk consciousness it becomes more subtile, pliant, colorful, adaptable, in a word, from a rather stiff workmanlike mold in which the art, which is first crude and tentative, becomes severe and self-conscious, it gradually works itself free from trammels of form to the point where the verbal and phrasal art is swallowed up in the swing and flow of thought. Such, in a remarkable degree, was the literary progress traceable in the Book of Proverbs.

> John F. Genung. *A Guidebook to the Biblical Literature* (Boston, Ginn, 1919), pp. 455–56

Poetry in parallelism is not exclusive to the Semites; it is found everywhere, from the "primitive" tribes of Africa to the highest circles of culture, like Chinese civilization. I would seek its origin in a dialogic or antiphonal improvisation. At seasonal festivals involving marriage ceremonies among the East Asians, choirs of boys and girls sing to each other in parallelistic fashion. Among the Finno-Ugric people, folksingers, sitting in twos, one facing the other, knee to knee, taking each other's hands, sway their bodies one toward the other to the rhythm of the melody and sing together the parallel rhymed couplets of a saga. The Bible, too, frequently (e.g., Exod. 34:18; Judg. 5:11; I Sam. 18:7; 21:12; Isa. 27:2) tells of two voices answering one another in song, so that the founder of biblical poetics, Robert Lowth, was even of the opinion that among the Hebrews nearly every song was, in one form or another, dialogic in structure. I allow myself to suppose that the source of the "proverb," a concentrated parallelistic pattern, is dialogic: one speaker says one line and his partner answers him, be it by way of contrast, by way of solution, by way of completion, but in any case in the form of paralleling. Unlike in China, though, where parallelism reaches its most exquisite development in a literary game that requires the players to fashion a two-part sentence by adding a sentence that is parallel word for word, in Israel we observe a different process, which merits attention. Among the possible types of response first place is taken by the contrastive response, and in this form is embodied the fundamental contrast that constitutes the essence of Hebrew proverbial poetry: the struggle between "wisdom," knowing the ways of God, and "foolishness," the name for deviating from this way. This struggle is the greatest theme in the Book of Proverbs, a theme that within its homogeneity is richly variegated in an amazing number of major themes, all of which relate to the central theme, directly or in a roundabout way.

Hebrew proverbial poetry absorbed a great deal from the wisdom literature of the ancient world in general and the rich literature of Egypt in particular, sometimes actually translating from it. Yet the decisive factor in spiritual history, innovation within borrowing, is revealed even here. The maxims of Egypt and Babylonia, when they were transferred into an essentially different spiritual milieu, the domain of an array of "wise men," knowers of God set against "fools," refusing to know him, evolve into something of an entirely different purpose. Here and only here is the vital contrast elevated, with the aid of the proverb form, to give expression to a struggle whose scene is the whole world and whose time is all history.

> Martin Buber. *Darko shel miqra'* (Jerusalem, Bialik Institute, 1964), pp. 338–39†

The Book of Proverbs is, as [Hilaire] Duesberg [*Les scribes inspirés*, 2d ed., 1966, p. 265] remarked, in itself a *comédie humaine*: a host of characters appear in its pages, and these are the characters and situations of the real world. It is true that they also are usually painted in black and white: such is the nature of the proverb, which distils and abstracts real life into a tiny compass. Nevertheless they are extremely varied: not merely do we have the obvious contrasts between the fool and the wise, the righteous and the wicked, but we find the street gang of youths, the loitering prostitute and the weak young man, the thief, the adulterer, the husband absent on business, the farmer, the sluggard, the dishonest trader, the strict father, the poor and the rich, the counsellor, the debtor and the creditor, the royal messenger and many more characters taken from life.

> Roger N. Whybray. *The Succession Narrative* (London, SCM, 1968), pp. 79–80

The first nine chapters of Proverbs clearly represent a more complex kind of artistic design than the rest of the book. There is much more reliance on bigger units. Equally refreshing is the variety of literary devices used to convey the wisdom theme. And there is a unifying theme, poetic texture, narrative viewpoint, and structure to this block of chapters. Although it would be accurate to call these chapters a miscellany, or collection of separate poems, it is a miscellany possessing a high degree of unity.

These nine chapters are carefully structured as a series of corresponding conflicts. The effect is that of a plot. The conflicts include wisdom (a lady) against the harlot, the good man against the evil man, life against death, wisdom against folly, and wisdom against evil. This series of conflicts sets up the necessity of choice between the competing sets of values. The "son" of the series, and by extension the reader, is constantly enjoined to choose one thing over another. Choice between conflicting forces thus lends plot structure to the piece. It is another chapter in the overriding plot of the Bible—the conflict between good and evil.

The group of chapters has its own unifying topic—wisdom. Within this single subject, various subordinate themes appear, including the origin of wisdom, the benefits of wisdom, the tragic results of rejecting widsom for folly (an indirect way of praising wisdom), the necessity to choose wisdom, and the characteristics and acts of wisdom.

There is also a unifying viewpoint and tone. The repeated addresses to "my son" give these chapters a single viewpoint. We have a strong sense of a single narrator throughout the chapters, something we do not have in the rest of the book or in the typical collection of proverbs. The narrator is always depicted as a wise authority figure. . . . The effect is to support the impression of a father addressing a son with urgently needed information. Unity of tone comes from the repeated imperative statements, which serve to stress the authority of the speaker, the necessity for choice, or the urgency of the situation.

Unity of poetic texture is achieved through the use of recurrent images and symbols, which bind the various smaller units into an artistic whole. These repeated images include the woman (Wisdom and the harlot), the son, jewel imagery, the path or way, and wisdom, whether as a conceptual image or a personified quality.

In the midst of all this unity, the writer has incorporated a diversity of literary techinques. In fact, the artistry of the author is seen as much in his ability to handle a variety of forms as it is in his achievement of unity. There is synonymous parallelism as well as the antithetical proverb. Other forms include the lyric poem, the dramatic monologue, the encomium, narrative, and the dramatized scene. The writer seldom relies solely on the sentence proverb, usually managing to present a larger poetic unit. . . .

Wisdom, a personified abstraction pictured as a lady, is one of two main characters in the opening chapters of Proverbs. She is the grand antagonist to the harlot or the strange woman, thus providing part of the narrative conflict of the work. She is usually pictured as calling people, especially "the son," to pursue wisdom. Examples include her monologue warning people against the neglect of wisdom (1:20–33) and her call to seek wisdom (Prov. 8).

The other woman who is vying for the allegiance of "the son" is "the loose woman," also called "the harlot" and "the strange woman." There is an ambiguity about the identity of the loose woman in these chapters. Some references describe her quite literally as a source of sexual temptation, while others seem to suggest that she is a symbol for all types of sin and folly, as the figure of the harlot often is in biblical literature. Many of these passages have a double meaning, referring to sin in general and to sexual infidelity or promiscuity in particular [e.g., 5:5, 6, 8]. . . . Proverbs 5:15–23 contrasts the immoral woman to the ideal of faithful wedded love in a passage that sums up much of the biblical teaching about the beauty and privacy of sexual love in its God-ordained state. Other monologues in which the father warns against sexual and spiritual adultery include Proverbs 6:20–35 and Proverbs 7:6–23, a story of temptation and seduction which is the most elaborate narrative in the book of Proverbs.

The lady named Wisdom is also sometimes described in terms appropriate to romantic love, thereby maintaining the balance and contrast of the work. . . .

The conflict between Wisdom and the foolish woman reaches its climax in chapter 9. The first six verses describe the feast that Wisdom prepares for the people of the town. The invitation to the feast of Wisdom is dramatized and uses the same images that have been used earlier in the seductions of the loose woman (Prov. 9:4–5). . . .

Verses 13 and 18 balance the feast of Wisdom with a description of the feast that "a foolish woman" prepares for the people of the town. She, too, extends an alluring invitation to passers-by from "the high places of the town," just as the maids of Wisdom had done (v. 3). Part of her invitation is a verbatim repetition of the invitation uttered by the maids of Wisdom: "Whoever is simple, let him turn in here!" (v. 16). The speech also repeats the images of bread and drink, but this time the addition of modifying words makes the feast a perversion of the feast of wisdom: "Stolen water is sweet, and bread eaten in secret is pleasant" (v. 17). The bold juxtaposition of the two feasts and the accompanying invitations concludes this unit on a note of vivid conflict and reinforces the theme that moral choice between wisdom and folly is a basic reality of life.

Leland Ryken. *The Literature of the Bible* (Grand Rapids, Mich., Zondervan, 1974), pp. 245–46, 248–49

Many biblical proverbs are similar in construction to what Northrop Frye has called the "literal structure of poetry," that is, "metaphor appears in its literal shape, which is simple juxtaposition" [*Anatomy of Criticism*, 1971, p. 123]. Considered in that light, Ezra Pound's "In a Station of the Metro" is constructed like a biblical proverb. . . . Compare [it with]:

> Deep waters
> The words of a man's mouth (Prov. 18:4).

> A gold ring in a snout of a pig
> A lovely woman lacking discretion (Prov. 11:22).

Such simple juxtaposition lies at the base of all biblical metaphor. The juxtaposition of the two things is not an artistic rhetorical embellishment of something already understood. Proverb formation is a process of discovery: man listens and looks "to discover whether in the tangle of events something like conformity to law, an order, cannot be here and there discerned." [Gerhard von Rad. *Old Testament Theology*, 1962, I, 418]. The actual juxtaposing of words by a proverb-maker is, therefore, as [Hans-Jürgen] Hermission observes, "not primarily an illustration of an insight, but a *winning* of an insight" [*Studien zur israelitischen Spruchweisheit*, 1968, p. 150].

Many proverbs are made up of more complex juxtaposing. Two-line proverbs with each line made up of two items are especially common. The two lines form various kinds of parallelism as in poetry generally (see Prov. 10:11; 25:13). A favorite type of juxtaposition (frequently as emblematic parallelism) sets a human action or behavioral characteristic alongside some phenomenon in nature: "The north wind brings forth rain; / And a backbiting tongue, angry looks" (25:23); "Like clouds and wind without rain / Is a man who boasts of a gift he does not give" (25:14). A few proverbs cluster together three or four items in order to make one point: "A crucible for silver / A furnace for gold / the Lord for testing the heart" (Prov. 17:3; cf. 26:1, 21). That form, called a *priamel*, sets forth a series of concrete images in order to say something about the final item in the series.

The nouns and nominal forms that make up a proverb keep the elements of a proverb discrete and unrelated. Each thing remains separated syntactically. A subject may be viewed from more than one angle, but it is not unified into a larger vision. In contrast to biblical stories, which are connected into larger and larger narrative patterns until they subsume the whole of existence in one grand narrative from creation to the eschaton, proverbs remain independent of one another.

Nevertheless, proverbs are capable of a certain kind of generalization without losing their specific concreteness. Consider the following proverb (not from the Bible) which arose from observing the drinking habits of a horse: "You can lead a horse to water, but you can't make him drink." Without losing its specific references to horses and their drinking habits, this proverb can be extended to many different situations, none of which involves horses or their drinking. The proverb-maker observes a specific commonplace incident and creates his aphorism, but he sees through the specific incident to a fundamental relationship common to that one and many others. Relationships between concrete references then gain the potential for becoming metaphoric images applicable to a variety of situations. The following proverbs make certain observations about honey:

> If you have found honey, eat only enough for you,
> lest you be sated with it and vomit it. —Prov. 25:16

> He who is sated loathes honey,
> but to one who is hungry everything bitter is sweet. —Prov. 27:7

The concrete images of honey, desirability, fullness, and emptiness are juxtaposed in such a way as to maximize their metaphoric potential, to lay bare certain structural relationships.

Proverbs thus discover order and make new connections in the tangle of events that make up human existence, but their form resists the construction of one grand vision.

Leonard L. Thompson. *Introducing Biblical Literature* (Englewood Cliffs, N.J., Prentice-Hall, 1978), pp. 163–65

PSALMS

And may not I presume a little further to show the reasonableness of this word *vates*, and say that the holy David's Psalms are a divine poem? If I do, I shall not do it without the testimony of great learned men, both ancient and modern. But even the name of Psalms will speak for me, which, being interpreted, is nothing but Songs; then, that it is fully written in metre, as all learned Hebricians agree, although the rules be not yet fully found; lastly and principally, his handling his prophecy, which is merely poetical. For what else is the awaking his musical instruments, the often and free changing of persons, his notable prosopopoeias, when he maketh you, as it were, see God coming in His majesty, his telling of the beasts' joyfulness and hills' leaping [cf. Ps. 114:4], but a heavenly poesy, wherein almost he showeth himself a passionate lover of that unspeakable and everlasting beauty to be seen by the eyes of the mind, only cleared by faith? But truly now having named him, I fear I seem to profane that holy name, applying it to poetry, which is among us thrown down to so ridiculous an estimation. But they that with quiet judgments will look a little deeper into it, shall find the end and working of it such as, being rightly applied, deserveth not to be scourged out of the church of God. [1595]

Sir Philip Sidney. *The Defense of Poesy.* Ed. by Albert S. Cook (Boston, Ginn, 1890), p. 6

As the *Psalmes* are excellent in regard of the *Author* and *Matter* of them; so, are they also in respect of their *Forme*. For, they are in *Verse*, & *Verse* of sundry kinds; wherein there is also greater varietie of expression, then can be found in any one volume of *Poesie*, whether you have respect to the nature of the *Poesie*, as it is *Heroicall*, Tragicall, Lyricall, & such like; or, to his manner of setting forth those things he purposeth: which is some time by way of complaint, some time petitionarily, some time in one fashion, and some time in an other; as I have alreadie showne you in one of the Chapters aforegoing. And, in my opinion, it addeth somewhat to their dignitie, that they doe by a sweete and extraordinary kind of speaking, seeke to ravish the minde with the love of God; and through the delicate Harmony of words, so allure men unto his praises, that, notwithstanding the tediousnesse which flesh and blood findeth in that exercise, they are by degrees wont to doe it with some good measure of chearefulnesse. Yea, the Prophet hath so mixed his wholesome precepts, and those necessary doctrines which seeme austere to carnall men, with the pleasing Harmony of *Numbers*, that they are received with much better attention.

George Wither. *A Preparation to the Psalter* (London, Printed by N. Okes, 1619), p. 127

In order to feel the beauty even of the finest Psalms, we must transport ourselves into the age, in which they were written, and return to its simplicity of feeling. As most of the Psalms are prayers, so that childlike submission of the heart is necessary to the proper use of them, which the Orientals require in their religious ceremonies and prayers, that silent admiration of God and his works, which sometimes rises into rapture, and sometimes sinks the mind to the deepest abasement. The song hurries from thought to thought, as from mountain to mountain. It touches the springs of emotion rapidly but deeply, and is fond of repeating the impression. It paints its objects only by rapid sketches. All lyric poetry, in which pastoral innocence and rural sentiments prevail, requires a calm and quiet mind; its beauties can produce no effect upon a sophisticated and scoffing one. As the heaven pictures itself only in the clear calm sea, so we see the gentle wave of emotion describe its circles only in the tranquil soul. [1783]

Johann Gottfried von Herder. *The Spirit of Hebrew Poetry*. Vol. II. Tr. from the German by James Marsh (Burlington, Vt., Edward Smith, 1833), pp. 245–46

But there is no more wonderful poetry of the emotional order than the psalms of David and his compeers relating to their own trials and agonies, their loves and hates and adoration. As we agonize and triumph with a supreme lyrical nature, its egoism becomes holy and sublime. The stress of human feeling is intense in such poetry as that of the sixth Psalm, where the lyrist is weary with groaning, and waters the couch with his tears, exclaiming, "But thou, O Lord, how long?" and that of the thirteenth, when he laments: "How long wilt thou forget me, O Lord? Forever?" and in successive personal psalms wherein the singer, whether David or another, avows his trust in the Deity, praying above all to overcome his enemies and to have his greatness increased. These petitions, of course, do not reach the lyrical splendor of the psalms of praise and worship: "The heavens declare the glory of God" [19], "The earth is the Lord's and the fulness thereof" [24]; and those of Moses—"He that dwelleth in the secret place of the Most High" [91], and its immediate successors. But the Hebrew, in those strains where he communes with God alone, other protectors having failed him, is at the climax of emotional song.

Modern self-expression is not so direct and simple. We doubt the passion of one who wears his heart upon his sleeve. The naïveté of the Davidic lyre is beyond question, and so is the superb unrestraint of the Hebrew prophecy and paeans. We feel the stress of human nature in its articulate moods. This gives to the poetry of the Scriptures an attribute possessed only by the most creative and impersonal literature of other tongues,—that of universality. Again, it was all designed for music, by the poets of a musical race; and the psalms were arranged by the first composers,—the leaders of the royal choir. It retains forever the fresh tone of an epoch when lyrical composition was the normal form of expression. Then its rhythm is free, unrestrained, in extreme opposition to that of classical and modern verse, relying merely upon antiphony, alliteration, and parallelism. Technical abandon, allied with directness of conception and faithful revelation of human life, makes for universality; makes of the Hebrew Scriptures a Bible, a world's book that can be translated into all tongues with surpassing effect, notably into a language almost as direct and elemental as its own, that of our Anglo-Saxons in its Jacobean strength and clarity.

> Edmund C. Stedman. *The Nature and Elements of Poetry* (Boston, Houghton Mifflin, 1895), pp. 84–85

But, in spite of this double loss, in the passage from verse to prose, and from Hebrew to English, the poetry of the Psalms is so real and vital and imperishable that every reader feels its beauty and power.

It retains but one outward element of poetic form. This is that balancing of the parts of a sentence, one against another, to which Bishop Lowth first gave the familiar name of "parallelism." The effect of this simple artifice, learned from Nature herself, is singularly pleasant and powerful. It is the rise and fall of the fountain, the ebb and flow of the tide, tone and overtone of the chiming bell. The twofold utterance seems to bear the thought onward like the wings of a bird. A German writer compares it very exquisitely to "the heaving and sinking of the troubled heart." . . .

The Psalms are rightly called lyrics because they are concerned with the immediate and imaginative expression of real feeling. It is the personal and emotional note that predominates. They are inward, confessional, intense; outpourings of the quickened spirit; self-revelations of the heart. . . .

But the Psalms breathe a spirit of human fellowship even when they are most intensely personal. The poet rejoices or mourns, in solitude it may be, but not alone. He is one of the people. He is conscious always of the ties that bind him to his brother men. Compare the intense selfishness of the modern hymn: "I can but perish if I go; / I am resolved to try; / For if I stay away, I know / I shall forever die," with the generous penitence of the Fifty-first Psalm: "Then will I teach transgressors thy ways; / And sinners shall be converted unto thee." . . .

We must recognize the varying poetic quality of the Psalms. There are some, like the Twenty-seventh, the Forty-second, the Forty-sixth, the Sixty-third, the Ninety-first, the Ninety-sixth, the One Hundred and Third, the One Hundred and Thirty-ninth, which are among the noblest poems of the world. Others move on a lower level, and show the traces of effort and constraint. There are also manifest alterations and interpolations, which are not always improvements. . . .

But the most essential thing in the appreciation of the poetry of the Psalms is the recognition of the three great qualities which distinguish it, and are evidences, not only of sublime genius, but also of spiritual inspiration. The first of these is the deep and genuine love of nature. . . . [In it] they see and hear the handwriting and the voice of God. It is his presence that makes the world sublime and beautiful. The direct, piercing, elevating sense of his presence simplifies, enlarges, and ennobles their style, and makes it different from other nature-poetry. They never lose themselves, like Theocritus and Wordsworth and Shelley and Tennyson, in the contemplation and description of natural beauty. They see it, but they always sweep swiftly beyond it. Compare, for example, a modern versified translation ["An Ode," by Joseph Addison] with the Psalm itself: "The spacious firmament on high, / With all the blue ethereal sky / And spangled heavens, a shining frame, / Their Great Original proclaim." Addison's descriptive epithets betray a conscious effort to make a splendid picture. But the psalmist felt no need of this; a larger impulse lifted him at once into "the grand style": "The heavens declare the glory of God; / And the firmament sheweth his handiwork" [Ps. 19:1]. The second quality of the poetry of the Psalms is their passionate sense of the beauty of holiness. Keats was undoubtedly right in his suggestion that the poet must always see truth in the form of beauty. . . . The third quality of the Psalms is their intense joy in God.

Henry Van Dyke. In The Bible as Literature, by Richard
G. Moulton et al. (New York, Crowell, 1896), pp. 94,
96–101

There is religious poetry among other nations—often far surpassing that of Israel in sustained reflection on the mysteries of life, and dramatic representations of the conflict of the individual with the inexorable decrees of fate—but in no other religious literature do we find ourselves in such close and intimate touch with God. The poets of Greece and Babylonia "feel after God." To the pure-eyed seers of Israel He was as luminously self-evident a Being as their own selves. . . . And this vital contact with God it is which gives that literature its perennial freshness and inspiration. We may know more of the Eternal than even the loftiest souls in Israel. But such was the immediacy of their feeling of God, and their power to express that feeling, that their lyrical utterances remain the classics of devotion. The Christian world still gives voice to its faith and hope and joy in God through the rapturous strains of the "sweet singers of Israel." And the best of our hymns have caught their glow at this altar.

Of this distinctively religious poetry of Israel the finest gems are found in the Psalter, which has been aptly described as "the heart of the Bible" [Martin Luther, *Preface to the Psalter*, 1528]. . . .

The literary quality of the Psalter varies with its mood. There are utterances of gloom and depression that hardly rise from the depths. And many of the later Psalms are stiff and stereotyped in expression, often mere cantos from older songs. In general, the language is simple and natural; for the Psalms represent mainly the feelings of the common worshipper. But when inspired by devout imagination or holy wrath, they are lit up by the glow of genuine poetry. The more lyrical parts of the Psalter—*e.g.* the many-toned "Psalms of David," the joyful Pilgrim Songs, and the lofty patriotic odes of Asaph and the "sons of Korah"—are alive with spiritual freshness, vigour and fire, and radiant with colour and imagery. Even the conventional notes of the later Books, the "new songs" and Hallelujahs which proclaim the righteous reign of Jahweh, are sustained on a plane of calm dignity and majesty that no other religious song approaches.

Alex. R. Gordon. *The Poets of the Old Testament* (New York, Hodder and Stoughton, 1912), pp. 97–98, 118

The one art in which they excelled sprang from and in turn laid hold on the mind of the common people. It was the art of sacred lyric poetry, which when it became steady and self-conscious took the names by which we know it—for the instrumental specification of *mizmor* is exactly paralleled by lyric (*lurikos*), "for the lyre"; and "praises," being the uprise of the heart to God, are the most buoyant and heartfelt subject matter for such expression. In a word, the Psalms embody the thoughts and feelings that the nation through all its history could sing; that is, put into the most spontaneous form of expression. How truly these lyrics give voice to the deep music of human nature is evident in the fact that the Book of Psalms has become, by translation or virtual paraphrase, the hymn book of a whole world. To say that these lyrics are the Hebrew *religious* poetry—as if they must needs be separated from poems of other sentiment, "And lovers' songs be turned to holy psalms,"—is in fact no differentiation except in modern estimate. Secular and religious were not dissociated in ancient thought or emotion; all was religious among people who lived in the conscious presence of a personal and accessible God.

John F. Genung. *A Guidebook to the Biblical Literature* (Boston, Ginn, 1919), pp. 433–34

A Psalm is a didactic lyric; the singer has had experiences and he expresses these, addressing Jehovah, in a lyric outburst. But he does so with a didactic purpose; he has learned in suffering and now he would teach others in song. But in this Song of David [Ps. 18] there are differences. The psalmist, in the nature of the case, is humble towards his God; he has been disciplined and he knows it; it is his purpose to show it. David praises, thanks and glorifies Jehovah, but he is not in the least humble about it. It all goes very subtly to glorify David. Jehovah, it is true, has stooped to him and magnified him, but David has done his part. He has been loyal to Jehovah, blameless, clean of hands; he knows that and he tells Jehovah that. The two of them, Jehovah and David, are apart by themselves, holding together, almost one might say against the rest of the world. Jehovah meets people as they meet Him; he has done all these things for David, with David, because of David's attitude to Him. It is all so simple and naive that we hardly notice the tremendous assurance of it. It is great religious poetry, but it is also utterly unregenerate. It holds possibilities for future development, but there is not a scrap of new-heart nonsense about David himself. He is a perfectly self-satisfied realist; with Jehovah he can meet the world. He has, in fact, so met it.

So much may be said for the spirit of the song. As to the language and form there are similar resemblances and differences. The Psalms tend to be abstract in expression, vague, even trite. When they use concrete words and phrases they are apt to give the impression that these are in a conventional language, are clichés. The words were alive once; now they are dead. We know exactly the same thing in the language of our hymns. But the words in the song of David are concrete throughout and alive throughout. It is as though he were using them in this way for the first time. Perhaps he was. But certainly he was putting on them the stamp of the great poet, making them look as though they were so used for the first time. And the same thing holds of the form, especially of the relation of the verses one to another. In that respect the Psalms are almost always formless; the verses do not link each with the other. If we were given the verses of a Psalm on separate slips of paper we could not possibly rearrange them in their original order. There are no links. But in this song of David's, verse with verse is linked; the verses can be paragraphed and the sequence of ideas traced and fixed.

So, at every point—spirit, language, structure—this song is original and the later Psalms show conventional imitation. And this leaves us with the question, Are there any other Davidic songs in the Psalter?—a question to which no absolute answer is possible. But it is quite safe to say that the only even approximate test must be this of reality, originality, vitality.

Duncan B. MacDonald. The Hebrew Literary Genius
(Princeton, N.J., Princeton University Press, 1933),
pp. 48–49

Most emphatically the Psalms must be read as poems; as lyrics, with all the licenses and all the formalities, the hyperboles, the emotional rather than logical connections, which are proper to lyrical poetry. They must be read as poems if they are to be understood; no less than French must be read as French or English as English. Otherwise we shall miss what is in them and think we see what is not.

Their chief formal characteristic, the most obvious element of pattern, is fortunately one that survives in translation. Most readers will know that I mean what the scholars call "parallelism"; that is, the practice of saying the same thing twice in different words. A perfect example is "He that dwelleth in heaven shall laugh them to scorn: the Lord shall have them in derision" (2:4). . . . In reality it is a very pure example of what all pattern, and therefore all art, involves. The principle of art has been defined by someone as "the same in the other." . . . "Parallelism" is the characteristically Hebrew form of the same in the other, but it occurs in many English poets too: for example, in [Christopher] Marlowe's "Cut is the branch that might have grown full straight / And burned is Apollo's laurel bough" [*Doctor Faustus*, Act 5, 5320–21]. . . . Of course, the parallelism is often partially concealed on purpose (as the balances between masses in a picture may be something far subtler than complete symmetry). And of course other and more complex patterns may be worked in across it, as in Psalm 119, or in 107 with its refrain.

C. S. Lewis. Reflections on the Psalms (New York, Harcourt, Brace, 1958), pp. 3–4

As a matter of fact, such exceptions as Psalms 73 and 49 with the other cases of the "I" of the poet, confirm the observation that the psalm writer is most of all himself and most genuine when he hides wholly behind the worshipper and enters completely into him and his situation, whether the worshipper represents the congregation (the people) or the individual Israelite in the typical situation of sorrow or joy.

When the psalmist then calls in agony out of the deep, or jubilantly gives thanks for experienced deliverance, he is the worshipper. His psalm is completely personal and gives expression to his innermost ego, precisely because he is a representative of a corporate personality, because his innermost soul is united with the congregation and its individual members in sorrow and joy. He knows them, lives in them, and knows what they feel, in their response to the demands of the situation. He feels the same, has perhaps many times felt it on his own behalf. Therefore he reaches the height of his artistic ability when he feels that now it is the soul of Israel and that of the typical Israelite that vibrates in his lamentation or his praise. For this reason we feel the personal heart-beat of this cult poetry not less strongly in the sad melancholic "we-psalm," Psalm 90, than in the mighty expressions of God's omniscience in Psalm 139. In both cases the poet has identified himself with another, in Psalm 90 with the congregation, in Psalm 139 with someone suffering from illness or struck by another disaster. Thereby he has found the most genuine expressions for his own personality.

Sigmund Mowinckel. The Psalms in Israel's Worship Vol. II. Tr. by D. R. ap-Thomas (Oxford, England, Basil Blackwell, 1962), p. 140

The Hebrew Psalms articulate in simple primary images the human need for confession, prayer, and trust. As a literary document, they provide the prototype for that special kind of subjective poetry in which the soul addresses itself to a personal God who deals with His creatures in love and justice. He is represented as the Shepherd (23, 80), the confidence of the everlasting hills (87, 121); at the same time, he is seated in the heavens (2), and by the voice of his thunder he causes the hills to skip like rams (114). He is the great water-giver who "causes the grass to grow for the cattle and herb for the service of man" (104), and by analogy, he is also the giver of spiritual water "satisfying the longing soul, and filling the hungry soul with goodness" (107). He appoints the light of the sun (104), and by the same token, he "sows" light for the righteous and gladness for the upright in heart (97).

The Psalms are often spoken of as lyric poetry, and compared to the lyric poetry of other nations, for instance that of England in the Romantic Period. Such a definition has more value than most definitions of this kind. The Hebrew poet singing a song of praise, "Sing unto the Lord a new song"—is engaged in just that spontaneous overflow of powerful and melodious feeling which we are told is the essence of lyrical poetry. But it is necessary to bear in mind a certain phenomenological difference between the lyric poems of the English romantics and the typical Hebrew Psalm: the former is essentially monologue, the latter is essentially dialogue. The *Sitz im Leben* of the romantic poet, is symbolized by the lines of Wordsworth,

> Behold her, single in the field,
> Yon solitary Highland Lass!
> Reaping and singing by herself;
> Stop here or gently pass! ["The Solitary Reaper"]

The solitary reaper does not answer nor does the poet address her; on the contrary, she is herself the symbol of the poet's own essential isolation. The romantic poet will often commune with Nature, but this is communion, not dialogue. There is blending, the abolition of separateness—again Wordsworth's stoical pantheism is typical of this tendency—but there is no distinct confrontation of self with an autonomous outer reality; there is no *dramatic* encounter. This is perhaps the reason why the romantic poets in England were unable to write true drama. Byron's *Cain* is, like his lyrics, essentially monologue.

Now, the Psalms are typically a song for two voices addressing one another in the intimate drama of the covenant-relation, the covenant that is to say as the bond between the soul and God. They are not so much the spontaneous overflow of powerful feelings as, to use the title of one of [Joseph] Hall's later devotional tracts, a *Susurrium cum Deo*. In such whispered dialogue the human speaker does not fill the overflowing vale with his sole unaccompanied voice, nor does he abandon his personality by a contemplative act of mystical self-effacement. He and his divine interlocutor remain confronting each other to the last, separate, and yet held together by indestructible bonds:

> O Lord, my God, I cried out to thee,
> And thou hast healed me [Ps.30:2].

Both the cry and the answered consolation are made real in the poem. There is a call and a response, giving to the poem a dramatic movement. A Psalm such as 61 or 130 will begin "out of the depths" of trouble and hopelessness and as a result of the exchange of vows, or of prayer and acceptance, which the Psalm celebrates, it will end on a note of comfort and assurance. This is typical movement. In this respect it is an active rather than a contemplative type of lyric poetry; it involves a movement through dialogue from one position to another.

Harold Fisch. Jerusalem and Albion (New York, Schocken, 1964), pp. 58–59

The essential feature of the dynamic psalm consists in the fact that a change of mood is going on within the poet, a change that is reflected in the psalm. What happens is that the poet begins the psalm in the mood of sadness, depression, despair, or fear; usually, in fact, it is a blend of these various moods. At the end of the psalm his mood has changed; it is one of hope, faith, confidence. Often it seems as if the poet who composed the end of the psalm was a different man from the one who composed the beginning. Indeed, they are different, yet they are the same person. What happens is that a change has occurred within the Psalmist during the composition of the psalm. He has been transformed; or better, he has transformed himself from a despairing and anxious man into one of hope and faith.

The dynamic psalm shows the inner struggle within the poet to rid himself of despair and to arrive at hope. Thus we find that the movement takes on the following form: it starts in some despair, changes to some hope, then returns to deeper despair, and reacts with more hope; eventually it arrives at the very deepest despair and only at this point is the despair really overcome. The mood has definitely changed, and in the following verses of the psalm there is no experience of despair, except as a receding memory. The psalm is the expression of a struggle, a movement, an active process occurring within a person; while in the one-mood psalm the poet wants to confirm an existing feeling, in the dynamic psalm his aim is to transform himself in the process of saying the psalm. The psalm is a document of the victory of hope over despair. It also documents an important fact: that only when the frightened, despairing person experiences the full depth of his despair can he "return," can he liberate himself from despair and achieve hope. As long as the full despair has not been experienced, he cannot really overcome it. He may overcome it for a while, only to fall back into it after a time. The cure of despair is not achieved by encouraging thoughts, not even by feeling *part* of the despair; it is achieved by the seeming paradox that despair *can be overcome only if it has been fully experienced.* . . .

Some examples of dynamic psalms [are the 6th, 8th, 90th, and 22nd, perhaps the most beautiful of this group].

The movement of the dynamic psalms has continued in the later Jewish tradition and found its most distinct and beautiful expression two thousand years later in the songs of Hasidism. Many of these songs, which were usually sung by the

Hasidic master together with his adherents on Saturday afternoons, have exactly the same inner movement as the dynamic psalms of the Bible. They begin in a mood of sadness and end in enthusiastic joy; this movement is, in fact, often repeated in the following way: first, the song itself has a movement which leads from sadness to joy. Secondly, the song is repeated many times, and each repetition is more joyful than the previous one; at the end, the *whole* song has become a hymn of joy. A good example is the famous "Rav's Nigun," the song created by R. Schneur Zalman, the founder of the Habad branch of Hasidim. It consists of three movements, beginning with sadness and ending in joy.

Erich Fromm. *You Shall Be as Gods* (New York, Holt, Rinehart and Winston, 1966), pp. 207–8, 220–21

All that is clear is that this vast and varied collection, to which there seems no parallel in any other literature, took the name of David from its chief writer, embodying Psalms 1 and 2 as a preface or introduction, and amalgamated with Levitical and Temple Songs. . . . [p. 125] We have thus a collection of lyrics, in which are embedded from time to time fragments of epic and historical elements, adapted through a very long period of liturgical uses. Their scale of emotions is not a wide one. Most of them concentrate on the attributes of God in all His aspects; but mainly on His righteousness. The complaints against Him, and they are many, do not doubt His omnipotence, but cry out against the slow, sometimes infinitely deferred, processes of His justice. That concern may be national, as in the lamentations of the exiles; or social, as in the stress on the miseries of the poor; or personal, as in the outcries of the poet in depression, sickness, poverty. Much of this outcry is concerned with the problem of Job: Why do the wicked flourish? The answers oscillate between assurance and ultimate justice, and seeming despair. . . . [p. 125]

The *righteous* and the *wicked* are set in a continuous antithetical conflict, which is expressed in a wide range of imagery. . . . "I have seen the wicked in great power, and spreading himself like a green bay tree" (37:35), but also "The righteous shall flourish like a palm-tree: he shall grow like a cedar in Lebanon" (92:12). . . . [pp. 125–26]

The characteristics of the imagery of the Psalms are commensurate with the imaginative pressure of such lyrics. They range over a narrow but intense field. The tree by the waters, the chaff on the threshing-floor; the weapons of war, sword, spear and buckler; the snares of nets, and the concealed pit in which his enemies seek to entrap the poet. God's justice is like sudden arrows. . . . [p. 127]

The Psalms, like Job, draw on the wonders of nature with a peculiar felicity and freshness; which comes, as always in poetry, from the sense of engagement with a living world. . . . "He shall come down like rain upon the mown grass: as showers that water the earth" (72:6), which recalls so vividly the intricate and lovely scents of the grass and the reviving land. . . . [pp. 127–28]

Perhaps, those Psalms which are of most concern today—always within the terms which I have postulated—are those which communicate, with vitality and simplicity, the poet's intense joy in nature. . . . "As the hart panteth after the water brooks . . ."(42); "God is our refuge and strength . . ." (46); . . . "He that dwelleth in the secret place of the most High" (91); Bless the Lord, O my Soul . . ." (104). We should include the Love Song or Epithalamium (45) for its exquisite imagery; together with the incomparable nineteenth and twenty-third. [pp. 141–42]

T. R. Henn. *The Bible as Literature* (New York, Oxford University Press, 1970)

One of the characteristics of the psalms is the intensity and range of the feelings they express. There are no drab grays and pale pinks and mauves. Black and white and flaming red and gleaming green are the colors on the canvas. There are no inhibitions about expressing the deepest (and sometimes most questionable) feelings. To make the sudden transition from praising the perfection of the visible world to pleading that certain unnamed persons be evicted from it is not too startling, if one takes into account the psychological and emotional candor of these ancient poets and the people whose innermost longing and hatred they expressed. They take human feeling as it is, and do not try to prettify it. The Book of Psalms is a vast repository of accurate insights into what it means to be a human being. There are the heights and the depths, the glories and the horrors; hope and despair, joy and desolation. To read the psalms is to explore one's own hidden life and feelings.

The psalms are part of the world's greatest inheritance of enduring poetry. In these poems, humanity is set in the midst of a world that is unmistakably real and solid. It is described in ways that speak not merely to the mind but to all the senses. But it does more than depict the outer world; it explores the inner one. We are led psalm by psalm, line by line, to join hands across the gulf of time with the authors of these poems. What they were is what we are.

Chad Walsh. *A Rich Feast: Encountering the Bible* (New York, Harper & Row, 1981), pp. 12–13

Rape of Tamar. *See* Tamar, Rape of

RUTH

Ruth the gleaner ranks among the most charming characters of sacred history, and the book that treats of her is one of the most poetic in the Bible. . . . A tale that is so bathed in the richness of poesy is, of course, no "history" in the strict sense but rather a poetic tale. Moreover, historical writing of the ancient period has as its subject state events, kings, and public figures; folk tradition, however, takes pleasure in telling about the small events that take place in the bosom of the family. And a historian is unable to tell about the nocturnal scene between Ruth and Boaz—a scene that took place in secret and that was to remain secret—because it cannot be known credibly and reliably. Furthermore, the narrator specifically differentiates his own period from the time when the story took place ("in former time," 4:7); he does not claim to be a contemporary of that "former time." . . .

If there is any occasion to discuss the art of narration in the Old Testament, it is surely to be found in the story of Ruth. We may distinguish among the Hebrew tales two kinds that are clearly recognizable by the extent of their range: either quite short ones, as, for example, the story of the Tower of Babel, which comprises only a few verses and hence narrates the entire action with the greatest possible brevity; or, besides those, more detailed stories that stem from a later, more developed practice of the art, and that in part take in a very wide expanse. An example of that is the Joseph legend. The story of Ruth belongs very clearly to this second category. Very few and simple events are here narrated, events that the narrator—if he had wished—could have reported in few words. Thus one sees that what is important to him is not so much the actual reporting of information but rather the depiction of the situations and the delineation of the characters.

Further, whereas the old practice of the art reports essentially only facts and presents to the reader's view what can be graphically perceived, but is very sparing where speech is concerned, here the bulk of the book is filled with direct speech. Through such an extensive use of conversation there ultimately develops a new genre that we may best term "novella." The Italian novellas of the Renaissance, source of the modern ones, also originated in fairy tales or legendary material extensively elaborated upon in the interest of character description. One is therefore justified in speaking of a Ruth novella. Here too the purpose of the many speeches is clearly that of character exposition. Occasionally the author tells indirectly through such speeches how he himself views the events. Thus Boaz praises Ruth's loyalty, and thus the people of the village in the end praise Ruth, Boaz, and Naomi—somewhat like the chorus in Greek tragedy that pronounces the public judgment. One must note such passages in order not to miss the ancient understanding of the story. The narrator does not inject his own views, and in the older stories of the Old Testament they are not to be found at all.

Goethe aptly characterizes the tale according to its nature as an "idyl." Simple peasant conditions are in the background—"the fragrance of the field that Yahweh has blessed" is wafted thence to us. . . .

The story moves forward slowly, peacefully, and in a quiet way. It has no cognizance of evil people; we are well disposed to all the chief characters, and even the minor characters Orpah and the kinsman are only less admirable, not wicked. . . . Yet the tale has a few powerful notes as well, to keep it from melting away in emotion. Naomi is an intelligent woman and knows that feminine charm, placed in the right light, conquers the heart of even a serious man. And Boaz would like to possess not only the woman but the field as well. . . .

At the same time, the story is of a religious nature. To be sure, God does not intervene in the action at any specific place; no miracle occurs, and everything runs its course naturally; nevertheless, the Deity holds the strings in his hand and "rules well over everything." Not without pleasure will one see how the thought that man must do his part as well is combined with this faith in God's rule. Ruth obtains her new husband through Naomi's womanly sagacity and through God's grace! The tale of Ruth shares with the saga of the wooing of Rebecca and especially with the Joseph story this faith in providence as it is brought to bear in particular upon family history. Similar in tone also are the tale of Samuel's birth and the tale of Tobias. These beautiful stories reveal to us how tender was the family life Israel led in ancient and in later times.

> Hermann Gunkel. *Reden und Aufsätze* (Göttingen,
> Vandenhoeck & Ruprecht, 1913), pp. 65, 84–87†

I suppose the best pastorals in secular literature are the first, those by Theocritus. Yet even the Sicilian masterpieces are inferior to a specimen found in the Bible, the book of Ruth. This wonderful idyl of the farm, told in an impeccable style by the old Hebrew writer, must forever remain supreme and unapproachable. The economy of words is striking; in the narrative of David's great-grandmother, there is not a superfluous sentence. The suppressed passion in this tale has been felt by all intelligent readers; and Keats, with his genius for beauty of feeling and beauty of tone, has arrested the lonely figure of Ruth in the grain-field, where she stands in immortal loveliness like the images on the Greek urn.

> Perhaps the self-same song that found a path
> Through the sad heart of Ruth, when sick for home,
> She stood in tears amid the alien corn.
>
> ["Ode to a Nightingale"]

> William Lyon Phelps. *Reading the Bible* (New York,
> Macmillan, 1919), p. 31

The Book of Ruth is one of the best short stories ever written. Originally propaganda, the purpose is so concealed in the perfection of its art and the art is so exquisite that it survives for quite other reasons than the one which caused it to be written. It is a plea for tolerance. . . . Was ever social bigotry more gently or more effectively rebuked? The story is what Goethe called it, "the daintiest of love idyls," but the love is not between a man and a woman, but between a mother-in-law and her daughter-in-law!—a theme which has certainly not been overworked in fiction. Notice its further peculiarities: it is a story without a villain, there is no analysis of character, no description of scenery, and the moral teaching is brought out by the whole action of the narrative and not appended.

The atmosphere is golden and serene, yet dramatic situations are not wanting. Only an artist of elevated spirit could have handled the scene of Ruth's midnight talk with Boaz so delicately. How suggestively and through how many chapters would one of our sex-drenched novels have treated the situation! There is one passage in the tale that is immortal through its sheer perfection of phrase:

> Intreat me not to leave thee, and to return from following after thee; for whither thou goest, I will go; and where thou lodgest, I will lodge; thy people shall be my people, and thy God my God; where thou diest will I die, and there will I be buried; the Lord do so to me and more also, if aught but death part thee and me (1:16–17).

Here prose certainly has the flame and the form of poetry. It has been suggested that this is a quotation from an ancient folk-song. But if so, the author was a true poet. It is not necessary to make the assumption, for the fine mind that wrote the prose narrative was quite capable of attaining this level of expression. We have the parallelism of poetry, also its rhythmic movement. The translators have not only preserved these, but they have perfected the balance of the sentences. Notice in the first half the two "I will's," changed in the last half to "will I," thus perfecting the form to fit the nobility of the thought.

Charles A. Dinsmore. *The English Bible as Literature*
(Boston, Houghton Mifflin, 1931), pp. 251–52

This restrained exultation of whispering hearts is what in this simple ancient story has charmed generations—and not just in the dramatic moments. There is charm here to plain nuance, to discourse that makes no pretensions to fancy speech. The nobility in the voices turns the simplest remark to poetry, to something immutable and unalterable. From the first encounter between Boaz and Ruth, when Ruth's grace touches this high-born citizen and he encourages her with the counsel, "Do not go to glean in the field of another, do not pass from this one" [2:8], to the burning scene of the innocent love story, when the man of the threshing-floor trembles at the happiness that has come to him in his unconsciousness in the dark of night, fussing over and praising this woman who has done a soldier a good turn . . . up until the entire practical discussion, when he marches steadily toward his goal and takes on a cool exterior in doing fair business, up until he wins this jewel—every utterance here is saturated with the same clarity of nuance and the same restraint of voice that constitute the charm of the biblical epic; it is as though precisely by means of economy in speech this hearty fullness is achieved, a fullness unattainable by the glaring hexameters of Homer, which use speech profusely, which enjoy speech for its own sake. . . .

Someone has said that the vitality of a literary work can be discerned in the passion to imitate it that it arouses in us. Whenever in the reading of a book there rises in us an impulse to write something similar, it is a sign that it has not lost its vibrancy and its growth has not abated.

From this standpoint the Scroll of Ruth is perhaps the most vibrant [part] of the scriptural epic. With all its simplicity, it still stimulates, arouses the action and the desire to write "something similar." There is in the candor of this little idyl something that charms us more than any mystery. How did it sprout? How was the concision of expression, with such a full content, achieved to such perfection? And how can such a fine composition in general be written—the description of the parting at the Moab border, the return to Bethlehem, the field of harvesters, and the walk to the threshing-floor? Is it not significant that we, who know quite a bit about the art of writing, fail at it, whereas this marvelous artist wrote naïvely and did not omit a thing, every phrase as though it sprouted by itself, without the slightest difficulty of expression—all natural, and yet all bearing the stamp of artistic perfection? . . .

What could be added to what is here narrated in a few laconic verses that exhaust the essence, verses that never yellow, that never age, whose odor never sours? Two women standing on the border of Moab and Judah, alone, bereft, orphaned, who have given up happiness forever, who have nothing left in life but love, their ultimate devotion to each other, are enveloped in such a light that it would almost be a sin to add to it. . . .

There is no doubt that the author of this scroll used the great wisdom of an artist when he opposed to Naomi and Ruth, who are full of heart, the man of restraint, the "nobleman" [Boaz], who could control his emotions. It was also wise that the author did not deny him a certain hint of tenderness, which the reader senses and knows how to appreciate.

> Jacob Fichman. ʿArugot (Jerusalem, Bialik Institute, 1954), pp. 282–86†

The initial impression one receives, even after only a casual reading of the story of Ruth, is that of picturesqueness. Scene after scene flashes its portrait of action upon the screen of the reader's mind with quick effect. Such episodes as the farewell scene in Moab, the arrival at Bethlehem, Ruth's gleaning in the field of Boaz with his corps of male and female harvesters, the dramatic act played out at the threshing-floor, the transaction at the city gate in the presence of the elders, and Naomi's caress of the child born to Ruth and Boaz, are so vivid and realistic that no one has any difficulty in picturing them to himself.

Recall the no less picturesque, though more extended and detailed, story of Joseph. It too has its multiple scenes leading to the unhappy experiences of separation, thence through the long hard lane of slavery to personal advancement and triumph, and finally to a joyful reunion with father and brethren in Egypt. To the empirico-logical mind which thinks in terms of experience and endeavors to transmit its thoughts in living story form, these narratives are like silent movies with colloquial script written beneath the portrayal of each successive event. It must be remembered, however, that the Joseph story concerns primarily a person, and only secondarily reflects the life situation of a family, while the book of Ruth details the experience of a family first, although its three main characters receive significant emphasis on occasion.

Another characteristic of the book of Ruth going hand in hand with its pictur-esqueness is its consciseness. While this is more or less true of all Old Testament stories, this quality appears to be especially focused here. The following state-ments will demonstrate the point. "In the day when the Judges were judging" [1:1] recalls the moving panorama of life sketched in the book of Judges, ampli-fied and illustrated by archaeological exploration. "Orpah kissed her mother-in-law, but Ruth clave unto her" [1:14] describes a touching experience so simply and clearly that details would mar its appeal and detract from its effectiveness. It is doubtful whether the account of any other scene in Ruth, or anywhere else in the Bible, is superior to this one in force, vitality, and pathos. "Is this Naomi?" [1:19] speaks paragraphs to the thoughtful reader. All the changes which time and sorrow had wrought are expressed in this three-word exclamation.

2:7, though the text is not altogether clear, throws a flood of light upon the character of the maiden who was so admirably playing her part in the mainte-nance of the name and family of her husband and her father-in-law. "Blessed be thou of the Lord, my daughter" [3:10] indicates the manifest recognition by Boaz of his duty and right, and his willingness to exercise both on behalf of so just a cause as that which Ruth was pleading by her act at the threshing-floor. "So Boaz took Ruth, and she became his wife" [4:13] pictures the marriage of the couple with its joyous celebration, its blessings, and the glad heart of Naomi who had been so active in arranging the marriage here described. Other expressions in this literary gem are of equal importance in illustrating the principle of conciseness and picturesqueness.

Along with the stylistic features just set forth must be mentioned another, namely, the completeness of the whole story in itself. In spite of its seeming lack of detail, there is an amazingly well-rounded unity of narrative, including every essential necessary to the story and ruthlessly excluding any irrelevancies militat-ing against the purpose and plan of the author.

Jacob M. Myers. *The Linguistic and Literary Form of
the Book of Ruth* (Leiden, Brill, 1955), pp. 4–6

More and more I become convinced that the great key to the reading of Hebraic literature is sensitivity to pattern, and nowhere is response to patterning more im-portant than in Ruth. The whole of chapter 1 is concerned with establishing a dominant pattern for the work, which is first given indirectly in various manifes-tations and then, near the end of the chapter, given overtly. This controlling pat-tern can be stated abstractly as emptiness-fullness. The first example is in verse 1: "there was a *famine in the land*." That is, with respect to physical nature, the land itself, emptiness is dearth and famine, and the implied opposite, of course, is plenty. In verse 3 occurs a second manifestation, again in negative form: "And Elimelech Naomi's husband died; *and she was left*, and her two sons." Here is the same theme on the social level: fullness is the complete and harmonious fam-ily, and emptiness is the loneliness of the widow. In the verse cited, Naomi's de-privation is only partial, and purposely so, for the artist wants the complete desolation two verses on to strike with greater force: "And Mahlon and Chilion died also both of them; and *the woman was left of her two sons and her husband.*" Stricken, Naomi yearns to fulfill completely the pattern she intuitively recognizes by dismissing her daughters-in-law, so that in its exterior appearances her life will reflect her interior state of total emptiness. In this attempt at dismissal appears the third manifestation of the pattern:

> And Naomi said, Turn again, my daughters: why will ye go with me? are there yet any more sons in my womb, that they may be your husbands? Turn again, my daughters, *go your way; for I am too old to have an husband.* If I should say, I have hope, if I should have an husband also to-night, and should also bear sons; Would ye tarry for them till they were grown? (11–13).

Here the theme is seen on a deeper and more personal level, emptiness presented as the barrenness of an old woman as over against the fullness of bearing.

Donald F. Rauber. Journal of Biblical Literature.
March, 1970, p. 29

The story of Ruth is as subdued as the accounts of Samson are raucous. I have wondered if its unknown author were perhaps a woman, for it has a delicacy that seems to me feminine. We should notice, first of all, against a persistent modern theory that no fiction can exist unless it depicts a conflict, that Ruth is devoid of it. Those who speak of the story as a series of vignettes are on the right track, for what takes place in Ruth is the unfolding narration of *subsequent* incidents, rather than *consequent* ones. . . . [pp. 25–26]

The theme of the book is the noble character of the girl, Ruth, who was of alien, disreputably alien, stock. That this should be the theme of a Hebrew book, and the book make its way into Scripture, surely more than overbalances the passages elsewhere which express scorn for and hostility to the Moabites. . . . [p. 31] As to the character study, the girl Ruth is examined with some thoroughness, for we move from the point at which we might suspect her earnestness through to our being shown the full convincing measure of it. What must impress us most of all is the restraint in the narration, in that this quiet little story deals with the potentially explosive matter of the background of the heroine. The story would have lacked all its force had it been about an equally worthy Hebrew girl. The account, then, is of a "convert," whose background rendered her sincerity suspect but whose character emerged as completely beyond reproach, and whose name became linked in tradition with Rachel and Leah, the wives of the Patriarch Jacob.

The story is a simple one in the sense that it is not plotted, nor does it have any ups and downs, nor any dramatic climax. Its appeal lies in the attractiveness of the people, Naomi, Ruth, and Boaz, and of the residents of Bethlehem. Indeed, we are shown an ideal, almost unrealistic, picture of a happy community, peopled by worthy persons, benignly guided by the Deity. [pp. 31–32]

Samuel Sandmel. The Enjoyment of Scripture (New
York, Oxford University Press, 1972)

The very structure which [Hermann] Gunkel described so well—whereby swift strokes of the brush establish the situation in the introduction and in the transitions, while the main scenes move at a much more leisurely pace—is a comprehensive indicator. No words are used that are unnecessary in the introduction, precisely because the pace is so fast, and therefore the hearer of the tale must take cognizance of such an apparently unimportant group of four Hebrew words as "and they dwelt there about ten years." These are ten years of childless marriage, and ten years when property ownership back in Bethlehem can become scrambled, and ten years during which Naomi can reach the age when she can have no more children. But these are ten years which do not require ten words to describe, because that is not where the action must lie.

On the other hand, the scene at the threshing floor and the scene at the city gate need some protraction, for they are full of good-hearted and rather robust suspense. The storyteller gets Ruth to the threshing floor in 3:6, but must have her wait, as it were, while Boaz eats and drinks and has his heart get merry and goes to lie down in the corner of the threshing floor. The hearer is waiting with her; this maneuver is no joke, and it has to be brought off correctly. Likewise, the scene at the city gate is one which is suspenseful. As a whole, this scene, as well as the previous surprise announcement that there even exists a nearer kinsman, is an example of the familiar retarding motif of good storytelling; but, even within that scene at the gate, the lengthy style of the speeches of Boaz serves to draw out the tension.

However, the storyteller is not toying with us. It is important that Boaz get right to this business. While Ruth is talking with her mother-in-law at the end of chapter 3, the storyteller signals a quick pace to Boaz's action by using contemporaneity. I take the beginning of 4:1, *ûvō'az 'ālâ*, as indicative by its word order not only of a change in subject but of a corresponding action to Ruth's departure from the threshing floor.

The timing and tempo of the story, then, are striking evidence of its artistry. [Luis] Alonso-Schökel also calls attention to the way in which precision of detail and color makes for vividness at those moments when vividness is required. Again, there is more to such parts of an Israelite story than just the barely necessary words. Several examples suggest themselves as places where the story's camera eye rests languidly on a momentary vignette. Thus the scene of the leave-taking in Moab where twice the women stop to weep and much must be made of the argument to persuade at least Orpah to stay at home. Thus the splendid portrayal of the little meal at the midday break in the fields, where Ruth is asked to join the others and to dip her morsel in the *homets*—whatever that really is—and receives the special heap of parched grain which is sufficient not only for herself but also for a supply to be taken home to her mother-in-law. There is purpose to all this, as the storyteller evokes the character of the personages and binds them together, but there is just good storytelling also. Consider as another example here the detail of 3:3, where Naomi instructs Ruth in the preparations for her visit to the threshing floor, "Wash yourself, and anoint yourself, and put on your raiment."

Vividness and color are employed where they are most needed, and it is interesting to contrast the instances cited (to which must be added the vivid scene at the city gate) with what might after all be thought of as the whole point of the book—namely, the birth of the baby. Five swift syntactical units and the whole business is over: "And Boaz took Ruth, and she became his wife, and he went in to her, and Yahweh gave her conception, and she bore a son" [4:13]. That's all! This may be the point of all that has gone before, but the fun, the tension, the pathos, the excitement have been in getting the hearer or reader there!

> Edward F. Campbell, Jr. In *Light unto My Path*. Ed. by
> Howard N. Bream et al. (Philadelphia, Temple Univer-
> sity Press, 1974), pp. 94–95

The Scroll of Ruth is the most perfect narrative of the Bible, and its principles of composition are common, more or less, to all the narratives of the Bible. These narratives include a framework of the word of God and its fulfillment, a concentric structure, repetitions of key words and linking words, numerical patterns, wordplays, echo (of preceding tales), and anticipation (of later ones). . . .

Adhering to the principle of preserving the concentric structure, and with special attention to unity of time, place, and character, I would divide the book as follows:

1. *Death and return*—Chapter 1
   A. Ten years of death in Moab ([vv.] 1–6);
   B. Ruth's clinging to Naomi and Orpah's return ([vv.] 7–19a);
   C. Naomi laments her bereavement before the townswomen ([vv.] 19b–22).

2. *In Boaz's field*—Chapter 2
   D. Naomi approves Ruth's plan to glean in fields ([vv.] 1–3);
   E. Ruth finds favor with Boaz ([vv.] 4–18a);
   F. Naomi and Ruth evaluate the meeting ([vv.] 18b–23).

3. *On Boaz's threshing-floor*—Chapter 3
   D. Ruth accepts Naomi's plan to go to the threshing-floor ([vv.] 1–6);
   E. Ruth finds favor with Boaz ([vv.] 7–15);
   F. Naomi and Ruth evaluate the meeting ([vv.] 16–18).

4. *Renewal of life in birth*—Chapter 4
   B. The redemption of Ruth by Boaz and the withdrawal of the unnamed redeemer ([vv.] 1–12);
   C. The townswomen celebrate the birth of Naomi's grandson ([vv.] 13–17);
   A. The birth of ten generations in Israel.

Before us are two designs artfully intertwined, one symmetrical and the other advancing toward its climax. The opening and closing chapters are based upon a symmetrical structure in which the beginning of the opening chapter parallels the end of the closing chapter, and the other chapters match, so that the internal divisions match in all parts (ABC—DEF—DEF—BCA). The first three chapters are parallel to one another in that three-part dialogue appears in the central unit of each of them. The fourth, concluding chapter opens with a unit in which there are eight parts, and proceeds with a gradual constriction of the amount of dialogue until its final disappearance in the last unit. . . .

In its language and themes, the Scroll of Ruth is connected with the books of Genesis, Judges, and Samuel. The approximately fifteen parallels to Genesis 24 prove that the theme of the Scroll is "The Way God Couples the Young Widow with the Bachelor Hero." Ruth's devotion to the family of Elimelech rescues the line of Perez from oblivion in the seventh generation, the one of special significance (Ruth 4:18–21; see Gen. 4:23f. [Lamech the murderer]; 5:21f. [Enoch "for God has taken him"]), and supports the line's continuity up to the birth of David in the tenth generation, to which, too, great significance is attached (Ruth 4:22; see Gen. 5:28f. [Noah]; 11:26 [Abraham]). Like Abraham, Ruth left her native land and her father's house to journey into the unknown (Gen. 12:1; Ruth 2:11). Her refusal to separate from Naomi, claiming that even death would not "separate" them, signifies the reunification of the lines of Lot and Abraham, whose paths "separated" beforehand (Gen. 13:9–11).

Bezalel Porten. Beth Mikra. Jan.–Mar., 1977, pp. 224–25, 227†

Since Hebrew is not the second language of most of the educated world, the verbal virtuosity of the Scroll of Ruth is difficult to demonstrate and the average reader must take it on faith. It is nonetheless a nice irony that the poverty of Hebrew, whose vocabulary is mainly expanded by fusion and vocalic change, can achieve assonance, homophony, and alliteration impossible in English. The Scroll of Ruth pivots, as it were, on four words and inflections thereof: go, stay, return, redeem. Among English poets only Blake, in the *Songs* attains such spareness and simplicity. . . .

Like all biblical stories, this one niether lingers nor moralizes, but records without stridency despair, courage, loyalty, love, and hope. It develops character, builds and resolves tension, and looks both backward and forward, its final verses not so much an ending as a continuation. Of greater formal significance, it is constructed like a sonata, whose central themes of death and restoration are restated and reworked so that form is inseparable from content: the two major melodies or narrative threads, are played on verbal instruments that precisely match and further the action.

The resemblance to a classical sonata is exact. The first half is an exposition of the subject of death (in various forms: of the land, of husband and sons, of a family name), with a transitional passage toward the other theme, restoration; the second half develops the idea of restoration, recapitulates both themes, and adds a coda. The first, third, and fourth chapters—statement and recapitulation—are of similar length; the second chapter, leading to and expanding upon restoration, is longer than the others. Like the same movement in a sonata, it is written andante, is the most richly modulated, and has the most to do. Even so, this whole sonata-narrative is fully orchestrated in the space of eighty-five Hebrew verses, or a six-sonnet sequence with a verse left over.

In a kind of anticipatory counterpoint, Chapter 1 states the major theme of death and couples it with the minor one of return, which heralds restoration. Less forthrightly, but with the insistence of a chord played in the bass, the theme of waiting is inserted, and will recur throughout the book, either opening or closing the succeeding chapters. It mediates between death and restoration. [Rainer Maria] Rilke says in one of the *Duino Elegies* that "staying is nowhere"; here staying or waiting is God-decreed, analogous to prayer, implying acquiescence and belief in the ultimate magnanimity of the Lord. While the great themes of death and restoration can be said to be in the tonic key, the supplementary theme of waiting is in the minor, always pulsing beneath the primary music.

Thus the first chapter uses, repeats, and modifies three of the four words that move the narrative from Bethlehem to Moab and back, that engineer both a marriage and a conversion, and that bring forth a historic child. They went to Moab; they stayed; they returned to Bethlehem. Eight times in twenty-two verses the word "go" or a variation of it appears; once, "stay" (a concept, however, that is reinforced by synonyms); twelve times, "return." In Hebrew a single verb can do the work of several, both by inflection and nuance. Thus the word "restore," besides being one of the two major themes, is also "return," inflected. To the undisturbed root an intensifier is added. Even more subtly, "stay" (more commonly translated "sit" in modern Hebrew) plays upon "return"; the key sounds are identical, approximated in English by the words "sojourn" and "journey." And best of all, perhaps, the Hebrew word for "seven" employs two of the same key letters as "stay," in the same order, and becomes, in Chapter 4, a holy, even an oracular, number.

Evelyn Strouse and Bezalel Porten. Commentary. Feb.,
1979, pp. 63–64

Once it is agreed that Ruth is modeled after a folktale pattern, it becomes possible to draw conclusions that are applicable to any literature of the same genre. As an artistic creation, even when it depends on factual occurrences, the folktale is completely satisfying, for it nurtures no expectation that is ultimately left unfulfilled. From its opening scene, when either "villainy" or "lack" are posed as challenges to the *hero*, the tale progresses on a course that is precharted in the audience's consciousness. No complications are introduced which are left unresolved; no character is given a role that remains ambiguous. *Heroes* find their mates, *villains* meet their fates, *dispatchers* find their ultimate reward, and *donors* fulfill their obligations. It is not surprising, therefore, that as a tale that hews closer to folktale patterns than most Biblical narratives, Ruth has constantly found favor in the eyes of a variegated audience. It is not merely that Ruth is brave and loyal, for other Old Testament heroines are equally valorous; it is not just that Boaz is kinder than other Biblical ancestors; it is not even that Naomi is more deserving of God's ultimate favor than other matriarchs; it is simply that these protagonists fully carry out assignments that were perfected generations before Ruth. Moreover, because a folktale leaves nothing that is unresolved, it becomes a self-contained entity. It is unnessary, therefore, for a folktale to be burdened either by a historical background or by a sequel meant to link it with datable narratives. Thus, unlike other Biblical narratives that gain by, indeed depend on, a historical setting, Ruth could easily be lifted out of the period of the Judges and still be appreciated as a superb work of art.

> Jack M. Sasson. *Ruth: A New Translation with a Philological Commentary and a Formalist-Folklorist Interpretation* (Baltimore, Johns Hopkins University Press, 1979), p. 216.

Whilst recent literature includes some valuable comments on the structure of the Ruth-narrative . . . there have been few attempts to apply the formal categories of [Roland] Barthes and [Claude] Lévi-Strauss to a story which in its design and symmetry seems ideally suited to such treatment. There is a larger symmetry to be considered also, viz., that revealed when the Book of Ruth is placed beside the parallel narratives of Lot, Abraham and the daughters of Lot (Gen. 13 and 19) and of Judah and Tamar (Gen. 38). The present study will be concerned with the larger symmetry of what I shall call the Ruth-corpus. The justification for this is not only in the striking parallels between these stories . . . but in the fact that they are all episodes in the history of a single family. Lot is the father of Moab and thus the ancestor of Ruth, whilst Judah is the father of Perez and thus the ancestor of Boaz. Another way of putting it would be to say that we have here the story of a single clan (that of Abraham and his nephew Lot) which separates (Gen. 13:11) at an early stage and is then reunited in the persons of Ruth and Boaz. . . .

The structuralist will, as a matter of principle, seek to be as inclusive as possible, rejoicing when he can bring together many stories under one single "code." In seeking to establish it, he will be undeterred by the differences in cultural setting or historical period between the various stories. . . . Enlightenment is not sought from the individual text or *parole*, but from the *langue* or constitutive grammar of many texts. . . .

It will be readily seen that all three narratives have a common starting-point. There is a departure involving a breaking of family ties. Lot departs from Abraham (Gen. 13:11); Judah descends from his brothers (Gen. 38:1); and Elimelech leaves his home town for the foreign country of Moab (Ruth 1:1). The "descent" in each case is followed by disaster—for Lot the destruction of the new environment in a violent overthrow; for Judah the loss of his wife and two sons; and the deaths of Elimelech and his two sons in the book of Ruth. The parallels continue. All three stories exhibit the same ʿ*agunah*-theme (the term is from Ruth 1:13). It is the theme of the woman abandoned or widowed and unable, as a result, to continue the line of the generations. And the solution in each case is along the same lines. A father or father-figure becomes responsible for the perpetuation of the family, although the initiative in all three narratives is taken by the widow/ daughter herself who secretly or by guile offers herself to the "father."

The parallels, which are more numerous and more detailed than indicated in the previous paragraph, are set out in the following table [not reproduced here] which is designed to reveal the structure of the corpus. Read horizontally from left to right the table exhibits the syntagm or nexus of relationships common to all three stories. This is the basis of the synchronic analysis of the corpus. It will be seen that along this axis we have a division into eight columns, each expressing a different term in the dialectical structure [Descent, Disaster, Agunah-Theme/Abandonment, Redemption, the Bed-trick, the Celebration, the Levirate Union, the Issue]. I have suggested further that these eight columns consist in fact of four antithetical pairs or couples. The first pair brings together dialectically the notion of material improvement and tragic loss, for the descent had been for the purpose of bettering the family's condition, but the opposite of this had been the result. The second pair exhibits the contrast of widowhood (or loneliness) and redemption. The third pair, which I have entitled respectively, the "Bed-Trick" and the "Celebration," involves a contrast between the privacy and secrecy of the woman's behaviour and the more public, unrestrained behaviour of the man. The final pair of columns exhibits the contrast within the kinship pattern of ban and blessing. The violation of the gravest sexual taboos yields in the case of Lot a fruitful outcome. The violation is slightly less serious in the case of Judah and Tamar (Judah is only the father-in-law) but it is there nevertheless. In the Book of Ruth it has been muted and transformed into a union sanctioned by established custom. But the sense of there being a legal difficulty to be overcome is strong in chapter 4 of the book. . . .

The synchronic pattern is capable of a high degree of abstraction, and the advantage of abstract formulae is that they make it possible to see the relevance of the structure to a wider group of narratives than those comprised in the corpus. We have spoken of the 'agunah-theme which is specific to the corpus: we could have expressed this more abstractly as an antinomy of separation and togetherness. Instead of speaking in descriptive and psychological language of the secrecy and guile of the woman contrasted with the joviality and openness of the man, we could speak of an antinomy of restraint and unrestraint, the closed and the open. Ultimately, we are concerned with the articulation of a dialectical pattern of order and disorder, life and death, fullness and emptiness. In fact the latter antinomy is explicit in Ruth as several commentators have pointed out. "I went away full, and the Lord has brought me back empty" (Ruth 1:21). Later on, Boaz gives Ruth six measures of barley so that she will not return empty-handed to her mother-in-law; and finally there is the fulfillment of Naomi with the birth of Obed. It does not require much ingenuity to see the relevance of these patterns to a host of narratives (for instance, those of Sarah and Abraham and of Hannah, the mother of Samuel). A line is renewed which appeared to be extinct.

Harold Fisch. *Vetus Testamentum*. Oct., 1982, pp. 427–32

SAMSON

Perhaps the most admirable example of folklore humor in the Bible, and one of the best in any literature, is the fascinating story of Samson [Judg. 13–16], who is not only portrayed as rioting in practical jokes, but also as being a genuine wit. The disasters which mark his life and the tragedy with which it concludes only serve to bring out more clearly the frolicsome spirit of the man. . . . The pathos of Samson's folly need not deter us from appreciating the humor of his performances. This accretion of tales around the memory of a popular hero is one of the most delicious bits of literary art in the Bible or out of it, and has furnished poets and dramatists with one of the most fruitful themes upon which they could engage their talents. The wit of Samson's riddle, propounded as a wager at his own wedding feast is obvious to all as soon as the circumstances which originated it are apprehended: "Out of the eater came forth meat, and out of the strong came forth sweetness" [14:14]. One can see the sunny-haired giant gleefully felicitating himself on the impossibility of his competitors ever guessing the secret of the honey in the lion's carcass. The way in which he paid the wager, when it had been lost through the treachery of his bride, illustrates the man's sense of humor: "And he went down to Ashkelon, and slew thirty men of them, and took their spoil, and gave change of garments unto them which expounded the riddle" [14:19]. One can imagine him smacking his lips over the grim jest of making his enemies pay his debt of honor. . . .

The drastic quality of Samson's humor appears again in the episode of the three hundred foxes sent scurrying through the cornfields of the Philistines with firebrands tied to their tails. . . . In all his feats of prodigious strength and agility the same humorous feeling is discoverable. His snapping the cords with which his enemies have bound him for delivery into the hands of the Philistines, his carrying off the gates of Gaza and depositing them upon the hill before Hebron—in fact, all the adventures which signalize his stormy career are shot through with a mischievous spirit of fun. He evidently luxuriates in his vindictive buffoonery. Nor is this wanton gladness absent from his unfortunate experiences with his Philistine paramour. Each time he fools her about the secret of his strength laughter shakes his ponderous frame and mockery pours from his lips. He revels in the deception of which she is the pouting victim. When finally he surrenders to the blandishments of Delilah, and compasses his own ruin by telling the truth about himself, the first impression upon his mind seems to be scarcely more serious than that the biter has been bitten at last. The joke is on him: "He wist not [did not know] that the Lord was departed from him" [16:20]. When the fatality of his situation draws upon him his inveterate humor still survives. His position is deplorable enough—a blind slave making sport for his hereditary foes. Nevertheless he will extract a morbid gratification from his misfortunes. He will add a climax to all his rude jokes upon his enemies by making them die with him. He pulls down the building in which they are making merry and they perish like cattle. The very grotesqueness of it mitigates the gloom of the catastrophe. . . . The writer of the narrative records with ill-concealed satisfaction: "So the dead which he slew at his death were more than they which he slew in his life" [16:30].

George P. Eckman. *The Literary Primacy of the Bible* (New York, Methodist Book Concern, 1915), pp. 111–14

He has the roughness and irresponsibility of the hero of a picaresque novel, and is the prototype of Gil Blas and his ilk. Moral sense is utterly lacking in him, his pranks are horseplay, his humor simple and racy and smacking of the soil. But in spite of these apparent crudities the stories make a tremendous appeal even to modern readers, for they are trenchant and have the ring of reality.

At first glance the cycle seems episodic and inconsequent, with the same lack of cohesion apparent in the Abraham cycle. Unlike those of the Jacob or Joseph series, the separate stories do not seem to grow out of one another, but rather to follow in haphazard order, but further reading will show that though no effort is apparent, there is very definite artistry in the tightening of interest and increase of intensity which culminate in the final tragedy. . . . There is first the long story of Samson and the woman of Timnah, told in some detail, and setting forth the predominant traits of the hero—his susceptibility to feminine wiles and his great strength. The story is full of rough humor, some of which has lost its point to modern days, but some of which is still appealing. The riddle which Samson asks, though not good, since the answer could not be guessed by anyone who did not know the special circumstances, is in keeping with that primitive fondness for riddles that has its place in the development of every literature. This story is capped with a short one which dwells on Samson's strength alone, and is followed by another reminiscence of his amatory adventures that ends with an account of his superhuman physical prowess still more exaggerated. Finally, before interest can flag, and when his characteristics have been firmly fixed in the minds of the audience, comes the capping tale, told at some length, and showing Samson, the victim of his passions, triumphing at last by means of his strength. When the cycle is considered from this viewpoint of structure and technique, it stands out at once as a rarely perfect creation. The first story introduces Samson with his strength of body and weakness of moral fiber, the two short episodes that follow act both as a point of rest and of suspension, keeping up the interest and emphasizing certain necessary details, and then, with the stage all set for the *dénouement,* the final tragedy is set forth in full, grim irony replacing the broad humor of the earlier tales.

The story, like the story of Jacob, is one of the world's great triumphs of character delineation. Samson is the first of the long literary line of big, simple, kindly animals, earthy and boisterous, slow to be aroused, but terrible in his anger because of his great body, and destined because of his unbridled passions to be the tool of women. He was a survival from some past and simpler generation, dropped in a complex modern environment and unable to adapt himself to its customs and manners. Instead of staying in the mountains where he was at home, he was constantly dragged by his desires into complex situations with which his naïve childishness could not cope. The woman of Timnah and the harlot merely created awkward situations out of which he extricated himself by brute force. But Delilah was of a different type, and in her hands Samson was helpless. The author uses few words to describe her gradual undermining of his defenses: with infinite subtlety she persists in her questionings, until finally, wearied by her importunities, he yields, and satisfied at last that now he will have peace, sleeps with his head in her lap. But the real center of interest in the story is not his amorousness, but his strength, and this rises triumphant in the end, when Samson, to be avenged of only one of his two eyes, overcomes the Philistines.

Brooke Peters Church. *The Israel Saga* (New York, Macmillan, 1932), pp. 240–43

In the middle of the book of Judges, Chapters 13 to 16 inclusive, is told one of the most fascinating stories in the Old Testament, the story of Samson. Upon a first reading it cannot fail to have a puzzling, even bewildering effect because it is so obviously a mixture of conflicting and inconsistent themes, a kind of potpourri of the holy and the extremely secular, of crude talk and mean tricks, of cajolery and deceit, of incredible tales of physical prowess and of cruelty to animals, of harlots and other designing women, of death by burning, by slaughter, and by falling pillars, of loose behaviour on the one hand and noble patriotism on the other, of a wedding, a heavenly vision, a riddle, and a tragedy — and all these in the brief space of four chapters. The first conclusion drawn from such an odd mass of seemingly unrelated material is that of diversity of origin. The vision of an angel to a barren woman hardly bears much relationship to the slaying of one thousand Philistines with the jawbone of an ass. And a child who has been solemnly ordained and dedicated to God from the day of his conception hardly acts in keeping with his high and holy mission in life when he sets the tails of three hundred foxes on fire as a revengeful means of consuming Philistine corn, vineyards, and olive trees!

This conclusion of quite different sources for these interesting, if ill-assorted, tales is a safe one. Although Samson is alleged in two different places in his story to have judged Israel twenty years, he is clearly not to be associated with leaders such as Moses, Joshua, Jephthah, and Gideon. His story belongs, in fact, not among the partly historical narratives of the judges of Israel, but instead to that type of literature common to all peoples and known as the folk tale. The stories concerning him and his chimerical behaviour made up a cycle of such tales which existed perhaps for centuries before they were at last written down and which were doubtless told by wandering storytellers to country people. Nor is Samson an epic hero such as Achilles in the *Iliad,* for instance. Nor does he possess the dignity of Joseph in the Jacob-Joseph saga. In spite of his valiant death, he is not actually of valiant mold, at least until that moment. Instead he is the typical folk hero, brawling and blustering, astonishing simple country people by his amazing feats and delighting them by his quite unrefined manners and his physical freshness and strength. He is, in a word, the Paul Bunyan of the children of Israel in their early days.

> Mary Ellen Chase. *The Bible and the Common Reader.*
> Rev. ed. (New York, Macmillan, 1952), pp. 117–18

The story as a whole resembles a sort of upside-down arc, with its high points at either end, and in the middle its low points. It opens on a high note, festive and wonderful, sowing in our hearts an expectation of great things to come. But Samson "descends" [Judg. 14:1] to Timnah. This wild man slides down into the vale of alien love, alien company, alien deeds. The heavenly blessing from on high is trampled in the low-lying abyss below. In the wake of the drum roll comes the clamor [Exod. 32:18], and from it the path turns back and upward toward the heroic and tragic end.

Greatly significant is the last verse, which seems like a detail that leads neither up nor down: "His kinsmen and the entire household of his father went down, bore him up, raised and buried him between Zareah and Eshtaol, in the gravesite of Manoah, his father" [Judg. 16:31]. Place of burial and manner of burial are not matters of import in the Bible. Samson was gathered to the gravesite of his forefathers, as was fitting. The last verse informs us that the Bible's final judgment on Samson is favor, not wrath. And thus the place is again emphasized: "between Zareah and Eshtaol," where the spirit of God had first come over him, teaching us that Samson's cleansed finale reaches the level of his pure beginning.

The story of Samson is a biblical tragedy, altogether the reverse of Greek tragedy. A predetermined fate does not bring the man to ruin; on the contrary, divine intention is always for the good, especially with regard to a man with a mission; ruination is nothing but the fruit of human choice. A man is free to choose between good and evil, as it is said in the Book of Deuteronomy. "Choose!"— this is the Bible's instruction to man, including the man on whose forehead is a mark of destiny. Even the chosen one must choose. . . . Every human tragedy in the Bible, including the tragedy of all humanity, descends not from above to below; rather, it irrupts and ascends from below and reaches up to the divine throne.

> Avraham Kariv. *Shivʿat ʿammudei hattenakh* (Tel Aviv,
> Am Oved, 1968), pp. 73–74†

Samson in a sense epitomizes the judges. He is, like Israel, a special child of God. He also is, like Israel, immature, opportunistic, rash. His weakness for women culminates in the loss of strength through the wiles of Delilah—like Israel, he has played the harlot once too often. He is enticed, as Israel is enticed; the source of his strength is taken from him, as God, the strength of Israel, removes himself to punish the Israelites; he is overcome, bound, and subdued, as Israel is sold into the power of her enemies and driven into the hills and mountains. Samson's blindness seems to symbolize and crystallize the blindness of Israel when it gives in to temptation and weakness and does evil in the sight of the Lord. Samson suffers literally the darkness which the Israelites suffer figuratively when they turn away from God and are forced to live in caves and dens, when their highways are unoccupied, their villages empty. But as the strength and favor of God are renewed repeatedly to the Israelites, so Samson's God-given strength returns in a natural manner; indeed, so natural is the return—"The hair of his head began to grow again after it had been shaved" (v. 22)—that it suggests, like the coming of dawn after night, how natural it is for God to give Israel new strength against its enemies.

> Kenneth R. R. Gros Louis. *Literary Interpretations of Biblical Narratives* (Nashville, Abingdon Press, 1974), pp. 161–62

Certain important motifs link the Samson saga with kindred texts within Israel's literary corpus. These portray a barren wife, a mighty hero meeting his nemesis in a woman, a quest for a deity's secret name, a death wish, loss of charisma, and a terror over theophany. An author, or several perceptive writers, freely drew upon the full range of stylistic devices that constituted *belles lettres* in ancient Israel.

In addition, the author chose a unifying theme, the choice between filial devotion and erotic attachment, that gave the stories unity and audience appeal. His treatment of this highly explosive issue demonstrated sensitivity and conviction.

The story combines tragic and comic elements with tremendous effect. Samson's *penchant* for foreign women drove him closer and closer to dark death, until at last he led an innocent lad into the same darkness. The lovely Timnite bride labored valiantly to escape a fiery death; eventually she fell victim to her own people's fury. Innocent Askelonites died at the hands of an angry Samson, whom they had neither befriended nor offended. But ludicrous episodes also occur, and thus prevent the taking of the saga too seriously. Still, tragic and comic elements give way before a stronger impulse—a tendency to lift one's eyes toward the heavens.

The Samson saga explores certain ambiguities of reality. It refuses to offer simple solutions for complex problems like endogamy and exogamy, human freedom and divine destiny, eros and charisma. Instead, the story depicts life as it transpired. As a result, Samson is neither saint nor sinner. Early Christian scholars labored much to turn him into a saint, despite his amorous conduct, violent personality, and suicide. In time he became a tragic hero, secular once again, but endowed with considerably more reflective powers. John Milton advanced the tradition even more; in *Samson Agonistes* the hero waged heroic warfare against temptation and triumphed in his final act.

James L. Crenshaw. *Samson* (Atlanta, John Knox Press, 1978), pp. 149–50

It has been long noted that the episodes of the Book of Judges conform to a clearly delineated cyclic structure. [Julius] Wellhausen reduced the pattern to the following scheme: Israel rebels, Israel is afflicted by God, Israel turns to God, Israel is granted peace [*Prolegomena to the History of Ancient Israel*, 1957, p. 231]. It has been further observed that the narrative of Samson runs along the same thematic lines as the entire Book of Judges. The parallels between the stories of Samson and Israel hold even more remarkably when one considers them in detail. In fact, the Samson story not only runs parallel to the story of Israel, whereby Samson would "typify" or "function as a symbol for" Israel. The story of Samson makes contact and assimilates with the story of Israel at several critical junctures. Reading the narrative as a riddle, one comes to a startling realization: Samson *is* Israel. The riddle can be solved: What appears to be Samson is the people Israel; what appears as the Naziriteship of Samson is the Israelite covenant. This interpretation, when carried through the text, accounts for and renders meaningful most if not all of the anomalies in the narrative. . . .

In the end, a thoughtful reader should be able to perceive this latent meaning of the Samson story. The text transmits here the history of Israel's backsliding, affliction, and ultimate hope by indirection, disguised as it were as the story of Samson the Judge. The narrative draws the reader in slowly, shapes his or her responses, and little by little discloses the veiled message. By postponing the revelation the narrative stores up its full power of surprise and unleashes it in a final sudden rush of recognition. The Samson story resembles in this respect the parable of Nathan the Prophet (II Sam. 12:1ff.). The parable alludes unmistakably to David's misappropriation of Bathsheba. But because it is masked by what appears to be a story about anonymous characters, David does not grasp its true significance until Nathan provides the solution (v. 7): "You are the man." Israel, not being an individual obsessed with protecting his ego, is capable, upon reflection, of identifying itself with Samson without being told the solution. But in order to facilitate the interpretation, the text, as we have seen, sprinkles transparent allusions to its reference throughout the narrative. . . .

Our understanding of the Samson story is *one* of its latent meanings, one that is not superimposed but answers to the stimuli of the text itself and reads the text in one of its own formative patterns, that of the riddle.

Edward L. Greenstein. *Prooftexts*. Sept., 1981, pp. 247, 253–55

Samson's life story is in its present embodiment a biographical narrative, a story in which "one unitary character stands at the center of all the chapters. . . . This character is surrounded by secondary characters who serve him as guides and aides or who lay obstacles across his path, a path whose beginning is usually his birth and whose end is the grave. This character generally maintains reciprocal relations with his sociohistorical environment" [Y. Even, *Millon munaḥei hassiporet,* Jerusalem 1978, pp. 27–28]. In this case the reciprocal relations with the environment are most intensive, for all the scenes revolve around the struggles between Samson and the Philistines, struggles that erupt in the wake of his relations with women.

The events are all interconnected, not only through the nexus of time but through the nexus of situation and outcome; the first event engenders a chain reaction, the following events cause additional repercussions, and so forth.

The situational nexus between the various events that the narrator has fashioned—even though it partly wavers at times—distinguishes this narrative from the picaresque, despite clear lines of similarity between it and the stories within that genre. . . . The picaresque narrative, in contrast to this story, "lacks a unity of plot spread over the length of one axis, for the only unifying factor is the protagonist, who performs various deeds or who falls victim to the machinations of others, and in whom the connective principle among the chapters is the flow of time in the sense of one thing following after the other, and not necessarily one (thing following) from the other" [*ibid.*, p. 26].

Lord Raglan compiled a comparative study of hero stories from different cultures (Oedipus, Zeus, Hercules, Romulus, Theseus, Moses, Elijah, King Arthur, etc.). Every one of these heroes earned "points" according to the number of "pure type" elements that appear in his biography. The type has implications for the degree of historicity of the traditions: As the character hews more to the type, we subtract from the historical credibility of the traditions concerning him.

Of the twenty-two points of the complete, "pure" type we find in the character of Samson the following points:

Number 3: His father is related to his mother (even though it is not explicitly said that Manoah's wife hails from the Danite family).

Number 4: The circumstances of his conception are not routine (the mother was barren; she was visited by the spirit of God, who sent his angel to bring the good tidings).

Number 5: The hero is reckoned as a son of a god (this point does not appear in the Bible because the story has been adapted to a monotheistic belief, but in the birth account we have uncovered a process of demythologization whose origin, so it seems, is in a story in which the wife is impregnated by a god).

Number 11: Preceding his marriage there is a victory over a predatory beast (the lion).

Number 13: The hero is made king (according to the editorial framework Samson became a judge, a savior of Israel).

Number 16: Later on he loses the affection of the gods (the Lord departs from him after his Nazirite vow is broken).

Number 18: His death is not a routine death (he brings death upon himself with his own hands; the passage about his death is formulated as a paradox: precisely then he kills more enemies than he killed during his life).

Number 20: His children—if he has any—are not his successors (Samson has no children).

In the biographical story of Samson the classic paradigm could not be kept because of the need to tailor the traditions both to the religion of Israel and to the sociopolitical framework of the period of the Judges. Therefore it is not said that he was a son of God, an attempt by his father to slay him is not depicted, he is not king, his wife is not a princess, and so on.

Yair Zakovitch. *Ḥayyei shimshon* (Jerusalem, Magnes Press, 1982), pp. 230–31†

SAMUEL

It is the misfortune of this great man that his writings have come down to us within the bounds of an ecclesiastical canon of Holy Scripture; otherwise students of the humanities would hardly continue to ignore a prose which, for combined simplicity and distinction, has remained unmatched in the literature of the world, and which the progressive sophistication of mankind has long since rendered forever unapproachable.

William R. Arnold. *Ephod and Ark* (Cambridge, Mass., Harvard University Press, 1917), p. 118

The people of Israel produced not only poetical narratives, but also a highly developed historical literature. Portions of this are preserved for us in II Samuel and in scattered passages of the other narrative books. This literature has an amazing objectivity. Owing to this really astounding objectivity the work of the Hebrew historian far surpasses anything produced elsewhere in the ancient East. Only by the great historians among the Greeks has he ever been excelled. "Hebrew civilization," says Eduard Meyer, "alone of all the other (ancient Eastern) civilizations, really stands on the same intellectual level as the Greek" [*Die Israeliten und Ihre Nachbarstämme,* 1906, p. 486]. The pictures have been painted in such true colours that Hebrew history, incomplete as our knowledge of it is, is more familiar to us than the history of any other people of the ancient East. Everywhere else in the East the annals of history were written in the service of despots, whereas in Israel there prevailed a spirit of freedom which refused to fall slavishly in the dust before the king, but depicted faithfully both him and his doings. Even the legends provide us with an abundance of historical information, revealing clearly the internal conditions of the nation, its religion, its customs, its laws, and its social relationships.

There are two respects in which these historical narratives, like the poetical narratives already discussed, have a great superiority over all modern literature of the same kind. These are *the simplicity of their conceptions* and their *power of depicting details*.

Hermann Gunkel. *What Remains of the Old Testament, and Other Essays*. Tr. from the German by A. K. Dallas (New York, Macmillan, 1928), pp. 30–31

The two books of Samuel, also made up of material from different and some-times conflicting cycles, perhaps contain more actual fact than any book that goes before. Here is another great literary enterprise that is epic. It would be hard to find anywhere a greater narrative. Eli, Samuel, Saul, David, Goliath, the witch of Endor, around whom is written one of the best stories of the supernatu-ral, Jonathan the true friend, Joab, Uriah, Bathsheba, Nathan, Absalom and other characters are depicted and played up against each other with a sureness of touch, technique, and fidelity never surpassed. Scenes and events are handled with the utmost sincerity and with graphic power. And here, as is generally the case in the Bible, all this is accomplished with the fewest words. Where we need six or ten thousand words to tell a story, those old writers did it better with a few hundred. Sometimes our boasted speed and efficiency break down. The books of Kings contain much that is equal to Samuel, but as a whole they are not quite up to its level.

Hilary G. Richardson. *Life and The Book* (New York, Macmillan, 1929), p. 210

Characteristic of [I Samuel], a book rich in striking episodes (the story of Han-nah, the revelation of God to Samuel, the battle of David and Goliath, and espe-cially the scene at En Dor and the fall of Saul and his sons on Gilboa), is the in-cessant struggle, be it open or covert, between Samuel and Saul, between Saul and David; a struggle for kingship, the twilight of the declining judge whose net is still spread over life; a psychological quilt of conflicts of heart, of amity and enmity, which sometimes cannot be distinguished. After [the Book of] Judges this is a more settled book, more modern from a human standpoint, as though epic and drama were intermixed here. The drama of Samuel and Saul, that of Saul and David to this day attract poets to treat them, to go back and embroider new visions on this tapestry. However, one cannot darken the magic of these sto-ries even in great poetic compositions. Herein is the secret of the ancients: some-thing incised in powerful line drawings on a stone tablet with an unbending chisel. . . .

The Second Book of Samuel contains, apart from the conflicts between the House of Saul and the House of David, almost exclusively the sequence of events about King David. Those who arranged the Bible concluded the first part with the description of the bitter end of Israel's first king, who fell, he and his sons, on Mount Gilboa. II Samuel tells of the victories of David, who succeeded in overpowering the enemy, in expanding the borders of Israel. However, the per-sonal life of the pursued David was more full of poetry than the life of the man who sat firmly on his throne. In I Samuel not only was the era of Saul completed; the youth of David was also completed, the romantic stage of his life, the one filled with adventure and wonder, was completed. He no longer alternately rises and falls—from a humble shepherd to a lauded national hero, from the son-in-law of the king, husband of the king's daughter, to a fugitive from Saul in the wilderness with a band of malcontents. Now he reaches the kingship—at first King over Judah, and soon over all the tribes of Israel. Indeed, the legendary magic of his name alone becomes hereafter an eternal magic. . . .

With regard to the personal life of the king, this is in no way a happy book. We would rather see David hiding from a pursuing Saul, making peace with him, then, torn apart by jealousy, pursuing him again, than see him in a palace full of domestic treachery. When he reached the kingship, something in David's character softened. The king at times reveals himself as a paterfamilias more than he reveals himself as a ruler; he offers reason for praise and he offers reason for derogation, too. From now on it is the spirit of Joab that sweeps over the kingdom.

Is it not he, despite the magic of David, who is the main hero in this book?

Jacob Fichman. *'Arugot* (Jerusalem, Bialik Institute, 1954), pp. 256–58†

When we look at the Book of Samuel from the human perspective, it is a thoroughly tragic book. Not one of the book's characters escapes tragedy. All the ties and connections between the main characters and the secondary characters (Eli-Samuel, Samuel-Saul, Saul-David, Jonathan-David, and Michal-David, too), even with the pleasant parts that play on their heartstrings, have a tragic tone. One person serves the cup of tribulation to the very person to whom he is attached. The boy Samuel, the child heralded by Eli and his protégé, heralds to Eli the calamity that will bring an end to his household. Beneath the protective wings of Eli Samuel grew up and was equipped for prophecy; yet the lad's first prophecy clipped Eli's gray head with black wings, throwing his last days in the shadow of his household's and his priestly dynasty's end. A similar chain of events occurs between Samuel and Saul. It was Samuel who raised up Saul from anonymity, anointed him king, and pressed the kiss of grandeur upon his forehead. It was he, too, who was privileged to herald to him that God rejected him, and in the resumption of his miserable mission Samuel feared for his life at Saul's hands ("If Saul hears, he will slay me"—I Sam. 16:2). The same thing is true of Saul and David. From the house of Saul love and hate, grandeur and deathtraps showered upon David. For love is as fierce as death—Jonathan's love for David; jealousy is as hard as Sheol [Song 8:6]—Saul's jealousy of David. There are no two troubles like this love and this jealousy. Jealousy sought to save the house of Saul at the cost of David's life, and love saved David's life at the cost of the house of Saul. What makes Jonathan's love so sublime is that his eyes were open to the consequences. Jonathan's love for David is wondrous because of the sacrifice, the tragedy in it. From such threads is woven the fabric of characters about whom the Book of Samuel tells.

Avraham Kariv. *Shiv'at 'ammudei hattenakh* (Tel Aviv, Am Oved, 1968), pp. 76–77†

The quality of the first encounter between Samuel and Saul is strikingly expressive of the personality of the aging priest. We are told that God had revealed to Samuel the day before the full details of Saul's coming, informing him that this young man was to be the Lord's anointed. Samuel was therefore ready to receive him. His need to be fully prepared for this event by advance information from God may reflect his own insecurity in regard to this first step in his displacement. The tone of the divine revelation is one of directness and intimacy, as of two close friends communicating with each other. God says, "Tomorrow about this time I will send thee a man out of the land of Benjamin, and thou shalt anoint him to be prince over My people Israel, and he shall save My people out of the hand of the Philistines; for I have looked upon My people, because their cry is come unto Me" [I Sam. 9:16]. The specific role that Saul is to play as military leader is here clearly defined.

The simplicity of God's message to Samuel and the manner in which the latter informs Saul of his destiny show a considerable contrast. The unsuspecting hero of the little drama about to unfold, accompanied by a servant, is in the quest of his father's strayed donkeys. The two men, finding themselves at the town where Samuel resided, plan to utilize the priest's reputation as a seer and inquire of him where the donkeys might be found. . . . Samuel then displays his powers as a clairvoyant, telling Saul of a series of incidents that would occur as he proceeded upon his homeward journey. The Bible then says, "And it was so, that when he turned his back to go from Samuel, God gave him another heart; and all those signs came to pass that day" [10:9].

The tone pervading this narration is one that emphasizes the importance of Samuel himself. It is he, the powerful leader, *the man of God,* who with dramatic suddenness, without any initial preparation for Saul of what is to happen, elevates the unknown son of a farmer to the high position of the Lord's anointed.

The abruptness with which Samuel initially presents himself to Saul as the man of power and reveals to the bewildered stranger the high destiny in store for him has a dramatic quality. Its unconscious purpose may have been to overwhelm the younger man and place him at once psychologically under Samuel's influence. The words, "And I will tell thee all that is in thy heart" [9:19], emphasize his prophetic ability. The magical words spoken by Samuel, "On whom is all the desire of Israel? Is it not on thee and on all thy father's house?" [9:20] have a seductive quality. They must have had a powerful impact upon the unsophisticated Saul, bringing forth the only verbal response recorded of him in this entire story. The Bible says, "And Saul answered and said: Am not I a Benjamite, of the smallest of the tribes of Israel? and my family the least of all the families of the tribe of Benjamin? wherefore then speakest thou to me after this manner?" [9:21] . . .

While ostensibly the selection of Saul was made by God, psychologically we must view this choice as an act of Samuel's, in response to the obligation he had undertaken. Indeed, the old priest behaves throughout in the *grand manner,* making it clear in every word and gesture that it is indeed he who is thus omnipotently creating a king out of a simple peasant. . . .

Probably the most significant factor that influenced Samuel's choice was the unconscious one of narcissistic identification. Saul must have represented the priest's own idealized self, or ego ideal, on a physical basis. The younger man may have reminded Samuel of how he once looked himself or of how he had wanted to look.

> Dorothy F. Zeligs. *Psychoanalysis and the Bible* (New York, Bloch, 1974), pp. 112–15

SAUL

As a straight ghost story [King Saul's meeting with the Witch of Endor (I Sam. 28)] could hardly be better told, and Charles Lamb has left on record the effect which it produced on his childish mind. It is reduced to the utmost simplicity and in that is its strength. "And the woman said unto Saul, 'Elohim did I see coming up from the earth.'" She means that through the beaten clay floor of her house something ascended from the spirit world. "And he said to her, 'What is his form?' and she said, 'An old man is coming up and he is covered over with a mantle.'" That was enough for Saul; he recognized the familiar figure of the aged Samuel with his mantle drawn over his head. For us, in trying to reach the Hebrew feeling for the Weird, the significant thing here is that the world of spirits is in immediate contact with our world of sense. There is no journey between; space does not exist; spirit and its world are as close to us as our own bodies. The only touch left of physical relation is that the ghost comes up; but folklore ghosts always do. "Why has thou brought me up," says Samuel, "disquieting me?"—literally, "making me quiver." But the story is evidently cut to the bone. With the appearance of Samuel, something told the woman that it was Saul himself who had come to seek her aid. Like a modern "medium" she was prepared to summon any spirit from the vasty deep, but like a modern "medium," too, she gained knowledge with their coming. Yet it is possible that something has dropped out at that point just as it is probable that Samuel's message has been expanded. He is too loquacious for a true ghost.

> Duncan B. MacDonald. *The Hebrew Literary Genius* (Princeton, N.J., Princeton University Press, 1933), p. 155

If one reads with imaginative vision and with fresh insight the pathetic and bitter account of his life, he emerges actually a nobler personality than David and even a far more appealing one. . . . There seems no doubt that Saul was an able king, who through the force of his personality united his people as David was at first unable to do. Nor was he ever confronted as was David with rebellions against him. Nor is there any question as to his capacities as a leader against the Philistines. But from the beginning of his reign one tragedy follows another because of his impetuous nature, the "fatal flaws" of pride and jealousy on the one hand and of superabundant love on the other. . . .

Throughout the mounting train of gloomy and fatal incidents which mark the downfall of Saul, one is conscious of the innate bigness of his nature. Headstrong and impulsive though he is, he is, at least before his madness, rarely cruel in an age of cruelty and never personally ambitious. Although he is superstitious and fanatical in temperament and even in mind, he is devoted to God with a single-mindedness which increases the pathos of his rejection by Samuel because of his premature burnt offering at Michmash, and of his bitter cry at Endor: *God is departed from me and answereth me no more* [I Sam. 28:15]. His disobedience in sparing both the spoil taken from the Amalekites and Agag, their king, presents him actually in a much nobler light than that surrounding the enraged Samuel, who again rejects him in the name of God before he proceeds himself to hew in pieces the wretched Agag. He is quick to acknowledge guilt and to ask forgiveness; to admire bravery in others; and to be ready to sacrifice even his son Jonathan when God casts the lot against him.

Mary Ellen Chase. *The Bible and the Common Reader.*
Rev. ed. (New York, Macmillan, 1952), pp. 121–24

It is not the national aspect of this tragedy, however, that engages the author's attention, but the human aspect. He describes in detail the tortuous course of the relations between Saul and David and the dead end at which they arrive, and as we read we feel the inevitability of these developments and the fact that there is no way out. Naturally, if Saul had killed David there would have been no tragedy, and if David had killed Saul and taken his place the tragedy would have been cheap and simple, just as it would have been very cheap and simple if the clash between them had become an open war for the throne. The tragedy lies in the fact that both Saul and David are directed and do not determine their own destinies, and when one of them tries to determine his fate—as, for instance, when Saul attempts to kill David—it is clear that he will fail, because he is acting in opposition to the purpose of the puller of the strings. If matters seem to be determined by fate, it should be remembered that it is Samuel, the emissary of God, who activates this fate. It is not fate that is the hidden force acting in the Biblical narrative, but God, and the question of the significance of the way of man in the Bible is the question of the ways of Providence. But the purposes of Providence are hidden and far off, and it acts here in the same way as fate in the Greek tragedy. The tragedy is painful because Saul's decline is not gradual or the result of old age, like those of Eli, Samuel and David; Saul collapses under the weight of the evil spirit while he is yet in his full strength, and up to his last moment he is described as being in full possession of his powers. The tragedy is painful because it is not understood, and it is not understood because it is not a war between good and evil; both Saul and David are very human and win our sympathy: we do not know which of them to blame, or with which of them we sympathize more, for we have caught a glimpse of something mysterious and terrifying which is beyond good and evil.

Zvi Adar. *The Biblical Narrative* (Jerusalem, Department of Education and Culture, World Zionist Organization, 1959), pp. 234–35

The tragic irony of the Saul story, as our narrator wished us to see it, lies in the disparities between the demand on Saul and Saul's capacity to meet it, and between what Saul understood of his role and what by divine oracle we are given to understand of it. It lies in the difference between his perception of himself and others' perception of him. The narrator judges Saul adversely. That is the way with Old Testament narrators; they are never content merely to state facts. But the narrator conveys by the way he constructs the story that Saul could have achieved a positive judgment. When that possibility had passed, decline and failure were inexorable. . . .

We have in the Saul story a masterpiece of structure, dramatic order and suspense, and tragic irony. Someday, someone will turn the story of Saul into a great tragedy for the stage. He will have to fill in characters and dialogue, and he will have to make explicit in speech and action much that the narrator has left implicit. But he will not have to alter a single episode. Then perhaps Saul will be recognized as a tragic figure of the same stature as Oedipus or Othello.

Edwin M. Good. *Irony in the Old Testament* (London, SPCK, 1965), pp. 79–80

In the present form of the book of I Samuel the figure of Saul has been swallowed up first by Samuel and then by David. Rather than standing as the focal point of the complex of narratives that tells of his rise to kingship and subsequent destruction, he is made to appear first as a graphic illustration of all that is wrong with kingship from the point of view of Samuel and prophetic circles and then as the rejected king and a foil against which the elected king David shines. Yet, there are moments when the figure of Saul breaks through with a strength and compelling immediacy. The stern figure of Samuel cannot wholly eclipse the appeal and vast potential of the young man when first met, nor can the attractive David overshadow the poignancy of Saul's last days and the stature he attains in his death.

Scholars have followed the lead of the tradition in their treatment of I Samuel, generally dividing the book into two parts: one dealing with *Samuel* and Saul (I Sam. 1–15), the other dealing with *David* and Saul (I Sam. 16–31 and on into II Sam.). However, the figure of Saul is at the heart of both segments and binds them together. It is the thesis of this essay that attention to the way in which Saul is presented in I Sam. 9–31 will reveal a significant structure in these chapters that has not received the notice it deserves. The following outline of I Sam 9–31 will set forth the structure and provide a basis for discussion of it:

Introduction: Saul as a man of heroic potential (I Sam. 9:1–2).

Part I: Saul becomes king over Israel (I Sam. 9–14).
   A. The first encounter with Samuel: announcement of future greatness
      (I Sam. 9:3–10:16).
   B. The first constructive phase of his kingship: public acknowledgment
      and initial success (I Sam. 10:17–11:15).
   C. The first destructive phase: hints of disintegration (I Sam. 13–14).

Part II: The disintegration of Saul and his kingship (I Sam. 15–27).
   A. The second encounter with Samuel: announcement of divine rejection
      (I Sam. 15:1–16:13).
   B. The second constructive phase: David enters Saul's court and fights his
      wars (I Sam. 16:14–19:10).
   C. The second destructive phase: Saul's disintegration (I Sam. 19:11–28:2).

Finale: The last days of king Saul (I Sam. 28–31).
   A. The third encounter with Samuel: announcement of defeat and death
      (I Sam. 28:3–25).
   B. A merging of destructive and constructive phases: the death and burial
      of Saul (I Sam. 29–31 and especially ch. 31).

After a brief introduction to Saul I Samuel 9–31 tells in three parts the story of this man as he moves from initial success to the final dissolution of his kingship and death, only then granting him renewed stature. While at times the figure of Saul vanishes from view, especially in the later chapters when attention centers on David (e.g., I Sam. 25, 27, 29–30), he reappears again at critical points that underscore the structural framework for I Samuel 9–31. Some general observations on this outline will be followed by more detailed comments on its several parts.

Attention must first be called to the fact that the figure of Samuel serves a distinctive literary function throughout the narrative. He appears three times, at the outset of each part, and announces privately what is, in fact, to be worked out publicly in that segment of the narrative.

A second overarching pattern may also be seen informing the three parts of the narrative. In parts I and II, after the private encounter with Samuel, there follows a segment that can be described as constructive, that is, one in which Saul realizes some success (I.B and II.B): the Ammonite threat to Jabesh-gilead is overcome and Saul is made king; the Philistine threat is thwarted and David enters Saul's court and family. This constructive phase is followed in each part by one that is destructive or at least bears the seeds of destruction (I.C and II.C): his first encounter with the Philistines results in only partial victory and future tensions between father and son, king and subjects, and Saul and his God are foreshadowed.

W. Lee Humphreys. *Journal for the Study of the Old Testament*. Feb., 1978, pp. 18–19

The story makes much of Saul's jealousy—at times a desperate, insane, even violent, jealousy—and there are more than a few hints of rashness in his action, though the action most commonly cited in this respect, the imposition of the fast in chapter 14, can equally be seen as an expression of deep piety or the cautious exercise of kingly responsibility.

The motif of jealousy prompts comparison with Shakespeare's *Othello* where we see this mind-warping emotion distort a fine leader's perception of things and lead him to reject and destroy an innocent person, the one, indeed, who most loves him. The biblical story's treatment of the theme, similar in many respects, is yet significantly different. For example, Desdemona, the object of Othello's jealousy, is essentially loyal to Othello and innocent of the charge of adulterous conspiracy (though it *is* possible to play her as more ambiguously motivated in her dealings with her husband and Iago). Similarly David is shown to be innocent, though charged with treasonable intentions: he makes no overt claim to the throne, does not fight against Saul, and refuses to "raise his hand against" him, even when it is in his power to do so, and effectively at that.

Jonathan, the object of Saul's anger (anger which is triggered by his jealousy of David), is likewise shown to be acting in good faith, attempting to mediate between his father and his (as he sees it) wronged friend. On the other hand, both characters are in fact much more ambiguously placed vis-à-vis Saul than ever Desdemona is vis-à-vis Othello. Jonathan does, in fact, deal (conspire, make a league?—22:8) with David behind Saul's back, and he ends by abdicating as heir to the throne in favour of David, thus effectively destroying Saul's dynastic hopes. David's position is more subtle. We (the readers) know that David is to replace Saul, according to Yahweh's plan, but Saul only knows that he, Saul, has been rejected and that a "neighbour" has already been designated his successor. Thus David, through his success as a leader ("Saul has slain his thousands, and David his tens of thousands"), naturally presents himself, in Saul's view, as a potential rival, perhaps *the* designated successor. Othello is fed by Iago (and "chance"?) a series of (false) clues pointing to a (nonexistent) threat; Saul, on the contrary, is faced with (genuine) clues to a (real) threat. Thus his attitude to David poses a moral conundrum for the reader, for his violent jealousy, objectionable as it is, nevertheless happens to be right on target.

David M. Gunn. The Fate of King Saul (Sheffield, England, JSOT Press, 1980), pp. 116–17

No wonder he captured the fancy of great poets, painters, composers. Rembrandt and Holbein, Byron and Rilke, Lamartine, Handel, D. H. Lawrence, and André Gide were all inspired by the tragic nobility, the romantic gravity of his singular yet exemplary destiny. More than any king who followed, Saul has intrigued creative spirits. Even more than David, whose impact was greater both historically and metaphysically, Saul attracts anyone who approaches Judaism from esthetic and ethical viewpoints. David and his conquests make us proud, but it is Saul and his failures that fascinate us. More complex than David, more tormented and tortured, Saul lifts us to mountain heights and then drops us into the abyss. Few personalities experienced as many metamorphoses, dramas, or breakdowns as Saul; few destinies ever followed as fast a rhythm, or had as many vicissitudes in rapid succession. Few men knew such glory, and few lost it for such absurd reasons.

Elie Wiesel. Five Biblical Portraits (Notre Dame, Ind., University of Notre Dame Press, 1981), p. 74

Saul is the one great tragic hero of the Bible: not only physically taller than any of his subjects (I Sam. 9:2), he is an able ruler and by his standards a fair-minded one. But he seems to do nothing right. He spares his enemy King Agag out of human decency, only to be told that in not killing him he is cheating Samuel's ferocious god out of a sacrifice, and that this will never be forgiven by a deity who "is not a man, that he should repent" (I Sam. 15:29). One can of course rationalize this episode, or any other episode, if one is interested in rationalizing. It seems to me that the narrator has not simply made the elementary though very common error of identifying God with the devil, but, by a kind of inspired blundering, has managed to add the one element that makes the story of Saul genuinely tragic. This is the suggestion of malice within the divine nature, a suggestion that is perhaps essential to all great tragedy. Saul becomes a doomed man from then on, with intermittent fits of melancholy and of frantic but futile efforts to rid himself of the threat from David. In the Witch of Endor scene he finally turns to the occult powers that he himself had forbidden consultation with, and disaster and death follow. The terrible and inevitable degeneration will remind the modern reader that Shakespeare must have studied the account of Saul with considerable care before writing *Macbeth*.

Northrop Frye. The Great Code: The Bible and Literature (New York, Harcourt Brace Jovanovich, 1982), pp. 181–82

SONG AT THE SEA

The passage of the Red Sea produced the most ancient and sonorous song of triumph, which we have in this language. It is a choral ode, one voice describing perhaps the acts themselves, those of the chorus striking in and as it were re-echoing the sentiment. Its structure is simple, full of alliteration and rhyme, which I could not give in our language without doing violence to it, for the Hebrew, from the simplicity of its forms, is full of such harmonious correspondencies [sic] of sound. Flowing and prolonged words but few in number float upon the air, and terminate for the most part in an obscure monosyllabic sound, that formed perhaps the burden of the chorus. . . .

This song, of which I have given but a feeble echo, gave their tone to the triumphal songs of the Hebrews, as the song of Deborah and the 68th Psalm evince. The rhythmical movement is animated by the same caesuras and cadences and by the same lively correspondencies of sound. The frequent exclamations, the oft recurring "Praise to Jehovah! / Sing praises to Jehovah!" the excitations addressed to the hearers, or the singers themselves, which at intervals interrupt, or rather animate the current of thoughts anew, form as it were the stave, on which the historical song is arranged. [1783]

> Johann Gottfried von Herder. *The Spirit of Hebrew Poetry.* Vol. II. Tr. from the German by James Marsh (Burlington, Vt., Edward Smith, 1833), pp. 65, 67–68

"And with the blast of thy nostrils" [Exod. 15:8]. Nothing can be grander than the image here employed. It signifies, that the gathering together of the mighty waters was an immediate act of divine power: the poet, therefore, represents the Deity as actually emitting from his nostrils the wind, which produced an effect never before, nor since, witnessed by man. The figure, too, sustains in the imagination the idea of Almighty wrath previously expressed—the inflated nostril, from which the blast of God's vengeance was ejected, conveying a distinct and emphatic notion of active anger. It is a singularly forcible picture, heaping upon the plastic imagination a crowd of vigorous ideas, rising out of, and fructifying from, this single but prolific root. We seem to have the whole process of sublime destruction brought at once before the mind by a waving, as it were, of the poet's mystical wand.

> The waters were gathered together,
> The floods stood upright as an heap,
> And the depths were congealed [Ibid.].

Here is a beautiful gradation of sense. The waters were not only raised up, like a wall, on the right hand and on the left, but were consolidated at the same moment; they were gathered together, and thus fixed, for the time, in a condition so contrary to their natural tendency, that the depths of the sea were disclosed, and a path left for "the ransomed to pass over." The waters were arrested in their channel, and ceased to flow, being actually congealed, but recoiled upon the pursuing host, who had dared to oppose the authority of the Most High. The whole description is eminently picturesque. I know nothing in ancient or modern poetry that, for force of impression, can surpass the line—"And the depths were congealed in the heart of the sea."

> John Hobart Caunter. *The Poetry of the Pentateuch.* Vol. I (London, E. Churton, 1839), pp. 280–81

Some scholars in our generation have made this song [Exod. 15] out to [have been written at a] much later time than that of Moses, saying first that he would not be likely to compose it spontaneously at the time. But this . . . should not trouble us at all because this song (like all the songs of the Bible) is not bound by the shackles of meter and rhyme; rather, it is entirely free discourse, following the spirit and impulse of the poet, as we have found Jacob and Moses reciting their blessings at the moment of their deaths, and as David recited several psalms while his spirit was tormented in his flights from Saul and Absalom. . . . [Scholars] have also questioned the probability of all Israel learning the song in short time so that they could sing it, and this is valid. Indeed, the Rabbis (Babylonian Talmud *Sota* 30b) were already divided on how [the Israelites] sang at the sea. To my mind, Moses said: "Let me sing of the Lord, for he is exalted, exalted, horse and its rider has he thrown into the sea" (v. 1), and Israel answered: "Horse and its rider has he thrown into the sea." Moses said: "My strength and my force is Yah, and he has become my salvation" (v. 2), and Israel answered: "Horse and its rider has he thrown into the sea"; and so on after each verse (and sometimes after half a verse) Israel answered with none other than these words: "Horse and its rider has he thrown into the sea." It was easy for the people to learn those words by heart. We find an analogue to this in the psalm "Praise the Lord for he is good, for his devotion is forever" (Ps. 136), where the words "For his devotion is forever" are duplicated in every verse; and so in the Song of Deborah (Judg. 5) we may say that the people would respond after each verse: "Bless the Lord!" and so in the Song of David, according to the second edition, which is the version in the Book of Psalms, chapter 18, which seems to have been emended for singing in the Holy Temple, I would claim that they would answer after each verse: "Let me love the Lord, my strength!" From this it follows for these three songs written in this special form of brick on slab and slab on brick that from the beginning, after each verse were written the words that they would answer, such as [Judg. 5:2–3]:

> For [the Lord's] requiting Israel,
> For the people's volunteering, Bless the Lord!
> Hear, O kings,
> Give ear, O rulers, Bless the Lord!

And if you say: If so, why wasn't Psalm 136 written brick on slab like these three songs? Your answer is at hand: There it was not possible to do so, for the response is after every verset. [1871]

Samuel David Luzzatto. *Perush ShaDaL 'al ḥamisha ḥumshei tora*. Ed. P. Schlesinger (Tel Aviv, Dvir, 1965), pp. 274–75†

The ode most nearly resembling . . . [the one] of Deborah is the Song of Moses and Miriam at the Red Sea. Here again the mode of performance is exactly indicated. The first verse says, "Then sang Moses and the Children of Israel this song"; the twentieth verse adds: "And Miriam, the prophetess, the sister of Aaron, took a timbrel in her hand; and all the women went out after her with timbrels and with dances. And Miriam answered them, Sing ye to the Lord, for he

hath triumphed gloriously; the horse and his rider hath he thrown into the sea."
The natural interpretation of these verses taken together is that the words last
quoted are a refrain, and to be sung by Miriam and the Women; while the body of
the Song was for Moses and the Men. The refrain would be repeated at the close
of each stanza. The structure suggests a prelude and three stanzas, each of which
commences with an apostrophe to God, and then deals with the subject of the deliverance. A further examination of these strophes reveals *augmenting,* as a
mode of lyric movement; not only do the successive strophes increase in the
number of their lines, but they bring out the incident with more and more fulness. The first merely refers to the event: the hosts cast into the sea and sinking
like a stone. The second stanza becomes a picture full of powerful details: floods
standing on heaps and depths congealed, the enemy already counting his spoils,
the single blast of wind, and the sinking like lead. But when the incident is
touched by the third strophe we have, not details, but consequences. The event is
stretched to take in all that will follow from it: the guiding through the wilderness
thus wonderfully opened to them, the terror falling upon the inhabitants of
Canaan and the kings that lie in the way, the bringing in and planting in the
mountain of inheritance—all poetically realised in the moment of this the first
step. To describe the movement of the whole ode we may say that the prelude introduces the great deliverance with a shock that is like a plunge, and the augmenting strophes follow like ripples widening to the furthest bound that imagination can go.

Richard G. Moulton. *The Literary Study of the Bible.*
Rev. ed. (Boston, Heath, 1899), pp. 142–43

It is as exciting and elevated as anything of its kind to be found in the world's
great literatures. It would unquestionably be difficult to discover anywhere so
marvelous an adaptation of the sound and movement of the verse to its meaning
as exists here. If it is as old as tradition claims and many of the critics acknowledge it to be, then the beginning of Hebrew poetry must lie in the remotest past.
For we can not detect in the specimen under consideration a trace of rawness or
an echo of the pains of growth and maturing. It stands before us full fledged, exhibiting to perfection the essential elements of Hebrew poetic composition. To
begin with it is alive, restless as the waves that flung themselves roaring on the
enemy. It is spontaneous, thrown out, as it were, all in a breath. Not a word in it
stands still but is tumbling on another's neck, not a clause but is short and quick.
Stich follows upon stich like a succession of waves to form the characteristic and
effective Biblical parallelism. The descriptions are picturesque, the imagery
vivid, the diction sonorous and studded with figures of speech, particularly with
that of alliteration, the language, as far as meager knowledge of the Hebrew
vocabulary and idiom permits us to judge, is at times archaic and exotic. The
poem's opening verse is unforgettable. It strikes us as if the unprecedented event
that had occurred at the sea's edge had itself opened its mouth to speak. It breaks
upon us with the startling suddenness with which those who actually witnessed

the amazing and swift end of the enemy must have begun to sing, when they awakened to consciousness and realized what had happened. It would be hard to believe that it was a composition of later years, an offspring of pale recollections, so instinct is it with the turmoil of life and reality. The other verses are equally fresh and nervous, containing not the stories of actions, but the actions themselves. "Wonderfully sublime," Bishop Lowth designated verses 9 and 10, in which the Pharaoh's unexpected ruin is brought into powerful relief by his arrogance and fury. But why attempt illustrations when the whole poem is literally crammed with excellencies. For whether they depict horse and rider, or God's powerful right hand or His consuming wrath, or the enemy's sinking as lead or melting away terror-stricken, everywhere the rolling waves of sound, flowed on with the same rhythmic cadence, the rising to joy and gratitude in the presence of victory, to the breathless expression of awe in the presence of God's might. . . .

The primary aim was not to compose a beautiful song. It was to glorify God, to celebrate the fulfillment of His promise to the Patriarchs, namely, that He would redeem Israel from Egypt and establish them in Canaan. What happened to Pharaoh and his charioteers is a matter of secondary importance. There is no singing here of arms and men or revenging oneself on the enemy. The fate of the Egyptians is significant only as an attestation of God's power and what He had already done for Israel, and even more a guarantee of the wonders yet to come. The poet has no thought for order, coherence, symmetry. He let his words fall as they list, concerned only with the end in view. He is obsessed with God, with whom he begins and ends. "I will sing to the LORD . . . The LORD shall reign for ever and ever!" That is his theme, and into this theme his every word and line and image fit. And it is from the unparalleled majesty of the theme that flow the logic, beauty and sublimity of his song.

Solomon Goldman. From Slavery to Freedom (New York, Abelard Schuman, 1958), pp. 26–27, 356–57

Song of Deborah. See Deborah, Song of

SONG OF SONGS

Consider'd as a meerly human Composition, 'tis the most beautiful of the kind that was ever written. 'Twas surely composed by the sweetest Singer of *Israel*. The Passion of Love was never touch'd in so fine and delicate a Manner. In Softness it surpasses Anacreon, Ovid, or Catullus. In Ease, Simplicity, and the Variety of Comparisons Theocritus, Himself falls short of it. We are carried thro' inchanted Regions, something like those Seats of feigned Love by the Poets, where new and delightful Prospects ever entertain Us, and the Scene is perpetually shifting from one agreeable View to another. No part of Poetry is more pleasing than the Descriptive, no Descriptions charm more than those taken from rural Life, and of all rural Descriptions These are some of the most easy and natural. Here the Spring approaches with reviveing Beauty, *The Winter is past, the Rain is over and gone, the time of the Singing of Birds is come, and the Voice of the Turtle is heard in the Land* [2:11, 12]. . . .

The Lineaments also of the human Mind are beautifully drawn, and the Passions themselves painted to the Life. In what strong Colours has He pictured the Vehemence of Love and Jealousy! *Love is strong as Death, Jealousy is cruel as the Grave* [8:6]. . . . The Spouse is describ'd with that Violence, yet that Tenderness of Affection, We may well say, *her Love is wonderful passing the Love of Women* [II Sam. 1:26]. With how elegant an Abruptness does She begin the Dialogue? *Let him kiss me with the kisses of his mouth!* [1:2] . . .

Surely the Author of this beautiful Love-Poem, was the softest of Poets, as well as the wisest of Men.

> John Husbands. Preface to *A Miscellany of Poems by Several Hands* (Oxford, J. Husbands, 1731), sigs. 12ʳ–13ᵛ

From an artistic point of view, it is to be observed that the characters are clearly distinguished from one another, and are consistent throughout. The permanent element in the poem are the "Daughters of Jerusalem" (1:5; 2:7; 3:5; 5:8, 16; 8:4)—i.e. no doubt the ladies of the Court, who play a part somewhat like that of the chorus in a Greek play. . . . The principal character is, of course, the Shulamite maiden, a paragon of modesty and beauty, who awakens the reader's interest in the first chapter, and engrosses it till the end. . . . The speeches attributed to the king are somewhat stiff and formal; those of the lover, on the contrary, breathe a warm and devoted affection. . . .

The poem can hardly be said to exhibit a "plot" in the modern sense of the term; the action is terminated, not by a favourable combination of circumstances, but by the heroine's own inflexible fidelity and virtue. . . .

The poetry of the Song is exquisite. The movement is graceful and light; the imagery is beautiful, and singularly picturesque; the author revels among the delights of the country; one scene after another is brought before us—doves hiding in the clefts of the rocks (2:14) . . . gazelles leaping over the mountains (2:9) . . . flowers with bright hues or richly-scented perfume are ever supplying the poet with a fresh picture or comparison.

> Samuel R. Driver. *An Introduction to the Literature of the Old Testament*. 10th ed., rev. and enl. (New York, Scribner's, 1903), pp. 446–47

The arbitrary ascribing of the religious significance, though in the eyes of many a devotee, a blessed theory, is not particularly interesting to the sincere student of the work as a piece of monumental Hebraic literature, a thing which though indeed symbolic, has its best claim thereto in its immediate and direct structure.

Love is its theme, human love, divinely human. It is neither a mystic-religious nor a purely erotic writing, however; but something more interesting and with a better claim to the immortality which has preserved it through the centuries. It is an epithalamium, or marriage-song, carrying out with haunting perfection the theme of the triumph of love. It might be called a little "morality" on the motive of love-loyalty. . . .

The dramatic idea has vaguely occurred to many, but was finally and quite desperately, dismissed by the majority, in favor at last of a rather disconnected series of love-lyrics, with no continuity except the general unity of theme. [Ernest] Renan, however, bold and sensitive student brought the parts into directly joined dialogue, dividing by natural denouements into scenes and acts. He has added nothing, taken away nothing; . . .

With the removal of the crust of theology, the antique drama is seen in all its honest outlines, immortally young and fresh as the newly-discovered frescoes under the ages' covering of dust and smoke. These characters are as clearly and effectively defined one against another as our more subtly juxtaposed types of to-day. Only the ancient way of treating them seems to us naively abrupt and inconsequent. But the peculiar quality of each is retained intact throughout, and the unity of the whole, as depending on the furtherance of one motive, may be said to be well maintained. . . . The shepherd will be remembered for his frank and steadfast wooing, so richly embellished with every fancy and allusion to nature, while the vine-dresser herself stands forth supreme in her beauty through all the passing centuries, the ever-longed-for, never-won, yet all-yielding flower of life—incarnation and symbol—the complete love of woman when she knows her inmost soul.

Ruby Archer. Poet Lore. Mar. 1907, pp. 97–98, 106

It is the first of all the love poems in the world, and I would sooner have written it than the whole of the rest of literature. How it got into the Canon of Holy Scripture is a puzzle, for it is pure sexual passion without the least trace of religious sentiment, all the more beautiful for that. [1917]

Wilfrid S. Blunt. My Diaries. Vol. II (New York, Alfred A. Knopf, 1923), p. 169

The tissue of the book, as the title intimates, is superlatively lyric, the loftiest reach of Hebrew song. It is the lyric mood, with its singleness and intensity of emotional states, that is throughout the controlling element. All along, however, a quasi-dramatic element supervenes, a suggestion of scene and personation, which tempts the reader to search for a coordinated plot but with elusive results. To make a built drama of it, or even something analogous to an Elizabethan masque, calls for too much artifice of interpretation; it does not justify itself against the next expositor. The Hebrew genius, at its freest in the impassioned lyric, was lame and clumsy in the dramatic; the Book of Job has to some extent evinced that. We can, however, call the book before us a lyric cycle. Somewhat

like the libretto of a cantata, it is a series of lyric moods, called forth by conflicting interests or desires, and moving in music to a firm lyric situation, which latter embodies the underlying purpose of the whole. Thus, while not unobservant
of dramatic concatenation, its parts remain true to the dictum later laid down by
Milton that a living poem should be "simple, sensuous, impassioned." It lets the
passion of pure and invincible love sing its own story.

John F. Genung. *A Guidebook to the Biblical Literature*
(Boston, Ginn, 1919), pp. 486–87

[The songs] do not represent grandiose poetry like the Symposium in Job or like
the Nature Poems added as a third stratum to the Book of Job; they betray no profound thought nor striking originality as do the reflections of Koheleth. They are
certainly not to be compared with the exquisite and sublime poetry of the Psalms,
nor are they literary gems such as are many of the sayings in the Book of Proverbs. They must be taken for what they are intended—simple little songs that
make their appeal by their genuine reflection of the folk spirit exercising itself on
a theme of thoroughly human and therefore of universal appeal. . . .

[As love lyrics, they] form one of the most precious as well as one of the
most charming legacies of the remote past. They afford us a picture of a phase of
life which is only occasionally touched upon in the pages of the Bible—
sometimes in the Book of Proverbs, and here and there in the tales of Genesis,
but nowhere with the grace and the poetic glow of the Song of Songs.

Morris Jastrow. Foreword to *The Song of Songs* (Philadelphia, Lippincott, 1921), p. 13

The full power of nature . . . suffuses the love poetry that finds a wondrous expression in this little book—a book that is so different from the remaining poetic
books of the Bible both in form and in content. Its charms are in this integration
with nature, in the great intoxication of blossoming, in the great longings for the
full happiness of land, and most especially in the acknowledgment that it is no
sin for us to listen to the voice of our blood; in the acknowledgment that love is a
foremost grace, a foremost privilege, and "scorn be unto" the man [Song 8:7]
who renounces it. Were it not for the Song of Songs we would not really be acquainted with the ancient Israelite man who took upon himself no other sovereign
than the sovereignty of the heart.

The unique charm of the Song of Songs lies in the fact that love and nature
are so firmly interlaid that there are times when we cannot tell what intoxicates
us more, the marvels of nature or the sparks of love. There is no discriminating
here between the light of love and the light of nature; the two blend and dissolve
into one another. The voice of the beloved joins with the voice of the turtledove
that is heard, as autumn passes, with the bright buds that appeared in the land.
The pleasures of youth sprouted at the same time as the grapevine and the date,
which gave off their fragrance, beckoning us to go out to the field, to lodge for
the night in the villages—to celebrate a festival of the blooming that covers the

ground. For the whole land is touched and with it the heart of man is touched, ripe for love, ripe for happiness. . . .

In the eight little chapters of the Song of Songs are assembled bits of Hebrew folk poetry very different from ancient Israelite poetry. Here there is neither the rebuke of chastisement nor words of appeasement and consolation. It is a primitive voice. It is spring in the world, spring bursting with all its might; there is no stopping it and no standing in its way. All the forces of life unite and pour out their dominion over man, who is set face to face before the powers. Love is here the most potent embodiment of the forces of existence that burst from their hiding places.

They forever amaze us, these fugitive voices of the heart of ancient man, who was naïve in nature and never had to think that love, with all its naïveté and warmth, took on such a complete sanctity in his soul. . . .

Out of the poetry the world of creation lights up, a world both exposed and closed at the same time. How few things are narrated here! And even so, each solitary line seems to fill a world of space. A slight event, even the hint of an event, immediately conjures up an image, bringing us near to the heart of the vision. The little suntanned shepherdess, whose brothers, sons of her mother, made her guard of the orchards and then grumbled at her when she failed to guard her orchard and went off to find him whom she loved—she is evidently only ethereal, insubstantial in her entrance. But these few etched lines immediately form in our hearts the graceful character of the naïve, perplexed girl, a stranger in her mother's house, presented alone in a wreath of happiness and pain and fear, before the world of spring rising and storming about her. And in the midst of her happiness she sees herself abandoned and pained.

The narrative restraint of the book actually pains us. How can we find out what has happened here? What became of the orchard girl straying lovesick in the fields, seeking out her beloved in the shepherds' pastures, all aflame, embarrassed as she passes by the flocks of her friends? In effect, almost nothing will be told. But all the time we are accompanying the girl who searches for her beloved in bewilderment along the lighted anxiety path of love. None of the world's elaborate tales of sorrow about love can touch our hearts like the wail of this girl whose beloved had been so close that her soul would move at his command; and yet at one moment she prentends not to know him, at another she treats him cruelly, and he slips away without knowing that for many restless nights she had waited for him, prayed for him, and listened for his footsteps from across the mountains. Here is a universal clue to the riddle of love, to the secret of its restlessness and hesitations, to that peculiar rebelliousness that attacks the soul of lovers and hurts them, that out of an abundance of love puts them to the test— with pain and regret afterward. All the charms and tribulations of love of which the poets of the world and the later great poets of Israel knew how to tell and sing are already alluded to in the chapters of this little *poema*. . . .

There has been so much controversy over the book's structure, literary genre, nature, and content that the multiplicity of opinions and arguments threaten to blur the picture entirely. Scholars make efforts to reveal the unity of the book as a complete poetic composition by means of conjectures and incisive syntheses and analyses. But any naïve reader senses the common light, the common sensibility in this work. The same basic nuance of expression, of music, of perception, the nuance that is the secret of its charm, cannot be disintegrated by any deletions or rearrangements. This is the power of authentic poetry: Every part of it maintains the power of the whole, of all its combinations. Every verse in the Song of Songs is a bright thread in the embroidery of the entire poem, and at the same time it gives off its own light. Hasn't this been identified as the power of every verse of prophecy, that while it seems separate from its fellows it is tied to them by a thousand unseen threads? . . .

Anyone for whom this poetry has become a part of his soul does not need to know whether it is an idyllic epic, as Goethe conceived, an anthology of folk songs, or a dramatic play. He tastes in it the flavor of all the poetic genres as one. There is no doubt that in this composition there is a mixture of the various elements that are in all ancient poetry, but with added power and grace. It is the grace of nature, which knows not the bounds and genres of poetics, which flows simultaneously through all the channels and simultaneously takes the shape of all poetic forms that reverberate with the whole and with every individual link in it. Doesn't the charm of the Song of Songs' grace rest in the fact that we walk through it as though on the floor of a thick, untrodden forest, breathing the scented grasses, the branches of the shrubbery growing wildly into one another, the patches of blue never ceasing to wink through the lattices of its bright eyes?

Jacob Fichman, 'Arugot (Jerusalem, Bialik Institute, 1954), pp. 272–75, 277–78, 280†

Had we not received a tradition that King Solomon wrote this Song, we would say that a *woman* composed it. The book of the Song of Songs is a female composition, written from the point of view of the woman, not the man. In the majority of verses it is the woman who speaks, who acts, and, most importantly, who reflects; the book is conveyed to us for the most part out of the rumination of the woman and not the man.

This will become immediately clear if we scan the book element by element: The first element is *repeating verses*. Into the book, like a golden thread, have been woven verses repeated twice or three times, and according to biblical style, they unify the book. *All these verses are the woman's and not the man's.* For example, "His left hand is under my head . . ." in chapters 2 and 8; or "My beloved is mine and I am his" in chapters 2, 6, 7; Or "I have sworn you, O daughters of Jerusalem, by the gazelles or by the hinds of the field, that you not arouse or rouse love until it be fulfilled" in chapters 2, 3, 8. . . .

The second element, which is the most poetic and original in the book, is the presence of highly dramatic scenes in which the Shulamite depicts herself speaking or meeting with her beloved or others, such as the daughters of Jerusalem or the watchmen roving through the city, on the affairs of her love, and she tells us what was said or done at those meetings. . . .

Besides these two, there are other elements in the book of the Song of Songs, especially descriptions of the bodies of the two lovers, dialogue between them—or the lovers' praises to their counterpart—or *songs having fixed openings,* such as the songs beginning with "Who is this coming (observed) . . ." in 3:6; 8:5; or "Behold, you are fair . . ." (1:15; 4:1; 6:4)—compare the stereotypical openings in the songbooks of the Yemenites. . . . These elements are apparently popular and conventional in the nation, while the first two are the product of the poet and inspiration. . . .

In addition, it should be said that the entire *atmosphere* in the book of the Song of Songs is female; there is here an air of a circle of women, or, as it is said a few times in the book, of "my mother's house." The father is not mentioned once, but mention of the mother, the mother of both the male lover and his "companion," occurs frequently. Even in those places where the parents' affection for their daughter is described, where we expect the father in particular to be mentioned, it says: "She is her mother's one, her progenitress' favorite" (Song 6:9). . . . The friends of the male beloved, too, are mentioned only *twice* and in the third person, while the speaker addresses the *daughters* of Jerusalem, or the *daughters* of Zion, no fewer than seven times. . . .

If we attend to the *linguistic allusions* expressed in a verse, we will find that the text itself brings this out; at the end of the Garden of Eden story in the book of Genesis, there appear the imprecations by which Adam, Eve, and the serpent were cursed. The curse of Eve is "To your man will be your dependence, and he will rule over you" [Gen. 3:16]. A woman's desire, her dependence upon her husband, is what subordinates her to him. But in the book of the Song of Songs the Shulamite says: "I am my beloved's, and his dependence is upon me" [Song 7:11]. In other words, she reverses what is said in the book of Genesis, as though she feels that what is said there in that early book no longer expresses the relations of men and women in her generation.

Shelomo Dov Goitein. *'Omanut hassippur bammiqra'*
(Jerusalem, Jewish Agency Aliyah and Youth Division,
1957), pp. 106, 108–9†

The work is an unabashed commentary on the sentiment of Proverbs 30:18–19, "three things are too wonderful for me, four I do not understand . . . the way of a man with a maid." There is no mystery about the book in its essential outlines. It is a series of poems describing the delights of human love and written with Oriental sensuousness. . . . The poems exalt the psychophysical union of men and women, albeit with a trace of romanticism that is at times airily adolescent. Yet it expresses throughout a fundamental Hebraic feeling about the unalloyed wonder and the essential rightness of the man-woman relationship.

But before it could find acceptance in the Jewish canon, the work had to be interpreted allegorically of God and Israel. The way was open for this line of interpretation ever since Hosea had set forth the union of Yahweh and his people under the marriage symbol. . . .

The traditional alternative to the allegorical dodge has been the dramatic interpretation, which assumes that the work is a dramatic integrity, in parts consisting of the speeches of the three principal characters: Solomon, a shepherd, and a maiden. . . . There is no sustained dialogue and not even as much evidence of staging as in the case of Job, where the dramatic interpretation is also fallacious. . . .

The view that the Song is an anthology of lyric poems has, until very recently, held the virtually uncontested lead in modern criticism. . . . In recent scholarship the cult-mythical theory of the Song of Songs has been advanced with much ingenuity. Basically its advocates claim that the work does not refer to human love at all but to the sacred marriage of a god and goddess as celebrated in many of the Near Eastern cults, notably Tammuz worship. Later the songs were spiritualized for monotheistic consumption by replacing the goddess with the figure of Israel, the Bride of Yahweh. . . . When held uncompromisingly, the cult-mythical theory turns out to be only a somewhat more sophisticated form of the allegorical interpretation.

The Song is as near to Romanticism as the Old Testament gets. In fact, here alone is nature considered as a phenomenon in its own right, a world evocative to the senses, aesthetically delightful, mirroring and echoing the lovers' raptures. . . . The bucolic playfulness of Theocritus, the breathless ecstasy of Keats and the Brownings, need no apology when they appear in the Old Testament. The Song of Songs serves as a welcome reminder that the Hebrews were men like ourselves, that their quest for God and God's choice of them did not nullify their passionate love of life and their simple rejoicing in the sexuality of the race.

> Norman K. Gottwald. *A Light to the Nations: An Introduction to the Old Testament* (New York, Harper, 1959), pp. 491–94

Rhetoric knows special triumphs in the Song of Songs. For with whatever persuasion one approaches or leaves the Song, one must deal with it rhetorically. The speech of this greatest of biblical poems is highly artificial. It is packed with rhetorical figures. Some of them are marvelously lucid in themselves but hopelessly opaque in context. Some are of an intrinsic opacity that makes any translation of meaning questionable: One must seize these by an ironclad intuition and hold them by a conviction of the same metal. All the figures, no matter what their surface simplicity or complexity, are remote, abstruse, patently of an ambiguity of circumstance or characterization that will allow no less than two meanings and will often permit a half-dozen or more, going as far as the rhetorical training, the human experience, and the poetic graces of the reader can take him.

One cannot fight shy of rhetoric in the Song of Songs. Whether one sees the book as an unparalleled flight of mysticism or a paean of praise of sexual union, it works its way in terms of rhetoric. It calls a cheek a cheek, a breast a breast, and an eye an eye. But it also calls a cheek a piece of pomegranate, a breast a young roe, an eye a weapon that wounds, and brings up among the heavy artillery of love one hair on the neck. It does not hesitate to compare the whole neck to "the tower of David, which is built with bulwarks," a thousand small round shields hanging on it, "all the armour of valiant men" (4:4)—the literal-minded can perhaps be forgiven for seeing in this formidable piece of anatomy something less than a comely object.

Barry Ulanov. *The Bridge*. Vol. 4, 1961–62, p. 89

It is inspired by the joyous spirit of a healthy normal youth with its happy optimism, its gaiety, its love of good-natured fun. This is a feature of the Song which has been overlooked by its commentators. They have invested the Song with a serious edifying character which does not fit it at all. It abounds in playfulness, in gentle raillery and fun, mingled with touching sentiments of love and tenderness. Only as playful banter can be rationally explained the grotesque description by the lover to the damsel of her neck as "like the tower of David built for an armoury", of her nose "as the tower of Lebanon which looketh toward Damascus", and of her head like mount Carmel (4:4, 7:5, 6), and similar comical comparisons of her other limbs. Pure fun is also the lover's offer to take the damsel to the high mountain tops of the Lebanon in order to frighten the little girl with the horrid lions in their dens and the tigers in the mountains (4:8), or the charming comparison of the damsel's figure to the lofty slender palm tree which he would climb up and take hold of the boughs and enjoy (a mixed metaphor) the vine clusters of her breasts and the apples' smell of her nose (7:7–8).

Similarly the damsel displays a vein of fun and gaiety in various parts of the Song. In the opening she demands from the swain: "Draw me, we will run after thee" (1:4). When she charges the daughters of Jerusalem by an oath, it is not a solemn oath by the Deity or even by their life, as usual in the Bible, but a merry oath by the roes and hinds of the field (2:7, etc.). In the banqueting house she is seized with a sickness and demands to be stayed with flagons and to be comforted with apples, for it is only a sickness of love (2:4–5). She talks of her lover leaping upon the mountains, skipping upon the hills, for he is like a roe and a young hart, and when he reaches her home he looks furtively through the windows and peeps through the lattices (2:8–9). She tells a long and sad tale of her ill-treatment by the town's watchmen in the darkness of the night when she was searching for her lost lover, and when the daughters of Jerusalem, moved to pity by her suffering, offer to help her in the search of her incomparable lover if she would tell them whither the lover had gone she answers merrily that the lover had only gone into his garden to pick flowers (5:2–6:2). To the complaint of her brothers of the difficulty of finding her a husband because she has no breasts and is like a wall, she retorts that she is indeed like a wall with her big breasts for its towers (8:10). All this playfulness and merriment in the Song is the natural product of the healthy and happy youthfulness of its actors. Finally to the youth of its actors may be largely ascribed the remarkable love of the Song for the landscape and all its variegated beauty and wealth, its mountains and hills, its gardens and vineyards, its trees and flowers, its fruits and wine and oil and honey, and above all the unexampled profusion of its scents and perfumes which fill the Song from beginning to end.

M. H. Segal. *Vetus Testamentum*. Oct., 1962 pp. 480–81

To judge from contemporary literature, the easiest books of the Bible for modern man to appreciate, in his completely secular society, are Job and the Song of Songs. The reason is obvious. They are not what he thinks of as religious. . . .

There are almost as many interpretations of the Song of Songs as there are interpreters. . . . The mythic interpretation of the Song of Songs which I prefer, and suspect might even be true, greatly resembles Marcel Granet's *Festivals and Songs of Ancient China,* his essential and revolutionary interpretation of the *Shi Ching,* the Chinese *Book of Odes*. There are several contemporary biblical critics who share this interpretation, which is: the Song of Songs is a collection of dance lyrics for group marriage, which were sung as young men and maidens danced in the fields and vineyards at the corn harvest festival, and when the water was turned from the irrigation ditches into the runnels between the rows of grape-vines, and finally at the grape harvest. . . .

An understanding of the background of the Song of Songs not only makes the poems themselves far more thrilling, but it restores to a central place in our conceptions of the world as holy, the sanctification of the communion of man and woman, of the people in community, of mankind and the earth from which he is made, and of earth and heaven.

Last but not least, the songs of the Song of Songs are very simply among the most beautiful love songs in all the literatures of the world, not to mention their contemporaneity—"I am black, but comely, O ye daughters of Jerusalem" [1:5].

Kenneth Rexroth. *Saturday Review of Literature*. April 26, 1969, p. 16

[It] is a notable example of how one love poet solved the problem of depicting romantic, sexual love in literature. On the one hand, the poet avoids the pitfall of allowing the love to evaporate into an abstraction by continually making physical attractiveness the main ingredient of the romantic relationship. On the other hand, the poet avoids pornography by consistently choosing to portray the sexual love that is his subject through the use of symbolism. The result is that we get a strong impression of the sexual attractiveness of the lovers and the value of their physical love without being asked to picture the physical details of their relationship.

Leland Ryken. *The Literature of the Bible* (Grand Rapids, Mich., Zondervan, 1974), p. 230

The influence of the Song of Songs loomed large in the history of world literature. The European love lyric has rarely equaled its naïveté and immediacy of expression. In Hebrew literature it was regarded with special reverence after the revered Rabbi Akiba interpreted it as an allegory of love between God and Israel and declared that "all the books in Scripture are holy but the Song of Songs is the holy of holies" (Mishnah, *Yadayim* 3:5).

Eisig Silberschlag. In *The Princeton Encyclopedia of Poetry and Poetics*. Ed. by Alex Preminger et al. Enl. ed. (Princeton, N.J., Princeton University Press, 1974), p. 339

It looms incongruously over the remainder of the Bible, a joyous and self-confident collection of ecstatic love lyrics which seem so far removed from Israel's tortured history in the days of the Divided Kingdom, and yet so worldly and so firmly rooted in the matrix of the people's daily life. The lovers call to one another in their richly-laden metaphors which, unlike Ezekiel's pointed reverie of man-made objects, mingle indiscriminately similes of human-made and natural: "Your lips are like a scarlet thread . . . Your cheeks are like the halves of pomegranates. . . . Your breasts are like two fawns . . ." (4:3–5); "His cheeks are like spice-beds . . . and his lips are lilies . . . and his arms are rounded gold inlaid with jewels, and his body is a work of ivory encrusted with sapphires, and his legs are alabaster columns set on golden bases. . . ." (5:13–15). Here we find a world transformed by youthful love, a world where king and peasant can confront each other in complete equality, a world in which the artificial and the natural are in perfect harmony, a world in which the woman and the man are siblings. And a woman unabashedly aggressive and outspoken, and a man possessed more than he endeavors to possess—things seem topsy-turvy. This book of canticles is polymorphously perverse. Sexuality inhabits all of nature and society, and occupies no single privileged locus of the human body. Words of love emerge ubiquitously animating, and ubiquitously erogenous. Yet nowhere is the male-female polarity more perfectly embodied. It is this exemplar, above all, that we must keep in mind when we conceive the possibility of sexual polarity devoid of sexual exploitation. And we must keep in mind, as well, that when we conjure up this possibility, we instantaneously revise not just the female-male relationship but the foundations of society itself. The world of Canticles, however, is by no means to be thought of as a Paradise. It represents a model of the culmination in development of civilized society itself, a bold incorporation of (and not retreat to) nature's bounty. The lovers in this song remain pre-eminently civilized, pre-eminently barbarized, in one. Not for nothing is this song recited every Sabbath and at Passover. This harmonious interpenetration of the works of nature and culture is the blueprint for the next degree of human evolution.

Joel Rosenberg. *Response*. Winter, 1975–76, pp. 84–85

If the Song [of Songs] is not a structural unity, what kind of compilation is it? I maintain that it is a collection of lyric love poems. But what exactly do we mean by "lyric"? The terms "lyric" and "lyrical" are surely among the more impressionistic words in our language; we seem to use them as much to characterize and praise as to specifiy and distinguish. Yet we do have certain things in mind when we call a work "lyrical," and it may be worth exploring both the more apparent and the less obvious senses of the term in order to see how they apply to the Song.

If lyric verse is distinguished from narrative and dramatic verse primarily by length and scope, all the poems in the Song would have to be seen as lyrics. So too, if we think of the lyric as sensual, the exquisitely rich imagery of the Song would certainly qualify the Song as lyrical poetry. . . .

Brevity, sensuality, and musicality, however, do not suffice to define the lyric. The lyric tends to be a subjective form, expressive of *personal* feeling toward specific subject matter and addressed to a *particular* listener. The speaker of the lyric is usually an individual I-speaker, although, as we shall see shortly, more than one voice may sometimes speak a lyric. The subject matter of the lyric can vary widely: it may be simple or complex, commonplace or extraordinary, secular or religious, public or private. And the audience of the lyric (by which I mean the listener whom the speaker addresses, not necessarily the readership of the poem) may be almost anyone—a relation, a friend, a beloved, a stranger, God, or the self. To see what kinds of lyrics comprise the Song, it may prove useful to examine the Song's various speakers in relation to their subject matter and audience.

For example, in the various poems of the Song in which a lover speaks to or about a beloved, there is present, to use Martin Buber's phrase, an I-Thou relationship. This relationship is most evident when the speaker directly addresses the beloved, but it may still be felt when the beloved is spoken of only in the third person. In other kinds of poems in the Song, however—those whose subject matter is erotic but which do not focus primarily on the beloved or the personal love relationship—the I-Thou relationship may be subordinate or absent. The presence or absence, and relative prominence, of the I-Thou relationship may therefore provide a means of distinguishing different types of love lyrics in the Song.

> Marcia Falk. *Love Lyrics from the Bible* (Sheffield, England, Almond Press, 1982), pp. 71–72 [slightly revised by the author]

TAMAR, RAPE OF

Chapter 13 [of II Sam.] begins with a brutal and premeditated act of violence, the rape of a virgin, an act condemned as $n^e v \bar{a} l \bar{a}$—wanton or outrageous folly in Israel. We observe what a great part sex plays in the whole narrative. There is much passion but very little love. And while the external events may signify simply the removal of the oldest son, heir presumptive to the throne, such a plot could have been forwarded with much less trouble and detail than is here displayed. Indeed, we quickly note the care with which each move of the affair is recounted, as well as the fact that events move without a pause to the end of chapter 14. So we must look deeper. The death of David's child by Bathsheba was the direct result of YHWH's displeasure, we were told in 12:14. Yet chapter 13 and its sequel form a far truer consequence of David's undisciplined act, for here he could not control the passions of his sons, any more than his own. He seems even to have entered as accomplice into their passions and schemes, for David played the "Joab" to Amnon's "David," by sending Tamar to his bedside, though he must have seen through the simple plan. It is difficult to believe that David, himself the author of much subtler intrigues, would have been completely taken in by such transparent designs as this one and Absalom's conspiracies in 13:23–27 and 15:7f.

A number of commentators have remarked on the reserve and reticence with which our author treats scenes such as the present one. And yet we note the deliberate detail, the slowed pace of action, and the concentration upon particulars. The story makes use of the technique of repetition: first Jonadab advised Amnon to feign illness and ask David to send Tamar to feed him; then Amnon did so. Next, David relayed the message to Tamar, and finally she came to prepare the cakes for her half-brother. Each time the details of word and action are repeated. Even then, the tale is delayed while we are treated to a minute account of her preparation of the delicacies—she took dough and kneaded it, patted out the cakes and fried them, brought the pan and dumped out the tasty dish for Amnon. Still the inevitable is put off—Amnon would not eat with his retainers looking on. They were dismissed, and Tamar was again asked to bring the cakes into his private chamber. Why this insistent detail, when the reader knows what will happen from the first words of Jonadab? Surely it is the art of the narrator, who intends us to have no doubt at all about the dark side of the human soul. There is no moralizing here, no editorial comment upon the deed. But we are forced to listen to the deliberate, inevitable progression of events leading to the act itself. In like manner we have already heard of the succession of events which forced David —if we may speak in such terms— to take the extreme step of murdering Uriah, and we are about to hear of Absalom's revenge, which he brooded over for two full years. Now all of these details could hardly have been known to the author, be he Abiathar, Ahimaaz, or some other figure close to the court but unknown to us. Only Amnon and Tamar were present at the climax of chapter 13—and even if Tamar had revealed all to her brother Absalom or some other, it is immediately apparent that the story and the dialogue have been carefully shaped to meet the needs of the story-teller. This is far from denying that the events took place, either in this episode or elsewhere. It simply emphasizes the painstaking care with which the author moulded his material. Indeed, the "faithfulness" of his account could hardly be greater, for he tells us that immediately "Amnon felt an exceedingly violent hatred for her; indeed the hatred with which he hated her was even greater than the love with which he had loved her. So Amnon snapped at her, 'Up! Get out!'" When she refused, and told him that this would be even worse than what he had already done to her, he ordered his servant to "Get this thing (Z'ōt) out of my sight outside, and bolt the door after her!" (II Sam. 13:15–17). One could hardly express more clearly Amnon's revulsion at his act, or the fact that he had treated his half-sister as a thing, not as a person.

When David heard of it, he was characteristically very angry, but he did nothing. Absalom, however, had taken matters into his own hands, and determined to murder the man who stood between him and the throne. Another violent act was then reported to David, who again resorted to open lament but took no action, passively condoning the deed. Once again the king was humiliated in the sight of all his courtiers, in that he lay helplessly grieving for Amnon on the ground, the victim of his sons' lawless acts. Most remarkable of all, when his nephew Jonadab spoke up, as if in all innocence, to announce that only Amnon of the king's sons was dead, since Absalom had plotted to kill him ever since the abuse of Tamar, the king was silent. We might have expected David to ask how he knew so much about it, but he did nothing of the sort.

Jared J. Jackson. *Canadian Journal of Theology*, 11, 3, 1965, pp. 189–91

Following the dramatic events [of II Sam. 13] the narrative ends in tranquillity: Tamar sits desolate in the house of her brother Absalom; David is very angry but he will not lift a finger; and even Absalom refrains from any concrete action. This tranquillity, however, exists only on the surface; beneath the surface, in the heart of Absalom, as the narrator hints, are disquiet and agitation. And this disquiet and agitation will blow up and come to expression in action at a later stage. In what is said at the end of verse 22, "For Absalom hated Amnon on account of his having raped his sister, Tamar," there is something of a preparation and transition to what will come afterward. But the reader will deal with this only after the fact. At this point it seems that Absalom's hatred is resolved in his silence toward Amnon, and there is nothing to compel any additional expression of this hatred. For this reason Absalom's act of revenge two years later comes as a complete surprise (not as in the story of Dinah, where the revenge comes as no surprise to the reader, as the narrator has opened his eyes beforehand in saying that Jacob's sons spoke with Shechem and Hamor *deceitfully*—Gen. 34:13).

With a comprehensive, summary view of the Amnon and Tamar narrative in its totality, the following characteristic features strike the eye:

The narrator knows all, but he does not make known to us all that he knows. He is a first-hand witness to the secret consultation between Amnon and Jonadab, and he is an eyewitness to the act of rape, at which no one was present but Amnon and Tamar themselves. His unlimited knowledge is expressed especially in the large number of interior views that are found in the narrative: "he loved her" ([v.] 1), "Amnon was upset" ([v.] 2), "it was beyond Amnon" ([v.] 2), "he did not desire" ([vv.] 14, 16), "Amnon hated her a very great hatred, for the hatred that he hated her was greater than the love which he loved her" ([v.] 15), "he was very angry" ([v.] 21), "for Absalom hated Amnon" ([v.] 22). Such a large concentration of direct information from the narrator concerning the internal state of the characters is unusual in biblical narrative, and it impresses its stamp upon the narrative before us. This information about the feelings and desires of the characters assists us in interpreting their behavior correctly: For example, without the information that after the rape Amnon hated Tamar a very great hatred, we would certainly have difficulty in making sense of her banishment from the house. Yet, in other stories in the Bible, too, it is sometimes difficult to explain the behavior of the characters, and even so direct information is generally scarce concerning the personal motives, aspirations, and passions that engendered the behavior. It is not just that in our story the amount of internal information is great, but that by means of it is conveyed a comparison between two feelings, between the power of Amnon's love for Tamar and the power of his hatred toward her—a comparison that is not necessary for understanding the external behavior of Amnon.

It must be concluded that our story attributes importance to the internal lives of the characters, beyond what is routine in the narratives of the Bible, and that feelings attain in it a position and status on a par with external behavior and not below it.

> Shimeon Bar-Efrat. *Ha'itsuv ha'omanuti shel hassippur bammiqra'* (Tel Aviv, Sifriat Poalim, 1979), pp. 229–30†

The author [of II Sam. 13] has made use of a variety of means toward one end: to present Amnon as totally guilty, and indirectly to prepare a positive groundwork, or a reservoir of sympathy, for the shaping of the character Absalom. . . .

The narrator selected the circumstance of premediated and degrading rape, behind which stands one and only one character—Amnon. . . .

The chronological thread of the plot is the rape. The scenes that build the plot revolve around the act of rape. The first two scenes [vv. 3–7] describe the stage of *planning* and negate any possibility of a sudden, one-time storm of passion. The *execution*—scene three [vv. 8–18]—underscores the cruelty and lack of consideration of Amnon. This scene is itself constructed of several stages so that following the stage of the rape appears the stage of banishment, and the narrator takes pains to emphasize—by means of Tamar's words (v. 16)—that the stage of banishment, and not the stage of the rape, constitutes the climax of Amnon's degrading behavior. Presenting the banishment stage as more severe than the rape stage reinforces the impression of cruelty, the violation of law and lack of consideration in Amnon's behavior. The fourth scene [vv. 19–20] and the words of the conclusion [vv. 21–22] are devoted to the presentation of the *reactions*. Tamar's reaction magnifies the dimension of humiliation and obscenity. The reactions of David and Absalom arouse in the reader the sense of an absence of appropriate response. Similarly, the organization of the plot sequence in a structure of three [scenes] plus a [climactic] fourth emphasizes the importance that the author attaches especially to the reaction stage. . . .

In the shaping of the characters Tamar and Amnon there is an inverse correlation: The more that Amnon's character is drawn in a negative way, the more the character of Tamar stands out as positive. Despite her intelligence and integrity, she does not manage to save herself, and this fact emphasizes the advantage of force. Because these emphases contravene the norms of biblical morality, whoever perpetrates them automatically turns into a negative character. . . .

The delineation of details such as Amnon's house, Tamar's house, Amnon's bedroom, and the presence of men in the room produces the feeling that Amnon calculated the stages in planning the rape. In the first stage Tamar's going to Amnon's house arouses no suspicion because additional people were in the house. The conditions for the rape were created only in the second stage, when Amnon departed from the limits of Jonadab's advice, removed everyone from his presence, and invited Tamar to his bedroom to feed him his diet. The expulsion of Tamar and the description of locking the door behind her also underscore the brutality in Amnon's behavior. These details emphasize that everything connected to the rape plan and to what happens afterward is connected to Amnon alone.

The control of the flow of time in which the story is told teaches that the author preferred to prolong and detail precisely the scene of rape and the scene of Tamar's banishment, which highlight the guilt of Amnon. Thus, even the dimension of time contributes to building up a negative assessment of Amnon by expanding the negative aspects. . . .

The details of the narrator's own exposition [vv. 1–2] oppose to each other [two hypotheses about Amnon's love: an] innocent announcement of love in the family (v. 1) and details that combine into an array of broad hints about the strange nature of this love (v. 2). The narrator has presented to the reader two hypotheses, between which the reader must decide in the course of reading, as the narrator himself has already decided in no small measure in favor of the second hypothesis and laid bare the techniques of his influence: selection of words ("to become sick," "to do something to her"), judgments of his own ("she was a virgin"), syntactic structures (circumstantial clause and its embedding), direct characterization of the character's action (v. 2a), and penetration of thoughts (v. 2b). The unbalanced presentation of the hypotheses lays bare the narrator's viewpoint, and any additional information that the reader receives supports preference for the second hypothesis and demolition of the first. After the first two scenes Amnon is portrayed as a schemer, on account of his handling of Jonadab's advice and in light of the correlation between Jonadab's statement and David's interpretation (using the technique of repetition). After the rape scene and the banishment the reader has no doubts about the preference of the second hypothesis. The narrator's words of judgment (v. 15) make it clear that the dubious love that was announced in the first verse turned to great hatred. The existence of the two opposed hypotheses and the gradual demolition of the first hypothesis is a way of magnifying the guilt of Amnon. Retrospective deliberation on what happens strengthens this conclusion. The reader discovers after the fact that Amnon's love for Tamar was impetuous love and that Amnon was a heartless man of lust who was not punished for his actions.

Yairah Amit. Ha-sifrut. July, 1983, pp. 84–85†

In preparation for the crime, episode one [II Sam. 13:1–3] presents the characters and their circumstances; episode two [vv. 4–5] reports a scheme devised for the prince by his advisor; and episode three [vv. 6–9] enlists the authority of the king. Circular structures organize these first two units while the third builds on a chain of command and response. . . .

Following the transitional phrase, a ring composition introduces the characters around a description of circumstances (13:1–3). Within this structure, circular patterns reflect the whole. At the beginning come three children of David. First named is Absalom, the third son, whose presence hovers over the entire tale, though he himself appears only near the end. Last is Amnon, the firstborn, whose desire initiates the action. Between these two males stands the female who relates to each of them and also has her own identity. Sister to Absalom and object of desire to Amnon, this beautiful woman is Tamar. The circular arrangement of the verse centers upon her:

> To Absalom, *Son of David,*
> > a sister beautiful, with the name Tamar,
> and desired her *Amnon, son of David.* (13:1)

Two males surround a female. As the story unfolds, they move between protecting and polluting, supporting and seducing, comforting and capturing her. Further, these sons of David compete with each other through the beautiful woman. . . .

[In vv. 4–5] Jonadab is indeed cunning. Having elicited from Amnon a confession that seeks license, he schemes to gratify the prince. The skills of a counselor he employs to promote illness. He would use the father to overcome the obstacle of the brother and secure the sister. Around Amnon, then, his speeches weave a net of friendship that ensnares Tamar, Absalom, and David. With its own ring structure, this second episode bears emphatically the message of the first: Tamar is trapped. . . .

In this central unit [vv.9–18], form and content yield a flawed chiasmus that embodies irreparable damage for the characters. Amnon's commands and various responses to them mark the beginning and the end. Within the *inclusio* Amnon and Tamar are the sole participants. In the first half come his command and her response, followed by a conversation between the two. In the corresponding section of the second half, their conversation collapses into his command and her response. The rape itself constitutes the center of the chiasmus. This design verifies the message of the preceding circular patterns: Tamar is entrapped for rape.

a   Amnon's command to the servants and their response (13:9de)
   b   Amnon's command to Tamar and her response (13:10–11a)
      c   Conversation between Amnon and Tamar(13:11b–14a)
         d   Rape (13:14b–15b)
      c'–b'   Conversation between Amnon and Tamar:
         Amnon's command to Tamar and her response (13:15c–16)
a'   Amnon's command to a servant and his response (13:17–18). . . .

Rape is the center of the chiasmus. Quickly, though with emphasis, the deed unfolds. Third-person narration distances the terror while reporting it. "He was stronger than she; thus he raped her and laid her" (13:14b). All three verbs come from the preceding section. The one who "grabbed (*hzq*) hold of her" (13:11) is truly "stronger (*hzq*) than she." "Do not violate (*'nh*) me," she had pleaded (13:12); so "he raped (*'nh*) her." "Lie (*shkb*) with me," he had ordered (13:11); now "he lay (*shkb*)" not, however, with her because the Hebrew omits the preposition to stress his brutality. "He laid her." If the repetition of verbs confirm the predictability of Amnon's act, the direct object *her* underscores cruelty beyond the expected. The deed is done. . . .

With the rape concluded, the plot moves to the aftermath: a meeting between Tamar and Absalom, a report on David, and a concluding description of characters and circumstances. These three episodes correspond, though with notable differences, to the three episodes before the crime. The first two units parallel in content and order the two immediately preceding the crime. The third episode returns to the opening verse of the story, thereby completing an overall ring composition (i.e., A, B, C, D, B', C', A').

Phyllis Trible. Texts of Terror (Philadelphia, Fortress
Press, 1984), pp. 37–38, 41–42, 43, 46, 49

Tamar and Judah. *See* Joseph: Judah and Tamar

Ten Commandments. *See* Exodus: The Ten Commandments

Tower of Babel. *See* Babel, Tower of

Part 4
APOCRYPHA

ECCLESIASTICUS

A very ancient Author, whose Book would be regarded by our Modern Wits as one of the most shining Tracts of Morality that is extant, if it appeared under the name of a *Confucius,* or of any celebrated *Grecian* philosopher: I mean the little Apocryphal Treatise entitled, *The Wisdom of the Son of Sirach.* How finely has he described the Art of making Friends by an obliging and affable Behaviour? . . . And with what Strokes of Nature (I could almost say of Humour) has he described the Behaviour of a treacherous and self-interested Friend [6:7–12]? . . . I do not remember to have met with any Saying that has pleased me more than that of a Friend's being the Medicine of Life [6:16], to express the Efficacy of Friendship in healing the Pains and Anguish which naturally cleave to our Existence in this World. . . . There is another Saying in the same Author which would have been very much admired in an Heathen Writer: *Forsake not an old Friend, for the new is not comparable to him: A new Friend is as new Wine; when it is old thou shalt drink it with Pleasure* [9:10]. With what Strength of Allusion and Force of Thought, has he described the Breaches and Violations of Friendship [22:20–22]? . . . We may observe in this and several other Precepts in this Author, those little familiar Instances and Illustrations which are so much admired in the moral Writings of *Horace* and *Epictetus.* [May 18, 1711]

Joseph Addison. *The Spectator.* No. 68 (London, Printed for S. Buckley and J. Tonson, 1712), pp. 387–89

Jesus the son of Sirach writes, with the radiance of the canonical Hebrew Bible shining behind him, with keen literary appreciation of its beauty and truth; and yet with the fervor not of a reformer, like Ecclesiastes and the author of Job, nor yet of an ardent and impassioned missionary, like the second Isaiah; rather of a bookman and dilettant, who sits cosily in his library far from the noise of the world, and in his refined tastes is inclined to despise the common man "whose talk," as he says, "is of bullocks." So his book, as compared to the original scripture, is a mild, reflected radiance, like moonlight to sunlight; it does not seem, in the passion of a vital issue, so to get down to close grips with the inner heart-throbs of men.

The character of the mashal, or aphorism form, prevailing in the book, answers also to this bookish, as it were academic character. . . . Here in Ecclesiasticus, for the most part, the mashal has become a kind of short essay, wherein several aspects of the thought are given, or wherein the imagery is not entirely illustrative but revelled in, so to say, for its own sake. In sum we may say, the mashal is in complete running order, graceful, finished, smoothly constructed, —with the fire taken out, the edge a little blunted. . . .

The most notable parts of the book, perhaps, are toward the end; where there occurs a noble Hymn of Praise on the Works of Creation; and following that a really unique and original kind of scripture, a Praise of Famous Men. "Let us now praise famous men," the author begins, "and our fathers that begat us". . . .

> John F. Genung. *The Hebrew Literature of Wisdom in the Light of To-day* (Boston, Houghton Mifflin, 1906), pp. 274–75, 277–78

The style of our author is sufficiently described when it is recognized as the gradual transition from the stiffness of the gnomic sentence to the flowing rhetoric which delights to accumulate parallel sentences as an end in itself. Imagery and other striking forms of expression abound. The sway of unjust wrath is its downfall; a proud heart has rooted a plant of wickedness in its owner; he who refuses to confess his sins forces the current of the river; self-will dries up the soul like a withering tree; aged feet climbing up a sandy way make an image for a man weighted with an unworthy wife. The gossiping fool "travails" with his news; again it is said: "Has thou heard a word? let it die with thee: be of good courage, it will not burst thee" [19:10]. The images of the spark, the whip, the hedge, are effectively applied to the tongue (28:12); the impalpable dream is touched with a profusion of shadowy comparisons.

> Dreams give wings to fools. As one that catcheth at a shadow,
> and followeth after the wind, so is he that setteth his mind on
> dreams. The vision of dreams is as this thing against that, the like-
> ness of a face over against a face.

The most figurative writing is to be found in the encomium on the Works of the Lord (42:15). The falling snow is like the lighting of the locust, the hoar frost congeals as points of thorns; the cold north wind devours the mountains, burns up the wild, and consumes the green herb as fire; as it passes, every gathering together of waters puts on as it were a breastplate.

Resemblances in Ecclesiasticus to other literature will strike every reader; they may not be defined enough to afford a basis of argument, but they will awaken a curious interest. One would have felt sure that the suggestion of gratitude as a sense of favours to come was the product of modern cynicism: but the son of Sirach urges this gravely: "He that requiteth good turns is mindful of that which cometh afterward" (3:31).

It is a far cry from Bacon to Martin Tupper: yet Ecclesiasticus has affinities with both. In English literature it was Bacon that developed into Tupper: Ecclesiasticus represents a progression which is as if Tupper developed into Bacon.

To those who like their literary food spiced with humour it may be said that the son of Sirach makes the nearest approach to humour in a literature which the absence of that quality distinguishes from the other greatest literatures of the world. Formal philosophy has at least an historic interest in the widening survey of life which yet stops short of the questioning of life's difficulties. And the reader sensitive to literary form cannot fail to feel attracted by a work presenting such varieties of form: from the unit proverbs still collected to fill gaps, through the intermediary epigrams and maxims, to sonnets and monologues having the charm of highest poetry, and essays and encomia which, over and above the force of their shrewd and reverent thought, offer the constant attraction of watching a style in the act of developing.

Richard G. Moulton. *The Modern Reader's Bible* (New York, Macmillan, 1907), pp. 1468–69

This latecomer in God's vineyard mastered many literary forms which his predecessors had employed. Like the author of the first major section in Proverbs, Sirach used the didactic essay to great advantage. A single saying no longer sufficed to encapsulate the message Sirach hoped to communicate concerning any given subject. Instead, exposition became the normal mode of discourse. In the oldest collections of proverbs, the teachers had been satisfied with stimulating others to think through the implications of a given proverb, even at the risk of misinterpretation. Sirach resembles interpreters who rely upon others for the original material which they endeavor to illuminate by means of their highly trained critical faculties. Rarely did he permit a proverb to appear without any interpretation. Occasionally he did set one saying alongside another to provide contrasting descriptions, for example, of poverty and wealth; in the same manner that the earliest sages had done (13:3; cf. 20:5–6; 11:11–13).

The topics which Sirach chose to discuss are wide-ranging, although some subjects occur several times and give the impression of special fondness on the teacher's part. Like others before him, Sirach reflected often upon the danger posed by evil women. . . . Sirach was almost equally fascinated with the subject of death, which he treated with considerable depth and occasional humor, particularly when alluding to an inscription on a tombstone which read: "Mine today, and yours tomorrow." . . .

Occasionally, Sirach becomes a poet, using exquisite images (clouds fly out like birds, icicles form like pointed stakes, ice settles on every pool as though the water were putting on a breastplate).

James L. Crenshaw. *Old Testament Wisdom* (Atlanta, John Knox Press, 1981), pp. 160–61, 169

JUDITH

Some people think this is not an account of historical events [*Geschichte*] but rather a beautiful religious fiction [*Gedicht*] by a holy and ingenious man who wanted to sketch and depict therein the fortunes of the whole Jewish people and the victory God always miraculously granted them over all their enemies. This would be similar to the way Solomon in his Song poetizes and sings of a bride, yet means thereby not some specific person or event but the whole people of Israel. . . . Such an interpretation strikes my fancy, and I think that the poet deliberately and painstakingly inserted the errors of time and name in order to remind the reader that the book should be taken and understood as that kind of a sacred, religious, composition. . . . It may even be that in those days they dramatized literature like this, just as among us the Passion and other sacred stories are performed. In a common presentation or play they conceivably wanted to teach their people and youth to trust God, to be righteous, and to hope in God for all help and comfort, in every need, against all enemies, etc. [1534]

> Martin Luther. *Luther's Works,* American edition. Vol. XXXV. Ed. by Helmut T. Lehmann (St. Louis, Mo., Concordia/Philadelphia, Muhlenberg, 1960), pp. 338–39

Now, as in many other cases of noble history, apocryphal and other, I do not in the least care how far the literal facts are true. The conception of facts, and the idea of Jewish womanhood, are there, grand and real as a marble statue—possession for all ages. And you will feel, after you have read this piece of history, or epic poetry, with honourable care, that there is somewhat more to be thought of and pictured in Judith, than painters have mostly found it in them to show you: that she is not merely the Jewish Delilah to the Assyrian Samson; but the mightiest, purest, brightest type of high passion in severe womanhood offered to our human memory.

> John Ruskin. *Mornings in Florence.* Vol. III (Orpington, Kent, England, George Allen, 1875), pp. 60–61

The chief literary defect of the book is the lack of simplicity: the gorgeous Oriental *mise en scène,* the turgid style, the patent exaggerations, the stately pomp and ceremony throughout, unrelieved by a sense of humor, give to the book a baroque rather than a classic appearance. A comparison of the story of Judith's deed in prose (12:10–13:10) or in verse (16:6–9) with the similar assassination of a foe by Jael, as sung in Deborah's ode (Judg. 5:24–27) or told in simple prose (Judg. 4:17–22), is a contrast between the extravagantly ornate and the superbly natural, between sophistication and unadorned reality, between conscious and unconscious art.

Despite such literary blemishes, which are more or less characteristic of the period of Hebrew literature in which the book was written, the Book of Judith is a good example of an ancient short story. Even if the plot was previously known, the author displays considerable originality in working out the details, in injecting his patriotism and faith into the narrative, and in creating an imaginary, magnificent, historical background. His characters, in spite of their heroic stature, have psychological reality: Nebuchadnezzar, the imperial monarch whose ambition does not stop at world domination, but aspires to divine honors; Holofernes, the successful general to whom overconfidence and self-assurance bring sudden disaster; Judith, in whom noble devotion to God and nation is combined with feminine wiles, refined seductiveness, and unscrupulous resolve. With surprising candor, the author contrasts the assurance of the Ammonite Achior, who is certain that the Jews are unconquerable unless they have sinned against their God (5:5–21), with the abject terror of the Jews, who preferred surrender to defeat (7:19–28), and the weakness of their leaders, whose faint hope in divine help did not enable them to overcome the cowardly despair of the masses (7:30f.; cf. 8:28–31) and thus provoked Judith's indignation (8:11–27).

The author was utterly sincere when he presented Judith as his ideal, and her deed as a heroic act approved by God—nay, God's own deed for the salvation of his people through her hand (13:11, 14, 18; 16:6; cf. 8:33; 9:10, 13). But at this point the verdict of readers is not always in agreement with the author's, and as in the case of the Book of Esther extreme praise and extreme abuse have been poured out upon the book.

Robert H. Pfeiffer. *History of New Testament Times, with an Introduction to the Apocrypha* (New York, Harper, 1949), pp. 299–300

With chapter 10 begins what some critics consider the center of the story. This center is no doubt the best part and a masterpiece of narrative art in Hebrew literature. It is this section which gives greatness to the book, fame to its author and popularity to the story among readers, writers, and artists. From the moment Judith prepares herself and exits from the town until she comes back to tell her story, the narrator displays all his craft of plotting, suspense, character description, irony, vividness, emotional intensity, mixture of comedy and tragedy.

The rules of the art demand that the reader does not know the outcome, or at least how it is achieved. At new readings one will enjoy watching the cleverness of the whole development of specific details. A Jewish reader knew that the end would be a happy one: first, because that is expected from a Hebrew story; second, because the narrator has announced it with sufficient if discreet clarity. In 4:13 we read: "The Lord heard their prayer and pitied their distress," in which Exodus 2:24–25 clearly resounds. While in Exodus the call of Moses follows immediately, here the situation worsens before a savior is sent. The expectation becomes a conviction at the sight of the assuredness of Judith in 8:32: "I am going to do a deed which will be remembered among our people for all generations." The author feels no need to state at the end of chapter 9 that the Lord heard her prayer.

However at the same time he is disclosing the success, he is building up the reader's ignorance as to the way: "I am going to do *a deed*. . . . But do not try to find out my plan; I will not tell you until I have accomplished what I mean to do" (8:32, 34). Between the lines the author speaks to the reader: "I will not tell you until it is accomplished." If the ignorance of the authorities is not necessary for the plan to succeed, the ignorance of the reader is required.

A second factor sustains interest and curiosity: the five day limit. It has both a theological and a narrative function. It is theological because to put a limit on God is to tempt him. Tempting God is a theological category "Who are you to tempt God" (8:12). The mayor of the city has joined the old and pitiful tradition of Israel going back to the days in the desert. Moreover, since the mayor is bound by oath and cannot break it, the five day limit becomes a challenge to Judith and is an added factor of suspense. . . .

And so, with a sense of expectation we enter chapter 10. The author seems to enjoy mocking our expectations. Only five days to carry out her plan, and the lady leisurely spends her precious hours to make herself up. Against the Hebrew tradition of economy, this series of nine or ten minute actions is simply extravagant. Is the author grinning at our expense? Yes, and he is planting a clue for subsequent action.

If the mourning of Judith was also a lament for the destitution of her people, so her festive attire anticipates their salvation. "Awake, awake, put on your strength, O Zion, put on your beautiful garments, O Jerusalem the holy city . . . shake yourself from the dust, arise" (Isaiah 52:1–2). . . . A major key of exultation opens the new section, in sharp contrast to the somber preceding scenes. Judith's recovered beauty is almost a "symbolic action" of salvation. The tone of 13:11ff. will confirm this.

Judith's beauty becomes the leitmotif of the next section, by its dramatic effect on onlookers and admirers. After the first mention made by the narrator, her beauty receives the homage of successive groups of men. It evokes the stupor of Bethulia's elders (10:7); the admiration of the sentries (10:14); and it perturbs the discipline of the encampment (10:18). This beauty begins to be blinding and fateful: "Turn away your eyes from me, for they disturb me" (Song 6:5). Next it causes the amazement of the higher ranks, until it reaches the general. In this moment the most beautiful face bows to the earth and covers itself. . . . It was a sweeping, conquering campaign, telescoping and reversing the campaign of Holofornes. In one short journey she has reached the head of the greatest army, the heart of its commander.

> Luis Alonso-Schökel. In *Narrative Structures in the Book of Judith* (Berkeley, Cal., Center for Hermeneutical Studies in Hellenistic and Modern Culture, University of California, 1975), pp. 5–7

Compositional analysis demonstrates that all sixteen chapters of the narrative fulfill important structural roles in the whole of an intricate two-part composition.

This study shows that to excerpt a few verses or chapters from Part II about the deed of the woman Judith is to do violence to the whole of the story. To abbreviate the story by excluding or compressing the first chapters is to tell a story which differs in important ways from the one told by the author. Abbreviation makes the story into an heroic tale which is much easier than the full story. Part II, the tale of the woman Judith, entertains and even inspires us, but alone it does not confront us with hard choices. By watching Judith's model responses, we are somewhat distanced from the reality of the struggle involved in identifying the God of our own lives. The experience of the story is harder if first we agonize with the Israelites over the threat of the approaching enemy, reason with them as they try every way they know to get God's help, and finally come with them to the brink of apostasy. They decide that slavery is better than death, but they are not comfortable with their choice. It produces great depression (cf. 7:32). Their choice is one based on the conviction that they have no alternative. Judith's emergence from the very midst of the community neutralizes their mistaken notion that they have no hope. Her conviction that the God of Israel is a God free from human manipulation corrects and transforms their fear. To avoid Part I of the Book of Judith is to miss the opportunity to learn what the people of Bethulia seemingly have learned about their God and about proper worship by the end of chapter 16. In the end, they have a triumphant song of praise to sing, but this comes only after considerable struggle. . . .

For all the seriousness of its subject, the story of Judith is replete with lighthearted touches of comedy. That a woman as punctiliously pious as Judith does some of the things that she does, surely pokes fun at stodgy notions of propriety and proper religious behavior. And is it not high comedy to make Nebuchadnezzar an Assyrian and put him into an already destroyed capital city where he tells in detail his "secret" plan and gives an order to his chief general which the latter soundly disregards? The three-day, three hundred mile journey of the Assyrian forces, and the putting of sackcloth on everything in sight, including the cattle, must also be added to the list of humorous details. Surely Holofernes' four-day wait before trying to seduce Judith, his falling across the bed in a drunken stupor when finally he has his chance, and Judith's pausing to pray before chopping off his head are acts which satirize standard behavior in such settings. These and numerous other details and incidents suggest that comedy and satire are important dimensions of the Book of Judith.

An adequate treatment of Judith as comedy or satire would require lengthy study. While this is not the place for such discussion, it is appropriate to raise as an issue meriting further study the question of humor as a conventional narrative technique in ancient story-telling. Just as the architectural structure of the story is "classical" in the sense that it is patterned on repetitions characteristic of finely crafted biblical stories, so too humor of the type found in stories like Judith, Job, Jonah, Ruth, Esther, and Tobit may share common characteristics. They all exhibit finely proportioned literary structures, they all have happy endings, and they indeed all use comic touches to provoke profound theological realizations.

To be sure, in the Book of Judith humor is a potent tool used to describe unfolding dimensions of the relationship between Yahweh and the people of Israel.

Toni Craven. Artistry and Faith in the Book of Judith
(Chico, Cal., Scholars Press, 1983), pp. 113–16

TOBIT

What was said about the book of Judith may also be said about this book of Tobit. If the events really happened, then it is a fine and holy history. But if they are
all made up, then it is indeed a very beautiful, wholesome, and useful fiction or
drama by a gifted poet. It may even be assumed that beautiful compositions and
plays like this were common among the Jews. On their festivals and sabbaths
they steeped themselves in them; and through them, especially in times of peace
and good government, they liked to instill God's Word and work into their young
people. For they had outstanding people—prophets, bards, poets, and the like
—who in all sorts of ways diligently set forth the Word of God.

It may even be that the Greeks picked up from the Jews their art of presenting
comedies and tragedies, as well as a lot of other wisdom and worship, etc. For
Judith presents a good, serious, heroic tragedy, and Tobit presents a fine, delightful, devout comedy. [1534]

Martin Luther. Luther's Works. American edition. Vol.
XXXV. Ed. by Helmut T. Lehmann (St. Louis, Mo.,
Concordia/Philadelphia, Muhlenberg, 1960), p. 345

It is of uncertain origin, but certainly very late, and might justly be classed as
work of a decadent period. Like many works of decadence it has a charm of its
own, and is unique in that it is one of the earliest known examples, if not the earliest, of the short novel, written primarily for amusement. . . .

The author leaves nothing to be inferred by the reader . . . [and] ties up every
loose end with a meticulous care amounting almost to absurdity, rigidly balancing every incident with its completion. The little dog goes out and returns; the
grave is dug and filled up; the debt is duly collected despite the complications
added to the plot by Tobias' marriage; prayers are timed to rise together. It is as
though a parallel were drawn at every turn, but unlike the earlier writers, the author of Tobit does not trust his structure and feels obliged to draw the reader's attention to it. Nevertheless, the structure itself is remarkable: there are two separate threads of plot, one having its origin in Tobit's career at Nineveh, the other
in Sarah's strange misfortune in faraway Ecbatana, and this dual plan is used definitely to prepare the climax. In the story of Sodom and Gomorrah the scene is
shifted from the oaks of Mamre to the wicked city on the plain, but always with

the angel at hand to fuse the two scenes into one personal experience. In the Joseph cycle there is the dual picture of Joseph in Egypt and his brothers in their Palestinian home, but here the blood relationship reduces the plot to a narrative of the diverse adventures of a numerous family. Only in Tobit are there two utterly disconnected elements of story brought together at the end to furnish a climax, a construction rare enough in early literature to stand as a landmark.

The structure is evidence of the author's art, but his art is self-conscious and yet immature, and the sure touch in character drawing is gone also. Save for Tobit and Anna, not an individual stands out; Tobias, Raphael, Sarah, are mere shadows moving through the events of the story.

> Brooke Peters Church. *The Israel Saga* (New York,
> Macmillan, 1932), pp. 294, 297–99

[The story of] Tobit is pious and moral but its comedy and pathos have a familiar and contemporary flavor. Carried into exile, Tobit will not eat the bread of the gentile, he remembers God with all his heart, he defies the law of the land in observing the divine law, and gives burial to the dead of his nation. But when his son Tobias sets forth on his errand with the disguised angel his dog follows them. The presence of that dog on such an errand is a characteristic touch of Jewish wit. And the poor bride persecuted by the demon Ashmodai—seven times married she remains a virgin—is saved only because Tobias is instructed to make a dreadful stink by burning fish in the bridal chamber to rout the demon. The story is both touching and funny. Obstinate, righteous, sententious Tobit is a charming old man. His prayers are heard; an angel is sent, but the dog, trotting after the angel, is also slyly introduced—and the burning of fish. Some two thousand years later, in the stories of Isaac Babel and Bashevis Singer, the world and the works of mankind are seen in an oddly tilted perspective very similar to that of Tobit.

> Saul Bellow, Introduction to *Great Jewish Short Stories*
> (New York, Dell, 1963), p. 9

Piety, magic, dead bodies, a nagging wife, a faithful dog, a demon lover, and a happy ending—there is something for everyone in Tobit. The genius of the anonymous author lay in his ability to unite history, autobiography, prayers, maxims, and pagan folklore into a didactic short story. . . .

The story embodies a variety of literary forms. The historical setting (1:2) is given in the formal style of official records. Like Ruth, Jonah, and Judith, the tale is set in the remote past, the author seeking literary effect by calling up famous names from former times. Tobit's affliction and his plea for death take the form of autobiography (1:2–3:6). His "deathbed" counsel to his son (4:5–19) and Raphael's final words (12:6–10) are series of maxims. And Tobit's and Sara's pleas for death (3:2–6 and 3:11–15), like Tobit's final praise of the God who remembered him (13:1–18), are moving prayers.

Tobit weaves all these elements into a story based on two folk tales. In "The Grateful Dead," a dead man rewards the person who provides a decent burial. In

"The Dangerous Bride," potential husbands of a desirable woman perish under mysterious circumstances. By establishing the characters as exiles in ancient Nineveh, the author of Tobit could transform the "Grateful Dead/Dangerous Bride" narrative into a vehicle for instruction in Judaism.

Though it embodies many differing features, the story has a notable unity. The anguish of Sara parallels that of Tobit. Tobit and Raguel have each an only child and strong concern for the levirate tradition [the custom of marriage by a man to his brother's widow]. The angel Raphael is opposed by the demon Asmodeus. The healing power of fish entrails provides a happy ending for both families. And underlying all the drama and humor and supernatural magic is the character of Tobit, an exemplary Jew with complete and active faith in the God of his fathers.

> Charles W. Harwell and Daniel McDonald. *The Bible: A Literary Survey*. Ed. by Harwell and McDonald (Indianapolis, Bobbs-Merrill, 1975), p. 180

Folklore has had its impact on Tobit. An obvious folk tale is the story of the bewitched bride. Sarah's string of seven unfortunate husbands is calculated to introduce God's intervention through Raphael and so unite the two plagued families.

Another contribution from folklore is the colorful Ahiqar who enjoyed a reputation for wisdom in the ancient Near East. . . . Although Ahiqar is mentioned only four times in the book, his presence lends an atmosphere of ancient wisdom to the story. . . .

The most obvious influence on the book is the Old Testament itself. The author clearly dialogues with his scriptural heritage and adapts it to the needs of his audience. For example, the wedding night in chapter 8 is a blend of Genesis 2 and Israel's prayer style. The quest for a bride for Tobias in chapters 6, 7 is modelled on the quest for a bride for Isaac in Genesis 24. Prophetic texts, such as Isaiah 60, exert a considerable influence on the description of the new Jerusalem (see chapter 13). . . . Tobit may be called "Deuteronomy Revisited" since the story reflects the living out of the covenant implications of that book.

Angels and demons add to the color and theological message of the story. Genesis 18–19 is an example of angels in disguise who demonstrate God's ongoing concern with his created world. In Tobit, however, the angel has a proper name—Raphael. The author develops angelic intervention against demons by having Raphael interact against the wicked Asmodeus. Angelology/demonology is a significant departure from Judith where only humans occupy center stage and thus control the destiny of others.

As in Esther and especially Judith, there are certain incongruities which rule out sober history as the literary genre. . . . Some see Tobit as the union of wisdom and an edifying or didactic story. Others suggest popular romance. Unlike Esther and especially Judith, it does not have something of an historical nucleus to qualify it as an historical novel. Perhaps it is best to label it a religious novel whose aim is to teach and edify. This would account for the emphasis on wisdom and traditional practices such as prayer and almsgiving.

John Craghan. *Esther, Judith, Tobit, Jonah, Ruth* (Wilmington, Del., Michael Glazier, 1982), pp. 131–33

WISDOM OF SOLOMON

The style is very unequal; it is often pompous and turgid, as well as tedious and diffuse, and abounds in epithets, directly contrary to the practice of the Hebrews; it is however sometimes temperate, poetical and sublime. The construction is occasionally sententious, and tolerably accurate in that respect, so as to discover very plainly that the author had the old Hebrew poetry for his model, though he fell far short of its beauty and sublimity. The economy of the work is still more faulty; he continues the prayers of Solomon from the ninth chapter to the very end of the book; and they consequently take up more than one-half of the whole. But beside the tediousness of such an harangue, he indulges in too great a subtilty of disquisition upon abstruse subjects, and mingles many things very foreign to the nature of an address to the Deity: and after all, the subject itself is brought to no perfect conclusion. [1753]

Robert Lowth. *Lectures on the Sacred Poetry of the Hebrews.* Vol. II. Tr. from the Latin by G. Gregory (London, Printed for J. Johnson, 1787), p. 179

This book is a philosophy of the vital elements of character; a kind of large parable of history, presenting in veiled form the author's judgment of the spiritual conditions around him and their working tendencies. And the fact that this purports to be the Wisdom of Solomon is an interesting Nemesis of historical criticism; for the historic Solomon it was who made such wreck of his higher nature by becoming entangled in Egyptian alliances and idolatry. . . . One prominent part of the book is an idealized description, put into Solomon's own mouth, of his youth, and his prayer for wisdom, and his experience of Wisdom's inner saving power. We have an analogue to this in modern literature in Tennyson's "Idylls of the King". . . .

[As to the author's style], in his hands the form of the mashal has reached the farthest possible remove from the terse, crisp couplet of the beginning of Wisdom. Here it consists of a nucleus assertion, like the text of a sermon; which assertion is then enlarged upon: drawn out in endless amplification and we must say dilution, phrase upon phrase, detail upon detail, rolling out the idea so thin that we begin to wonder if a thing that flows so glibly can ever stop. He is evidently much enamored of his own literary fluency. But mere fluency is not the worst of it. The amplification has taken the reins into its own hands, and spreads out at its own sweet will, no longer thinking primarily of the truth, but only of the picture and the rhythm. We see this here in his fatally fluent portrayal of Ecclesiastes' supposably bad involvements and propensities.

John F. Genung. *The Hebrew Literature of Wisdom in the Light of To-day* (Boston, Houghton Mifflin, 1906), pp. 282, 286

As frequently in eloquent orations, the tone tends to rise in a gradual crescendo from pianissimo to fortissimo. The book begins with a quiet, earnest exhortation in chapter 1; passes to the wicked Jews' lyrical outburst, abounding in metaphors, in chapter 2; subsides again in the objective contrast between the pious and the wicked in chapters 3–4, which culminates in the dramatic scene of the last judgment (far more tempestuous than Dan. 7) in chapter 5. Similarly the second part of the book begins again with a calm exhortation (chapter 6) and with Solomon's reminiscences (7:1–21), rising to a lyrical praise of Wisdom in general (7:22–8:1), and as Solomon's beloved comrade in particular (8:2–21), and culminating in an eloquent prayer (chapter 9). The third part, in spite of some brilliant though fantastic pieces (such as the nightmare of the Egyptian darkness in chapter 17), is decidedly inferior in literary quality to the other two: it combines argumentation with rhetorical outbursts, history and apocalypse, logic and fantasy, and does not rise to an oratorical climax like the other two (although there is a crescendo from 10:1–11:19 to 11:20–12:27, and to 13–15; 16–19). In fact, the conclusion (19:22) is so abrupt and pedestrian that some critics have surmised that the original end of the book is lost.

In style as well as in thought the author amalgamates Israel and Hellas. In the list of literary forms given above, the first ones are Hebrew, the last ones (sorites, syncrisis, definition, and catalogues) are Greek. Aiming to be an apology for Judaism as a way of salvation, the book is modeled both after Proverbs 1–9 and after the diatribe. The poetry of the book (well sustained in chapters 1-5; 9; sporadic elsewhere, though more prevalent in 6–8; 10–12 than in 13–19, which are mostly prose) is a blend of Hebrew parallelism and Greek prosody, and at times is truly impressive. . . .

The author's rhetorical skill appears also in the musical effects achieved deliberately through the order and choice of words, through assonance, rhyme, alliteration, paronomasia, and other devices. . . .

His sophisticated literary elegance may be noticed by comparing, for instance, his vignette of the idolmaker (13:11–19) with that of the Second Isaiah (44:13–20), which served as his model. Here (13:11–15), and occasionally elsewhere (12:3–7, 8–11, 27; 17:14f., 17, 18f. [LXX 17:13f., 16, 17f.]), the author discloses his ability to construct in the Greek manner elaborate sentences including subordinate clauses, although usually he adopts the simpler Hebrew structure in which brief sentences are co-ordinated. . . .

The style of the author runs the gamut from the sober exhortation in chapter 1 to the lyrical eloquence of chapter 8; from the realistic description of a carpenter (13:11–19) or a potter (15:7–9) at work making idols to the fantastic description of the horrors of darkness in chapter 17; from philosophical arguments (like the cosmological proof of God's existence in 13:1–5, or the explanation of the origin of death in 2:23f.; cf. 1:13f.) to impassioned denunciations of the heathen (14:22–28) and praises of wisdom (7:22–29; 8:4–8).

From the literary point of view, the best parts of the book are those written under the compulsion of a stirring emotion (as in the fine passage 3:1–9). The intensity of feeling expresses itself in eloquent, lyrical, imaginative language. The most brilliant use of metaphor and simile occurs in the elegies on the vanity of human life in general (2:2–5) or of the wicked's lot in particular (5:7–14); less musically lyrical is the image of God's panoply (5:17–22). Elsewhere metaphors appear only sporadically (3:6f., 15; 4:3–5; 11:22; 15:10; 16:29; 18:4, 16; 19:9, 18) or not at all (in chapters 1, 6–10, 12–14 in particular). The author vividly personifies wisdom (chapters 6–9; cf. Prov. 8) and the divine *lógos* (18:15f.), without, however, conceiving either one as an actual person distinct from God. Of the numerous antitheses in the book the most apt and vivid shows how futile it is to pray to idols (13:18f.). . . .

In summing up, we may say that, despite some literary blemishes (particularly evident to modern readers in Chapters 10–19) and the rhetorical prolixity that at times fails to conceal vagueness of thought, Wisdom is "the most beautiful of all late Jewish [i.e., ca. 150 B.C.E.–100 C.E.] writings" (R. Reitzenstein, *Zwei religionsgeschichtliche Fragen*, 1901, p. 109).

Robert H. Pfeiffer. *History of New Testament Times, with an Introduction to the Apocrypha* (New York, Harper, 1949), pp. 330–34

COPYRIGHT ACKNOWLEDGMENTS

600

HARPER & ROW PUBLISHERS, INC. For permission to quote excerpts from the following books: *Introduction to the Old Testament* by Robert H. Pfeiffer (1941). *The Hills Beyond* by Thomas Wolfe (1941). *The Book of Books* by Solomon Goldman (1948). *The Prophetic Faith* by Martin Buber (1949), translated by Carlyle Witton-Davies. *In the Beginning* by Solomon Goldman (1949). *History of New Testament Times, with an Introduction to the Apocrypha* by Robert H. Pfeiffer (1949). *Symbols and Society*, edited by Lyman Bryson et al. (1955). *The Books of the Old Testament* by Robert H. Pfeiffer (1957). *A Light to the Nations* by Norman K. Gottwald (1959). *The Modern Reader's Guide to the Bible* by Harold H. Watts (1959). *The Jews*, Volume I, edited by Louis Finkelstein (1960). *The Prophets* by Abraham Joshua Heschel (1962). *The Message of the Prophets* by Gerhard von Rad, translated by D. M. G. Stalker (1972). *A Rich Feast: Encountering the Bible* by Chad Walsh (1981). *The Story of the Stories* by Dan Jacobson (1982).

HARVARD THEOLOGICAL REVIEW. For permission to quote an excerpt by Stephen A. Geller from the *Harvard Theological Review*, January 1982.

HARVARD UNIVERSITY PRESS. For permission to quote from the following books: *Ephod and Ark* by William R. Arnold (1917). *Biblical Motifs*, edited by Alexander Altmann (1966). *Early Christian Rhetoric* by Amos N. Wilder. Copyright 1971 by the President and Fellows of Harvard College. *Canaanite Myth and Hebrew Epic* by Frank Moore Cross (1973).

A.M. HEATH LTD. For permission to quote an excerpt from *The Story of the Stories* by Dan Jacobson (1982). Used by permission of Dan Jacobson and Secker & Warburg Ltd.

HEBREW UNION COLLEGE. For permission to quote excerpts from the *Hebrew Union College Annual*, 23 (1950–51), by William F. Albright; and 51 (1980), by Michael V. Fox.

DELBERT R. HILLERS. For permission to quote an excerpt from his article in *Zeitschrift für alttestamentliche Wissenschaft* 77 (1965).

HOLT, RINEHART & WINSTON/CBS, INC. For permission to quote excerpts from the following books: *How to Read the Bible* by Edgar J. Goodspeed (1946). *The Golden Years* by Brooke Peters Church (1947). *The Forgotten Language* (1951) and *You Shall Be as Gods* (1966) by Erich Fromm.

HOUGHTON MIFFLIN CO. For permission to quote excerpts from the following books: *The English Bible as Literature* by Charles A. Dinsmore (1931). Copyright 1931 by Charles A. Dinsmore. Copyright renewed 1959 by Union & New Haven Trust Company. *Essays in Appreciation* by John Livingston Lowes. Copyright 1936 by J. L. Lowes. Copyright renewed 1964 by John Wilbur Lowes. All used by permission of Houghton Mifflin Company.

HUMAN SCIENCES PRESS. For permission to quote an excerpt from *Moses: A Psychoanalytic Study* by Dorothy F. Zeligs (1985).

Martin Greenberg with Hannah Arendt, edited by Max Brod. Copyright 1949. *Four Strange Books of the Bible* by Elias Bickerman (1967). *Text and Texture* by Michael Fishbane (1979). *In the Beginning* by Everett Fox (1983).

SCHOLARS PRESS. For permission to reprint an excerpt by James Muilenburg, "The Literary Approach: The Old Testament in Hebrew Literature," from *Journal of the National Association of Biblical Instructors* 1 (1933). Copyright 1933 by the American Academy of Religion. Reprinted by permission of Scholars Press on behalf of the American Academy of Religion.

SETON HALL UNIVERSITY, INSTITUTE OF JUDAEO-CHRISTIAN STUDIES. For permission to quote an excerpt by Barry Ulanov from *The Bridge* 4 (1961/62). Used by permission.

SIFRIAT POALIM. For permission to quote excerpts by Shimeon Bar-Efrat from *Ha'itsuv ha'omanuti shel hassippur bammiqra'* (1979). Used by permission.

SOCIETY OF AUTHORS. For permission to quote excerpts from the following books: *The Adventures of the Black Girl in Her Search for God* by Bernard Shaw (Dodd, Mead & Company, Inc., copyright 1933). *The Problem of Style* by John Middleton Murry (Humphrey Milford, copyright 1922). By permission of the Society of Authors as the literary representative of the Bernard Shaw Estate and the Estate of John Middleton Murry.

SOCIETY OF BIBLICAL LITERATURE. For permission to quote excerpts from the following books: *Biblical Structuralism* by Robert M. Polzin (Fortress Press and Scholars Press, 1977). *The Book of Esther* by Sandra Beth Berg (Scholars Press, 1979). *Encounter with the Text*, edited by Martin J. Buss (Fortress Press and Scholars Press, 1979), excerpt by John G. Gammie. *The Biblical Mosaic*, edited by Robert M. Polzin and Eugene Rothman (Fortress Press, 1982), excerpt by Geoffrey Hartman. *Artistry and Faith in the Book of Judith* by Toni Craven (Scholars Press, 1983). *The Workings of Old Testament Narrative* by Peter D. Miscall (Fortress Press and Scholars Press, 1983). For permission to quote excerpts from the following articles in the *Journal of Biblical Literature*: James A. Montgomery in September 1945; Donald F. Rauber in March 1970; Robert Gordis in March 1976; Jerome T. Walsh in June 1977; Alan J. Hauser in March 1980; Robert L. Cohn in September 1982. For permission to quote excerpts from the following articles in *Semeia*: David M. Gunn in 3 (1975); James G. Williams in 8 (1977).

SOUNDINGS. For permission to quote an excerpt from James Crenshaw, "Journey into Oblivion," *Soundings*, Summer 1975, pages 251–52.

SOUTHERN METHODIST UNIVERSITY PRESS. For permission to quote an excerpt by Charles F. Kraft from *A Stubborn Faith*, edited by Edward C. Hobbs (1956).

EVELYN STROUSE. For permission to quote an excerpt from an article in *Commentary*, February 1979.

INDEX TO CRITICS